Study Guide
with
Quicken® *Business Law Partner* ® 3.0 CD–ROM
to Accompany
West's Business Law
Alternate Edition
Text & Summarized Cases—Legal, Ethical, Regulatory, and International Environment
Seventh Edition

GAYLORD A. JENTZ
Herbert D. Kelleher
Professor in Business Law
University of Texas at Austin

ROGER LeROY MILLER
Institute for University Studies
Arlington, Texas

FRANK B. CROSS
Associate Director,
Center for Legal and Regulatory Studies
University of Texas at Austin

Prepared by

Barbara E. Behr
Member of
New York State Bar
Pennsylvania State Bar

James A Bernstein
Jorden Burt
Berenson and Johnson, LLP
Washington, D.C.

Susan Bernstein
Member of
Maryland State Bar

WEST
WEST EDUCATIONAL PUBLISHING COMPANY
An International Thomson Publishing Company

Publisher/Team Director: Jack Calhoun
Senior Acquisitions Editor: Rob Dewey
Acquisitions Editor: Scott Person
Developmental Editor: Jan Lamar
Production Editor: Bill Stryker
Marketing Manager: Michael Worls

ISBN: 0–324–00410–9

1 2 3 4 5 6 7 G P 3 2 1 0 9 8 7

Printed in the United States of America

I(T)P®

International Thomson Publishing
West Educational Publishing is an ITP Company.
The ITP trademark is used under license.

TABLE OF CONTENTS

Preface

The function of this *Study Guide* is to assist you in your efforts to grasp the fundamental principles of law developed in *West's Business Law (Alternate Edition): Text, Cases, Legal, Ethical, Regulatory, and International Environment (Seventh Edition)* by Kenneth W. Clarkson, Roger LeRoy Miller, Gaylord A. Jentz, and Frank B. Cross.

Students approaching the subject of business law tend to be overwhelmed because of the unfamiliar terms and the apparently countless number of legal rules that they are expected to understand. This *Study Guide* highlights important concepts and terminology and provides a framework for organizing your studying. This structured approach should reduce anxiety and eliminate confusion. With this in mind, the materials in the *Study Guide* have been developed in order to give you a variety of learning tools so that you can do your studying in an organized fashion.

It is assumed, of course, that you will be attending and attentive in classes as well as reading and referring to the textbook and relevant appendices while using these supplementary materials.

Included in the *Study Guide* are the following:

1. **Unit Summaries** — Brief overview of the areas of law covered in each of the eleven units.

2. **Chapter Introductions** — Short summaries of the topics covered in each of the chapters. The introductions preview and tie together the concepts presented in more detail in the textbook and the chapter outlines provided in this *Study Guide*.

3. **Things to Keep in Mind** — Reminders of important principles. A difficult concept may be clarified or reiterated; relevant principles that are developed in earlier chapters may be recalled; and explanations may be given for terminology or items, the significance of which may have been overlooked.

4. **Chapter Outlines** — Detailed systematic reviews of legal principles presented in the textbook.

5. **Key Words and Phrases** — A list of significant terms that are discussed in the textbook.

6. **Fill-in Questions** — The function of these questions is to enable you to determine whether or not you have become familiar with major and/or difficult concepts and important terminology. Suggested answers to these questions are available in a separate Answer Key.

7. **Multiple Choice Questions** — Suitable for self-testing. The degrees of difficulty of the questions vary. Answers to the questions are available in the separate Answer Key.

8. In several chapters, there also are **other types of objective questions** that may help you in applying legal principles to business situations. Answers to these questions also are available in the separate Answer Key.

9. A section containing **Uniform CPA Business Law and Professional Responsibilities Examination Information** for accounting majors who contemplate sitting for the CPA Examination.

For their helpful and varied contributions, we are indebted to our editor, Jan Lamar of West Publishing Company/ITP, our readers, Christopher Rider (Johns Hopkins '98) and Jonathan Fuller (Cornell '97), and the many students whom we have encountered and for whom we have great respect.

Barbara E. Behr
James A Bernstein
Susan Bernstein

UNIT ONE:
THE LEGAL ENVIRONMENT OF BUSINESS

Business activities do not exist in a vacuum. Rather, they are conducted in a world in which there are any number of other influences and concerns, all of which affect business. One such important influence is law, for it permeates the manner in which business is organized and conducted. For this reason, it is essential that people who engage in business activities have familiarity with the legal environment in which business is conducted. The material in the textbook is meant to expose the readers to many of the underlying legal concepts and rules that create this legal environment of business.

The purpose of the chapters in Unit One is to furnish you with a foundation for your continued study of law as it relates to business and to introduce you to what have become traditional topics for students in business law and legal studies courses, such as contracts and commercial transactions (covered in subsequent units). The first chapter in Unit One, therefore, is devoted to material dealing with philosophies and approaches to the law, as well as to sources and classifications of law. Because ethics and social responsibility play important roles in both law and business, the authors introduce them in Chapter 2. (Note that following each Unit in the book, there is a section entitled "Focus on Ethics," and that there are discussions of relevant ethical issues interspersed throughout the text.)

The third and fourth chapters provide an overview of the legal and court systems in the United States. In Chapter 5, the focus is on the constitutional bases for the regulation of business in this country. The following three chapters deal with torts (civil wrongs) that are most frequent in business, intellectual property (such as trademarks, patents, and copyrights), computer and cyberspace law, areas of substantive law of importance to most people, including businesspersons. Concluding the Unit are chapters relating to criminal law and comparative law.

Chapter 1
Introduction to Law and Legal Reasoning

This introductory chapter contains discussions of the nature and origins of law in the United States and the methods that are used in order to find relevant legal principles in cases, statutes, and administrative regulations.

THINGS TO KEEP IN MIND

An important function of law is that it provide stability and certainty. Knowledge of the legal principles that govern relationships among parties engaging in commercial transactions is important when making business decisions. Businesspersons, who have this knowledge, realize how they are expected to conduct themselves and can predict how those with whom they deal will behave in the future.

OUTLINE

I.   What is law? — Enforceable rules governing relationships among individuals and relationships between individuals and their society.

    A. Natural law and positive law.

        1. Positive law is the established law of a particular society at a particular point in time.

        2. The natural law tradition — There are inherent moral and ethical principles that are universal and higher than positive law.

        3. Legal positivism — Positive law is the highest law and must be obeyed until it is changed in an orderly manner through the recognized lawmaking process.

    B. Legal realism — Law is not a set of abstract rules that can be applied uniformly to all cases involving similar facts.

        1. Judges' unique personalities, value systems, and intellects affect their interpretation of decisions in previous cases and their reasoning in the particular cases that they are deciding.

2. No two cases, however similar, are exactly the same; judges should tailor their decisions to the specific circumstances of the cases that they are deciding and consider social and economic realities.

3. The Uniform Commercial Code (UCC) emphasizes practicality, flexibility, reasonability, and customary trade practices and thus reflects the influence of legal realism.

C. Judicial interpretation of the law.

1. A function of the courts is to interpret and apply the law.

2. Because legal rules tend to be expressed in general terms, courts have flexibility; to some extent, judges decisions are affected by the judges' values and judicial philosophies.

II. The common law tradition.

A. Much of the law in the United States is derived from the English common law, a body of general rules developed by judges prescribing social conduct.

B. Early English courts.

1. Courts of law and remedies at law.

a. Remedies are provided by courts in order to recover a right or redress a wrong.

b. Remedies at law that historically were provided by courts of law to plaintiffs (persons bringing lawsuits) included possession of land, possession of items of value, and money as compensation for damage incurred by plaintiff.

2. Courts of equity and remedies in equity.

a. Decisions by courts of equity are based upon fairness and justice.

b. In England, individuals who were unable to obtain adequate remedies in courts of law petitioned the king for relief.

c. Often, the king's chancellor made decisions; later, courts of equity (chancery) were established.

d. Equitable relief may be available when the remedy at law is inadequate or unavailable or will result in hardship.
   1) Decree of specific performance — An order directing a party to perform a particular act as promised in a contract.
   2) Injunction — An order directing a party to refrain from doing a particular act.

       3) Rescission — A court may rescind (cancel) or abolish duties created by an agreement and return the parties to the positions that the parties would have been in if they had not entered into the agreement.

    e. Courts of equity use discretion in granting remedies in equity and are guided by equitable maxims:
      1) A person who seeks equity must do equity.
      2) When there is equal equity, the law must prevail.
      3) A person who seeks equitable relief must have clean hands.
      4) Equity will not suffer a right to exist without a remedy — equity will not permit a right for relief for a civil wrong to exist without providing a remedy.
      5) Equity is more concerned with substance than form (legal technicalities).
      6) Equity aids the vigilant, but not those who rest on their rights.
        a) The equitable doctrine of laches — Those petitioning for equitable relief must do so within a reasonable period of time.
        b) Today, statutes of limitations prescribe the period of time within which a person must begin a lawsuit.

C. Legal and equitable remedies today.

  1. Most states have combined courts of law and equity so that plaintiffs or petitioners may request, and courts may grant, either legal or equitable relief, or both.

  2. There still are distinctions between law and equity with regard to procedure, remedies, and the right to a jury trial that exist when the legal remedy of compensatory damages is sought, but not in a case in which equitable relief is sought.

D. The doctrine of *stare decisis*.

  1. Common law is judge-made law because, when deciding present cases, judges stand by (adhere to and apply) general principles of law that were established in previously decided cases; these earlier cases serve as legal precedents for current cases.

  2. Case precedents and case reports.

    a. Courts use past decisions as precedents in adjudicating cases before them when the current cases are based upon the same or similar fact situations.

    b. Today, decisions in cases are published in reporters (reports).

  3. *Stare decisis* and the common law tradition.

    a. Because of the doctrine of *stare decisis*, a decision made by the highest state court on a particular issue is followed by the lower state courts in later cases, and a decision made by the United States Supreme Court relating to a given issue is binding on all inferior courts in future cases in which the same issue is raised.

    b. Case precedents, statutes, and other laws are binding authorities that must be followed by courts.

    c. The doctrine of *stare decisis* results in efficiency in the courts and the stability, certainty, and predictability of law.

4. Departures from precedent — Sometimes, a court may overturn a precedent because of changes in technology, knowledge, business practices, or society's attitudes, or because a statute changes the prior rule or, in rare instances, the court determines that an error was made in a prior case.

5. When there is no precedent upon which to base a decision in a case of first impression, or there are conflicting precedents, a court may consider legal principles and policies underlying previous decisions or existing statutes, fairness, social values, customs, public policy, and data and concepts drawn from the social sciences.

E. *Stare decisis* and legal reasoning.

1. Legal reasoning is the thought process that is expressed by a court in arriving at its decision in a case when it determines the applicable law and applies that law to the facts in a particular case.

2. Basic steps in legal reasoning — Ask the following questions:

    a. What are the key (important) facts that may have been alleged (or claimed) by the plaintiff (and possibly refuted by the defendant who has raised defenses)?

    b. What are the legal issues?

    c. What are the relevant rules of law (precedents) that apply in this case?

    d. How do the relevant rules of law apply to the particular facts and circumstances of this case? Are there earlier cases that are on point because the facts are similar to the facts in the current case?

    e. What conclusion should be drawn in deciding the legal issues posed in the particular case based upon the answers to these questions?

3. Forms of legal reasoning.

    a. Deductive reasoning — A court's opinion may be in the form of a syllogism relying upon a major premise, a minor premise, and a conclusion.

        b. Linear reasoning — A court's opinion may be in the form of a logical progression of connected points that leads to a conclusion.

        c. Reasoning by analogy — A court may compare facts in the case at hand to facts in similar earlier cases.

    F. There is no one "right" answer.

        1. Good arguments often can be made to support each side of a controversy.

        2. Because legal rules are expressed in general terms, judges have flexibility in interpreting and applying the law; to some extent, the personal beliefs and philosophies of judges affect the process of legal reasoning.

III. Sources of law in the United States.

    A. Primary sources of law in the United States include constitutions and statutes (codified law), regulations adopted by administrative agencies, and case law.

    B. There also are secondary sources of law, such as encyclopedias, treatises, law reviews, and respected compilation of legal principles.

    C. Constitutional law.

        1. The United States Constitution and the constitutions of the states provide for the organization, powers, and limitations of their respective governments.

        2. The United States Constitution is the supreme law of the land — Any statutory or case law rule that is contrary to the U.S. Constitution will not be enforced. [See Appendix B and Chapter 5.]

        3. The Tenth Amendment to the U.S. Constitution reserves all power not given to the federal government to the states or to the people.

        4. State constitutions are the supreme law within the states' geographic areas if they do not conflict with the U.S. Constitution or a federal statute.

    D. Statutory law.

        1. Statutes are laws enacted by legislative bodies.

        2. Ordinances are laws, rules, or orders governing local matters that have been adopted by municipalities, counties, or other governmental subdivisions.

        3. Uniform laws.

            a. In order to promote uniformity and reform, the National Conference of Commissioners on Uniform State Laws drafts proposals for comprehensive codes of law concerning specific subject areas, which the legislative bodies in the various states may adopt as statutes.

    b. A state legislature may adopt a uniform act with changes, modifications, and/or deletions.

4. The Uniform Commercial Code (UCC).   [See Appendix C and Units Two, Three, Four, and Five.]

    a. The UCC is statutory law that has been enacted in all the states in the United States (at least in part), the District of Columbia, and the Virgin Islands. (Note that the entire UCC has not been enacted in Louisiana.)

    b. The UCC is a major source of commercial law that relates to business.

    c. In general, the UCC does not change basic principles, but provides an internally consistent, organized, modern body of clearly stated uniform rules relating to business transactions.

E. Administrative law. [See Chapter 44.]

1. Administrative agencies are created by legislative bodies through enabling legislation and are empowered to exercise specific governmental powers by issuing rules, orders, and regulations that affect business firms.

2. Some federal administrative agencies are part of the executive branch; others are independent regulatory agencies (e.g., the Federal Trade Commission, the Securities and Exchange Commission, and the Federal Communications Commission).

3. There may be parallel administrative agencies at the state and local levels.

4. Administrative law is an area of public law that covers the conduct, powers, and procedures of federal and state governmental agencies.

F. Case law and common law doctrines.

1. The body of rules of law announced in court decisions, including interpretations of provisions in constitutions, statutes, and regulations, as well as precedents in past cases, is referred to as judge-made law, common law, or case law.

2. The relationship between the common law and statutory law.

    a. Case law is distinguishable from statutory (codified) law that has been enacted by legislative bodies.

    b. In areas that are not covered by statutory law, common law governs.

      c. Some statutes codify what had been common law rules; in interpreting such a statute, a court may use common law as a guide in determining the intentions of the legislators.

      d. Statutory and case law may vary among the states.

    3. Restatements of the Law.

      a. The American Law Institute publishes compilations of case law rules in a number of areas of law, such as contracts, torts, agency, and property.

      b. Restatements contain summaries of case law in the various states; Restatements are important secondary reference sources, but do not have the force of law.

IV. Civil law versus criminal law.

  A. Civil law.

    1. Rules dealing with rights and duties that exist between persons or between citizens and their government (excluding the duty not to commit crimes).

    2. In a civil case, a private party (the plaintiff) who sues another person (the defendant) must prove his or her case with a preponderance of evidence in order to obtain a remedy from the court.

  B. Criminal law.

    1. Criminal acts are wrongs committed against the public as a whole; crimes are defined and prohibited in statutes.

    2. In a criminal case, a defendant is prosecuted by the state which must prove its case beyond a reasonable doubt in order for penalties to be imposed.

  C. There are other classifications of law.

    1. Substantive law defines and describes legal rights, relationships, and obligations among persons, whereas procedural law deals with the methods and means of enforcing substantive legal rights.

    2. Public law is law that affects relationships between persons and their government (which represents the interests of society) and includes constitutional, criminal, administrative, and tax law, whereas private law relates to legal relationships among persons.

V. How to find primary sources of law.

  A. Finding statutory law.

1. Statutes are compiled in codified form so that laws relating to a particular subject are found in titles that are subdivided into sections in organized compilations of statutes.

2. A citation for a statute indicates where the particular law can be found; for example, 15 U.S.C. §1 means that the statute is codified in Title 15 of the *United States Code* at Section 1.

3. Commercial publications, such as the *United States Code Annotated* (U.S.C.A.), include notes relating to court decisions in which courts have interpreted sections of the statutes and other information.

B. Finding administrative law — Rules and regulations adopted by federal administrative agencies similarly are compiled in the *Code of Federal Regulations* (C.F.R.) in titles that are subdivided into sections.

C. Finding case law.

1. The typical three tier court system consists of trial courts, in which evidence is presented, and one or more levels of appellate (or reviewing) courts.

2. State court decisions.

 a. Reporters containing state court decisions — Appellate court decisions are published in reports (or reporters), the volumes of which are numbered consecutively.

 b. West Publishing Company also compiles opinions of state appellate courts in regional units of the *National Reporter System.*

 c. Case citations — A typical citation for a case includes the title of the case (i.e., the names of the parties), the volume number of the reporter, an abbreviation of the reporter, the page number, the year in which the decision was made, and the court in which the case was decided.

3. Federal court decisions.

 a. Cases decided in the federal district courts (trial courts) are published in West's *Federal Supplement*, and opinions from the courts of appeals for the various circuits (intermediate appellate courts) are published in West's *Federal Reporter.*

 b. Decisions of the U.S. Supreme Court are published in the official *United States Reports*, West's *Supreme Court Reporter*, and the *Lawyers' Edition of the Supreme Court Reports.*

4. Old case law.

5. Case digests and legal encyclopedias.

VI.   How to read and understand case law.

    A. Case titles — indicate the names of the parties.

    B. Terminology.

       1. Parties to lawsuits.

          a. The plaintiff (or petitioner) is the party initiating the action or lawsuit and the defendant (or respondent) is the party against whom the action or suit is brought.

          b. Appellate cases.
             1) The appellant is the party who appeals a case to an appellate court; sometimes the appellant is referred to as the petitioner.
             2) The appellee is the party against whom an appeal is taken; sometimes the appellee is referred to as the respondent.

       2. Judges and justices — Designation given to those who administer law in courts.

       3. Decisions and opinions.

          a. Unanimous opinion — Written by one judge with whom all of the judges agree.

          b. Majority opinion — Written by one judge with whom more than half the court agrees.

          c. Dissenting opinion — Minority opinion.

          d. Concurring opinion — Opinion of a judge who agrees with decision of other judges, but whose reasons are different.

          e. A *per curiam* opinion is an opinion of the court or a statement of the court's disposition of a case without a written opinion; an *en banc* decision is an opinion in a case decided by all the judges sitting as members of an appellate court.

       4. Abbreviations.

    C. A sample court case.

KEY WORDS AND PHRASES IN TEXT

law	legal positivism
positive law	legal realism
natural law	judicial interpretation

common law (case law)

remedy

courts of law and remedies at law

compensatory money damages

courts of equity and remedies in equity

chancellor

specific performance

injunction

rescission of a contractual obligation

equitable maxims

plaintiff (petitioner)

defendant (respondent)

defenses

laches

statutes of limitations

stare decisis

legal precedent

binding authorities

case on point

case of first impression

public policy

legal reasoning

allege

deductive (syllogistic) reasoning

linear reasoning

reasoning by analogy

United States Constitution

state constitutions

constitutional law

statutory law

local ordinances

uniform laws

Uniform Commercial Code (UCC)

administrative law

administrative agencies

executive agencies

independent regulatory agencies

Restatements of the Law

civil law

breach of (failure to comply with) a duty

criminal law

primary sources of law

United States Code

Code of Federal Regulations

trial court

appellate (reviewing) court

reporters (reports)

case citation

parallel citation

case title

appellant (petitioner)

appellee (respondent)

judges and justices

court opinion

unanimous, majority, concurring,
   and dissenting opinions

per curiam opinion

en banc decision

FILL-IN QUESTIONS

1. Common (or case) law refers to the rules of law that have been developed over time by _____, who decide cases based upon general principles of law which have been established in similar cases in the past.

2. When a court bases its decision on precedents that have been established in earlier cases, the court is following the doctrine of _____.

3. Rules of law that are enacted by a legislative body, such as the Congress of the United States, are referred to as _____ law. Rules of law that are announced in court decisions are called _____ law.

4. The _____ is a model statute that states uniform rules relating to business transactions. It has been adopted in whole or in part by the _____ bodies in the states, the District of Columbia, and the Virgin Islands.

5. Today, in the United States, primary sources of law include the U.S. Constitution, constitutions that have been adopted in the states, _____ that have been enacted by the U.S. Congress and state legislative bodies, local _____, administrative agencies' rules, regulations and rulings, and _____ law.

6. Jones intentionally took Smith's automobile. Because Jones committed a wrong against the public (society), he may be prosecuted for a _____. Because Jones interfered with Smith's rights in his property, Jones has committed a tort, which is a _____ wrong.

7. The title of a United States Supreme Court case is *Meritor Savings Bank, FSB v. Vinson*. Meritor Savings Bank, FSB was the _____ and Vinson was the _____.

MULTIPLE CHOICE QUESTIONS

1. "Law" governs relationships between:
   A. persons, including natural persons and corporations.
   B. natural persons, but **not** relationships between corporations.
   C. people, but **not** relationships between people and the government.
   D. people, but **not** relationships between the federal government and the states.

2. Legal precedents are rules of law that are established by:
   A. federal and state constitutions.
   B. legislatures when they enact statutes.
   C. courts when they decide cases.
   D. legislatures when they enact statutes and courts when they decide cases.

3. The doctrine of *stare decisis*:
   A. is followed usually by judges when they make decisions.
   B. enables judges to make fairer decisions.
   C. results in consistency in the law.
   D. All of the above are correct.

4. The doctrine of *stare decisis*:
   A. only applies to decisions of the United States Supreme Court.
   B. only applies to decisions made by the highest appellate courts in the states of the United States.
   C. is applied when lower courts of a state follow precedents established by the highest appellate court of that state.
   D. no longer is applied by state courts in the United States.

5. A basic characteristic of case law (common law) is that:
   A. statutes are derived from case law.
   B. case law establishes precedents for other courts to follow when similar controversies are litigated.
   C. case law eliminates the need to apply antiquated doctrines, such as *stare decisis*.
   D. in the United States, all case law is codified in statutes.

6. When a petitioner brings an action in equity:
    A. a remedy that a court may give is an injunction in order to prevent an injury.
    B. a remedy that a court may give is money in order to compensate an injured party.
    C. the distinction between law and equity has no relevance today.
    D. a court will not apply the doctrine of *stare decisis*.

7. A source of law in the legal system of the United States would include:
    A. the United States Constitution.
    B. state statutes.
    C. local ordinances.
    D. court decisions.
    E. All of the above are sources of law.

8. In general, current principles of business law:
    A. are considered to be part of civil law.
    B. are codified to some extent in the Uniform Commercial Code.
    C. have been developed in cases decided by state courts.
    D. All of the above are correct.

9. In 1978, the highest state court ruled in the case of *Moyer v. Quitt* that a promise to make a gift is **not** enforceable. A similar case, *Casius v. Smite*, is being decided today by a court in the same state. Because the court will apply the doctrine of *stare decisis* in deciding the Casius case:
    A. the court will enforce a promise to make a gift.
    B. the court will **not** enforce a promise to make a gift.
    C. it is **not** possible to tell how the court will decide the case since the Moyer case has nothing in common with the Casius case.
    D. it is **not** possible to tell how the court will decide the case since the Moyer case is not a precedent for the Casius case.

The following information is given for questions 10, 11, 12, and 13. Note that you will need to use logic and reasoning skills in order to answer the questions. The United States brought a civil action against Container Corp. of America, and others, asserting that the corporation violated Section 1 of the Sherman Act, a federal antitrust law. The lower court's decision was appealed to the United States Supreme Court by the United States. Justices Marshall, Harlan, and Stewart agreed with the lower court, but five Justices disagreed with the lower court decision. Justice Fortas agreed with the result of the Supreme Court's decision, but he wrote a separate opinion in which he emphasized a particular point. The opinion of the court was written by Justice Douglas and is found in volume 438 of the United States Supreme Court Reports at page 422. It is a 1978 case.

10. The case can be classified as one involving:
    A. criminal law.
    B. an action in equity.
    C. statutory law.
    D. legal realism.

11. Container Corp. of America was:

    A. the plaintiff in the original case and the defendant in the appeal to the United States Supreme Court.

    B. the respondent in the original case and the defendant in the appeal to the United States Supreme Court.

    C. the defendant in the original case and the appellant in the appeal to the United States Supreme Court.

    D. the defendant in the original case and the appellee in the appeal to the United States Supreme Court.

12.   The official citation for the case is:
    A. U.S. v. Container Corp. of America, et al., 422 U.S. S. Ct. Dec. 438 (1978).
    B. U.S. v. Container Corp. of America, et al., 438 U.S. 422 (1978).
    C. Container Corp. of America, et al. v. U.S., 438 U.S. 422 (1978).
    D. Container Corp. of America, et al. v. U.S., 438 1978 S. Ct. Rep. 422.

13.   The following statement is **false:**
    A. The decision of the lower court was reversed.
    B. Justice Douglas wrote the majority opinion and Justice Fortas the dissenting opinion.
    C. Justice Fortas wrote a concurring opinion and was a member of the majority.
    D. The dissenting Justices were Marshall, Harlan, and Stewart.

Chapter 2
Business Ethics

This chapter provides an introduction to business ethics and a framework for analyzing business decisions and activities in light of ethical values and goals. The nature of business ethics, the relationship between ethics and the law, and approaches to ethical reasoning are discussed. A theme in the chapter is the problem of balancing profit maximization goals with ethical duties that are owed to various groups, such as employees and consumers, as well as to society as a whole.

THINGS TO KEEP IN MIND

Business law is based upon the premise that people act in an ethical manner when dealing with one another. You will observe in other Chapters that people are expected to honor contractual commitments, cooperate with each other in the performance of contracts, act reasonably and in good faith, and exercise care in their undertakings.

OUTLINE

I.   What is ethics?

   A. Ethics is the study of what constitutes "right and wrong" behavior and is a branch of philosophy that focuses on the rational basis for conduct and the fairness, justice, or rightness of a person's action.

   B. Morals are universal guidelines that may emanate from religious concepts or other sources, and determine a person's actions and character and, therefore, affect that person's ethics.

II. The nature of business ethics.

   A. Business ethics deals with what constitutes "right or wrong" behavior in the conduct of business activities and how moral principles are applied by business-persons when they engage in such activities.

   B. Duty-based ethics may be derived from revealed truths, such as religious beliefs, and philosophical inquiries concerning the nature of "right," fair, and just behavior.

      1. Religious ethical standards — In the United States, religious (Judeo-Christian) tradition establishes absolute duties to act in accordance with

ethical standards and requires compassionate treatment of others.

2. Kantian ethics — Immanuel Kant identified general guiding principles for moral behavior based upon what he believed to be the fundamental nature of human beings.

   a. Human beings are qualitatively different from other physical objects.

   b. Human beings are endowed with moral integrity and the capacity to reason and conduct their affairs rationally; their thoughts and actions, therefore, should be respected.

   c. Kant's categorical imperative — Individuals should objectively evaluate their actions in light of the consequences that would follow if everyone in society acted in the same way.

3. The principle of rights.

   a. Duty-based ethical standards imply that, because human beings have certain duties, human beings also have reciprocal basic rights.

   b. Failure to comply with an ethical duty is not justified even if the motive is benevolent or the consequences are desirable — "The ends cannot justify the means."

   c. In order to respect the rights of other people, a person making an ethical business decision must consider how the decision affects others.

C. Outcomes-based ethics: Utilitarianism.

1. Utilitarianism is associated with Jeremy Bentham and John Stuart Mill.

2. Utilitarianism is outcome oriented — The consequences of any given action determine what is ethical. ("The ends justify the means.")

3. An action is morally correct whenever it produces the greatest amount of good for the greatest number of people who are affected by the act.

4. Application of the theory that an action is good if it results in the greatest amount of positive benefits for the greatest number of individuals requires:

   a. A determination of those individuals whose well-being will be affected by the action;

   b. An assessment (cost-benefit analysis) of the negative and positive effects of alternative actions on these individuals; and

   c. A choice among alternative actions that will produce maximum utility to society.

5. The objective quantification approach of utilitarianism tends to reduce human welfare to plus and minus signs and has been used to justify human costs that many people find unacceptable.

III. Ethical decision making.

A. If a business firm determines that a given course of action is profitable, the firm then should evaluate if the undertaking is also legal and ethical.

B. Is the contemplated action legal?

1. Laws regulating business — Business firms are expected to know the law, including relevant statutes and rules and regulations issued by administrative agencies, and, therefore, should obtain legal advice before making important business decisions.

2. "Gray" areas in the law — Sometimes, it is difficult to predict how a court or administrative agency may interpret and apply a statute or regulation.

C. Is the contemplated action ethical?

1. Often, law itself is an expression of society's ethical values so that some ethical decisions are made for members of society; compliance with the law is the moral minimum.

2. Codes of ethics.

    a. Because not all ethical requirements are codified, some conduct may not be legally wrongful even though it might be unethical.

    b. Firms establish ethical policies and standards to guide executives, managers, and employees in the business decision-making process.

3. Establishing ethical priorities.

    a. Business decisions affect a number of groups, including the firm's owners, employees, suppliers, consumers, and the greater community.

    b. A firm that adopts a utilitarian perspective by giving equal weight to the interests of each group may make an ethical decision that is different from a decision made by a firm with a duty-based or rights-based perspective.

4. Maximum versus optimum profits — Today, many firms sacrifice some profits in order to aim for optimum profits, the maximum profits that can be realized by complying with legal and ethical standards.

6. Public opinion and business ethics — In order to protect their goodwill and reputations, business firms that are faced with ethical dilemmas are attentive to public opinion as expressed by the media and public interest groups.

D. Ethical decision making and the corporate environment.

   1. Normally, a single corporate officer or manager may provide some input but does not have complete control over the collective decision-making process.

   2. The nature of the corporate environment may obstruct ethical decision making by corporate decision makers who are shielded from personal responsibility, accountability, and the consequences of their individual decisions when decisions are made collectively.

IV. Ethical issues in business.

A. Ethical issues, such as those relating to employment, may be internal to a firm; ethical issues, such as those involving consumer welfare, are external issues.

B. Employment relationships. [See Chapters 35 and 36.]

   1. Employers are obligated by law to provide a safe workplace and pay a minimum wage and are prohibited by statutes from discriminating against an existing or potential employee because of race, color, national origin, gender, pregnancy, religion, age, or disability.

   2. Employees wish to be free of harassment by co-workers and to have their personal integrity and privacy rights respected by their employers.

   3. In addition to complying with statutory obligations, employers have ethical responsibilities to their employees; sometimes, employers are faced with conflicts between their ethical and legal duties.

   4. Sexual harassment versus wrongful discharge.

      a. Federal law and the Equal Employment Opportunity Commission guidelines impose duties on employers to take "immediate and appropriate corrective" actions when employees report sexual abuses to superiors.

      b. Some state statutes and many employment agreements prohibit employers from discharging employees without "just cause."

      c. Employees who have been discharged because they have sexually harassed co-workers have sued for wrongful discharge (being fired without good cause or for discriminatory reasons).

      d. An employer may attempt to avoid liability for sexual harassment or wrongful discharge by adopting a harassment policy establishing procedures and corrective actions that are to be followed when an employee initiates a harassment complaint.

   5. Corporate restructuring and employee welfare.

      a. Conflict between maintaining the profitability of the firm and the ethical duty to employees who have loyally served the firm over time arises when making a decision to replace long-term, highly paid employees with younger employees who are willing to work at lower salaries.

      b. An employer cannot breach a contract of employment or violate the Age Discrimination in Employment Act (ADEA).

  C. Consumer welfare. [See Chapters 8 and 25.]

    1. Although consumer protection laws have been enacted to prevent the distribution of unsafe or unhealthy products, the marketing of certain products may not be prohibited by these laws; marketing such products, however, may be unethical.

    2. In some cases, the issue is: At what point does a manufacturer's responsibility for the safety of consumers end and consumers' responsibility begin?

    3. Product misuse — An ethical issue arises when a substantial number of consumers are injured by using product in a way that it was not intended to be used.

    4. Duty to warn — Manufacturers and sellers of goods are required to warn consumers of risks that are associated with misuse of their products; this duty to warn does not apply when the particular risk is "open and obvious."

V.   The ever-changing ethical landscape — What is ethical, fair, just, or right in a given situation varies from person to person and from group to group as well as over time.

KEY WORDS AND PHRASES IN TEXT

ethics	"gray areas"
business ethics	moral minimum
ethical reasoning	codes of ethics
duty-based ethics	maximum profits
Kant's categorical imperative	optimum profits
outcomes-based ethics (utilitarianism)	sexual harassment
principle of rights	wrongful discharge
cost-benefit analysis	corporate environment

FILL-IN QUESTIONS

1.   Ethics is a branch of _____ that focuses on morality and the ways in which moral principles are applied to daily life. A person is making an ethical decision if he or she considers the _____, justice, or rightness of an action.

2. Because law may reflect society's ethical values and principles, many, but not all, ethical decisions are made for us when we comply with the law. For example, often criminal laws are expressions of ethical principles when these laws represent a social _____ or the shared beliefs of the members of society. Even though a particular act is not prohibited by a criminal statute, the act may still be _____.

3. One applying a duty-based ethical standard would say that the _____ may never justify the "means" under any circumstances. For example, traditionally in the United States, a person has a duty not to take property that belongs to another person. Taking an automatic pistol from its owner, therefore, is never justified.

4. One applying a utilitarian ethical standard would say that the _____ may justify the "means" under some circumstances. For example, traditionally in the United States, a person has a duty not to take property that belongs to another person. Taking an automatic pistol from its owner, therefore, may be _____ if the owner is pointing the pistol at a group of children in a classroom.

5. Kant's philosophy is classified as being duty-based. It is based upon the idea that the consequences of a person's actions are to be judged in terms of what would be the results if everyone in society acted in the _____.

6. People who engage in business rely upon their individual ethical standards in order to guide them when they are involved in business activities. In the corporate environment, however, one person may not be the only decision maker because decisions are made _____. As a result, a single individual may not be _____ for the actions of the corporation.

MULTIPLE CHOICE QUESTIONS

1. When a person is deciding that he or she will act in a particular way because it is morally right or just, he or she is making an ethical decision and will probably ask:
   A. Should I act this way because it is the fair or just thing to do?
   B. Should I act this way because I have been told to do so by my parents?
   C. Is there any law that requires that I act this way?
   D. Is there any law that prohibits me from acting this way?

2. Ordinarily, the decision to produce leather gloves with fur linings may not be an ethical one because it is based upon the manufacturer's analysis of the demand for and supply of such gloves. People may, however, argue that:
   A. If everyone kills animals, the skins and furs of which are used for the gloves, Kant's "categorical imperative" would be violated, and the manufacturer of the gloves is engaging in an unethical business activity.
   B. One has an absolute ethical duty **not** to kill animals other than for food.
   C. The killing of animals is morally wrong because the present loss of the animals will result in the future reduction of food for society.
   D. Each of the above may be true depending upon one's personal ethical standards.

3. The Acme Corporation has substantial accumulated profits. In determining whether to make a distribution of profits to the shareholders in the form of dividends or to retain the profits in order to expand the corporation's operations and/or increase the compensation that the corporation pays to its employees, the directors have a primary duty to:
    A. the shareholders to maximize short-run profits and, therefore, must declare a dividend.
    B. the shareholders to maximize long-run profits and, therefore, must use the current profits for purposes of expansion.
    C. the firm's employees and, therefore, must increase the wages and salaries that it pays to the employees.
    D. the shareholders to maximize profits, but must act in good faith in exercising their discretion when determining the best use to be made of accumulated profits.

Questions 4, 5, 6 , and 7 are based upon the following fact situation: Smith engages in the business of selling automobiles. He employs four people as salespersons: Asher, who is 42 years old and has worked for him for 18 years and whose salary is $55,000; Broom, who is 38 years old and has worked for him for 15 years and whose salary is $50,000: Carlton, who is a 25 year old male; and Daughty, who is a 25 year old female. Carlton and Daughty began working on the same day and receive the same salary of $25,000. Asher and Broom are excellent salespersons. In the past year, sales of automobiles have dropped and, as a result ,Smith's revenue and profits have fallen. Smith, therefore, contemplates reducing the number of salespersons whom he employs. In answering questions 4, 5, 6, and 7, assume that Smith is acting in a socially responsible manner when he determines that he will jeopardize the financial well-being of his business enterprise if he does not reduce the payroll.

4. In resolving the conflict between profit-making goals and ethical duties owed to his employees, which of the following question(s) should Smith try to answer?
    A. Does the duty that I owe to Asher and Broom, who have loyally worked for me for much longer than Carlton and Daughty, take precedence over my self interest in reducing cost?
    B. Should I offer Asher a financial incentive to retire? What would be a "just" or "fair" amount to give him?
    C. Should I discuss my financial difficulty with the four salespersons and ask if they will consider taking a reduction in their salaries until auto sales "pick up"? Would a 10% reduction be "fair"?
    D. All of the questions would be relevant to Smith's analysis.

5. If Smith believes that his ethical duty to his employees is more important than his duty to society, he will analyze his dilemma by reasoning that:
    A. The best solution is to discharge Broom and retain Carlton and Daughty. If I do this, I will reduce my costs by $50,000 and society will be harmed less because only one person will be unemployed.
    B. The best solution is to retain Broom and discharge Carlton and Daughty. If I do this, I will reduce my costs by $50,000 and retain a long-term loyal employee, even though society will be harmed because two people will be unemployed.
    C. The best solution is to put all four names in a hat and discharge the person whose name is drawn.

D. The best solution is to retain all the employees and incur a loss until I am insolvent at which time I will discharge all four employees.

6. If Smith believes that his ethical duty to society is more important than his duty to his employees, he will analyze his dilemma by reasoning that:
   A. The best solution is to discharge Broom and retain Asher, Carlton, and Daughty. If I do this, I will reduce my costs by $50,000, and society will be harmed less because only one person will be unemployed.
   B. The best solution is to retain Broom and discharge Carlton and Daughty. If I do this, I will reduce my costs by $50,000 and retain a long-term, loyal employee, even though society will be harmed because two people will be unemployed.
   C. The best solution is to discharge Carlton and retain Daughty because Daughty is a member of a protected class.
   D. The best solution is to retain all the employees and incur a loss until I am insolvent, at which time I will be able to discharge all four employees under the federal bankruptcy law.

7. Which of the following statements is correct?
   A. Even though some people might believe that Smith has made an unethical decision, a decision by Smith to discharge Asher does **not** violate the Age Discrimination in Employment Act.
   B. Even though some people might believe that Smith has made an unethical decision, a decision by Smith to discharge Broom does **not** violate the Age Discrimination in Employment Act.
   C. Even though some people might believe that Smith has made an unethical decision, a decision by Smith to discharge Asher and Broom does **not** violate the Age Discrimination in Employment Act.
   D. Smith does **not** have to make an ethical choice because he can solve the problem by discharging Carlton and Daughty.

8. United States laws impose more onerous safety obligations on owners of vessels registered under the U.S. flag than do the regulations of other countries. For example, all safety rules must be printed in English on U.S. flag ships. Which of the following reasons for registering a ship in Portugal would be the most persuasive to an ethical ship-owner that is a resident of the U.S.?
   A. Because a ship-owner can avoid expensive compliance with U.S. regulations, a ship-owner whose vessel is registered in Portugal can make more money.
   B. Because a ship-owner can avoid expensive compliance with U.S. regulations, a ship-owner whose vessel is registered in Portugal can make more money and will, therefore, pay more taxes to the U.S.
   C. A ship-owner whose vessel is registered in Portugal has the option of complying with those U.S. regulations that the ship-owner believes are important and yet can make more money because the ship-owner can avoid compliance with those U.S. regulations that it believes are unreasonable.
   D. A ship-owner whose vessel is registered in the U.S. and complies with all the regulations, including the printing of safety instructions in English, has no social responsibility to print safety instructions in Portuguese, the language in which all of its seamen are fluent.

Chapter 3
Courts and Alternative Dispute Resolution

An important source of law in the United States is case law — the rules of conduct that are determined by judges when they make decisions in cases that have been brought before them by parties who are involved in controversies. The way in which cases get to appropriate courts so that disputes can be adjudicated is the subject of this chapter. Often, the legal principles that become part of the body of law with which businesspersons will be concerned have been established by appellate courts. Material in this chapter deals with the federal and state court systems, and judicial and alternative methods of resolving disputes.

THINGS TO KEEP IN MIND

Normally, people recognize and properly perform their legal obligations or duties. In those instances in which a controversy arises between parties, one of the parties (the plaintiff in a civil action) may initiate a case in a court. Frequently, however, the issues between parties are settled or resolved without recourse to the courts.

OUTLINE

I.   The judiciary's role in American government.

    A. Judicial review — The judicial branch of government has the power to determine the constitutionality of actions taken by the legislative and executive branches of government.

    B. The federal courts have the power to determine the constitutionality of an Act of Congress (statutory law); this power of judicial review was established in the case of *Marbury v. Madison.*

    C. The federal courts have the power to determine if a state constitution or statute complies with the United States Constitution.

    D. The federal courts have the power to determine the constitutionality of action taken by the executive branch (e.g., *U.S. v. Nixon).*

II. Basic judicial requirements.

    A. Jurisdiction — The power or authority of a court to hear and decide a case.

        1. The court must have jurisdiction over the subject matter as well as the persons and/or property involved in the dispute when a case is before the court.

2. Jurisdiction over persons.

    a. Jurisdiction over the person (*in personam* jurisdiction) is required before a court can enter a judgment against a party in an action.

    b. Jurisdiction over persons is obtained when parties, who are residents of the state and/or can be served within the territorial boundaries of the state, are given notice that they are involved in suits (usually, by service of a summons).

    c. Long arm statutes.
        1) Long arm statutes enable state courts to obtain jurisdiction over persons who have committed wrongs even if those persons are non-residents and are outside the state.
        2) The nonresident must have had some minimum contacts with the state, or the cause of action (the subject matter of the action or lawsuit) must have arisen in the state.

    d. A corporation is considered to be a resident of a state in which it is incorporated, or has an office, or does intrastate business.

3. Jurisdiction over property.

    a. Jurisdiction over property or "over the thing" is also known as *in rem* jurisdiction.

    b. In a proceeding concerning property, the property must be within the territorial boundaries of the court in which the proceeding is brought.

4. Jurisdiction over subject matter.

    a. Limited (or special) jurisdiction.
        1) Some courts can hear only cases that deal with certain specified subject matters.
        2) Examples — Probate, family matters, small claims, and traffic violations.

    b. General jurisdiction — A court with general jurisdiction has the power to hear all kinds of controversies, except those that are appropriate for courts having limited jurisdiction.

5. Original and appellate jurisdiction.

    a. A court that has original jurisdiction is a trial court (a court of first instance) in which lawsuits begin, trials take place, and evidence is presented.

    b. A court that has appellate jurisdiction has the power to review decisions (as to law) that were made by lower courts.

6. Jurisdiction of the federal courts.

    a. The constitutional boundaries of federal judicial power.
        1) Article III of the United States Constitution provides that the judicial power of the United States is vested in the Supreme Court and in inferior courts that Congress may create [Section 1], and extends to cases in law and equity arising under the United States Constitution, statutes, and treaties [Section 2].
        2) Congress can control the number, kinds, and jurisdiction of federal courts, and the courts can promulgate rules narrowing the types of cases that they will hear.

    b. Federal questions.
        1) A federal question arises if a plaintiff's cause of action is based upon the United States Constitution, a treaty, or a federal statute.
        2) If a federal question is raised, the lawsuit can be commenced in a District Court, which is a federal court having original jurisdiction.

    c. Diversity of citizenship.
        1) Federal courts may have concurrent jurisdiction with state courts in civil suits when there is diversity of citizenship and the amount in controversy exceeds $75,000.
        2) Diversity of citizenship exists when:
            a) One or more of the parties is an individual (natural person) who is a citizen of or resides in a state that is different than that of another party to the controversy;
            b) One of the parties is a foreign country or a citizen of a foreign country; or
            c) One or more of the parties is a corporation which is incorporated in or has its principal place of business in a state which is different than that of another party to the controversy.

7. Exclusive versus concurrent jurisdiction.

    a. Concurrent jurisdiction exists when both federal and state courts have the power to hear and decide a case.
        1) The case can be commenced in either a federal or state court.
        2) Typically, this is so when there is diversity of citizenship.

    b. A court has exclusive jurisdiction if no other court has the power to hear a case.
        1) Federal courts have exclusive jurisdiction in cases involving federal crimes, bankruptcy, patents and copyrights, claims against the United States, admiralty (maritime) law, and other federal causes of action as provided for by statutes.
        2) The United States Supreme Court has exclusive jurisdiction when there is a dispute between two or more states.

3) State courts have exclusive jurisdiction in cases involving certain subject matters, such as violation of state criminal laws, divorce, and adoption.

B. Venue — The geographic area (defined in a statute) in which a particular court that has jurisdiction over the subject matter may hear and decide a case because the incident leading to the suit (the cause of action) occurred in the area or the litigants (the parties to the suit) reside in the area.

   1. A particular court may have power only to hear and decide cases that arose within its venue.

   2. There may be a change of venue in a criminal case when the defendant's rights to a fair and impartial trial have been impaired.

C. Standing to sue.

   1. An active party in a lawsuit is a litigant (i.e., a plaintiff or defendant).

   2. A person (the plaintiff) is a proper party to bring a suit if he or she has standing to sue — a legally protected and tangible interest at stake in the litigation.

   3. If a plaintiff lacks standing to sue, the court will not address the issue of whether or not there is a justiciable (real and not merely hypothetical) controversy.

III. The state and federal court systems.

A. State court systems — Most states have three levels of courts: trial courts, intermediate appellate courts, and courts of final appeal.

   1. Trial courts — Courts having original jurisdiction in which evidence is presented by the parties so that a judgment in a civil action or a verdict in a criminal prosecution can be entered on the record.

      a. Limited jurisdiction trial courts.
         1) May be referred to as special inferior trial courts or minor judiciary courts.
         2) Examples — Domestic relations (family) courts, local municipal courts, probate (surrogate) courts, small claims courts, traffic courts, and justice of the peace (magistrate) courts.

      b. General jurisdiction trial courts.
         1) May be called county, district, common pleas, superior, circuit, etc., courts.
         2) Trial courts having general jurisdiction hear all types of cases other than those handled in courts having limited jurisdiction.

    c. A trial court judge decides questions of law and a jury (if there is one) decides questions of fact; if there is no jury, the judge is the trier of both the law and the facts.

  2. Courts of appeal.

    a. In some states, a trial court that has general jurisdiction also may have appellate jurisdiction to hear appeals from a trial court, which has limited jurisdiction.

    b. Most, if not all, appellate courts are multi-judge tribunals.

    c. An appellate court has jurisdiction to review decisions of trial courts (based only upon the record of the case) in order to determine whether or not a trial court made an error as to law (questions of law) or procedure, but does not have the power to review questions of facts.

    d. Frequently, intermediate appellate courts are called courts of appeal.

    e. An appellate court may reverse a decision of a lower court if the lower court's decision was erroneous, in which case, ordinarily, the higher court will remand (send back) the case to the lower court; it is more usual, however, that the appellate court affirms the decision of the lower court.

  3. State supreme (highest) court.

    a. In a number of states, the highest courts are called supreme courts.

    b. Decisions of the highest court are final as to state law; if a federal constitutional issue is involved in a decision made by the highest court in a state, however, the decision may be appealed to the United States Supreme Court.

B. The federal court system.

  1. The United States Constitution provides for the creation of a Supreme Court and gives Congress power to create "inferior," or lower, courts [Article III, Section 1 and Article I, Section 8].

  2. Federal judges and the nine Justices of the United States Supreme Court are appointed by the President, with the advice and consent of the Senate [U.S. Constitution, Article III].

  3. United States District Courts.

    a. District Courts are federal trial courts with general original jurisdiction that have been created by Congress.

b. At the present time, there are 91 judicial districts and hundreds of district court judges.

4. There are other federal trial courts that have original limited jurisdiction, such as the U.S. Tax Court, U.S. Bankruptcy Courts, and the U.S. Claims Court (which hears suits against the United States), as well as administrative agencies that have judicial powers.

5. United States Courts of Appeals.

a. The Courts of Appeals for the twelve judicial circuits (one of which is the District of Columbia) have appellate jurisdiction to review cases decided by District Courts, other federal trial courts, and some administrative agencies.

b. The Court of Appeals for the Federal Circuit has limited appellate jurisdiction to hear cases relating to patents, claims against the United States, international trade, and some federal agencies.

c. Usually, a panel of three judges of a Court of Appeals will hear a case, but sometimes the entire court will sit *en banc* to hear an appeal.

6. The United States Supreme Court.

a. The Supreme Court is a constitutionally created court, provided for in Article III of the U.S. Constitution.

b. In a few rare instances (such as disputes among two or more states), the U.S. Supreme Court has original jurisdiction [Article III, Section 2].

c. Usually, the Supreme Court hears appeals from the Courts of Appeals for the various federal circuits and from the highest courts of the states when constitutional questions are raised.

d. The Supreme Court has discretion to determine whether or not it will hear an appeal, and it is the final arbiter of the Constitution and federal law.

7. How cases reach the Supreme Court.

a. Original jurisdiction.
   1) The United States Supreme Court has original exclusive jurisdiction in cases involving controversies between two or more states.
   2) The Supreme Court also has original concurrent jurisdiction in cases involving ambassadors or other public officials of foreign countries; controversies between the U.S. and a state; and controversies between a state and a citizen of another state or a foreign country.

b. Appellate jurisdiction.

    1)   A party does not have a right to appeal to the U.S. Supreme Court, but must request that the Court issue a writ of *certiorari* directing the lower court to send the Supreme Court the record of the case for review.

    2)   The Supreme Court may issue a writ of *certiorari* when:

        a)   An important constitutional issue is raised.

        b)   A court has decided a federal question that previously had not been determined by the Supreme Court.

        c)   The decisions of two or more federal Courts of Appeals are inconsistent with each other.

        d)   An appellate court has held that a federal law is invalid or has upheld a state law that has been challenged as violating federal law.

    3)   Most petitions for writs of *certiorari* are denied; denial is not necessarily considered to be a decision on the merits or agreement with the lower court.

    4)   The rule of four — A writ of *certiorari* is not issued unless approved of by four Justices.

IV. Alternative dispute resolution (ADR).

A. There are various methods for settling and resolving disputes outside the court system that save the time, expense, and publicity of litigation.

B. Negotiation.

    1. Negotiation is an informal process in which disputing parties come together, with or without attorneys, in an effort to settle differences.

    2. Mini-trials — A mini-trial is a private proceeding in which the attorneys argue the parties' cases often in the presence of a neutral third person who gives an opinion as to how the case most likely would be decided by a court.

    3. Early neutral case evaluation by a third party whose evaluation of the merits of the parties' positions is meant to facilitate a settlement of the dispute.

    4. In a summary jury trial (SJT), the parties present their evidence and arguments before a jury, which gives a nonbinding decision; after the decision, the parties are required to engage in negotiations.

    5. Voluntary conciliation occurs when a neutral third person assists the parties to reconcile their dispute by carrying proposals from one party to the other when the parties refuse to negotiate directly.

C. Mediation — A form of assisted negotiation in which the parties voluntarily meet with a neutral third person, a mediator (or a panel of mediators).

1. The mediator's role — A mediator plays an active role in negotiating a dispute by meeting with the parties, together and separately, and proposing a solution or alternative solutions.

2. The advantages of mediation.

    a. Mediation is not adversarial and reduces antagonism between the parties.

    b. Mediation is used successfully in labor and spousal disputes.

D. Arbitration.

1. Arbitration is more formal than negotiation, conciliation, and mediation, but is less formal than a judicial proceeding.

2. Court-mandated ADR.

    a. Federal courts refer cases for nonbinding arbitration.

    b. In many states, arbitration is an integrated part of the judicial procedure for settling civil disputes so that cases in which the amounts in controversy are less than certain specified sums are heard by arbitrators.

3. The arbitration process.

    a. Parties who have a dispute may voluntarily agree to have their dispute arbitrated by a third person, an arbitrator (or a panel of three arbitrators).

    b. Usually, arbitrators have expertise in the subject matter involved in the dispute.

    c. Parties, who submit to arbitration, agree to adhere to the decision (the award) of the arbitrator.

    d. Awards that have been made by arbitrators are enforced by the courts; usually, a court only reviews matters relating to law and accepts the finding of facts made by the arbitrator.

    e. Arbitration is a less formal, speedier, and less expensive alternative to having controversies resolved through the court system.

4. Arbitration clauses and statutes — State statutes and the Federal Arbitration Act provide for enforcement of arbitration clauses in contracts which state that, if the parties have an existing dispute or subsequently have a dispute, the parties will submit their disputes to arbitration.

5. The enforcement of arbitration agreements.

a. If a party to an agreement containing an arbitration clause refuses to submit to arbitration, a court will issue an order (for specific performance) compelling arbitration when the controversy is one that is arbitrable.

b. If parties have agreed to submit disputes to arbitration, a court may stay (suspend) or dismiss a judicial proceeding that is commenced by one of the parties.

6. Arbitrability.

a. Today, there is a strong public policy favoring enforcement of pre-dispute agreements providing for arbitration of future disputes between parties because:
1) Courts are reluctant to interfere with contracts that are voluntarily formed (freedom of contract); and
2) Alternative methods of dispute settlement are encouraged as a means of reducing heavy caseloads in the courts.

b. Arbitration statutes establish a policy favoring resolution of disputes by arbitration when parties have agreed to do so, except when there is a clear legislative "intent to preclude enforcement of arbitration agreements."

7. A court may set aside an arbitration award when:

a. The arbitrator exhibited bad faith or misconduct by refusing to hear relevant evidence, acted in a way that substantially prejudiced the rights of one of the parties, or clearly evidenced bias or partiality.

b. The arbitrator made an error as to law or exceeded his or her powers.

c. Enforcement of the award would result in the commission of a crime or violate a strong public policy.

E. Providers of ADR services include the American Arbitration Association, governmental agencies, and private organizations.

KEY WORDS AND PHRASES IN TEXT

judicial review
jurisdiction
jurisdiction over the person (*in personam*)
long arm statute
jurisdiction over property (*in rem*)
jurisdiction over subject matter
jurisdiction of federal courts
diversity of citizenship
exclusive jurisdiction
bankruptcy court

federal question
concurrent jurisdiction
venue
standing to sue
justiciable controversy
general jurisdiction
limited jurisdiction
trial courts with original jurisdiction
questions of law
questions of fact

trial courts having limited jurisdiction
probate courts
small claims courts
appellate jurisdiction
litigation
the federal court system
United States District Courts
United States Courts of Appeals
United States Supreme Court
writ of *certiorari*
rule of four
alternative dispute resolution (ADR)
court-mandated ADR

negotiation
mini-trials
neutral case evaluation
summary jury trial (SJT)
conciliation
mediation
arbitration
arbitration process
arbitration award
arbitration clauses and statutes
arbitrability
American Arbitration Association (AAA)

FILL-IN QUESTIONS

1. The power of a court to hear and decide a case is termed _____.

2. A court has _____ jurisdiction over the party who brings a case (the plaintiff). In order for the court's decision to be effective with regard to the other party to the controversy (the defendant), the court must have _____ jurisdiction over that person as well.

3. A long arm statute enables a state court to obtain jurisdiction over a nonresident when the nonresident has sufficient _____ with the state. This requirement is met, for example, when a corporation that is incorporated in the state of Delaware operates a factory in the state of Washington. As a result, a court in the state of _____ can exercise jurisdiction over the Delaware corporation in a case brought by an injured employee against the corporation.

4. Courts that have power to hear and to make determinations in cases involving most kinds of controversies, without regard to the subject matter, have _____ jurisdiction. Federal courts that have this type of jurisdiction include the _____.

5. Some courts have limited jurisdiction because they hear and make decisions only in cases dealing with particular specified subject matters. Federal courts, such as the _____ _____, have limited jurisdiction.

6. A court possessing the power to review decisions rendered by lower courts (which have original jurisdiction) has _____ jurisdiction. Federal court having such power include the _____. In the federal court system, the _____ is a court with original, general jurisdiction.

7. The power of a court to determine the constitutionality of a statute that was passed by the _____ branch of government, or an action that was taken by the executive branch, is referred to as the power of _____ .

8. Rather than resort to the courts for resolution of a civil dispute, parties may turn to _____ (ADR). The parties may agree to discuss the dispute in the presence of a third person, a _____, who will informally assist them in settling their disagreement; or the parties may agree to submit their dispute to _____, in which case one or more experts, called _____, will hear the dispute and render a legally binding decision.

MULTIPLE CHOICE QUESTIONS

1. A court having original jurisdiction would be the appropriate court in which to commence an action involving:
   A. the commission of a crime.
   B. a contract.
   C. a corporation.
   D. All of the above are correct.

2. A court having appellate jurisdiction would be the appropriate court in which to commence an action involving:

	The commission of a crime	A contract
A.	Yes	Yes
B.	Yes	No
C.	No	Yes
D.	No	No

3. An important function of the federal district courts is to:
   A. hear cases involving state criminal violations when a defendant asks for a change of venue.
   B. hear cases when there is diversity of citizenship or when federal questions are in controversy.
   C. hear appeals from state trial courts.
   D. review decisions made by intermediate state appellate courts.

4. A case in which one of the parties is a resident of Pennsylvania and the other party is a resident of Arkansas may be commenced in:
   A. an appropriate Pennsylvania or Arkansas court and then appealed as a matter of right to a U.S. (Circuit) Court of Appeals.
   B. a federal District Court because there is diversity of citizenship.
   C. a federal District Court if the amount in controversy exceeds $75,000.
   D. a U.S. (Circuit) Court of Appeals if the amount in controversy exceeds $75,000.

5. The United States Claims Court is a federal court that has:
   A. original, general jurisdiction.
   B. original, limited jurisdiction.

C. appellate jurisdiction over bankruptcy matters.

D. general, appellate jurisdiction.

6. The United States Court of Appeals for the Federal Circuit is::

A. a trial court that has original and appellate jurisdiction.

B. a court that has limited appellate jurisdiction.

C. a court that is provided for expressly in the United States Constitution.

D. a court that hears appeals from state trial courts.

7. Today, the power of the United States Supreme Court to review the constitutionality of Acts of Congress:

A. is well established.

B. has been successfully challenged because it was based upon the old decision of the Supreme Court in *Marbury v. Madison*.

C. does not exist because the doctrine of judicial review gives courts power to review only judicial decisions and actions of the executive branch.

D. is no longer available because of the 1981 Federal Reorganization Act that was passed by Congress.

8. A litigant has a right to appeal from a decision rendered by a state trial court:

A. to a court having original jurisdiction.

B. to a federal Court of Appeals.

C. when an error as to a fact has been made.

D. when an error as to law has been made.

9. Parties to a contract may agree that they will submit any disputes that may arise in the future to an arbitrator rather than commence a lawsuit. Which of the following statements is **false**?

A. A hearing before an arbitrator is similar to a trial, but is not conducted with the same formality as a trial before a court.

B. The arbitrator's decision is referred to as an award.

C. A court will enforce the arbitration agreement by compelling a party to submit a dispute to arbitration.

D. A court will never set aside a decision made by an arbitrator.

10. An arbitrator's award will be enforced by a court:

A. following a rehearing of the factual evidence by the court.

B. unless the arbitration award was contrary to law.

C unless the procedures followed by the arbitrator were the same as those used in the court.

D. only if the court has equity jurisdiction.

Chapter 4
Court Procedures

In the United States, the system of justice is adversarial. The parties to a civil dispute (the litigants), who usually are represented by attorneys, present their cases in a court proceeding or hearing that is presided over by a judge. The litigants in a civil case are the plaintiff, who initiates the proceedings, action, or lawsuit, and the defendant, the party against whom the action or suit is brought. Lawyers act as advocates for their clients. The judge acts in an impartial manner and is responsible for making determinations as to the appropriate law to be applied. The procedures that are used in a typical civil case are discussed and illustrated in this chapter.

Increasingly, businesspeople find themselves dealing with attorneys and litigation. The information in this chapter is meant to give you some knowledge of the rules under which the judicial system operates in the event that you become a party or are otherwise involved in litigation.

THINGS TO KEEP IN MIND

1. The purposes of the rules of civil procedure include assuring each litigant an opportunity to present his or her case in an orderly manner and removing the element of surprise.

2. A motion is a formal request to the court that the court make a decision as a matter of law. A decision that is made by a trial court judge granting or denying a motion may be appealed because it is a decision based upon law. Motions may be made before, during, and after a trial.

OUTLINE

I. Procedural rules.

    A. Procedural requirements, as to what must be done and at which stage in civil litigation (as opposed to criminal) process it is to be done, are set forth in rules of civil procedure.

    B. The Federal Rules of Civil Procedure (FRCP) govern civil trials in federal district courts.

    C. Each state has its own procedural rules that apply in the courts within the state, and each court has its own local rules that supplement the state rules of procedure.

II. Consulting with an attorney.

   A. Litigation is costly in terms of time and money.

   B. Legal fees.

      1. Fees are based upon the difficulty of the legal matter, the experience and skill of the attorney, and the amount of time and cost involved.

      2. Expenses covering filing charges and costs that directly relate to the case are not included in an attorney's fee.

      3. Types of fees.

         a. Fixed fees for performance of specified services.

         b. Hourly fees for expenditures of time.

         c. Contingent fees are specified, fixed percentages of clients' recoveries.

   C. Settlement considerations — Usually, there will be an initial meeting between a potential client and an attorney, during which the client and attorney discuss what may be necessary in order to resolve the dispute.

   D. A retainer agreement may be entered into by the attorney and client and a retainer fee paid by the client.

III. Pretrial procedures.

   A. The pleadings.

      1. The pleadings are documents that are filed with the court and served on (i.e., properly delivered to) opposing parties; pleadings give factual information regarding the claims of the parties and the issues involved in the case.

      2. The plaintiff's complaint (which may be called a petition or declaration).

         a. The complaint is filed by the plaintiff with the clerk of the court having original jurisdiction over the subject matter of the case.

         b. Contents — Statement of facts:
            1) Explanation of jurisdiction of the court.
            2) Basis for the plaintiff's cause of action entitling plaintiff to a remedy.
            3) Remedy that the plaintiff seeks.

         c. Service of process — A copy of the complaint with a summons (a direction to answer the complaint and to appear in court) is served on (i.e., delivered to) the defendant by a person who is not a party to the litigation and may be a sheriff or a deputy sheriff or other process server.

  1) Serving corporate defendants.
    a) Legal process (the summons and complaint) may be served on a corporate officer or registered agent of the corporation.
    b) The names and addresses of the registered agents are stated by corporations in documents filed in the secretary of state's offices in the states in which corporations are incorporated and in states in which corporations conduct intrastate business.
  2) Waiver of formal service of process — The FRCP provide that a defendant in a federal case may waive service in order to lengthen the defendant's response time from 20 to 60 days.

3. The defendant's response — The answer.

  a. In an answer (which becomes part of the pleadings), the defendant admits, denies, or otherwise challenges the legal validity of the plaintiff's claim.
    1) An answer may contain a counterclaim (or cross-complaint) in which the defendant sets forth his or her own claim or cause of action against the plaintiff.
    2) An answer may contain affirmative defenses if the defendant raises new facts showing that the plaintiff's case should be dismissed.

  b. The answer is filed by the defendant with the clerk of the court and a copy is served on the plaintiff.

4. The reply — Plaintiff may respond to issues raised in the answer by filing a reply with the clerk of the court and serving a copy of the reply on the defendant.

B. Dismissals and judgments before trial.

  1. The parties may negotiate a settlement or make pretrial motions in order to have a case dismissed.

  2. A motion is filed with the court and a notice of motion is serve on, or sent to, the opposing party.

  3. Motion to dismiss (or, in some states, demurrer).

    a Defendant asserts that the plaintiff has not stated a claim upon which relief can be granted (i.e., even if the alleged facts are true, defendant is not liable).

    b. Defendant may make a motion to dismiss based upon the court's lack of subject matter or personal jurisdiction, improper venue, etc.
      1) If the motion is granted:
        a) Defendant does not have to answer the complaint.
        b) Plaintiff may amend complaint — If a plaintiff does not amend the complaint, judgment will be entered against the plaintiff.

2) If the motion is not granted, the defendant is given an extension of time within which to answer the complaint.

c. Plaintiff may make a motion to dismiss if parties have reached an out-of-court settlement.

4. Motion for judgment on the pleadings — Either the plaintiff or the defendant or both may assert that, based upon the pleadings, there is no issue requiring a trial.

5. Motion for summary judgment — May be made by either or both parties.

a. A motion for summary judgment will be granted if there are no genuine questions of fact and the only questions are questions of law.

b. In considering a motion for summary judgment, the court may take into account evidence outside the pleadings, including affidavits (i.e., sworn statements refuting claims).

C. Discovery — Procedural devices for obtaining information before trial.

1. The purposes of discovery are to preserve evidence and testimony from witnesses (who might not be available at, or whose memories may fade before, the time of a trial) and to prevent surprises.

2. Depositions — Sworn testimony of witnesses given before and recorded by an authorized court official.

3. Interrogatories — Written questions submitted by one party to be answered in writing by another party to the litigation.

4. Request for admissions — Written requests made by one party that the other party admit the truth of certain matters involved in the case.

5. Request for documents, objects, and entry upon land.

6. Request for physical and mental examinations, which are subject to the right of privacy of the person being examined.

D. Pretrial conference.

1. Informal discussion between the judge and attorneys for the parties may be initiated by a party or the court.

2. The purpose of a pretrial hearing is to identify the matters that are in dispute and to plan the course of the trial.

E. The right to a jury trial.

1. Jurors are triers of facts and the judge is the trier of law; if there is no jury, the judge determines the facts as well as the law.

2. A person's right to have a jury trial may be limited.

   a. In a federal court, a party has a right to a jury trial in a suit at common law when the amount in controversy is more than twenty dollars [U.S. Constitution, Seventh Amendment].

   b. States have similar guarantees, but may have a higher dollar restriction.

   c. The right to a jury trial may be waived.

   d. In general, a person does not have a right to a jury trial in a case that is based upon an equitable cause of action.

   e. In some states, a jury may be composed of fewer than twelve people.

F. Jury selection.

   1. Jurors are selected from the rolls of voters and/or property owners.

   2. *Voir dire.* — Oral *voir dire* examination of prospective jurors is conducted in order to determine if a potential juror is biased or has any connection with a party to the action or a witness.

   3. Challenges during *voir dire.*

      a. Each party has a specified number of preemptory challenges, and each party also may challenge prospective jurors for cause.

      b. Prospective jurors may not be excluded based on discriminatory criteria.

   4. Alternate jurors are also chosen and seated if a juror has to be excused during a trial.

IV. The trial.

A. Rules of evidence govern the admissibility of evidence at a trial.

   1. Relevance.

      a. Relevant evidence is evidence that tends to prove or disprove a material fact that is in question or to establish the degree of probability of a fact.

      b. Relevant evidence may be excluded if its probative value is outweighed by other important considerations or its admission would detract, distract, or mislead the jury.

2. Hearsay evidence is testimony about a statement made by another person and usually is not admissible.

B. Opening statements are made by attorneys for the parties.

C. Examination of witnesses is conducted in accordance with rules of evidence.

1. Plaintiff's witnesses are first questioned by plaintiff's attorney in direct examination and then by defendant's attorney in cross-examination; plaintiff's attorney may conduct redirect examination followed by defendant's attorney in recross-examination.

2. Defendant's attorney may make a motion for a directed verdict (or, as it is called in the federal courts, a judgment as a matter of law) on the ground that, as a matter of law, the plaintiff has failed to present enough evidence to support the plaintiff's claim (a *prima facie* case).

3. Defendant's witnesses are next questioned by defendant's attorney in direct examination and then by plaintiff's attorney in cross-examination; defendant's attorney may conduct redirect examination followed by plaintiff's attorney in recross-examination.

4. Plaintiff's attorney may offer rebuttal, additional evidence to refute defendant's case; defendant's attorney may refute rebuttal in a rejoinder.

D. Closing argument — Each party's attorney presents a closing argument.

E. Jury instructions — The judge gives instructions (charges) to the jury as to the applicable law.

F. The jury's verdict.

1. The burden of proof.

a. In a civil action, a plaintiff must prove his or her case with a preponderance of evidence (i.e., evidence that is of greater weight or more convincing than that of the defendant).

b. This is different from the burden of proof in a criminal case, in which the state must prove the defendant's guilt beyond a reasonable doubt.

c. In some civil cases, plaintiff must prove his or her case by clear and convincing evidence.

2. After the jury deliberates and reaches a decision, the jury returns a verdict.

V. Posttrial motions.

A. Usually, the party who wins the case makes a motion for a judgment in accordance with the verdict.

B. Motion for new trial — Will be granted if the judge determines that the jury was in error, additional evidence is discovered, or that there was prejudicial conduct by participant or prejudicial error by the judge.

C. Motion for judgment notwithstanding the verdict (N.O.V.) — Will be granted if the judge determines that, even if the evidence is viewed in the light most favorable to the other party, the jury should not have found the verdict that it did.

D. The court enters judgment in favor of the "winning" party on the record.

VI. The appeal.

A. Filing the appeal — Either or both parties may appeal to a court having appellate jurisdiction by filing a notice of appeal with the clerk of the trial court.

   1. If there is an appeal, the party who appeals is called the appellant, or petitioner, and the other party is referred to as the appellee, or respondent.

   2. Record on appeal (including copies of pleadings, transcript of trial testimony, exhibits, rulings on motions, arguments of counsel, instructions or charge to jury, jury verdict, posttrial motions, and the order for judgment) is filed with the clerk of the appellate court.

   3. Typically, the appellant will also file an abstract and brief (containing a statement of the facts, the issues, the lower court's ruling and the arguments of the appellant supported by applicable statutory and/or case law); the appellee files an answering brief.

B. Appellate review.

   1. An appellate court does not hear any evidence but bases its decision upon the record, abstract, briefs, and oral argument of the attorneys.

   2. Usually, an appellate court affirms the lower court's decision, but it may reverse the lower court decision and/or remand the case (return the case to the trial court for a new trial or entry of an appropriate judgment) or modify the trial court's decision.

F. Higher appellate courts.

   1. A "losing party" may appeal the decision of an intermediate appellate court to the highest state court by filing a petition.

   2. Often, such petitions are denied.

   3. If the petition is granted, then the parties will file briefs, etc. with the court.

4. The highest state appellate court may affirm or reverse the decision of the intermediate appellate court and/or remand the case to the trial court for a new trial or entry of an appropriate judgment.

5. Only if a federal issue is raised, and then rarely in a civil case, will the United States Supreme Court consider a petition for a writ of *certiorari*.

VII. Enforcing the judgment — Methods of ensuring that the prevailing party receives the court's judgment are discussed in Chapter 31.

KEY WORDS AND PHRASES IN TEXT

adversarial system of justice
Federal Rules of Civil Procedure (FRCP)
state rules of procedure
types of legal fees (fixed, hourly, and
    contingent fees)
retainer agreement
pleadings
complaint
summons
service of legal process
registered agent of corporation
default judgment
motion to dismiss (demurrer)
answer
counterclaim
affirmative defense
reply
pretrial motion
motion for judgment on the pleadings
motion for summary judgment
affidavit
discovery
depositions and interrogatories
requests for admissions
requests for documents, objects, and
    entry upon land
requests for physical and
    mental examinations
pretrial conference
jury trial

jury selection
voir dire
preemptory challenge
challenge for cause
rules of evidence
relevant evidence
hearsay evidence
opening statements
direct examination
cross-examination
redirect and recross-examination
motion for directed verdict
prima facie case
rebuttal and rejoinder
closing arguments
burden of proof
preponderance of evidence
clear and convincing evidence
verdict
motion for new trial
judgment notwithstanding the verdict
    (judgment N.O.V.)
appeal
appellant (petitioner)
appellee (respondent)
brief
abstract
appellate review
affirm, reverse, and/or remand
reversible error

FILL-IN QUESTIONS

1. In the United States, there is a long-standing policy that the doors of the courts should be open to the people who have controversies in order that parties to disputes, which are otherwise not resolved, may avail themselves of the court system. It is referred to as an _____ system of justice in the sense that one person (who usually is called the _____) brings an action or lawsuit against another person (who usually is referred to as the _____).

2. Rules of _____ define how the parties to litigation are to proceed in order to bring cases to the courts and the process that will be followed when a case proceeds through the judicial system.

3. The party initiating a legal proceeding is called the _____. He or she commences the action by _____ _____.

4. In order for a court's decision to be effective with regard to parties to a controversy, a court must have jurisdiction over the litigants. By commencing an action or lawsuit, a _____ gives the court *in personam* jurisdiction over himself or herself. Jurisdiction over the defendant is conferred on the court when the defendant is properly served with a _____ and complaint.

5. A civil case is commenced when a _____ is filed with the court by the plaintiff. After the defendant is served with a summons and a copy of the _____, the defendant has a period of time within which to respond by filing an _____, a copy of which is delivered to the defendant or the defendant's attorney.

6. The complaint (in which the plaintiff states the facts upon which the plaintiff's cause of action is based and the remedy which the plaintiff is asking the court to grant) and the answer (in which the defendant responds) are referred to as the _____.

7. In order to save time and to limit the issues of a civil case being litigated, the parties may use pretrial procedures. For example, the defendant, who claims that the plaintiff has not stated a cause of action upon which relief can be granted, will make a motion _____. Either party desiring to preserve the testimony of a witness who will be unable to appear in court may request that a _____ be taken during the discovery process.

8. If there is a jury trial, the jury determines the _____ alleged in the case and the judge who presides at the trial determines and instructs the jury as to the _____. The judge's instructions to the jury as to the appropriate _____ is often called a charge.

9. Oral _____ examination of prospective jurors is conducted in order to determine if prospective jurors are biased or have any connections with a party to the action or to witnesses.

MULTIPLE CHOICE QUESTIONS

1. In a civil action, the party who is initiating the action must file in the court in which the action is being commenced:
   A. a summons.
   B. a summons and complaint.
   C. a complaint.
   D. a petition for a writ of certiorari.

2. The pleadings in a civil case include information about the parties' assertions and claims. The pleadings consist of the:

   I.   summons.
   II. complaint.
   III. answer.

   A. I and II.
   B. II.
   C. III.
   D. II and III.

3. In connection with a controversy brought to court, the term, "legal pleadings," refers to:
   A. the complaint filed by the plaintiff and the answer filed by the defendant.
   B. the reply filed by the defendant and complaint filed by the plaintiff.
   C. the trial of a case in court, with or without a jury.
   D. the procedure required in order to appeal a case to an appellate court after a trial.

4. During the pretrial period, a defendant who has received a complaint may make a motion to dismiss because:
   A. the plaintiff has failed to state a cause of action for which a court can give a remedy.
   B. the court does not have jurisdiction to hear the dispute.
   C. the defendant was not properly served with the summons and complaint.
   D. Each of the answers above is correct.

5. Processes for obtaining information before a trial begins are referred to as discovery and include:

   I.   interrogatories.
   II. depositions.
   III. preemptory challenges.

   A. II.
   B. III.
   C. I and II.
   D. I, II, and III.

6. During the pretrial period, a defendant who has received a complaint and not made a motion to dismiss is required to file an answer with the court.
   A. In the defendant's answer, the defendant may deny the allegations set forth in the complaint but **cannot** include a claim against the plaintiff.

B. If the defendant admits the allegations set forth in the complaint, the defendant **cannot** raise additional facts in order to assert an affirmative defense.

C. If the defendant does **not** file an answer, a default judgment may be entered against the defendant.

D. In the defendant's answer, the defendant may make a motion for a directed verdict.

7. The right to a jury in a trial held in a United States District Court:
   A. is provided for in the Federal Rules of Federal Procedure.
   B. is guaranteed in the Seventh Amendment to the United States Constitution if the amount in controversy is more than twenty dollars.
   C. is guaranteed in Article III of the United States Constitution if the amount in controversy is more than twenty dollars.
   D. may **not** be waived by a party.

8. In order for a civil court to enter a judgment in the plaintiff's favor:
   A. the plaintiff must prove his or her case with a preponderance of evidence.
   B. the plaintiff must prove his or her case beyond a reasonable doubt.
   C. the defendant must prove his or her case with a preponderance of evidence.
   D. the defendant must prove his or her case with clear and convincing evidence.

9. A litigant has a right to appeal from a decision rendered by a trial court:
   A. to a court having original jurisdiction.
   B. and on appeal the litigant may cross-examine witnesses.
   C. when an error as to a fact has been made.
   D. when an error as to law has been made.

10. A party in a civil law suit may appeal a decision made by a trial court by filing a notice of appeal with the clerk of the trial court. On appeal, the party seeking the review of the trial court's decision is referred to as:
    A. the plaintiff.
    B. the appellant or petitioner.
    C. the appellee or respondent.
    D. the judgment defendant.

Chapter 5
Constitutional Authority to Regulate Business

The Constitution of the United States of America is the supreme, or highest, law in this country [Article VI, Paragraph 2]. At the time of the ratification of the Constitution in 1788, the existing states delegated a portion of their sovereignty (the supreme power that nations possess) to the newly created national government. In this chapter, the focus is on those constitutional provisions that have an effect upon the legal environment in which business is conducted. The chapter includes an introduction to the Constitution and constitutional law, followed by sections relating to governmental powers that are derived from the Constitution and to Amendments to the Constitution that have significance for the conduct and regulation of business.

The Constitution is reproduced in Appendix B of the textbook.

THINGS TO KEEP IN MIND

1. The meanings of various provisions in the Constitution have been interpreted by the courts in tens of thousands of cases. (Samples of some of these decisions are presented in the text.)

2. Each state has a state constitution that also provides for distributing governmental powers among three branches of government. Many provisions in state constitutions are similar to those in the United States Constitution.

OUTLINE

I. The constitutional powers of government.

    A. Federalism —The Constitution addresses the relationship between the United States government and the states (and among the states) by providing for the division of governmental powers between the central (national) government and the states.

        1. The federal government has only those powers that are conferred upon it by the Constitution, which is a grant, or delegation, of enumerated powers or authority from the states to the federal government that the states established.

        2. The national government can exercise only those powers that expressly are conferred upon the government or may be implied (or inferred) because such

powers are necessary and proper for carrying out the government's expressly enumerated powers.

3. Any powers that are neither delegated to the national government nor prohibited by the Constitution are retained by the states or the people [Tenth Amendment].

4. Any rights which are not enumerated in the Constitution are reserved to the people [Ninth Amendment].

B. Separation of powers.

1. The Constitution provides for a government that is composed of three branches.

   a. The legislative branch [Article I] — Congress is empowered to make laws by enacting legislation (United States statutes).

   b. The executive branch [Article II] — The President has the duty to execute, or carry out, the laws of the United States.

   c. The judicial branch [Article III] — The power to hear and determine controversies arising out of the laws of the United States is vested in the United States Supreme Court and the inferior courts that are established by Congress.

2. Checks and balances system — Governmental functions are balanced (or distributed) among the three branches, each of which has checks on the other two branches.

   a. One branch may not exercise power that has been conferred upon another branch of government.

   b. Each branch has power, however, to check (or limit) the action of the other two branches.

C. Congress has power to legislate in areas that have importance for business [Article I, Section 8].

1. Congress has express power to make laws dealing with certain enumerated matters, such as interstate commerce and taxation [Article I, Section 8, Paragraphs 1 through 17].

2. Congress has implied power "to make all Laws which shall be necessary and proper for carrying into Execution" its express powers [Article I, Section 8, Paragraph 18].

D. The commerce clause — Congress may regulate commerce with other nations (and the Indian tribes) and among the states [Article I, Section 8, Paragraph 3].

1. Commerce among the states means interstate commerce.

2. Congress is not empowered to pass statutes regulating purely intrastate commerce (business that is conducted within a state).

3. The breadth of the commerce clause.

   a. The U.S. Supreme Court has held that intrastate activities that affect interstate commerce are subject to federal regulation.

   b. The Supreme Court has upheld the application of federal statutes to wholly local activities when the activities substantially affect interstate commerce.

4. The regulatory powers of the states.

   a. States possess police powers in order to protect the public health, safety, morals, and general welfare of their citizens.

   b. If a state statute imposes a substantial burden on interstate commerce, the statute may be held by a court to violate the U.S. Constitution.

   c. In general, there is a presumption that a state regulatory law is a valid and constitutional exercise of the police power by the state.

E. The supremacy clause [Article VI].

   1. State laws that conflict with the U.S. Constitution or federal statutes will not be enforced.

   2. Sometimes, the federal government and the states have concurrent or shared powers. If Congress, however, has chosen to act exclusively in regulating certain activities, the federal statute preempts, or takes precedence over, the state law.

F. The taxing and spending powers.

   1. The taxing power — Congress has the "power to impose and collect taxes, duties, imposts and excises" in order to raise revenue [Article I, Section 8, Paragraph 1].

      a. Duties, imposts and excises must be apportioned uniformly throughout the United States.

      b. Congress cannot tax exports [Article I, Section 9].

      c. Although the power of Congress to impose a uniform direct or individual tax originally was restricted in the Constitution [Article I, Sections 1 and 9], the Sixteenth Amendment gave Congress authority to impose an income tax without apportionment among the states.

    d. Congress may not regulate indirectly by taxation an activity that Congress is not authorized to regulate directly.

2. The spending power.

    a. Congress has the power to spend revenues (collected by the federal government) in order to pay the "debts and provide for the common defense and general welfare" [Article I, Section 8, Paragraph 1].

    b. Federal funds can be spent in order to carry out the enumerated powers of Congress and other worthwhile objectives.

II. Business and the Bill of Rights [Amendments I through X].

A. The Bill of Rights — The first ten amendments to the U.S. Constitution protect the rights of people against interference or intrusion by the federal government.

B. Many of the constitutionally protected rights, which are provided for in the Bill of Rights, apply to legal entities, such as corporations, as well as to natural persons.

C. The Fourteenth Amendment, which provides that the states "shall not deprive any person of life, liberty, or property, without due process of law," has been interpreted to mean that the states also cannot interfere with the rights guaranteed by the Bill of Rights.

D. The First Amendment protects the freedom of religion, speech, and the press and the rights of the people to assembly peaceably and to petition the government.

1. Freedom of speech.

    a. Freedom of speech is not absolute.

    b. Symbolic speech — Nonverbal expressions, such as gestures and articles of clothing, have been protected by the First Amendment.

    c. Commercial speech — Advertising and other speech by business firms.
       1) Commercial speech, such as advertising, is protected by the First Amendment to a lesser extent than noncommercial speech.
       2) A restriction on commercial speech is valid as long as the restriction:
          a) Seeks to implement a substantial government interest;
          b) Directly advances that interest; and
          c) Goes no further than necessary in order to accomplish its objective.

         d.   Corporate political speech — The U.S. Supreme Court has held that a state statute prohibiting corporations from using corporate funds to support political candidates was constitutional.

            1)   Corporate contributions constitute a form of political speech and, therefore, protected by the First Amendment.

            2)   A state, however, may limit corporations from making such contributions in the interest of preserving the fairness of political debate by ensuring that the wealth of corporations does not give them potentially unfair advantages over other voters.

         e.   Unprotected speech — The First Amendment does not protect defamation (libel, if it is written, or slander, if it is oral) or lewd and obscene speech.

   2.   Freedom of religion.

         a.   The separation of church and state — "The establishment clause."

            1)   Neither the national nor a state government may establish any one religion.

            2)   A governmental regulation that places a significant burden on religion is unconstitutional.

            3)   Government must make accommodations to all religions.

         b.   The free exercise of religion — Government cannot prohibit the free exercise of religious practices.

            1)   Government cannot infringe upon the free exercise of religion unless there is a compelling state interest in doing so.

            2)   Statutes prohibiting discrimination against persons because of their religion may require that private employers make reasonable accommodations for the religious practices of employees, unless doing so would cause undue hardships to the employers' business interests.

E.   Self-incrimination — The Fifth Amendment guarantees that a person cannot be compelled to incriminate himself or herself in a criminal case.

   1.   A person cannot be forced to give evidence (oral testimony or production of incriminating objects or documents) that may subject him or her to prosecution for a crime.

   2.   The guarantee against self-incrimination does not extend to legal entities (corporations and partnerships) which are not treated as natural persons.

F.   Searches and seizures — The Fourth Amendment prohibits unreasonable searches and seizures.

   1.   Search warrants and probable cause.

         a.   Federal, state, and local officers may not stop, search, or seize a person or his or her property without immediate justification, unless a warrant to do so has been obtained.

      b. Federal, state and local officers are required to obtain warrants in order to search or seize a person or property.

         1) Warrants may not be issued without showing that probable cause, or justification, exists to believe that a crime has been or is being committed.

         2) A warrant must fully describe the person or place to be searched and/or the person or property to be seized.

   2. Searches and seizures in the business context.

      a. An unannounced government inspection cannot be conducted without a warrant that was obtained with justification by showing the existence of a general and neutral enforcement plan.

      b. Warrants are required to examine and obtain records of business firms that are clients of lawyers and accountants when the records are in the hands of the firms' lawyers and accountants

III.   Other constitutional protections.

  A. The privileges and immunities clause — "The Citizens of each State shall be entitled to all Privileges and Immunities of Citizens in the several States" [Article IV, Section 2, first paragraph].

    1. If certain rights, benefits and advantages are given to residents of a state, that state must afford the same rights, benefits, and advantages to nonresidents of the state.

    2. A state may discriminate against nonresidents who engage in basic and essential activities within the state's boundaries if:

      a. There is a substantial reasons for treating nonresidents differently than the state treats its own residents; and

      b. The reason for the discrimination is closely related to the state's purpose in adopting a statute or regulation.

    3. The Fourteenth Amendment provides that no "state shall make or enforce any law which shall abridge the privileges and immunities of citizens of the United States" and protects U.S. citizens from infringement of certain rights by states.

  B. The full faith and credit clause — "Full faith and credit shall be given in each State to the public Acts, Records, and judicial Proceedings of every other State" [Article IV, Section 1].

    1. This clause applies to civil matters.

2. Official records (e.g., deeds and judgments) in one state, must be recognized, honored, and enforced in other states.

3. A court in a state that is deciding a case involving a cause of action that arose in another state must apply principles of law found in the statutes and judicial decisions of the state in which the cause of action arose.

C. Due process — No person may be deprived "of life, liberty, or property, without due process of law" by the national government [Fifth Amendment] or a state [Fourteenth Amendment].

1. Procedural due process — Any governmental action, which amounts to a taking of life, liberty, or property, must be conducted in a fair, nonarbitrary, and nondiscriminatory manner.

2. Substantive due process — The content (or substance) of legislation or regulations must be in harmony with the U.S. Constitution.

a. Economic (business related) regulations, therefore, merely must relate rationally to a legitimate governmental purpose.

b. If a law or governmental action limits a fundamental right, the law or action must be necessary in order to promote a compelling or overriding public interest.

D. Equal protection — A person may not be denied "the equal protection of the laws" [Fourteenth Amendment].

1. Because the Fifth Amendment due process clause has been interpreted as including the concept of equal protection of the laws, the prohibition against denial of this protection extends to the federal government as well as the state governments.

2. Governments cannot impose burdens or legal obligations upon some people and not on others (e.g., establish classifications) unless there is a rational reason based upon legitimate governmental interests to distinguish among the different groups of people.

3. When a law distinguishes between classes or individuals, a court applies three standards to determine if the distinction is discriminatory.

a. "Strict scrutiny" is applied to any law that affects a fundamental right.

b. "Intermediate scrutiny" is applied when the issue in a case involves gender or birth legitimacy.

c. The "rational basis" test is applied when there is a legitimate governmental interest that may outweigh an individual right.

E. Privacy rights — The Ninth Amendment provides that just because the rights of people (such as the right to privacy) are not protected specifically by (or enumerated in) the U.S. Constitution does not mean that the people do not have such rights.

IV. Constitutional law in cyberspace — The spread of Internet communications has led to new inquiries involving basic constitutional rights.

A. Regulating online obscenity — The Communications Decency Act makes it a criminal offense to make obscene images available to minors.

B. Cryptography and constitutional protection — The increase in computer use has been accompanied by protection of different forms of coded data.

1. Encrypted data and criminal law — It is unclear whether or not a government can compel disclosure of computer encrypting information.

2. Encryption source codes and free speech.

a. The International Traffic in Arms Regulations requires any firm that wishes to export encryption software or products containing encryption components to obtain a license.

b. The U.S. District Court for the Northern District of California ruled (in 1996) that a cryptographic code is a protected form of speech.

C. Free speech and unwanted electronic mail.

1. Electronic leaflets — The issue of whether or not the right of free speech applies to transmission of "electronic leaflets" is unresolved.

2. Courts may be asked to determine if unwanted electronic mail is protected or if it can be regulated.

3. Other issues — See Chapters 9 and 45.

KEY WORDS AND PHRASES IN TEXT

United States Constitution
amend
federal form of government
separation of powers
branches of government
executive branch
legislative branch
judicial branch
checks and balances
enumerated power of Congress

commerce clause
interstate commerce
intrastate commerce
police power
supremacy clause
preemption of area for regulation
        by federal government
taxing power
spending power
Bill of Rights

right to privacy

freedom of speech

defamatory speech (libel and slander)

symbolic speech

political speech

commercial speech

unprotected speech

freedom of religion

establishment (of religion) clause

free exercise of religion

reasonable accommodation

privilege against self-incrimination

unreasonable searches and seizures

search warrant

probable cause

privileges and immunities clause

full faith and credit clause

due process clause

procedural due process

substantive due process

equal protection clause

strict scrutiny

intermediate scrutiny

rational basis test

FILL-IN QUESTIONS

1. The structure of government in the United States is based upon the concept of federalism. As a result, some governmental _____ are exercised by the United States government and others by the _____.

2. The Tenth Amendment provides that those powers which have neither been delegated to the United States government nor prohibited by the Constitution, are retained by the _____ or the people.

3. The United States Constitution provides for the division of governmental functions among three branches of government. The power to enact statutes is given to the _____ branch, composed of the Senate and _____ _____. The executive branch is responsible for executing the laws of the United States. The functions of the executive branch are performed by the _____. The third branch is the _____ which is composed of the courts.

4. The first ten amendments to the Constitution are know as the _____.

5. The enumerated powers of Congress are set forth in Article I, Section 8 of the United States Constitution. They include the power to regulate _____ with foreign countries, with the Indian tribes, and among the several _____, and the power to raise revenue through taxation. Import taxes, duties, and excise taxes must be _____ throughout the United States.

6. The right to be free from _____ searches and seizures is protected by the Fourth Amendment. This amendment also provides that search warrants and arrest orders shall only be issued after law enforcement officials establish that there is _____ cause to believe that the search or arrest is justified. It also provides that the premises to be searched or the _____ or _____ to be seized must be described fully.

7. The Fifth Amendment prohibits double jeopardy and guarantees that a _____ cannot be compelled to testify against himself or herself. This

privilege against self-incrimination does not extend to artificial organizations or entities, such as _____ and _____.

8. In the future, courts may be required to decide if unwanted electronic mail should have the same _____ as other forms of speech.

MULTIPLE CHOICE QUESTIONS

1. The Constitution of the United States was a delegation of power by the states to the federal government. As a result:
   A. all governmental powers are exercised by the federal government.
   B. only the federal government has the power to impose an income tax.
   C. the states delegated their "police powers" to the national government.
   D. the states retain some sovereignty.

2. Certain enumerated powers, including the power to regulate interstate and foreign commerce and the power to tax in order to raise revenue to pay the expenses of government, were delegated to the Congress of the United States by the:
   A. states of the United States.
   B. United States Supreme Court.
   C. Bill of Rights.
   D. Fourteenth Amendment to the United States Constitution.

3. The President of the United States **cannot** establish a law which regulates interstate commerce because:
   A. the power to legislate is vested in Congress.
   B. of the concept of separation of powers among the branches of government.
   C. Congress has been given the express power to regulate commerce among the several states.
   D. All of the answers above are correct.

4. The executive branch of government has certain "checks" on the other branches of government. For this reason, the President has the power to:
   A. veto an Act of Congress.
   B. remove a member of Congress from his or her position.
   C. overrule a decision of a federal court.
   D. enter into a treaty with a foreign nation.

5. Because of the interstate commerce clause found in Article I, Section 8 of the Constitution, Congress has the power to regulate:
   A. the weight of trucks on interstate highways.
   B. the manufacture of automobiles with specified safety features.
   C. the activities of real estate brokers who are licensed in the state of Louisiana if the brokers' activities substantially affect interstate commerce.
   D. All of the answers above are correct.

6. Laws providing for taxes on products that are being imported into the United States may be enacted by:

A. a state legislature with the approval of the governor.
B. treaties entered into with other nations by the President without the consent of the United States Congress.
C. the United States Congress with the approval of the President.
D. None of the answers above is correct.

7. Laws providing for taxes on products that are being exported from the United States may be enacted by:
A. a state legislature with the approval of the governor.
B. treaties entered into with other nations by the President without the consent of the United States Congress.
C. the United States Congress with the approval of the President.
D. None of the answers above is correct.

8. When Congress passes a statute that is approved by the President relating to a subject over which the states and the federal government have concurrent power:
A. an existing state law that contains similar provisions automatically is invalid.
B. a state law is invalid only if Congress has expressly stated in the legislation that the federal statute is meant to preempt state laws relating to the same subject matter.
C. the federal law preempts state statutes if Congress indicated that Congress intended that the federal law was to supersede state law.
D. Congressional action cannot supersede state statutes when both the federal and state governments have concurrent power.

9. The police power of state governments:
A. was granted to the states in the United States Constitution.
B. was granted to the states in an Act of Congress.
C. is limited to enacting and enforcing statutes relating to crimes.
D. is the basis for state statutes regulating public health.

10. A state statute prohibits restaurants from employing people with contagious diseases as food handlers. If a case involving the statute arises, the court is likely to rule that:
A. the state has power to enact such a statute and its enforcement does not violate the interstate commerce clause of the United States Constitution.
B. a federal statute to similar effect preempts the state law.
C. the state statute is unconstitutional because enforcement of the law results in a substantial burden on interstate commerce.
D. the state statute is contrary to the due process clause in the Fourteenth Amendment of the United States Constitution.

11. The Fifth Amendment to the Constitution of the United States provides that no person shall "be deprived of life, liberty, or property, without due process of law." This provision:
A. also is contained in the Fourteenth Amendment which protects people from actions by state governments that violate the rights specified in the Bill of Rights.
B. is superseded by the Fourteenth Amendment.

    C. means that, as long as a statute is procedurally fair, the statute can be enforced even though it is substantively unfair.

    D. means that Congress cannot impose an excise tax.

12. Although most speech is protected by the Constitution, the federal government may regulate:

    A. computer generated photographs of naked men that are published on the Internet.

    B. the use of computer encryption.

    C. the publication of access codes.

    D. All of the answers above are correct.

13. A state may regulate:

    A. waste entering that state from another state by taxing the out-of-state waste.

    B. statements on package labels on products produced in other states.

    C. computer games on the Internet that include sexual content and are aimed at children.

    D. The contents of newspapers.

Chapter 6
Torts and Strict Liability

A tort is a civil wrong, other than a breach of contract, committed against a person or a person's property. As members of society, we each have rights to be free from unjustified interference by other people with our legally recognized interests. Because of tort law, tangible interests (such as a person's interest in being free from bodily harm and in being able to use and to enjoy his or her property) and intangible interests (such as privacy, family and other relationships, reputation, and dignity) are protected. As members of society, we also have reciprocal obligations, or duties, to avoid interfering with other people's recognized rights and interests. A tort is committed when there is a breach of a duty that is owed by the wrongdoer or tortfeasor (the defendant) to the injured party (the plaintiff), and that breach is the proximate cause of the injury incurred by the plaintiff. Conduct may be tortious because of an intentional act or because of a failure to exercise reasonable care. In some instances, strict tort liability is imposed without regard to fault.

THINGS TO KEEP IN MIND

1. A function of the law of torts is to compensate an injured party whose legally recognized interests have been interfered with by another person (the tortfeasor) so that responsibility for a loss caused by the wrongful conduct of the tortfeasor is borne by the wrongdoer (the tortfeasor), rather than the victim.

2. In order to recover for a tort, a plaintiff must show that the defendant's breach of duty not to harm the plaintiff was the direct cause of the plaintiff's injury.

3. If a plaintiff is alleging that a defendant was negligent, it is not necessary to show that the defendant's conduct was intentional. If liability is imposed because of strict liability, it is not necessary to establish the wrongful intent or negligence of the defendant.

OUTLINE

I.   The basis of tort law.

    A. Torts and crimes compared.

        1. A crime is a public wrong committed against the state, or society as a whole, and is defined in a statute — If the state (which prosecutes the alleged

criminal) is successful in proving that the defendant committed the crime, a penalty (e.g., imprisonment and/or a fine) is imposed.

2. A tort is a civil wrong consisting of unreasonable, wrongful conduct by one person (the tortfeasor) that results in an injury to the person or property of another person and for which the tortfeasor should compensate the injured person.

   a. The injured party brings a civil action or suit against the tortfeasor.

   b. If the injured party proves that a tort was committed by the defendant, a judgment is entered against the defendant who usually will be required to pay monetary damages to the injured party.

3. A wrongful act may be both a crime and a tort; if so, the wrongdoer may be prosecuted by the state for the criminal wrong as well as sued by the victim for the tort, the civil wrong.

4. Some wrongful acts are crimes but not torts; other wrongful acts may be tortious but are not treated as criminal wrongs.

B. Torts and breaches of contract compared.

1. When parties form contracts, they make promises concerning their future conduct and, therefore, create their own obligations; breaches of contracts occur if parties to contracts fail to carry out obligations (duties) that were created by the parties themselves.

2. Torts are violations, or breaches of, duties that are imposed by law.

3. Punitive damages may be awarded by a court in a tort case, but punitive damages rarely are given as a remedy in a breach of contract case.

4. In some cases, a person (e.g., a professional) may be liable both for a breach of contract and the tort of negligence for a failure to perform duties properly.

C. Categories of torts:

1. Intentional torts — An intentional tort is committed when a tortfeasor willfully commits an act which causes damage to another person's interests (i.e., the defendant's breach of the duty to refrain from intentionally harming others persons was the proximate cause of the injury to the plaintiff or to the plaintiff's property).

2. Unintentional torts.

   a. Negligence — Negligence occurs when a tortfeasor's careless act injures another person or his or her property (i.e., the defendant's breach of the duty to exercise reasonable care was the proximate cause of an injury to the plaintiff or to the plaintiff's property).

    b. Nuisance — Unreasonable and substantial interferences with the health, safety, comfort, or rights of other people to use or enjoy their property.

    c. Strict tort liability — Liability may be imposed, without regard to fault, upon those who engage in certain activities, the consequence of which is harm to other people.

II. Intentional torts against persons.

  A. An intentional tort is committed if the tortfeasor consciously intended to perform an act that results in an interference with the person, property, or business interests of another person in a way that is not permitted by law.

    1. One is assumed to intend the normal consequences of one's acts; as long as the plaintiff shows that the tortfeasor intended to do the act, it is not necessary to show that the defendant actually intended to injure the plaintiff or intended to cause the particular injury which the plaintiff sustained.

    2. The plaintiff must have incurred an injury, loss, harm, or a wrong to or invasion of a protected interest; it is not necessary that the injury be a physical or financial one.

  B. Assault and battery.

    1. Assault — An intentional, unexcused act that creates in another person a reasonable apprehension or fear of immediate harmful or offensive conduct. (The interest that is protected is freedom from apprehension of harmful or offensive contact.)

    2. Battery — An intentional unexcused, harmful, or offensive physical contact. (The interest that is protected is freedom from interference with personal security and safety.)

    3. Compensation — An injured party, who proves that there was an intentional, offensive contact, may be compensated for physical harm, emotional harm, and/or loss of reputation.

    4. Defenses to assault and battery.

      a. Consent negates the wrongful nature of the conduct, and, therefore, liability for any normal damage.

      b. Self-defense — A person is privileged to use whatever force is reasonably necessary to prevent real or apparent harmful, offensive contact.

    c. Defense of others — A person can act in a reasonable manner in order to protect others who are in real or apparent danger of being harmed.

    d. Defense of property — A person can use reasonable, but not excessive, force in order to protect his or her possession of property.

C. False imprisonment — Unreasonable, intentional, and present confinement, restraint, or detention of a person without justification. (The interest protected is the freedom to move without restraint.)

    1. The confinement may be due to physical barriers, physical restraints, or threats of physical force, to which the detained person does not agree.

    2. Merchant protection statutes — Reasonable detention of a suspected shoplifter is permissible if there is justified or probable cause to believe that the suspect is taking or interfering with a merchant's property.

D. Intentional infliction of emotional distress — Extreme and outrageous conduct that exceeds the bounds of decency accepted by society and which results in severe emotional or mental pain, anxiety, or distress.

E. Defamation — Breach of the duty to refrain from making false statements that harm another person's good reputation, esteem, or respect by holding the person up to contempt, ridicule, or hatred.

    1. Slander — Oral defamatory statements or utterances.

    2. Libel — Written defamatory statements or communications.

    3. The publication requirement — The defamation must have been communicated to a person other than the defamed party.

    4. Damages for defamation.

        a. General damages compensate the plaintiff for disgrace or dishonor in the community, humiliation, injured reputation, emotional stress, and other general harm.

        b. Special damages may be awarded for libel; special damages may be awarded for slander, only when the plaintiff incurred an actual economic or monetary loss.

        c. Statements that are slander *per se* (in and of themselves) — Proof of actual damage is not required if the statement was made that a person has a loathsome communicable disease, committed improprieties while engaging in a profession or trade, committed or has been imprisoned for a serious crime, or that an unmarried woman is unchaste.

    5. Defenses to defamation:

    a. Truth of the statement is an absolute defense.

    b. Privileged speech.
       1) An absolute privilege or immunity is given for communications made in judicial and legislative proceedings.
       2) A qualified privilege exists when there is a common interest between the person who makes the statement and the person to whom the statement is communicated or by a person writing a letter of recommendation or evaluation of an employee.

    c. Public figures, such as government officials and employees or people in the public limelight, must prove that the defamatory statements were made with actual malice (i.e., with knowledge of their falsity or reckless disregard of the truth).

  6. Online defamation.

    a. Defamatory statements made over the Internet are accessible to other people and, therefore, probably actionable libel.

    b. Defamatory statements made in "chat boxes" or "virtual rooms" may be treated as slander.

F. Invasion of the right to privacy.

  1. Use of a person's name, picture, or other likeness without permission for commercial purposes.

  2. Intrusion upon a person's affairs or seclusion.

  3. Public disclosure of information placing a person in a false light.

  4. Public disclosure of private facts about an individual that an ordinary person would find objectionable.

G. Fraudulent misrepresentation. [Additional explanation is found in Chapter 16.]

  1. Elements:

    a. Misrepresentation of facts with knowledge that the representation is false or a representation that is made with reckless disregard for the truth;

    b. Intent to induce another person to rely upon the misrepresentation;

    c. Justifiable, reasonable reliance on the misrepresentation by the deceived party;

    d. Damage suffered by the deceived party as a result of his or her reliance on the misrepresentation; and

e. Causal connection between the misrepresentation and the injury incurred by the deceived party.

2. Puffery, or seller's talk, is distinguishable from actionable fraud.

III. Intentional torts against property.

A. Trespass to land (real property).

1. Real property consists of land, things below the surface, and things that are affixed to the land.

2. The tort of trespass occurs when there is a wrongful interference with another person's exclusive right to possession of real property by entering onto the land, causing anything or anyone to enter onto the land, remaining on the land, or permitting anything to remain on the land, even though there is no actual harm to the land.

3. Trespass criteria, rights, and duties — The trespasser is liable for damage caused to the property.

a. The trespasser assumes the risk of injury and cannot recover from the owner for personal injuries; today, in many states, there are exceptions to this common law rule:
1) Attractive nuisance doctrine.
2) In some cases, owners have a duty to warn of dangerous conditions.

b. An owner has the right to remove the trespasser by using reasonable force and the right to remove another person's property using reasonable care.

4. Defenses against trespass to land include consent.

B. Trespass to personal property.

1. Personal property, or personalty, consists of all things, other than real property, that are capable of being owned.

2. Trespass occurs when there is a wrongful interference with another person's exclusive right to possession and enjoyment of tangible (moveable) personal property.

C. Conversion — Wrongful taking and retention of personal property, to which a person has no right, with the intent of exercising dominion or control over the property in a manner that is inconsistent with the rights of another person.

1. Wrongdoer is liable for the value of the property.

2. A purchaser of stolen goods is liable for conversion to the true owner of the property.

3. Defenses to conversion include superior title or right to possession and necessity.

IV. Negligence.

A. Unintentional failure to exercise reasonable care under the circumstances, so that a foreseeable risk to another person is created, resulting in an injury to the plaintiff.

B. Elements of negligence.

1. The duty of care and its breach.

   a. Each person owes a duty of exercising reasonable care so as to avoid harming other people.

   b. A breach of the duty occurs when a person fails to exercise reasonable care.

   c. Whether or not a person's act, or failure to act, is unreasonable depends upon the nature of the act, the manner in which the act is performed, the nature of the injury, and the social usefulness of the act.

   d. The reasonable person standard — The factual question that is asked is: how would an objective, reasonable person act under the circumstances?

   e. Duty of landowners — Landowners are required to use reasonable care to prevent injuries to people who come upon their land.
      1) A landlord, who rents to tenants, owes a duty of care to tenants and the tenant's guests.
      2) Business firms, which invite people to come upon their premises, owe duties to protect business invitees against foreseeable risks about which the business firms know or should have known.

   f. Duty of professionals.
      1) A person who has superior knowledge, skill, or intelligence is held to a higher standard of care than other people.
      2) A person who provides professional services may be liable for malpractice if he or she violates the duty of care.

   g. No duty to rescue — Although there may be an ethical duty to do so, the duty of exercising reasonable care does not extend to warning or rescuing people in danger.

2. The injury requirement and damages.

    a. The plaintiff must have incurred a legally recognized injury in the form of a loss, a wrong, or an invasion of a protected interest.

    b. The plaintiff, who has suffered an injury, will receive the remedy of compensatory damages and may recover punitive damages.

3. Causation — The plaintiff's injury must have been caused by the defendant's failure to exercise reasonable care.

    a. Causation in fact.
       1) The "but for test" — The defendant's breach of duty to exercise reasonable care was a cause of the plaintiff's injury if the injury would not have occurred "but for" the defendant's act.
       2) The "substantial factor test" — When the defendant's act occurs in conjunction with another event, and each of the events would cause the plaintiff's injury, the defendant's act is a cause of the injury if the defendant's act was a "substantial factor" in bringing about the injury.

    b. Proximate cause (legal cause).
       1) A negligent defendant's responsibility and liability extend only to anticipated, foreseeable consequences of his or her acts and to those people who foreseeably may be injured if he or she is careless.
       2) Foreseeability test — A victim can recover damages only upon proving that, under the circumstances, a reasonable person would have foreseen a risk of injury to the particular victim.

C. Defenses to negligence.

1. Assumption of the risk — Plaintiff, expressly or impliedly, knowingly, and voluntarily placed himself or herself in a situation involving risk.

2. Superseding intervening cause.

    a. If a subsequent, unforeseen event or force was the cause of the injured party's damage, the causal connection between the original negligence of the wrongdoer and the victim's injury is broken, and liability may not be imposed upon the negligent party.

    b. A negligent party is not relieved of liability if an intervening occurrence is foreseeable. It is considered to be foreseeable that:
       1) A person who has been personally injured because of a wrongdoer's tortious act may develop a subsequent disease, illness, or reaction, or receive improper medical care.
       2) A person whose property is endangered may be injured in an attempt to protect the property.
       3) A person who is physically endangered may take defensive action.
       4) Rescuers may attempt to aid an imperiled victim and be harmed.

2. Contributory and comparative negligence.

   a. In the few states, in which the common law theory of contributory negligence is applied, a plaintiff whose own negligence contributed to his or her own (the plaintiff's) injury cannot recover from a negligent defendant.
     1) The injured party bears the entire burden of his or her financial loss.
     2) Last clear chance doctrine — A negligent plaintiff may be able to recover if the negligent defendant had the "last clear chance" to prevent injury to the plaintiff.

   b. Comparative negligence — This doctrine has been adopted in most states and applies when the plaintiff's negligence contributed to his or her own injuries.
     1) The amount of damages is apportioned between the plaintiff and defendant (based upon the relative fault of each of the parties) so that the plaintiff's damages are reduced by a percentage representing the degree of the plaintiff's contributing fault.
     2) In some states, a plaintiff cannot recover if the plaintiff's negligence was equal to or greater than the negligence of the defendant; in some states, a plaintiff cannot recover if the plaintiff's negligence exceeded the negligence of the defendant; in other states, a plaintiff can recover even if the plaintiff's negligence exceeded that of the defendant.

D. An enhanced-injury theory may apply when there are separate events (an initial event and a second event that caused a more severe injury).

E. Special negligence doctrines and statutes.

1. *Res ipsa loquitur* ("the facts speak for themselves" or "the thing speaks for itself").

   a. Usually, the plaintiff has the burden of proving that the defendant was negligent.

   b. The burden, however, may be shifted to the defendant, who must prove that he or she was not negligent, when there is an inference, or presumption, of the defendant's negligence because of the *res ipsa loquitur* doctrine.

   c. *Res ipsa loquitur* may apply when:
     1) The event is one that ordinarily does not occur in the absence of negligence;
     2) The event was caused by an agency or instrumentality within the exclusive control of the defendant;
     3) The event must not have been due to any voluntary action or contribution on the part of the plaintiff; and
     4) In some states, the evidence available to explain the event must be more accessible to the defendant than to the plaintiff.

2. Negligence *per se* (in and of itself) — A defendant may be liable because of negligence *per se* (as a matter of law) if the defendant has been found guilty of a crime, the commission of which injured the plaintiff.

3. "Danger invites rescue" doctrine — A tortfeasor also may be liable for injuries suffered by a third person in attempting to rescue or aid a party who is in danger because of the wrongful conduct of the tortfeasor.

4. Special negligence statutes.

    a. Good Samaritan statutes relieve people, who voluntarily come to the aid of others, from liability for negligence.

    b. Dram shop acts impose liability on sellers and/or servers of alcoholic beverages to third parties who are injured because of the intoxicated condition of the buyer; in some states, similar liability is imposed upon social hosts who serve intoxicating beverages.

V. Strict liability — Liability without fault and without regard to a defendant's intent or exercise of reasonable care.

A. Origins of strict liability — In the English case of *Rylands v. Fletcher* (1868), the rule was established that, if a person uses his or her real property in a "nonnatural" or abnormal manner, creating a peril to others, that person is liable for resulting injuries to other people, without regard to his or her intentional conduct, creation of a nuisance, or negligence.

B. Abnormally dangerous activities — People who engage in dangerous activities that create an extraordinary risk of harm are liable in tort for injuries sustained by anyone who suffers as a result of the activity if:

1. The activity involves a high degree of risk that cannot be guarded against completely even with the exercise of reasonable or extraordinary care;

2. The risk is one that involves potentially serious harm; and

3. The activity is one that is not commonly performed in the geographic area.

C. Other applications of strict tort liability.

1. Owners of animals may be liable to people who are harmed by the animals.

2. Manufacturers of products are held strictly liable for damages for injuries caused by their products in many states. [See Chapter 8.]

3. Strict liability is imposed upon certain bailees who are given possession of goods in conjunction with contracts of bailments. [See Chapter 49.]

4. Employers are strictly liable to their employees for injuries sustained in the ordinary course of their employment under workers' compensation statutes. [See Chapters 35.]

5. Employers and principals are strictly liable for torts committed by employees and agents who are acting within the ordinary course of their employment. [See Chapters 34 and 35.]

KEY WORDS AND PHRASES IN TEXT

torts
compensatory damages
punitive damages
intentional torts
tortfeasor
assault and battery
defense of consent
self-defense
defense of others
defense of property
false imprisonment
defense of probable cause
infliction of emotional distress
actionable
defamation
slander
libel
publication of defamatory communication
privileged speech (and communications)
public figures
actual malice
slander *per se*
truth as an absolute defense
invasion of the right to privacy
fraudulent misrepresentation or fraud
puffery (seller's talk)
trespass to land (real property)

trespass to personal property (personalty)
conversion
negligence
duty of (exercising reasonable) care
reasonable person standard
breach of duty of care
business invitees
duties of professionals
malpractice
legally recognized injury
causation in fact
proximate cause
foreseeability
assumption of the risk
superseding intervening cause
contributory negligence
comparative negligence
last clear chance
res ipsa loquitur
negligence *per se*
danger invites rescue doctrine
Good Samaritan statutes
dram shop acts
strict liability
abnormally dangerous activities
product liability

FILL-IN QUESTIONS

1. A _____ is a civil wrong for which an injured party may recover damages from a person who has caused a personal, physical injury or who has harmed another person's property interests.

2. Some torts are intentional torts because the defendant intended to commit a particular act. Intentional torts, such as defamation and battery, are wrongs against the

_____. Other torts, such as trespass and conversion, are wrongs against _____.

3. An _____ occurs if one person threatens to inflict immediate bodily harm on another person who, therefore, reasonably becomes fearful or apprehensive that he or she will incur physical harm. If the threatened act is performed intentionally and results in harmful or offensive physical contact, the tort of _____ has been committed. In either or both instances, it is possible that the defendant may raise a defense, such as: _____, self-defense, _____, or _____.

4. _____ is the unjustified intentional restraint or confinement of a person. A merchant who suspects that a customer is shoplifting may detain the customer without liability if there is probable cause to believe that the customer has taken the merchant's goods and the detention is conducted in a _____ manner and for a _____ period of time.

5. One who makes false and defamatory statements about another person may be liable for the tort of libel, if the statement is _____, or slander, if the statement is made _____. Usually, in an action based upon defamation, _____ is an absolute defense.

6. A person is liable for the tort of negligence if he or she causes an injury to the person or property of another person because of a failure to exercise the _____ that a reasonable person would exercise. There are, however, defenses that can be raised by a defendant in an action based on negligence. Such defenses include supervening (intervening) cause, _____.

7. Strict tort liability may be imposed upon a person who engages in an abnormally _____ that has a high degree of risk which cannot be guarded against completely and normally is not conducted in the community or geographic area.

MULTIPLE CHOICE QUESTIONS

1. A tort action may be based upon:
   A. negligence.
   B. an intentionally caused injury.
   C. strict liability.
   D. All of the answers above are correct.

2. The following is a tort:
   A. a breach of duty (owed by one person to another) which produces an injury, even though the person who breached the duty did not actually know that he or she owed a duty.
   B. a breach of duty (owed by one person to another), which was provided for by a contract, so that he or she knew that a duty was owed to the other party.
   C. a crime that results in no injury to another party, such as "running a stop sign" when no other car or person is in the vicinity.

  D. All of the above are torts.

3. If John punches Jim without provocation, John has committed:
  A. assault.
  B. an assault and a battery.
  C. a nuisance.
  D. negligence.

4. A store owner observed that a woman in a black coat took merchandise from a shelf and placed it into a shopping bag that the woman was carrying. The store owner did not see the woman's face. At the time, there were five female customers in the store who were wearing black coats and carrying shopping bags. The store owner will **not** be liable for false imprisonment:
  A. if the store owner detains all five women, who were wearing black coats and carrying shopping bags, and questions the women in his office for three hours. This is so because the store owner has probable cause to believe that one of the women has taken the merchandise.
  B. if he stops and detains one woman for five minutes after the woman has left the store, and the woman admits that she took the merchandise and did not pay for the merchandise.
  C. if the store owner locks the doors to the store and detains all the customers for ten minutes. This is so because the store owner is justified in believing that one of the customers has been shoplifting.
  D. if the store owner locks the doors to the store and detains all the customers for ten minutes in a state that has enacted a merchant protection statute.

5. A person commits the tort of trespass to real property without a defense when she:
  A. parks her car in another person's driveway in order to attend a party at that person's home.
  B. recovers her car which she left on the owner's property after attending a party at the owner's home.
  C. drives into another person's driveway, after skidding on ice and, therefore, losing control of her car.
  D. parks her car in a neighbor's driveway because there is no room in her own driveway.

6. Mr. House's home was destroyed by a fire, which had been caused by Pyro when Pyro knocked over a kerosene heater that House had placed in front of the entrance to his home.
  A. Pyro can successfully raise the defense of contributory or comparative negligence if Pyro is sued for negligence by House.
  B. Pyro can successfully raise the defense of assumption of the risk if Pyro is sued for an intentional tort by House.
  C. Pyro is strictly liable to House for the tort of arson.
  D. Pyro is **not** liable to House for the tort of trespass if House invited him into his home, and House did **not** incur a personal injury.

Questions 7 and 8 are based on the following fact situation: Donna was driving in an erratic manner on an interstate highway at a speed of eighty miles per hour when she was observed by police officers. The police officers put on their siren and sped after her. Donna became "flustered" when she realized that the police officers were trying to stop her. Donna, therefore, carelessly put pressure on the accelerator, rather than the brake, causing her car to collide with Victoria's vehicle. As a result, Victoria's property was damaged, and Victoria suffered personal injuries.

7.   Victoria may successfully sue:
     A. the police officers who are strictly liable for the personal injuries suffered by Victoria.
     B. the police officers and Donna for false imprisonment because Victoria was unable to extricate herself from the wreckage for ten minutes.
     C. Donna, who, as a result of her failure to exercise reasonable care, caused both property damage and personal injuries to Victoria.
     D. Donna, who, as a result of her failure to exercise reasonable care, is liable to Victoria for the property damage but not for Victoria's personal injuries.

8.   If Victoria sues Donna, Donna may:
     A. successfully raise the defense of comparative negligence (or contributory negligence) if Victoria was also speeding and driving in an erratic manner.
     B. win the case because the action of the police officers was a superseding, intervening event that broke the causal connection between Donna's negligence and Victoria's injuries.
     C. successfully raise the defense of assumption of the risk because a person who drives on an interstate highway assumes the risk of injury.
     D. **not** raise any defense because her conduct was the basis for Victoria's suit based on an intentional tort.

9.   In a state following the comparative negligence doctrine, a plaintiff, who incurred $100,000 in damages but is found to have been ten percent contributorily negligent, would be entitled to:
     A. recover $90,000 as damages in a civil suit.
     B. recover $100,000 as damages in a civil suit.
     C. recover $10,000 as damages in a civil suit.
     D. no recovery of damages in a civil suit.

10. A building contractor was constructing a new store on Main Street and used a small amount of dynamite in order to blast a large rock formation. Ingersoll's car, which was parked a block away, was demolished by a large boulder that was catapulted through the air by the blast. Which of the following statements is correct?
     A. The building contractor is relieved of liability to Ingersoll because the contractor used extraordinary care in order to prevent harm to property in the vicinity.
     B. Because Ingersoll saw that the building contractor was using dynamite when she parked her car, Ingersoll assumed the risk of the car being damaged.
     C. The contractor is liable to Ingersoll for the tort of trespass to property.
     D. The building contractor is strictly liable to Ingersoll for the damage to Ingersoll's car even though no personal, physical injury was incurred by Ingersoll.

Chapter 7
Basic Business Torts

There is a strong public policy favoring the free private enterprise system and competition in business in the United States. Competition, however, must be conducted fairly. For this reason, certain types of intentional conduct engaged in by business firms are treated as being wrongful. This is so when the activities are contrary to accepted ideas of fair methods of competing and doing business. In some cases, wrongful interference with the business rights of other people or firms is tortious. The business torts discussed in this chapter include interference with contractual and other business relationships, appropriation, disparagement, and business defamation in "cyberspace." The concluding section of the chapter addresses business fraud under the Racketeer Influenced and Corrupt Organizations Act (RICO). This federal statute provides that violators of RICO can be held liable in civil suits to injured parties as well as criminally liable.

THINGS TO KEEP IN MIND

Certain unfair practices, such as restraints of trade, price discrimination, and unfair labor practices, also are prohibited by statutes that provide for both criminal and civil liability. See Chapters 47 and 35.

OUTLINE

I.   Wrongful interference.

    A. Intentionally interfering with the business rights of others may be wrongful and, therefore, a tort; the interests being protected may be based upon a contractual or noncontractual relationship.

    B. Wrongful interference with a contractual relationship — Elements:

        1. A valid, enforceable contract must have existed between two parties, one of whom is the plaintiff;

        2. A third person (the defendant/tortfeasor) must have known that the contract existed; and

        3. The third person (the tortfeasor) intentionally must have induced or caused one of the parties to the contract not to perform his or her contractual duties

(i.e., a breach of contract, which is not a tort) in order to advance the economic, or financial interests of the third person (the tortfeasor).

C. Wrongful interference with a business relationship.

   1. Use of abusive or predatory business practices, not for the purpose of making a profit or advancing a fair legitimate business interest, but rather in order to interfere with or injure another person's business relationship or prospective economic advantage.

   2. Elements:

      a. A business relationship (which need not be based upon a contract) must have existed between the plaintiff and another person or persons;

      b. The defendant, without justification, must have interfered intentionally with the relationship in a manner that was unfair according to contemporary business standards; and

      c. The plaintiff must have been damaged (i.e., sustained a recognized injury) as a result of the defendant's interference with the relationship.

D. Defenses to wrongful interference — Some activities that have the effect of interfering with business interests of competitors are permissible and, therefore, not tortious.

   1. Normal and fair competitive attempts to attract customers, such as aggressive marketing and advertising strategies, are permitted.

   2. Unless there is an associated illegal activity or a statutory prohibition, it is permissible to cut prices, give discounts or rebates, negotiate secretly behind a rival's back, refuse to do business with a competitor, or refuse to deal with other people until they stop doing business with a competitor.

II. Appropriation — The use of a person's name, likeness, or identifying characteristics, without permission and for the benefit of the user, is an interference with the right to privacy, which includes the right to the exclusive use of one's identity.

III. Disparagement of property.

A. Slander of quality (trade libel) — Unprivileged publication of economically injurious falsehoods about another person's products.

   1. Plaintiff must show that a third person refrained from dealing with the plaintiff because of the disparaging publication.

   2. Plaintiff also must show that publication of the injurious false statement was the proximate cause of actual pecuniary loss or damage to the plaintiff.

B. Slander of title — Unprivileged publication of injurious, untrue statements about the title to property that results in financial loss to the owner of the property.

IV. Business defamation in cyberspace.

 A. Defamation includes:

 1. Libel or slander that injures a person in his or her profession, business, or trade or adversely affects a business entity's credit rating, prestige, business character, or dealings with others.

 2. Unprivileged publication of injurious derogatory or disparaging false information that injures another person's business reputation and prospects for future advantageous business relationships.

 B. Online service providers (OSPs) are liable for defamatory statements that they publish, but not necessarily liable for defamatory statements generated by third party users of their services.

 C. The status of online service providers.

 1. Usually, an OSP that distributes defamatory material is not liable, unless it knew or had reason to know of the defamatory content of the material.

 2. An OSP that publishes a defamatory statement is republishing, or repeating, the statement and, therefore, may be liable for defamation.

 3. An OSP that holds itself out as exercising editorial control may be considered to be a publisher and, therefore, liable for defamation.

 D. The Communications Decency Act of 1996 [See Chapter 5.] — The Act regulates the transmission of obscene and pornographic material but specifically does not consider OSPs to be publishers.

V. Racketeer Influenced and Corrupt Organizations Act (RICO).

 A. Criminal and civil liability are provided for in RICO, a federal statute, the purpose of which was to curb the entry of organized crime into legitimate business enterprises.

 B. Activities prohibited by RICO.

 1. It is a federal crime to use income obtained from a pattern of racketeering activities to purchase any interest in an enterprise; to acquire or maintain an interest in an enterprise through a pattern of racketeering activity; to conduct or participate in the affairs of an enterprise through a pattern of racketeering activity; or to conspire to do any of these things.

2. RICO incorporates by reference twenty-six federal crimes (such as securities fraud and mail fraud) and nine state felonies (such as gambling, arson, and extortion).

C. Civil liability under RICO.

1. The United States government may seek civil penalties, including divestiture of a defendant's interest in a business enterprise or dissolution of a business firm.

2. People who also have been injured may bring civil suits and may recover treble damages (three times the amount of the actual damages), costs, and reasonable attorney's fees.

3. In interpreting RICO, courts have held that:

   a. Commercial fraud may be treated as a racketeering activity.

   b. An injured party can recover in a civil RICO suit, even if the defendant was not convicted of a RICO violation.

   c. An injured party must establish that there was a "pattern of racketeering activity." (This has been interpreted to mean continuity of the prohibited activity over a substantial period of time.)

   c. An economic motive is not a requisite for RICO liability.

   d. An employer may be liable for a RICO violation perpetrated by an employee when the employer derived some benefit from the violation.

KEY WORDS AND PHRASES IN TEXT

business torts
unfair competition
wrongful interference with a
        contractual relationship
wrongful interference with a
        business relationship
competitive conduct distinguished
        from predatory activity
appropriation

disparagement of property
slander of quality (trade libel)
slander of title
defamation in cyberspace
online service provider (OSP)
Racketeer Influenced and Corrupt
        Organizations Act (RICO)
treble damages
pattern of racketeering activity

FILL-IN QUESTIONS

1.   There is a strong public policy in the United States favoring free _____.
     Some types of business conduct are viewed as wrongful, however, because such
     conduct is unfair and not in accordance with accepted standards for those engaging in

business. For this reason, tort liability may be imposed upon a person who intentionally disturbs and interferes with business relationships that exist between other people whether or not those relationships are based upon _____.

2. A person is liable in _____ for wrongfully interfering with a contractual relationship between other people when he, she, or it knew that a valid, enforceable contract existed between the parties to the contract, and he, she, or it _____ caused or induced one of the parties to the contract to violate the terms of the contractual agreement.

3. Super Sales, Inc. knew that Everett had a two-year contract of employment with IT Corp. when Super Sales, Inc. willfully (intentionally) induced Everett to resign from his position as sales manager for the IT Corp. in order to assume a similar position (at a higher salary) with Super Sales, Inc. IT Corp. may recover from Everett for breach of the employment contract. In addition, IT Corp. may also recover from Super Sales, Inc. for the tort of _____, because (a) Super Sales, Inc. knew that a valid and enforceable _____ existed between Everett and _____ , and (b) Super Sales, Inc. induced Everett to repudiate the terms of his contract with his employer in order to advance its own pecuniary interests.

4. Disparagement of property is an intentional tort that occurs when economically injurious, _____ statements are made about another person's property or products. An unprivileged publication of a false statement relating to another person's goods or products that proximately results in a financial or pecuniary loss is referred to as _____. An unprivileged publication of a false statement relating to another person's legal ownership of property that results in a financial or pecuniary loss is referred to as _____.

5. Munston and Nagle are competing sellers of automotive parts. On Monday, Munston placed an advertisement in the local newspaper in which it was falsely stated that the auto batteries sold in Nagle's store were defective. On Wednesday, Munston placed an advertisement in the newspaper in which it was falsely stated that the tires available for sale in Nagle's store had been stolen. Because of the advertisement in the newspaper on Monday, Nagle may sue Munston for the intentional tort of _____. Because of the advertisement in the newspaper on Wednesday, Nagle may sue Munston for the tort of _____. Nagle will have to show in both cases that, as a proximate result of Munston's actions, he incurred an actual _____ loss.

6. Hoop Corporation and RBA, Inc. are business competitors. The president of Hoop Corporation gives an antique car to Olsen, who is an employee of RBA, Inc., in exchange for a list of RBA, Inc.'s customers. RBA, Inc. may sue Hoop Corporation in a civil suit based upon tort because Hoop Corporation has intentionally interfered with the _____ relationship that RBA, Inc. has with its employee, Olsen.

MULTIPLE CHOICE QUESTIONS

1. In order to induce Luton to lend Sterling $10,000, Sterling promised to repay the loan and told Luton that Sterling was the owner of a money-making machine but needed funds to buy paper. Luton has not been repaid and brings a lawsuit against Sterling based on tort.
    A. Luton's contributory negligence will prevent Luton from recovery for an intentional tort.
    B. Luton will **not** be able to recover for the tort of fraud because Luton's reliance on the representation made by Sterling was unreasonable.
    C. Luton will **not** be able to recover for the tort of fraud because Sterling's representation did not result in any injury to Luton.
    D. Luton will be able to recover for the tort of interference with a contractual relationship.

2. In April 1997, Sanders entered into a valid, enforceable contract with the owners of the Bumblebees, a professional soccer team, and agreed to act as coach for two years. New State University had a soccer team with a record of one win and twenty losses in the past two seasons. As a result, attendance at its games was poor and gate receipts were almost zero. In March 1998, New State University offered Sanders a position as head soccer coach at a salary that was triple what he was receiving from the Bumblebees. Sanders accepted the offer and subsequently refused to perform his coaching duties for the Bumblebees. The Bumblebees may recover from:
    A. Sanders for the tort of failing to carry out his contractual duties.
    B. Sanders because of strict liability.
    C. New State University because it wrongfully interfered with a contractual relationship.
    D. New State University in tort only if it had exercised bad faith or acted with malice.

Questions 3 and 4 are based on the following fact situation: Archibald was an architect. Reginald, a local businessman, employed Archibald to prepare plans for a new building. Reginald was dissatisfied with the plans. Reginald orally told Columbo that buildings, for which Archibald prepared the plans, were unsafe. As a result, Columbo canceled a contract that she had with Archibald. In addition, Reginald posted a message on his home page, in which he stated that Archibald was not properly licensed. Architectural Online Service copied Reginald's message and distributed the false statement that Archibald was not properly licensed to engage in the profession.

3. Archibald can successfully sue Reginald for the tort of:
    A. defamation.
    B. slander.
    C. maliciously interfering with business relationships.
    D. All of the answers above are correct.

4. Which of the following statements is correct?
    A. Archibald will be successful if he sues Columbo for the tort of breach of contract.
    B. Archibald will be successful if he sues Reginald for slander based upon the oral statement made by Reginald to Columbo.

C. The message posted on Reginald's home page was **not** defamatory.

D. Because Architectural Online Service merely copied the false statement made by Reginald, Architectural Online Service is **not** liable for defamation.

5. The Racketeer Influenced and Corrupt Organizations Act (RICO) is a federal statute which:

A. provides that plaintiffs in civil actions, who prove that defendants have violated RICO, may recover treble damages.

B. requires that the government prove that violators of RICO engaged in the offenses for which they are being prosecuted in conjunction with organized criminals.

C. requires that plaintiffs in civil actions prove that violators of RICO engaged in the offenses for which they are being prosecuted in conjunction with organized criminals.

D. provides that a civil action can be brought by an injured person against a corporate violator of RICO for dissolution of the corporation.

6. KYQ Co. has been convicted under RICO (Racketeer Influenced and Corrupt Organizations Act) of using income derived from racketeering activities to purchase an interest in the LZR Corporation. Zebra, a shareholder in LZR Corporation, can establish that he has incurred a one million dollar loss because of KYQ Co.'s wrongful activities and has had to pay attorneys' fees. Zebra may bring a civil suit and recover a maximum of:

I.   One million dollars.
II.   One million dollars and atttorneys' fees.
III. Three million dollars.
IV.   Three million dollars and attorneys' fees.

A. I.
B. II.
C. III.
D. IV.

Chapter 8
Product Liability

If a manufactured product is defective, the product may be the cause of personal or property injuries to the purchaser or a third person, such as another user of the item or a bystander. Typically, the product was the subject matter in a chain of numerous sales transactions and, as a result, many sellers may have potential liability to those injured by the defective item. Who bears the burden of liability is determined by the theory of law upon which the injured person bases his or her cause of action. Liability for defective products may be imposed based upon the tort of negligence, the intentional tort of misrepresentation, and, in many states, strict tort liability. In addition, liability may be based upon the contract theory of warranty that is discussed in Chapter 25.

The diagram below illustrates the numerous potential parties. Some may be parties because they have been injured and are plaintiffs; others may be parties because they were in the "chain" of purchases and sales. Note that often it is the remote user or bystander, rather than the ultimate buyer, who will seek to impose liability on one of the sellers in the vertical chain of sales.

Producer of component part

↓

Manufacturer of product that caused damage because of defect

↓

Wholesaler or other distributor of product

↓

Retail seller of product

↓

Buyer of product from retail seller

↓

Remote injured party

> Second-hand purchaser
>
> Donee or guest in home
>
> Lessee or other user
>
> Bystander

THINGS TO KEEP IN MIND

1. In the diagram, those in the vertical chain are potential defendants. The retail buyer and remote parties represent potential plaintiffs. The retail buyer may be a defendant as well as a plaintiff.

2. In many states, people who are injured because of defective products also may recover from the manufacturers and other sellers for injuries caused by the defects in the products based upon warranty theories that are discussed in Chapter 25. For this reason, people who have been injured by products rely upon multiple theories of law and include all potentially liable parties in their lawsuits.

OUTLINE

I.   Negligence.

    A. Negligence is an area of tort law. [See Chapter 6.]

    B. In an action based upon the defendant's negligence, the plaintiff must prove that:

       1. The defendant owed a duty to exercise the degree of care that a reasonable, prudent person would exercise under the circumstances;

       2. There was a breach of the duty to exercise due (reasonable) care by the defendant;

       3. The plaintiff incurred a legally recognizable injury; and

       4. The breach by the defendant of the duty to exercise due (reasonable) care was the proximate cause of plaintiff's injury.

    C. In order to recover against a manufacturer (as well as any other seller of the product) for an injury that resulted from a defective product based upon the tort theory of negligence, the plaintiff must prove that:

       1. A duty of exercising care was owed by the defendant;

          a. A manufacturer must exercise due care in the design of a product, selection of the materials used in producing the product, utilizing appropriate production processes, assembling and testing the product, placing adequate warnings on the label, and inspecting the product; and

          b. It must have been foreseeable to the manufacturer that, unless the product was carefully made, the product would be unreasonably dangerous when used in the expected manner;

       2. The manufacturer failed to exercise due care;

       3. The plaintiff was injured; and

4. The manufacturer's failure to exercise due care was the proximate cause of the plaintiff's injury.

D. Privity of contract not required.

1. In an action based upon the tort of negligence, an injured party need not show that privity of contract existed between the injured party and the defendant; the injured party, therefore, need not be a buyer of the product.

2. A manufacturer of a defective product is liable to any person who the manufacturer should expect to be endangered by the negligently made product.

E. Violation of statutory duty.

1. Federal and state statutes impose duties upon manufacturers of goods that are purchased for consumption with regard to labeling, advertising, selling, etc.

2. A violation of such a statutory duty may be treated as negligence *per se* (inherently, or in and of itself, a failure to exercise reasonable care).

II. Misrepresentation — See also Chapters 6 and 16.

A. Fraudulent misrepresentation — A buyer who is injured, because the buyer reasonably relied upon a representation of a material fact that was false and intentionally or recklessly made in order to induce a contract, may recover for the tort of fraud.

B. In contrast to tort actions based upon negligence and strict liability, the plaintiff in a suit based upon fraudulent misrepresentation does not have to show that the product was defective or malfunctioned.

C. Nonfraudulent misrepresentation — In many jurisdictions, if a misrepresentation of a material fact is innocently made by a seller, without the intention of deceiving a buyer, the buyer also may recover in tort for the injuries that the buyer incurred because of the misrepresentation.

III. Strict liability — See also Chapter 6.

A. The strict tort liability theory is suggested in Restatement (Second) of Torts and is used in some cases in order to impose liability upon manufacturers and other sellers of defective products without regard to their intentional conduct or their failure to exercise reasonable care.

B. In some states, a seller may not be liable for property damage or economic losses.

C. The Restatement of Torts — Section 402A, which currently is being revised for the Restatement (Third) of Torts.

1. The injured party does not have to establish privity of contract and may be a bystander.

2. The injured party does not have to prove that the defendant failed to exercise reasonable care as the injured party would have to establish in an action based upon negligence.

3. Public policy reasons for adoption of strict liability theory.

   a. Consumers should be protected from unsafe products.

   b. Manufacturers and distributors should not escape liability merely because they are not in privity of contract with an injured party who is harmed when a defective product is used.

   c. Manufacturers and other sellers of products are in better positions to prevent and to bear the costs associated with injuries caused by their products than are the injured parties or society because the costs ultimately can be passed on to all consumers in the form of higher prices.

D. Requirements of strict product liability summarized — An injured party (including a bystander) has a cause of action (based upon strict liability) against the seller of a defective product if the injured party can show that:

1. The product was in a defective condition when it was sold by the defendant;

2. The defendant normally engaged in the business of selling the product;

3. The defect caused the product to be unreasonably dangerous to the user or consumer, or to his or her property, when the product was used for its ordinary purpose (in most states);

4. The plaintiff incurred a physical (personal) injury or property damage because of the use or consumption of the product;

5. The defective condition was the proximate cause of the plaintiff's injury or damage; and

6. The product reached the plaintiff without any substantial change in the product's condition after its sale by the defendant.

E. Product defects and strict liability claims — A product may be unreasonably dangerous to the buyer, user, consumer, or other people because of a:

1. Flaw in the manufacturing process.

2. Design defect.

a. A plaintiff must show that a safer, feasible, alternative design was available, but the defendant failed to use it.

b. A defendant may show that the benefits of the design outweighed the risks of the design.

c. Factors that may be considered include the product's utility and desirability, availability of other safer products, prior identification of the danger, obviousness of the danger, normal expectation of danger, probability of injury, avoidability of injury, reasonable foreseeability of misuse, and viability of eliminating the danger without appreciably impairing the product's function or greatly increasing its price.

3. Inadequate warning — A supplier of a product has a duty to warn users of product-associated risks and dangers including harm that can result from the misuse of the product.

F. Market-share liability — In some jurisdictions, when a plaintiff is unable to prove which of many sellers of a harmful product supplied the particular product that caused plaintiff's injury, industry-wide liability may be imposed and allocated based upon the respective market shares of multiple sellers of the product.

G. Other applications of strict liability.

1. Strict liability has been imposed upon suppliers of component parts and lessors of goods.

2. Lessees of goods can recover based upon strict liability or breach of an implied warranty that the leased goods will be fit for the duration of the lease.

3. Crashworthiness doctrine — May apply in cases involving motor vehicles.

a. Liability is imposed upon manufacturers for injuries sustained because of defects in motor vehicles during the ordinary use of the vehicles; some courts have held that ordinary use does not include involvement in a collision.

b. In some states, liability has been imposed for defects in the design or construction of motor vehicles that increase the extent of injuries to a passenger in the event that an accident occurs, even though the defect was not the cause of the accident.

IV. Defenses to product liability claims.

A. A defendant in a product liability suit may raise defenses by asserting that the requisites for the particular tort have not been proven by the plaintiff.

B. Assumption of the risk [See Chapter 6] — Defendant must establish that:

1. The plaintiff voluntarily exposed himself or herself to the possibility of harm, while realizing the potential danger caused by the defective condition;

2. The plaintiff knew and appreciated the risk created by the defect; and

3. The plaintiff's decision to undertake the known risk was unreasonable.

C. Product misuse.

   1. The plaintiff used the product for a purpose for which the product was not intended.

   2. If the misuse of a product is reasonably foreseeable, the seller must take steps to guard against the misuse.

D. Comparative Negligence [See Chapter 6.] — In many states, the intentional conduct or negligence of a plaintiff (that contributed to the injury for which the plaintiff seeks damages) may be considered in apportioning liability and damages in an action based upon strict liability.

E. Commonly known dangers.

   1. Manufacturers do not have to warn users of common dangers associated with their products.

   2. Manufacturers do not have to warn users of specific dangers about which the users should have knowledge because of their expertise, training, and experience.

F. Federal preemption.

   1. In areas of law in which both the federal government (usually, because of the interstate commerce clause discussed in Chapter 5) and state governments (because of the police power) have concurrent jurisdiction, federal regulations may preempt, or prevail, over state law.

   2. The United States Supreme Court has determined that, if the clear intention of the Congress (based upon the wording of the statute and the legislative history) is to act exclusively in an area in which there is concurrent power, the federal law prevails; if not, state law is applied.

   3. *Cipollone v. Liggett Group, Inc.* is an example of a case based upon state law relating to fraudulent misrepresentation, in which the Supreme Court held that the state law was outside the scope of federal law and, therefore, was not preempted by federal law.

G. Statutes of limitations and repose. [See Chapter 1.]

1. Statute of limitations — An action or suit must be commenced within a specified period of time after the cause of action accrued.

    a. A cause of action accrues when damage occurs.

    b. The running of the time period may be tolled (suspended) until the injury is discovered or should have been discovered.

2. Statute of repose.

    a. Limits the time within which a plaintiff may file a product liability suit.

    b. The typical statute of repose begins to run at an earlier date (e.g., date of manufacture or sale) but for a longer period than a statute of limitations.

KEY WORDS AND PHRASES IN TEXT

product liability
negligence
due care
privity of contract is not required
     between parties in a tort action
bystander
violation of statutory duty
negligence *per se*
fraudulent and nonfraudulent
     (innocent) misrepresentation
strict liability in tort
Restatement (Second) of Torts,
     Section 402A
liability to bystanders
unreasonably dangerous product

flaw in manufacturing process
design defect
inadequate warning
market-share liability
crashworthiness doctrine
defenses to product liability
assumption of the risk
product misuse
comparative negligence (or fault)
commonly known dangers
knowledgeable user
federal preemption
statutes of limitation
statutes of repose

FILL-IN QUESTIONS

1. _____ generally refers to the liability of sellers, manufacturers, and distributors of goods to buyers of the goods and other people who have incurred injuries caused by the products.

2. A buyer of goods that prove to be defective may bring an action against the seller, with whom the buyer contracted, based on a contract theory if the buyer can show that there was a breach of an express or implied warranty. If the buyer bases his or her cause of action on tort, the buyer will have to establish that the seller was either _____ or strictly liable.

3. If a seller of goods made false representations concerning the goods that induced the buyer to purchase the goods, the buyer may recover from the seller based on the tort

theory of fraud in the inducement if the buyer reasonably _____ _____ and was _____.

4. A person, who was not a purchaser of a manufactured product but who was injured by the product, may recover from the manufacturer of the product in an action based upon the tort of negligence. The injured person does not have to show that there was _____ of contract with the manufacturer. The injured person, however, must establish that the manufacturer failed to exercise _____ and that the manufacturer's failure to exercise _____ was the proximate cause of his or her injury.

5. Based on the tort doctrine of strict liability, any person who is injured by a manufactured product, including the buyer, a bystander, or remote user, may successfully recover from the manufacturer or other seller of the item by establishing that he or she was injured by the product, which was defective, and that

_____
_____
_____.

MULTIPLE CHOICE QUESTIONS

1. In order to establish a cause of action against a seller of a defective product based upon the tort of negligence for injuries that result from the use of the defective product, the injured person must prove the elements of the tort of negligence. The injured party, therefore, must prove that the seller:
    A. was aware of the defect in the product.
    B. sold the product to the injured party.
    C. failed to exercise reasonable care.
    D. was the manufacturer of the product.

2. In order to establish a cause of action against a seller of a product based upon the tort of fraudulent misrepresentation for injuries resulting from the use of the product, one of the elements that the injured person must prove is that:
    A. the product was defective.
    B. the seller intentionally represented that there were no defects in the product or the seller concealed a defect in the product.
    C. the seller made a representation that, in the seller's opinion, the product would not malfunction.
    D. the seller failed to exercise reasonable care.

3. Roger, the owner of a sailboat that had a leak, stated to Beutell that there were no leaks in the boat. Beutell bought the sailboat from Roger. When Beutell was about to use the boat, he discovered the leak. In order to recover from Roger in a suit based upon fraudulent misrepresentation, Beutell must prove that:
    A. he incurred personal injuries when he used the sailboat.
    B. Roger failed to exercise reasonable care in making repairs to the sailboat.
    C. he reasonably relied on Roger's statement that there were no leaks in the sailboat.
    D. the leak in the sailboat caused the boat to be unreasonably dangerous.

4. In order to establish a cause of action against a seller of a defective product based upon strict tort liability for personal injuries that result from the use of the defective product, one of the elements that the injured person must prove is that the seller:
    A. was aware of the defect in the product.
    B. sold the product to the injured party.
    C. failed to exercise reasonable care.
    D. sold the product in a defective condition.
    (This question has been adapted from objective question #44 on the Uniform CPA Examination, November 1995.)

Questions 5 and 6 are based on the following fact situation: Thirsty purchased a 75¢ bottle of soda, manufactured by the Soke Company, at a neighborhood grocery store. Thirsty took the bottle home, where he drank some and shared the rest with Parched. Thirsty and Parched became violently ill because they swallowed slivers of glass that were in the bottle of soda. The grocery store and Soke Company exercised extraordinary care to prevent such an occurrence.

5. The grocery store would be liable to:
    A. Parched based upon strict tort liability even though Parched did not buy the soda from the grocery store.
    B. Thirsty only, because there was privity of contract between the grocery store and Thirsty.
    C. Thirsty for the tort of negligence.
    D. Parched for the tort of negligence.

6. With regard to the liability of Soke Company, which of the following statements is **incorrect?**
    A. Soke Company is liable to Thirsty and Parched in tort, even though soda normally is not a hazardous product.
    B. Soke Company is liable to Thirsty and Parched in tort, even though the company exercised a high degree of care.
    C. Soke Company is **not** liable to Thirsty and Parched for the tort of negligence because Soke Company used due care in the manufacture of its product in order to insure that the product was safe when used for the purpose for which the product was intended.
    D. Soke Company is **not** liable to Thirsty and Parched in tort because a reasonable person would have inspected the bottle and its contents before consuming the soda.

7. Acro bought a set of Goodmonth tires from Tyre, a dealer in tires. The tires were put on Acro's delivery truck. After the truck had been driven 200 miles on the new tires, one of the tires blew out causing the truck to go out of control. As a result, the truck was completely wrecked and Ernest, the driver employed by Acro, was injured as was Innocent, the driver of the automobile into which Acro's truck collided. Neither Ernest nor Innocent was negligent.
    A. Tyre is the only party who is liable in tort to Acro.
    B. Goodmonth is liable in tort for personal injuries incurred by Ernest.
    C. Goodmonth is **not** liable in tort for personal injuries incurred by Innocent.
    D. Tyre is relieved of any liability because he did not manufacture the defective tire.

8. Evans incurred an injury due to the malfunctioning of a power tool that he had purchased at a local hardware store. The tool was manufactured by Cautious Tool Company. Evans has commenced an action against the hardware store and Cautious Tool Company based upon strict tort liability. Which of the following statements is correct?

   A. Privity of contract will **not** be a valid defense against Evans in his lawsuit.
   B. Evans' suit against the hardware store will be dismissed because the hardware store was not at fault.
   C. Cautious Tool Company will **not** be liable to Evans if the company manufactured the tool in a nonnegligent manner.
   D. Evans' lawsuit will be dismissed because strict liability has not been applied in product liability cases in most jurisdictions.

   (This question has been adapted from objective question #55, Uniform CPA Examination, November 1983.)

9. Dieffenbacher is suing the manufacturer, the wholesaler, and the retailer for bodily personal injuries suffered by her as a result of using a lawnmower that she had purchased. Under the theory of strict tort liability:

   A. lack of privity of contract will be an absolute bar insofar as the wholesaler is concerned if the wholesaler did not have a reasonable opportunity to inspect the lawnmower.
   B. comparative (or contributory) negligence on the part of Dieffenbacher will always be a bar to recovery.
   C. the manufacturer will avoid liability if the manufacturer can show that it followed the custom of the industry.
   D. Dieffenbacher may recover despite the fact that she cannot show negligence was involved.

   (This question has been adapted from objective question #60 on the Uniform CPA Examination, November 1983.)

10. Kaye leased a new automobile from R&R Rent A Car in August. In October, while operating the car in a correct, safe, and lawful manner, Kaye was injured when the auto crashed into a highway divider. The crash occurred because the brakes on the auto failed to operate properly. Kaye has brought a tort action based upon strict liability against the manufacturer and R&R Rent A Car. Based upon recent trends in the law:

    A. Kaye may be able to recover from either the manufacturer or R&R Rent A Car even though Kaye had leased, rather than purchased, the automobile.
    B. Kaye may be able to recover from R&R Rent A Car even though Kaye had leased, rather than purchased, the automobile, but Kaye may not recover from the manufacturer with whom he did **not** have privity of contract.
    C. Kaye will have to establish that the automobile was extraordinarily dangerous.
    D. Kaye may be able to recover from the manufacturer even though R&R Rent A Car had made modifications on the automobile at Kaye's request.

Chapter 9
Intellectual Property and Cyberlaw

Intellectual property consists of legally recognized rights associated with creations of the human mind, such as trademarks, trade names, patents, and copyrights. This chapter begins with a discussion of the laws that have been designed to reward inventive and artistic creativity and thus protect these forms of intangible property. Article I, Section 8 of the United States Constitution, authorizing Congress to pass laws "To promote the Progress of Science and useful Arts, by securing for limited Times to Authors and Inventors the exclusive right to their respective Writings and Discoveries." Laws enacted in accordance with this constitutional provision are based upon the concept that those who have used their minds, intelligence, and creative and mental powers should have the right to enjoy the fruits of their own labors.

Section five (V) of this chapter discusses the laws that have evolved over time in order to adapt to changing conditions brought about by new technologies. In recent years, computers have revolutionized the way in which business is conducted, but have posed difficult questions for legislators and the courts when it comes to protection of intellectual rights associated with computer software and use of the Internet. In some cases, existing statutory and case law have been applied to computer software and Internet use; in other instances, statutes have been amended or new legislation created in order to serve the needs of a computerized society.

The Chapter concludes with a section relating to international protection for intellectual property.

THINGS TO KEEP IN MIND

Today, the law dealing with protection of intellectual property as it relates to computer technology is in a period of evolution. On the horizon, there are other new technologies, such as artificial intelligence and robotics, that will affect the manner in which tomorrow's business will be conducted. One might ask how the law will grow and be shaped in order to handle the challenges to be posed by these technologies.

OUTLINE

I. Trademarks and related property.

    A. A trademark is a distinctive identifying mark, symbol, design, device, motto, or emblem that a manufacturer imprints or affixes to goods so as to distinguish the goods from those of other manufacturers and merchants.

B. Trademark registration.

1. Trademarks are protected from infringement at common law and by statutes, such as the Lanham Trademark Act of 1946 and state trademark laws.

2. Trademarks can be registered with the U.S. Patent and Trademark Office.

   a. The mark can be register if the applicant currently is using the mark or intends to use the mark within six months. (The six-month period may be extended for 30 months.)

   b. Registration is renewable between the fifth and sixth year after initial registration and, thereafter, every ten years (or 20 years for marks registered before 1990).

   c. The symbol ® used by a registrant indicates that the mark is registered.

3. Trademark infringement occurs when a person intentionally or unintentionally copies, uses, or imitates a trademark without permission and, therefore, misleads potential purchasers as to the origin of goods.

C. Distinctiveness of mark — A trademark must be distinctive so that consumers identify the manufacturer of the goods and can differentiate among competing products.

1. Strong marks — Words that are uncommon, fanciful, arbitrary, or suggestive are the most distinctive and, therefore, strong marks.

2. Secondary meaning — Descriptive words, geographic terms, personal names, and colors cannot be trademarked unless they have acquired secondary meanings (because they are associated in the public mind with the products) or are used in a fanciful or arbitrary ways.

3. Generic terms.

   a. Trademark protection may be lost if the mark acquires a generic meaning so that the mark is used to refer to the product generally, rather than the particular goods of the registrant.

   b. Words that have acquired a broader meaning are protected only to the extent that consumers might be deceived.

D. The Federal Trademark Dilution Act of 1995 — The Act is similar to laws adopted in half of the states and prohibits unauthorized use of marks, which are identical or similar to distinctive, well-known marks, on noncompeting goods and services.

E. Trade dress infringement refers to the misuse of a distinctive product's or service's overall appearance or image.

F. Service, certification, and collective marks.

1. A service mark is used in order to distinguish the services of one person from those of another person and may be registered in the same manner as a trademark.

2. Certification marks are used in connection with the products or services of one or more persons, other than the owner, in order to certify the region in which the goods are produced, the materials used, the mode of manufacture, the quality, or the accuracy of the goods or services.

3. Collective marks are used by cooperatives and other organizations for purposes of identifying the sources of products and services.

G. Trade names.

1. A trade name is the name or designation of a person, partnership, corporation, or firm that is adopted and used when engaging in business.

2. The purpose of using a trade name is to avoid consumer confusion and to secure to the first user the benefits of the name's association with the first user's reputation and goodwill.

3. Common law liability is imposed upon a person or firm that uses a name that is the same or deceptively similar to the trade name of another business enterprise.

4. Protection is afforded to trade names that contain words that are unusual or fancifully used, but not to names that are merely descriptive of the product.

II. Patents.

A. A patent is a grant from the government that gives an inventor the exclusive right to make, use, and sell an invention for 20 years from the date of filing the application for the patent by the inventor with the Patent and Trademark Office.

1. Design patents are given for shorter periods of time (fourteen years).

2. In order to be patentable, the invention, discovery, or design must be new, genuine, useful, and nonobvious in the light of the technology of the time.

B. Patent infringement.

1. Infringement occurs when a person copies the patented invention, design, or process without being licensed (given the right) to do so by the patent holder.

2. Because of the complexity of issues in patent infringement cases, the U.S. Supreme Court ruled that judges should interpret the scope and nature of patent claims before instructing juries about other issues.

C. Patents for software.

    1. A mathematical formula, abstract idea, law of nature, etc. is not patentable.

    2. Computer software or programs, which automate procedures that can be manually performed, are not patentable because such software and programs are not novel and nonobvious.

    3. A process, however, that incorporates a computer program containing a known mathematical equation may be patented.

III. Copyrights.

A. A copyright is an exclusive right granted to an author or originator of a literary or other creative or artistic work in accordance with the federal Copyright Act.

B. Copyright protection is given for the life of the author plus 50 years or, in the case of a publishing house, 75 years from date of publication or 100 years from the date of creation, whichever comes first; copyrights may be registered in the Copyright Office of the Library of Congress.

C. What is protected expression?

    1. Literary, musical, dramatic, choreographic, pictorial, graphic, sculptural, sound, and audiovisual works as well as computer software and architectural plans are copyrightable.

    2. The work must be original and in some tangible, expressed form (i.e., "fixed in a durable medium" from which the work can be perceived, reproduced, or communicated).

    3. Copyright protection is not given to an "idea, procedure, process, system, method of operation, concept, principle, or discovery regardless of the form in which it is described, explained, illustrated, or embodied" [Copyright Act, Section 102].

    4. The expression of an idea, concept, etc. cannot be copyrighted if the idea and the expression of the idea, etc. are inseparable.

    5. Anything that is not an original expression, such as facts (other than compilations of facts), page numbers, or mathematical calculations, cannot be copyrighted.

D. Copyright infringement.

    1. Infringement occurs when there is a direct or contributory copying or reproduction of an entire work in the same or a substantially similar form, or of a substantial portion of the original work without permission of the copyright holder.

2. Liability for infringement.

    a. Willful infringers may be criminally liable.

    b. Civil remedies include actual damages plus the infringer's profits, or statutory damages of up to $100,000, and injunctive relief.

3. "Fair use" of reproduction of copyright material is permitted "for purposes of criticism, comment, news reporting, teaching, scholarship, or research" [Copyright Act, Section 107].

E. Copyright protection for software.

1. The Computer Software Copyright Act (1980) provides for the copyrighting of computer programs.

2. A computer program is defined as a "set of statements or instructions to be used directly or indirectly in a computer in order to bring about a certain result."

3. Both a computer program's source code (which is readable by humans) and the binary-language object code (which is only readable by computers) may be copyrighted.

4. Based upon case law, copyright protection has been expanded to cover the overall concept of a program, including the program's structure, sequence, and organization.

5. Based upon case law, the "look and feel" aspects of a program (the general appearance, command structure, video images, menus, windows, and other screen displays) are not protected under the 1980 Act.

F. Protection for mask works (the series of images related to the pattern formed by the multiple layers of a semiconductor chip product).

1. The Semiconductor Chip Protection Act provides that the owner of a mask work that is fixed in the product may register the mask work with the U.S. Copyright Office within two years of initially taking commercial advantage of the mask work.

2. Registration assures to the owner the exclusive ten-year right to reproduce, import, or distribute the mask work or a semiconductor chip product containing the mask work.

IV. Trade secrets.

A. A trade secret may consist of a unique formula, pattern, device, manufacturing process, or compilation of information, such as customer lists, which gives the developer of the secret an advantage over competitors, and which is not in the public domain, but is known only by its owner and the owner's employees to whom, of necessity, it must be confided.

B. Common law protection of trade secrets extends to ideas and their expression.

C. Liability is imposed upon a person who obtains and misappropriates the secret by breach of confidence, contract, industrial espionage, or any improper means.

D. The Economic Espionage Act of 1996 makes the theft of a trade secret a federal crime. [See Chapter 10.]

V.   Cyberlaw: protecting intellectual property in cyberspace.

A. The unique nature of the Internet raises unique legal questions and issues.

B. Trademark protection on the Internet — Domain names.

1. Domain names are Internet addresses that enable people to access sites on the World Wide Web.

2. Domain name registration.

a. Domain names are registered with Network Solutions, Inc. (which acts on behalf of the Internet Network Information Center).

b. A person seeking registration must state that:
1) The registrant's use of the name will not infringe on the intellectual property rights of any other party;
2) The registrant intends to use the name on "a regular basis on the Internet;" and
3) The registrant's use of the name will not be unlawful.

3. Trademark infringement — The unauthorized use of another person's mark in a domain name may be trademark infringement.

4. Trademark dilution — Commercial use of another person's mark that dilutes the mark's distinctiveness and "cybersquatting" are actionable by the holder of the trademark under the Federal Trademark Dilution Act of 1995.

C. Patents for cyberproducts.

1. Cyberproducts include data-compression, information linking, and retrieval software and encryption programs.

2. Patent holders may protect themselves by giving limited licenses to others (licensees) and restricting the purposes for which the cyberproducts can be used.

D. Copyrights in cyberspace.

1. Online issues include:

    a. Is storage of Internet material copyright infringement?

    b. Is downloading a musical recording placed on the Internet a misuse of copyrighted material?

    c. Is surfing or browsing the Internet "fair use" of copyrighted material?

2. Online copyright liability of providers, such as Internet access services and bulletin board service operators, for copyright infringement (pirating) by its customers may depend upon answers to questions, such as:

    a. Does the pirating have a commercial effect on the copyright owner?

    b. Does the service provider encourage infringement?

    c. Is the customer's use of the material commercial or private?

VI. International protection for intellectual property.

A. Often, inventors apply simultaneously for patents in several countries, the patent laws of which may vary as to what may be patented, the period of time after application before the patent is granted, and the protection that is afforded to the patent holder.

B. The United States is a party to the Berne Convention.

1. If a citizen of a country which is a member of the Berne Convention writes a book, the copyright must be recognized by other signatory countries.

2. If a citizen of a country that is not a member of the Berne Convention writes a book and first publishes the book in a country that has signed the Convention, the copyright must be recognized by other signatory countries.

C. The Trade-Related Aspects of Intellectual Property Rights (TRIPS) Agreement.

1. The TRIPS agreement establishes standards for the international protection of intellectual property rights, including patents, trademarks, and copyrights for books, films, computer programs, and music.

2. Member nations have agreed not to discriminate against foreign owners of intellectual property rights and to assure that legal procedures are available for such owners to bring infringement actions.

D. Cyberspace issues — The World Intellectual Property Organization (WIPO) is attempting to update international law to reduce international piracy of intellectual property.

KEY WORDS AND PHRASES IN TEXT

intellectual property
trademark
Lanham Trademark Act
trademark registration
trademark infringement
strong trademarks
Federal Trademark Dilution Act
trade dress
service, certification, and collective
        marks
trade name
patent
patent infringement

patents for computer software
copyright
copyright infringement
fair use of copyrighted material
Computer Software Copyright Act
trade secrets
cyberlaw
domain names
patents for cyberproducts
Berne Convention
Trade-Related Aspects of Intellectual
        Property Rights (TRIPS)
        Agreement

FILL-IN QUESTIONS

1. The power to enact patent and copyright laws was conferred upon the Congress in Section 8 of Article 1 of the United States _____.

2. A _____ is a grant from the government that secures to an inventor the exclusive right to make, use, and sell an invention. The applicant must show that the invention is genuine, novel, _____, and not _____ in the light of current technology.

3. Liability for patent infringement may be incurred by a person who copies and reproduces an invention of a product or process that has been registered properly with _____. The patent holder's exclusive right to make, use, and sell his or her invention is protected for _____ years from the date the patent holder's application was filed.

4. A _____ is a grant from the government to an author or originator of a literary or artistic production whose work is fixed in a tangible means of expression.

5. Copyright protection extends for the life of the author plus _____ years if a natural person is the holder of the copyright.

6. A person who, without authorization, copies a distinctive registered mark, design, or symbol that is affixed by a manufacturer to its product may be liable for _____ infringement.

7. In general, computer software is not patentable because a computer program is based upon a mathematical equation or formula, and a computer program is not considered to be _____ and not obvious. If, however, the computer program is incorporated into a process that is original, _____, and not obvious, the process using the program is patentable.

MULTIPLE CHOICE QUESTIONS

1. Ian has invented a new product. If Ian has applied for and received a patent from the Patent and Trademark Office in the Department of Commerce:
    A. Ian was granted the patent because he was able to show that his invention was genuine, novel, useful, and nonobvious.
    B. Ian's patent protection will continue for the period of time during which Ian uses and manufactures the invention.
    C. Ian's patent protection will not begin until Ian uses the invention or until he gives a license to another person to use the invention.
    D. Ian's patent will also cover any future modifications to the patented product, so that Ian will not subsequently have to apply for a new patent for an improvement to the product.

2. Strictland manufactures and sells security alarm devices that Strictland invented but has not patented:
    A. Strictland **cannot** recover in tort from E, an employee, who copied and sold devices to buyers, because Strictland failed to obtain a patent on her invention.
    B. Strictland **cannot** recover in tort from F, one of her salespersons, who gave a copy of Strictland's list of customers to Security Plus, Inc., a competitor of Strictland's, for $20,000.
    C. Strictland can recover from Security Plus, Inc., a competitor, which induced G, a key employee of Strictland, to leave Strictland's employment and work for Security Plus, because Security Plus has tortiously interfered with a contractual relationship.
    D. Strictland can recover from Security Plus, Inc., a competitor, for copyright infringement, if Security Plus, Inc. has reproduced security alarm devices that are exact replicas of those produced by Strictland.

3. Cameron has developed a computer program that may be incorporated into a manufacturing process for producing basketballs. Which of the following things may Cameron patent?

	The computer program	The manufacturing process	The basketball
A.	Yes	Yes	Yes
B.	Yes	Yes	No
C.	Yes	No	No
D.	No	Yes	No

4. Information relating to the copyright for the *Seventh Edition* of *West's Business Law* is found on the back of the title page of your textbook. After reading the information, you know that:
    A. the publisher's copyright will expire after the death of all of the authors of the textbook.
    B. the publisher's copyright will expire fifty years after the death of one of the authors of the textbook.
    C. the publisher's copyright will expire fifty years after the death of the last surviving author of the textbook.

D. the publisher's copyright will expire seventy-five years after the date of publication of the textbook.

5. Copy Kat makes multiple copies of five chapters of a book. Which of the following statements is correct?
   A. If Copy Kat is a professor who distributes the copies to his students for educational purposes, he probably will **not** be liable to the copyright holder for copyright infringement.
   B. If Copy Kat is a professor who sells the copies to his students but clearly indicates the name of the author and publisher, he probably will **not** be liable to the copyright holder for copyright infringement.
   C. If Copy Kat makes fewer than one hundred copies, reproduction of the material is permitted because of the doctrine of "fair use."
   D. If the book was published thirty years ago, Copy Kat will probably **not** be liable to the copyright holder for copyright infringement.

6. The D Corp. manufactures chewing gum which is packaged in a wrapper that is an exact copy of the wrapper which P Gum, Inc. uses for its product and contains a replica of P Gum, Inc.'s trademark. Today, P Gum, Inc. will probably be successful if it sues the D Corp.:
   A. whether or not P Gum, Inc. can prove that D. Corp. consciously and fraudulently intended to deceive potential customers.
   B. because customer confusion can easily be shown since the two wrappers are exactly the same.
   C. for trademark infringement.
   D. All of the statements above are correct.

Chapter 10
Criminal Law and Procedures

Crimes are wrongful offenses committed against society. The elements of each specific crime and the penalties that are imposed upon people who are found guilty of the crime are defined by statute. Usually, a crime consists of commission or omission of an act with criminal intent. Material in this chapter relates to crimes that affect business, including so called "white-collar" crimes that may be committed in the course of legitimate business activities.

In the United States, a person who is accused of having committed a crime is prosecuted by the government but is presumed to be innocent until he or she is proven to be guilty beyond a reasonable doubt. In some instances, a person who has a valid defense may be excused from, or relieved of, criminal responsibility. Under our system of laws, a person accused of a crime is afforded certain safeguards by the federal and state constitutions. As explained in this chapter, much of criminal procedural law is based upon the concept that defendants are entitled to due process and the protection of their rights in criminal prosecutions.

There also have been difficulties in applying traditional criminal law to wrongful acts associated with computer and Internet usage. For this reason, new criminal statutes have been enacted in order to ensure that certain forms of computer abuse (which otherwise would fall outside the traditional definitions of existing crimes) are criminal wrongs.

THINGS TO KEEP IN MIND

One act may be both a criminal and a civil wrong. The state is a party in the criminal prosecution; the injured party is the plaintiff in the civil action based on tort. If the accused person is found guilty of the crime beyond a reasonable doubt, he or she will be punished. If a defendant in a civil action is found, by a preponderance of evidence, to have committed a tort, the defendant will be required to compensate the plaintiff who was injured because the tortious conduct.

OUTLINE

I.   Classification of crimes — Crimes may be classified based upon their seriousness; often, the seriousness of crimes is reflected in the punishment provided for in statutes.

     A. Treason — See the United States Constitution, Article III, Section 3.

B. Felonies.

    1. Felonies are crimes that are punishable by death or imprisonment in a state (or federal) penitentiary for more than one year.

    2. Felonies can be divided into different degrees based upon the seriousness of the crime; for example, the Model Penal Code provides for four degrees of felonies:

        a. Capital felonies for which the maximum penalty is execution.

        b. First degree felonies with a maximum penalty of life imprisonment.

        c. Second degree felonies with a maximum penalty of ten years in prison.

        d. Third degree felonies with a maximum penalty of five years in prison.

C. Misdemeanors are less serious crimes that typically are punishable by imprisonment for less than one year in local jails and/or fines.

D. Offenses are violations that sometimes are referred to as petty offenses and are punishable by fine and/or possible brief imprisonment.

II. The essentials of criminal liability — Most crimes consist of a combination of performance (or commission) of a prohibited act and specific criminal intent.

A. The criminal act (*actus reus*, or guilty act) — The particular criminal behavior for each crime is defined by statute and may be an act or an omission (failure to act).

B. State of mind.

    1. Criminal intent or state of mind (*mens rea*) is an element of most crimes.

    2. Wrongful criminal intent may be based upon criminal purpose, knowledge and awareness, recklessness, or negligence, or be inferred because a person is presumed to intend the proximate and natural consequences of his or her own acts.

III. Criminal procedures.

A. Constitutional safeguards — Most of the guarantees found in Amendments to the United States Constitution apply to the states as well as to the federal government by virtue of the Fourteenth Amendment. (State constitutions also contain similar provisions.)

    1. Fourth Amendment — Provides protection from unreasonable searches and seizures and issuance of warrants without probable cause.

2. Fifth Amendment — Prohibits self-incrimination and double jeopardy and guarantees due process of law.

3. Sixth Amendment — Guarantees speedy, public trial by jury, and the right to be informed of charges, confront the accused, subpoena witnesses, and have the assistance of an attorney.

4. Eighth Amendment — Prohibits excessive bail and fines and cruel and unusual punishment.

5. Judicial interpretations — The U.S. Supreme Court has interpreted and applied these Constitutional guarantees:

   a. The exclusionary rule — Evidence obtained in violation of the rights spelled out in the Fourth, Fifth, and Sixth Amendments and evidence that is derived from the wrongfully obtained evidence cannot be used against a defendant in a criminal prosecution.

   b. The *Miranda* rule — A person who is being arrested must be informed of his or her constitutional rights (*Miranda v. Arizona*, 1966).

   c. The erosion of the *Miranda* rule — Exceptions to the *Miranda* rule have reduced some of the rights afforded to an accused person (e.g., a "public safety" exception and the admission of certain statements made during the "routine booking" of the defendant).

B. Criminal process.

1. Arrest — A warrant based upon a showing of probable cause that the accused person committed, or is about to commit a crime, is required, unless probable cause and urgent time constraints reasonably justify immediate arrest.

2. Indictment or information — An indictment is issued by a grand jury or an information is issued by a magistrate (a public official vested with judicial authority) if there is sufficient evidence to justify formally charging a defendant with a specified crime and bringing the defendant to trial for the crime.

3. Trial — The state must prove guilt beyond a reasonable doubt; this is a higher standard than the standard of a preponderance of evidence that is required in a civil case.

C. Federal sentencing guidelines.

1. When imposing a sentence on a defendant who was found guilty of a federal crime, the judge must select a sentence from within the specified range of possible penalties for the particular crime.

2. Sentencing guidelines are specified for crimes committed by corporations and corporate employees who have committed "white collar crimes" (discussed later in this chapter) and criminal violations of laws dealing with employment (Chapters 35 and 36), securities (Chapter 43), and antitrust (Chapter 47).

3. In determining a sentence, a judge may consider the defendant's history of past violations, cooperation with federal investigators, and the extent to which the firm has undertaken procedures to prevent criminal activities by employees.

IV. Crimes affecting business.

A. Some crimes that affect business are referred to as "white collar crimes."

B. Forgery — Fraudulent making or materially altering an instrument or document so as to change the rights and/or liability of another person.

C. Robbery — Unlawful taking (theft) of personal property of another person with force or intimidation.

D. Burglary — Breaking and entering a dwelling or other structure with the intent to commit a felony.

E. Larceny — The wrongful or fraudulent taking and carrying away of personal property (theft) of another person without the use of force or threats.

1. *Grand larceny* (a felony) — The value of the property is greater than a statutorily fixed threshold amount.

2. *Petit larceny* (a misdemeanor) — The value of the property is less than that set for grand larceny.

3. Larceny is a crime of theft in which the subject matter is tangible personal property; thefts of intangible personal property and services also are crimes.

F. Obtaining goods by false pretenses.

G. Receiving stolen goods.

H. Embezzlement — Fraudulent misappropriation or conversion of property or money by a person to whom the property or money originally was entrusted.

I. Arson.

1. Willful and malicious burning of a building (and, in some states, personal property) of another person.

2. Statutes also make it a crime to burn property in order to defraud insurers.

J. Mail and wire fraud — Because of a federal statute, it is a crime to mail a writing for the purposes of executing an organized scheme to defraud.

K. Bribery.

    1. Bribery of public officials — Tender of something of value to a governmental official with the intent of influencing the official to act in a manner that serves a private interest; accepting a bribe is also a crime.

    2. Commercial bribery.

        a. Intentionally offering a payment of money or something of value in order to obtain proprietary information, secure new business, or "cover up" defects in a product.

        b. Examples include "kickbacks" and "payoffs" to employees of competitors and other activities while engaging in industrial espionage.

    3. Bribery of foreign officials — The Foreign Corrupt Practices Act is discussed in Chapter 55.

L. Bankruptcy fraud — Usually, bankruptcy fraud and similar other crimes involve attempts to shield assets from a court, and thus from creditors. [See Chapter 32.]

M. Money laundering.

    1. Money is "laundered" when cash and profits derived from illegal activities (dirty money) are invested in legitimate business firms whose subsequent profits are distributed to investors (clean money).

    2. Placement of profits derived from illegal transactions in financial institutions is limited because banks and other financial institutions in the United States must report currency transactions of more than $10,000.

N. Insider trading — Insiders, who are individuals possessing material, nonpublic information about corporations whose securities are issued and/or traded publicly, may be prosecuted for securities law violations if they engage in trading (buying or selling) of the corporate securities without making certain disclosures. [See Chapter 43.]

O. The theft of trade secrets — The Economic Espionage Act of 1996 makes it a federal crime to buy or possess trade secrets belonging to another person, knowing that the trade secrets were stolen or otherwise acquired without the owner's authorization.

P. Computer crime — A computer crime refers to a wrongful act that is directed against a computer and/or its parts, a wrongful use of a computer as an instrument of a crime (computer-assisted crime), or an abusive use of a computer.

1. Types of computer crime.

    a. Financial crimes — Altering computer records and/or conducting unauthorized financial transactions by accessing a computer.

    b. Theft of computer equipment (hardware) and theft of goods with the use of computer are subject to the same criminal laws as are thefts of other tangible property.

    c. Vandalism and destructive programming (e.g., dissemination a "virus").

    d. Software piracy — See also Chapter 9.
        1) Computer software piracy is a crime in most states.
        2) A 1990 federal statute prohibits the renting, leasing, or lending of computer software without express consent of the copyright holder.

    e. Theft of data or services.
        1) The unauthorized use of another person's computer system or data stored in another person's computer system may not be larceny, which encompasses a physical taking and carrying away of property from the possession of another person (i.e., theft of tangible property).
        2) A person who, without authorization, uses another person's computer system or data stored in another person's computer system may be prosecuted for the crime of theft of services or the crime of larceny in states which broadly construe such criminal statutes.

2. Prosecuting computer crime.

    a. The Counterfeit Access Device and Computer Fraud and Abuse Act makes it a crime knowingly to access a computer in order to:
        1) Obtain restricted government information with the intent of using the information to injure the United States or aid a foreign nation.
        2) Obtain information contained in a financial institution's financial records or in a consumer reporting agency's files relating to consumers.
        3) Use, modify, destroy, or prevent the authorized use of a computer operated for or on behalf of the federal government, or to disclose the information that such a computer contains.

    b. Computer crime is difficult to detect and often there is a considerable lapse of time before the crime is detected and/or a determination made as to the person who committed the crime.

    c. A particular form of computer abuse may not fall within the statutory definition of a crime.

Q. Criminal RICO violations.

1. The purpose of the Racketeer Influenced and Corrupt Organizations Act (RICO), a federal statute, was to curb the entry of organized crime into legitimate business enterprises.

2. Liability in cases involving white-collar crimes has been imposed based upon RICO. (Civil RICO violations are discussed in Chapter 7.)

3. It is a federal crime to use income obtained from a pattern of racketeering activities to purchase any interest in an enterprise; to acquire or maintain an interest in an enterprise through a pattern of racketeering activity; to conduct or participate in the affairs of an enterprise through a pattern of racketeering activity; or to conspire to do any of these things.

4. RICO incorporates by reference federal crimes (such as securities fraud and mail fraud) and state felonies (including gambling, arson, and extortion).

V. Defenses to criminal liability — Defenses are conditions that relieve a defendant of liability for commission of a crime.

A. A criminal defendant may show that the government did not prove the elements of the crime beyond a reasonable doubt because there is reasonable doubt that:

1. The crime was committed (e.g., no *corpus delicti*) or that the particular defendant committed the crime because the defendant did not commit the specific act for which the defendant was accused (e.g., the defendant has an alibi because the defendant was at another place at the time that the crime was committed); or

2. The defendant did not have the requisite criminal intent.

   a. Infancy — States have statutes providing that certain minors are treated as lacking the necessary moral sense to be capable of knowing right from wrong. (The statutes and their applications vary among the states.)

   b. Intoxication.
      1) Involuntary intoxication is a defense to a crime if the perpetrator was unable to understand that the act committed was wrong.
      2) Voluntary intoxication is a defense only if it prevented the perpetrator from having the necessary intent.

   c. Insanity — Different standards are applied among the states.
      1) As a result of mental disease or defect, the defendant lacked the mental capacity to appreciate the wrongfulness of his or her conduct or to conform his or her conduct to the requirements of the law.
      2) The person accused of a crime did not appreciate the nature of the act or know that it was wrong.
      3) The person accused of the crime committed the criminal act because of an "irresistible impulse."

B. A criminal defendant may show that he or she has a defense that is recognized in the courts.

    1. Mistake.
        a. In general, ignorance or mistake of law is no excuse.

        b. In some states, when a statute has been enacted making an act, which previously was lawful, illegal, and the new statute has not been publicized, mistake of law may be raised as a defense.

    2. Consent of the victim may cancel the harm that is intended to be prevented; some crimes (e.g., murder and drug use), however, are not negated by the victim's consent.

    3. Duress — A wrongful threat of imminent serious bodily harm that is of a greater degree than the harm committed by the defendant.

    4. Justifiable use of reasonably necessary force.

        a. Self-defense or defense of other people.

        b. Defense of dwelling or other property.

        c. Prevention of a violent or serious crime.

    5. Entrapment — Law enforcement officer's or other government agent's encouragement induced the defendant to commit a criminal act that the defendant was not predisposed to commit.

    6. Statute of limitations — Statutes restrict prosecution after expiration of a stated period of time.

    7. Immunity — An agreement not to prosecute, or to prosecute for a less serious offense, may be granted by the state in exchange for information.

C. In addition, the defendant may raise a defense that his or her constitutionally protected rights were violated. [See above at III. A.]

See Chapters 40 and 41 in Unit Eight regarding criminal liability of corporations and other entities, and their responsible persons and employees.

KEY WORDS AND PHRASES IN TEXT

crime
felonies
capital offenses
misdemeanors and (petty) offenses
elements of a crime

act of commission or omission
commission of a prohibited act
    (*actus reus* or guilty act)
wrongful state of mind
    (*mens rea* or guilty mind)

criminal purpose and/or knowledge
criminal recklessness or negligence
guilt beyond a reasonable doubt
unreasonable searches and seizures
warrants for searches and seizures
due process of law
double jeopardy
speedy public trial by jury
right to confront witnesses
right to legal counsel
excessive bail or fine
cruel and unusual punishment
exclusionary rule
the *Miranda* rule and its erosion
probable cause
indictment by grand jury
information (formal accusation)
burden of proof in criminal trials
federal sentencing guidelines
white-collar crimes
forgery
robbery
burglary
larceny
obtaining goods by false pretenses

receiving stolen goods
embezzlement
arson
mail and wire fraud
bribery
bankruptcy fraud
money laundering
insider trading
theft of trade secrets
computer crime
Racketeer Influenced and Corrupt
     Organization Act (RICO)
defenses to criminal liability
infancy
voluntary and involuntary intoxication
insanity
mistake of law and mistake of fact
consent
duress
justifiable use of force
self-defense
entrapment
statutes of limitations
immunity
plea bargaining

FILL-IN QUESTIONS

1.   A crime is a public _____ which is defined by statute. The person who is accused of committing a crime is the defendant in a criminal prosecution brought by _____.

2.   A crime punishable by imprisonment for more than one year is considered to be a _____. Other crimes are classified as _____.

3.   In order to be found guilty of a particular crime, a person must have performed or committed, a specified _____ (or, in some cases, failed to perform a required _____) with the requisite specified criminal state of mind or intent. Criminal intent may be based upon purpose, knowledge and awareness, _____, or be implied.

4.   An accused person is protected against _____ by the Fourth Amendment and against _____ by the Eighth Amendment of the United States Constitution.

5. A prohibition against the issuance of a warrant without probable cause is provided by the Fourth Amendment of the United States Constitution and prohibitions against _____ by the Fifth Amendment.

6. The Sixth Amendment guarantees a person accused of a crime _____ _____.

7. Crimes involving the theft of property include burglary (breaking and entering into a dwelling, building, or other structure with the intention of committing a crime), robbery (_____) and _____ (wrongful taking of property without force with the intention of depriving the owner of the possession or use of the property).

8. When Todd, the accountant for CCC Corp., uses CCC Corp.'s pension funds in order to pay a personal gambling debt, Todd has probably committed the crime of _____.

9. If an accused person can show that he or she committed a criminal act while insane or because of duress, the accused person has a valid _____ which relieves him or her of criminal responsibility.

10. There is a presumption that a person who is accused of having committed a crime, is _____ until he or she has been found _____ beyond a reasonable doubt.

11. A person, who physically takes a PC (personal computer) from its owner's possession and uses it for her own purposes, may be prosecuted for a _____ of theft, such as larceny, because the PC is a form of tangible property. If, however, a person uses another person's PC, without physically removing it from the owner's possession, she may **not** be prosecuted for larceny in a state in which the _____ of larceny is defined as the "taking of tangible property."

12. A person, who physically takes a PC (personal computer) from its owner's possession and uses it for her own purposes, may be liable for an intentional tort, such as conversion, because of the wrongful taking and retention of the PC, which is considered to be a form of tangible _____ property. If a person uses another person's PC without permission, but without physically removing it from the owner's possession, she may be liable for the intentional tort of _____ to personal property, a wrongful interference with another person's exclusive right to possession and enjoyment of personal property.

MULTIPLE CHOICE QUESTIONS

1. A crime is considered to be a felony if it is:
   A. a federal offense.
   B. punishable by death or imprisonment for more than a year.
   C. punishable by a fine or imprisonment for less than a year.
   D. so stated by a grand jury in its indictment.

2.   Least serious crimes are referred to as:
     A. felonies.
     B. misdemeanors.
     C. civil wrongs.
     D. torts.

3.   A person who is accused of having committed a crime must be proven guilty:
     A. beyond a reasonable doubt.
     B. by substantially reasonable evidence.
     C. with a preponderance of evidence.
     D. by a majority of the jurors.

4.   A policeman stopped a college student, who was running down the street with a smoking revolver in his hand, searched and arrested the student without first having obtained a warrant:
     A. The absolute right to be free from a search and seizure has been violated.
     B. The right to be free from an unreasonable search and seizures has been violated, if an indictment had not been previously issued by a grand jury or an information issued by a magistrate.
     C. The right to be free from an unreasonable search and seizure has been violated.
     D. The right to be free from an unreasonable search and seizure has **not** been violated even if a warrant had not been obtained previously from a judicial body.

5.   Under the "*Miranda* rule," an arrested person has the right:
     A. to a trial by a jury of twelve peers.
     B. to a lawyer when the case is appealed.
     C. to remain silent.
     D. to make a free telephone call.

6.   Which of the following statements is **false**?
     A. Crimes are offenses against society as a whole.
     B. Defendants in criminal cases are prosecuted by the state in which the crime occurred.
     C. An objective in a criminal case is to compensate a person who was injured because a crime.
     D. Commission of an act that is a federal crime is not necessarily also a state crime.

7.   C.P. Desprite has been subtly altering a client's books of account and, as a result. has been able to add about $400 a month to his own income. When it is discovered that he has taken and used the money, he probably will be prosecuted for the crime of:
     A. forgery.
     B. conversion.
     C. entrapment.
     D. embezzlement.

8.   A defendant who is being prosecuted for the crimes of assault and battery, having hit another person with a baseball bat, would most likely be successful in defending against the charge by showing that:

A. she had to strike the other person in order to prevent what she thought was a deadly threat to her life.

B. she honestly believed that the law allowed her to strike another person under the circumstances.

C. she felt morally justified in striking another person, even though she knew that society objected to such conduct.

D. because of the actions of undercover police officers, she felt trapped and, therefore, struck one of the officers.

E. All of the above would be good defenses.

9. One act may be the basis for prosecution for the commission of more than one crime. For example, if C breaks into V's home while V is away and steals a television set, C may be found guilty of the crimes of:

A. burglary and robbery.

B. battery and misappropriation.

C. burglary and larceny.

D. arson and larceny.

10. One act may be the basis for a criminal prosecution by the state and a civil lawsuit by the victim. For example, if an employee takes $600 from his employer's cash register, without the knowledge or permission of his employer, the employee may be sued by the employer for the tort of:

A. conversion and prosecuted for the crime of embezzlement.

B. conversion and prosecuted for the crime of burglary.

C. larceny and prosecuted for the crime of burglary.

D. fraud and prosecuted for the crime of deceit.

11. Jones shot and wounded Smith. Jones may:

A. be charged with premeditated homicide, or murder, if Jones' mental state was such that she deliberately intended to kill Smith.

B. be charged with a crime but **not** sued civilly by Smith.

C. **not** be found guilty of a crime. if she establishes that she had reasonable justification.

D. **not** be found guilty of a crime, if she establishes that Smith consented to be shot.

12. Aggent, an undercover narcotics police officer, approached Pushor, who on several past occasions was observed selling illegal drugs. Aggent negotiated with Pushor for the purchase of a substance, the sale of which is prohibited by state law. After buying the substance, Aggent arrested Pushor. At his trial, Pushor raises the defense of entrapment. The defense of entrapment probably will prove to be:

A. ineffective because Pushor was seventeen years of age at the time of the sale to Aggent.

B. ineffective because Pushor was predisposed to commit the crime.

C. effective because of the use of duress by Aggent.

D. effective because Aggent induced Pushor to make the sale.

13. In 1997, Joker, a bank employee, obtained a loan from the bank. The loan has not been repaid. Joker accesses the bank's computer and changes the information in the

bank's records so that the records now state that the loan was repaid. Joker may be prosecuted for:

A. the crime of mail fraud by the United States.

B. a violation of the Counterfeit Access Device and Computer Fraud and Abuse Act by the United States.

C. a violation of the Counterfeit Access Device and Computer Fraud and Abuse Act by the state in which the bank is located.

D. the tort of conversion and the crime of robbery by the state in which the bank is located.

14. Bezellor, a bank employee, accessed the bank's computer and perused data that was stored in the computer's files. Bezellor found information about Victim, a customer of the bank, that, if published in a newspaper, would be detrimental to Victim. Bezellor wrote a letter to Victim threatening to give the information to a newspaper unless Victim paid Bezellor $10,000. Bezellor may be prosecuted and convicted for the crimes of:

A. robbery and larceny.

B. embezzlement and computer battery.

C. extortion and mail fraud.

D. computer robbery and copyright infringement.

Chapter 11
Comparative Law

The business activities and ultimate success of American companies doing business outside the United States depend upon both international law and national law. International law is the body of law that governs relations among nations and between citizens of different countries. National law is the law of a particular nation.

In this chapter, the authors contrast two important types of national schemes for creating law — the common law system and the civil law system. The common law system is the basis for development of legal principles by judges in making determinations in cases in the United States and some other countries, such as Great Britain and Canada. The civil law system sometimes is referred to as continental law and is founded upon codification of rules of law. The civil law system is the basis for law in many parts of the world. Material in the chapter deals with areas of law of major concern to business enterprises that are operating abroad. Topics covered include contracts, torts, and employment law.

THINGS TO KEEP IN MIND

Traditions and legal systems vary from nation to nation. Certain legal concepts and principles of substantive law relating to business law, such as contracts, torts, and employment, however, may be common to many nations. In order for a firm organized in the United States to succeed when conducting business abroad, the firm's officers first must familiarize themselves with the traditions, legal system, and laws of the foreign country in which the firm intends to operate.

OUTLINE

I.   Doing business abroad.

    A. Officers and employees of American firms engaging in transnational business operations should have knowledge about the culture, economy, and business climate of foreign countries in which the firms propose to operate or are operating.

    B. Language and communication.

       1. The meanings of certain English words may be quite different from their meanings when these words are translated into another language.

2. Nonverbal language (e.g., facial expressions, body movements, and gestures) and connotations associated with certain colors and numbers vary from culture to culture.

C. Perceptions of time — Northern Europeans and Americans consider punctuality to be crucial, but businesspersons in many Latin American, Middle Eastern, and Asian countries have more flexible attitudes toward time.

D. Management styles — It is thought that American and European managers employ a direct, pragmatic, and competitive style, that Latin American managers tend to be more humanistic and indirect, and that Asian managers may be less direct and attempt to avoid confrontations.

E. Ethics — While many important ethical principles are common to virtually all countries, significant differences exist due to varied cultures and religions.

1. Consumption of alcoholic beverages and certain foods is forbidden by the Koran in Islamic countries.

2. Gift-giving or bribery?

a. In some countries, gift-giving is a common practice among contracting companies or between firms and the local government.

b. Gift-giving may be considered unethical and illegal bribery that is prohibited by the Foreign Corrupt Practices Act (FCPA) if engaged in by U.S. firms. [See Chapters 10 and 55.]

3. Women in business — The role played by women and members of certain minority groups may pose dilemmas for U.S. firms operating abroad.

a. Certain Islamic and Asian countries reject any role for professional women so that the presence of women in a commercial transaction may be considered offensive.

b. Title VII of the Civil Rights Act of 1964 (prohibiting discrimination in employment) may conflict with foreign customs; many U.S. firms remain reluctant to assign women and certain other people to work in some countries. [See Chapter 36.]

II. Comparative legal systems.

A. American companies doing business in a foreign country are subject to the jurisdiction and laws of that country.

B. Constitutional foundations.

1. Usually, the foundation of a country's legal system is set forth in a governing document (a constitution) or a series of fundamental documents

(e.g., the United Kingdom's Magna Carta, Bill of Rights of 1689, and other documents) providing for the exercise of legislative, executive, and judicial powers by different branches of government.

2. Some nations have federal systems, in which governmental powers are divided between national and provincial governments, while other nations have centralized or unitary governmental systems.

3. The constitutions of some countries, including the U.S., provide for judicial review of legislative action. [See Chapter 3 regarding the power of the courts to determine the constitutionality of legislation.]

4. Unlike the U.S., some nations have specialized commercial law courts that deal with business disputes.

C. Common law and civil law systems.

1. Common law systems — In a common law system, courts develop the rules governing certain areas of law independently; judge-made law exists in addition to statutes enacted by legislative bodies. [See Chapter 1.]

   a. The common law principle of *stare decisis* obligates judges to follow precedential decisions in their jurisdictions; occasionally, courts may modify or overturn past precedents.

   b. Common law systems exist in countries that once were parts of the British Empire, including Australia, Canada, India, and the U.S.

2. Civil law systems — In nations following the civil law system, the only official source of law is a statutory code.

   a. In this context, the term, "civil law," refers to codified law, an orderly grouping of legal principles enacted into law by a legislature or governing body, rather than to civil as opposed to criminal law (as discussed in Chapter 1).

   b. Courts are required to interpret the statutory code, which, in theory, sets forth all the principles needed for the legal system, and apply those rules to individual cases; courts may not depart from the code and develop their own laws.

   c. Most continental European nations and Latin American, African, and Asian countries have civil law systems. [This system originated with the Twelve Tables of Rome (451-450 B.C.) and well known examples include the French Napoleonic Code (*Code Napoleon*, 1807 as amended), the Spanish Commercial Code (1885), the Japanese Commercial Code (1890), and the German Commercial Code (1900).]

3. Legal (ommon law and civil law) systems compared.

a. In the U.S., criminal law is codified law because crimes are defined in statutes; this is true of all law in civil law systems.

b. Most civil law systems permit the nation's judiciary to interpret the civil law codes.

4. Judges in common law nations have produced different common law principles; for instance, while both the U.S. and India derive their legal traditions from England, rules of law governing contracts differ in some respects between these countries.

5. The laws in nations with civil law systems vary; for instance, the French civil code sets forth general principles of law as compared to the German code which is extremely specific and lengthy.

6. Ingredients of the civil law system are found in predominantly Muslim countries; the civil codes, however, are based upon religious Islamic directives (*shari'a*) making these codes more difficult to alter.

D. Judges and procedures — The primary function of judges in almost all countries is the resolution of disputes, but the characteristics and qualifications of judges may vary.

1. In the U.S., judges normally do not actively participate in a trial; in many other countries, however, judges are more involved in trial proceedings and often question witnesses.

2. Legal procedures vary from country to country.

E. Lawyers and litigation — In other countries, lawyers play dissimilar roles, and there are disparities regarding perceptions of the functions of lawyers.

1. In the U.S., an attorney serves as an advocate of his or her client's interests; in China, lawyers are obligated to advance the interests of the government.

2. While it is not unusual for American firms to include lawyers and accountants on their negotiating teams, in foreign settings, the presence of these professionals may cause the other side to suspect duplicity.

3. Tort litigation tends to be more extensive in common law systems, and the U.S., in particular, is perceived to be overly litigious with a court system overburdened by lawsuits, many of which may be frivolous in nature, due in part to the large number of lawyers in the U.S.

III. National laws compared.

A. Virtually all nations have laws governing contracts, torts, intellectual property, and other areas that impact on firms doing business abroad; while the basic principles of these laws may be similar, there are significant variations in their practical applications and effects.

B. Tort law.

1. A tort is a civil wrong that causes an injury to a person or a person's property and for which the law provides a remedy; a tort may be the result of an intentional or unintentional (e.g., negligence) act. [See Chapters 6 and 7.]

2. Typically, tort law in a nation that has a common law system is based upon case law.

3. The civil law codes of different nations do not uniformly define what constitutes a tort, and the application of tort law may vary among nations, even when the statutory languages is similar. [See Exhibit 11-4.]

4. There are other significant differences among nations regarding tort law that may affect firms doing business abroad.

   a. Failure to act — The liability imposed by foreign law for omissions, or failures to act (e.g., breach of the duty to rescue), varies.

   b. Damages — The method of calculating damages differs among nations.

   c. Statutes of limitations — The deadlines for filing lawsuits as well as the burdens of proof required in tort lawsuits vary.

5. Product liability. [See Chapters 8 and 25.]

   a. Courts in the U.S. often apply principles of strict tort liability in suits involving defective goods; as a result, there are only limited defenses that can be raised by sellers of such products in such suits.

   b. Courts in other nations recognize certain defenses in cases involving defective products.

C. Contract law.

1. The United Nations Convention on Contracts for the International Sale of Goods (CISG) applies to many transactions involving the sales of goods between firms that are located in different countries. [See Chapter 21.]

   a. The CISG applies only to transactions involving firms in countries that are signatories to the CISG and only if the parties have not otherwise agreed in their contracts.

   b. When a transaction involves firms in countries that are not signatories to the CISG, the parties need to determine which nation's laws govern any disputes arising under the contract; the parties may stipulate that the CISG or the law of a particular nation will govern potential disputes.

2. Basic contract requirements in the United States — A contract is an agreement that can be enforced in a court because certain requisites are present.

3. In other nations, the requirements are similar, but there are differences regarding specific aspects of the requirements — Some of these differences are pointed out below.

   a. Agreement — In all countries, contract formation is based upon an offer and an acceptance but there are variations among nations with regard to what constitutes an offer and acceptance.
      1) In the U.S., usually, an offer can be revoked (canceled or withdrawn) before the offer is accepted. [See Chapter 13.]
         a) The German Civil Code has detailed provisions governing contracts, one of which is that a written offer must be held open for a reasonable period of time unless the offer specifically states otherwise; if an oral offer is not accepted immediately, the offer terminates so that it no longer can be effectively accepted.
         b) In Mexico, the commercial code is similar to the UCC, but special rules apply to offer and acceptance; for example, if the duration of an offer is not specified, the offer is deemed to be held open for three days in addition to the time necessary for the offer and acceptance to be sent through the mail.
      2) In the U.S., the rule that important terms of a contract be definite has been relaxed particularly as it applies to mercantile transactions. [See Chapters 13 and 21.]
         a) This is also true in Mexico.
         b) In other countries, such as Saudi Arabia, there are strict requirements regarding the definiteness of terms of a contract.

   b. Consideration.
      1) Under U.S. law, something having legal value must be exchanged for a contractual promise in order for a contract to be legally binding. [See Chapters 14 and 48.]
      2) As is true in most civil law countries, the exchange of consideration is not necessary in order to create a binding contract in Germany.
      3) Traditional common law principles of contract law that are similar to those in the U.S. are codified in India; unlike the law in the U.S., however, past consideration is sufficient to support a contractual promise.

   c. Legality — Contracts that provide for the performance of illegal acts are not recognized as valid contracts because they are void and unenforceable. [See Chapter 17.]
      1) In Islamic countries, contracts for the sale of certain products, such as alcohol and pork, are illegal.

2) In the People's Republic of China, certain contracts are void unless formal approval by the central or a provincial government is obtained.

d. Remedies for breach of contract — See Chapters 1, 19, and 24.
   1) In the U.S. and many other countries, the normal remedy for a breach of contract is the legal remedy of damages to compensate the nonbreaching party for losses that result from a breach.
   2) In the U.S., equitable remedies, such as specific performance, are not available unless the legal remedy of money damages is inadequate.
   3) In Germany and other countries, the typical remedy for breach of contract is specific performance; damages are available only after notice and use of prescribed procedures to obtain performance.

e. Defenses can be raised by parties to contracts if certain requirements for contracts are not met.
   1) In the U.S. and other countries, certain types of contracts must be evidenced by signed writings, but other contracts are enforceable even if they are oral. [See Chapter 17.]
      a) The CISG and the laws in many nations do not require written contracts. [See Chapter 21.]
      b) In Saudi Arabia, although contracts are not required to be in writing, written contracts which are formally witnessed are encouraged.
   2) Lack of genuine assent because of fraud or duress commonly is recognized as a defense. [See Chapter 16.]
   3) Adequacy of consideration. [See Chapter 14.]
      a) In the U.S., the adequacy (or value) of the consideration exchanged for a contractual promise is not questioned unless it is grossly inadequate or is evidence of lack of genuine assent.
      b) On the other hand, parties can raise defenses relating to the adequacy of consideration in other countries.

D. Employment law.

1. In the U.S., the traditional employment-at-will doctrine, permitting employers to "fire" employees for any reason or no reason at all, has been changing so that, today, there are restrictions in some states. [See Chapter 35.]

2. Modifications of the at-will doctrine — Many countries impose requirements on employers before the employers can discharge employees.

   a. France.
      1) The doctrine of *abus de droit* (abuse of a right) prohibits employers from firing workers for illness, unionization, political beliefs, etc.
      2) The Dismissal Law of 1973 provides that an employer can discharge an employee, who was hired for an indefinite term, only for genuine

and serious cause or economic factors and also establishes procedural requirements.

   b.   Poland — Under the Polish labor law, employment is predominantly "at-will" and either party may terminate the employment relationship at any time; usually, notice is required.

3.   Wages and benefits.

   a.   Although wage rates may be lower in other nations, employers in other countries are required to provide certain fringe benefits.

   b.   For example, in Mexico, employers are required to give a minimum amount of paid vacation time, annual bonuses, and training courses.

4.   Income security and workers' compensation — As is true in the U.S., many nations have laws providing for social security and unemployment benefits and requiring employers to compensate employees for work-related injuries. [See Chapter 35.]

5.   Equal employment opportunity [Chapter 36] — United States laws that prohibit an employer from discriminating against job applicants or employees based upon race, color, gender, national origin, religion, age, or disability apply to a U.S. firm operating abroad, unless to do so would violate the laws of the other nation (the foreign laws exception).

6.   Employment termination — In many countries, there are restrictions on discharging employees; examples include:

   a.   France — See above at III. D. 2. a.

   b.   Egypt — An employer can discharge an employee who was hired for an indefinite term only if the employee committed a serious offense, and the employer must submit a proposal for termination to a committee composed of representatives of the union and government.

   c.   Taiwan — An employer may discharge a worker for economic reasons or if the worker is not capable of performing the assigned work, but advanced notice and severance pay must be given to the employee.

IV.   The European Union (EU).

A.   Current members (which have entered into and adhere to a multinational agreement) are Austria, Belgium, Denmark, Finland, France, Germany, Greece, Ireland, Italy, Luxembourg, the Netherlands, Portugal, Spain, Sweden, and the United Kingdom.

B. The EU has eliminated many tariffs and private restrictive agreements among its members and promotes free trade, competition, and movement of workers, goods, and capital among the member nations.

C. The elected Assembly (Parliament) oversees the EU Commission that proposes regulations (binding directives) to the Council of Ministers (which coordinates economic policies); the European Court of Justice (ECJ) can review each nation's court decisions and is the ultimate authority on EU law.

D. Directives of the EU govern antitrust, corporate, securities, product liability, and environmental protection law.

V. Expanding overseas business opportunities. [See also Chapter 55.]

A. In recent years, the risk that a foreign government will nationalize private business ventures and impose restrictions on repatriation of profits has diminished.

B. In many countries, national companies that had been run by the government as monopolies have been privatized.

KEY WORDS AND PHRASES IN TEXT

international law
national law
Koran
Foreign Corrupt Practices Act
Title VII of the Civil Rights Act
    of 1964
federal system
unitary system
constitution
Magna Carta
judicial review
common law system
civil law system
stare decisis

Napoleonic Code
commercial codes
shari'a
requirements of contracts
Convention for the International
    Sale of Goods (CISG)
employment-at-will doctrine
abus de droit (abuse of rights)
European Union (EU)
EU Council of Ministers
European Court of Justice
nationalization
repatriation
privatization

FILL-IN QUESTIONS

1. The _____ of 1977 prohibits _____ firms from offering payments or gifts to officials of foreign nations in order to secure favorable contracts, but does not prohibit payments to minor government officials for purposes of facilitating necessary paperwork relating to a transaction.

2.   Some nations have _____ systems, in which governmental powers are divided between national and provincial governments, while other nations have centralized governments, called _____ systems.

3.   The _____ principle of *stare decisis* obligates _____ to follow decisions made in previously decided cases in their jurisdictions.

4.   In a _____ system, the only official source of law is a statutory code. The term, _____, thus, refers not to civil as opposed to criminal law, but to codified law, an orderly grouping of legal principles enacted into law by a legislative or governing body.

5.   The law of contracts as it relates to transactions involving sales of goods when the buyer and seller are citizens of different countries has been internationalized because of the United Nations _____ which, as of 1997, has been ratified by 38 countries, including the United States.

6.   Traditionally in the U.S., details of _____ relationships have been left to negotiations between employers and employees with little governmental interference. Under the _____ doctrine in the U.S., an employer may discharge an employee who has been hired for an indefinite term. In many other countries, restrictions are imposed on employers who wish to discharge such employees.

7.   The economic integration of western Europe has been the result of the formation of the _____, which was created by Belgium, France, Italy, Luxembourg, the Netherlands, and West Germany when these countries agreed to the 1957 Treaty of Rome in order to reduce trade barriers. Since that time, the number of member nations has expanded because Austria, Denmark, Finland, Greece, Ireland, Portugal, Spain, Sweden, and the United Kingdom have also joined in what is now referred to as the _____.

8.   The purchase of an entire business enterprise that had been owned and operated by a government is referred to as _____.

MULTIPLE CHOICE QUESTIONS

1.   The Noodles Company, a Delaware corporation, wants to do business in Mongolia and proposes to send Rob Smith, a vice-president of the firm, to Ulaanbatar, the capital of Mongolia, to open a Mongolian branch office. In order to be successful in the venture, it will be necessary for Mr. Smith to become knowledgeable about certain matters, such as:
     A. the legal system and laws of Mongolia.
     B. the language and culture of Mongolia.
     C. the firm's obligations under the Foreign Corrupt Practices Act of 1977.
     D. All of the answers above are correct.

2. Because of the principle of *stare decisis*, a Canadian judge, who is deciding a case for which there is no precedent in Canada, might examine and follow a decision made by a court in the:

	United States.	United Kingdom of Britain and Northern Ireland.
A.	Yes.	No.
B.	No.	Yes.
C.	Yes.	Yes.
D.	No.	No.

3. Which of the following is **not** indicative of a civil law system?
   A. The Napoleonic Code.
   B. The Magna Carta.
   C. The Japanese Commercial Code.
   D. All of the answers above are correct.

4. Aeroheed, Inc., a California corporation that manufactures passenger jet planes, is attempting to "win" a contract to build ten large passenger aircraft from the aviation ministry of Sapan, a country in Asia with a civil law system. The aviation minister in the Sapanese government has contacted Aeroheed's president and has told her that Aeroheed will be awarded the contract if Aeroheed makes a five million dollar contribution to the aviation minister's political party. If Aeroheed makes this contribution, which of the following statements most likely is correct?
   A. Sapan need **not** grant the contract to Aeroheed because Sapan is **not** a signatory to the United Nations Convention for the International Sale of Goods.
   B. Aeroheed's contribution probably violates the Foreign Corrupt Practices Act of 1977.
   C. Sapan need **not** award the contract to Aeroheed because Sapan has a civil law system and the U.S. has a common law system.
   D. Because gift-giving is a common practice in Sapan, the Aeroheed contribution is **not** prohibited by the Foreign Corrupt Practices Act of 1977.

5. The European Union Council of Ministers issues a directive on environmental law that requires all vehicles produced in EU-member nations to be free of certain polluting emissions. Which of the following statements is correct?
   A. The directive defines EU law in this area and is binding on EU-member nations.
   B. Because the directive has **not** been reviewed by the European Court of Justice, the directive is **not** binding on EU-member nations.
   C. Before the directive can be binding on all EU-member nations, the directive must be approved by the highest court in each of the EU-member nations.
   D. Before the directive can be binding on all EU-member nations, the directive must be approved by the EU Commission.

6. United States companies that engage in business abroad may be subject to certain risks because:
   A. a foreign government might nationalize private business ventures and may, or may not, compensate the owners.

B. a foreign country may impose restrictions on the ability of U.S. companies to repatriate their profits.

C. a foreign country may not effectively enforce its own intellectual property protection laws.

D. All of the answers above are correct.

7. Mykey Shoes, Inc. is a Delaware corporation that operates a factory in Ryland, an African country whose employment laws adhere to the doctrine of *abus de droit*. The factory manager may discharge or dismiss a factory employee:

A. for no reason at all.

B. who is disliked by the factory manager because the employee is left-handed.

C. because the employee burned down the factory.

D. for being a member of the Ryland shoe workers' union.

UNIT TWO:
CONTRACTS

The objective of Unit Two is to help you understand concepts of contract law that are the foundation upon which other areas of law relating to business are superimposed. The law of contracts deals with promises that have been made by parties who voluntarily have entered into private agreements. A contract is an agreement made by two or more parties, containing a promise or set of promises to perform or refrain from performing some act or acts, that will be enforced by a court. Contracts create expectations that the parties to the contracts will act in an agreed-upon manner. Contract law provides the framework for assuring that those expectations will be realized or remedies provided if they are not.

In the chapters in this unit, you will be learning about the rules that have been adopted relating to the rights and duties of the parties to such agreements, how contracts are formed and discharged, and what happens when parties fail to carry out the promises that they have made.

The principles of contract law have been developed by state courts. Although there are some variations among the states, in general, there is a substantial amount of similarity in the case law throughout the United States. The *Restatement of the Law of Contracts* (currently in a second edition), prepared by the American Law Institute, is a systematic compilation of the common law principles that are applicable to contracts. The *Restatement* often is cited by courts in their decisions, but note that the *Restatement* is neither a statute nor is the *Restatement* binding on the courts.

Some of the rules of contract law have been codified in statutes. For example, contracts for sales and leases of goods are governed by Articles 2 and 2A of the Uniform Commercial Code (UCC). The UCC is reproduced in Appendix C of the textbook.

Chapter 12
Nature and Terminology

A contract is a legal relationship between two or more competent parties who agree that each of the parties will act in some specified lawful manner. A contract exists when, in exchange for a promise given by one party (the promisor), the other party (the promisee) performs an act, refrains from performing an act, or makes a promise. Contractual promises may be made orally, or in writing, or even be inferred from the conduct of the parties. Usually, contractual promises are executed, or carried out, by the parties so that recourse to the courts is not necessary.

Contract law is the body of legal rules that relate to the formation, discharge, and breach of legally enforceable promises. In order to understand the principles of contract law discussed in the subsequent chapters in this unit, it is important that you become familiar with the basic concepts, terminology, and the rules of interpretation of contracts that are presented in this chapter.

THINGS TO KEEP IN MIND

A promise is an undertaking or commitment to do something, or refrain from doing something, in the future. The person making a promise is called the promisor and the person to whom the promise is made is referred to as the promisee. For example, you (the promisor) may promise to give ten dollars to another person (the promisee) tomorrow, or make a promise not to eat any candy for a week. If nothing is given in exchange for your promise, your promise will not be treated as a contractual promise, and you will not be penalized if you fail to pay the ten dollars or eat candy at some point during the week. On the other hand, suppose that the person to whom you made the promise to pay the ten dollars, or the promise to refrain from eating candy for a week, agreed that, in exchange for your promise, he or she would give you a book. Because something has been given or promised in exchange for your promise, the agreement is considered to be a contract. If you fail to carry out your promise, there is a breach of the contract, for which you may be liable to the promisee.

OUTLINE

I.   The function of contract law.

   A. Contracts create expectations as to how parties to agreements will conduct themselves in the future; usually, parties comply with their contractual obligations.

B. Contract law deals with the formation and enforcement of agreements between parties and is based upon the principle that "agreements shall be kept."

C. If a party to a valid contract does not carry out a promise, a court will enforce the contract and provide some form of relief or a remedy to the nonbreaching party.

D. Contract law provides stability and predictability and is the foundation upon which more specialized areas of the law are built.

II. Freedom of contract and freedom from contract.

A. Article I, Section 10 of the U.S. Constitution recognizes the rights of people to enter freely into contractual arrangements, and, therefore, provides that "no state shall pass any law impairing the obligations of contracts" (i.e., a state cannot change the existing contractual rights and duties of parties to valid contracts).

B. In general, people may freely enter into contracts unless the terms are contrary to law or public policy. [See Chapter 17.]

C. Changes in the law have occurred imposing restrictions on the manner of contracting and the terms that are allowed in contractual agreements.

III. The basic requirements of a contract.

A. In order to form a valid, enforceable contract, certain elements or requisites must be present.

B. Major elements:

1. Agreement — The mutual assent and agreement of the parties must be evidenced by an offer and an acceptance of the offer.

2. Consideration — Legally sufficient and bargained-for consideration (i.e., something that has legal value) must be exchanged for contractual promises.

3. Contractual capacity — There must be two or more parties who are recognized as being legally competent to enter into contracts.

4. Legality — The purpose and subject matter of the contract must not be contrary to law or public policy.

C. In addition, the following requisites (that typically are raised as defenses to the enforceability of an otherwise valid contract) must be met:

1. Genuineness of assent — The assent of the parties must be real, genuine, and voluntarily given; a contract may not be formed as a result of fraud, mistake, undue influence, or duress.

2. Form — The agreement must be in the form that is required by law if one is prescribed by statute (e.g., a signed writing).

IV. The objective theory or contracts.

A. A party's intention to enter into a legally-binding agreement is considered by a court in determining if a contract has been formed and should be enforced.

B. The apparent intention of a party to enter into a contract is determined by the objective, outward manifestation of that party's assent as such assent would be interpreted by a reasonable person, rather than by that party's own secret, subjective intentions.

C. Objective factors include (1) the conduct of the party, (2) the words spoken or written by the party, and (3) the circumstances surrounding the transaction.

V. Types of contracts.

A. Contract may be classified based upon the nature of the promises made by the parties (unilateral or bilateral); the manner in which the assent of the parties is given (express or implied); the necessity of compliance with a statute requiring a special formality (formal or informal); the stage of the performance of the parties' contractual obligations (executed or executory); and the legal validity and enforceablity of the contract (valid and enforceable, void, voidable, or unenforceable).

B. Bilateral versus unilateral contracts.

1. Bilateral contract — Reciprocal promises are exchanged by the parties so that the promise of one party is exchanged for the promise of the other.

2. Unilateral contract — One party makes a promise in exchange for the other party's actually performing some act (performance) or refraining from performing some act (forbearance).

    a. Usually, a unilateral contract is proposed by a promisor/offeror, who makes an offer consisting of a promise which is exchanged for actual performance so that, in order to accept, the promisee/offeree must complete performance of the required act.

    b. Occasionally, the issue in cases involving unilateral contracts is whether or not the offeror/promisor may revoke (cancel, terminate, or abrogate) the offer after the promisee begins his or her performance but before that performance is completed by the promisee. [See Chapter 13.]
       1) Traditional view — Offeror/promisor can revoke an offer at any time prior to completion of full performance.
       2) Modern view — Offeror/promisor may not revoke after offeree/promisee begins performance.

C. Express versus implied contracts.

1. Express contract — The terms of the agreement are stated explicitly in oral or written words.

2. Implied-in-fact or implied contract — The terms of the agreement are inferred from the conduct of the parties.

3. A contract may be a mixture of an express contract and an implied-in-fact contract when some contract terms are expressed in words but other terms are implied.

4. A court may hold that an implied contract was formed when:

    a. One party (the plaintiff) furnished services or property to the other party (the defendant);

    b. The plaintiff expected to be paid for that service or property, and the defendant knew or should have known that payment was expected; and

    c. The defendant had a chance to reject the services or property but did not do so.

D. Quasi contracts (sometimes referred to as contracts implied in law) are fictional contracts created by courts and imposed on parties in the interests of fairness and justice, and, therefore, are equitable, rather than contractual, in nature.

1. An obligation to pay the reasonable value for a benefit conferred or received may be imposed by a court in order to avoid unjust enrichment and to achieve justice although there actually is no contractual duty to pay.

2. Quasi contracts are based upon the doctrines of unjust enrichment and *quantum meruit* ("as much as he deserves").

3. A limitation on the doctrine of quasi contract — The person receiving the benefit is not liable in quasi contract or because of the doctrine of *quantum meruit* when the benefit was conferred unnecessarily or conferred because of misconduct or carelessness.

4. When an actual express or implied-in-fact contract exists, the doctrine is not applied because remedies for a breach of contract are available. [See Chapter 20.]

E. Formal versus informal contracts.

1. Formal contracts.

    a. A special formality is prescribed for their creation or formation.

    b. Examples include negotiable instruments, such as checks, and promises under seal at common law.

2. Informal contracts — Simple contracts that are based upon their substance and for which no special formality is required.

F. Executed versus executory contracts.

1. Executed contracts are contracts that have been completely performed by all parties.

2. Executory contracts are contracts that have not been fully performed by one or more parties.

G. Valid, void, voidable, and unenforceable contracts.

1. Valid contract — All of the elements that are necessary in order to form a contract are present.

2. Void contract.

a. Agreement has no legal effect and is not really a contract.

b. Examples: A party was adjudicated by a court to be mentally incompetent or the subject matter and purpose of the agreement are illegal.

3. Voidable contract.

a. One or more of the parties has the option either (1) to avoid his or her contractual obligation or (2) to ratify the contract.

b. Examples: a party was a minor who lacked full contractual capacity or the assent of a party was not real and genuine. [See Chapters 15 and 16.]

4. Unenforceable contract.

a. A contract that cannot be proven in the manner required by statutory law.

b. Examples: the statute of limitations bars enforcement; or a promise, which is required by the statute of frauds to be in writing, was made orally. [See Chapter 17.]

VI. Interpretation of contracts.

A. Over time, the courts have developed guidelines for determining the meaning of terms in a disputed contract so as to give effect to the contract that the parties made. The objective of the rules of interpretation is to determine the intent of the parties from the language used in their agreement.

B. The plain meaning rule — When the words used in a writing are plain, clear, unequivocal, and unambiguous, their meaning will be determined from the face of the written document alone and a court will not consider extrinsic evidence (evidence that is not contained in the writing itself).

C. Interpretation of ambiguous terms — Other rules of interpretation are used if the words used in a writing are ambiguous or not clear, in which case, extrinsic evidence may be admissible in a court to clarify the intent of the parties.

1. The interpretation which results in a reasonable, effective, and legal contract is preferred over one that results in an unreasonable, ineffective, or illegal agreement.

2. A writing will be interpreted as a whole; all writings that are part of the same transaction will be interpreted together; and words will not be taken out of the context in which the words are used.

3. Terms that were the subject of separate negotiation will be given greater consideration than standardized terms and terms that were not negotiated separately.

4. A word will be given its ordinary, commonly accepted meaning, and a technical term will be given its technical meaning, unless the parties clearly intended something else.

5. Specific terms will be given greater consideration than general language.

6. Handwritten words prevail over typewritten words, and typewritten words prevail over preprinted words.

7. When multiple meanings of language are possible, the language will be interpreted most strongly against the party who chose the words.

8. The court will admit evidence of usage in trade, prior dealings, and course of performance. [See Chapter 21.]

KEY WORDS AND PHRASES IN TEXT

contract
promise
breach of contract
promisor
promisee
objective theory of contracts
freedom of contract
freedom from contract
basic requirements of a contract
agreement (offer and acceptance)
legally sufficient and bargained-
    for consideration

contractual capacity
legality
genuiness of assent
form of contract
offeror
offeree
bilateral contract
unilateral contract
express contract
implied-in-fact (or implied) contract
quasi contract (implied in law contract)
unjust enrichment

quantum meruit
formal contract
contract under seal
informal (or simple) contract
executed contract
executory contract
valid contract

void contract
voidable contract
unenforceable contract
rules of interpretation
plain meaning rule
extrinsic evidence

FILL-IN QUESTIONS

1. A contract is a legal relationship created when _____ competent, consenting parties agree to perform or refrain from performing a legal act.

2. The requirements, or elements, of a contract are _____ _____ _____.

3. When words are used to create and define the terms of a contract, the parties have formed _____ contract. When the parties have used conduct, rather than words, they have entered into _____ contract.

4. A _____ contract consists of reciprocal promises. A unilateral contract consists of an exchange of a promise for _____.

5. If all the parties to a contract have completely performed their contractual promises, the contract is referred to as an _____ contract. If one or more of the parties has not completed his or her performance, the contract is said to be an _____ contract.

6. If the meaning of words in a writing setting forth the terms of a contract do not clearly express the _____ of the parties to the contract, a court will use rules of interpretation in order to clarify the terms of the agreement. For example, if two interpretations of terms in a written agreement are possible, one of which results in the contract being void because of illegality, and the other resulting in the contract being legal and valid, the interpretation that results in a _____ contract will be used by a court.

MULTIPLE CHOICE QUESTIONS

1. A unilateral contract:
    A. is a promise to perform an act.
    B. consists of mutual promises to act.
    C. consists of a promise to act exchanged for performance of an act.
    D. is one that is binding on one of the parties only.

2. A bilateral contract exists if:
    A. a promise to perform is exchanged for performance.

    B.   a promise of forbearance is exchanged for performance.

    C.   a promise to perform is exchanged for a promise of forbearance.

    D.   performance is exchanged for forbearance.

3.   Amin says to Bernard: "I will pay you ten dollars if you change the flat tire on my car." Bernard changes the flat tire.

    A.   A unilateral contract is created so that Amin must pay Bernard ten dollars.

    B.   A bilateral contract is created so that Amin must pay Bernard ten dollars.

    C.   A formal contract is created so that Amin must pay Bernard ten dollars.

    D.   No enforceable contract results.

4.   Dill says to Houk: "If you promise to paint my car, I promise to pay you two hundred dollars." Houk then says, "It's a deal; I promise to paint the car." This creates:

    A.   an express, unilateral contract.

    B.   an express, bilateral contract.

    C.   an implied-in-fact, unilateral contract.

    D.   an implied-in-fact, bilateral contract

5.   An implied-in-fact contract can be defined as one:

    A.   that lacks one or more elements of a true contract, but which may nevertheless be enforced by courts if it is in the best interests of the parties to do so.

    B.   that is formed entirely without the use of words.

    C.   in which the intentions of the contracting parties are inferred by the courts in large part from the parties' conduct and surrounding circumstances.

    D.   in which the intentions of the contracting parties are expressed with the use of words.

6.   A contract implied in law can be defined as one:

    A.   that is the same as an implied-in-fact contract.

    B.   in which one of the parties would be unjustly enriched even though he or she had not consented to the conferring of a benefit.

    C.   in which the intentions of one or all of the parties is inferred from their conduct and surrounding circumstances rather than words.

    D.   that has been fully performed by all of the parties.

7.   Don requests and accepts the services of Herr, an accountant, without agreeing to pay a specified fee for the services. As to the compensation which Herr is to receive, there is:

    A.   a formal contract.

    B.   an express contract.

    C.   an implied-in-fact contract.

    D.   a contract implied in law.

8.   An executed contract is a contract that:

    A.   involves more than two parties.

    B.   will be enforced unless one of the parties elects to disaffirm the contract.

    C.   is yet to be completely performed.

    D.   has been completely performed.

9. An executory contract is a contract that:
   A. has been completely performed.
   B. is yet to be completely performed.
   C. will **not** be recognized as enforceable by the courts.
   D. is illegal and will **not** be enforced by the courts.

10. An agreement to commit arson by burning down a building is an example of a:
    A. valid and enforceable contract.
    B. express, voidable contract.
    C. voidable, implied-in-fact contract.
    D. void and unenforceable contract.

11. Hughes and Ikes entered into a written contract for the sale of equipment by Hughes to Ikes for $10,000 to be paid for by Ikes in six months. In the preprinted form supplied by Hughes, there was a statement to the effect that "interest at the rate of 18% will be charged." This statement was crossed out and followed by the following handwritten statement: "Ikes will pay Hughes $10,800 six months from the date of this contract."
    A. Because current trade usage is to charge 22% interest, a court will find that Ikes will have to pay $1,100 as interest.
    B. A court will interpret the written contract and find that Ikes will have to pay $900 as interest.
    C. A court will interpret the written contract and find that Ikes will have to pay $800 as interest.
    D. A court will hold that Ikes does **not** have to pay any interest.

MATCHING QUESTIONS

There has been an automobile accident in which April, May, and June incurred injuries. April, May, and June were brought to a hospital. April, who was conscious, signed a written agreement in which she promises to pay the hospital for medical services and supplies. May, who was conscious, but unable to write her signature because of fractures, nodded her head up and down when asked if she agreed to the rendering of services and promised to pay for the medical services and supplies furnished at the hospital. June was unconscious when she arrived at the hospital. The hospital furnished medical services and supplies to June. The hospital submitted bills to April, May, and June, all of whom have recovered from their injuries because of the services provided by the hospital. April, May, and June have refused to pay the hospital bills.

Select from the list in the right hand column the two bases for the hospital recovering for the failure of each of the persons, who is named in questions 1, 2, and 3, to pay for the services and supplies that were furnished by the hospital.

1. April: _____ _____   A. The contract is an express contract.
2. May: _____ _____   B. The contract is an implied-in fact contract.
3. June: _____ _____   C. Quasi contract.
                               D. The contract is an executed bilateral contract.
                               E. The contract is an executory bilateral contract.
                               F. There is no contract.

Chapter 13
Agreement

In order for there to be a valid and enforceable contract, there must be an agreement that reflects the mutual assent of the parties to the terms of the contract. The parties are the offeror, the one who makes an offer, and the offeree, the person to whom the offer is made. The offeror and offeree must indicate or manifest their present, objective willingness and intention to assent to the same terms regarding their respective rights and duties. Agreement is evidenced by the process of offer and acceptance — an offer, or proposal, must have been made by the offeror and an acceptance given by the offeree.

The offeror shows and communicates his or her intention to agree to the material terms of the offer by using words or such conduct as would indicate to a reasonable person an intention to be bound by these terms. This is important because the terms of the offer will become the terms of the contract if the offeree accepts and agrees to the terms. The important terms are: the identification of the parties, the identification of the subject matter, the consideration (or "price" to be paid), and the time for performance. When the offeree accepts the offer by exhibiting his or her intention to be bound to the same terms, a contract is formed. At that point in time, the parties have shown their objective, mutual assent.

THINGS TO KEEP IN MIND

The parties may contemplate either (1) a unilateral contract, which provides that actual performance of an act or actual forbearance is exchanged by one party (usually, the offeree) for a promise by the other party (usually, the offeror) to perform an act or refrain from doing a particular thing, or (2) a bilateral contract, in which case both the offeror and offeree make promises relating to their future conduct.

OUTLINE

I.   Requirements of the offer.

    A. The offeror shows his or her objective assent when he or she communicates a proposal (the offer) to the offeree, setting forth with reasonable clarity, definiteness, and certainty the material terms to which he or she is presently, objectively agreeing and intending to be bound.

    B. Intention.

        1. The offeror must manifest his or her objective, serious intention to be bound by the terms of the offer.

2. The words and/or conduct used by the offeror must be such that, under the circumstances, a reasonable person would be warranted in believing that an agreement was intended by the offeror.

3. A reasonable person would understand that a proposal that is made in obvious jest, anger, or undue excitement is not intended to be an offer to enter into a contract.

4. It is necessary to distinguish offers from:

   a. Expressions of opinion and statements of intent to make future offers;

   b. Preliminary negotiations, requests to negotiate, and invitations soliciting bids or offers; and

   c. Advertisements, catalogues, circulars, and price lists that usually are considered to be invitations to the recipients to make offers to the advertiser.

   d. Requests of auctioneers for bids at auctions [UCC 2-328].
      1) Unless the auction is explicitly stated to be without reserve, the goods being auctioned may be withdrawn by the seller at any time before the sale is closed, and the goods do not have to be be sold to the highest bidder.
      2) A bidder is considered to be an offeror; the bidder may withdraw or revoke his or her bid, and the auctioneer may reject a bid or all bids.
      3) A contract for the sale of the goods is formed when the auctioneer brings down the hammer.
      4) In auctions with reserve, the seller may retain the right to reject the sale, even after the hammer falls, if the audience at the auction is notified that a sale of the goods is not final until confirmed by the seller.

   e. Agreements to agree at a future date — Today, some courts may enforce such agreements if the parties clearly intended to be bound.

C. Definiteness of terms.

   1. In the offer, the material, important terms that must be expressed explicitly or reasonably inferred are:

      a. The identification of the parties;

      b. The identification of the subject matter (which may be goods, services, or land) and, when appropriate, the quantity;

      c. The consideration (or "price" to be paid); and

      d. The time for payment, delivery or other performance by the parties.

2. All of the material terms of what will become the contract must be indicated in the offer with clarity, definiteness, and certainty or a means stated in the offer by which one or more of the terms will be made definite or precise.

3. The offeror may provide that one or more of the terms are to be made more definite by the offeree, by a third person, or by reference to an outside standard.

4. Sometimes, courts are willing to supply missing reasonable terms when the parties have clearly manifested their intent to form a contract and such terms do not conflict with the intent of the parties.

5. Terms of a modified contract also must be reasonably definite to enable a court to determine if there has been a breach.

D. Communication.

1. The offeror must have the intention of making the terms known to the offeree and those terms must be received by the offeree so that the offeree has knowledge of the terms of the offer.

2. An offer may be made to a specific offeree to whom it is communicated.

3. A public offer, such as an offer for a reward, is treated as communicated to those people who have knowledge of such an offer.

II. Termination of the offer.

A. Termination by actions of the parties.

1. Revocation of the offer by the offeror.

   a. In general, an offer may be revoked (withdrawn or repudiated) by the offeror at any time before acceptance, expressly or by acts that are inconsistent with the existence of the offer and are known to the offeree.

   b. A revocation must be communicated to the offeree.
      1) The revocation, therefore, must be received by the offeree prior to the offeree's acceptance.
      2) A revocation is effective if the offeree indirectly learns of the revocation.

   c. An offer to a specific offeree is effectively terminated when the revocation is received by the offeree.

   d. A public offer is effectively terminated when the revocation is communicated in the same manner as that used in order to make the offer.

   e. Irrevocable offers.

1) Option contracts.
   a) An option contract is a separate contract that exists when an offeror promises to hold an offer open (i.e., not revoke the offer), and the offeree accepts the offer for the option contract and gives consideration for this promise to the offeror.
   b) The offer is irrevocable for the period of time that is stated or, if no period is stated, for a reasonable period of time.
   c) Death or incompetency of the offeror or the offeree does not terminate the offer, unless the offeror's personal performance is essential to the fulfillment of the contract.
2) Merchants' firm offers are provided for in the UCC in Section 2-205.
   a) A written offer for the purchase or sale of goods, made and signed by a merchant dealing in those goods, in which the merchant promises to hold the offer open, is irrevocable for the specified period of time (not exceeding three months) or, if no time is specified, a reasonable period of time. [See Chapter 21.]
   b) The offer is irrevocable even if consideration is not given by the offeree as long as the period of time is less than three months.
3) Detrimental reliance — Because of the doctrine of promissory estoppel, an offeror may be estopped (i.e., barred or precluded) from revoking an offer when an offeree detrimentally changed his or her position in justifiable reliance on the offer. [See Chapter 14.]
4) Offers to enter into unilateral contracts.
   a) Traditional view — Offer to enter into a unilateral contract may be revoked by offeror even though the offeree has begun, but not completed, performance of the act(s) necessary to accept offer.
   b) Modern views — Restatement of Contracts, Second, Section 45.
      (1) Offeror may not revoke offer if offeree has substantially performed.
      (2) Offeror may not revoke offer for a reasonable period of time after offeree begins performance.
      (3) Some courts have held that the offeror may revoke offer but must pay for any benefit conferred upon the offeror.

2. Rejection of the offer by the offeree.

   a. Offeree demonstrates his or her intention not to accept offer.

   b. In order to terminate an offer effectively, a rejection must be communicated to and, therefore, be received by the offeror or the offeror's agent.

   c. An inquiry made by an offeree is distinguishable from a rejection and does not terminate offer.

3. Counteroffer by the offeree.

   a. A counteroffer is a rejection of an offer and the simultaneous making of a new offer. (The counteroffer may, or may not, be accepted by the original offeror.)

      b. A counteroffer terminates the original offer.

      c. Mirror image rule.
         1) Offeree's acceptance must exactly match the offeror's offer.
         2) A communication from the offeree that contains a material change in or addition to the terms of the original offer is a counteroffer, which terminates the original offer. [See Chapter 21 regarding UCC provisions relaxing the mirror image rule.]

B. Termination by operation of law.

   1. If an offer is terminated by operation of law because of lapse of time, destruction of the subject matter, death or incompetency of the offeror or offeree, or supervening illegality of the proposed contract, communication giving notice of the happening of the event is not necessary.

   2. Lapse of time.

      a. If the duration of an offer is stated in the offer, the offer terminates automatically after expiration of the stated period of time.

      b. If the duration of an offer is not stated in an offer, the offer lapses after a period of time that is reasonable under the circumstances.

   3. Destruction of the subject matter of the offer before the offer is accepted.

   4. Death or incompetency of the offeror or offeree before the offer is accepted.

      a. The death or an adjudication by a court of incompetency of a party terminates an offer.

      b. Exception — Irrevocable offers (e.g., option contracts and firm offers).

   5. Supervening illegality of the proposed contract as a result of legislation or judicial decision.

III. Acceptance.

A. The offeree accepts the offer when the offeree unequivocally and voluntarily manifests his or her willingness and intention to assent to the terms of the offer.

   1. Acceptance must be given by the person to whom the offer was directed or by his or her agent.

   2. In general, once the parties have entered into an option contract, the offeree can transfer his or her right to accept to another person.

   3. When the offer is made jointly to two or more persons, acceptance must be given by all of them.

B. Unequivocal acceptance — The acceptance must positively, unconditionally, and unequivocally accord to the terms of the offer.

C. Silence as acceptance.

1. Ordinarily, the offeree must exhibit his or her agreement to be bound with words or other overt conduct, and silence cannot constitute an acceptance.

2. Silence is not considered to be an acceptance unless the offeror indicates that he or she will assume that the offeree is accepting the offer if the offeree does not reject it, and:

   a. The offeree accepts the benefit of the offered services or goods when the offeree had an opportunity to reject the offered services or goods and knew that such services or goods were offered with the expectation of compensation;

   b. There was a similar prior course of dealings; or

   c. The offeree exercised dominion over the subject matter. (This does not apply to unsolicited merchandise sent through the mail.)

D. Communication of acceptance.

1. If a unilateral contract is contemplated, acceptance is effective when the performance (or forbearance) is completed; notification of the acceptance is not necessary unless the offeror requests such notice or has no adequate means of determining if the requested act has been performed or such notice is required by law. [See also Chapter 21.]

2. If a bilateral contract is contemplated, acceptance is effective when the offeree gives the requisite promise; the offeree must use reasonable efforts to communicate the acceptance to the offeror.

E. Mode and timeliness of acceptance of offers for bilateral contracts.

1. An acceptance is timely if the acceptance is effective before the offer has terminated.

2. Authorized means of communicating acceptance.

   a. If the mode of communicating the acceptance is specified expressly in the offer by the offeror, an acceptance is effective when the acceptance is dispatched or sent in the manner expressly authorized by the offeror, even if the communication is not received by the offeror (the mailbox or deposited acceptance rule).

   b. If the means of communicating the acceptance is not specified by the offeror, acceptance is effective when the acceptance is sent, if it is sent by using an impliedly authorized means of communication.
   1) Offeree uses the same mode of communication as was used by the offeror for communicating the offer or uses a faster means of communication.
   2) Offeree uses any customary or reasonable mode of communication.

3. Acceptance is not effective until the acceptance is received by the offeror if the acceptance is sent in a manner that is not authorized expressly or impliedly by the offeror.

4. Exceptions to the rule that acceptance is effective when dispatched by using an expressly or impliedly authorized means of communication — Acceptance is not effective until acceptance is received by the offeror if:

   a. Acceptance is improperly sent — For example, if acceptance is mailed, the letter is not correctly addressed or does not have the correct postage.

   b. The offeror included a condition in the offer that acceptance will not be effective until the acceptance is received by the offeror.

   c. The offeree sends a rejection and later sends an acceptance; in this case, the first communication received by the offeror will be effective.

F. A contract is created at the moment that the acceptance is effective.

IV. Contract formation in an electronic age.

A. Courts have extended traditional contract law principles to offers and acceptances made through nontraditional and new modes of communication, including fax (facsimile) machines and the Internet.

B. Faxed offers and acceptances.

   1. A signature on a faxed document is considered to be legally binding, unless an "original" signature specifically is required.

   2. When an acceptance is faxed to the offeror's office, but the acceptance is not received in a timely fashion or is lost, the acceptance is not effective upon dispatch. (The acceptance is effective when it is received by the offeror.)

   3. If the offeror did not receive a faxed acceptance because the offeror's fax machine was out of paper, and the offeree had reason to know or suspect that the offeror did not receive the faxed acceptance, a court might hold that the faxed acceptance was not effective.

   4. If an offer is faxed to an offeree's office, but the offeree is not aware that the offer has been received, a court might not consider the offer to have been

effectively communicated, unless the offeree had agreed to the fax method of communication or there had been a pattern of conduct reflecting acquiescence to the fax method of communication.

C. The validity of online "click-on" acceptances on the Internet is an emerging area of law and probably depends upon whether or not the offeree's conduct was meant to be an intentional acceptance. [See Chapter 21.]

KEY WORDS AND PHRASES IN TEXT

agreement
mutual assent
offer
offeror and offeree
objective intention to be bound
offers distinguished from expressions
    of opinions, intentions, invitations,
    preliminary negotiations, catalogs,
    and advertisements
auctions
definiteness of terms of offer
    (and, therefore, contract)
communication of offer to offeree
offers for rewards
terminations of offers by actions of
    parties
revocation of offer (by offeror)
irrevocable offers
option contract
merchant's firm offer

detrimental reliance on an offer
promissory estoppel
estop
rejection of offer (by offeree)
counteroffer (by offeree)
"mirror image rule"
termination of offers by operation of law
termination of offer because of lapse
    of time, destruction of subject
    matter, or illegality
termination of offer because of death or
    incompetency of offeror or offeree
acceptance
unequivocal acceptance
silence generally does not operate as
    an acceptance
communication of acceptance
implied means of acceptance
"mailbox (or deposited acceptance) rule"
faxed offers and acceptances

FILL-IN QUESTIONS

1. In order to form a contract, it is essential that the parties manifest their mutual assent to the terms of their agreement. The assent of the offeror is evidenced by communication of the terms of the offeror's _____ to the offeree. The contract will exist when the offeree shows his or her assent by _____ the offeror's terms.

2. The person, who is making a proposal or offer is called the _____, and the person to whom an offer is made is referred to as the _____.

3. In order for the parties to a contract to know what performance is expected of them, certain important terms must be expressed clearly in their contract or be capable of being reasonably inferred from their contract. These terms, therefore, must also be set forth with definiteness in the offer, and include: the identification of the _____; the identification of the _____, which may be

services, goods, or other property; the _____, or price to be paid; and the time when performance, payment, or delivery is to be made.

4. In general, an offeror has the power to terminate or _____ an offer before it has been accepted. If, however, the offeror promises not to withdraw the offer for six months and the offeree pays the offeror ten dollars, the offeror cannot _____ the offer during the six months because the parties have entered into a valid, enforceable _____ contract.

5. A merchant, who makes an offer to sell specified goods and also promises in a signed writing to hold the offer open for two weeks, cannot _____ the offer during the two-week period, even though the offeree gave no consideration, because the merchant offeror has made a _____ offer. If the merchant offeror's signed written promise was to hold the offer open for four-months, however, the merchant offeror can withdraw the offer during the four month period if no consideration was given by the offeree for the _____ offer.

6. A communication from the offeree to the offeror in which the offeree states that he or she does not wish to accept an offer is called a _____ and effectively terminates the offer. A communication from the offeree to the offeror in which the offeree sets forth terms that are different from the terms contained in the original offer is considered to be a _____, which also effectively terminates the original offer.

7. An offer is terminated at the expiration of the period of time that is specified by the offeror in the offer or, if the duration of the offer is not specified explicitly in the offer, after _____ has elapsed. An offer also is terminated by operation of law if one of the parties has _____ or been adjudicated by a court as incompetent, the _____ has been destroyed, or a statute has been enacted which makes performance of the contract illegal.

MULTIPLE CHOICE QUESTIONS

1. The general rule is that a person who responds to an advertisement by stating that he or she will purchased advertised goods at the advertised price is:
    A. making an inquiry or invitation to the advertiser asking that an offer be made.
    B. making a counteroffer, which is a rejection of the advertiser's offer.
    C. making an offer to buy the goods from the advertiser.
    D. accepting the advertiser's offer for the sale of the goods.

2. The following advertisement appeared in a newspaper:

    Brand new bicycles: Worth up to $100! Our price $25! Limited number available.

    This advertisement would be considered to be:
    A. an invitation to make an offer.
    B. an offer to a unilateral contract.
    C. an offer to a bilateral contract.
    D. a contract.

3.   The following advertisement appeared in a newspaper:

     One new 10 speed green mountain bike manufactured by Rockies Bikes, Inc., catalog number 10 SMB 50. available for $50.00. Be the first to call 234-5678.

     This advertisement would be considered to be:
     A. an invitation to make an offer.
     B. an offer to a unilateral contract.
     C. an offer to a bilateral contract.
     D. a contract.

4.   In order for an offer to be effective, the following requirement or requirements must be met:
     A. the terms of the offer must be communicated to the offeree.
     B. the material terms of the offer must be reasonably definite, clear, and certain.
     C. the offeror must show objectively that he or she intends to be bound by the terms of the offer.
     D. A and B above are correct.
     E. A, B, and C above are correct.

5.   The ABC Auto Sales Co. sent the following telegram to Ford Motor Company:

     "We need ten automobiles as soon as possible. Ship to ABC Auto Sales Co."

     A. The telegram contains an offer.
     B. Acceptance by Ford Motor Company will not take place until receipt of the automobiles by ABC Auto Sales Co.
     C. The telegram is too indefinite and uncertain to constitute an offer.
     D. The telegram creates a contract.

6.   When goods are placed on sale at an ordinary auction, a contract is formed at the moment that:
     A. the auctioneer shows the goods.
     B. the highest bid is made.
     C. the auctioneer brings down the hammer.
     D. the highest bidder pays for the goods.

7.   Which of the following statements concerning the effectiveness of an offeror's revocation and an offeree's rejection of an offer generally is correct?

	An offeror's revocation is effective when it is:	An offeree's rejection is effective when it is:
A.	sent by the offeror.	received by the offeror.
B.	received by the offeree.	sent by the offeree.
C.	sent by the offeror.	sent by the offeree.
D.	received by the offeree.	received by the offeror.

     (This question has been adapted from question #1-22, Uniform CPA Examination, May 1989.)

8.   A communication by the offeree setting forth terms that are different from those contained in the original offer is considered to:

A. be a counteroffer and, therefore, a rejection.
B. result in a binding contract.
C. keep the original offer open.
D. create a unilateral contract.

9. An outstanding offer to sell a tract of real property is terminated at the time that:
    A. the buyer mails a rejection of the offer if the original offer was sent by mail.
    B. the buyer learns of the sale of the property to a third person.
    C. the buyer learns of the seller's death.
    D. the seller mails a revocation of the original offer if the offer was sent by mail.

10. John writes a letter to Bill in which he offers to sell his motorcycle to Bill for $1,000. John may revoke his offer:
    A. after the expiration of one week.
    B. at any time before Bill sends an acceptance to John.
    C. at any time before John receives an acceptance from Bill.
    D. at no time because the offer is in writing.

11. If no time is specified by the offeror as to when an offer will terminate, the offer lapses after the expiration of a reasonable period of time. What is a reasonable period of time depends on:
    A. the nature of the subject matter.
    B. the period of time within which the offeror's purpose can be effected.
    C. the prior course of dealings of the parties.
    D. All of the answers above are correct.

12. An offer is terminated:
    A. by the expiration of a reasonable period of time although a specified period of duration is stated in the offer.
    B. by the expiration of a reasonable period of time when no specified period of duration is stated in the offer.
    C. when the offer is not rejected by the offeree.
    D. within a reasonable period of time after the offeror and offeree separate if the offer had been oral.

13. In order to be effective, if the United States postal service is used:
    A. an offer must be received by an offeree and a rejection sent by an offeree.
    B. an offer must be received by an offeree and a revocation received by an offeror.
    C. an acceptance must be received by an offeror and a revocation received by an offeree.
    D. an acceptance must be sent by an offeree and a revocation received by an offeree.

14. A letter of revocation of an offer to enter into a contract is effective when it is:
    A. written and signed by the offeror.
    B. deposited in the mail by the offeror.
    C. received by the offeror.
    D. received by the offeree.

15. On March 1, Sam made an offer to sell his horse, Star, for $10,000 to Bill. Star was stolen on March 5 and still is missing. Bill and Sam have entered into a contract for the sale of Star, if Bill:
    A. accepted Sam's offer in a letter that was mailed on March 4 and received by Bill on March 6.
    B. sent a fax to Sam's office on March 6, in which he stated that he accepted Sam's offer, even though the fax was not received because of Sam's failure to connect the fax machine.
    C. sent a fax to Sam's office on March 6, in which he stated that he accepted Sam's offer and Bill received and read the fax.
    D. mailed a rejection on March 4 that was received by Sam on March 7, but Bill faxed an acceptance on March 5 that was received and read by Sam on March 6.

Chapter 14
Consideration

In order for a contractual promise to be enforceable, the promise must be supported by legally sufficient consideration so that there is a bargained-for exchange by the parties. The party making the promise, the promisor, must receive a legal benefit (something that he or she does not already have a right to receive), or the promisee, the party to whom the promise is made, must incur a legal detriment (give up something that he or she has a right to keep), or both. Consideration is given, therefore, if something that is recognized as having legal value is given in exchange for the promise. If consideration is not given for a promise, there is no contract.

THINGS TO KEEP IN MIND

The issue of lack of consideration arises when a promisee sues a promisor who has failed to carry out a promise and the promisor raises the defense that no consideration was given in exchange for the promise. There is a lack of consideration if:

1. The promisor receives nothing having legal value, and/or
2. The promisee does not give up, or promise to give up, a legal right by doing something that the promisee has a right not to do or by refraining from doing something that the promisee has a right to do.

OUTLINE

I. Legal sufficiency of consideration.

A. Parties to a contract.

1. Promisor — The party who makes a promise to do or refrain from doing something.

2. Promisee — The party who receives a promise.

3. If, as illustrated in the diagram below, a unilateral contract is contemplated, only one party (A) is the promisor. The other party (B) is the promisee.

$$A \xrightarrow{\text{promise made by A}} B$$
(promisor)   (promisee)

4. If a bilateral contract is contemplated, as illustrated in the following diagram, promises are exchanged by the parties. Each party, therefore, is a promisor as to the promise which he or she makes and a promisee as to the promise which he or she receives. Each promise must be supported by consideration.

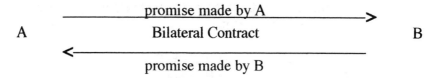

B. There must be a presently bargained-for exchange between the parties. Consideration may be thought of as the "price" paid by the promisee for a promise so that mutual obligations are present.

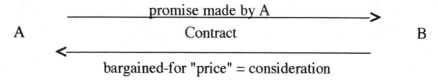

C. Legally sufficient consideration exists when either the promisee incurs a legal detriment, or the promisor receives a legal benefit, or both.

1. A legal detriment is incurred by a promisee if the promisee does one of the following:

   a. Actually gives up something that he or she (the promisee) has a prior legal right to keep in the case of a unilateral contract. This is illustrated in the diagram below:

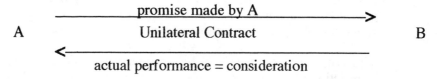

   b. Actually refrains or forbears from doing something that he or she (the promisee) has a prior legal right to do in the case of a unilateral contract. This is illustrated in the diagram below:

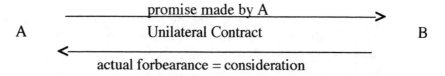

   c. Promises to surrender something that he or she (the promisee) has a right to retain. This is illustrated in the following diagram of a bilateral contract:

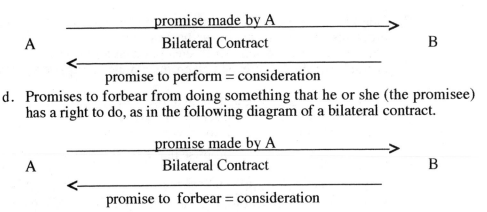

d. Promises to forbear from doing something that he or she (the promisee) has a right to do, as in the following diagram of a bilateral contract.

2. A legal benefit is received by a promisor if the promisor received something to which he or she is not entitled, but for the contract.

3. It is not necessary that an economic or material loss be incurred by the promisee or that an economic or material benefit be received by the promisor. All that is necessary is a surrender or receipt of a prior legal right.

II. Adequacy of consideration.

   A. In general, because of the doctrine of freedom of contract, the relative value of the consideration given by contracting parties is not examined by the courts.

   B. Exceptions to the rule that adequacy of consideration, or the fairness of the bargain, will not be examined by a court:

      1. The fact that the relative value of consideration given by one party is greater than the consideration given by the other party may be evidence that the assent of one party was not genuine or voluntarily given, or may be a reflection of a party's incompetency or lack of full contractual capacity.

      2. The consideration received by one party was grossly inadequate and the transaction was unconscionable (an equitable principle). [See Chapter 16.]

III. Contracts that lack consideration.

   A. Preexisting duty.

      1. Doing something that one already has a duty to do, or promising to do what one already has a legal duty to do, is not legally sufficient consideration for another person's promise.

         a. The promisee does not incur a legal detriment if the promisee is doing something that the promisee already is required to do.

         b. The promisor does not receive a legal benefit if the promisor already has a right to receive the promisee's performance or forbearance.

2. One has a preexisting duty imposed by law not to commit a crime or tort; a promise to refrain from committing an illegal or tortious act, therefore, is not consideration for another person's promise to pay money, or a promise to perform some other act, or a promise to refrain from doing something.

3. Performing an existing contractual duty or promising to carry out an existing contractual obligation cannot be consideration for another person's promise to pay additional money or to otherwise perform.

4. Consideration is present, however, if in addition to performing a preexisting duty, the promisee does something or promises to do something that the promisee otherwise is not required to do.

5. Exceptions to the preexisting duty rule.

    a. Unforeseen difficulties.
        1) Sometimes, a promise to pay additional consideration, or compensation, is enforceable if unknown, unanticipated, unforeseen difficulties arise causing the burden of performance to increase greatly.
        2) In states in which the unforeseen difficulties exception is recognized, the exception usually is applied in limited situations, such as construction contracts.

    b. Rescission and new contract.
        1) Rescission means that a contract is canceled or unmade so as to return the contracting parties to the positions they were in before the contract was formed.
        2) If a contract is completely executory because neither party has performed, the parties mutually may agree to rescind, or cancel, the contract.
        3) Thereafter, the parties are free to enter into a new contract that may have the same or different terms.

    c. Modification of existing contract — If a contract is executed in part by one of the parties, and the party who has not performed gives new consideration, the parties may modify, or change, the terms of the contract.
        1) Some states have enacted statutes providing that, if the modification is in a signed writing, the modification will be enforceable without new consideration.
        2) Sale of goods — Section 2-209(1) of the UCC provides that a modification of a contract for the sale of goods is enforceable without consideration.

B. Past consideration — Past consideration is no consideration because there is no presently bargained-for exchange. (You can bargain for something to take place now or in the future, but not for something that already has occurred.)

C. Promises that are based upon moral duties are not enforceable because a moral obligation is not considered to be legally sufficient consideration.

IV. Problem areas concerning consideration.

    A. Uncertain performance.

        1. An illusory promise is one that appears to be a promise but is not really an undertaking to do anything.

        2. A promise that solely depends upon the discretion, whim, or wish of the promisor is illusory.

        3. An unconditional "option-to-cancel" clause.

            a. If the right to cancel is absolute and unconditional, the contract is illusory.

            b. If the right to cancel is conditioned upon the happening of some event, the contract is enforceable.

    B. Settlement of claims.

        1. A promise to pay or actual payment of part of a mature, liquidated, undisputed debt is not consideration for a creditor's release of a debtor's obligation to pay the remaining balance.

        2. Accord and satisfaction — Used in order to extinguish an obligation.

            a. An accord is a new agreement entered into by a debtor and creditor; an accord provides that the debtor promises to give something, other than that which was originally agreed upon, in exchange for the creditor's acceptance of the debtor's performance in full satisfaction of the original debt.

            b. Satisfaction occurs when the accord is executed (i.e., consideration is given when the new or different performance is rendered by the debtor).

            c. A debtor and creditor may settle an outstanding obligation by entering into an accord and satisfaction if the original debt is not mature, or not liquidated, and/or the obligation to pay or the amount of the debt is disputed.

                1) Liquidated debt.

                    a) The amount of the debt is ascertained, fixed, agreed-upon, and settled, and the amount is an exact sum of money or a sum that is capable of being made definite by computation.

                    b) Accord and satisfaction does not apply to a liquidated debt — Acceptance of a sum that is less than the entire amount of a liquidated debt is not satisfaction because no consideration is given by the debtor who already has a preexisting obligation to pay the entire debt.

                2) Unliquidated debt.

a) The amount of the debt is not ascertained, fixed, agreed-upon, settled, or computable, or reasonable persons may differ over the amount that is owed.

b) Accord and satisfaction does apply to an unliquidated debt — Consideration is exchanged because each party gives up a legal right to contest the amount in dispute.

d. A debtor and creditor may settle an outstanding obligation by entering into an accord (new agreement) and satisfaction (performance of new terms) if additional consideration is given or if the debt is not mature (the obligation to pay is not yet due).

3. Release.

a. A release is a relinquishment of a right or discharge of an obligation or claim that one person has against another person.

b. A release is binding and bars any additional recovery beyond the terms stated in the release if:
1) The release was obtained and given in good faith.
2) In some states, the release is in a signed writing.
3) Consideration is given for the release or, if the transaction is covered by the UCC [Section 1-107], there is a written waiver or renunciation signed by an aggrieved party; the effect is to discharge the other party's liability for a breach, even though consideration is not given.

4. Covenant not to sue.

a. A covenant not to sue is a promise by a person, who has a right to bring an action or sue, that he or she will not sue in order to enforce such right of action.

b. A covenant not to sue is enforceable if it is obtained and given in good faith, supported by consideration, and, in some states, be evidenced by a signed writing.

C. Promises enforceable without consideration.

1. In the past, consideration was not necessary if a promise was in a writing to which a seal was affixed.

2. Promises to pay debts barred by a statute of limitations.

a. Statutes provide that a person (e.g., a creditor) who has a cause of action must commence the action, or sue, within a specified period of time; after the statutory period of time has expired, the aggrieved party is barred from suing because the contract is unenforceable.

b. A new promise by a debtor to pay a debt, even though technically the promise is not supported by new consideration, will extend the period of time provided for in the statute of limitations so that the new promise is enforceable by the creditor.

c. If a debtor makes a partial payment of a debt after the statutory period has run, it is implied that the debtor acknowledges the existence of the debt, and the creditor can sue thereafter for the balance of the debt.

d. In some states, the new promise made by the debtor to pay the debt must be in a writing that is signed by the debtor.

3. Detrimental reliance, or promissory estoppel.

   a. In those states in which the doctrine has been adopted, a promisor will be estopped (or prevented) from raising the defense that consideration was not given for a gratuitous promise.

   b. A court will enforce an otherwise unenforceable promise in order to avoid an injustice, if:
      1) A promise is made to induce a promisee to act in a particular way;
      2) The promisor can foresee that the promisee will justifiably rely upon the promise;
      3) The promisee substantially and detrimentally changes his or her position in the foreseeable manner and incurs damage because of his or her (the promisee's) reasonable reliance upon the promise; and
      4) Injustice can be avoided only by enforcing the promise.

4. Charitable subscriptions.

   a. On the basis of traditional contract law, promises to make gifts to religious, educational, charitable, or other nonprofit organizations are not supported by legally sufficient consideration.

   b. Today, such charitable subscriptions are enforced based upon different theories.
      1) Consideration may be found if the charitable organization made a promise that the gift would be used for a specific purpose.
      2) Consideration may be found because each promisor's promise is made in consideration for the promises made by other donors.
      3) Some courts apply the doctrine of promissory estoppel and, therefore, enforce charitable subscriptions.
      4) Some courts enforce the promises because of public policy.

5. Other statutory exceptions.

   a. UCC provisions — In addition to Section 2-209, relating to modification of contracts for the sale of goods [See above at III. A. 5], Section 1-107, providing for signed written waivers or renunciation of claims [See above at IV. B. 3.], and Section 2-205 dealing with merchants' firm offers [See Chapter 13], Article 3 establishes rules for negotiable instruments (formal contracts), which may be issued and transferred without consideration [See Unit 4].

b. The Model Written Obligations Act and similar state statutes provide that certain promises contained in signed writings are enforceable even though these promises are not exchanged for consideration.

KEY WORDS AND PHRASES IN TEXT

consideration
legally sufficient value
bargained-for exchange
performance of an act
forbearance (refraining from
     doing something)
promisor
promisee
legally detrimental to promisee
legally beneficial to promisor
adequacy of consideration ("fairness" of
    bargain usually is not relevant)
unconscionable
preexisting duty
unforeseen difficulties

mutual rescission of contract
modification of existing contract
past consideration
uncertain performance
illusory promise
option-to-cancel clause
settlement of claims
accord and satisfaction
liquidated debt distinguished from
     unliquidated debt
release
covenant not to sue
debts barred by a statute of limitations
detrimental reliance or promissory estoppel
enforceability of charitable subscriptions

FILL-IN QUESTIONS

1. Sufficient legal consideration exists if the promisor receives a legal _____ or the promisee incurs a legal _____ in exchange for a contractual promise.

2. _____ means refraining from doing something and may be the bargained-for exchange for a contractual promise and, therefore, legally sufficient _____.

3. Johnson promises to pay ABC Video Games $500 if it promises to close its video arcade before 7:00 p.m. every day for one year. ABC Video Games has given _____ legal consideration for Johnson's promise because promising to _____ from doing something, which one has a legal right to do, is consideration for a contractual promise.

4. A promise to perform an act that a person is already legally obligated to perform (or legally obligated to forbear or refrain from doing) is not considered to be sufficient _____ for another person's promise. This is referred to as the _____ duty rule.

5. Two months ago, Rory promised to pay Ella $900 in exchange for Ella's promise to refrain from shoplifting for one month. Ella abstained from shoplifting for more than a month and now wishes to enforce Rory's promise to pay her the $900. Rory's promise is not enforceable because his promise was not bargained-for in exchange for _____ consideration. Ella, the promisee, did not incur a legal detriment because she merely did that which she had a _____ duty imposed by statute to do. Rory, the promisor, did not receive a legal _____ because he already had a legal right to know that Ella was not violating a criminal statute.

6. Six months ago, Rose and Ed entered into a contract for the construction of a garage at Rose's home. Rose had agreed to pay Ed $3,000 and Ed agreed to build the garage according to specifications, but Ed has not built the garage. Last month, Rose promised to pay Ed an additional $400 in exchange for Ed's promise to construct the garage in accordance with their prior contract. Ed will not be able to enforce Rose's promise to pay the additional $400 because this promise was not bargained-for in exchange for _____ consideration. Ed, the promisee, did not incur a legal detriment because he merely did that which he had a _____ duty imposed by contract to do. Rose, the promisor, did not receive a legal _____ because she already had a contractual right to receive Ed's performance.

7. A promise to buy all the widgets that one wishes to buy in exchange for a promise to sell all such widgets is _____ and not supported by_____.
    A promise to buy all the widgets one may require or need in exchange for a promise to sell all such widgets is supported by _____.

8. The common law rule is that payment of a lesser sum of money by a debtor is not sufficient consideration for a promise by a creditor to release the debtor from his or her obligation to pay a mature, _____, undisputed debt in a greater sum.

MULTIPLE CHOICE QUESTIONS

1. The common law doctrine of consideration:
    A. recognizes that forbearance from doing something that one has a legal right to do constitutes consideration.
    B. requires a roughly equal exchange of something that has legal value by the parties to a contract.
    C. requires only that the promisee receive something of value.
    D. has been abrogated completely by statutes in a majority of states.

2. Consideration for a promise must be either a detriment to the:
    A. offeror or a legal benefit to the offeree.
    B. offeree or a legal benefit to the offeror.
    C. promisee or a legal benefit to the promisor.
    D. promisor or a legal benefit to the promisee.

3. The following is an example of a binding and enforceable promise:

    A. an agreement by a manufacturer to agree to make a contract in the future with a retailer.

    B. a promise by a grandmother to give a grandchild a $10,000 bequest in her will.

    C. a promise to a friend to obtain a free ticket for admission to a rap concert.

    D. None of the answers above is correct.

4.   Aunt told Nephew: "If you go to Europe and spend the summer there, I will reimburse you for all the expenses that you incur." Nephew went to Europe for the summer, but Aunt refused to reimburse Nephew for his expenses. If Nephew sues Aunt, the court will probably hold that Nephew may:

    A. recover because Aunt made a promise to make a gift.

    B. recover because Nephew incurred a legal detriment.

    C. **not** recover because Aunt received no legal benefit.

    D. **not** recover because Nephew received a legal benefit.

5.   As a general rule, when a creditor accepts a payment of money from a debtor and promises to release the debtor from any further liability, the creditor is legally bound by his/her promise to release the debtor:

    A. only if the debtor can clearly prove that the promise was made (regardless of other circumstances).

    B. only if the original debt was a mature, liquidated, and undisputed debt.

    C. only if the original debt was not a mature, liquidated, or undisputed debt.

    D. as long as the statute of limitations had not run before the payment was made (regardless of other circumstances).

6.   The doctrine of promissory estoppel:

    A. requires legal consideration in order to be effective.

    B. results in an irrevocable offer.

    C. applies to the sale of goods when one of the parties is a merchant.

    D. allows enforcement of a promise in the absence of consideration.

7.   A promise to buy such quantity of goods as one may wish is:

    A. an illusory promise.

    B. a valid contract.

    C. sufficient consideration for a promise to sell such quantity.

    D. sufficient consideration because the promisee is incurring a detriment.

8.   Which of the following agreements is **not** enforceable?

    A. An agreement between a seller of goods and a buyer to alter the place of delivery prior to performance of the contract.

    B. An agreement by a seller to supply to a buyer all the flour the buyer needs to run his bakery for one year at a set price per pound although the total amount is not precisely established at the time the agreement is entered.

    C. An agreement between a buyer and seller for delivery of specified goods in six months that gives the buyer the right to cancel at anytime within the six months.

    D. None of the answers above is correct.

9.   Best Buy Sneaker Co. has entered into a contract to purchase all of the shoe laces that Best Buy Sneaker Co. may require at a price of fifty-five cents each for six months

from the Last Lace Corp; and Last Lace Corp. agreed to sell all of the shoe laces that Best Buy might require during that time at a price of fifty-five cents. The contract is:
A. void because of illegality.
B. valid and enforceable.
C. voidable because no place of delivery is stated.
D. enforceable by Last Lace Corp. only.

10. Two armed men robbed the First National Bank of Metropolis. A reward of $10,000 was offered by the bank to anyone who gave information leading to the arrest and conviction of the perpetrators of the robbery. On the basis of information furnished by a bank employee, a local law enforcement officer, and a bank customer, the robbers were apprehended and convicted. The employee, the law enforcemet officer, and the customer applied for the reward. The reward should be given to:
A. the bank employee.
B. the local law enforcement officer.
C. the bank customer.
D. the bank employee, the local law enforcement officer, and the bank customer.

11. Today in most states, although no consideration is given, a written promise to pay a debt will be enforceable when:
A. the promise is to pay a debt that is mature, but there is a dispute as to the amount of the debt.
B. the promise is to pay a debt that is barred by the statute of limitations.
C. the promise is to pay a mature, liquidated, undisputed debt, but the promisee agrees to and actually gives the promisor an apple.
D. All of the answers above are correct.

12. Cochran purchased a television set from the Acme Appliance Store. One of the terms of sale was that the Acme Appliance Store would service the television set without charge within 24 hours after Cochran advised the store that the set was not functioning properly during the first year following the purchase. Two months after the sale there was a loss of sound. Cochran called the store promptly, but was advised that a serviceperson could not be sent to Cochran's home for a week. Cochran promised to pay twenty-five dollars if a serviceperson was sent the next day because Cochran desperately wanted to watch the World Series. A serviceperson was sent and the difficulty was corrected. Acme Appliance Store sent Cochran a bill for twenty-five dollars.
A. Cochran will **not** have to pay the bill because the store was obligated to send the serviceperson.
B. Cochran will **not** have to pay the bill, but will have to pay the reasonable value for the services rendered.
C. Cochran will have to pay the bill because the store can show that the cost of sending the serviceperson was twenty-five dollars.
D. Cochran will have to pay the bill because it was the fifth time Cochran called the store in order to request service.

13. Stellar brought a lawsuit against Comet ten years after Stellar and Comet entered into an oral contract and eight years after there was a breach of the contract by Comet.

Comet raises the statute of limitations as a defense. Which of the following allegations would be most important to Comet's defense?

A. There was no written evidence that Stellar and Comet had entered into a contract.

B. The action was **not** brought in a timely manner because, allegedly, the contract was entered into ten years before the commencement of the lawsuit.

C. The action was **not** brought in a timely manner because, allegedly, the contract was breached eight years prior to the commencement of the lawsuit.

D. Comet's promise was to deliver one copy of *West's Business Law* to Stellar.

(This question has been adapted from question #1-22, Uniform CPA Examination, November 1993.)

Chapter 15
Capacity

People are presumed to be sufficiently and fully competent to enter into contracts unless they are considered to be at disadvantages (that may affect the relative bargaining power of the contracting parties) when dealing with others because of their young age, mental impairment, intoxication, or other disability that is recognized by law. Contracts made by persons who have been adjudicated by courts to be mentally incompetent are void. Contracts that have been entered into by parties who are minors, intoxicated, or mentally incompetent (but not yet so adjudicated) are voidable by the party lacking full competency.

THINGS TO KEEP IN MIND

Usually, a contract that is made by a person who lacks capacity is voidable. As a result, the party who does not have full contractual capacity has a number of options. He or she may:

1. Enforce the contract by suing on it; or
2. Avoid his or her contractual obligations by bringing an action for rescission (cancellation of the contract); or
3. When sued on the contract by the other party, raise the defense that the contract is voidable because of his or her lack of full capacity.

The other contracting party who is fully competent may not avoid the contract.

OUTLINE

I.   Minors.

A. Statutes prescribe the age of majority; in most states, it is eighteen.

B. Minor's right to disaffirm.

1. Usually, a minor can enter into any contract that an adult can, unless it would result in the violation of a statute prohibiting a minor from being a party to a particular certain type of contract (e.g., a contract for the sale of alcoholic beverages).

2. Most contracts entered into by a minor are voidable at the option of the minor who may, therefore, disaffirm or avoid his or her contractual obligations.

a. Minors may disaffirm contracts during minority and for a reasonable period of time after attaining the age of majority.

b. Words or conduct can be used by a minor who is disaffirming his or her contractual obligations.

c. Minors may not disaffirm if a contract has been approved by a court or, in some states because of statute, if the contract is for:
   1) Life or medical insurance.
   2) An educational loan.
   3) Medical care.
   4) Marriage.
   5) Enlistment in armed forces.
   6) Transportation by common carrier.
   7) Business purposes, and the minor is engaged in business.

d. In most states, a conveyance of real property by a minor cannot be disaffirmed until the minor has reached the age of majority.

e. A minor who is exercising his or her right of disaffirmance must disaffirm the entire contract.

f. The contract is voidable by the minor, but not by the adult.

3. Executed versus executory contracts — If a minor fails to disaffirm a contract within a reasonable time after reaching the age of majority:

   a. A fully performed, executed contract is presumed to be ratified by the minor and, therefore, binding on the minor.

   b. An executory contract (a contract that is not yet fully performed by both parties) is treated as disaffirmed by the minor and, therefore, not binding on the minor.

4. Minor's obligations on disaffirmance.

   a. The general rule is that if a minor disaffirms, each party must make restitution by returning the consideration received from the other party.

   b. Executory contracts that have not been performed by either party:
      1) Minor may disaffirm the executory contract — As the minor received nothing from the other party, there is no need to make restitution.
      2) Majority rule — Continued silence after a minor reaches the age of majority is treated as disaffirmance of the executory contract.

   c. Executed contracts — Minor may disaffirm an executed contract.
      1) The adult with whom a minor has contracted must make restitution by returning any consideration received from the minor to the minor.

    2) If goods were sold by a minor to an adult, who resold the goods to an innocent good faith purchaser, the purchaser will not be required to return the goods to the minor; the adult, with whom the minor dealt, must pay the minor the equivalent value of goods [UCC Section 2-403(1)].

    3) The minor must return consideration received from the adult.

       a) The majority rule is that the minor must make restitution only if the minor is able to do so.

       b) In some states:

          (1) By statute, a deduction is made for damage, deterioration, and depreciation.

          (2) The minor must pay the reasonable value for the benefit that was conferred.

5. Misrepresentation of age.

    a. In most states, if a minor has misrepresented his or her age in order to induce another person to enter into a contract, the minor may disaffirm the contract.

       1) In some states, the other party may disaffirm the contract because he or she was induced to enter into contract because of the misrepresentation.

       2) In some states, the other party may not disaffirm the contract because the indirect effect would be to enforce the contract against the minor.

    b. Other states have different rules in instances when a minor has made a misrepresentation of age:

       1) Contract is not voidable by the minor because of a statute.

       2) Contract is voidable by the minor, but the minor must pay the reasonable value for benefits that were conferred.

       3) The minor will be estopped from showing his or her lack of capacity.

6. Emancipation — Express or implied, absolute or conditional, total or partial, relinquishment by parent of the legal right to exercise control over the minor and the parental duties of providing care for the minor.

7. Liability for necessaries.

    a. Necessaries include food, clothing, shelter, medical services rendered for a minor's protection, and, in some cases, education and services that are necessary so that the minor can earn a living and maintain his or her financial and social status.

    b. A minor may disaffirm a contract for necessaries that are not provided by a parent or guardian but is liable in quasi contract for the reasonable value of necessaries that were furnished to the minor.

8. Insurance and loans.

a. In some states, minors are prohibited from disaffirming contracts for life or medical insurance; in other states, minors may disaffirm insurance contracts, but recovery is limited to the value of the paid premiums less the insurer's actual cost of protecting the minor under the policy.

b. In general, a loan is not considered to be a necessary, even if the money is spent on necessaries; if the loan, however, is made for the express purpose of enabling a minor to buy necessaries, and the lender makes sure that the money is so spent, the minor is obligated to repay the loan.

C. Ratification — A contract will be enforceable if the minor indicates an intention to be bound by the contract after reaching the age of majority.

1. Express ratification — A ratification may be an oral or written.

2. Implied ratification — A ratification may be implied based upon the minor's conduct that indicates satisfaction with the contract because the minor retains the consideration, or continues to accept the benefits or to perform his or her obligations.

D. Nonvoidable contracts.

1. Statutes restrict minors' ability to disaffirm certain contracts and require that minors perform their legal duties.

2. Some contracts cannot be avoided by minors as a matter of public policy.

E. Liability for torts — A minor is liable for torts unless the minor is very young or the enforcement of tort liability has the indirect effect of also enforcing a contract that the minor has disaffirmed.

F. Parents' liability.

1. A parent is not liable for performance of a contract made by his or her minor child unless the parent personally obligated himself or herself as a party to the contract, or the contract was for necessaries which the parent had failed to furnish.

2. Parents are not liable for torts committed by their minor children, but may be liable for negligence in failing to exercise control over their minor children, or because of statutes or case law that impose such legal responsibilities on parents.

II. Intoxicated persons.

A. A contract is voidable if it was made by a person who was so intoxicated that his or her judgment was impaired and he or she did not comprehend the nature of the transaction and the legal consequences of entering into the contract.

B. A contract may be disaffirmed at the option of an intoxicated person (even if the intoxication was voluntary) while the person is intoxicated or within a reasonable time after he or she becomes sober.

  1. Restitution must be made by both parties.

  2. An intoxicated person cannot disaffirm if a third person would be injured.

  3. An intoxicated person must pay the reasonable value for necessaries that were furnished.

C. A contract may be ratified expressly or impliedly after the intoxicated person regains sobriety.

III.   Mentally incompetent persons.

A. A person is considered mentally incompetent if his or her judgment is impaired because that person cannot understand or comprehend the nature and effect of a particular transaction.

B. If a person is declared judicially incompetent, his or her contracts are void.

C. A contract that is made by a person who is mentally incompetent (but has not been so adjudicated) is voidable by the mentally incompetent person while he or she is mentally incompetent, or within a reasonable time after regaining mental competency, or by his or her guardian or other representative.

D. A contract for necessaries may be disaffirmed, but the mentally incompetent party is liable for the reasonable value of necessaries furnished.

E. A contract that is made by a mentally incompetent person may be ratified by that person when he or she is mentally competent and lucid or by a guardian appointed by a court.

IV.   Aliens.

A. In general, citizens of other countries who are in the United States legally have contractual capacity and their contracts are valid.

B. Enemy aliens and illegal aliens have limited contractual capacity, so that such aliens usually cannot enforce contracts against citizens of this country.

KEY WORDS AND PHRASES IN TEXT

contractual capacity (or competency)	disaffirmance
minors	duty of restitution
age of majority	misrepresentation of age
minors' rights to disaffirm	emancipation

quasi contract liability for necessaries
express ratification
implied ratification
nonvoidable contract
liability of minors for torts

parents' liability
intoxicated persons
mentally incompetent persons
lucid interval
aliens

FILL-IN QUESTIONS

1. If a minor or mentally incompetent person or intoxicated person makes a contract with another person who does not have a contractual disability, the contract is _____. The one who lacks capacity may _____ the contract, but the other fully competent party may not do so.

2. During his or her minority, a minor may _____ a contract to which he or she was a party.

3. A minor who has been furnished with necessaries, such as _____ _____, must make restitution if the minor is rescinding the contract by paying _____ for the benefits received.

4. A minor may not effectively ratify a contract that he or she has entered into until the minor attains the age of _____ or within a reasonable period of time thereafter.

5. A person who is mentally incompetent because _____ _____ may disaffirm his or her contract. If such a person is adjudicated to be incompetent, his or her contracts are _____.

MULTIPLE CHOICE QUESTIONS

1. The following term best describes a contract entered into by a minor:
   A. illegal.
   B. void.
   C. voidable.
   D. unenforceable.

2. A contract between a minor and an adult may be disaffirmed by:
   A. only the minor.
   B. only the adult.
   C. only the minor's parent or guardian.
   D. either party.

3. Ted is sixteen years old. If Ted signs a written agreement to buy a bicycle from Cindi's Cycle Shop, Ted's right to disaffirm the contract will:
   A. require Cindi's Cycle Shop to deal with all minors.

B. **not** alter the fact that Cindi's Cycle Shop is bound by the terms of the contract.

C. **not** be effective because, in Ted's case, the bicycle is considered to be a necessary.

D. give Cindi's Cycle Shop the right to disaffirm the contract even though Cindi's Cycle Shop is owned by an adult.

4. When she was seventeen years of age, Mary purchased an automobile from AAA Car Sales for $12,000, to be paid for in 36 monthly installments. Two years later, the car was totally demolished in an accident and Mary failed to make the last eleven payments. AAA Car Sales sued Mary to recover these eleven payments. In a state in which the age of majority is eighteen, a court will probably hold for:

A. Mary, because Mary was a minor at the time of the purchase and may disaffirm contracts that she made when she was a minor.

B. Mary, because the contract was nullified when the automobile was demolished.

C. AAA Car Sales, because Mary ratified the contract by making several payments after she reached her eighteenth birthday.

D. AAA Car Sales, but the amount of recovery will be limited because the automobile was demolished.

5. An item which would be considered to be a necessary if purchased by a minor is:

A. a winter jacket.

B. a pizzaburger.

C. a filling in a tooth.

D. All of the answers above are correct.

6. A minor may disaffirm a contract for the purchase of goods that the minor entered into with an adult:

A. for the furnishing of the goods only if the goods are not necessaries.

B. for the furnishing of the goods even if the goods are necessaries.

C. before the minor reaches the age of eighteen because, as a result of a federal statute, the age of majority has been established at eighteen years of age.

D. before he has reached the age of majority as may the adult with whom he has contracted even if the goods are necessaries.

7. Courts of equity may deny relief to a minor who is a party to a contract if the minor has:

A. disaffirmed the contract.

B. purchased necessaries.

C. misrepresented his or her age.

D. Any of the answers above is correct.

8. Civil liability arising out of a tort committed by a minor:

A. may be disaffirmed much like contractual liability because of common law principles.

B. may be disaffirmed much like contractual liability because of statutory law.

C. may be disaffirmed under common law principles, but only if the wrongful act (the tort) was not a crime.

D. as a general rule, may **not** be disaffirmed at all.

9. A person, who was a minor when he or she entered into a contract, may ratify the executed contract upon reaching the age of majority in any of the following ways **except** by:
   A. failing to disaffirm the contract within a reasonable period of time after reaching the age of majority.
   B. orally ratifying the entire contract.
   C. affirming in writing some, but not all, of the terms of the contract.
   D. acting in a manner that indicates his or her satisfaction with the contract.
   [This question is adapted from questions #1-21, Uniform CPA Examination, May 1991, and #1-13, Uniform CPA Examination, May 1993.]

10. The contracts of a person, who, in fact, is mentally incompetent but not so adjudicated by a court, may be ratified by:
   A. the mentally incompetent person when he or she is competent.
   B. the mentally incompetent person when he or she is competent or mentally incompetent.
   C. the other party to the contract so as to bind the mentally incompetent person.
   D. the mentally incompetent person only if the contract is for the furnishing of necessaries.

11. A person has been adjudicated to be mentally incompetent by a court. Two months later, that person agrees to purchase a CB radio from the Radio Palace for $700. The contract for the sale of the CB radio is:
   A. voidable.
   B. void.
   C. voidable.
   D. illegal.

OTHER OBJECTIVE QUESTIONS: MATCHING QUESTIONS

Ace Auto Store enters into contracts for the sales of automotive parts to Michael, Arianne, Delphia, and Euphrade. Michael, who is not a citizen of the United States, is in this country legally. Arianne, who also is not a citizen of the United States, is in this country illegally. Delphia, a citizen of the United States, is sixteen years of age. Before she entered into the contract with Ace Auto Store, Euphrade, a citizen of the United States, was adjudicated as incompetent, and Freeze was appointed by the court at Euphrade's guardian.

After each of the names of the parties, who are listed in the left hand column, select from the list in the right hand column the reason (if any) for each of these parties disaffirming the contract that was entered into with Ace Auto Store for the purchase of automotive parts.

1. Michael: _____
2. Arianne: _____
3. Delphia: _____
4. Euphrade: _____
5. Freeze: _____

A. The contract is void because one party is an illegal alien.
B. The contract is voidable because one party is a legal alien.
C. The contract is void because one party is a minor.
D. The contract is voidable because one party is a minor.
E. The contract is void because one party has been adjudicated as mentally incompetent.
F. There is no basis for disaffirmance because the contract is valid and enforceable.

OTHER OBJECTIVE QUESTIONS: YES-NO QUESTIONS

Ace Auto Store wishes to disaffirm the contracts with Michael, Arianne, Delphia, and Euphrade. In the space provided, state **yes** if Ace Auto Store may disaffirm the contract with the listed party, or **no** if Ace Auto Store cannot disaffirm the contract with the listed party.

6.   Michael: _____
7.   Arianne: _____
8.   Delphia: _____
9.   Euphrade: _____

Chapter 16
Genuineness of Assent

Objectively, the parties to a contract may have agreed to the same terms, but subjectively the assent of one or all of the parties may not have been real or genuine or voluntarily given because of mistake, fraud, misrepresentation, undue influence, or duress. Ordinarily, if a party is coerced or induced to assent to the terms of a contract to which the party would not have agreed had he or she known the true circumstances, the contract is voidable. As indicated in this chapter, there also are situations involving lack of genuine assent in which contracts may be treated as void because of circumstances surrounding their formation.

THINGS TO KEEP IN MIND

Usually, a contract that is made by a person, who was prevented from freely exercising his or her own will when assenting to the agreement, is voidable by the party whose assent was not real, genuine, or voluntary. That party, therefore, may do one of the following:

    a. Enforce the contract by suing for enforcement of the contract; or

    b. Disaffirm the contract by bringing an action for rescission (cancellation of the contract) or, in a case of fraud, undue influence, or duress, sue for damages for the wrongful, tortious conduct of the other contracting party; or

    c. Raise the defense that the contract was voidable because of lack of genuine assent in the event that he or she is sued on the contract by the other party for a breach of the contract.

OUTLINE

I.   Mistakes.

    A. A mistake of fact is an error or unconscious ignorance or forgetfulness of a past or present occurrence or event; a fact is material, if it is very important or essential and a moving influence in causing a person to enter into a contract.

    B. Mistake as to material facts are distinguished from mistakes of judgment as to value or quality; value is a matter of opinion and is not a fact.

    C. Unilateral mistakes — If only one party to a contract has made a mistake concerning a material fact, usually that party cannot disaffirm the contract unless:

1. The other party was responsible for the mistake being made or knew of the mistake or should have known of the mistake and failed to correct the mistake; or

2. In some states, the mistake was made because of an inadvertent mathematical error, and the mistaken party was not grossly negligent.

D. Mutual mistake of material fact.

1. If both parties have made a mistake concerning a material fact, the contract may be voidable at the option of either party.

2. If the mistake relates to the existence of the subject matter that is essential for performance of the contract, a court may find that there is no objective mutual assent and the contract, therefore, is void and unenforceable by either party.

E. Mutual mistake of value — A mutual mistake as to the quality or value of something or a future contingency does not result in a voidable contract. (Note that value varies from person to person, time to time, and place to place.)

II. Fraudulent misrepresentation.

A. Fraud in the inducement — A contract is voidable if a party was damaged by being induced to enter into a contract (that he or she otherwise would not have made) because he or she reasonably relied upon a false representation of a material fact.

B. Elements of fraud.

1. Misrepresentation of a material fact has occurred.

a. A false representation of a material past or present fact was made; a fact is material or important if it is a moving influence that causes a person to enter into a contract.

b. In general, representations of future events, predictions, promises, opinions (except those made by experts, who have superior knowledge), and puffery are not treated as representations of fact.

c. Misrepresentation by conduct — Conduct, including concealment that prevents the deceived party from learning the truth about a material fact, may be treated as a false representation or a material fact.

d. Misrepresentation of law.
   1) There is a presumption that people know the law of the state in which they reside; for this reason, normally, a misrepresentation regarding state or local law does not entitle a contracting party to relief.
   2) A misrepresentation of law may be fraudulent if it was:

        a) Made to a person who is not a resident of the state whose law was misrepresented; or

        b) Made by a lawyer or a person who is presumed to know the law because of his or her occupation.

   e. Misrepresentation by silence — Usually, there is no duty to inform a contracting party of facts and a party to a contract may remain silent with the following exceptions:

       1) A seller must disclose serious latent defects or problems that are not readily discoverable but which cause the subject matter of a contract to be dangerous.

       2) A seller, who has superior knowledge, may not conceal facts when the seller knows that the other party lacks knowledge.

       3) When a party has previously misstated a material fact and later realizes that he or she made a misstatement, he or she is required to make a correction.

       4) When parties have a fiduciary or confidential relationship, the party with knowledge of relevant facts has an obligation to disclose them to the other party.

       5) Statutes, such as the federal Truth in Lending Act, require disclosure of certain relevant facts. [See Chapter 45.]

2. Intent to deceive.

   a. Misrepresentation was made by a person who had knowledge that it was false and with the intent to deceive (*scienter*, or guilty knowledge).

   b. Knowledge of the falsity of a representation may be inferred from the circumstances surrounding the transaction.

   c. If a misrepresentation was made by a person with reckless disregard or indifference to its truth or falsity, he or she may be treated as having had knowledge that the representation was false.

   d. Intent to deceive may exist when a statement is made based upon personal knowledge or investigation and the person making the representation lacked such knowledge or did not make an investigation.

   e. The evidence that a misrepresentation was made with intent to induce the deceived person to enter into a contract is the fact that the contract actually was formed.

3. Reliance on the misrepresentation — Reliance must have been such that a reasonable person would have been justified in relying upon the misrepresentation.

   a. The representation must have dealt with an important fact, but the fact that was misrepresented need not have been the only factor that caused a party to enter into the particular contract.

    b. Reliance is not reasonable if evidence to easily disprove the representation is readily available by using ordinary senses of sight, hearing, etc.

   4. Injury to the innocent party — The contract would not have been formed or would have been more valuable if the representation had been true.

    a. In some states, in an action for rescission, actual damages need not be established because the parties are returned to the positions that they were in before the contract was formed.

    b. In an action for damages, proof of injury is required. A court may award punitive or exemplary damages in addition to compensatory damages.

  C. Fraud in the execution — If a party has been led to believe that an act, which that person is performing, is something other than executing a contract, that person's assent is not objectively given, and any contract that appears to have been formed is void. (Typically, an innocent person signs a writing believing that it is something other than terms of a contract.)

III. Nonfraudulent misrepresentation.

  A. Innocent misrepresentation — If a person unintentionally makes a representation without knowledge of its falsity, a party to a contract, who relied upon the representation and was damaged, may rescind the contract, but usually may not recover compensatory damages.

  B. Negligent misrepresentation — If a person fails to exercise reasonable care in uncovering or disclosing a material fact, or does not use the skill or competence that his or her business or profession requires and, therefore, makes a negligent misrepresentation, he or she will be considered to have made a fraudulent misrepresentation intentionally.

IV. Undue influence.

  A. When a party, who is in a dominant position because of a confidential relationship, secures an unfair advantage in a contract with a weaker, dominated party, the contract is voidable and may be disaffirmed by the dominated party, who was unable to use his or her free will.

  B. There is a rebuttable presumption of undue influence when the parties are in a familial or other fiduciary relationship based upon trust and confidence, and the contract is extremely unfair to the dominated party.

  C. The presumption may be rebutted by showing that a full disclosure was made, the consideration that was received was adequate, and/or competent, independent advice was received by the weaker party before completing the transaction.

V. Duress.

A. When a party is coerced into entering into a contract because of the actual wrongful use of force or a wrongful threat of force (e.g., blackmail or extortion), that party's assent is not voluntary, and the contract is voidable.

B. Assent must have been induced because of fear or apprehension of:

1. Bodily injury to the contracting party or a member of his or her family.

2. Criminal prosecution of (but not commencement of civil litigation against) the party to the contract or a member of his or her family.

3. Harm to the property or business interests of the contracting party (economic duress).

C. A contract may be void if the contract resulted from extreme duress.

VI. Adhesion contracts and unconscionability.

A. An adhesion contract arises when one party who has overwhelming bargaining power takes such unfair advantage of the other party that the latter party has no choice but either to adhere to the dictated terms or to do without a particular good or service.

B. This may be a "take-it or-leave-it" situation in which the adhering party has no opportunity to negotiate the terms of the contract.

C. Clauses or provisions in standard form contracts written by one of the parties, who had greater bargaining power, may not be enforced if enforcement would be unfair or oppressive and, therefore, unconscionable.

D. A contract for the sale of goods may be held to be unenforceable because of unconscionability [UCC Section 2-302].

KEY WORDS AND PHRASES IN TEXT

genuiness of assent	fiduciary relationship
mistake as to facts	intent to deceive
unilateral mistake as to a material fact	*scienter* (guilty knowledge)
mutual (bilateral) mistake of material fact	justifiable reliance on misrepresentation
mistakes in value	injury to the innocent (deceived) party
fraudulent misrepresentation	punitive (exemplary) damages
elements of fraud	innocent misrepresentation
misrepresentation of material fact	negligent misrepresentation
puffery	undue influence
misrepresentation of law	duress
silence as a misrepresentation	adhesion contract
fraudulent concealment	unconscionability

FILL-IN QUESTIONS

1. A party, whose assent was not real or genuine when that party entered into a contract, may enforce the contract against the other party, or he or she may _____ the contract because the contract is usually treated as being _____ rather than void.

2. A contract may be rescinded if there has been a _____ mistake concerning a material fact rather than a _____ mistake.

3. If a party to a contract makes a misrepresentation of a material fact with knowledge that the representation is false and the other party to the contract incurs an _____ because of his or her reasonable and justifiable _____ upon the representation, the contract may be disaffirmed by the innocent party because of fraud in the inducement.

4. A statement of _____ usually is **not** treated as a representation of fact unless the statement is made by an expert or a person who has superior knowledge because of his or her profession or occupation.

5. Joan agreed to sell, and Mary agreed to buy, a painting valued at $10,000 for one hundred dollars. Joan, who is ninety-nine years of age, may be able to disaffirm the contract if she can show that mental coercion was employed by Mary, who was a relative or a fiduciary. In other words, _____ was used to obtain Joan's assent.

MULTIPLE CHOICE QUESTIONS

1. A court will rescind a contract if:
    A. the parties made a mutual mistake concerning the existence of the subject matter.
    B. the parties made a mutual mistake concerning the value of the subject matter.
    C. one of the parties a misrepresentation concerning the value of the subject matter.
    D. All of the answers above are correct.

2. S was the owner of a sailboat, which he offered to sell to B for $23,000. On the day before B accepted the offer by telegram, the boat was stolen.
    A. There is no contract between S and B because there was a mistake as to the existence of the subject matter.
    B. There is no contract between S and B because there was a mistake as to the identity of the subject matter.
    C. There is a contract between S and B, but the contract may be disaffirmed by S.
    D. There is a contract between S and B, but the contract may be disaffirmed by B.

3. If fraud in the inducement is to be used as the basis for rescission of a contract, the defendant must have made a misrepresentation relating to some material past or existing fact:
    A. with knowledge that the misrepresentation was **not** true.
    B. in order to induce the plaintiff to enter the contract.

C. upon which the plaintiff reasonably relied.

D. All of the answers above are correct.

4. A necessary element to be shown in an action brought to recover damages for fraud in the inducement is that the defendant:

A. misrepresented a material fact.

B. innocently misrepresented a material fact.

C. intentionally misrepresented a material fact.

D. All of the answers above are correct.

5. When one of the parties to a contract induces the other party to enter into the agreement by making a misrepresentation of a material fact with the intention of deceiving the other party to the agreement, the contract may be:

A. rescinded by the party who made the misrepresentation.

B. rescinded by the deceived party who relied upon the representation.

C. rescinded by a court only if the misrepresentation was made orally or in writing.

D. All of the answers above are correct.

6. A seller is obligated to disclose to the buyer:

A. all defects concerning the subject matter of the sale.

B. serious hidden defects concerning the subject matter of the sale.

C. obvious defects concerning the subject matter of the sale.

D. no defects concerning the subject matter of the sale.

7. Whittier, a used car dealer, persuaded Montgomery to buy a 1982 Cadillac! by telling Montgomery, "This baby is going to be a collector's item — you can't lose!" This is an example of:

A. a fraudulent misrepresentation of fact.

B. a negligent mistake of fact.

C. puffery.

D. undue influence.

8. Ellen painted over a number of damaged areas in chairs that she sold to Van. Such conduct might be the basis for an action for the tort of fraud:

A. in the inducement even though Ellen made no verbal misstatements with regard to the chairs.

B. in the inducement only if Ellen made a verbal misstatement with regard to the chairs.

C. despite the fact that the defects in the chairs were minor and did not result in the chairs being dangerous.

D. but Van has no basis for rescission of the contract for the sale of the chairs.

9. When a court decides that a person should not be required to perform a contract that was entered into involuntarily, the court may be referring to:

A. a felony.

B. duress or undue influence.

C. a mistake as to value.

D. a misinterpretation of law.

10. A fiduciary is one occupying a confidential relationship with another person. If a fiduciary uses the relationship to induce another person to enter into a contract, the fiduciary:
    A. will be considered as having used duress.
    B. will be considered as having used duress if the resulting contract is grossly unfair.
    C. will be considered as having used undue influence if the resulting contract is grossly unfair.
    D. will be considered as having used duress if he or she has made an intentional misrepresentation of a material fact.

11. Fly claimed that Guy owed him two hundred dollars. Guy insisted that he did not owe Fly any money. Fly told Guy: "If you don't pay me the two hundred dollars, I'll beat you up!" Guy immediately wrote a check for two hundred dollars payable to Fly and gave the check to Fly. Soon after leaving Fly, Guy stopped payment on the check. The bank upon which the check was drawn refused to honor it.
    A. Fly will **not** be successful in a suit to make Guy pay because Fly used a fraudulent misrepresentation in order to obtain Guy's assent.
    B. Fly will **not** be successful in a suit to make Guy pay because Fly used duress in order to obtain Guy's assent.
    C. Fly will be successful in a suit to make Guy pay because Guy objectively manifested his genuine assent to the agreement.
    D. Fly will be successful in a suit to make Guy pay because Guy justifiably agreed to the terms of the contract.

Chapter 17
Legality and the Statute of Frauds

Two very different aspects of contract law are covered in this chapter — the requirement that contracts have legal purposes and subject matters (in the first section), and the requirement that certain types of contractual promises be evidenced by signed writings (in the later section). Notice that the effect of a failure of the parties to comply with these requisites differs — illegal agreements are void, whereas contracts that are required by statutes to be written and signed are not void, but merely unenforceable.

As first discussed in this Chapter, if an act to be performed or the purpose of an agreement is criminal, tortious, or contrary to public policy, the agreement is treated as an illegal bargain. Such bargains are considered to be void and, therefore, really not contracts. As a general rule, courts will neither enforce illegal bargains nor give remedies for their breach.

The final portions of the chapter deal with the form in which contractual promises are embodied. Although it is advantageous to do so, contracts generally need not be reduced to writing in order to bind the parties. Because of statutes, however, some contracts must be evidenced by writings that are signed by the parties against whom these contracts are to be enforced. These statutes are commonly referred to as Statutes of Frauds and are civil, rather than criminal, in nature. Whether or not contracts are required by statutes to be evidenced by signed writings, contracts frequently are in such form. If a document is regarded as an integration of the agreement of the parties to it, other evidence, which changes the effect of the writing, is not admissible because of the parol evidence rule, the topic of the concluding section in this chapter.

THINGS TO KEEP IN MIND REGARDING LEGALITY

Public morality and ideas as to what is considered to be wrongful conduct are reflected in statutes and policies. Although there is considerable uniformity in the United States, these laws and policies vary over time and from place to place.

THINGS TO KEEP IN MIND REGARDING THE STATUTE OF FRAUDS

1. The Statute of Frauds does not require a formal document. Usually, all that is necessary is a signed memorandum indicating the essential terms.

2. If a contract does not comply with the Statute of Frauds, the contract is unenforceable, rather than void or voidable. This means that the contract cannot be proven in the manner required by law.

3. Ordinarily, the Statute of Frauds is raised as a defense. If the issue is not raised, an oral contract will be enforced.

OUTLINE

I.   Legality.

    A. Contracts contrary to statute.

        1. Usury.

            a. Usury statutes fix the maximum lawful (contract) rate of interest that can be charged for a loan of money; the rates vary from state to state and over time.

            b. The lawful rate of interest prescribed by the usury law is distinguishable from the judgment rate of interest and the legal rate of interest.
                1) Judgment rate — The rate fixed by statute that is applied when monetary damages are awarded in a judgment; interest accrues from the date of the judgment until the judgment is paid.
                2) Legal rate — The rate fixed by statute that is to be applied when parties to a contract intend that interest is to be paid, but fail to state the amount or rate of interest. (If no legal rate is specified in a statute, the legal rate is the same as the judgment rate of interest.)

            c. Exceptions.
                1) Usury laws do not apply to corporate borrowers.
                2) Statutes often allow higher rates of interest for small loans and/or permit discounting for loans of less than one year.
                3) Usury laws generally do not apply to sales of goods on credit.
                    a) Retail sales installment loans, retail charge agreements, and revolving charge accounts.
                    b) Other statutes restrict the amount of interest that can be charged in particular types of transactions.

            d. If more than the statutory lawful maximum rate is charged, the effect varies from state to state.
                1) Transaction is void as to excess interest only;
                2) Transaction is void as to interest, but not as to principal; or
                3) Entire transaction is tainted by usury and, therefore, void as to principal and interest.

            e. In some states, the maximum rate of interest that may be charged is a floating rate because the rate is dependent upon the cost of capital in a specified market (e.g., certain U.S. Treasury notes).

        2. Gambling.

            a. Gambling (or wagering) involves creation of risk and distribution of property by chance among persons who have given consideration in order to participate.

    b. In some states, certain forms of gambling, such as lotteries and casino and horse racing gambling, are permitted by statute.

    c. Some states, in which gambling is prohibited, will not enforce gambling debts incurred in other states.

    d. Agreements involving gambling are distinguishable from:
      1) Futures contracts (contracts for the future purchases or sales of commodities) and stock option contracts as well as purchases of securities (such as corporate stock) on margin.
      2) Contracts for insurance which provide for shifting existing risks from policyholders, who have insurable interests, to insurance companies.
      3) Games of skill.

3. Sabbath (Sunday or blue) laws.

    a. The nature of statutes restricting contracting on Sunday varies as does the enforcement of these statutes.

    b. If a statute prohibits formation or performance of a contract on a Sunday, contracts made or performable on Sunday are illegal, void, and unenforceable; in some states, contracts may be entered into on Sunday, but performance is prohibited except for labors of charity or necessity.

    c. Sunday laws have been held to be unconstitutional in a number of states.

4. Licensing statutes.

    a. Statutes require that licenses be obtained in order to engage in certain trades, professions, or businesses.

    b. Enforceability of contracts made by unlicensed persons.
      1) Some statutes expressly provide that contracts which are made by unlicensed persons are void and unenforceable.
      2) If the object of a statute is regulatory (to protect the public from unauthorized practitioners), contracts made by unlicensed persons are void and unenforceable.
      3) If the purpose of a statute is merely to raise revenue, contracts made by unlicensed persons are enforceable.

5. Contracts to commit crimes.

    a. Agreements providing for commissions of crimes are illegal and void.

    b. If the purpose or performance of the contract becomes illegal because of enactment of statute after the contract has been entered into, the parties are discharged from their obligations by operation of law because of impossibility of performance. [See Chapter 19.]

B. Contracts contrary to public policy.

1. An agreement that injures an established interest of society or has a negative effect on society is considered to be contrary to public policy and, therefore, is void and will not be enforced.

2. Contracts in restraint of trade (anticompetitive agreements that adversely affect the public because they are intended to reduce competition) are governed by state and federal antitrust laws. [See Chapter 47.]

3. Covenants (promises) not to compete.

   a. If two or more parties enter into an agreement in which they exchange mutual promises not to compete with each other and their only objective is to restrict competition, the agreement is void because it is against a strong public policy favoring free, fair competition.

   b. An ancillary (subsidiary) promise, or covenant, not to compete will be enforced if the promise is reasonable (no more extensive than necessary under the circumstances to protect a legitimate business, property, or other valuable interest of the promisee).

   c. Contract for the sale of an ongoing business (including goodwill) — The reasonableness of an ancillary restrictive covenant is determined by the nature of the business, period of duration, and geographic area covered.

   d. Restrictive covenants in employment contracts.
      1) An ancillary covenant is enforceable if the covenant is not excessive in scope or duration.
      2) Statutes in some states prohibit restraint of trade clauses in employment contracts.

4. Unconscionable contracts or clauses.

   a. A contract may be procedurally unconscionable because of inconspicuous print, unintelligible language, or lack of opportunity to read or to ask questions about its meaning.

   b. Adhesion contracts and unconscionability — See Chapter 16.
      1) A contract may be unconscionable if one party (the dominant party), who is receiving an unusually greater benefit, has superior bargaining power over the adhering party in a "take it or leave it" situation; if the bargain is oppressive, overly harsh, or grossly unfair, a court may hold that the unconscionable provision, or the entire contract, is void.
      2) Courts may refuse to enforce unconscionable contracts or clauses in contracts for the sale of goods [UCC Sections 2-302 and 2-719], the lease of goods [UCC Section 2A-108], and consumer loans [Uniform Consumer Credit Code Sections 5.108 and 1.107].

    c. Contracts or clauses may be substantively unconscionable because they are oppressive or overly harsh and "shock the conscience" of the court.

5. Exculpatory clauses.

    a. An exculpatory clause, containing a promise to relieve another person from potential liability based upon tort, without regard to fault, will be strictly construed or may be held to violate public policy.

    b. Exculpatory clauses in employment contracts and lease agreements for the rental of commercial or residential property often are held to be contrary to public policy.

    c. In general, an exculpatory clause is not enforced when the party seeking its enforcement engages in a business that is important to the public (e.g., public utilities, common carriers, banks, etc.).

    d. Exculpatory clauses have been enforced when parties seeking their enforcement are not engaging in businesses that are essential to the public.

    e. An exculpatory clause, which limits liability for harm occurring outside the promisee's control or ordinary course of business or limits the amount of liability, may be enforced.

6. Discriminatory contracts — Promises to discriminate based upon color, race, religion, national origin, or gender are unenforceable because they violate statutes and are contrary to public policy.

7. Contracts for the commission of a tort — A contract that requires a party to commit a tort (a civil wrong) is contrary to public policy and void.

8. Contracts conflicting with (injuring) public service.

    a. Public officials cannot enter into contracts that cause a conflict of interest between their official duties and their private interests or that otherwise interfere with their official duties.

    b. Promises to pay legislators or other public officials for taking certain action are against public policy, but may be distinguished from lobbying activities.

9. Agreements obstructing the legal process.

    a. Agreements that are intended to delay, prevent, or obstruct the legal process, such as concealing commission of a crime, suppressing evidence, promising not to prosecute, and jury tampering, are illegal.

    b. Today, an agreement to submit a dispute to arbitration, rather than engage in litigation, or to a court in a specified jurisdiction (a forum-selection clause) is not treated as contrary to the public policy of maintaining access to the courts.

C. Effect of illegality.

1. The general rule is that an illegal agreement is void, and, therefore, a court will not aid either party by enforcing the agreement or giving a remedy for breach of the agreement.

2. Exceptions to the general rule.

   a. Justifiable ignorance of the facts that caused the agreement to be illegal.

   b. A member of a class intended to be protected by a statute prohibiting a specific activity (e.g., state "blue sky laws" regulating the sale of securities and statutes regulating the sale of insurance) may recover the consideration or the funds that he or she paid as a party to the contract.

   c. Withdrawal from an illegal agreement before illegal performance is rendered.

   d. Illegal contract induced by fraud, duress, or undue influence — If parties are not equally at fault (**not** *in pari delicto*), the party, who was induced to enter into an illegal bargain because of fraud, duress, or undue influence, may recover the consideration that was paid to the guilty party.

3. Severable, or divisible, contracts.

   a. A severable contract contains distinct promises that are each exchanged for separate consideration.

   b. Courts will enforce legal provisions of a contract if the illegal portions of the contract can be severed.

II. The Statute of Frauds.

A. In order to be enforceable, some contractual promises must be evidenced by writings that are signed by the parties against whom the promises are being enforced (the parties being charged) or their authorized agents.

B. Contracts that must be in writing in order to be enforceable — Contracts that "fall under" or "fall within" the Statute of Frauds.

1. Contracts involving interests in land.

   a. Realty or real property includes the land itself, physical objects that are permanently attached to the ground, things contained beneath its surface, and fixtures that have become part of the realty.

    b. Other interests in land include mortgages and leases. [See Unit 10.]

    c. Contract may be taken out of the Statute of Frauds because of:
      1) Full performance of oral contract by one or both parties.
      2) Substantial part performance by a purchaser if the purchaser's action is explainable only as being pursuant to a contract.
        a) Part payment of consideration;
        b) Taking possession; and
        c) Making substantial improvements in reliance on oral contract.

2. The one-year rule — Contracts that cannot by their own terms be performed within one year.

    a. Possibility of performance — If performance is possible within one year, even if performance is highly improbable, an oral contract is enforceable.

    b. The year begins to run from the day after the contract is made, and not from the date upon which performance is to begin.

    c. If time for performance is of uncertain duration, but depends upon some contingency that may occur within a year, an oral contract is enforceable.

    d. Even if performance actually takes more than one year, an oral contract is enforceable as long as performance was possible within one year.

3. Collateral promises — Secondary (ancillary) promises by third parties to answer for obligations of others who are primary parties to contracts.

    a. A secondary, collateral promise to answer for a debt of another person, or to discharge the duties of another person, if that person (the principal obligor) does not carry out his or her primary promise to perform, is illustrated in the following diagram.

b. A promise is within the Statute of Frauds and must be in a signed writing if:
   1) The promise is made to the obligee (rather than the principal obligor) by a person who is not presently liable for the debt or who does not have a present duty to perform.
   2) The liability of the guarantor is secondary and collateral to that of the principal obligor and is conditioned on the failure of the principal obligor to perform.

c. Primary versus secondary obligations.
   1) A guarantor is a third party who makes a secondary, conditional promise to fulfill an obligation of a principal party (who is primarily liable), if the principal obligor does not perform; the guarantor's promise is a conditional promise that is within the Statute of Frauds and must be in a signed writing.
   2) A surety is a third party who makes a primary promise along with the principal obligor; the surety's promise is a primary promise that is not within the Statute of Frauds and is enforceable even if it is oral.

d. If a secondary promise of a third person (guarantor) is made to the person to whom the primary obligation is owed (i.e., the obligee or creditor), the promise is within the Statute of Frauds. If the secondary promise is made to the primary obligor (i.e., the debtor), however, the promise is not within the Statute of Frauds.

e. "Main purpose rule" exception — If the main purpose or leading object of the secondary promisor (the guarantor) is to protect his or her own interest or to obtain a material benefit, an oral promise is enforceable.

f. Estate debts — A promise by an executor or administrator of the estate of a deceased person (a decedent) personally to pay a debt of the decedent's estate must be in writing in order to be enforceable.

4. Promises made in consideration of marriage — Unilateral promises to pay money or give property in exchange for promises to marry and prenuptial (antenuptual) agreements must be in signed writings to be enforceable.

5. Contracts for the sale of goods — See Chapter 21.

   a. In order for a contract for the sale of goods for a price of $500 or more to be enforceable, there must be a writing indicating that a contract was made by the parties and that writing must be signed by the party to be charged [UCC Section 2-201].

   b. Exceptions:
      1) Goods made specially to order — Goods, which are not ordinarily suitable for resale, that are to be specially manufactured for the buyer by the seller, who has begun production of the goods.

> 2) Confirmation of an oral contract between merchants — If the contract for the sale of goods is between merchants, and either party, within a reasonable period of time, sends a written confirmation of an oral agreement to which the other party fails to object within ten days.
> 3) Partial performance — Seller accepts payment for goods or buyer accepts delivery of the goods [UCC Section 2-201(3)(c)].
> 4) Admissions — An admission in pleadings or in court that a contract was made [UCC Section 2-201(3)(b)].

   c. Proposed revisions of the UCC do not contain this "Statute of Frauds" provision; this will conform the law in the U.S. with international law.

6. Other UCC provisions:

   a. Contracts for sales of securities [UCC Section 8-319] — Statute of Frauds is satisfied by payment and/or delivery and acceptance of securities by buyer, or by a written confirmation.

   b. Security agreements [UCC Section 9-203].

   c. Contracts for sale of miscellaneous personal property when the price is more than $5,000 [UCC Section 1-206].

C. Exceptions to the Statute of Frauds.

1. Partial performance of contracts for the sale of an interest in land (See above at II. B. 1. c.) amd for the sale of goods (See above at II. B. 5. c.)

2. Admissions — See above at II. B. 5. c.

3. Promissory estoppel — A court may use the doctrine of promissory estoppel (detrimental reliance) to permit recovery under an oral contract, which would otherwise be unenforceable because of the Statute of Frauds, if the reliance of a promisee was foreseeable to the party making the oral promise and if injustice can be avoided only by enforcing the promise. [See Chapter 14.]

D. Sufficiency of the writing.

1. Memorandum or other writing evidencing the contract need only contain the basic, essential terms of the contract.

   a. Contract for sale of goods — Quantity must be indicated.

   b. Other contracts — Parties, subject matter, consideration, and any other essential terms must be indicated with reasonable certainty.

   c. Contract for sale of land — In some states, writing must contain price and description of the property.

2. Writing must be signed somewhere by the party against whom enforcement is sought (the party to be charged) or his or her authorized agent.

3. It appears that courts are ruling that a facsimile (fax) copy of a document satisfies the Statute of Frauds requirements.

III. The parol evidence rule.

A. If a written instrument is regarded by the parties as their complete, final, integrated agreement, other oral or written extraneous evidence is inadmissible for purposes of changing, altering, or contradicting the effect of the writing.

B. Parol evidence is admitted to supplement the written agreement or to show:

1. A subsequent modification of the writing.

2. The contract was void or voidable.

3. The meaning of ambiguous or vague language.

4. The writing was incomplete.

5. A prior course of dealings, course of performance, or a usage in trade in a contract for the sale of goods [UCC Sections 1-205 and 2-202]. See Chapter 21.

6. Contract was subject to orally agreed-upon conditions.

7. Obvious or gross typographical or clerical errors that clearly do not represent the agreement of the parties.

8. Another separate contract with a different subject matter.

KEY WORDS AND PHRASES IN TEXT

usury
gambling (creation of risk)
Sabbath (Sunday or blue) laws
licensing statutes
contracts contrary to public policy
restraint of trade
anticompetitive agreement
covenant not to compete
unconscionable bargain
adhesion contract
exculpatory clause
discriminatory contract
contract conflicting with public service

agreement obstructing legal process
parties *in pari delicto*
justifiable ignorance of facts
members of protected class
blue sky law
severable, or divisible, contract
Statute of Frauds
enforceability of contracts
contract for sale of an interest in land
the one-year rule
collateral, secondary promise to pay
   debts or discharge another
   person's obligations

guarantor
guaranty as differentiated from surety
main purpose rule
prenuptial (antenuptial) agreement
contracts for the sale of goods at a
     price of $500 or more

partial performance of oral contract
promissory estoppel
admissions
parol evidence rule
integrated contract (agreement)

FILL-IN QUESTIONS

1.   Agreements that violate _____ or _____ are illegal bargains and, therefore, void and unenforceable.

2.   _____ statutes provide the maximum rate of interest that lawfully may be charged for a loan of money.

3.   Assume that a state statute prohibits a lender from charging interest of more than twenty percent per year on a loan of money. Larry made a loan of one hundred dollars to Bob, and Bob agreed that he would repay the one hundred dollars in a year and give Larry an additional forty dollars. At the time of repayment, Bob will have to pay Larry _____.

4.   Contracts that provide for the creation of risk are _____ contracts and are illegal in most states. Contracts that provide for _____ risk, such as contracts of insurance, are legal.

5.   A promise not to compete with another person is termed a _____. The promise will be enforced if the promise is _____ and no more extensive than necessary to protect a property interest of the promisee.

6.   A clause in a contract that provides that one party to the contract will be relieved of any liability to the other without regard to fault or negligence may be unenforceable because this clause is an unconscionable _____ clause.

7.   Promises that are required by the Statute of Frauds to be in writing and signed by the party against whom such promises are being enforced include those _____
_____
_____.

8.   Johnson said to the manager of a local store: "If Cooper does not pay for his purchases this month, I will pay for them." Johnson's promise is unenforceable because the Statute of Frauds requires that a promise _____
_____ must be in writing and signed by the promisor. If Johnson told the manager of the store that he would pay for the purchases made by Clark, Johnson's employee, Johnson's promise would be enforceable because _____
_____ and, therefore, is **not** within the Statute of Frauds.

9. The essential terms of a contract for the sale of goods, when the price is $_____ or more, are required to be in a writing that is signed by the party against whom enforcement is sought.

10. The parol evidence rule provides that if a written instrument is regarded by the parties as a complete, integrated statement of their agreement, other oral or written statements, agreements, or promises are _____ for the purposes of adding to, deleting from, changing, altering, or contradicting the effect of the writing, which is the final expression of the rights and duties of the parties.

11. Parol evidence is admissible to show that a contract is _____ because of illegality, fraud in the execution, mistake as to the existence of the subject matter, or judicially determined incapacity. Parol evidence is also admissible to show that a contract is _____ because of lack of capacity (minority, mental incompetency, intoxication), fraud in the inducement, misrepresentation, mutual mistakes of fact, duress, or undue influence.

12. With regard to a written contract, oral evidence is admissible to prove that the writing was **not** intended as the entire agreement of the parties or to prove

_____

_____.

MULTIPLE CHOICE QUESTIONS

1. An agreement to engage in an illegal act, such as robbing a bank, is an example of a:
    A. void contract.
    B. voidable contract.
    C. valid contract.
    D. quasi contract.

2. *In pari delicto* means that:
    A. one of the parties to an agreement is guiltier than the other party.
    B. one of the parties to an agreement is a member of a class meant to be protected by a statute.
    C. both of the parties to an agreement are equally at fault.
    D. both of the parties to an agreement like to eat delicious food.

3. A transaction will be found to be usurious if the following has occurred:
    A. a lender makes a loan of money to a borrower.
    B. the borrower is required to repay the loan.
    C. a sum of money, in excess of the interest allowed by statute, is to be paid by the borrower to the lender.
    D. All of the above must have occurred.

4. The Fit Finance Co. made a loan of $1,200 to Bart, a borrower, who agreed to repay the $1,200 in two years and to make monthly payments of $50 until the due date of the loan. Bart made no monthly payments, and Bart did **not** repay the $1,200 two years after receiving the loan. In **some states**, Fit Finance Co. is entitled to receive:

    A. nothing from Bart.
    B. $1,200 from Bart.
    C. $1,200 in addition to the lawful rate of interest from Bart.
    D. All of the answers above are correct.

5.   Bettor and Gambling attend a baseball game in a state in which all gambling is illegal and make a bet on the outcome of the game. Bettor withdraws from the wager when the sixth inning begins. Bettor's withdrawal:
    A. is **not** effective without Gambling's consent.
    B. does **not** prevent Gambling from enforcing their agreement.
    C. is effective because Bettor withdraws from the wager before the conclusion of the illegal act.
    D. is effective only if the team upon which Bettor bets is ahead at the time that Bettor withdraws from the wager.

6.   An insurance contract is **not** treated as an illegal gambling contract:
    A. because all states have statutes that so provide.
    B. because it provides for shifting an existing risk as opposed to creating a risk.
    C. unless the premium paid bears no reasonable relationship to the value of the insured property.
    D. unless the contract is for life insurance and the life insured is that of a child who is less than eighteen years of age.

7.   Contracts that are entered into by a person who has **not** complied with a statute which requires a license for the practice of a business, trade, or profession:
    A. may be enforced by the unlicensed party if the licensing statute is a revenue-raising statute rather than a regulatory one.
    B. may be enforced by the unlicensed party if the licensing statute is a regulatory statute rather than a revenue-raising statute.
    C. may be enforced by the unlicensed party unless the statute states that such contracts are unenforceable.
    D. may be enforced by the unlicensed party as long as the contracts are reasonable and not injurious to the other party to the contract.

8.   An attorney, who has been admitted to practice law in North Dakota but **not** in Missouri, performs legal services and conducts a trial for a client in Missouri.
    A. The client will be required to pay the attorney a fee for the legal services performed.
    B. The client will be required to pay the attorney a fee for the legal services performed and for conducting the trial.
    C. The attorney **cannot** collect a fee for performing the legal services, but can collect a fee for conducting the trial.
    D. The attorney **cannot** collect a fee for any legal services performed in Missouri.

9.   Reale Proper is a real estate broker licensed in New Jersey. Reale Proper concludes a contract for the sale of land in Pennsylvania, in which Reale Proper is **not** licensed. Reale Proper:
    A. does **not** have a right to collect the commission for the sale of the land.
    B. is entitled to receive a commission for concluding the sale of the land.

C. is entitled to receive a commission for concluding the sale of the land even though she does **not** have the right to keep the commission.

D. is entitled to receive a commission for concluding the sale of the land if she obtains a license in Pennsylvania after the sale is completed.

10. Smith purchased the Tiny Department Store from Timothy. All of the terms of the sale were contained in a writing signed by Smith and Timothy. One of the terms provided that Timothy would **not** engage in the same business for ten years within a radius of five hundred miles of the Tiny Department Store. One year later, Timothy opened the Huge Department Store a half mile from the Tiny Department Store.

A. Timothy has **not** breached the covenant because Timothy did **not** use his own name or the word "Tiny" at his new store.

B. The contract is unenforceable because the parties failed to comply with the Statute of Frauds.

C. The restrictive covenant that Timothy made is contrary to public policy and is, therefore, illegal and void.

D. The restrictive covenant that Timothy made is neither illegal nor void.

11. Jacobs purchased the Warehard Hardware Store from Ware for $5,000,000. All of the terms of the sale were contained in a writing that was signed by Jacobs and Ware. One term provided that Ware would **not** engage in the same business for six months within one mile of the Warehard Store. Five months later Ware opened the Quick Hardware Store two blocks from the Warehard Store.

A. Jacobs can obtain an injunction because Ware has violated the terms of the contract.

B. Jacobs **cannot** obtain an order for specific performance of the contract because the contract contains an illegal restraint of trade.

C. This is an example of a restraint of trade that is unreasonable and, therefore, illegal and void.

D. The contract violated the federal antitrust laws.

12. Which of the following is void and unenforceable because the subject matter is illegal?

A. A restrictive covenant in an employment contract prohibiting an employee from using the employer's trade secrets.

B. An employer's promise **not** to press embezzlement charges against an employee who makes restitution.

C. A contingent fee charged by an attorney to represent a plaintiff in a civil case.

D. An arbitration clause in a contract for automobile insurance.

(This question has been adapted from objective question #22 on the Uniform CPA Examination, November 1990.)

13. The Statute of Frauds requires that certain contracts be in writing and signed by the party against whom the contracts are being enforced. If such a contract does **not** comply with the Statute of Frauds, the contract is:

A. voidable.

B. void.

C. unenforceable.

D. illegal.

14. The Statute of Frauds:
    A. is an old English statute that has no relevance today.
    B. applies to all contracts that, by their terms, require the payment of $500 or more.
    C. defines what constitutes fraudulent conduct by a party in inducing another to enter a contractual relationship.
    D. requires that a contract for the sale of an unimproved piece of real property for $80 be in writing.

15. Philo Stine owns ten acres of land on which there is a large house. Which of the following contracts that Philo Stine contemplates entering into would **not** have to be evidenced by a signed writing in order to satisfy the Statute of Frauds?
    A. An agreement with Picasso to paint the house for $15,000.
    B. A two-year lease of the house and one acre of land to Lolita for $20,000.
    C. A four-month easement over the land to Monet for $20.
    D. The right to remove stones from one acre of land for two months to Vladimir for $60.

16. A contract must be in writing and signed by the party to be charged if the contract provides for:
    A. a sale of goods when the price is more than $300.
    B. a lease of equipment for more than one month.
    C. a promise made to a third party to answer for the default of another person.
    D. a promise made to a debtor to answer for the debtor's debt to another person.

17. The section of the Statute of Frauds dealing with suretyship and guaranty refers to:
    A. promises to pay debts of other people.
    B. contracts for the sale of securities.
    C. contracts for the sale of real property.
    D. mutual promises to marry.

18. On November 1, Richards orally agreed to employ Everett for one year as a clerk at a salary of $600 per week. Everett began working a week later and performed satisfactorily. On December 20 of that year, Richards terminated Everett's employment because of business reversals. Everett is suing Richards for damages for breach of contract.
    A. Everett will be successful if, on November 1, the parties had **not** fixed the date upon which Everett was to begin work.
    B. Everett will be successful if, on November 1, the parties had fixed November 8 as the date upon which Everett was to begin work.
    C. Whether or not the agreement stated the date upon which employment was to commence, the agreement will **not** affect the outcome of the lawsuit.
    D. Because the salary to be paid was more than $500 per week, Everett will **not** be successful because the agreement was **not** in writing.

19. Marco Manufacturing Co. orally agreed to sell, and the Reed Retail Store orally agreed to buy, $20,000 worth of merchandise.
    A. If Marco fails to deliver the merchandise and Reed fails to pay the $20,000, Reed can enforce the contract against Marco.

B. If Marco fails to deliver the merchandise and Reed fails to pay the $20,000, Marco can enforce the contract against Reed.

C. If Marco delivers the merchandise, and Reed accepts the merchandise, the contract can be enforced by Marco against Reed.

D. The Statute of Frauds does **not** apply to a sale of goods between merchants, and the contract is, therefore, enforceable.

20. The parol evidence rule:
   A. requires that certain contracts be in writing or evidenced by a writing in order to be enforceable.
   B. relates to evidence that may be offered if a prisoner wishes to be released from prison before the expiration date of her sentence.
   C. prevents the introduction of oral testimony to alter the terms of a written contract.
   D. applies to a contract for the sale of miscellaneous personal property when the price is more than $500.

21. Gordon and Henry entered into a contract for the sale of goods. All of the terms were reduced to writing. Gordon is attempting to introduce another writing in evidence. Under which of the following circumstances will Gordon **not** be able to introduce the evidence?
   A. The evidence relates to another agreement between the parties concerning a different subject matter.
   B. The written contract indicates that the agreement was intended as the "entire contract" between the parties and the point is covered in detail.
   C. The evidence relates to statements made by Henry, to which Gordon assented, that the contract for the sale of goods would become effective if the price of gasoline rose to two dollars per gallon.
   D. The written contract contains an obvious typographical error concerning the point in issue.

22. Which of the following offers of proof are **not** admissible under the parol evidence rule when a written contract is intended to be the complete agreement of the parties?
   I.   Proof of the existence of a subsequent oral modification of the contract.
   II. Proof of the existence of a prior oral agreement that contradicts the written agreement.

   A. I. only.
   B. II. only.
   C. Both I. and II.
   D. Neither I. nor II.
   (This question appeared as objective question #24 on the Uniform CPA Examination, November 1993.)

23. Karla and Victor entered into a contract for the delivery of goods, all of the terms of which were reduced to writing. Karla is attempting to introduce oral evidence. She will be prevented from doing so if the evidence relates to:
   A. a mistake concerning the value of the goods.
   B. the subject matter of the contract, which was heroin.
   C. another agreement concerning a loan of money.
   D. a modification of the contract made a week after the writing of the contract.

Chapter 18
Third Party Rights

As a result of entering into a contract with one another, the parties to a private contract have reciprocal rights and obligations and, therefore, create a relationship with each other. This relationship between the parties to a contract is referred to as privity of contract. Normally, other people who are not parties to the agreement lack privity of contract and, therefore, have no contractual rights that a court will recognize.

A party to an existing contract may transfer rights that he or she has to a stranger to the contract (an assignment of rights) or delegate performance of his or her duties to a third person (a delegation of duties). Sometimes, a contract between two parties may involve a third party who has rights or assumes obligations. The parties to a contract may expressly provide that a benefit is to be conferred upon a person who is not a party to the contract. This type of agreement is referred to as a third party beneficiary contract.

THINGS TO KEEP IN MIND

1. The person to whom performance is to be given under the terms of a contract has a "right" to receive that performance. This "right" may be assigned. The one who is required by a contract to render performance has a "duty" to perform. This "duty" may be delegated.

2. In a third party beneficiary situation there is only one contract. When there is an assignment of rights and/or delegation of duties, however, there are two relevant contracts. The assignment or delegation occurs after the original contract was formed.

OUTLINE

I. Assignments and delegations.

   A. Assignments of rights.

      1. As illustrated in the following diagram, an assignment is an act whereby one party to an existing valid contract (the assignor) transfers the rights that he or she has to another person (the assignee), who is a stranger to the original contract, but who may enforce the contract after the assignment.

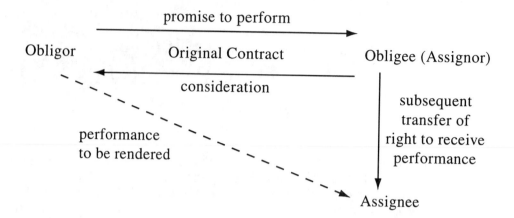

2. Effect of assignments — An assignment is a transfer of rights from an assignor (a party to the contract who has rights) to an assignee who can enforce the rights against the obligor, the party to the original contract who has an obligation to render some specified performance.

   a. Following an unconditional assignment, the assignor no longer has the right to receive the performance from the obligor.

   b. The assignee has a right to receive the performance of the obligor, the party to the original contract who promised to perform.
      1) An assignee can enforce the contract against the obligor.
      2) An assignee takes the claim subject to all defenses available against the assignor (the original obligee) even if consideration was given for the assignment.

   c. The obligor has a duty to perform in the manner specified in the original contract; the obligor, however, may assert defenses, which the obligor could have asserted against the assignor, against the assignee.

   d. Note that a waiver of rights clause in the original contract providing that, if there is an assignment, the obligor agrees not to assert any defenses, which the obligor might have, is strictly construed.

3. How assignments function — Assignments of contractual rights, including rights to receive payments of money, are used in order to finance business operations and transactions.

4. Form of the assignment.

   a. No special formality is necessary in order to make an effective assignment.

   b. An assignment may be oral, unless the Statute of Frauds or another statute requires that evidence of the assignment be in writing.

5. Consideration — Legally sufficient consideration need not be given in order to make an assignment.

 a. If consideration is given by the assignee, normally, the assignor cannot revoke the assignment.

 b. If no consideration is given by the assignee, the assignment is a gratuitous assignment that may be canceled or revoked by:
 1) An assignor who gives notice of revocation to the assignee;
 2) A subsequent assignment of the same rights by the assignor to another third party; or
 3) The death or bankruptcy of the assignor.

 c. A promise to make a future assignment must be supported by consideration in order for the promise to be effective.

6. In general, the right to receive the payment of money or the delivery of goods or a deed to real property may be assigned without the assent of the obligor, who has the obligation to pay the money or deliver the goods or the deed.

7. Rights that cannot be assigned.

 a. Statutes expressly prohibit certain assignments of rights to payments of money; examples include future workers' compensation benefits and pensions because of military service.

 b. The right to receive personal or confidential services may not be assigned without the consent of the person who is to perform the services (the obligor); the right to receive payment for personal services may be assigned after the services are rendered.

 c. A contract right cannot be assigned if the assignment will materially increase or alter the risk or the duties of the obligor.
 1) An obligee who is making an assignment may not change the nature of the obligor's performance (which the obligee has a right to receive) in a manner that increases the burden or risk to the obligor, without the assent of the obligor.
 2) Claims for injuries due to torts may not be assigned prior to entry of a judgment.
 3) Rights of an insured against an insurer may not be assigned prior to an actual insured casualty loss. [See Chapter 52.]
 4) See also UCC Section 2-210(2).

 d. A right cannot be assigned if there is a reasonable prohibition against assignment in a contract —See I. A. 8. directly below.

8. Anti-assignment clauses — The general rule is that, if a contract expressly provides that a right cannot be assigned, that right cannot be transferred by assignment.

a. Exceptions — Anti-assignment clauses are not enforced in the following situations:

1) A contract cannot prohibit the assignment of the right to receive money because such a restriction discourages the free flow of money and credit.

2) Parties cannot provide in a contract that rights in real property are nonassignable because restraints against alienation often are contrary to public policy.

3) The assignments of negotiable instruments cannot be prohibited. (See Chapter 26 in Unit Four.)

4) Even if there is a prohibition against assignment in a contract for the sale of goods, the right to receive damages for breach of contract or payment of an account that is owed may be assigned [UCC Section 2-210].

b. Restrictions on the power to assign contract rights operate only against the parties; these restrictions are not effective to prevent assignment by operation of law.

c. Frequently, anti-assignment clauses are found in leases.

d. A due-on-sale provision in a mortgage provides that a purchaser of mortgaged real property cannot assume the mortgage without the consent of the mortgagee (lender) and that repayment of the entire loan is accelerated if the real property is sold.

e. Insurance policies often provide that, if a policyholder attempts to make an assignment before a loss is incurred, the policy is void.

9. Notice of assignment.

a. Although it is not legally necessary to give notice of assignment to an obligor, it is wise to do so.

b. Problems that arise if notice of the assignment is not given.

1) Which assignee has priority if an assignor has made successive assignments of the same rights to multiple assignees, each of whom takes the assignment in good faith and gives consideration for it? This is illustrated in the diagram below.

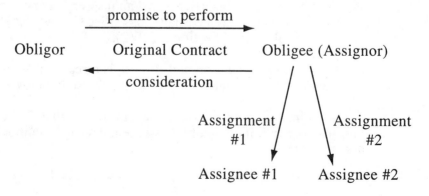

      a) Once an obligee makes an unrevoked assignment of all the rights that the obligee possesses, a subsequent assignment of the same rights by the obligee to another assignee is wrongful.

      b) In some states, the assignee who takes an assignment first prevails, even if that assignee did not give notice of the assignment to the obligor before a subsequent assignment to another assignee.

      c) In other states, the assignee who first notifies the obligor of an assignment will prevail.

  2) If notice of an assignment is not given, the obligor will render his or her performance to the assignor.

      a) The obligor is discharged and, therefore, the assignee will have right to recover only from the assignor.

      b) If notice of an assignment is given, the obligor is not discharged if the obligor renders performance to the assignor, and the assignee has a right to recover from the obligor.

10. Multiple assignments.

  a. An obligee may make partial assignments of his or her rights — For example, if the obligee has a right to receive one hundred dollars ($100) from the obligor, the obligee may assign the right to receive thirty dollars ($30) to one third party, twenty dollars ($20) to another third party, and retain the right to receive fifty dollars ($50).

  b. An assignee may make a subassignment by reassigning the contract rights to another person.

B. Delegations of duties.

  1. As illustrated in the following diagram, a party to a contract may transfer, or delegate, his or her contractual obligation to perform an act.

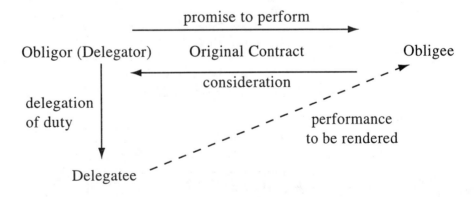

  2. Performance of duties that do not require personal skills, talents, credit, etc., may be delegated by an obligor.

    a. In the event that the delegatee fails to perform, the delegator of the duty is not relieved of the obligation owed to the obligee to perform.

    b. No special form is required to make a valid delegation of duties; all that is required is that the delegator express an intention to make the delegation.

3. Duties that cannot be delegated.

    a. Personal duties that depend upon the skill or talents of the obligor may not be delegated without the assent of the party to whom performance is to be rendered.

    b. When special trust has been placed in the obligor, the obligor may not delegate his or her duties.

    c. When performance by a third party will vary materially from the performance expected by the obligee, duties may not be delegated.

    d. Usually, when a contract expressly restricts either party's right to delegate duties, the expressed contractual prohibition will be enforced.

4. Effect of delegation — A delegation is a transfer of duties (obligations) from a delegator to a delegatee.

    a. The obligee, who has a right to receive performance, can enforce this right against the delegator (the party to the original contract who has an obligation to render some specified performance) or the delegatee to whom the obligation to perform was transferred.

    b. If a delegatee fails to perform, the obligee may recover for breach of contract from either:
      1) The obligor with whom the obligee had contracted; or alternatively;
      2) The delegatee — The obligee is treated as a third party creditor beneficiary of the contract formed by the obligor (delegator) and delegatee. (See the following illustration and discussion of third party beneficiary contracts at II. below.)

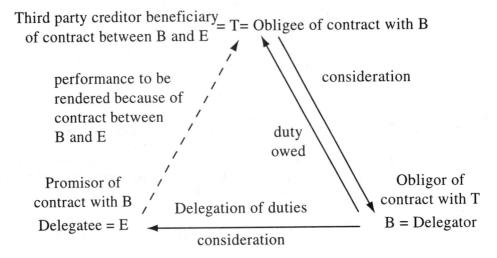

C. Assignment of "all rights."

    1. When general words are used in an assignment, the modern view is to construe the assignment as implying that there is both an assignment of rights (by the assignor) and a delegation of duties (by the assignor/delegator) and an assumption (by the assignee/delegatee) of duties.

    2. There is a distinction between an assignment with an accompanying delegation of duties on the one hand, and a novation, the effect of which is to discharge a party to a contract, on the other hand. [See Chapter 19.]

II.   Third party beneficiaries.

A. As illustrated in the accompanying diagram, the third party beneficiary is a stranger to the contractual relationship between the parties to the contract; the third party beneficiary makes no promises and gives no consideration to the promisor, who is to render performance, but the intention of the parties (the promisor and the promisee) is to confer a benefit upon the third party.

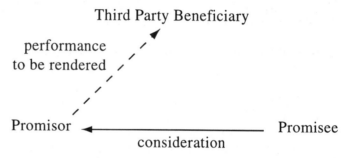

B. Types of intended beneficiaries — An intended beneficiary has legally recognized rights and, therefore, may enforce the contractual promise by directly suing the promisor for breach of contract if the promise is not carried out.

    1. Creditor beneficiary — The promisee's intention is to discharge an obligation owed to a third party by having the promisor, with whom the promisee contracts, render performance to the third party.

    2. Donee beneficiary — The promisee's intention is to confer a gift upon a third party by having the promisor, with whom the promisee contracts, render performance to the third party.

    3. Any other intended beneficiary may enforce the promise.

C. The vesting of an intended beneficiary's rights.

    1. An intended beneficiary (such as a donee or creditor beneficiary) has a legal right to enforce the contract against the promisor only after the beneficiary's rights vest.

    a. The beneficiary's rights vest when the rights are effective and cannot be taken away.

    b. Note that a creditor beneficiary also has rights against his or her debtor, the promisee.

2. The third party intended beneficiary's rights vest so that the original contracting parties cannot modify, alter, change, rescind, or terminate the contract when the beneficiary:

    a. Learns of and manifests assent to the contract; or

    b. Sues on the contract; or

    c. Materially alters or changes his or her position in detrimental reliance on the contract.

3. The third party beneficiary acquires rights subject to the right of the promisor to raise defenses, which the promisor might have against the promisee, against the beneficiary.

4. If the parties to the contract expressly reserve the right to cancel, rescind, or modify the contract, the intended third party beneficiary is subject to any change, rescission, or cancellation.

D. Intended versus incidental beneficiaries.

1. A person who is to receive an incidental benefit from the performance of a contract may not enforce the contract if there was no intent to confer a benefit upon him or her.

2. A person is considered to be an intended beneficiary if a reasonable person in the position of the beneficiary would believe that the promisee intended to confer the right to enforce the contract upon the beneficiary.

3. Factors that may indicate that a third party is an intended (rather than an incidental) beneficiary of the contract include:

    a. Performance is rendered directly to the third party.

    b. The third party has the right to control the details of performance.

    c. The third party is designated expressly as the beneficiary in the contract.

KEY WORDS AND PHRASES IN TEXT

privity of contract	assignor
assignment of (contract) rights	assignee

obligor

obligee

gratuitous assignment

rights that cannot be assigned

right to receive personal services

anti-assignment clause

restraint against alienation

notice of assignment

delegation of (contractual) duties

delegator and delegatee of duties

assignment of "all rights"

intended third party beneficiary

third party creditor beneficiary

third party donee beneficiary

vesting of rights of intended beneficiary

incidental beneficiary

FILL-IN QUESTIONS

1. Usually, a person who is not a party to a contract cannot enforce the contract because he or she lacks _____ of contract.

2. If one person transfers to another person the rights that he or she has because of a contract, he or she has made an _____. The transferor of rights is called the _____ and the transferee is called the _____.

3. The performance of duties that are not personal in nature may be _____ by the party who, under the terms of a contract, is required to render performance to the other contracting party.

4. In general, the parties to a contract may assign rights, which they have because of the contract, to strangers to the contract, unless (1) there is a _____ against assignment; (2) there is an anti-assignment clause in the contract; (3) the contract requires the performance of personal services or duties; or (4) as a result of the assignment, the duties of the obligor will be _____.

5. If the parties to a contract expressly agree that one of the parties is to render his or her performance to a third party, the person to whom the performance is to be rendered may be an intended beneficiary, such as a third party _____ or a _____ beneficiary.

6. Adams and Brady have made an agreement that provides that Adams will pay Brady $50 each week for twelve weeks in exchange for Brady's promise to cut the grass on Cotton's and Delmer's property. If Delmer is a friend of Adams, Delmer will be treated as a third party _____ beneficiary because Adams intends to give him a gift of having his grass cut. If Adams owes Cotton $600, Cotton will be treated as a third party _____ beneficiary. Both Cotton and Delmer can enforce the contract. Nailer, a neighbor of Cotton's, will also benefit from the performance of the contract. Nailer, however, is merely an _____ beneficiary and cannot enforce the contract against Brady.

MULTIPLE CHOICE QUESTIONS

1. On April 4, the Barnes Store sold $100 worth of merchandise on credit to Ames, who promised that she would pay the Barnes Store $100 on May 1. On April 6, the store assigned its right to be paid to the Careful Credit Corp.for $90.

A. Careful Credit Corp. may **not** assign its rights to Doubtful Claims Inc.

B. Careful Credit Corp. may **not** enforce Ames' promise to pay the $100 because Ames did not consent to the assignment.

C. If Ames returns the merchandise to the Barnes Store which accepts the merchandise on April 8, Ames can raise a good defense when Careful Credit Corp. sues her for the $100 after May 1.

D. Because the Barnes Store is a merchant, the store is prohibited from assigning its right to be paid by Ames until May 1 when the $100 is due and owing.

2.   The right to recover under a fire insurance policy may be assigned:
A. by the insured at any time.
B. by the insured after the policy has been in force for a reasonable period of time without incurring a loss.
C. after a fire when the duty of the insurer to pay is fixed.
D. never.

3.   Simple Oil Distributing Co. contracted with Vital Service Station to supply Vital's gasoline requirements for one year, estimated to be one million gallons, at a price of twenty cents above the price per gallon paid by Simple. All of the terms of the contract were reduced to writing. Simple was having difficulty obtaining gas supplies and, therefore, agreed with Best Oil Corp. that Best would "take over" Simple's contract with Vital by supplying Vital's requirements and receiving payment therefor from Vital.

A. Simple was **not** obligated to deliver gasoline to Vital if Simple was unable to obtain supplies because the quantity of gasoline to be delivered and the price were uncertain.

B. Simple has effectively assigned its rights and delegated its duties under the terms of its contract with Vital to Best.

C. Simple **cannot** assign its right to be paid by Vital to Best without the assent of Vital.

D. Simple is effectively released from any further obligation to perform under the terms of the contract with Vital.

4.   Manson orally agreed to sell his truck to Jackson, who orally promised to pay Manson $510 within one week and $800 one year after delivery of the truck. Prior to delivering the truck, Manson orally assigned his right to be paid to Thompson.

A. Thompson **cannot** enforce Jackson's agreement because the Statute of Frauds provision in the UCC requires that the contract and the assignment be in writing.

B. Thompson **cannot** enforce Jackson's agreement because Thompson gave no consideration to Manson for the assignment.

C. Thompson **cannot** enforce Jackson's agreement because Jackson did not assent to the assignment by Manson.

D. Thompson can enforce Jackson's agreement.

5.   Rawson has a contract with Green, the owner of a professional basketball team, to play basketball for Green's team for one year. In most states:

A. Green may assign his contractual rights to the owner of another basketball team without Rawson's consent.

    B. Rawson may delegate his duty to play basketball and assign his right to be paid to Hubbard without Green's consent if Hubbard is a better basketball player than Rawson.

    C. Rawson may assign his right to be paid for playing basketball, without Green's consent, after Rawson has rendered his performance.

    D. Rawson may **not** assign any rights or delegate any duties, which Rawson has as a result of being a party to the contract with Green, to another person.

6.   A life insurance policy, which provides that, upon the death of the insured, the insurance proceeds are to be paid to a creditor of the insured, is:

    A. illegal.

    B. a third party creditor beneficiary contract.

    C. a third party donee beneficiary contract.

    D. a contract for the assignment of rights and the delegation of duties.

7.   Roberts took out a $10,000 life insurance policy on her own life with ABC Insurance Company and named Sanders as the beneficiary. Roberts paid all the premiums until her untimely death a year later. The insurance company has not paid Sanders who, therefore, is suing the insurance company.

    A. Sanders is entitled to the payment of the $10,000 because Sanders is a third party donee beneficiary.

    B. If Roberts made misrepresentations concerning material facts in the application for insurance, the ABC Insurance Company can successfully raise the defense against Sanders that the contract was voidable because of fraud or misrepresentations.

    C. Although Sanders gave no consideration and was not a party to the contract between Roberts and ABC Insurance Company, Sanders is a proper party to enforce the insurance contract.

    D. All of the answers above are correct.

8.   A has agreed to pay B $3,000 if B promises to paint C's house.

    A. If C gave no consideration to A or B, then C has no standing to sue B because there is lack of privity of contract between B and C.

    B. If C gave no consideration to A or B, then C will be treated as a third party donee beneficiary and may enforce the contract against B.

    C. Because C is a third party beneficiary, C may enforce the contract against B, who will be barred from raising any defenses against C that he (B) could have raised against A.

    D. C is an assignee because A effectively transferred his (A's) rights to have his (A's) house painted by B.

9.   Hendon owed Borhan $200. On Monday, Hendon gave $200 to Katz, who promised to give the money to Borhan on the following Friday in order to discharge Hendon's debt. Katz did not deliver the money to Borhan. Borhan, a third party creditor beneficiary, will be successful if she sues Katz:

    A. because the parties to a contract that provided for conferring a benefit upon a third person cannot terminate their agreement if the third person learns of the original contract and detrimentally changes his or her position in reliance upon the contract.

B. even though Hendon and Katz altered their agreement on Wednesday before Borhan learned of the agreement that Hendon and Katz had entered and before Borhan gave her consent to the alteration of that agreement.

C. even though Hendon and Katz altered their contract on Tuesday before Borhan materially changed her position in detrimental reliance on the contract.

D. because the parties to a contract that provides for conferring a benefit upon a third person lack the power to alter or terminate their contract after they confer a benefit upon the third person.

10. The Acme Construction Co. contracted with Granite City to build a new court house. It was foreseeable that blasting would be necessary and Acme, therefore, promised in its contract with the city that it (Acme) would pay for "any and all property damage caused by the blasting."

A. MacDonald, a homeowner, can recover from Acme for damage to his home caused by the blasting because MacDonald is an incidental beneficiary.

B. Naughton, a homeowner, **cannot** recover from Acme for damage to her home caused by the blasting because Naughton is an incidental beneficiary.

C. Oppenheimer, a tourist, can recover for damage to her car caused by the blasting because Oppenheimer is a third party beneficiary.

D. Only Granite City can recover from Acme for damage to the city's property because the city was a party to the contract.

Chapter 19
Performance and Discharge

Most contractual duties are fully performed by parties to contracts so that the parties are discharged, or released, from any further contractual obligations and the contract, which is considered to be an executed contract, is, therefore, terminated. After their full performance, the parties know that they no longer owe any contractual duties to each other. As is explained in this chapter, even though a party does not perform a contractual obligation, he or she may be discharged because of the occurrence of a conditioning event or because of a breach of contract by the other contracting party. In addition, the contract and the parties to the contract may be discharged as a result of a subsequent agreement of the parties or by operation of law.

THINGS TO KEEP IN MIND

1. When a party to a contract fails to perform an absolute contractual promise, he or she (the breaching party) is not discharged, but is liable to the other party (the nonbreaching party) for breach of the contract. [The topic of remedies for breach of contract is the subject matter of Chapter 20.] The nonbreaching party is discharged and, therefore, excused from performing.

2. If a contractual promise is conditional and the conditioning event occurs, the promisor's duty to perform does not arise (in the case of a condition precedent) or is terminated (in the case of a condition subsequent) so that no liability attaches for failing to perform.

OUTLINE

I.   Conditions.

   A. A condition is a future uncertain event, the occurrence (or possibly, the nonoccurrence) of which changes, limits, precludes, gives rise to, or terminates a contractual duty or obligation.

   B. Types of conditions.

      1. Conditions precedent.

         a. A condition precedent is one that "precedes" the absolute duty of a party (or the parties) to perform as promised in a contract, so that the conditioning event must occur before performance by the promisor is required.

        b. If the condition precedent does not occur, the parties are discharged.

        c. Until the conditioning event occurs, the promisee has no right to receive performance; the contract is contingent upon (and not enforceable until) the occurrence of the conditioning event.

   2. Conditions subsequent.

        a. A condition subsequent is one that follows, or is subsequent to, the duty to perform as promised in a contract.

        b. The occurrence of the conditioning event extinguishes an existing contractual duty, so that the parties are discharged from their obligations.

   3. Substantively, the distinction between conditions precedent and subsequent is not important; for procedural purposes, however, the distinction is relevant.

        a. The party (usually the plaintiff) asserting that the other party has a duty to perform must plead and show that there was a condition precedent and that the condition precedent occurred so that he or she had a right to receive performance.

        b. The party (usually the defendant) asserting that he or she does not have a duty to perform must plead and prove that there was a condition subsequent and that the condition subsequent occurred so that he or she no longer has a duty to perform.

   4. Concurrent conditions — If there is a concurrent condition, the performance of each party is conditioned, or dependent, upon the simultaneous performance of the other party.

   5. Express and implied conditions — Conditions may be classified based upon the manner in which conditions arise.

        a. An express condition is a condition that is clearly stated and provided for in the contract by the parties. (Look for the words: if, provided, after, and when.)

        b. An implied-in-fact condition is one that is not expressed by the parties but is understood or inferred.

        c. An implied-in-law, or constructive, condition is one imposed by a court in order to achieve justice and fairness.

II.   Discharge by performance.

   A. Full, complete performance in the manner prescribed by the contract discharges the performing party.

B. Tender of complete performance — An unconditional offer to perform by a party who is ready, willing, and able to do so discharges the tendering party if his or her tender is not accepted.

C. Types of performance.

1. Complete performance.

   a. Complete performance includes strict, exact, and complete compliance with any express conditions.

   b. Failure to comply with an express condition and render the exact performance may discharge the party receiving the defective performance.

2. Substantial performance.

   a. Substantial part performance is good-faith performance that provides the important or essential benefits of the contract.

   b. Substantial part performance does not vary greatly from the performance that is promised in the contract, but is slightly less than that which reasonably could be expected.

   c. Effect of contractual conditions on discharge by performance.
      1) Strict compliance with express conditions is necessary.
      2) Substantial performance of constructive conditions is necessary.

   d. If the partial performance is accepted, the performing party can recover the value of his or her performance.

   e. If performance is substantial, but there is merely a minor or trivial deviation from a contractual obligation, and the deviation is not the result of bad faith, the performing party is discharged, but the performing party is liable for his or her failure to render complete performance. (See Chapter 20 for the measure of damages.)

   f. Partial performance that is not substantial performance is a breach of contract and results in the discharge of the party entitled to receive performance, but not in the discharge of the partially-performing party.

3. Performance to the satisfaction of one of the parties — The promise of one party to pay may be expressly conditioned on that party's personal satisfaction with the other party's performance.

   a. If personal taste, preferences, aesthetics, fancy, or comfort is involved, payment is excused if dissatisfaction is honest and in good faith, even though a reasonable person would have been satisfied.

b. If satisfaction relates to operative fitness, marketability, merchantability, or mechanical utility, payment is excused when dissatisfaction is honest and a reasonable person would have been dissatisfied.

4. Performance to the satisfaction of a third party — The promise of one party to pay may be expressly conditioned on a third party's personal satisfaction with the other party's performance, in which case the rules presented above in II. C. 3. also apply.

D. Material breach of contract.

1. A breach of contract is the nonperformance of a contractual duty.

2. A party who totally fails to perform is not discharged and is liable for damages for breach of contract. The other party, however, is discharged and need not hold himself or herself ready to perform.

3. If a party performs in part, but his or her performance does not amount to substantial part performance, then there is a material breach of contract.

a. The partially-performing party is not discharged and is liable for the material breach of contract.

b. The other party is discharged and need not hold himself or herself ready to perform.

4. If there is a minor, nonmaterial breach of contract, the breaching party is liable for damages if the breach is not cured. The nonbreaching party is not discharged and is required to perform.

E. Anticipatory repudiation of contract.

1. If a party repudiates a contract before that party is required to perform, the other party may sue immediately and does not have to remain ready to perform.

2. Reasons for treating anticipatory repudiation (or breach) as equivalent to a material breach:

a. Nonbreaching party should not be required to remain ready and willing to perform when the other party has refused to perform.

b. Nonbreaching party should have an opportunity to seek another similar contract elsewhere.

3. Under the UCC (Section 2-611), until the nonbreaching party treats the early repudiation as a breach of contract, the repudiating party can retract the anticipatory breach by giving proper notice and restoring the parties to their original positions.

4. The doctrine of anticipatory breach does not apply to a promise to pay a stated sum of money; the doctrine also does not apply to a unilateral contract or to a bilateral contract that is executory on one side only.

F. Time for performance.

1. If the time for performance is not stated, performance is to be rendered within a reasonable period of time.

2. The time requirement must be complied with if the parties expressly stipulate that time is of the essence (i.e., vital to performance).

3. If time for performance is stipulated, but not vital, performance prior to or within a few days of the stated time satisfies contract.

III. Discharge by agreement.

A. There may be a provision in the original contract for a possible agreement to discharge the contract.

B. Parties may enter into a new, subsequent, valid, and enforceable contract for the purpose of discharging the original contract.

1. Elements of contract, including real, mutual assent (offer and acceptance), consideration, and, if relevant, compliance with Statute of Frauds, must be present.

2. Discharge by rescission — The parties mutually agree to discharge and relieve each other of their contractual obligations.

a. If the original bilateral contract was executory, consideration is present because each party gives up existing rights.

b. If the original contract was a unilateral or a bilateral one that was executed by one party, new consideration must be given to the party who performed in exchange for his or her promise to relieve the non-performing party of his or her contractual duty to render the originally-promised performance.

c. Even if the original contract was in writing, an agreement to rescind the original contract may be oral except when the new agreement falls within the Statute of Frauds.

3. Discharge by substituted agreement.

a. Novation — The parties to an existing contract agree with a third person that the contractual duties and rights of one of the original parties will be assumed by the third person.

1) The third person is substituted for one of the original parties with the consent of the party entitled to receive the performance.
2) The original obligation of the prior party is extinguished, and the prior party is completely discharged.

b. Substituted agreement — Parties agree to enter a new agreement with different and inconsistent terms as a substitute for an original contract, which is expressly or impliedly discharged.

c. A compromise or settlement agreement, which is entered into by parties who have a bona fide dispute regarding an existing contract, expressly or impliedly discharges the obligations specified in the prior contract.

4. Discharge by accord and satisfaction.

a. An accord is an executory contract to perform some act in order to satisfy an existing contractual obligation; the parties agree that a different type of performance will be rendered by one party as satisfaction for his or her original obligation.

b. Satisfaction is the performance or execution of the accord agreement; the different act is actually performed by the obligor and accepted by the obligee, thus discharging the original contractual obligation.

c. Until the accord is satisfied, or carried out, the original contractual obligations are merely suspended; if the obligor refuses to perform as promised in the accord, the obligee may bring an action against the obligor based upon the original contract or may seek specific performance of the accord.

d. See also Chapter 14 dealing with consideration in connection with accord and satisfaction.

IV. Discharge by operation of law.

A. Alteration of the contract — If there is a material alteration of a written contract without consent, the contract is voidable by the party who was unaware of the change; he or she, therefore, has the option of treating the contract either as discharged or as enforceable in accordance with the original terms or with the terms as altered.

B. Statutes of limitations.

1. Statutes provide that a person who has a particular cause of action must bring his or her action or lawsuit within a specified period of time; for example, a party must sue within a specified number of years after a breach of contract has occurred.

2. Typically, there is a two-year to three-year statute of limitations for oral contracts and a four-year to five-year statute of limitations for written contracts; state statutes also bar enforcement of judgments after periods ranging from ten to twenty years.

3. The UCC provides for a four-year statute of limitations for an action based upon a breach of contract for the sale of goods; the parties in their original contract can provide for a shorter, but not a longer, period [Section 2-725].

4. Failure to commence an action or suit within the period of limitation bars access only to judicial remedies, but does not extinguish a debt or underlying obligation.

   a. A new promise to pay a debt or otherwise to perform (made either before or after the statute of limitations has run) will extend the statutory period even though no new consideration is given; many states, however, prescribe that such a promise be in writing. [See also Chapter 14.]

   b. A cause of action that is barred by a statute of limitations will be revived following partial performance.

C. Bankruptcy — Bankruptcy is covered in Chapter 32.

1. A discharge in bankruptcy operates as a release of a debtor from most debts and contractual obligations.

2. After a decree of discharge in bankruptcy is issued by a bankruptcy court, a partial payment by a debtor will not revive the obligation.

D. Impossibility or impracticability of performance.

1. Objective impossibility of performance — Performance may be objectively impossible because of the occurrence of a supervening, unforeseen event that occurs before performance is rendered; because of the impossibility, the parties to the contract are discharged.

   a. Death, serious illness, or incapacitation of a party who was to render personal services.

   b. Destruction of specific subject matter of contract.

   c. Change in law making performance illegal.

2. Commercial impracticability — Performance may be excused by a court if an extreme change in conditions (that was not reasonably foreseeable by the parties when the contract was formed) makes performance impracticable because performance will be extremely difficult, burdensome, or costly to render.

3. Frustration of purpose — A contract will be discharged upon the occurence of an unforeseen, supervening event that frustrates the purpose for which one of the parties entered the contract so that the value of the expected performance that he or she is to receive is destroyed.

4. Temporary impossibility — When performance is temporarily suspended because of an unexpected occurrence and subsequent circumstances make the suspended performance very difficult or substantially more burdensome, the parties may be discharged.

KEY WORDS AND PHRASES IN TEXT

discharge
conditions
condition precedent
condition subsequent
concurrent condition
express condition
implied-in-fact condition
tender of performance
complete performance
substantial part performance
performance to the satisfaction
    of a party to a contract
performance to the satisfaction
    of a third party
breach of contract

material breach of contract
anticipatory repudiation (breach)
discharge by agreement of parties
discharge by mutual rescission
novation
discharge by substituted agreement
settlement or compromise agreement
discharge by accord and satisfaction
discharge by operation of law
statute of limitations
discharge in bankruptcy
impossibility of performance
commercial impracticability
frustration of purpose
temporary impossibility

FILL-IN QUESTIONS

1. If parties to a contract agree that one of the parties will not be required to perform upon the happening of some event, their contract contains a condition _____. If, however, the parties agree that the occurrence of some event will terminate an existing contractual obligation, the contract contains a condition _____.

2. Karen promised to pay Trina $2,000 in exchange for Trina's promise to paint Karen's house in a color to be selected by Karen. The contract between Karen and Trina contains an express condition _____. If Karen does not select a color of paint, Trina is _____ from her obligation to paint the house.

3. National Sales Company is in the mail-order business. A customer may order goods from the company and, if so, promises to pay the purchase price for the merchandise. National Sales Company agrees that when goods ordered by a customer do not meet with the customer's satisfaction, the customer can return the merchandise within 15 days and will not be required to pay the purchase price. Contracts between National Sales Company and its customers, thus, contain express conditions _____. If Beth orders three blouses from National Sales Company and returns one blouse

within 15 days, she is _____ from her obligation to pay for the returned blouse. If Beth fails to pay for the two other blouses, she will be liable to the company for _____ of the contract.

4.   A party who renders or tenders _____ in the manner prescribed by a contract is discharged.

5.   A party to a contract is _____ if he or she renders complete performance. If a party substantially performs, he or she is _____, but is liable for the minor, trivial breach of contract. If, however, there is a material breach of contract because a party only partially performs, he or she is not _____, but the other party, to whom the breaching party owed a contractual duty, is _____.

6.   Sam agreed to sell 400 pens to Pam for $100. When Sam delivers the 400 pens, Sam is _____ and Pam is obligated to pay to Sam $100. If Sam delivers 396 pens, Sam is also _____. Pam, however, will not be _____ until she pays $100 for the pens, less a deduction (probably of $1) because there has been a minor, trivial breach of contract by Sam. If Sam delivers only 40 pens, he is not _____ because there has been a material breach of contract. Pam will not be required to pay for the pens because of Sam's material _____ of contract.

7.   The parties to a contract may subsequently agree to discharge and terminate their existing agreement by making a new contract. The new agreement may be an accord and satisfaction, _____, _____, settlement agreement or novation.

8.   Parties to a contract are discharged by operation of law if there has been a material alteration of a written contract by one party without the assent of the other party or _____ _____, or performance is impossible or commercially impracticable .

9.   A contract is discharged because of _____ if the subject matter has been destroyed or one of the parties who was to perform personal services has died.

MULTIPLE CHOICE QUESTIONS

1.   Aunt Alice promised to give her niece, Emily, $5,000 if Emily spends her two month summer vacation in Europe. Emily is legally entitled to the $5,000 if she:
  A. spends three weeks in Europe and works at home for the remainder of her vacation.
  B. spends two months in Mexico and Brazil.
  C. spends eight weeks in Europe.
  D. All of the answers above are correct.

2. On November 1, S and B entered into a written contract for the sale by S of a fully described tract of land for $20,000, delivery of the deed and payment by B to be due on December 1.
   A. If B advises S on November 15 that B no longer wishes to purchase the land and is repudiating the contract, S can successfully sue B for breach of contract on November 17.
   B. If S advises B on November 15 that S no longer wishes to sell the land and is repudiating the contract, B can successfully sue S for breach of contract on November 17.
   C. If B advises S on November 15 that B no longer wishes to purchase the land and is repudiating the contract, S can successfully sue B for anticipatory repudiation (breach) of contract on November 17.
   D. If S advises B on November 15 that S no longer wishes to sell the land and is repudiating the contact, B can successfully sue S for anticipatory repudiation (breach) of contract on November 17.

3. When a breach of contract is material, the nonbreaching party:
   A. is required to complete his or her performance before commencing an action for damages for the breach of contract.
   B. may recover damages for the breach of contract only if he or she had at least partially performed.
   C. is excused from performing his or her contractual duties and has a cause of action for damages caused by the breach of contract.
   D. is able to repudiate the contract if he or she pays the contract price for the partial performance rendered by the breaching party.

4. If a breach of contract is:
   A. material, the nonbreaching party may sue for damages but must perform his or her part of the contract.
   B. material, the nonbreaching party may **not** sue for damages if he or she has accepted the improper performance.
   C. minor, the nonbreaching party is excused from performing.
   D. minor, the nonbreaching party may sue for damages for the breach.

5. On July 10, Fred, the owner of a farm, contracted to sell 3,000 bushels of Grade A tomatoes on September 1 to the Prince Pizza Co. The tomatoes on Fred's farm were destroyed in a hail storm on August 8. If Fred fails to deliver 3,000 bushels of tomatoes on September 1:
   A. Prince Pizza Co. may successfully sue Fred for breach of contract.
   B. Fred is discharged because of a condition subsequent.
   C. Fred is discharged by operation of law because of impossibility.
   D. Prince Pizza Co. may successfully sue Fred for anticipatory repudiation of contract.

6. On June 1, Frank, the owner of a farm, contracted to sell 2,000 bushels of Grade A corn grown on his farm on August 10 to Careful Corn Canners, Inc. The corn on Frank's farm was destroyed by locusts on August 1. If Frank fails to deliver the 2,000 bushels of corn on August 10:

A. Careful Corn Canners, Inc. may successfully sue Frank for breach of contract.
B. Frank is discharged because of a condition subsequent.
C. Frank is discharged by operation of a law because of impossibility.
D. Careful Corn Canners, Inc. may successfully sue Frank for anticipatory repudiation of contract.

7. Larry rented a room from Mike along Main Street on a Saturday for the purpose of watching a parade. Mike knew that this was the reason for renting the room. Unfortunately, there was a bad snow storm and the parade was canceled. Mike has sued Larry for the rent. In most states, a court will determine that:
A. the contract is discharged because of impossibility.
B. the contract is discharged because of economic frustration.
C. the contract is discharged because of the occurrence of a conditioning event.
D. the contract is **not** discharged.

8. On March 1, Pick and Quick entered into a valid written contract that provided for the sale by Pick of 1,000 yo-yos to Quick for $1,000. All of the terms were clearly and unambiguously contained in the writing. A week later Pick delivered 400 yo-yos, but Pick has failed to deliver the remaining 600 yo-yos.
A. Pick is **not** discharged and is liable to Quick for a material breach of the contract.
B. Quick must remain ready, willing, and able to pay Pick the $1,000.
C. Even if Quick accepted the 400 yo-yos, Quick would **not** have to pay for these yo-yos because there has been a material breach of contract.
D. If Quick accepted the 400 yo-yos, Pick is discharged without liability and does **not** have to tender delivery of the remaining 600 yo-yos.

9. Don promised to pay Cathy $500 if Cathy painted Don's portrait.
A. If Cathy dies before completing the portrait, Cathy and Don are discharged.
B. If Ellen, Cathy, and Don agree that Ellen will paint the portrait and Don will pay Ellen rather than Cathy, the parties have entered a novation.
C. Cathy paints the portrait but Don fails to pay the $500. Cathy is discharged but Don is **not** discharged.
D. All of the answers above are correct.

10. Teller brought a law suit against Kerr ten years after an oral contract was made and eight years after there was a breach of the contract. Kerr raised the statute of limitations as a defense. Which of the following allegations would be most important to Kerr's defense?
A. The contract was oral.
B. The action was **not** brought in a timely manner because, allegedly, the contract was breached eight years prior to the commencement of the lawsuit.
C. The action was **not** brought in a timely manner because the contract was entered into ten years prior to the commencement of the lawsuit.
D. The contract could **not** be performed within one year from the date it was made.
[This question is adapted from objective question #22, Uniform CPA Examination, November 1993.]

Chapter 20
Breach of Contract and Remedies

A breach of contract occurs when a party fails to perform a contractual duty fully and correctly. The party to whom the duty is owned may sue the breaching party or bring an equitable action against the breaching party in order to enforce his or her rights and obtain an appropriate remedy (i.e., a remedy at law or a remedy in equity).

THINGS TO KEEP IN MIND

1. When there has been a breach of contract and the nonbreaching party sues, the remedy that usually will be afforded will be compensatory damages, a sum of money that will be adequate in order to put the nonbreaching party in the position that the nonbreaching party would have been in had there not been a breach of contract.

2. A contracting party who has been injured may seek an equitable remedy, such as rescission, restitution, specific performance, reformation, or a quasi contractual recovery. The general rule is that equitable remedies are **not** available if:

   a. Money damages are adequate, determinable, available, and will not result in hardship;

   b. The aggrieved party has shown bad faith or used fraud (the doctrine of clean hands);

   c. The aggrieved party has delayed unnecessarily in bringing an action (the doctrine of laches); or

   d. The court will have to supervise the execution of the remedy.

OUTLINE

I. Damages.

   A. A legal remedy — In a typical lawsuit, a court may order that a sum of money (compensatory damages) be paid to a person who has incurred an injury or loss by the person who caused the injury or loss.

   B. Types of damages.

      1. Compensatory damages. [See also Chapter 6.]

a. Compensatory damages are awarded to a nonbreaching party in order to compensate the nonbreaching party for the actual harm or loss of the bargain caused by the breach of contract.

b. The measure of damages usually is a factual question.
    1) How much money will place the plaintiff in as good a position as the plaintiff would have been in if the defendant had performed correctly?
    2) Usually, this amounts to the loss of normal, expected profit plus any sums previously paid and incidental expenses incurred by the nonbreaching party. (Incidental expenses may include sums that were paid to obtain comparable performance elsewhere.)
    3) The measurement of compensatory damages for breach of contract varies depending upon the type of contract and usually equals loss of profit plus any costs already incurred by the nonbreaching party in rendering performance.

c. Sale of goods — Compensatory damages for breach of a contract for the sale of goods is an amount equal to the difference between the contract price and the market price at the time and place for the tender of the goods [UCC 2-708 and 2-713].

d. Sale of land.
    1) Usually, compensatory damages for breach of a contract for the sale of real property is an amount equal to the difference between the contract price and the market price.
    2) Minority position: if there is a non-deliberate breach by the seller, the purchaser can recover any down payment plus expenses.

e. Construction contracts — Damages vary depending upon which party fails to perform and at what stage construction is when the breach occurs.
    1) Breach by owner (the person for whom the building was to be constructed).
        a) Before performance begins — Contractor recovers contract price less cost of materials and labor.
        b) During construction — Contractor recovers profits plus costs incurred in partially constructing building.
        c) After construction is completed — Contractor recovers contract price with interest.
    2) Breach by contractor.
        a) Before substantial completion — Compensatory damages equal cost of completion and reasonable compensation for delay.
        b) After substantial completion — Damages equal cost of completion if there is no substantial economic waste in completing the construction.
        c) After late completion — Damages equal loss of use.

f. Employment contracts.
    1) Breach by employer — Salary for unexpired term less earnings of the discharged employee from a job of similar nature, or, if such a

job is available, compensation that the discharged employee would have received if he or she had accepted the new position.

    2) Breach by employee — Cost of procuring replacement employee less contracted salary or wages.

2. Consequential (special) damages — Speculative, unforeseen, remote, indirect, or unexpected injuries or losses, which ordinarily do not flow from a breach of contract, are not recoverable unless, at the time the contract was formed, these injuries or losses were contemplated by (and, therefore, foreseeable to) the nonperforming party because the nonperforming party was given notice of the possibility of their occurrence and the special circumstances.

3. Punitive or exemplary damages — Unusual award by a court as punishment for willful, wanton, malicious (tortious) harm caused to a nonbreaching party and to deter wrongdoing.

4. Nominal damages — Inconsequential sum which establishes that the plaintiff has a cause of action but suffered only a technical injury with no measurable pecuniary loss.

C. Mitigation of damages.

1. An innocent, nonbreaching injured party must mitigate, or reduce, his or her actual damages if the injured party is able to do so.

2. Lessor is required to use reasonable means in order to find a new tenant.

3. An employee whose employment has been wrongfully terminated is required to use reasonable means in order to find a similar position elsewhere.

D. Liquidated damages versus penalties.

1. Liquidated damages clauses: Parties may provide in their contract that, in the event of a future default or breach of contract, a certain stated sum of money will be paid (or, if previously deposited, forfeited).

2. Courts will enforce a liquidated damages clause (rather than award compensatory damages) as long as the amount is not viewed as a penalty.

    a. At the time that the contract was entered into, it was apparent that damages would be difficult to estimate in the event of a breach.

    b. At the time that the contract was entered into, the amount appeared to be reasonable and not excessive.

    c. If the court determines that the amount is an excessive penalty, the court will not enforce the liquidated damages clause.

II. Rescission and restitution.

    A. Rescission means cancellation, annulment, or "undoing" of a contract.

        1. Parties to a contract mutually may agree to rescind or discharge their contract. [See Chapter 19.]

        2. If the assent of a party was not real or voluntarily given or a party lacked contractual capacity, that party unilaterally may rescind a contract or request the remedy of rescission from a court.

        3. A court may grant the remedy of rescission when there has been a material substantial breach of contract or a failure of consideration.

        4. Statutes may give contracting parties a right to rescind certain contracts.

    B. Restitution.

        1. Restitution means returning or restoring parties to the positions that the parties were in before entering into a contract.

        2. Usually, the remedy of restitution is given with rescission so that previously rendered consideration, or its equivalent value, is returned or reimbursed.

        3. Today, restitution also may be awarded in breach of contract, tort, and other actions at law or in equity.

III. Specific performance — An order by a court directing a person to render contractually promised performance.

    A. Specific performance will be granted when the injured party's legal remedy of money damages is inadequate (as is true if the subject matter of the contract is unique property) and the performance that is to be rendered is clear and unambiguous.

    B. Sale of land — Specific performance of a contract for the sale of land will be granted as a remedy because land is always considered to be unique property.

        1. Money damages, therefore, are inadequate to enable a buyer of real property to purchase the same property from another seller.

        2. Money damages, rather that specific performance, will be awarded if the buyer asks for the legal remedy, or the seller has sold the property to someone else.

    C. Contracts for personal services — Specific performance will not be granted when the performance to be rendered involves personal services.

1. Involuntary servitude is contrary to public policy and prohibited by the Thirteenth Amendment to the U.S. Constitution.

2. A court will not give a remedy that will require the court to monitor performance.

3. A court will not enforce a "positive covenant" (a promise to work for another person) in a contract of employment by issuing an order for specific performance; but a court may enforce a reasonable "negative covenant" (a promise not to work for another person) for a limited period of time by issuing an injunction (an order enjoining or restraining a person from doing some act).

IV.   Reformation.

A. A court may correct a written agreement so that the agreement will conform to the intentions of the parties.

B. Reformation, an equitable remedy, may be used when fraud, a mutual mistake, or a typographical error has occurred.

C. If an agreement contains a number of provisions, one of which is illegal, a court may reform the contract by deleting the illegal provision.

V.   Recovery based on quasi contract. [See Chapter 12.]

A. A court may require that a person who has received a benefit pay for the benefit that was conferred in order to prevent unjust enrichment (*quantum meruit*).

B. The person seeking a quasi contractual recovery must show that:

1. He or she has conferred a benefit on the other party;

2. He or she conferred the benefit with the reasonable expectation of being paid;

3. He or she did not act as a volunteer in conferring the benefit; and

4. The party receiving the benefit will be unjustly enriched if he or she retains the benefit without paying for the benefit.

VI.   Election of remedies.

A. In the past, a plaintiff was required to elect either a legal remedy (compensatory money damages) or equitable relief (exclusive relief).

B. Today, generally, both legal and equitable relief will be available if they are not inconsistent (cumulative relief).

C. The UCC eliminates the doctrine of election of remedies in contracts for the sale of goods; a buyer or seller may obtain both damages and an equitable remedy but may not duplicate any item of recovery. [Sections 2-703, 2-711, and 2-721.]

VII. Waiver of breach.

A. A nonbreaching party voluntarily may waive, relinquish, give up, or surrender a right that the nonbreaching party has to seek a remedy for breach of contract by accepting the defective performance of the other party.

B. Waiver of a breach of contract extends only to the matter waived; it does not extend to the whole contract or to additional or future breaches of the contract.

C. Waiver of a breach, however, will extend to subsequent defective performance if there was a pattern of conduct which would indicate to a reasonable person that similar defective performance in the future would be acceptable; in order to prevent this, the nonbreaching party should notify the breaching party that future defective performance will not be accepted.

D. Effect of waiver of a breach of contract.

1. Nonbreaching party cannot rescind the contract.

2. Breaching party remains liable to nonbreaching party for damages caused by defective or less than full performance.

VIII. Contract provisions limiting remedies.

A. Types of clauses.

1. An exculpatory clause provides that no damages can be recovered for certain types of breaches of contract; it absolves a party from liability for such breaches. [See Chapter 17.]

2. A clause may provide that, if there is a breach, damages will be limited to a specified amount.

3. A limitation-of-liability clause may restrict, or limit, the availability of certain remedies if there is a breach of contract.

B. Mutual assent to limitation required.

1. The provision must have been a term that was clearly stated and communicated by the offeror in the offer and was a term that was accepted by the offeree. [See Chapter 13.]

2. A provision in a writing (e.g., an offer containing a clause limiting liability or remedies) is considered to be communicated so that the recipient (who may have received, but not read, the writing) has notice of the provision if a

reasonable person would understand from the nature of the transaction and the surrounding circumstances that such a provision might be embodied in the writing.

C. Type of liability excluded.

1. Contractual limitations on liability, including limitations on the amount that can be recovered if there is a breach of contract and limitations as to remedies that will be available in the event of a breach of contract, will be enforced unless the limitations are unconscionable or the result of unequal bargaining power.

2. Provisions that will not be enforced:

   a. Exclusion of liability for criminal acts, other violations of law, or intentional torts, including fraud and/or gross negligence.

   b. Exclusion of liability for negligence when parties do not have equal bargaining power.

D. Sales of goods covered by the UCC. [See Chapter 24.]

1. If a contract for the sale of goods provides that one remedy (repair and replacement) is the sole and exclusive remedy available to the buyer, the provision is enforceable so long as it is not unconscionable [UCC 2-719(1)].

2. When circumstances cause an exclusive remedy or limited remedy to fail in its essential purpose, all other remedies provided for in the UCC are available [UCC 2-719(2)].

3. Consequential damages may be limited or excluded unless it is unconscionable to do so [UCC 2-719(3)].

KEY WORDS AND PHRASES IN TEXT

breach of contract
remedies at law (damages)
remedies in equity
compensatory damages
measure of compensatory damages
consequential (special) damages
punitive (exemplary) damages
penalties
nominal damages
mitigation of damages
liquidated damages
liquidated damages versus penalties

rescission
restitution
specific performance
reformation
quasi contract recovery
unjust enrichment
quantum meruit
election of remedies
waiver of breach of contract
pattern of conduct
exculpatory clauses
contractual provision limiting remedies

FILL-IN QUESTIONS

1. A plaintiff, who is suing a party with whom the plaintiff has entered into a contract, may recover _____ damages to compensate the plaintiff for the foreseeable injury sustained because of a breach of contract.

2. In an action based upon a breach of a contract for the sale of property, the measure of damages usually will be the difference between the _____ and the _____.

3. Smith agreed to sell his house to Baker for $70,000. Baker was unable to obtain a mortgage and, therefore, did not complete the purchase. The fair market value of the house was $64,000. If Smith sues Baker for breach of contract, Smith can recover _____ damages in the amount of $_____ because the appropriate measure of damages is the loss of profit, or the difference between the contract price and the _____.

4. Consequential, or _____, damages are those that indirectly flow from a _____ and are awarded only when such damages were, or should have been, reasonably foreseeable to the parties at the time that the contract was formed.

5. If a provision in a contract states that a certain sum of money will be forfeited by a party who fails to perform a contractual duty, the provision is referred to as a _____ clause and will be enforced as long as the amount _____.

6. _____ will be granted by a court if a minor, or a party whose assent was not real, wishes to disaffirm a voidable contract to which he or she was a party.

7. Equitable relief, such as rescission, _____, and quasi contract, will be granted if a legal remedy, such as compensatory damages, is unavailable or is _____.

8. Mark was 17 years of age when he entered into a written contract to buy a car. Because Mark was a minor, the contract for the purchase of the car is _____ by Mark. Two months later, Mark decided that he wished to return the car to the seller and get back the purchase price, which he had paid to the seller. Mark will seek the equitable remedies of _____ and _____.

MULTIPLE CHOICE QUESTIONS

1. In an action instituted by the seller based upon a refusal by a buyer to accept and pay for $100 worth of pencils, a court will probably:
   A. only award nominal damages.
   B. only award compensatory damages.
   C. grant a decree of specific performance.
   D. grant a decree of specific performance and compensatory damages.

2.   In an action based upon a breach of an employment contract by an employee, a court
      will probably:
      A. award nominal damages.
      B. award punitive damages.
      C. award compensatory damages.
      D. grant a decree of specific performance.

3.   Nominal damages refer to:
      A. a small sum of money awarded to a plaintiff, whose rights have been infringed
         upon as a result of a defendant's breach of contract, when the plaintiff incurred no
         actual loss.
      B. a specific sum of money that one party agrees to pay to another party in the event
         that he or she fails to perform in accordance with a major provision in a contract.
      C. an award by a court when it is determined that a liquidated damages clause in a
         contract is excessive because the amount of liquidated damages does not bear a
         reasonable relationship to the actual damage incurred.
      D. the difference between the contract price and the market price of goods which
         were the subject matter of a contract that has not been performed by either the
         buyer or seller of the goods.

4.   When a contract provision requires that a party, who fails to perform as agreed upon
      in a contract, pay a specified sum to the other party, the amount is referred to as:
      A. specific performance.
      B. nominal damages.
      C. liquidated damages.
      D. punitive damages.

5.   Sigma entered into a contract to sell 100 chairs to Beta. Beta repudiated the contract.
      Sigma then sold the chairs at a lower price to Chi. Sigma's action is known as:
      A. nominal damages.
      B. mitigation of damages.
      C. liquidation of damages.
      D. liquidating the damages.

6.   Master Manufacturing Co. contracted in writing with Accur Computer Services, Inc.
      for maintenance of Master's computer system. Master's manufacturing process
      depends upon its computer system operating properly at all times. A liquidated
      damages clause in the written agreement provided that Accur would pay $1,000 to
      Master for each day that Accur was late in responding to a request for services. On
      January 12, Master notified Accur that Master's computer system failed (bombed).
      Accur did not respond to Master's service request until January 16. If Master sues
      Accur based upon the liquidated damage provision of the contract, Master will:
      A. lose, because Accur's breach was not a material breach of the contract.
      B. lose, because liquidated damages provisions violate public policy.
      C. win, unless the liquidated damages provision is determined to be a penalty.
      D. win, because liquidated damages provisions are enforceable under all
      circumstances.
      (This question is adapted from Objective Question 1 - #25 on the Uniform CPA
      Examination, May 1993.)

7. Specific performance is:
    A. the remedy used when the subject matter of a contract is unique.
    B. the first remedy a court will grant if there is a breach of contract.
    C. used when a party has failed to mitigate damages.
    D. infrequently used in cases of breach of contracts for the sale of real property.

8. In an action based upon a breach of a contract:
    A. whenever possible, a court will require specific performance.
    B. if a party can be adequately compensated by money damages, that party will **not** be granted an injunction.
    C. the party to whom damage is done because of the breach will be awarded money damages only if the contract is rescinded.
    D. the party to whom damage is done because of the breach usually will be awarded money damages as well as rescission or an injunction.

9. The Grateful Living, a well-known group, entered into a contract and promised to perform at the Oldtown Fair. Later, because of receiving a more lucrative offer from New City, the Grateful Living refused to honor its commitment to Oldtown. If Oldtown commences an action against the group in a court, the court probably will:
    A. rescind the contract between The Grateful Living and Oldtown.
    B. enter judgment for Oldtown and award it compensatory damages.
    C. enter judgment for Oldtown and award it punitive damages.
    D. issue an order for specific performance because the subject matter of the contract is unique.

10. Cassie and Dave entered into a written agreement stipulating that Dave would deliver 100 tons of sand to Cassie within three (3) days. There was a mistake in the written document because the intentions of Cassie and Dave had been to provide that delivery would be within thirty (30) days. If Cassie insists upon delivery within three days, Dave would seek the remedy of:
    A. reformation.
    B. rescission.
    C. specific performance.
    D. punitive damages.

11. A person who incurs damage, because the party with whom he or she has contracted has failed to perform, has a duty to reduce his or her actual damages if possible. This is referred to as:
    A. making an election of remedies.
    B. limiting liability.
    C. liquidation of damages.
    D. mitigation damages.

12. Joshua contracted to sell a set of dueling pistols to John for $50,000. Both Joshua and John believed that the pistols had been owned by Aaron Burr. It is learned that they made a mutual mistake of fact and John wishes to avoid the contract. The most appropriate remedy is:
    A. nominal damages.
    B. compensatory damages.

C. rescission.

D. reformation.

13. Reynolds promised to sell 500 shares of stock in a specified corporation to Ingram for $10,000, but Reynolds has failed to deliver the stock certificates to Ingram. A court will issue a decree for specific performance, if it is established that:

A. Ingram used false representations of fact in order to induce Reynolds' assent to the contract.

B. the shares of stock are those of a corporation whose shares are publicly traded on a national stock exchange.

C. a provision of the contract stipulated that, if Reynolds did not deliver the stock certificates, Reynolds would pay Ingram $100, which was the foreseeable amount of damages that would be incurred.

D. the shares of stock are those of a small corporation that are not readily available for purchase.

UNIT THREE:
DOMESTIC AND INTERNATIONAL
SALES AND LEASE CONTRACTS

The objective of this unit is to familiarize you with business transactions involving tangible, moveable, personal property, or "goods." Much of the law relating to such transactions has been codified in the Uniform Commercial Code (UCC or the Code), an internally consistent, comprehensive statement of applicable basic principles of law. References are given in the chapters of this unit to sections of the UCC. The provisions of the Code are reproduced in Appendix C of the textbook.

The UCC has been adopted, at least in part, by the legislatures in all fifty states and in the District of Columbia and the Virgin Islands. You will probably observe that the Code is written in ordinary language with a minimum of "legalese." Because of this, people engaging in business are able to refer easily to the Code and to understand the rules of law that govern common business transactions.

The Code applies to most aspects of a commercial transaction when the subject matter is goods. It, therefore, does not relate to transactions involving real property or the performance of services, to which other statutes and case law apply. Included in Article 2 of the UCC (the focal point of Chapters 21 through 25) are rules relating to agreements for the sale of goods by original manufacturers, by wholesalers and other distributors and, ultimately, by retailers, who sell the goods to final consumers. Note that, if parties to sales contracts wish to vary the effect of some provisions of the UCC, the parties may agree to do so.

The UCC also contains provisions dealing with the transportation and storage of goods and the methods available for financing their purchase and for securing payment of the purchase price or other performance. These topics are covered in subsequent units of *West's Business Law* and this *Study Guide*.

For some time, it was questioned whether or not Article 2 (the Sales Article) applied to transactions in which goods were leased, as opposed to being sold. For this reason, a new Article (Article 2A) covering leases, was proposed and has been adopted in many states. As pointed out in in this unit, many of the sections in Article 2A are very similar to those in the Sales Article.

Frequently today, U.S. firms engage in international commercial transactions. Many international sales contracts are governed by the Convention on Contracts for the International Sale of Goods (CISG). Excerpts from the CISG are found in Appendix D of the textbook. Most of the principles of law set forth in the CISG are similar to those in the UCC, which applies to domestic sales contracts in the United States. There are, however, some important differences between the CISG and the UCC. Information relating to the rules governing international sales transactions, particularly when the rules vary from those in the UCC, are interspersed in many of the chapters in this Unit.

Unless otherwise noted, the Articles and Sections referenced in the chapters in this unit are to Articles and Sections in the UCC.

Chapter 21
The Formation of Sales and Lease Contracts

The law of sales deals with the rights and duties of the buyers and sellers of goods in the entire chain of purchases and sales from their original production to their ultimate purchase for consumption or other use. Transactions involving sales of goods for consideration are covered by Article 2 of the Uniform Commercial Code (UCC or the Code). Contracts for the leasing of goods are governed by Article 2A of the UCC. Because the UCC is a statute, its provisions have "priority over" case law. Recall from Chapter 1 that, in the event that there is conflict between case law and statutory (codified) law, the principles of law espoused in a statute prevail over rules found in judge-made, case law.

The UCC, which is reproduced in Appendix C of the textbook, is a model for legislation that has been adopted, at least in part, by all of the states in the United States, the District of Columbia, and the Virgin Islands. The UCC provides for flexibility and establishes standards of good faith and reasonableness for parties engaging in sales transactions. Provisions of the Code that change some of the rules of law with which you became familiar when you studied the law of contracts are highlighted in this and subsequent chapters. Note that revisions of Article 2, which may be adopted in the various states, have been proposed.

Increasingly, U.S. firms are engaging in international trade by buying and selling products in the global market. For this reason, the final section of the chapter is devoted to the Convention on Contracts for the International Sale of Goods (CISG), which governs international sales agreements. (Excerpts from the CISG are reproduced in Appendix D of the textbook.) Many of the rules set forth in the CISG are similar to those set forth in the Uniform Commercial Code. As explained in the text, there are, however, some important differences. In addition, contracts for international sales often contain important provisions relating to language and dispute resolution.

THINGS TO KEEP IN MIND

1. An agreement for the sale or lease of goods is a contract. All of the elements of a contract, therefore, must be present for it to be valid and enforceable. Some of the rules of contract law, however, are relaxed under the UCC.

2. Often special rules are applicable if one or, in some cases, both parties are merchants.

OUTLINE

I.   The Uniform Commercial Code.

    A. Origins of sales law and the UCC.

        1. The modern rules relating to sales of goods can be traced back to the Law Merchant (*Lex Mercatoria*), a system of rules, customs, and usages adopted and used by traders and merchants for centuries in order to settle disputes and enforce obligations.

        2. By the end of the seventeenth century, the Law Merchant had become part of the English common law and, therefore, was the foundation for state law in the United States.

        3. In this country, the need for consistent and uniform commercial law among the states first was addressed with the adoption of the Uniform Negotiable Instruments Law (1896) and the Uniform Sales Act (1906).

        4. In the 1940s, the National Conference of Commissioners on Uniform State Laws developed the Uniform Commercial Code (UCC, or the Code) into which a number of earlier uniform acts covering business transactions were incorporated. Over the years, there have been revisions of and additions to the Code.

    B. Comprehensive coverage of the UCC.

        1. The UCC provides a consistent and integrated framework of rules to deal with all phases of an entire commercial transaction relating to the sale or lease of goods and payment for the goods or the lease of the goods.

        2. Contracts for the sales of goods are the subject of Article 2; contracts for leases are covered by Article 2A, many of the provisions of which are the same as, or similar to, those in Article 2.

        3. Payments for goods may be handled by using commercial paper, such as checks and other negotiable instruments (Article 3), or letters of credit (Article 5). [See Unit Four.]

        4. Banks provide mechanisms for transferring and collecting commercial paper and electronic funds transfers — (Articles 4 and 4A). [See Chapter 29.]

        5. If credit is being extended to buyers of goods, the transactions may be secured transactions — Article 9. [See Chapter 30.]

        6. Storage and shipment of goods — Article 7. [See Chapter 49.]

7. Bulk transfers of goods are covered in Article 6, the repeal of which has been recommended by the Commissioners of Uniform State Laws, and revised for consideration by those states that have not repealed Article 6.

8. Investment securities — Article 8. [See Chapter 43.]

C. Periodic revision of the UCC.

1. As methods of conducting business change, the UCC has been, and continues to be, revised.

2. Current clarifying revisions of Article 2 of the UCC reflect changes in commercial practices.

II. The scope of Article 2 — The sale of goods.

A. If Article 2 of the UCC does not provide a rule regarding a particular issue, another statute or the common law of contracts applies.

B. Article 2 deals with goods (tangible, moveable, personal property) but not with real property, intangible personal property, and services.

C. What is a sale? — A sale is a present transfer by a seller to a buyer of ownership rights (title) to existing, identified goods for consideration, known as the price.

D. What are goods? — Goods are items that are tangible and moveable and have physical existence.

1. Goods associated with real estate [UCC 2-107] — Goods associated with real property that are covered by Article 2 include:

a. Minerals or similar natural resources that are found beneath the surface and are to be severed (removed) by the seller.

b. Growing crops and similar things attached to land that are to be severed by the buyer or seller.

c. Things attached to realty to be severed by the buyer or seller without material harm to the land.

2. Goods and services combined.

a. When a transaction combines a sale of goods and a rendering of services, the transaction is not covered by Article 2 if the dominant purpose and character of the contract is for services with the sale of goods incidentally involved.

b. Contracts for sales and services of computer software as well as food and beverages have been treated as contracts for sales of goods.

        c. Goods include unborn animals, rare coins, and other forms of money that are treated as commodities as well as items that are specially manufactured [UCC 2-105].

E. Who is a merchant? — Section 2-104 of the UCC provides that a merchant, to whom special rules apply, is a person who:

    1. Deals in goods of the kind involved in the transaction; or

    2. Holds himself or herself out, because of his or her occupation, as having knowledge and skills peculiar to the business or goods involved in the transaction; or

    3. Employs other people who are merchants to act on his or her behalf.

III.   The scope of Article 2A — Leases.

A. Article 2A of the UCC applies to transactions in which goods are leased, rather than sold, and to which neither Article 2 (Sales of Goods) nor Article 9 (Secured Transactions) apply.

B. Definition of a lease.

    1. A lease provides for the transfer of the right to possession and use of goods.

    2. The lease agreement is the bargain (the understanding) of the parties as expressed in their language and as implied from other circumstances, including course of dealings, usage of trade, and course of performance [UCC 2A-103(k)].

    3. The lessor is the person who sells the right to possession and use of goods under a lease [UCC 2A-103(p)] and the lessee is the person who acquires the right to possession and use of goods under a lease [UCC 2A-103(o)].

C. Consumer leases.

    1. A consumer lease is a lease for total payments of less than $25,000, involving a lessor, who engages in the business of leasing or selling (comparable to a "merchant" in Article 2), and a lessee, who leases the goods primarily for personal, family, or household purposes [UCC 2A-103(1)(e)].

    2. Different rules sometimes apply to consumer leases. For example, with regard to unconscionability, even if a lease is not unconscionable, a court can give relief if unconscionable conduct induced the consumer lessee to enter into a lease or occurred in the collection of a claim under the lease [UCC 2A-108(2)]; a court also can award attorneys' fees to the lessee, or to the lessor if the lessee's claim is groundless [UCC 2A-108(4)(a)].

D. Finance leases.

1. Lessor (financer) buys or leases goods from a supplier and leases or sub-leases the goods to the lessee [UCC 2A-103(g)].

2. Lessee's obligations are irrevocable and independent from those of the financer [UCC 2A-407].

IV. The formation of sales and lease contracts.

   A. Contract law principles apply to agreements for the sale of goods and the lease of goods unless modified by the Code; the UCC applies unless otherwise modified by the parties.

   B. Offer — See also Chapter 13.

      1. The moment at which a contract becomes effective may be undetermined. [UCC 2-204; 2A-204].

      2. Open terms — If it was the intention of the parties to form a contract, a contract will not fail for indefiniteness because some terms are left open.

         a. Open price term [UCC 2-305].
           1) If parties intended to form a contract, but did not set a price or provide a method by which the price was to be determined, the price will be the reasonable price at the time of delivery.
           2) If the buyer or seller is to set the price, he or she must do so in good faith.
           3) If the price is not fixed through the fault of one party, the other party may treat the contract as canceled or fix a reasonable price.

         b. Open payment term — If the terms of payment are not specified, payment is due at the time and place at which the buyer is to receive the goods [UCC 2-310(a)] and is to be made in cash or a commercially acceptable substitute for cash [UCC 2-511(2)].

         c. Open delivery term.
           1) When the place of delivery is not specified [UCC 2-308]:
              a) Goods are to be delivered at the seller's place of business or, if the seller has none, his or her residence.
              b) If the goods are at a location other than the seller's place of business, and both parties know this, goods are to be delivered at that location.
           2) When the time for delivery is not specified, the goods are to be delivered within a reasonable time [UCC 2-309].

         d. Duration of an ongoing contract — When no period of time is specified for the duration of a contract for delivery of goods, a party who is terminating the ongoing contract must give reasonable notice to the other party [UCC 2-309].

e. Options and cooperation regarding performance [UCC 2-311].
   1) If the particulars of performance are to be specified by one of the parties, such specifications must be made in good faith and within the limits of commercial reasonableness.
   2) Unless otherwise agreed, the seller selects arrangements for shipment and the buyer specifies the assortment of goods.

f. Open quantity terms — Requirements and output contracts.
   1) At the time that the parties enter into a requirements or output contract, the precise quantity of goods to be purchased or sold is not certain. The quantity is treated as sufficiently definite, however, because the expectation is that the actual amount bought or sold will be the amount as may occur in good faith and is a quantity that is reasonably related to normal or comparable prior requirements or output [UCC 2-306].
   2) Such agreements are not considered to be illusory because of lack of consideration.
   3) Requirements contracts.
      a) Consideration is given because the buyer agrees to purchase, and the seller agrees to sell, all or an amount up to a specified amount, that the buyer needs or requires, even though the exact amount is uncertain.
      b) The seller's promise is supported by sufficient consideration.
         (1) The seller gets the benefit of knowing that he or she has a market for at least some of his or her products.
         (2) The buyer incurs a detriment because he or she gives up the opportunity (a legal right) to purchase products from other sellers (possibly at lower prices).
      c) The buyer's promise is supported by sufficient consideration.
         (1) The buyer gets the benefit of knowing that he or she has a source of supply of the product that is necessary in order to operate his or her business.
         (2) The seller incurs a detriment because the seller gives up the opportunity (a legal right) to sell to other buyers (possibly at higher prices) until the obligation under the requirements contract is satisfied.
      d) The contract is illusory and, therefore, not binding, if the buyer agrees to purchase only the goods that he or she may wish, want, or desire.
   4) Output contracts.
      a)) The seller agrees to sell, and buyer agrees to purchase, all or up to a specified amount of the seller's output.
      b) The seller's promise is supported by sufficient consideration.
         (1) The seller gets the benefit of knowing that he or she has a market for his or her products.
         (2) The buyer incurs a detriment because the buyer gives up the opportunity (a legal right) to purchase products from other sellers (possibly at lower prices) until the buyer has purchased all of the particular seller's goods.

        c) The buyer's promise is supported by sufficient consideration.
            (1) The buyer gets the benefit of knowing that he or she has a source of supply of the product that is necessary in order to operate his or her business.
            (2) The seller incurs a detriment because the seller gives up the opportunity (a legal right) to sell to other buyers (possibly at higher prices).
        d) The contract is illusory if its terms permit the seller to sell to other purchasers or if seller's obligation to produce is based upon seller's wish, want, or desire.

    3. Merchant's firm offer [UCC 2-205; 2A-205].

        a. A written offer for the purchase, sale, or lease of goods, made and signed by a merchant dealing in those goods, in which the merchant gives assurances (promises) to hold the offer open, is irrevocable for the specified period of time (not exceeding three months) or, if no time is specified, a reasonable period of time.

        b. "'Signed' includes any symbol executed or adopted by a party with present intention to authenticate a writing" [UCC 1-201(39)].

        c. The offer is irrevocable even if consideration is not given by the offeree as long as the period of time is shorter than three months.

  C. Acceptance — See also Chapter 13.

    1. Methods of acceptance.

        a. An offeror can specify that acceptance be sent by using a particular means of communication; if the offeree uses an unauthorized (different) means of communication, an acceptance is effective when it is received.

        b. Any reasonable means [UCC 2-206(1); 2A-206(1)].
           1) If no mode for communication of acceptance is specified, any commercially reasonable means of transmission may be used.
           2) Normally, an acceptance is effective when it is sent.

        c. Promise to ship or prompt shipment [UCC 2-206(1)(b)].
           1) An offer to buy goods for current or prompt shipment is accepted when the seller promises to ship or promptly ships conforming goods.
           2) Shipment of nonconforming goods constitutes both an acceptance and a breach of contract.
           3) If the seller notifies the buyer that nonconforming goods are being shipped as an accommodation, the shipment is a counteroffer; a contract is formed if the buyer accepts the nonconforming goods.

2. Communication of acceptance — If an offeree to a unilateral contract does not notify the offeror within a reasonable period of time that the offeree is beginning performance, "the offeror may treat the offer as having lapsed before acceptance" [UCC 2-206(2); 2A-206(2)].

3. Additional terms — Offeree's communication to the offeror may state that the offeree intends to accept an offer but changes or adds a new term [UCC 2-207].

   a. Because of the common law "mirror image rule," a communication by an offeree of an "acceptance" that contains a different term is a counteroffer and, therefore, a rejection. (See Chapter 13.)

   b. A dispute, the "battle of the forms," may arise when there are discrepancies in the forms used by the seller and the buyer.
      1) Rule when seller or buyer is a nonmerchant — If either or both of the parties are not merchants, it is an effective acceptance of the terms which are agreed upon, and a proposal for the new or different terms.
      2) Rule when both parties are merchants — If the buyer and seller are merchants, the new or different terms become part of the contract unless:
         a) The offer expressly limits acceptance to only its terms; or
         b) The terms materially alter the offer (such that the terms result in hardship or surprise); or
         c) The offeror notifies the offeree of the offeror's objections to the terms within a reasonable period of time.

   c. Conditioned on offeror's assent — If offeree's communication containing changed or added term is conditioned on the offeror's assent to the changes, offeree's communication is treated as a counteroffer and, therefore, a rejection.

   d. Additional terms may be stricken — Additional written terms, to which the parties do not agree, may be stricken when the conduct of the parties indicates that the parties recognize the existence of a contract [UCC 2-207(3)].

D. Today, contracts for the sale or lease of goods may be created electronically. Some of the existing issues relating to electronic sales contracts are the subject matter of the Emerging Trends section in the Chapter in the textbook.

E. Consideration. (See also Chapter 14.)

1. Information relating to consideration for requirements and output contracts may be found above in the Outline for this Chapter at IV.B.2.f.

2. Modification of terms.

    a. Modification must be made in good faith — Consideration is not necessary if the change is made in good faith [UCC 2-209; 2A-208].

    b. When modification without consideration requires a writing — A signed writing is necessary if:
      1) Agreement of the parties provides that modification without consideration requires that the modification be evidenced by a writing; or
      2) The contract, as revised, is required to be in writing in order to be enforceable under the Statute of Frauds.

F. Statute of Frauds [UCC 2-201(1); 2A201(1)].

1. If there is a contract for the sale of goods and the price of the goods is $500 or more, or if there is a lease contract and the payment exceeds $1,000, the contract is not enforceable unless there is a writing that is signed by the party against whom enforcement is sought or by an authorized agent or broker of that party.

2. Sufficiency of the writing.

    a. Contract for the sale of goods — The writing or memorandum must indicate the parties, identify the goods that are the subject matter of the contract, and indicate the price and quantity, unless the method by which the price and/or quantity terms may be made definite are specified. (See above at IV. B. 2.)

    b. A contract for the lease of goods must identify and describe the leased goods and the important terms of the lease.

3. Special rules for contracts for the sale of goods between merchants — When the buyer and seller are merchants and have entered into an oral agreement, if one of the parties sends a written confirmation of their oral contract within a reasonable period of time, and the other party does not object within ten days, the contract is enforceable against both parties [UCC 2-201(2)].

4. Exceptions — A writing signed by the party against whom enforcement is sought is not required in the following situations:

    a. Specially manufactured goods — A contract for goods to be specially manufactured for a particular buyer or lessee when the goods are not suitable for resale or lease in the ordinary course of the seller's or lessor's business, and the seller or lessor has begun production or made a commitment to obtain the goods.

    b. Admissions — A party admits in pleadings, testimony, or court that the contract for the sale or lease of the goods had been formed.

      c. Partial performance — Payment for the goods and acceptance of payment by the seller or lessor or receipt and acceptance of the goods by the buyer or lessee.

G. Parol evidence [UCC 2-202; 2A-202].

    1. Even if a writing is a complete statement of the agreement of the parties, parol evidence (in the form of other writings or oral testimony) is admissible to explain or supplement the writing by showing trade usage, a course of dealings, or a course of performance that is not inconsistent with the terms of the writing.

    2. Consistent additional terms — Evidence of consistent (but not contradictory) additional terms may be admitted for purposes of clarification or removal of an ambiguity.

    3. Course of dealings — Prior conduct of the parties while engaging in similar transactions [UCC 1-205(1) and (3)].

    4. Usage of trade — Any regular or customary practice or method of dealing in the particular place, trade, or vocation, which a person is justified in expecting will be observed with regard to the transaction [UCC 1-205(2)].

    5. Course of performance — Subsequent conduct of the parties to a contract for the sale of goods, which is indicative of their intentions [UCC 2-208].

    6. Rules of construction [UCC 1-205(4); 2-208(2);2A-207(2)].

        a. Express terms, course of performance, course of dealing, and usage of trade, which do not contradict each other, are construed together.

        b. If such a construction is unreasonable, the order of priority is:
            1) Express terms.
            2) Course of performance.
            3) Course of dealing.
            4) Usage of trade.

H. Unconscionability — Contracts or severable contract provisions, which are grossly unfair or one-sided under the circumstances at the time, will not be enforced [UCC 2-302; 2A-108]. See also Chapter 17.

V.   Contracting for the international sale of goods — Contracts for the international sale of goods are governed by the United Nations Convention on Contracts for the International Sale of Goods (CISG) when the parties are residents of nations that have ratified the Convention.

    A. The CISG (Convention on Contracts for the International Sale of Goods) — See Appendix D for excerpts from the CISG.

1. Many of the provisions in the CISG are similar to those in the UCC.

2. The CISG is a treaty that the U.S. Senate has ratified — It is federal law and, because of the supremacy clause in the U.S. Constitution, has priority over state statutes, such as the UCC. [See Chapter 5.]

B. Applicability of the CISG.

1. Technically, the CISG applies only to sales contracts between entities located in countries that have ratified the CISG.

2. Parties to a contract may specifically agree that the law of a particular jurisdiction (such as the UCC as adopted in a specified state), rather than the CISG, will apply.

3. If parties have not agreed that the law in a specific jurisdiction will apply to their contract, the contract is governed by the CISG; if there is a conflict between a provision in the CISG and one in the UCC (as adopted in a particular state), then the CISG takes precedence.

4. The CISG applies only to commercial international sales of goods — The CISG does not apply to domestic sales or to sales of consumer goods.

C. A comparison of CISG and UCC provisions.

1. The mirror image rule — See also above at IV.C and Chapter 13.

   a. In general, an acceptance of an offer must conform exactly to the offer; if a reply to an offer does not so conform, it will be treated as a counter-offer and, therefore, a rejection.

   b. "A reply to an offer that purports to be an acceptance, but contains additions, limitations, or other modifications is a rejection of the offer and constitutes a counter-offer" [CISG, Article 19(1)].

   c. If the additions or different terms in such a reply "do not materially alter the terms of the offer" and the offeror does not promptly object to the discrepancy, the reply is treated as an acceptance [CISG, Article 19(2)].
      1) "The terms of the contract will be the terms of the offer with the modifications" [CISG, Article 19(2)].
      2) The phrase "not materially alter" has been narrowly construed.

2. Irrevocable offers — CISG, Article 16(2)

   a. An offer cannot be revoked if the offeror states that the offer is irrevocable or if the offeree reasonably relies on the offer as being irrevocable.

   b. There is no requirement that an irrevocable offer be in writing or that consideration be given by the offeree.

3. Statute of Frauds — CISG, Article 11.

   a. There is no requirement that contracts be evidenced by signed writings.

   b. The CISG conforms to the legal customs of most nations in which oral agreements are enforceable.

4. The necessity of a price term — Either the exact price must be stated or there must be an express provision that provides for determining the price [CISG, Articles 14(1) and 55].

5. Time of contract formation — A contract is formed when the acceptance is received by the offeror [CISG, Article 18(2)] or at the time that the offeree renders performance [CISG, Article 18(3)].

D. Special provisions in international contracts.

   1. Choice of language — A clause in the contract may designate the language by which the contract will be interpreted, provide for translation into another language and ratification of the translation by the parties, etc.

   2. Choice of forum — A forum-selection clause is a designation of the court (the forum) in which disputes are to be litigated.

      a. The forum does not have to be within a nation in which the parties are residents or citizens.

      b. A forum-selection clause will not be enforced if, as a result, a party will be denied an effective remedy, or, if the clause was the product of fraud or unconscionable conduct, causes substantial inconvenience to a party, or violates public policy.

   3. Choice of law.

      a. A choice-of-law clause is a designation of the law that will govern the relationship of the contracting parties.

      b. The CISG imposes no limitation regarding choice of law [Article 6].

      c. The Hague Convention on the Law Applicable to Contracts for the International Sale of Goods provides that, if no choice of law is specified by the parties, the contract will be governed by the law of the country in which the seller's place of business is located.

   4. *Force majeure* — A *force majeure* clause provides that a party is excused from liability for nonperformance if certain stated unexpected, unavoidable, natural, or other forces or events, which are beyond the control of the parties, occur.

KEY WORDS AND PHRASES IN TEXT

Law Merchant (*Lex Mercatoria*)
Article 2 of the Uniform Commercial
    Code (UCC)
goods (tangible, moveable personal property
contract for the sale of goods
goods associated with realty
transaction combining sale of goods and
    rendering of services
merchant
open terms
open price term
open payment term
open delivery term
requirements contract
output contract
merchant's firm offer
conforming goods
nonconforming goods
shipment of nonconforming goods
    as an accommodation
acceptance containing additional
    or different terms

mirror image rule
contract modification
statute of frauds
written confirmation between merchants
specially manufactured goods
partial performance
parol evidence rule
course of dealings
usage of trade
course of performance
unconscionability
lease of goods
lease agreement
lessor and lessee
consumer leases
finance leases
Convention on Contracts for the Inter-
    national Sale of Goods (CISG)
choice-of-language clause
forum-selection clause
choice-of-law clause
force majeure clause

FILL-IN QUESTIONS

1. Article 2 of the Uniform Commercial Code covers contracts for the sales of
    _____. Such a transaction provides for a _____ of title or
    ownership rights to existing, identified, tangible, moveable personal property for
    consideration known as the _____.

2. Article 2A of the Uniform Commercial Code covers contracts for the lease of
    _____. Such a transaction provides for a _____ of the right to
    possession and use of tangible, moveable personal property for a period of time in
    return for consideration.

3. Article 2 of the Uniform Commercial Code contains special rules if the parties to a
    contract are _____. For example, they are held to higher standards of
    good faith than other people. A _____ is a person who _____
    _____ or holds himself or herself out, because of his or her
    occupation, as having the special knowledge and skills peculiar to the business or
    goods involved in the transaction, or employs others with such knowledge and skills.

4. In order for an offer to be effective at common law, all of the material terms must be
    clear, definite, and certain. This rule is relaxed by the Uniform Commercial Code.
    For example, the _____, and in output and requirements contracts the

_____ of goods, which are the subject matter of a contract of sale, may be left open.

5. A buyer and seller may modify a contract for the sale of goods in good faith in order to change the date upon which the goods are to be delivered without any new _____. The modification must be in writing, and signed by the seller, in order to be enforceable by the buyer, if the contract, as modified, provided for the sale of goods at a price of $_____, or the agreement of the parties so provides.

6. If a merchant makes a written signed offer to buy or sell goods and gives an assurance that the offer will remain open, the offer is _____ for the specified period of time if a period is stated or, if no time is specified, for a _____ period of time.

7. In general, an acceptance, which includes one or more terms that are different from or in addition to the terms contained in an offer for the sale of goods, will be treated as an effective acceptance. If one or more of the parties is not a _____, the additional or changed terms will be construed as proposals for additions to or changes in the contract. Between _____, the additional or changed terms become part of the contract unless (1) the offer limits acceptance to the terms contained in the offer, or (2) the additional or changed terms _____, or (3) notification of objection to the additions or changes has been or is given within a reasonable time after notice of the addition or change is received.

8. With regard to contracts for the sale of goods, the general rule is that, if the price of the goods is _____, the contract is not enforceable unless there is a writing which evidences the contract between the parties and which is signed by the party against whom enforcement is sought.

9. The United Nations Convention on _____ _____ (CISG) governs agreements for the sale of goods when the buyers and sellers are located in different countries and those countries have ratified the CISG. Because the United States Senate has ratified the Convention, the Convention is considered to be a _____ of the United States. As such, it has priority over state law in the U.S. Unless the parties to an international contract for the sale of goods otherwise agree, disputes regarding their contract will be resolved by applying the rules set forth in provisions of the _____.

10. If a U.S. firm enters into a contract to sell specified clothing to a Mexican retail seller of clothing, the contract is governed by the CISG because the U.S. and Mexico have ratified the CISG and the contract provides for a _____ (nonconsumer) sale of goods. The CISG would not apply if there were a specific provision in the contract that another law would govern their transaction. A statement in their contract to the effect that "the provisions of the UCC as adopted in the State of New York, and _____ the CISG, shall apply" would, therefore, be effective.

11. If a U.S. firm enters into a contract to sell specified clothing to Suarez, a resident of Mexico, for personal use, the contract is not governed by the CISG because, although both the U.S. and Mexico have ratified the CISG, the contract provides for a _____ sale of goods.

12. Pursuant to the Convention on Contracts for the International Sale of Goods (CISG), an acceptance of an offer to enter into a contract for the sale of goods, which does not exactly conform to the offer because it provides for different price terms, will be treated as a _____. This rule is similar to the common law _____ rule in the U.S., but contrary to the rule that applies under the UCC when the parties are _____.

13. A provision in a contract for the sale of goods by a French manufacturer to a U.S. store to the effect that "any dispute arising under this agreement must be tried before the District Court of Essex County in the State of New Jersey," is referred to as a _____ clause.

MULTIPLE CHOICE QUESTIONS

1. A contract providing for the transfer of title to four automobile tires is **not** covered by Article 2 of the Uniform Commercial Code if:
   A. the bargained-for consideration is services to be performed by the recipient.
   B. there is no bargained-for consideration given by the recipient.
   C. the tires are to be specially manufactured for an antique fire engine.
   D. the price for the tires is less than $500.

2. Article 2 of the UCC applies to the sale of tangible, moveable personal property, including:
   A. minerals, if removed from realty by the buyer.
   B. things that are attached to realty, which are to be severed by the seller, without regard to the harm to the realty.
   C. things that are not yet in existence.
   D. unborn animals.

3. Polk owns 100 acres of woodland. He agrees to sell a specified amount of the timber growing on the land to the Lewiston Lumber Co. and the right to extract coal from the land to the Comet Coal Co. for one year.
   A. The transaction with Lewiston Lumber Co. involves a sale of goods if the timber is to be cut by Lewiston.
   B. The transaction with Comet Coal Co. does **not** involve a sale of goods.
   C. The transaction with Lewiston Lumber Co. involves a sale of goods if the timber is to be cut by Polk.
   D. All of the answers above are correct.

4. Ware orally contracts to specially manufacture two pairs of glasses with prescription lenses for Ohl for $600.
   A. The transaction is **not** covered by Article 2 of the Code because it provides for the sale of goods to be specially manufactured.

    B. The transaction is **not** covered by Article 2 of the Code because it is a contract for the performance of services.

    C. Although the agreed upon price is more than $500, the contract will be enforceable against Ohl because Ware sent a written confirmation of the agreement immediately and Ohl failed to object within ten days.

    D. Although the agreed upon price is more than $500, the contract will be enforceable against Ohl if Ware has begun grinding the lenses because the glasses are **not** suitable for resale in the ordinary course of business.

5.   If it is established that a buyer and seller had contractual intent, their contract will be enforced even though:

    A. the buyer had **not** communicated his or her assent to the seller's offer.

    B. it provides for the sale of an illegal substance.

    C. it calls for the sale of all the carpeting manufactured at the seller's plant for one year, despite the fact that the quantity of goods to be sold is indefinite.

    D. it calls for the sale of all carpeting that the buyer may wish to buy for one year because the quantity of goods to be sold is indefinite.

6.   Lee is the owner of a clothing store. On January 2, she called the Demarre Dress Manufacturing Co. and placed an order for 120 dresses, at a price of $50 per dress to be delivered on January 20. Lee refused to accept the dresses, which conformed to the contract, on January 20.

    A. Lee is liable to Demarre if Demarre sent a writing on January 3 confirming the agreement, and Lee received the January 3 communication but did not respond.

    B. Lee is liable to Demarre if Demarre sent a writing on January 3 stating that the price would be $55 per dress, and Lee received the January 3 communication but did not respond.

    C. Lee is liable to Demarre because the Statute of Frauds provision of the Code is **not** applicable when the buyer and seller of goods are both merchants.

    D. Lee is **not** liable to Demarre because the dresses were not delivered to her place of business.

7.   A merchant's offer to sell goods states that the offer will remain open and **not** be revoked by the seller. The offer is revocable:

    A. unless consideration is given by the buyer if the offer is oral.

    B. unless the period of time during which it is to be held open is stated in the offer.

    C. unless the offer is evidenced by a writing that is signed by the buyer.

    D. if the period of time during which it is held open is reasonable.

8.   Wright Box Corp. offered to sell 1,000 #4 cardboard boxes at a price of $200 to the Pomfert Packing Co. and stated that Wright Box Corp. would **not** withdraw the offer for one month.

    A. The offer is a firm offer and irrevocable, without consideration, for three months if it is in writing.

    B. The offer is a firm offer and irrevocable, without consideration, for the period stated if it is in writing.

    C. The offer is a firm offer and irrevocable, without consideration, for a reasonable period of time if it is oral.

D. Pomfert Packing Co. is bound by the agreement if it does **not** object within ten days.

9.   Kelso agrees to sell and Long agrees to buy 100 pounds of flour at a price to be determined by Kelso, the seller.
   A. The flour is to be delivered at Long's place of business, because the parties did **not** expressly state where it was to be delivered.
   B. There is no contract, because the parties did **not** agree to the place of delivery.
   C. There is no contract, because Long did **not** agree to a price.
   D. Long will be required to pay the price set in good faith by Kelso.

10. The United Nations Convention for the International Sale of Goods (CISG) applies to contracts for the sale of goods when the contracting parties are located in nations that have ratified the Convention. The contract is governed by the CISG if the seller engages in the business of selling goods and the buyer is purchasing the goods for purposes of:

	reselling the goods to consumers.	using the goods as components for products that it manufactures.	using the goods in his or her home.
A.	Yes	Yes	Yes
B.	Yes	Yes	No
C.	Yes	No	No
D.	No	Yes	No

Questions 11, 12, and 13 are based upon the following fact situation: Rite Box Corp. of Salem, Massachusetts orally offered to sell 5,000 #2 fully described cardboard boxes at a price of one dollar per box to a packing company located in Denmark and stated that Rite Box Corp. would not withdraw the offer for one month.

11. The offer is:
   A. irrevocable for one month.
   B. revocable if no consideration was given by the Danish firm.
   C. revocable because it was orally made by Rite Box Corp.
   D. revocable unless the Danish firm notifies Rite Box Corp. that it wishes to consider the offer for one month.

12. The packing company in Denmark sends a written reply within one month stating that it accepts the offer in accordance with Rite Box Corp.'s terms. A contract exists between the U.S. corporation and the Danish firm on the date on which:
   A. Rite Box Corp. sent its original offer.
   B. the Danish firm sent its acceptance.
   C. Rite Box Corp. receives the acceptance.
   D. Rite Box Corp. acknowledges receipt of the Danish firm's reply.

13. The packing company in Denmark sends a written reply within one month stating that it accepts the offer on condition that the quantity be increased to 6,000 boxes. Because the CISG applies to the transaction, the Rite Box Corp. and the packing company:

A. have **not** entered into a contract for the sale of boxes.
B. are parties to a contract for the sale of 6,000 boxes.
C. are parties to a contract for the sale of 5,000 boxes.
D. are parties to a contract for the sale of either 5,000 or 6,000 boxes, the precise number to be determined by the seller.

14. In a May 1 letter, Sales Emporium, a Phoenix, Arizona store, order 400 fully described cabinets at a price of $300 each from York Mfg. Co., located in York, Pennsylvania. York Mfg. Co. received the order on May 4. On May 5, York Mfg. Co. mailed a letter, in which it stated that the order would be filled and that the cabinets would be shipped within ten days. Sales Emporium received this letter on May 8. An effective acceptance was given by:
A. Sales Emporium on May 1.
B. Sales Emporium on May 3.
C. York Mfg. Co. on May 5.
D. York Mfg. Co. on May 8.

15. In a May 1 letter, Sales Emporium, a Phoenix, Arizona store, order 400 fully described cabinets at a price of $300 each from York Mfg. Co., located in York, United Kingdom. York Mfg. Co. received the order on May 4. On May 5, York Mfg. Co. mailed a letter, in which it stated that the order would be filled and that the cabinets would be shipped within ten days. Sales Emporium received this letter on May 8. An effective acceptance was given by:
A. Sales Emporium on May 1.
B. Sales Emporium on May 3.
C. York Mfg. Co. on May 5.
D. York Mfg. Co. on May 8.

16. A contract for the international sale of goods entered into between a U.S. seller and an Italian buyer contains a forum-selection clause, in which a New York trial court is specified, and a choice-of-law clause, in which English law is specified. The forum-selection clause is enforceable:
A. because one of the parties is located in New York.
B. because the seller is located in New York.
C. and the choice-of-law clause is enforceable.
D. but the choice-of-law clause is **not** enforceable because neither of the parties is located in England.

17. A contract for the international sale of goods entered into between a U.S. buyer, whose principal place of business is located in Florida, and a German seller contains a forum-selection clause, in which a trial court in Delaware, the buyer's state of incorporation, is specified. The contract, however, is silent with regard to the law to be applied if there is a dispute. In the event that a dispute arises and cannot be resolved by applying the CISG, the court will apply:
A. German law.
B. the UCC, as most recently revised.
C. Delaware law.
D. Florida law.

Chapter 22
Title, Risk, and Insurable Interest

For some purposes, such as taxation, inheritance, and creditors' rights, it is necessary to determine which party has title (rights of ownership) to the goods that are the subject matter of a contract for the sale of goods. In a transaction based upon a lease, title to the goods is retained by the lessor. The lessee receives the rights to the possession and use of the goods, but not the rights of ownership.

The concept of title does not have importance, however, in determining the rights and responsibilities of the parties to a sales or lease transaction under the Uniform Commercial Code (UCC). To a great extent, the concept of title to goods has been replaced by concepts of identification of goods to the contract, risk of loss, and insurable interest, which are explained in this chapter. These concepts affect the rights and liabilities of the parties in both sales and leases of goods transactions when the goods are damaged, destroyed, or lost as well as their rights to obtain insurance and the rights of their creditors.

THINGS TO KEEP IN MIND

1. The rules discussed in the chapter apply only if the parties have not specified in their contract when identification of the goods or transfer of the risk will occur.

2. Goods that are in existence usually are identified when the contract is made, at which time the buyer or lessee has an insurable interest, even though the buyer or lessee may have neither possession nor bear the risk of loss.

3. If a buyer or lessee has a contract right to receive goods that are not in existence (future goods), the earliest point in time, at which the buyer or lessee has an insurable interest or bears the risk of loss is when the goods come into existence and are identified to the contract.

OUTLINE

I. Identification.

    A. Identification of the goods is a designation of goods that are the subject matter of a contract for the sale of goods [UCC 2-501] or a lease of goods [UCC 2A-217].

    B. The parties may specify in their agreement when identification will occur.

C. If the parties do not so specify when identification of the goods will occur, the following rules apply.

   1. Existing goods — Identification of goods that are in existence and described in the contract occurs when the contract is made.

   2. Future goods are goods that are not in existence and identified. (A contract for the sale of future goods is a contract to sell or to lease.)

      a. If the goods are unborn animals or crops, the general rule is that identification occurs when the animals are conceived or the crops are planted or begin to grow.

      b. Other future goods are identified when the goods come into existence and are marked, shipped, or identified by the seller or lessor.

   3. Goods that are part of a larger mass.

      a. Identification occurs when the particular goods are marked, shipped, or designated by the seller or lessor.

      b. Fungible goods are goods, every unit of which is the equivalent of every other unit by nature, trade usage, or agreement of the parties [UCC 1-201].
        1) A number of people may be owners in common of undivided shares of fungible goods that are held in mass (in bulk).
        2) Fungible goods may be identified as a specified portion, weight, or quantity of the designated, larger mass without being separated physically from that mass [UCC 2-105(4)].

D. Identification determines when the buyer or lessee has a right to obtain insurance on the goods, recover from a third person who damages the goods, and, in some cases, obtain the goods from the seller or lessor.

II.   When title passes]UCC 2-401].

A. Title does not pass until goods are in existence and identified.

B. Parties may agree on the manner and conditions under which title passes.

C. If parties have not otherwise agreed, title passes to the buyer at the time and place the seller performs the physical delivery of the goods.

   1. Shipment contracts.

      a. When a seller is required or authorized to ship goods by carrier, but the contract does not require that the seller deliver the goods at the destination, title passes at the time and place of shipment.

  b. A contract is assumed to be a shipment contract if the contract does not provide otherwise.

 2. Destination contracts — When a seller is required to deliver goods at a particular destination, title passes when the goods are tendered at that destination.

 3. Delivery without movement of the goods.

  a. If the contract provides for delivery of a document of title by the seller, title passes at the time and place where the document is delivered.
   1) A bill of lading is a document of title that is issued and signed by a carrier and evidences receipt of the goods by the carrier and the terms of the contract for their transportation.
   2) A warehouse receipt is a document of title that is issued and signed by a warehouse and evidences receipt of the goods by the warehouse and the terms of the contract for their storage.

  b. When the contract does not provide for delivery of a document of title and delivery is to be made without movement of the goods:
   1) If the goods are identified, because the goods are segregated, marked, or designated by the seller as the goods to which the contract refers [UCC 2-509(1)(b)], title passes at the time and place the contract was made.
   2) If the goods are not identified, title does not pass until identification occurs.

D. Sales [UCC 2-402, 2-403] or leases [UCC 2A-303, 2A-304, 2A-305] by non-owners.

 1. A seller who does not possess full ownership rights has imperfect title.

 2. A seller of goods can transfer only the interest which the seller has to another person; a buyer acquires at least the title that the seller has.

 3. A lessee acquires whatever leasehold interest (the right to possess and use the goods) that the lessor has or has the power to transfer, subject to the lease contract.

 4. Void title.

  a. Even if a good faith purchaser (or lessee) gives value to a seller (or lessor) whose title is void, the purchaser (or lessee) does not acquire good title to (or a leasehold interest in) the goods.

  b. A real owner of goods has a right to reclaim stolen goods from a buyer or lessee.

 5. Voidable title.

    a. A seller (or lessor) may avoid or disaffirm a contract for the sale (or lease) of goods while the buyer (or lessee) has possession of the goods if the seller (or lessor) is a minor or if the buyer (or lessee) used fraud in order to induce the contract, etc.

    b. If the buyer has resold the goods to a good faith purchaser for value, the subsequent purchaser acquires valid title. The seller's only remedy is damages.

    c. If the buyer has resold the goods to a person who is not a good faith purchaser for value, the actual owner (the original seller) can reclaim the goods from the subsequent purchaser.

  6. The entrustment rule.

    a. If an owner of goods entrusts possession of the goods to a merchant who deals in those kinds of goods, the merchant has power to transfer owner's title to a purchaser in the ordinary course of business [UCC 2-403].

    b. If a lessor entrusts goods to a lessee, who is a merchant dealing in goods of that kind, and the lessee-merchant transfers the goods to a buyer or sublessee in the ordinary course of business, the buyer or sublessee acquires the rights that the lessor had in the goods [UCC 2A-305(2)].

III. Risk of loss.

  A. Risk of loss does not shift to a buyer until goods are in existence and identified.

  B. Parties may agree as to how and when risk of loss will shift to the buyer or lessee.

  C. Risk of loss passes in accordance with the following rules if the parties have not agreed otherwise.

    1. Delivery with movement of the goods — Carrier cases.

      a. Shipment contracts — Risk of loss passes to the buyer or lessee when goods are delivered to the carrier [UCC 2-509(1)(a); 2A-219(2)(a)].

      b. Destination contracts — Risk of loss passes to the buyer or lessee when the goods are tendered to the buyer at the specified destination [UCC 2-509(1)(b); 2A-219(2)(b)].

      c. Contract terms — The following terms are used when goods are being transported and indicate whether or not certain charges are included in the price of the goods to be paid by the buyer or lessee.
        1) F.O.B., free on board at a stated price [UCC 2-319(1)].

a) If location is the place of shipment, risk of loss passes when the seller puts the goods in the possession of the carrier.

b) If location is the place of destination, risk of loss passes when the seller tenders delivery of the goods.

2) F.A.S., free alongside a vessel at a named port [UCC 2-319(2)]; risk of loss passes when the goods are delivered alongside the ship.

3) C.I.F. (price includes cost of the goods, insurance, and freight charges) or C. & F. (price includes cost of the goods and freight but not insurance) requires that the seller put goods in the carrier's possession before risk of loss can pass to buyer [UCC 2-320].

4) Delivery ex-ship — The seller's obligations and risk of loss do not end until the goods are delivered and unloaded from the carrying vessel at the specified port of destination [UCC 2-322].

2. Delivery without movement of the goods.

a. If the seller or lessor is a merchant, risk of loss passes to the buyer or lessee when the buyer or lessee takes physical possession of the goods [UCC 2-509(3); 2A-219(2)(c)].

b. If the seller is not a merchant, risk of loss passes to the buyer upon tender of delivery of the goods [UCC 2-509(3)].

c. If a bailee is holding the goods for the seller and the goods are to be delivered without being moved, risk of loss passes to the buyer when:
   1) The buyer receives a negotiable document of title; or
   2) Bailee acknowledges the buyer's right to possession of the goods; or
   3) The buyer receives a nonnegotiable document of title and has had a reasonable period of time to present it to the bailee and demand the goods [UCC 2-509(2), 2-503(4)(b)].

d. If a bailee is holding the goods, risk of loss passes to the lessee upon acknowledgment by the bailee of the lessee's right to possession of the goods [UCC 2A-219(2)(b)].

D. Conditional sales — Parties may provide that the buyer has the privilege of returning conforming goods to the seller [UCC 2-326].

1. Sale or return — Goods are delivered primarily for resale.

a. Buyer may return some or all of the goods.

b. Title and risk of loss passes to the buyer when the buyer receives possession at the time of the sale.

c. Buyer bears expense and risk of return [UCC 2-327(2)].

d. Goods are subject to a buyer's creditors' claims while the goods are in possession of the buyer [UCC 2-326(2)].

2. Consignment — Owner of goods (consignor) delivers goods to a consignee for sale by the consignee [UCC 2-326(3)].

    a. If the consignee sells the goods, he or she pays consignor for the goods; if the goods are not sold, the consignee returns the goods to consignor.

    b. While goods are in consignee's possession, the consignee has title to the goods and the consignment is treated as a sale or return transaction.

3. Sale on approval — Goods are delivered primarily for use.

    a. Seller offers to sell goods and delivers possession (makes a bailment) of the goods to the buyer on a trial basis.

    b. Title and risk of loss remain with the seller until goods are accepted by the buyer.

    c. The buyer must exercise the right of returning goods within the specified time or, if none is specified, a reasonable time; the seller bears the expense of returning the goods and any risk [UCC 2-327(1)].

    d. Until goods are accepted by a buyer, the buyer's creditors have no rights with respect to the goods [UCC 2-326(2)].

E. Risk of loss when there is a breach of a contract for the sale or lease of goods [UCC 2-510; 2A-220].

    1. Breach of contract by the seller or lessor.

        a. If nonconforming goods are tendered by a seller (or lessor), and the defect is discovered immediately, risk of loss does not pass to the buyer (or lessee) until the defect is cured or the buyer (or lessee) knowingly accepts the nonconforming goods.

        b. If a defect in the goods is discovered after nonconforming goods are accepted, the buyer (or lessee) can revoke the acceptance. To the extent that the buyer (or lessee) is not covered by insurance, the seller (or lessor) bears the risk of loss.

    2. Breach of contract by the buyer or lessee.

        a. If goods are identified, the risk of loss shifts to the buyer (or lessee) for a commercially reasonable period of time after the seller (or lessor) learns of the buyer's breach.

        b. To the extent that a seller (or lessor) is not covered by insurance, the buyer (or lessee) bears the risk of loss.

IV. Insurable interest.

A. An insurable interest in property exists if a person will benefit from the continued existence of the property or incur a loss if the property is lost, damaged, or destroyed. (See Chapter 52.)

B. Insurable interest of the buyer [UCC 2-501(1)] or lessee [UCC 2A-218(1)].

   1. A buyer or lessee has an insurable interest in existing goods that have been identified as soon as a contract for sale or lease is made.

   2. A buyer or lessee has an insurable interest in future goods when the goods come into existence and are identified.

C. Insurable interest of the seller [UCC 2-501(2)] or lessee [UCC 2A-218(3)].

   1. A seller has an insurable interest in the goods as long as the seller retains title or, after title has passed, if the seller retains a security interest in the goods. (See Chapter 30 regarding security interests.)

   2. A lessor has an insurable interest in the goods until an option to buy the goods has been exercised by the lessee and the risk of loss has passed to the lessee.

D. Both the buyer (or lessee) and the seller (or lessor) can have an insurable interest in identical goods at the same time.

V. Bulk transfers — A bulk transfer is a transfer (usually a sale) in bulk of a major portion of assets, such as inventory, materials, furniture, fixtures, etc., that is not in the ordinary course of the transferor's business [UCC 6-102(1)].

A. The effect is to jeopardize creditors' ability to collect debts owed by a seller.

B. If the requirements of Article 6 are complied with, a buyer (transferee) acquires title to the goods free of all claims of the seller's (transferor's) creditors.

C. Requirements of Article 6 [UCC 6-104, 6-105].

   1. The seller (transferor) must furnish the buyer (transferee) with a list of all creditors, their addresses and the amounts due to them; the list must be signed and sworn to or affirmed by seller.

   2. The buyer and seller prepare a schedule of property that is being transferred.

   3. A buyer must preserve the list of creditors and the schedule of property for six months and permit their inspection by creditors or file them in a designated public place.

   4. The buyer must give notice of the proposed transfer to the seller's creditors at least ten days before sale so that the creditors can protect their own interests.

D. If the requirements of Article 6 are not complied with, property in the hands of the buyer (transferee) is subject to claims of the seller's (transferor's) creditors for one year; if the transfer was concealed, creditors have one year from date of disclosure within which to enforce their rights   [UCC 6-110].

F. Because of changing business methods and legal considerations, The National Conference of Commissioners on Uniform State Laws has recommended that states either repeal or revise Article 6.   [See Appendix C which contains "Alternative B" of Article 6.]

KEY WORDS AND PHRASES IN TEXT

title (ownership rights in goods)
contract for the sale or lease of goods
identification of goods
existing goods
future goods
identified goods
goods that are part of a larger mass
fungible goods
passage of title to goods
shipment contract
destination contract
tender of delivery
document of title
bill of lading
warehouse receipt

leasehold interest
void title
voidable title
good faith purchaser
entrustment
risk of loss
F.O.B., F.A.S., C.I.F., C. & F.,
      and delivery ex-ship
sale or return contract
consignment of goods
sale on approval contract
bailment
insurable interest
bulk transfer (UCC Article 6)

FILL-IN QUESTIONS

1.   When there is a contract for the sale of goods, identification of existing goods occurs at the time that _____.   When parties enter into a contract providing for the sale of future goods, identification of the goods that are not yet in existence does not take place until the goods come into existence and are properly _____, _____, or identified by the seller.

2.   If a buyer, who purchased goods for the buyer's own use, has a right to return conforming goods to the seller, the sale is a sale _____.   If the buyer purchased the goods for resale, the transaction is a sale _____.

3.   If the parties to a contract for the sale of goods do not indicate the place of delivery or the manner in which the goods are to be delivered, the place of delivery is the merchant _____.   In this case, the price of the goods does not include charges for _____, storage, or insurance.

4.   If parties have not agreed otherwise in their contract for the sale of existing goods to be delivered by a merchant seller to the buyer, title passes and the buyer has an

insurable interest at the time _____ , but the risk of loss is not transferred to the buyer until _____.

5. A contract for the sale of future goods that are to be shipped from the seller to the buyer may indicate which of the parties is to pay certain transportation and other charges. F.O.B. means _____ at a stated place. F.A.S. means _____ a vessel at a port. If the stated place is in the city or port, in which the buyer is located, the _____ must pay the shipping charges. These terms also are treated as delivery terms and determine when title and _____ shifts from the seller to the buyer.

6. C.I.F. indicates that the price of the goods includes the cost of the goods as well as _____. C.& F. indicates that the price of the goods includes their cost and _____. With both C.I.F. and C. & F. contracts, the risk of loss during shipment is borne by the _____.

7. If parties have agreed in their contract for the sale of future goods that the goods are to be shipped F.O.B. to a carrier in the city in which the seller maintains its business, it is a _____ contract. Title and risk of loss to the buyer will pass when the goods are _____, even though the buyer has _____ when the goods come into existence and are identified.

MULTIPLE CHOICE QUESTIONS

1. Frank lent his bicycle to his friend, Pat. Pat then sold the bicycle to Bob for a fair price. Bob did not know how Pat had acquired the bicycle. When Frank learned what Pat had done, he demanded that Bob return the bicycle to him.
   A. Frank can enforce his demand.
   B. Frank **cannot** enforce his demand, because he was not a minor.
   C. Frank can enforce his demand only if Pat was the owner of a bicycle store and Bob was a customer.
   D. Frank can enforce his demand only if Pat was insolvent at the time of the sale.

2. On Monday, Frankel purchased a bicycle for $150 from The Cycle Shop but left it with the seller so that some adjustments could be made. On Tuesday, Brady purchased the bicycle for $155 from The Cycle Shop without knowing that it was Frankel's property. The sale to Brady was:
   A. effective because The Cycle Shop's title was only voidable as a result of Frankel being a minor.
   B. effective because Frankel had entrusted the bicycle to The Cycle Shop, which dealt in bicycles.
   C. **not** effective because The Cycle Shop did not have title to the bicycle.
   D. **not** effective because The Cycle Shop's title was void.

3. Theeve stole two personal computers from the Own P C Store. He sold one to Abby for $1,000 and gave one to Beth as a gift.
   A. Own P C Store does **not** have a right to recover either the computer sold to Abby or the one given by Theeve to Beth.

B. Own P C Store has a right to recover both the computer sold to Abby and the one given by Theeve to Beth.

C. Own P C Store has a right to recover the computer that Theeve gave to Beth because Beth was **not** a purchaser for value, but the store cannot recover the computer purchased by Abby.

D. Own P C Store has the right to recover the computer that Theeve gave to Beth if Beth subsequently sold it to Carla for $1,010.

4. Under the Sales Article and the Lease Article of the UCC, which of the following factors is most important in determining who bares the risk of loss in contracts for the sale and lease of goods?
    A. Title to the goods.
    B. The method of shipping the goods.
    C. The shipping terms in the contract.
    D. How the goods were lost.
    (This question has been adapted from objective question #45 on the Uniform CPA Examination, November 1995.)

5. Under the Sales Article and the Lease Article of the UCC, in an F.O.B. place of shipment contract, the risk of loss passes to the buyer or lessee when the goods:
    A. are identified to the contract.
    B. are delivered to the carrier.
    C. are placed on the seller's or lessor's loading dock.
    D. reach the buyer's or lessee's loading dock.
    (This question has been adapted from objective question #46 on the Uniform CPA Examination, November 1995.)

6. Under a contract for a sale of goods, a buyer may return goods after the goods have been delivered but before the goods are accepted.
    A. If the goods are the kind that are used by the buyer, the buyer's creditors can make a claim with regard to the goods.
    B. If the goods are the kind that are used by the buyer and they are stolen, the risk of loss falls on the buyer.
    C. If the goods have been purchased for ultimate resale by the buyer, the buyer's creditors can make a claim with regard to the goods.
    D. If the goods have been purchased for ultimate resale by the buyer, the seller bears the expense of returning the goods when the buyer exercises his right of returning the goods.

7. Cey Corp. entered into a contract to sell parts to Deck, Ltd. The contract provided that the goods would be shipped "F.O.B. Cey Corp.'s warehouse." Cey Corp. shipped parts that were different from those specified in the contract. Deck, Ltd. rejected the parts. A few hours after Deck, Ltd. informed Cey Corp. that the parts were rejected, the goods were destroyed by a fire in Deck, Ltd.'s warehouse. Cey believes that the parts were conforming to the contract. Which of the following statements is correct?
    A. If the parts were conforming goods, risk of loss does **not** pass to the buyer, Deck, Ltd., until a reasonable period of time after the goods are delivered to Deck, Ltd.

B. If the parts were nonconforming goods, the buyer, Deck, Ltd., had the right to reject them, but the risk of loss remains with Deck, Ltd. until Cey Corp. takes possession of the parts.
C. If the parts were nonconforming goods, the seller, Cey Corp., will bear the risk of loss even though the contract was a shipment contract.
D. Without regard to whether or not the parts were conforming goods, the buyer, Deck, Ltd. will bear the loss because the contract was a shipment contract.

(This question has been adapted from objective question #44 on the Uniform CPA Examination, May 1990.)

8. Beyer, in Kansas City, Missouri, ordered 1,000 fully described pots and pans from Deelar, a wholesaler, in Pittsburgh, Pennsylvania. The pots and pans were in existence and to be shipped by truck. If the pots and pans were to be shipped:
A. F.O.B. Kansas City, but the goods were lost in transit, the risk of loss is borne by Beyer.
B. F.O.B. Kansas City, but the goods were lost in transit, the risk of loss is borne by Deelar.
C. C.I.F. and the goods were lost in transit, the risk of loss is borne by Deelar.
D. C. & F. and the goods were lost in transit, the risk of loss is borne by Deelar.

9. The New England Candy Co. of Boston, Massachusetts, contracted for the purchase of a stated quantity of sugar from Sweet Sugar Inc. of Louisiana. Assume that the contract provided that the sugar was to be shipped:
A. F.O.B. Boston. The expense of loading is borne by New England Candy Co.
B. F.A.S. Coastal Queen (a freighter), New Orleans. The expense of loading is borne by Sweet Sugar Inc.
C. ex-ship Boston. The expense of loading is borne by Sweet Sugar Inc.
D. C. & F. The expense of loading is borne by New England Candy Co.

10. Pulse Corp. maintained a warehouse where it stored its manufactured goods. Pulse received an order from Starr. Shortly after Pulse identified the goods to be shipped to Starr, but before moving the goods to the loading dock, a tornado destroyed the warehouse and its contents. With respect to the goods ordered by Starr, which of the following statements is correct?
A. Pulse Corp. had title and an insurable interest.
B. Starr had title and an insurable interest.
C. Pulse Corp. had title but **not** an insurable interest.
D. Starr had title but **not** an insurable interest.

(This question has been adapted from objective question #45 on the Uniform CPA Examination, May 1990)

11. Krupp owned a manufacturing business in a state in which the UCC Bulk Transfer Article has **not** been repealed. Krupp sold all of his business property to Stone. Caruso, a creditor of Krupp, will be able to reach some of this property because the bulk transfer was ineffective because:
A. a schedule of the property to be transferred was **not** filed with a court thirty days prior to the bulk transfer by Krupp or Stone.
B. the list of creditors and schedule of property that was transferred was **not** retained for two years after the bulk transfer.

C. although Stone did not know it, Krupp did **not** prepare a complete, accurate list of her creditors.

D. Stone did **not** request that Krupp supply him with a complete, accurate list of her creditors.

12. The provisions in the UCC Bulk Transfer Article:
    A. protect the creditors of the seller. As a general rule, if the Code is complied with, such creditors must look to the proceeds of the sale only.
    B. protect the creditors of the buyer. As a general rule, if the Code is **not** complied with, such creditors must look to the proceeds of the sale only.
    C. require that a list of creditors and a schedule of property be filed with a designated official of the state or county.
    D. must be complied with in order that the contract of sale be enforceable by a seller against a buyer.

Chapter 23
Performance of Sales and Lease Contracts

As is true of any contract, the parties to a contract for the sale or lease of goods assume certain express duties to perform in accordance with their agreement — the seller or lessor to transfer and deliver goods that conform to the contract and the buyer or lessee to accept and pay for the goods. In addition, the Uniform Commercial Code imposes obligations on each of the parties to exercise good faith in performing and to do nothing to impair the expectations of the other party that the contract will be duly performed.

THINGS TO KEEP IN MIND

1. Many of the seemingly intricate rules explained in this chapter are effective if the parties have used certain commercial terms with which you should become familiar. Often, if you give some thought to it, you will realize that the consequences of using a particular term are implicit from the wording of the term itself.

2. In the law relating to sales and leases, the word "delivery" does not necessarily mean a physical delivery of the goods. A seller or lessor is required to make goods available to the buyer or lessee. This may be accomplished by the tender of delivery of a document of title, rather than the goods themselves.

OUTLINE

I.   The good faith requirement.

    A. Standards of good faith and commercial reasonableness are read into every contract for the sale or lease of goods.

        1. Good faith "means honesty in fact in the conduct or transaction concerned" [UCC 1-201(19)].

        2. In the case of a merchant, good faith means honesty and "observance of reasonable standards of fair dealing" [UCC 2-103(1)(b)].

    B. Parties are expected to be cooperative and not to take advantage of each other — For example, if a party is to fill in particulars of performance, he or she must do so "in good faith and within limits set by commercial reasonableness" [UCC 2-311].

II.   Obligations of the seller or lessor.

A. It is the obligation of the seller or lessor to tender goods that conform to the contract to the buyer or lessee.

B. Tender of delivery by the seller or lessor must occur at a reasonable time and in a reasonable manner; a seller or lessor holding conforming goods must give reasonable notification to the buyer or lessee to enable the buyer or lessee to take delivery [UCC 2-503(1); 2A-508(1)].

C. Place of delivery. [See also Chapter 22.]

    1. Noncarrier cases — In situations in which the place of delivery is not specified and transportation by carrier is not required, the place of delivery is:

        a. The seller's place of business; if the seller has none, seller's residence.

        b. When the parties know that goods are at a location, other than the seller's place of business, delivery should be at that location.

        c. When the goods are held by a bailee, the seller tenders delivery of document which will enable the buyer to obtain goods [UCC 2-308].

    2. Carrier cases [UCC 2-319 through 2-322, 2-504, 2-509].

        a. Shipment contract — The seller must:
            1) Put goods in the carrier's possession;
            2) Make a reasonable contract for transportation of the goods;
            3) Deliver or tender to the buyer any documents necessary to enable the buyer to obtain possession of goods from the carrier; and
            4) Notify the buyer promptly of shipment.

        b. Destination contract — The seller must tender conforming goods at the specified destination.

        c. The time at which the seller's duty ends depends upon the specific type of delivery.
            1) F.O.B. — Seller's duty ends when goods are at the designated place.
            2) F.A.S. a named vessel — Seller's duty ends when goods are delivered to the dock and the seller obtains receipt (usually a bill of lading), which is tendered to the buyer (shipment contract).
            3) Delivery ex-ship (from the carrying vessel) — Seller's duty ends when the goods are unloaded (destination contract).
            4) C.I.F. — The seller is obligated to load goods, pay freight, obtain proper insurance, receipt and other necessary documents, prepare invoice, and tender all documents to the buyer.

D. The perfect tender rule [UCC 2-601; 2A-509].

1. In order to be entitled to payment, the seller or lessor is required to tender conforming goods in a manner that completely accords to the terms of the contract.

2. If the goods and/or tender do not conform to the contract, the buyer or lessee may reject all the goods or accept all the goods.

3. The buyer or lessee may accept one or more of the commercial units of the goods and reject the rest of the units. A commercial unit may be a single article, a set of articles, a quantity, or any other unit that is treated as a single whole (by trade usage) for purposes of sale, and division of which impairs the character of the unit, its market value, or its use [UCC 2-105(6); 2A-103(1)(c)].

E. Exceptions to the perfect tender rule.

1. Agreement of the parties — Buyer and seller (or lessee and lessor) may otherwise agree in order to arrive at an acceptable solution to the problem caused by a less than perfect tender.

2. Cure — The seller or lessor may repair, replace, or, in some cases, make a price adjustment for nonconforming goods.

   a. The buyer or lessee is required to disclose the nature of the defect.

   b. If the time for delivery has not expired, the seller or lessor is required merely to give notice of an intention to make a proper delivery and make such delivery within the time provided for in the contract.

   c. If the seller (or lessor) delivered nonconforming goods and reasonably believed that the buyer (or lessee) would accept a tender of non-conforming goods, but the buyer (or lessee) rejects the goods, the seller (or lessor) has a reasonable period of time within which to make proper delivery (cure) after giving notice to the buyer (or lessee), even though contracted time for delivery has expired [UCC 2-508; 2A-513].

3. Substitution of carriers.

   a. Seller may substitute a different means of delivery if, without fault of the seller, the agreed manner of delivery becomes impracticable or impossible to use [UCC 2-614].

   b. If there is no material delay or loss, the buyer may not reject the goods because of the inappropriate shipping arrangements [UCC 2-504].

4. Installment contracts [UCC 2-307, 2-612; 2A-510].

a. An installment contract is a single contract that requires or authorizes delivery in two or more separate lots to be separately accepted and paid for by the buyer or lessee.

b. Delivery of goods in installments may be contemplated in the contract or be necessary because of circumstances.

c. A buyer or lessee may reject a nonconforming installment which cannot be cured and which substantially impairs the value of the installment.

d. There is a breach of the entire contract if one or more nonconforming installments substantially impair the value of the entire contract.

5. Commercial impracticability — If performance of a contract is commercially impracticable because of an unforeseen, supervening occurrence that was not contemplated by the parties at the time of contracting, the failure to deliver the goods or a delay in the delivery does not constitute a breach [UCC 2-615; 2A-405].

a. Foreseeable versus unforeseeable contingencies — In order to fall within this exception, the event must have been so totally unexpected that the risk of the unexpected occurrence was not allocated by the contract or by custom in the trade or business.

b. Partial performance — If the unexpected event only partially affects the seller's or lessor's ability to perform, the buyer or lessee may accept or reject a fair and reasonable allocation of the performance (partial delivery of some of the goods) after the buyer or lessee has notice of the proposed allocation.

6. Destruction of identified goods [UCC 2-613; 2A-221].

a. If the identified goods are totally destroyed without fault of either party before risk of loss passes from seller to buyer, or lessor to lessee, the parties are excused from rendering performance.

b. If identified goods are partially destroyed, the buyer or lessee may treat the contract as canceled or accept the goods with a deduction from the contract price.

7. Assurance and cooperation [UCC 2-609, 2-311(3); 2A-401].

a. The right of assurance.
   1) If either party to a sales or lease contract has reasonable grounds to believe that the other party will not perform, that party may make a written demand for reasonable adequate assurance that due performance will be rendered.

2) Until such assurance is received, the party who has reasonable grounds for insecurity may suspend performance for which that party did not receive consideration.

b. The duty of cooperation — When one party's performance depends upon the other party's cooperation, and cooperation is not forthcoming, the party (which is willing to cooperate) can suspend performance.

III. Obligations of the buyer or lessee.

A. The buyer is obligated to accept the goods and to pay for the goods [UCC 2-301, 2-310, 2-607], and the lessee is obligated to accept the goods and pay the specified lease payment [UCC 2A-516] in accordance with the terms of the contract for sale or lease unless otherwise provided in the contract.

B. Payment — If no provision is made in the contract:

1. Unless a sale is made on credit, payment is to be made at the time and place that the goods are received by the buyer or lessee [UCC 2-301(a), 2-511; 2A-516(1)].

2. Payment can be in cash or another commercially acceptable medium [UCC 2-511].

3. If a sale is made on credit, the credit period begins on the date of shipment [UCC 2-310(d)].

C. Right of inspection [UCC 2-513; 2A-515].

1. The buyer or lessee has a right to inspect goods before making payment in order to determine that the goods conform to the contract unless the buyer or lessee has agreed to C.O.D. shipment or payment upon presentation of document of title.

a. Place, time, and manner of inspection must be reasonable.

b. Cost of inspection is borne by the buyer unless otherwise agreed.

2. Collect on delivery (C.O.D.) shipments.

a. If buyer has not agreed to a C.O.D. shipment, the buyer can reject the goods because the opportunity to inspect is lost.

b. If buyer agreed to a C.O.D. shipment, the buyer does not have the right to inspect the goods.

3. Payment due — Documents of title.

        a. Payment is due before inspection when a required document of title is received.

        b. This is the case when a bill of lading is tendered with a C.I.F. or C. & F. contract.

  D. Acceptance [UCC 2-606; 2A-515].

     1. Acceptance may be manifested expressly or by conduct when a buyer or lessee, who has had opportunity to inspect, indicates that the goods are conforming, or that the goods are acceptable despite nonconformity, or fails to reject the goods.

     2. In addition, acceptance of goods by a buyer occurs when the buyer performs an act that is inconsistent with the seller's ownership (e.g., uses or resells the goods).

     3. Partial acceptance [UCC 2-601; 2A-509].

        a. The buyer or lessee can make a partial acceptance if:
           1) The goods are nonconforming and the seller or lessor has failed to cure; or
           2) The goods are nonconforming and the nonconformity was not reasonably discoverable before acceptance.

        b. The buyer or lessee cannot make a partial acceptance of less than a commercial unit because acceptance of part of a commercial unit is an acceptance of the entire unit. (See above at II.D.3.)

IV. Anticipatory repudiation — If, before the time for performance, either party communicates to the other party an intention not to perform, the aggrieved party may:

  A. Wait for the other party to perform correctly or to retract the repudiation;

  B. Resort to an appropriate remedy; or

  C. Suspend his or her own performance [UCC 2-610; 2A-402].

V. Dealing with international contracts — The letter of credit.

  A. Letters of credit are financial devices that have been used for centuries in order to assure the performance of international sales contracts.

  B. A letter of credit issued by a bank may be used in order to facilitate an international business transaction.

  C. A letter of credit is a written engagement (a promise or statement) by a bank, made at the request of a customer of the bank, that the bank will honor orders or demands for payment upon compliance with the conditions specified in the letter of credit. [See UCC Article 5.]

D. The parties to a letter of credit [UCC 5-103].

1. Issuer — The bank (or other person) which issues a letter of credit.

2. Beneficiary — The person (e.g., the seller or lessor of goods) who is entitled to draw or demand payment under the terms of the letter of credit.

3. Account party (e.g., the buyer or lessee of goods) — The customer of the bank (which issues a letter of credit) who reimburses or promises to reimburse the issuer for the amount paid to the beneficiary.

4. Advising bank (typically, a correspondent bank) — The bank which gives notification of the issuance of a letter of credit by another bank and transmits information.

5. Paying bank (confirming bank) — The bank which engages that it will honor a letter of credit issued by another bank or engages that a letter of credit will be honored by the issuer or a third party.

E. The value of a letter of credit — The use of a letter of credit assures the seller or lessor (the beneficiary of a letter of credit) of payment and assures the buyer or lessee (the account party) that payment will not be made until the seller or lessor has complied with the terms and conditions of the letter of credit, including furnishing evidence that the goods have been shipped.

F. A letter of credit may be conditioned upon presentment by the seller or lessor of a document of title (e.g., a bill of lading) in which case it is called a documentary letter of credit and usually provides that it is subject to the Uniform Customs and Practice for Documentary Credit.

G. A letter of credit is independent of the underlying contract between the buyer and seller, or the lessee and the lessor, and protects both parties, the buyer and the seller, or the lessee and the lessor.

H. Compliance with a letter of credit.

1. The issuer has a duty to determine that documents presented by the beneficiary (the seller or lessor) comply with the terms of the letter of credit.

2. Traditionally, courts have required strict compliance; today, some courts require substantial or reasonable compliance.

KEY WORDS AND PHRASES IN TEXT

performance of sales and lease contracts	tender of delivery
good faith	conforming goods
commercial reasonableness	place of delivery in noncarrier cases
obligations of the seller or lessor	place of delivery in carrier cases

document of title
perfect tender rule
exceptions to the perfect tender rule
nonconforming goods
cure
substitution of carriers
installment contract
commercial impracticability
partial performance
destruction of identified goods
assurance of due performance
duty of cooperation
obligations of the buyer or lessee
payment by the buyer or lessee

right of inspection
C.O.D. shipment
payment due on receipt of
    document of title
acceptance of delivered goods
    by buyer or lessee
revocation of acceptance
partial acceptance
anticipatory repudiation
letter of credit
parties to letter of credit transaction
    (issuer, beneficiary, account party,
    advising bank, and paying bank)
documentary letter of credit

FILL-IN QUESTIONS

1. In order to perform, a seller is obligated to transfer and deliver goods _____ to the buyer, who has an obligation to accept and _____ the goods. If the parties have not specified otherwise, the seller's and buyer's obligations are to be rendered at the same time because they are _____ conditions.

2. If a seller is to deliver goods to a carrier under a shipment contract, the seller is required to (1) _____, (2) make a commercially reasonable contract for transportation, and (3) promptly notify the buyer.

3. Delivery F.A.S. and ex-ship are terms used when goods are to be transported by ship. If delivery is F.A.S. a named vessel, the seller's duty ends when the goods are _____ and the seller obtains a receipt that is duly tendered to the buyer. If the goods are to be delivered ex-ship, the seller's duty, risk, and expense continue until the goods are _____.

4. If a seller or lessor tenders goods that do not conform to the contract, the buyer or lessee has a number of options. The buyer or lessee may (1) _____ all of the goods, (2) _____, or (3) the buyer or lessee may accept one or more of the commercial units of the goods and reject the rest of the units.

5. When the parties have not indicated any terms of payment, but goods have been properly tendered for delivery by a seller, a buyer has an obligation to pay at the time and place the goods are _____ by using cash or _____ for payment.

6. If, before the date when his or her performance is due, one party to a contract for the sale or lease of goods indicates that he or she clearly does not intend to perform in accordance with the contract, an _____ or repudiation of the contract has occurred.

7.   A letter of credit is a written document that contains a promise or engagement by the _____ of the letter of credit to honor drafts, orders, or other demands for payment of money on behalf of the _____, who, in turn, promises to reimburse the _____ of the letter of credit. The _____ of the letter of credit is the party who is entitled to draw or demand payment under the terms of the letter of credit.

MULTIPLE CHOICE QUESTIONS

1.   Upon delivery of nonconforming goods, a buyer may:
     A. reject all of the goods.
     B. accept all of the goods.
     C. accept those commercial units that conform to the contract but reject other units.
     D. do any of the above.

2.   The New England Candy Co. of Boston, Massachusetts, contracted for the purchase of a stated quantity of sugar from Sweet Sugar Inc. of Louisiana. Assume that the contract provided that the sugar was to be shipped by sea, to arrive November 1.
     A. Assume that Sweet Sugar learns that shipment by truck will be less expensive and ships by truck, rather than by sea in accordance with the contract. New England Candy Co. may reject the goods, which arrived on October 30 in Boston because of the seller's failure to make a perfect tender.
     B. Assume that there is a hurricane off the coast of New Orleans and that Sweet Sugar, therefore, ships the sugar by truck, rather than by sea. New England Candy Co. may **not** reject the goods arriving on October 30 in Boston, because of Sweet Sugar's failure to perform in accordance with the contract.
     C. Assume that the goods arrived by ship in Boston on October 30 but were stolen from the vessel on October 31. New England Candy Co. bears the risk of the loss, even though Sweet Sugar failed to notify the buyer that the goods were being shipped.
     D. Assume that the goods arrived by ship in Boston on October 30, but were stolen from the vessel on October 31. Sweet Sugar bears the risk of loss, even though it sent and New England Candy received the bill of lading, through normal banking channels.

3.   Shuman Auto Parts Inc. entered into a contract for the sale of 3,000 spark plugs to Wright Auto Supplies Distribution Co. The 3,000 sparks plugs were marked, packaged, and held by Shuman at its plant. Wright was notified that the spark plugs were available. A week later, a fire occurred at Shuman's plant, and the spark plugs were destroyed.
     A. If no delivery terms were specified in the contract for the sale of the spark plugs, Shuman made a tender of delivery and has fully performed its contractual obligations.
     B. Shuman is excused from performing because identified goods were destroyed before the risk of loss was transferred to Wright.
     C. Both Shuman and Wright are excused from performing because of commercial impracticability.
     D. Wright may treat the contract as canceled because the goods have been destroyed.

4. The Bertown Bridge Club placed an order with McDonald for 100 decks of playing cards. No date was specified for delivery. A week later, McDonald tendered 100 decks of cards to the Bridge Club. The Bridge Club discovered that 50 of the decks were missing the ace of diamonds and immediately notified McDonald that the goods were nonconforming and unacceptable.
    A. McDonald's action may be treated as an anticipatory repudiation. The Bertown Bridge Club can, therefore, suspend its performance.
    B. The Bertown Bridge Club's action may be treated as an anticipatory repudiation. McDonald may, therefore, sue the Bridge Club for damages.
    C. McDonald will cure the defect by supplying the missing aces of diamonds within a reasonable period of time.
    D. McDonald will cure the defect by reducing the price of the fifty decks by three percent.

5. Selk and Buckingham had a contract for the sale of three personal computers that were delivered by the seller, Selk, in the manner prescribed by the contract. Buckingham has a right to inspect the computers before paying for them:
    A. unless Selk notified Buckingham that the personal computers did not conform to the contract because the computers were gray instead of blue and were being shipped as an accommodation.
    B. unless the contract specified that the computers were to be shipped C.O.D.
    C. only if the contract so provided.
    D. only if Buckingham accepts delivery of the computers at Selk's place of business.

6. In general, the buyer is deemed to have waived his right of inspection when an agreement for sale is:
    A. a shipment contract.
    B. a documentary sale.
    C. an identification.
    D. a destination contract.

7. Schain delivered ten window screens to Barton in the manner prescribed by the contract of sale and Barton paid for the screens.
    A. If Barton resells the screens to a third person, Barton will be treated as having accepted the screens.
    B. If Barton discovered that the screens were defective three months later, while she was putting them up, and notified Schain of the defect, Barton will **not** be treated as having accepted the screens.
    C. If Barton discovered that the screens were defective three months later, while putting them up, but did not notify Schain of the defect for six months, Barton will **not** be treated as having accepted the screens.
    D. If Barton inspected the screens when they were delivered, without noticing the defects, which became apparent when she put the screens up, Barton may **not** revoke her acceptance.

Questions 8 and 9 are based upon the following fact situation: TP Seller of Tokyo entered into a contract for the sale of goods to Best Buys, Inc. in Boston. The agreement required that Best Buys, Inc. provide TP Seller with a documentary letter of credit. Best Buys, Inc.

obtained a letter of credit from its bank in Boston, which faxed it to the Bank of Tokyo. TP Seller shipped the goods and obtained a bill of lading from the carrier.

8. In this transaction:
    A. TP Seller is the beneficiary of the letter of credit and Best Buys, Inc. is the issuer of the letter of credit.
    B. TP Seller is the beneficiary of the letter of credit and the Boston bank is the issuer of the letter of credit.
    C. Best Buys, Inc. is the account party and the Bank of Tokyo is the issuer of the letter of credit.
    D. Best Buys, Inc. is the account party and the issuer of the letter of credit.

9. At the earliest, TP Seller can receive payment from:
    A. the Boston bank after Best Buys, Inc. receives the goods.
    B. the Boston bank after the bill of lading is received by the bank.
    C. the Bank of Tokyo upon TP Seller's presentment of the bill of lading.
    D. the Bank of Tokyo after the Boston bank notifies the Bank of Tokyo that the bill of lading has been received by the Boston bank.

Chapter 24
Remedies for Breach of Sales and Lease Contracts

If one of the parties to a contract for the sale or lease of goods repudiates the contract, fails to properly perform, or becomes insolvent, a number of different remedies are available to the aggrieved party under the Uniform Commercial Code (UCC) and under the Convention for Contracts for the International Sale of Goods (CISG). The reason for the variety of remedies is to ensure that appropriate relief will be afforded to an aggrieved party in order to put that party in as good a position as he or she would have been in had the other party correctly performed [UCC 1-106]. In addition, if they wish, parties to contracts for the sale or lease of goods may create or provide their own remedies.

THINGS TO KEEP IN MIND

Some of the UCC remedies revolve around acceptance by a buyer or lessee of identified, conforming goods. Acceptance usually is signified by (1) receipt and retention of goods by a buyer or lessee after inspection reveals that the goods conform to the contract, (2) an indication by a buyer or lessee that the buyer or lessee will take nonconforming goods, or (3) the failure of a buyer or lessee to reject nonconforming goods.

OUTLINE

I.   Remedies of the seller or lessor.

    A. When the goods are in the possession of the seller or lessor.

        1. The right to cancel the contract.

           a. The seller or lessor can cancel the contract if the buyer or lessee wrongfully rejects goods, revokes an acceptance of conforming goods, fails to pay for goods, or repudiates the contract for the sale or lease of the goods [UCC 2-703; 2A-523].

           b. After a seller notifies a buyer, or a lessor notifies a lessee, of cancellation, all unperformed duties of the parties are terminated, and the seller or lessor may sue for breach of contract [UCC 2-106(4); 2A-505(1)].

        2. The right to withhold delivery — Seller or lessor may retain goods if:

a. There is a breach of contract by the buyer or lessee or the buyer or lessee repudiates part of the contract by wrongfully rejecting, revoking acceptance, or failing to make proper payment [UCC 2-703; 2A-523(1)].

b. Buyer or lessee is insolvent and does not pay in cash [UCC 2-702(1); 2A-525(1)].

3. The right to resell or dispose of the goods.

a. A seller or lessor, who has possession of the goods, can sell or lease the goods to another person, or otherwise dispose of the goods, if there is a breach of contract by a buyer or lessee, who wrongfully rejects the goods, revokes acceptance, fails to pay, or repudiates the contract [UCC 2-703, 2-706; 2A-523, 2A-527].

b. Unfinished goods [UCC 2-704(2); 2A-524(2)] — The seller or lessor must exercise reasonable commercial judgment in order to mitigate his or her loss by doing one of the following:
   1) Cease manufacturing the goods and resell for scrap or salvage value;
   2) Complete the manufacture of the goods, and then identify the goods to the contract; or
   3) Proceed in any other reasonable manner .

c. Resale by seller [UCC 2-706].
   1) The seller may recover the difference between the resale price and contract price as well as incidental damages from the buyer.
   2) The resale of the goods must be made in good faith in a commercially reasonable manner and may be public or private.
   3) The seller must give the buyer reasonable notice of the resale, unless the goods are perishable.
   4) A seller is not liable to a buyer for any profits made as a result of resale.
   5) A purchaser at the sale takes free of any claims of the buyer to the goods.

d. When a lessor leases the goods to another person, the lessor may recover from the original lessee:
   1) Any unpaid lease payments up to the beginning date of the new lease;
   2) The lease payments due under the original lease with the breaching lessee and the contract price with the new lessee; and
   3) Incidental damages [UCC 2A-527(2)].

4. The right to recover the purchase price [UCC 2-709, 2-710] or lease payments due [UCC 2A-529] — A seller may sue for the unpaid purchase price, or the lessor may sue for unpaid lease payments that are due, and for incidental damages, when:

a. The buyer or lessee accepted the goods and has not revoked acceptance.

      b. Conforming goods were lost or damaged after risk of loss passed to buyer or lessee.

      c. Breach of contract by the buyer or lessee occurred after the goods were identified, but the seller or lessor is unable to sell, lease, or otherwise dispose of the goods at a reasonable price.

   5. The right to recover damages [UCC 2-708; 2A-528].

      a. Usually, the measure of damages is the difference between the contract price and the market price at the time and place of tender of the goods (i.e., loss of expected profit).

      b. Incidental damages include commercially reasonable charges or expenses incurred by the seller (after the buyer's breach) in stopping delivery, transporting, and caring for goods [UCC 2-710; 2A-530].

B. When the goods are in transit (in the hands of a carrier or other bailee), the seller or lessor may stop the delivery of goods [UCC 2-705; 2A-526].

   1. If there has been a breach of the contract by the buyer or lessee, the seller or lessor may stop a carload or other large shipment.

   2. If the buyer or lessee is insolvent, the size of the shipment is immaterial.

   3. The seller or lessor must give timely notice to the bailee and pay any charges resulting from the stoppage.

   4. In a sales transaction, if the negotiable document of title issued by the bailee is not surrendered, the bailee is not required to obey the direction of the seller by stopping the delivery of the goods.

   5. Right to stop in transit ends when:

      a. The buyer or lessee receives the goods.
        1) Physical possession; or
        2) The bailee, other than a carrier, acknowledges to the buyer or lessee that the goods are held for the buyer or lessee.

      b. The carrier acknowledges to the buyer or lessee that the goods are held for the buyer or lessee for reshipment or storage.

      c. In a sales transaction, a negotiable document of title has been negotiated to the buyer.

C. When the goods are in the possession of the buyer or lessee.

1. After there is a breach of contract, the seller can sue the buyer for the purchase price, or the lessor can sue the lessee for the lease payment that is due (rent), and for incidental damages [UCC 2-709; 2A-529].

2. The right to reclaim the goods.

   a. When a seller (who contracted to sell the goods on credit) discovers that the buyer was insolvent at the time the buyer received the goods, the seller can demand return of the goods within ten days after the buyer's receipt of the goods [UCC 2-702(2) and (3)].
      1) The seller can reclaim goods at any time if the buyer made a written misrepresentation of solvency within three months prior to delivery of the goods.
      2) A seller's right to reclaim goods is lost if a buyer resold the goods to a buyer in the ordinary course of business or a good faith purchaser.
      3) Because the seller (who is reclaiming the goods) is given preferential treatment over other creditors of the buyer, the seller is barred from seeking other remedies.

   b. The lessor may reclaim leased goods that are in the lessee's possession after a default by the lessee [UCC 2A-525(2)].

3. Remedies after goods have been reclaimed [UCC 2-703; 2A-523] — The seller or lessor who has possession of the goods because of a proper stoppage in transit or reclamation has the following remedies:

   a. Cancel the contract.

   b. Retain the goods and recover damages.

   c. Resell or otherwise dispose of the goods and recover damages.

   d. Sue to recover the purchase price or lease payments due.

II. Remedies of the buyer or lessee.

   A. When the seller or lessor refuses to deliver the goods.

   1. The right to cancel (rescind) the contract [UCC 2-711(1); 2A-508(1)(a)].

      a. The buyer or lessee may cancel the contract if the seller or lessor wrongfully fails to make a proper delivery of the goods or repudiates the contract or if the buyer or lessee rightfully rejects or revokes acceptance of the goods.

      b. The right to cancel may be lost if the buyer delays in exercising that right.

      c. All unperformed duties of the parties are terminated, but the buyer or lessee may sue for a breach of contract that occured before cancellation.

2. The right to recover identified goods — If a seller or lessor is insolvent or becomes insolvent within ten days after receiving a full or partial payment, the buyer or lessee has the right to obtain the identified goods in the possession of the seller or lessor upon tendering any unpaid balance of the purchase or lease price [UCC 2-502; 2A-522].

3. The right to obtain specific performance — A decree for specific performance may be granted if the goods are unique or the buyer's or lessee's remedy at law is inadequate [UCC 2-716(1); 2A-521(1)].

4. The right of cover [UCC 2-712; 2A-518].

    a. A buyer (or lessee) may enter into a contract with another seller (or lessor) for the purchase (or lease) of goods in substitution for the goods due from the original seller (or lessor) with whom the buyer (or lessee) had a prior contract, if:
       1) The seller (or lessor) repudiated the contract or failed to deliver goods; or
       2) The buyer (or lessee) rightfully rejected or revoked acceptance of goods.

    b. The measure of damages is the difference between the cost of cover (i.e., the market price) and the contract price plus incidental and consequential damages.
       1) Incidental damages include reasonable expenses incurred in inspection, receipt, transportation, and charges, expenses, or commissions incurred in order to effect cover [UCC 2-715(1); 2A-520(1)].
       2) Consequential damages include foreseeable losses, of which the seller or lessor had reason to know at the time of contracting, and which could not reasonably be prevented by cover [UCC 2-715(2); 2A-520(2)].

    c. A buyer or lessee is not required to cover and may seek alternative remedy.

5. The right to replevy goods — The buyer or lessee may bring an action for replevin of identified goods in the possession of the seller or lessor, who is wrongfully withholding the goods, when the buyer or lessor is unable to effect cover (i.e., buy substitute goods in the market) [UCC 2-716(3); 2A-521(3)].

6. The right to recover damages.

    a. Nondelivery or repudiation of a sales contract — The measure of damages is the difference between the market price of the goods at the time that the buyer learned of the breach (at the place where the goods were to be delivered by the seller) and the contract price, plus any incidental and consequential damages, and less any expenses that were saved because of the seller's breach [UCC 2-713].

b. Nondelivery or repudiation of a lease — The measure of damages is the difference between the market rent on the date of default (at the place where the goods were to be tendered by the lessor) and the original contract rent computed for the remaining lease term, plus any incidental and consequential damages, and less any expenses that were saved because of the lessor's breach [UCC 2A-519].

B. When the seller or lessor delivers nonconforming goods.

1. The right to reject the goods.

   a. If the goods are nonconforming or improperly delivered, the buyer or lessee may:
      1) Reject all the goods; or
      2) Accept all the goods; or
      3) Accept one or more commercial unit or units and reject the remaining units [UCC 2-601; 2A-509].

   b. Timeliness and reasons for rejection required.
      1) A rejection must be within a reasonable time after delivery or tender of the goods and the seller or lessor must be given seasonable notification of the rejection [UCC 2-602(1); 2A-509(2)].
      2) The buyer or lessee must designate particular defects that are ascertainable by reasonable inspection [UCC 2-605; 2A-514].

   c. Duty of merchant buyers and lessees when goods are rejected.
      1) If a merchant buyer or lessee is rejecting goods rightfully, and the seller or lessor has no agent or place of business at the market of rejection, the buyer or lessee has a duty to follow the reasonable instructions of the seller or lessor with respect to the goods and to act in good faith [UCC 2-603; 2A-511].
      2) A merchant buyer or lessee is entitled to reimbursement for reasonable expenses.
      3) If the seller or lessor does not give the merchant buyer or lessee instructions:
         a) The buyer or lessee can resell goods that are perishable or threaten to decline in value quickly and is entitled to reimbursement for expenses [UCC 2-603(1); 2A-511(1)].
         b) If goods are not perishable, the buyer or lessee may store the goods or reship the goods to the seller or lessor at the seller's or lessor's expense [UCC 2-604; 2A-512].

2. Revocation of acceptance.

   a. Acceptance may be revoked by notifying seller or lessor of a breach within a reasonable period after the buyer or lessee discovers or should have discovered the breach [UCC 2-608; 2A-517].

    b. The buyer or lessee may revoke acceptance of a lot or commercial unit if a nonconformity substantially impairs the value of the lot or unit and:
   1) Acceptance was predicated on the reasonable assumption that the nonconformity would be cured, and it has not been seasonably cured; or
   2) Buyer or lessee did not discover the nonconformity, but the acceptance of the buyer or lessee was reasonably induced because of difficulty of discovery or assurances (of correct performance) made by the seller or lessor [UCC 2-608(1); 2A-517(1)].

    c. Notice of revocation required [UCC 2-608(2); 2A-517(4)].
   1) Notice of revocation must be given by a buyer to the seller (or a lessee to the lessor) within a reasonable period of time after the buyer (or lessee) discovers, or should have discovered, the grounds for revocation.
   2) Revocation must occur before the goods have undergone a substantial change that was not caused by their own defects.

3. Buyer's right to retain a security interest in the goods [UCC 2-711(3)].

    a. A buyer, who rightfully rejects goods or revokes acceptance and has possession or control of the goods, may enforce a security interest for any payments made and reasonable expenses incurred.

    b. Such a buyer is considered to be "a person in the position of the seller" and, therefore, may withhold delivery or stop delivery of the goods, resell the goods, and recover incidental damages [UCC 2-707].

    c. If a buyer resells the goods, the buyer must account to the seller for any excess over the amount of the security interest [UCC 2-706(6)].

4. The right to recover damages for breach when goods were accepted.

    a. In order to recover damages for a seller's or lessor's breach of contract or breach of warranty, a buyer or lessee who accepted nonconforming goods must notify the seller or lessor within a reasonable time after the defect was, or should have been, discovered, or within the period of time specified in the contract for notification [UCC 2-607(3); 2A-516(3)].

    b. The measures of damages.
   1) A buyer or lessee, who has accepted nonconforming goods and given notice to the seller or lessor, may recover for the loss "resulting in the ordinary course of events" from the seller's or lessor's breach "as determined in any manner which is reasonable" [UCC 2-714(1); § 2A-519(3)].
   2) A buyer or lessee, who has notified the seller or lessor, may deduct all or part of the damages resulting from the seller's or lessor's breach from the price which is due to the seller [UCC 2-717; 2A-516(1)].

3) The measure of damages for a breach of warranty is the difference between the value of the goods as accepted (at the time and place of acceptance) and the value that the goods would have had if the goods had been as warranted [UCC 2-714(2); 2A-519(4)]. (See Chapter 25 regarding breach of warranties.)

III.   Contractual provisions affecting remedies.

A. The parties to a sales or lease contract may expressly provide for additional remedies, substitute remedies, or a different measure of damages, as well as stipulate that a particular remedy is to be an exclusive or sole remedy [UCC 2-719(1); 2A-503(1)].

B. If circumstances cause the purpose of an exclusive remedy to fail, the aggrieved party may pursue remedies provided by the UCC [UCC 2-719(2); 2A-503(2)].

C. A limitation or exclusion of consequential damages will be enforced unless it is unconscionable [UCC 2-719(3); 2A-503(3)].

D. The amount to be paid as liquidated damages must be reasonable in light of the anticipated or actual loss caused by the breach of contract, the difficulty of proving the loss, and the inconvenience or nonfeasibility of obtaining an adequate remedy [UCC 2-718; 2A-504].

IV.   Lemon laws.

A. When an automobile, which is under warranty, has a defect that significantly affects its value or use, and the defect has not been remedied by the seller within a specified number of opportunities, the buyer has a right to a new car, replacement of defective parts, or return of all consideration paid.

B. Usually, disputes are heard by arbitration panels.

V.   Remedies for breaches of international sales contracts — Remedies provided for in the United Nations Convention on Contracts for the International Sale of Goods (CISG) are similar to those provided for in the UCC.

A. Damages for breach of contract consist of a sum equal to the foreseeable loss incurred as a consequence of the breach; normally, damages are the difference between the market price and the contract price (loss of profit) and may include foreseeable consequential damages [CISG Article 74].

B. A buyer may declare the contract avoided if the seller breaches the contract or fails to deliver the goods during the time specified in the contract or at such later date as may be agreed upon and fixed by the parties [CISG Article 49].

C. Seller may declare the contract avoided if the buyer breaches the contract, fails to accept delivery of the goods, or fails to pay for the goods [CISG Article 64].

D. Specific performance — If "one party is entitled to require performance of any obligation of the other party, a court is not bound to enter judgment for specific performance unless the court would do so under its own law in respect of similar contracts of sale not governed by" the CISG [CISG Article 28].

E. Parties are required to mitigate losses [CISG Article 77].

KEY WORDS AND PHRASES IN TEXT

remedies of the seller or lessor
cancellation of sales or lease contract
right to withhold delivery of goods
insolvent buyer or lessee
resale or other disposition of goods
right to recover purchase price
      or lease payments due
damages for breach of contract
stoppage of goods in transit
right to reclaim goods
incidental damages
remedies of the buyer or lessee
right to recover the goods
specific performance

cover
replevy (replevin of) goods
damages for nondelivery or repudiation
right to reject goods
timely, seasonable notice of rejection
merchant buyer or lessee
revocation of acceptance
damages for breach when goods accepted
buyer's right to security interest in goods
measure of damages
exclusive remedy
waiver of defenses
lemon laws
remedies provided for in the CISG

FILL-IN QUESTIONS

1. If there is a breach of contract by a buyer who wrongfully rejects goods, revokes a prior acceptance, fails to make a proper payment, repudiates part of a contract, or becomes insolvent, a seller has certain remedies and, therefore, the seller may

   _____

   or _____.

2. If a buyer of goods becomes insolvent, under certain circumstances, the seller may _____.

3. A seller can recover the contract price as compensatory damages if the buyer has not paid for the goods, which have been _____, or if the buyer has_____ the goods and the goods cannot be reasonably resold.

4. In most cases, when a seller has failed to deliver goods, the measure of the damages that the buyer can recover is the difference between _____ and the cost of cover in addition to any _____ or consequential damages.

5. When a lessor delivers goods that do not conform to the lease contract, in addition to having the right to revoke a prior acceptance, under some circumstances, the lessee has the right to _____ the goods or sue to recover _____.

6.   A stipulated damages clause is enforceable as a liquidated damages clause provided the amount (or formula) is _____ and approximately equal to the anticipated or actual harm caused by the breach of contract.

MULTIPLE CHOICE QUESTIONS

1.   Salisbury sold a refrigerator to Benton, who paid for it with a check. Benton stopped payment on the check before Salisbury cashed it.
     A. Salisbury has a right to take possession of and retain the refrigerator.
     B. Salisbury has the right to cover.
     C. Salisbury has the right to take and retain the refrigerator if the refrigerator is in the possession of a good faith purchaser in the ordinary course of Benton's business.
     D. Salisbury has the right to revoke Benton's acceptance.

2.   If there is a breach of contract for the sale of goods by the buyer, the seller may stop the delivery of the goods in the possession of a carrier when:
     A. the size of the shipment is a carload or less.
     B. the carrier acknowledged to the buyer that the carrier was holding the goods for the buyer as a warehouser.
     C. the seller gives timely notice to the carrier and surrenders a negotiable document of title to the carrier.
     D. a negotiable document of title has been negotiated to the buyer.

3.   Sassafras Distributors entered into a contract for the sale of goods to Blake. Blake refused to pay for the goods. Sassafras Distributors will **not** be able to recover the price for the goods if:
     A. Blake accepted the goods but wishes to return the goods.
     B. the goods were destroyed after the risk of loss passed to Blake.
     C. Blake refused to accept delivery of the goods and the goods were resold by Sassafras Distributors in the ordinary course of business.
     D. the goods were identified to the contract and Sassafras Distributors made a reasonable effort to resell the goods at a reasonable price but was unable to do so.

4.   Under the Leases Article of the UCC, which of the following rights is (are) available to a lessor when a lessee materially breaches a contract for the lease of goods?

	Right to cancel the contract	Right to recover damages
A.	Yes	Yes
B.	Yes	No
C.	No	Yes
D.	No	No

(This question has been adapted from objective question #50 on the Uniform CPA Examination, November 1995.)

5.   Crane Fabricators Corp. and Lucky Builders Co. agreed that Crane would custom manufacture a building crane and lease the crane to Lucky for three years. Lucky agreed to make annual lease payments of $50,000. After Crane manufactured the crane at a cost of $100,000, Lucky notified Crane that it no longer needed the crane.

Crane is holding the crane and has requested payments from Lucky. Crane has not been able to sell or lease or otherwise dispose of the crane. Crane has incurred storage charges of $3,000. If Lucky refuses to take delivery and make any lease payments, the maximum amount of damages that Crane will be able to recover is:
A. $50,000
B. $103,000.
C $150,000.
D. $153,000.

Questions 6 and 7 are based on the following fact situation: Boyer Office Supplies of Akron, Ohio entered into a contract to purchase 250 cases of blue paper for use in computer printers from Syllor Paper Co. of Duluth, Minnesota. The contract provided that the paper was to be shipped by truck F.O.B. Duluth by March 15.

6.   On March 10, Syllor Paper Co. marked and identified 250 cases of blue computer printer paper. On March 12, Boyer Office Supplies notified Syllor Paper Co. that it was repudiating the contract. Syllor Paper Co. has the right to:

	resell the paper.	cancel the contract.
A.	No	No
B.	No	Yes
C.	Yes	No
D.	Yes	Yes

7.   Syllor Paper Co. marked 250 cases of yellow computer printer paper. The 250 cases of yellow paper were delivered to a carrier in Duluth on March 13 and delivered to Boyer Office Supplies on March 15, at which time Boyer inspected the shipment and learned that it contained yellow, and not blue, paper. Boyer Officer Supplies has the right to:

	reject the goods.	obtain an order for specific performance.
A.	No	No
B.	No	Yes
C.	Yes	No
D.	Yes	Yes

8.   Under the UCC Sales Article, which of the following remedies would a buyer **not** have when a seller fails to transfer and deliver goods identified to the contract?
A. an order for specific performance.
B. punitive damages.
C. purchase substitute goods (cover).
D. replevy (obtain or recover) the goods.
(This question has been adapted from objective question #47 on the Uniform CPA Examination, May 1994.)

9.   In accordance with a contract for sale, Dainty Dish Manufacturers shipped 100 sets of dishes to M Mart Store. The shipment arrived on Monday, earlier than it was expected. The receiving department made a perfunctory examination of the dishes and put them in a storeroom. When ten sets of the dishes were taken from the storeroom

on Wednesday morning, it was discovered that the quality of the dishes was inferior to that specified in the contract. Which of the following statements is correct?

A. M Mart Store must retain the dishes, because M Mart Store accepted them and had an opportunity to inspect the dishes upon delivery.

B. M Mart Store's only remedy is to bring an action for rescission.

C. M Mart Store has no rights against Dainty Dish Manufacturers if the dishes are of merchantable quality.

D. M Mart Store can reject the dishes upon its subsequent discovery that the dishes are not in accordance with the contract specifications.

10. Under the Sales Article of the UCC, which of the following rights is (are) available to the buyer when a seller commits an anticipatory breach of contract?

	Demand assurance of performance	Cancel the contract	Collect punitive damages
A.	Yes	Yes	Yes
B.	Yes	Yes	No
C.	Yes	No	Yes
D.	No	Yes	No

(This question appeared as objective question #47 on the Uniform CPA Examination, November 1995.)

11. Under the Sales and Leases Articles of the UCC, which of the following statements regarding liquidated damages is (are) correct?

I. The injured party may collect any amount of liquidated damages provided for in the contract.

II. The seller or lessor may retain a deposit of up to $500 when a buyer or lessee defaults, even if there is no liquidated damages provision in the contract.

A. I only.

B. II only.

C. Both I and II.

D. Neither I nor II.

(This question has been adapted from objective question #49 on the Uniform CPA Examination, November 1995.)

Chapter 25
Sales and Lease Warranties

Sellers and lessors of goods make assurances, promises, and guaranties about the goods that they sell or lease. These assurances and promises are referred to as warranties. Warranties may be made expressly by sellers and lessors. Even though sellers and lessors may not expressly make warranties, it is inferred or implied that they are making certain promises, guaranties, or warranties about the goods. In the event that an assurance relating to the goods is not fulfilled, there is a breach of the warranty, for which a seller or lessor is liable. An injured person, therefore, may seek redress from the seller or lessor of the goods by relying upon the contractual theory of breach of warranty.

THINGS TO KEEP IN MIND

Manufactured items that were the subject matter of sales and lease contracts may prove to be defective or not fit for the normal or particular use for which the items were acquired. As a result, buyers, lessees, and other people may incur personal injuries or property damage. In addition to pursuing actions based upon tort law (discussed in Chapter 8), injured parties may bring actions against sellers and lessors of the products based upon the contract theory of breach of warranties.

OUTLINE

I. Warranty of title.

    A. In the usual case of a contract for the sale of goods, the seller makes a warranty, or assurance, that the seller has the right to sell the goods free of claims to the goods by other persons [UCC 2-312]. If the seller did not have such a right, there is a breach of the warranty, for which the seller is liable to the buyer.

    B. Good title — A seller warrants that the seller has valid title to the goods and that the transfer of title to the buyer is rightful [UCC 2-312(1)(a)].

    C. No liens.

        1. A seller warrants that there are no liens, security interests, or other encumbrances of which the buyer lacks knowledge [UCC 2-312(1)(b)].

        2. A lessor warrants that there are no claims of third parties that will interfere with the lessee's enjoyment of the leasehold interest [UCC 2A-211(1)].

D. No infringements [UCC 2-312(3); 2A-211(2)].

    1. A seller or lessor, who is a merchant, warrants that the goods are free from adverse copyright, patent, trademark, or similar claims.

    2. This warranty against infringement does not apply if the goods were made to the specifications of the buyer or lessee.

    3. A buyer or lessee (with the exception of a consumer lessee) who is sued for infringement must notify the seller in order to retain rights against the seller or lessor [UCC 2-607(3)(b) and (5)(b); 2A-516(3)(b) and (4)(b)].

E. Disclaimer of title warranty [UCC 2-312(2); 2A-214(4)].

    1. Warranty of title may be expressly excluded, disclaimed, or modified in a contract for the sale or lease of goods.

    2. The warranty of title is excluded if the sale occurs under circumstances that clearly indicate that no such assurances are being made by the seller.

II.   Express warranties [UCC 2-313; 2A-210].

A. Written or oral factual assertions, representations, affirmations, or promises relating to the quality, condition, description, or performance potential of the goods, which become "part of the basis of the bargain."

    1. The goods will conform to an affirmation of fact or promise that relates to the goods.

    2. The goods will conform to a description of the goods.

    3. The goods will conform to a sample or model of the goods.

    4. No particular words need to be used in order to create an express warranty.

B. Basis of the bargain.

    1. An affirmation or promise becomes the basis of the bargain if the natural tendency of the making of the affirmation or promise is to induce the buyer to purchase (or the lessee to lease) the goods, and may include affirmations made before, while, and immediately after entering the contract.

    2. The buyer or lessee does not have to show that he or she actually relied upon the affirmation or promise.

C. Statements of opinion and value [UCC 2-313(2); 2A-210(2)].

    1. Statements of opinion and value do not create express warranties as to the quality of the goods, unless the statements are made by experts.

2. In distinguishing warranties from puffing (seller's talk or exaggerated commendations), the reasonableness of the buyer's or the lessee's reliance upon the statement, the context within which the statement is made, the specificity of the statement, and whether the statement was made orally or in writing may be relevant.

D. In some cases, a seller or lessor may not make any express warranties, or may effectively disclaim those warranties that he or she has made by using unambiguous language to that effect in the contract for the sale or lease of goods.

III. Implied warranties.

A. Implied warranties arise because of the nature and circumstances of the transactions unless implied warranties are expressly excluded.

B. In an action based upon breach of an implied warranty, the buyer or lessee must show that the implied warranty existed, that the warranty was broken, and that the breach of warranty was the proximate cause of the damage sustained.

C. Implied warranty of merchantability [UCC 2-314; 2A-212].

   1. An implied warranty of merchantability is made by a merchant seller or lessor who deals in the kinds of goods that are the subject matter of the contract.

   2. Merchantable goods.

      a. Goods are merchantable if the goods are reasonably fit for the normal, ordinary purposes for which they generally are used.

      b. In order to be merchantable, the goods must:
         1) Be of average, fair, or medium grade or quality;
         2) Pass, without objection in the trade or market, for goods of the same description;
         3) Be adequately packaged and labeled as provided by the agreement;
         4) Conform to the affirmations of fact or promises made on the label or container; and
         5) Be of even quality and quantity in each unit and among all units.

   3. A merchant seller or lessor is absolutely liable for breach of the warranty of merchantability, without regard to whether the seller or lessor knew of or could have discovered a defect that caused the goods not to be reasonably fit for the ordinary purposes for which they are used.

   4. Merchantable food — A warranty of merchantability is made in a contract for the sale of food or drink for consumption on the premises or elsewhere and applies when a substance, which consumers would not reasonably expect to find in the food or beverage, is in the food or beverage.

D. Implied warranty of fitness for a particular purpose [UCC 2-315; 2A-213].

1. The seller or lessor, who may or may not be a merchant, warrants that the goods are fit for the particular purpose intended by the buyer.

2. The implied warranty of fitness for a particular purpose is made by a seller (or lessor) who has reason to know (but not necessarily actually know) the particular use for which the buyer is purchasing (or the lessee is leasing) the goods and that the buyer (or lessee) relies on the skill and judgment of the seller (or lessor) in selecting suitable goods.

E. Implied warranties of fitness for particular purpose and merchantability may both be included in a contract for the sale or lease of goods.

F. Implied warranty arising from course of dealing or trade usage — When both parties (the buyer and seller or the lessor and lessee) have knowledge of a well-recognized trade custom or a prior course of dealings, it may be implied that the parties intended that the trade usage or course of dealings apply to their contract for the sale or lease of goods [UCC 2-314(3); 2A-212(3)].

IV. Overlapping warranties [UCC 2-317; 2A-215].

A. More than one warranty may be made by a seller or lessor in a transaction.

B. If multiple warranties are consistent with each other, a buyer or lessee can sue the seller or lessor for breach of warranty based upon all of the warranties; the warranties are construed to be cumulative.

C. If multiple warranties are inconsistent, the intention of the parties will determine which will prevail. The following rules are used as guides in order to determine their intentions.

1. Technical specifications prevail over inconsistent models, samples, or general descriptions.

2. A "sample from an existing bulk" prevails over inconsistent general descriptions.

3. The implied warranty of fitness for a particular purpose takes precedence over express warranties.

4. Express warranties take precedence over implied warranties of title and merchantability.

V. Warranties and third parties.

A. Because of the common law doctrine of privity of contract, a person who has not consented to a contractual relationship neither acquires rights nor assumes obligations. [See Chapter 18.]

1. A person is liable for failure to carry out an obligation that is imposed because of a contract (including a breach of warranty) only to a party with whom he or she has privity of contract.

2. The common law rule regarding breach of an express or implied warranty by a seller was that the buyer could sue and recover from the buyer's seller, but an injured user of the goods or other remote non-contracting party, who was not in privity with the seller, could not sue the seller for the breach of warranty.

B. Courts in some states have held that warranties made by a seller extend to those persons who reasonably could be foreseen by a manufacturer as potential users of the manufactured item, and that warranties relating to food, drink, and other items, which, if they are deleterious, are dangerous to human life, extend to remote users.

C. The requirement of privity of contract has been modified in UCC Sections 2-318 and 2A-216; each state has the option of selecting one of three alternative provisions.

1. The effect is to make certain persons, such as family members, donees, and bystanders, third party beneficiaries of express and implied warranties that are made by sellers and lessors of the goods. [Third party beneficiaries are covered in Chapter 18.]

2. Warranties extend to any persons who are reasonably expected to use, consume, or be affected by the goods and who are injured (third party beneficiaries of warranties).

    a. Persons who are covered by UCC Sections 2-318 and 2A-216.
       1) Alternatives A and B extend only to natural persons.
       2) Alternative A is limited to natural persons who are members of the family or household or guests in the home of the purchaser.
       3) Alternative C extends to natural and other persons, such as corporations.

    b. Types of injuries covered by UCC Sections 2-318 and 2A-216.
       1) Alternatives A and B cover only those persons who incur personal injuries and, therefore, exclude property damage.
       2) Alternative C does not restrict coverage to personal injuries and, therefore, extends coverage to property damage.

VI. Warranty disclaimers.

A. Warranties may be excluded, disclaimed, or modified by the parties.

B. A buyer or lessee must be aware of the disclaimer at the time the contract is formed.

C. Express warranties.

   1. A seller or lessor may exclude express warranties by refraining from making promises or affirmations of fact relating to the goods.

   2. A seller or lessor may effectively disclaim those warranties which the seller or lessor has made with unambiguous language to that effect in the contract for the sale or lease of goods [UCC 2-316(1); 2A-214(1)].

D. Implied warranties [UCC 2-316; 2A-214] — Warranties of fitness for a particular purpose and merchantability may be disclaimed or modified by:

   1. Using expressions such as "as is" or "with all faults."

   2. A conspicuous disclaimer.

      a. A disclaimer of the warranty of fitness for particular purpose must be a written, conspicuous disclaimer, but does not have to refer to fitness.

      b. A disclaimer of the warranty of merchantability must use conspicuous language and include the word "merchantability," but need not be in writing.

   3. An inspection conducted by the buyer or lessee or a refusal by the buyer or lessee to examine the goods or a sample. (There is no warranty as to defects that a reasonable examination would reveal.)

   4. Trade usage, course of dealings, or course of performance.

E. Buyer's or lessee's examination of the goods.

   1. If a buyer or lessee has examined the goods or a sample of the goods as fully as the buyer or lessee desires or has refused to examine the goods, there is no implied warranty with respect to defects that a reasonable examination would reveal [UCC 2-316(3)(b); 2A-214(3)(b)].

   2. A seller or lessor is liable for breach of warranty for defects that an ordinary inspection would not reveal.

F. Unconscionability — A court may refuse to enforce a warranty disclaimer clause in a contract for the sale or lease of goods if the clause is unconscionable [UCC 2-302; 2A-108].

VII. Statute of limitations [UCC 2-725; 2A-506].

A. Actions for breach of contract brought under the UCC must be commenced within four years after the cause of action arose.

B. Parties may not extend the four year period but may reduce the period to not less than one year.

C. A cause of action for breach of warranty accrues when the seller or lessor makes tender of delivery, even though the buyer or lessee did not know of the defect.

D. When a warranty explicitly extends to the future performance of the goods, and discovery of a breach cannot be made until that future time, the cause of action accrues when the breach is or should be discovered [UCC 2-725(2)].

E. Causes of action based upon non-UCC claims are subject to applicable state statutes of limitations.

VIII. Magnuson-Moss Warranty Act.

A. The Magnuson-Moss Warranty Act is a federal statute that applies to express warranties made in consumer sales transactions.

B. An express warranty is any promise or affirmation of fact made by the seller to a consumer indicating:

1. The quality or performance of the product.

2. The product is either free of defects or will meet a specific level of performance over a period of time.

3. A written agreement to refund, repair, or replace the product if the product fails to meet written specifications.

C. If a seller makes an express written warranty, and the price is more than ten dollars, the warranty must be labeled as either full or limited.

D. A Federal Trade Commission regulation requires that, if the price of the goods is more than fifteen dollars, certain disclosures must be stated fully and conspicuously in a single document in "readily understood language."

E. Full warranty.

1. A full warranty provides for free repair or replacement of a defective part; if the defective part cannot be repaired within a reasonable time, the consumer has the choice of either a refund or a replacement without charge.

2. Limitations on consequential damages must be conspicuously stated.

3. Frequently, there is no time limit.

F. Limited warranty — A limited warranty is made when one of the minimum requirements for a full warranty is not met and the warranty must contain a conspicuous statement that the warrantor is giving a limited warranty.

G. Implied warranties are not covered under the Magnuson-Moss Warranty Act; the implied warranties of merchantability and fitness for a particular purpose cannot be disclaimed or modified in an express warranty that is made to a consumer.

IX. Warranties under the CISG [Article 35].

A. Although the term "warranty" is not used in the CISG, the concept is recognized.

B. The "seller must deliver goods which are of the quality, quantity, and description required by the contract and which are contained or packaged in the manner required by the contract" and, therefore, conform to the contract [Article 35(1)].

C. If goods are not merchantable or fit for the purpose for which the goods are intended, the "goods do not conform with the contract," unless the parties have otherwise agreed or "the buyer knew or could have been aware of" the lack of conformity [Article 35 (2) and 35 (3)].

KEY WORDS AND PHRASES IN TEXT

warranty
warranty of good title
warranty that there are no liens,
    encumbrances, or security interests
warranty that there are no infringements
    upon the rights of a third person
express warranty
basis of the bargain
implied warranty
implied warranty of merchantability
implied warranty of fitness for a
    particular purpose

implied warranty arising from course
    of dealings or trade usage
overlapping warranties
third party beneficiaries of warranties
warranty disclaimers and modifications
unconscionable disclaimers of warranty
statute of limitations (in UCC)
Magnuson-Moss Warranty Act
full warranties and limited warranties
CISG provisions relating to equivalent
    of warranties

FILL-IN QUESTIONS

1. Whether or not a seller of goods is a merchant, the seller impliedly warrants that the seller is transferring good title to the buyer, that the seller has the right to do so, and that the goods are free from any liens, security interests, or other _____. A seller, who is a merchant, also warrants against infringements. This means that the goods are free from adverse claims based upon patent, _____, trade name, or copyright infringement.

2. A seller, who makes a statement or representation concerning the quality of the goods that the seller sells, has made an _____ warranty if the assertion, statement or representation deals with a _____ characteristic of the goods, as distinguished from a statement of opinion or value or puffing.

3. Even though a seller of goods makes no express warranties concerning the quality of the goods that the seller is selling, it is implied that the goods are _____ and _____.

4. A merchant, who deals in the kinds of goods that are the subject matter of a sale to a consumer, makes an implied warranty of merchantability. The merchant warrants that the goods are (1) of the average or usual quality existing in the market, (2) _____, and (3) contained, packaged, and labeled as provided in the contract. A merchant seller may effectively disclaim or modify this implied warranty by using conspicuous language, which includes the word _____.

5. If the intentions of the parties are not clear as to whether or not an express warranty made by the seller was to take precedence over an inconsistent implied warranty, an implied warranty of _____ will prevail over an inconsistent express warranty. If, however, an express warranty is inconsistent with an implied warranty of merchantability or title, the _____ warranty will prevail over the inconsistent implied warranty of _____ or the warranty of good title.

6. Under the UCC today, a person who did not purchase a manufactured product but incurred a personal injury as a result of a defect in the product may recover from the seller, based upon a breach of an express or implied warranty because such a person is treated as a _____ of the contract for the sale of goods. In all states, however, such a person will have to show that he or she was a person who was reasonably expected to _____ or _____ the goods or be affected by the goods.

7. A lessee of goods that prove to be defective may bring an action against the lessor, with whom the lessee contracted, based upon contract if the lessee can show that there was a breach of an express or implied _____. If the lessee bases his or her cause of action on tort, the buyer will have to establish that the lessor was either _____ or strictly liable.

MULTIPLE CHOICE QUESTIONS

Some of the following questions require applications of principles of law that are covered in Chapters 8 and 24 as well as Chapter 25.

1. Edson purchased a radio from the Radio Store for cash. Later, Ogden, a competitor of the Radio Store, demanded that Edson turn over the radio to him because he (Ogden) could prove that the radio had been stolen from Ogden's store. Edson relinquished the radio to Ogden and demanded his money back from the Radio Store.
   A. Edson will **not** be able to get his money back because of the warranty that the goods were free from any claims of infringement.
   B. Edson will **not** be able to get his money back because the contract of sale provided that the seller make no express warranties.

C. Edson will be able to get his money back because of the breach of warranty of merchantability by the Radio Store.

D. Edson will be able to get his money back because of the breach of warranty of good title by the Radio Store.

2. Obedin owned and operated a precision machine manufacturing business. Kendall contracted with Obedin for the manufacture of a metal cutting machine for which Kendall supplied specifications. Obedin produced and delivered the machine, which conformed to the specifications, and Kendall paid the contract price. The machine performed satisfactorily. Six months after delivery of the machine to Kendall, Cuter Machine Tools brought an action against Obedin and Kendall for infringement of its patent rights. Kendall, in turn, brought an action against Obedin based upon breach of warranty. Kendall will **not** be successful if his action is based upon breach of:

A. an express warranty, because an implied warranty against infringement takes precedence over a conflicting express warranty.

B. an implied warranty against infringement, because the machine was made in accordance with specifications furnished by the buyer.

C. an implied warranty of good title, because an implied warranty of good title is displaced by an implied warranty against infringement when the seller is a merchant.

D. an implied warranty that the machine was free of liens or other encumbrances, because such a warranty is **not** made when goods are specially manufactured.

3. In a contract for the lease of goods, an express warranty is made by the lessor if:

A. the lessor represents that the goods will increase in value by at least 20 percent in two months.

B. the lessor states that, in the lessor's opinion, the goods will prove satisfactory for the lessee's purpose.

C. the lessor assures the lessee that the goods will be the same as a sample which the lessor exhibits.

D. the lessor says that the lessor's goods are better than the goods of the lessor's competitors.

4. Langer, who was not a merchant, sold a computer to Vannan for use in an educational project. Langer made no express warranties. Vannan claims and is able to show that the computer does not perform the operations needed for her project. Vannan, therefore, is suing Langer for breach of warranty. Vannan will probably be successful because Langer breached the implied warranty:

A. of merchantability.

B. of fitness for a particular purpose.

C. that the item sold was fit for the ordinary purpose for which computers normally are used.

D. that there were no security interests or other encumbrances that would interfere with Vannan's use of the computer.

Questions 5, 6, and 7 are based upon the following fact situation: Charlotte went to Katherine's store in order to purchase a new ladder so that she could paint the trim on her 15-foot ceilings. Charlotte asked to see a ladder manufactured by X, which Katherine showed her. Katherine also showed Charlotte a ladder manufactured by Y and one by Z. Katherine stated that she believed that the Y ladder was the "best buy" of the three and that the X ladder would not prove satisfactory for Charlotte's purposes. You are to assume that the entire transaction was conducted orally.

5.   Charlotte purchased the X ladder. She was injured when the ladder collapsed while she was painting the trim on her ceiling. With regard to a breach of warranty of fitness for a particular purpose, which of the following statements is true?
   A. There has been a breach of warranty of fitness, because Katherine knew the purpose for which Charlotte was making the purchase.
   B. There has been **no** breach of warranty of fitness, because Charlotte did not rely on Katherine's skill and judgment in making her selection.
   C. There has been no breach of warranty of fitness because Katherine used conspicuous language to exclude the warranty of fitness effectively.
   D. There has been a breach of warranty of fitness because the ladder was **not** fit for the normal purpose for which ladders are used.

6.   Charlotte purchased the Y ladder. Charlotte was injured when the ladder collapsed while she was painting the trim on her ceiling. With regard to a breach of warranty of merchantability, which of the following statements is true?
   A. There was a breach of the warranty of merchantability because the ladder was not reasonably fit for the purpose for which a person usually uses a ladder.
   B. A warranty of merchantability takes precedence over express warranties.
   C. Katherine effectively disclaimed the warranty of merchantability.
   D. Katherine's express statements created an express warranty of merchantability.

7.   Charlotte purchased the Z ladder. Charlotte was injured when the ladder collapsed while she was painting the trim on her ceiling.
   A. Katherine is **not** liable for breach of any warranties because she made no assertions or representations of facts concerning the Z ladder.
   B. An implied warranty of merchantability can be excluded expressly by contract if the seller is a nonmerchant, but **not** by Katherine because she was a merchant.
   C. An implied warranty of merchantability would have been excluded effectively if the defect had been revealed by Charlotte's inspection.
   D. A disclaimer of the warranty of merchantability by Katherine would **not** be effective unless the disclaimer was conspicuous and in a writing containing the word "merchantability."

8.   Thirsty purchased a 75¢ bottle of soda, manufactured by the Soke Company, at a neighborhood grocery store. Thirsty took the bottle home, where he drank some and shared the rest with Parched. Thirsty and Parched became violently ill because they swallowed slivers of glass that were in the bottle of soda. Which of the following statements is correct?
   A. Soke Company could have effectively disclaimed all liability to buyers and other consumers of its product by putting a carefully worded disclaimer on the label.
   B. Federal and state consumer product safety protection statutes do **not** apply to Soke Company, because normally soda is not a hazardous product.
   C. The Magnuson-Moss Warranty Act does **not** apply to Soke Company's liability to Parched or Thirsty.
   D. The Magnuson-Moss Warranty Act insures that the implied warranty of merchantability is extended to Parched as well as to Thirsty.

9. Freyberg became violently ill after eating a hamburger purchased at Speedy Burger Palace. It has been determined that Freyberg's illness was caused by a poisonous substance in the hamburger. As a result, the hamburger was unfit for human consumption. Freyberg is suing the Speedy Burger Palace. Freyberg's cause of action is based upon breaches of the implied warranties of merchantability and fitness for a particular purpose.

   A. Freyberg may base his cause of action upon either or both of the warranties.
   B. Freyberg may base his cause of action upon one of the warranties, but **not** upon both the warranties of merchantability and fitness for a particular purpose.
   C. The implied warranty of merchantability does **not** apply because Freyberg did not consume the hamburger at the Speedy Burger Palace, but rather ate it while seated in his own car.
   D. The implied warranty of fitness for a particular purpose does **not** apply because Speedy Burger Palace was not informed by Freyberg of the particular purpose for which Freyberg was purchasing the hamburger.

10. Huber purchased a case of beer from Beere's Beverages. Huber drank one can of the beer without any harmful effects and used the remainder of the beer to wash his car. As a result of this use of the beer, the paint on the car was permanently damaged.

    A. Beere's Beverages is liable to Huber for breach of the implied warranty of merchantability.
    B. Beere's Beverages is liable for breach of the implied warranty of fitness for a particular purpose.
    C. Beere's Beverages is **not** liable to Huber for breach of any implied warranties as to quality, because Beere's Beverages did not know the purpose for which Huber bought the beer, and Huber used the beer for an unusual purpose.
    D. Beere's Beverages is **not** liable for breach of any implied warranties as to quality because such warranties do not apply to food or drink.

11. Which of the following conditions must be met for an implied warranty of fitness for a particular purpose to arise in connection with a sale of goods?

       I. The warranty must be in writing.
       II. The seller must know that the buyer was relying on the seller in selecting the goods.

    A. I only.
    B. II only.
    C. Both I and II.
    D. Neither I nor II.
    (This question appeared as objective question #55 on the Uniform CPA Examination, May 1992.)

12. Mink sold Beaver twenty fur coats in accordance with a signed written contract. The contract contained no specific provisions regarding warranties of title but stated that the coats were sold to Beaver "with all faults and defects." Two of the coats that were sold to Beaver had been stolen and were reclaimed by the rightful owner. Which of the following is a correct statement?

    A. The implied warranty of title is eliminated by the parol evidence rule.

    B. The disclaimer "with all faults and defects" effectively negates any and all implied warranties.

    C. Beaver assumed the risk of Mink's title being void because there was no express warranty of good title.

    D. The contract automatically contained a warranty that good title was conveyed, which could only be excluded by specific language.

(This question has been adapted from objective question #52, Uniform CPA Examination, November 1983.)

13. Cautious T.V. Store wishes to exclude implied warranties as to quality from the store's future sales of television sets. The store can effectively do so by:

    A. selling only brand name merchandise.

    B. using a written contract form which conspicuously states that, "All warranty protection by Cautious T.V. Store is expressly excluded by the seller."

    C. using a written contract form which conspicuously states that, "There are no warranties which extend beyond the description contained in this contract of sale."

    D. using a written contract form which conspicuously states that, "The merchandise is sold as is and with all faults."

Questions 14 and 15 are based on the following fact situation: Tillie bought a new personal computer manufactured by the BMI Corp. from a retail seller of business equipment for $2,450. When she brought the computer home, she tested the keyboard by typing her name. As she touched the "L" key, all of the keys flew out of the keyboard severely injuring Tillie. On the written contract of sale, there was a conspicuous statement to the effect that: (1) The sale was covered only by the manufacturer's warranties; (2) the seller did not warrant that the computer and the keyboard were fit for the particular purpose intended by the buyer; and (3) the seller did not make any warranties as to the merchantability of the computer and keyboard. There was a conspicuous written twelve month warranty attached to the computer ,which promised that BMI Corp. would replace the computer and any parts if they proved to be defective.

14. With regard to the retail seller from whom Tillie purchased the computer and keyboard:

    A. the seller is liable to Tillie for breach of the warranty of merchantability.

    B. the seller is liable to Tillie for breach of the warranty of fitness for a particular purpose.

    C. the seller is **not** liable to Tillie for negligence if the seller can show that it exercised reasonable care.

    D. the seller is **not** liable to Tillie in tort for personal injuries but is liable for property damage.

15. The warranty statement attached to the computer:

    A. was binding on BMI Corp. and the retail seller with whom Tillie dealt.

    B. was binding on BMI Corp. only.

    C. does **not** have to comply with the Magnuson-Moss Warranty Act because the computer was purchased for Tillie's personal use.

    D. limits BMI Corp.'s liability to Tillie for personal injuries.

Questions 16 and 17 are based on the following fact situation: Fleur Sweater Co. purchased yarn from Scott Yarns, Inc., a manufacturer of yarn. The yarn was delivered, accepted, and paid for by the buyer, Fleur Sweater Co. The yarn was used to manufacture 5,000 sweaters, which were subsequently sold throughout the United States. Months after the sweaters had been sold to consumers, Fleur Sweater Co. began to receive complaints that, due to defects in the yarn, the sweaters were disintegrating. Fleur Sweater Co. notified Scott Yarns, Inc. that, unless Scott Yarns, Inc. came into the litigation, Scott Yarns, Inc. would be bound by any and all judicial determinations. Scott Yarns, Inc. has not responded.

16. Fleur Sweater Co. successfully can:
    A. sue Scott Yarns, Inc. for compensatory (money) damages, including the amounts consumers have recovered from Fleur Sweater Co.
    B. revoke its acceptance of the yarn.
    C. exercise its remedy of cover.
    D. All of the answers above are correct.

17. Which of the following statement is **false**?
    A. Scott Yarns, Inc. may join in the litigation.
    B. If Scott Yarns, Inc. does **not** come into the litigation, a judgment can be entered against Scott Yarns, Inc.
    C. If Scott Yarns, Inc. does **not** come into the litigation, but is subsequently sued by Fleur Sweater Co., Scott **cannot** re-litigate factual issues that are common to Fleur's action against Scott and the customers' actions against Fleur, when determinations of the issues were made in the customers' actions.
    D. If Fleur Sweater Co., defends in the action brought against it by its customers, but loses, it can later bring an action against Scott Yarns, Inc. even though Fleur Sweater Co. did **not** notify Scott Yarns, Inc. of the litigation brought against Fleur by its customers.

UNIT FOUR
NEGOTIABLE INSTRUMENTS

A variety of writings, or documents, are used to expedite commerce and trade. For example, money in the form of currency is used daily by most of us. Recall from the material in Unit Two that many contractual agreements are reduced to writing and often the rights of the parties are assignable. In addition, in order to facilitate the delivery of goods, documents of title are issued, and investment securities, such as stocks and bonds, are issued by business organizations and frequently bought and sold by investors. These writings all represent intangible personal property because a person who is in possession of these forms of writings has rights associated with ownership. Such documents are used in business because of the relative ease in transferring them.

Special kinds of paper, the subject of this unit, are referred to as commercial paper when the documents contain written promises or orders to pay money. Commercial paper is a form of intangible personal property representing contract rights. Commercial paper is easily transferable and is used in order to facilitate the conduct of business. You are probably familiar with checks, having received and used them in paying for goods and services. Checks are one type of commercial paper. In addition, there also are promissory notes, drafts, and certificates of deposit. Instruments such as these have been used in the business community for centuries and are discussed in Chapters 26 through 28. The ways in which funds are transferred and ultimate payments obtained by holders of commercial paper are covered in Chapter 29.

The principles of law governing commercial paper are codified in Article 3 of the Uniform Commercial Code (UCC). Articles 4 and 4A of the UCC deal with the transfer and collection of funds through the facilities of the banking system. Unless otherwise indicated, section citations in the chapters in Unit Four refer to sections in the UCC.

In 1990, substantial revisions were made in Articles 3 and 4 of the UCC. These revisions now have been adopted by most states. The UCC, as reproduced in Appendix C of the textbook, contains the revised versions of Articles 3 and 4 of the Code. References in the textbook and in this *Study Guide* also are to the revised Articles 3 and 4. Important changes in these Articles are pointed out in footnotes in the textbook. These changes are incorporated into the outlines for the chapters in this Unit of the *Study Guide*. (When references are made to such differences in the *Study Guide*, the unrevised UCC section numbers are provided.)

Chapter 26
Basic Concepts, Negotiability, and Transferability

Money is a medium of exchange used for purchasing goods, other forms of property, and services. When the term, money, is used, we usually think of paper currency and coins that are issued by the government. For convenience and safety, other forms of paper also are used in order to facilitate paying for property and services and borrowing funds.

Commercial paper has long been an integral part of business transactions. Centuries ago, commercial paper was used by traders and merchants whose customs and rules became part of the Law Merchant. Later, the Law Merchant was absorbed into the common law and eventually into codified law. Today, these principles of law are codified in all the states of the United States because those states have adopted Article 3 of the Uniform Commercial Code (UCC).

Most of the states have enacted the 1990 revisions of Article 3 of the UCC. Some states have not done so. The UCC, as reproduced in Appendix C, contains the revised version of Article 3. References in the textbook and in this *Study Guide* are to the revised Article 3. Important changes in Article 3 are pointed out in footnotes in the textbook and these changes are incorporated into the outline in this chapter of the *Study Guide*. (When references are made to such differences in the *Study Guide*, the UCC section numbers that are given refer to the unrevised UCC.)

Commercial paper, and particularly negotiable instruments, continue to play an important role in the relatively smooth functioning of business and the economy. The terminology associated with commercial paper and important underlying concepts relating to commercial paper are discussed in the beginning of this chapter.

Commercial paper may be negotiable or nonnegotiable. If commercial paper is not negotiable, the law of contracts applies. For example, when contract rights are assigned, defenses that could have been asserted by the obligor against the obligee (the assignor) also may be raised against the third party (the assignee) to whom the assignment was made. [See Chapter 18.] If the commercial paper is negotiable, unique, special rules that are found in Article 3 of the Code govern the rights and obligations of the parties to the negotiable instrument, as well as other people to whom the instrument may be transferred. As a result of these rules, negotiable promissory notes, certificates of deposit, drafts, and checks are freely transferable. Because negotiable instruments are readily acceptable as substitutes for money and credit, they are more desirable than nonnegotiable commercial paper.

The manner in which commercial paper is transferred depends first of all upon whether the paper is negotiable or nonnegotiable. If commercial paper is negotiable, it is transferred by negotiation; if the paper is nonnegotiable, transfer is by assignment. Negotiation of order paper is by delivery and indorsement. Bearer paper may be negotiated by delivery alone.

As discussed in this chapter, an indorsement has certain characteristics that are not mutually exclusive. Thus, an indorsement indicates (1) how a subsequent negotiation is to be effected (blank or special), (2) limitations on the liability of the indorser (qualified or unqualified), and (3) the type of interest being transferred (restrictive or nonrestrictive).

THINGS TO KEEP IN MIND

1. In order to understand the rules relating to negotiable instruments that are explained in Article 3 of the UCC, it is important to become familiar with the terminology presented in this chapter.

2. Commercial paper is treated as a negotiable instrument when it conforms to certain formal requisites, all of which must be found within the "four corners" of the writing. In order to be treated as a negotiable instrument, the paper must be in writing, signed by the maker or drawer, contain a single, unconditional promise or order to pay a fixed amount of money on demand or at a definite time in the future, and must be payable to the order of a specified, identified payee or to bearer [UCC 3-104(a)].

3. A person who signs his or her name on a negotiable instrument acquires liability to subsequent holders of the instrument.

4. No indorsement can change the negotiable character of commercial paper. If commercial paper is negotiable on its face, it remains a negotiable instrument even though it is transferred.

OUTLINE

I.   Article 3 and its revision.

A. Most of the states have adopted the 1990 revisions of UCC Article 3.

B. Article 4 of the UCC that governs bank deposits and collections of payments also was revised in order to reflect changes in Article 3.

C. Article 3 of the UCC prescribes the form in which commercial paper must be in order for the paper to be treated as a negotiable instrument and explains the rules that will apply when the commercial paper is transferred as well as the rights, obligations, and liability of parties to the negotiable instrument.

D. If commercial paper is negotiable, the paper is referred to as a negotiable instrument (or merely, as an instrument) and those who have possession of the instrument (as opposed to nonnegotiable commercial paper) have "extraordinary" rights; negotiable instruments, therefore, are thought of as having greater value than nonnegotiable commercial paper. [See VI. in this chapter.]

II.   The functions of instruments.

A.   For purposes of convenience and safety, commercial paper (in the form of a check) may be used as a substitute for money in payment of a monetary obligation.

B.   Commercial paper may be used as a credit device.

   1.   A person wishing to extend the time of payment for goods, services, or the use of money (a loan) may give a creditor a written instrument in the form of a promise to pay money or an order to pay money directed to a third person.

   2.   If the creditor wishes to have cash immediately, the creditor may sell the instrument received from the debtor, but the creditor may have to "pay for" the immediate cash by accepting a discount (paying interest in advance).

C.   In order to operate as a substitute for money or credit, the paper must be easily transferable with little danger of not being collectible; negotiable instruments are used for this reason.

III. Types of negotiable instruments.

A.   Negotiable instruments may be classified as orders (checks and drafts) or promises (promissory notes and certificates of deposit) to pay money.

B.   Negotiable instruments may be classified based upon when payment is to be made.

   1.   Demand or sight paper.

      a.   A demand instrument is payable whenever the instrument is presented for payment by the person who properly has possession of the instrument.

      b.   A check, by definition, is payable on demand; funds in checking accounts, therefore, are called demand deposits.

   2.   Time paper is paper that is payable at a time in the future.

C.   Drafts and checks (orders to pay).

   1.   Drafts [UCC 3-104(e)] — A draft is a written order, direction, or command made by one person (the drawer) to another person (the drawee) to pay a sum of money to a third person (the payee).

      a.   In the past, drafts were called bills of exchange.

      b.   Parties to a draft.
         1)   Drawer [UCC 3-103(a)(3)] — The person who issues the paper and directs or orders that a sum of money is to be paid.

        2) Drawee [UCC 3-103(a)(2)] — The person to whom the draft is directed, who is ordered to pay, and who already is, or may become, obligated to the drawer.

        3) Payee — The person to whom the money is to be paid.

        4) One person may be more than one party to a draft. (For example, the drawer also may be the drawee or the payee.)

  c. Time drafts and sight drafts.

        1) A time draft is a draft that is payable at a future time.

        2) A demand (or sight) draft is a draft that is payable when the holder presents the draft for payment. (A draft may be payable at a stated time after sight.)

  d. Drafts are used to collect accounts, to finance purchases of property and services, and to transfer funds.

  e. Types of drafts.

        1) Trade acceptance — A draft that is drawn by (and usually payable to) the seller of goods and is accepted by the buyer who is the drawee.

            a) The seller is the drawer and may also be payee.

            b) The buyer is the drawee who "accepts" (engages or promises that he or she will pay) the draft by placing his or her signature on the face of the paper.

            c) Usually, the draft is a time draft that is payable in the future.

        2) Banker's acceptance — A draft that is drawn on and accepted by a bank.

2. Checks. [See also Chapter 29.]

  a. A check is a demand draft that is drawn on a bank by a drawer (a customer of the bank) who has money on account at the drawee bank [UCC 3-104(f)].

  b. Particular types of checks.

        1) Cashier's check — A check drawn by a bank on itself so that the bank is the drawer and drawee; a cashier's check is treated as being accepted in advance [UCC 3-104(g)].

        2) Teller's check (bank draft) — A draft drawn by one bank on another bank or payable through or at another bank [UCC 3-104(h)].

        3) Traveler's check — An instrument that is designated by the term traveler's check (or a similar term) drawn on a financial institution and that requires the countersignature by the person whose specimen signature appears on the instrument [UCC 3-104(i)].

  c. An instrument may be a check even though it states that it is a "money order" [UCC 3-104(f)].

D. Promissory notes and CDs (promises to pay).

1. A promissory note (or simply, a note) is a written promise, signed by the promisor (the maker), to pay a sum of money to another person at a definite time or on demand [UCC 3-104(e)].

   a. Parties to a promissory note:
      1) Maker — The person who issues, signs, and is making the promise to pay money [UCC 3-103(a)(5)].
      2) Payee — The specified, identified party to whom the promise is made; as an alternative, a note may be issued to bearer.

   b. Promissory notes are substitutes for credit and are used to borrow money, to buy goods and other property, to obtain services, and as evidence of indebtedness.

   c. Types of promissory notes.
      1) Mortgage note — A promise to repay a loan of money that is secured by real property.
      2) Collateral note — A promise to pay money that is secured by personal property. [See Chapter 30.]
      3) Installment note — A promise to pay indebtedness in specified periodic installments.

2. Certificates of deposit (CDs).

   a. A certificate of deposit is an acknowledgment by a bank (the maker) of the receipt of money with a promise to repay the money with interest to the payee [UCC 3-104(j)].

   b. Small CDs are for amounts up to $100,000; large (jumbo) CDs are for amounts over $100,000.

IV. Requirements for negotiability [UCC 3-104(a)].

A. Written form [UCC 3-103(a)(6) and (9)] — The writing must be permanent, preservable, portable, moveable, and tangible.

B. Signatures — The writing must be signed by the maker of the note or CD [UCC 3-103(a)(5)] or the drawer of a draft or check [UCC 3-103(a)(3)].

   1. The word "signed" means any symbol or mark intended by the user to authenticate a writing [UCC 1-201(39)].

   2. A signature is made by the use of any name (which may be a trade name or assumed name) or by any word or mark instead of a written signature [UCC 3-401(b)].

   3. Placement of the signature — The signature need not appear at the bottom right hand corner of the writing (a subscription).

4. Signature by authorized representative — The signature may be placed on the instrument by an agent or other representative who has the authority to act for the maker, drawer, or indorser [UCC 3-401(a) and 3-402]. (See also Chapters 27 and 34.)

C. Unconditional promise or order to pay — The instrument must contain an express, absolute, unequivocal, unconditional promise or order to pay money.

1. Promise or order — UCC 3-103(a)(9) and (6).

   a. Promise — A promise is an express, affirmative undertaking or engagement and is necessary if the instrument is a promissory note.
      1) A mere acknowledgment of indebtedness (as in an IOU), without the inclusion of words such as "due on demand," does not satisfy this requisite.
      2) A certificate of deposit (CD) is a note of a bank in which the bank acknowledges receipt of a sum of money and indicates that the bank promises to repay the sum of money [UCC 3-104(j)].

   b. Order — An express, precise, mandatory instruction, direction, or command to the drawee (who is identified) is necessary if the instrument is a draft or check.

2. Unconditionality of promise or order — The holder (a person in possession of an instrument that is payable to bearer or, if the instrument is payable to an identified person, is that identified person) need not look outside of the paper in order to determine his or her (the holder's) right to payment [UCC 3-104(a) and 3-106].

   a. A promise or order is conditional, and, therefore, the paper is **not negotiable** when it states:
      1) An express condition to payment;
      2) That the promise or order is subject to or governed by another writing; or
      3) That the rights or obligations relating to the promise or order are stated in another writing [UCC 3-106(a)].

   b. A promise or order is not conditional, and, therefore, an instrument is **negotiable** if:
      1) It is subject to implied or constructive conditions, such as good faith.
      2) It states the consideration or transaction which gave rise to the instrument with words such as "as per contract" or "arising out of the sale of goods."
      3) It refers to another separate collateral agreement by using words such as "secured by a mortgage" or "secured by a security interest in certain property" [UCC 3-106(a) and (b)]. (These words make the paper "better.")

   c. Instruments that are payable out of a particular fund or source.

1) The instrument is **negotiable** if it is payable out of a particular fund or source in states that have adopted revised Article 3 [UCC 3-106(b)(ii)].

2) In states that have not adopted the revisions to Article 3, paper is not negotiable if the paper states that it is payable out of a particular fund or source, because payment depends upon the existence and sufficiency of the source of funds [UCC 3-105(2)(b)].

   a) Paper is **not negotiable** if words such as, "payable only from account number 3," "pay out of proceeds of sale," etc., are used.

   b) Paper is **negotiable** if:

   (1) It indicates a particular fund out of which reimbursement is to be made or an account is to be debited.

   (2) It is payable out of a particular fund when the paper is issued by a governmental body or agency to be paid out of specified revenue funds, or when the instrument is issued by a partnership, estate, or trust and is payable only out of that entity's assets.

D. A fixed amount of money — At the time that the holder receives the instrument, the holder must be able to know the present value of the instrument in terms of the existing medium of exchange.

1. The instrument must contain a promise or order to pay a fixed amount of money with regard to the principal [UCC 3-104(a)].

2. If interest is to be paid, the amount or rate of interest may be specified or ascertainable by reference to a statute, formula, or a source described in the instrument, and may be a variable (fluctuating) rate [UCC 3-112(b)].

3. In states that have not adopted the revisions in Article 3, the amount to be paid must be a "sum certain" in money [UCC 3-104(1)(b) and 3-106].

   a. At the time that the holder receives the instrument, the holder must be able to ascertain from the face the exact minimum amount that the holder will receive when the instrument is paid; and

   b. At the time or maturity, the holder must be able to determine the definite sum that the holder will be paid. The exact sum to be paid must be stated or capable of being made certain by computation from the face of the instrument.

   c. An instrument is negotiable if the instrument provides that it is to be paid:

   1) With stated interest or in stated installments.

      a) **Negotiable** if the instrument states that it is:

      (1) Payable with interest at the contract (lawful) rate or at the judgment or legal rate, if the statutory rate is not a fluctuating rate. (In some states (e.g., New York), unrevised UCC 3-106 has been amended to provide that an otherwise negotiable instrument is not nonnegotiable if it provides for

the payment of interest at a variable rate.)

    (2) Payable with interest, which is interpreted as the statutory legal (judgment) rate of interest [UCC 3-118(d)].

    b) **Nonnegotiable** if the instrument states that interest is to be payable at "prevailing" or "current bank rate."

2) With different stated interest rates before and after default or on a specified date; or

3) With reasonable court costs and attorney fees upon default in those states that permit such clauses; or

4) With a stated discount or additional sum if payment is made before or after the date fixed for payment.

4. Payable in money.

    a. Money is the "medium of exchange authorized or adopted by a domestic or foreign government as a part of its currency" [UCC 1-201(24)].

    b. If an instrument is payable in foreign currency, the instrument may be payable in equivalent United States dollars [UCC 3-107].

    c. If commercial paper provides for payment in a commodity (other than money) instead of or in addition to money, the paper is not negotiable.

E. Payable on demand or at a definite time.

1. Payable on demand — Payment is required whenever the instrument is presented for payment by the holder [UCC 3-108(a)].

    a. An instrument may specify that it is payable "at sight," "on demand," or "on presentment."

    b. If no date of payment is stipulated in an instrument, the instrument is payable on demand.

2. Payable at a definite time [UCC 3-108(b)] — The holder must be able to determine the latest possible date on which the instrument will be paid.

    a. An instrument is negotiable "if it is payable on elapse of a definite period of time after sight or acceptance or at a fixed date or dates or at a time or times readily ascertainable at the time the promise or order is issued, subject to rights of (1) prepayment, (2) acceleration, (3) extension at the option of the holder, or (4) extension to a further definite time at the option of the maker or acceptor or automatically upon or after a specified act or event" [UCC 3-108(b)].

    b. Acceleration clause — The instrument may state that the time for payment will be accelerated (advanced) upon the happening of some event, such as the failure of the obligor (who usually is the maker of a note) to make a payment of interest or an installment that is due.

    c. Extension clause — The instrument may state that the time for payment may be extended:
      1) To another stated date so that the outer limit of the time for payment is known. (Think of the instrument as being payable at the date to which it may be extended, but subject to acceleration to the earlier stated date.)
      2) At the option of the holder with no outer limit stated. (Think of the instrument as being demand paper after the specified maturity date.)

    d. An instrument is **not negotiable**:
      1) If it is payable upon the happening of an event the date of which is not certain (such as the arrival of a ship or death of a named person).
      2) If it is payable at a definite stated time, but the obligor (maker or drawee) has the option of indefinitely extending the date of payment.

F. Payable to order or to bearer — The words of negotiability.

  1. Order instrument.

    a. An order instrument is one that is payable to the order of an identified person or to an identified person or his or her order [UCC 3-109(b)].

    b. A promise or order to pay money is an order instrument on its face if it states:
      1) Pay to the order of a identified, specified payee (who may be the maker, drawee, or drawer); or pay to a named payee or his, her, or its order.
      2) Pay to the order of multiple payees together (jointly) or in the alternative.
      3) Pay to the order of an estate, trust, partnership, unincorporated association, etc.

  2. Bearer instrument.

    a. A bearer instrument is one that does not designate a specific payee [UCC 3-109(a)].

    b. A promise or order to pay money is a bearer instrument on its face if it states:
      1) Pay to bearer; pay to order of bearer; or pay to the order of an identified person or bearer (or his or hers assigns).
      2) Pay to cash or payroll or a similar designation.

    c. A bearer is any person who has physical possession of an instrument that is payable on the instrument's face to anyone, without a specific designation, or an instrument that has been indorsed to bearer or in blank. (A blank indorsement consists of only the indorser's signature.)

G. If an instrument is a draft or check, the drawee must be identified.

V.   Factors not affecting negotiability.

    A. An instrument is negotiable even though the instrument:

        1. Does not state the date of issue, unless such date is necessary in order to determine the date upon which payment is due [UCC 3-113(b)].

        2. Is postdated or antedated [UCC3-113(a)].

        3. Omits a statement of the consideration or the place where the instrument was drawn or is payable [UCC 3-111].

        4. Contains a statement that collateral is given [UCC 3-104(a)(3)(i) and 3-106(b)].

    B. Rules of interpretation.

        1. If there is a conflict between typewritten and preprinted words, the typewritten words control. If there is a conflict between handwritten words and those that are typed or preprinted, the handwritten words control [UCC 3-114].

        2. If there is a conflict between words and symbols, such as numbers that represent the words, the words control [UCC 3-114].

        3. If no place of payment is specified, an instrument is payable at the maker's or drawee's place of business or, when the maker or drawee has no place of business, at the maker's residence [UCC 3-111].

        4. If an instrument provides that the instrument is payable with interest, but the rate or an amount is not specified, the instrument is payable with interest at the judgment rate [UCC 3-112(b)].

    C. A promise or order, other than a check, containing a conspicuous statement that it is not negotiable or is not governed by Article 3, is not a negotiable instrument [UCC 3-104(d)]. (This is not true under unrevised Article 3.)

VI.   Transfer by assignment or negotiation.

    A. Transfer by assignment — The transfer of a nonnegotiable instrument is an assignment of contract rights. [See Chapter 18.]

        1. The transferor is an assignor and the transferee is an assignee.

        2. The delivery of nonnegotiable paper by a payee to another person is an assignment [UCC3-203(b)]; thereafter, an assignee may make a sub-assignment in order to transfer his or her rights to another person.

3. When a nonnegotiable instrument becomes due and payable, the obligor (i.e., the maker of a promissory note or the drawer of a draft) may raise any defenses, which the obligor could have asserted against the original obligee/assignor (usually the payee), against the assignee.

B. Transfer by negotiation.

1. In addition to being an assignment, the proper transfer of a negotiable instrument in order to make the recipient a holder is referred to as a negotiation [UCC 3-201(a)].

   a. A holder is the person who has possession of a negotiable instrument that is payable to bearer or, if the instrument is payable to an identified person, is that identified person [UCC 1-201(20)].

   b. A holder who is a holder in due course (HDC) may have more rights than his or her transferor.
      1) An HDC is a good faith holder to whom a negotiable instrument was transferred for value; who took the instrument without notice that the instrument was overdue or had been dishonored or that there were claims to or defenses against the instrument; and against whom certain defenses cannot be raised. [See Chapter 27.]
      2) When the negotiable instrument becomes due and payable, the obligor (the maker of a promissory note or the drawer of a draft) may not raise some of the defenses against the HDC which the obligor could have asserted against the original obligee (usually the payee).

   c. If a negotiable instrument is not properly negotiated, the transfer of the instrument is an assignment of rights, and any defenses that could have been asserted against the original maker of a note or the drawer of a draft may be raised against the transferee/holder.

2. A negotiation is a transfer that results in the transferee being a holder, a person in possession of a negotiable instrument, drawn or issued to his or her order or to bearer, or indorsed to him or her, or to his or her order, or to bearer, or in blank [UCC 1-201(20)].

3. The manner in which negotiation is effected depends upon whether the negotiable instrument is order or bearer paper [UCC 3-201].

   a. Issue of the instrument by maker or drawer — The rights of the parties to the initial transfer of an instrument (from the original maker or drawer to the person to whom the maker or drawer intended to be the recipient) are governed by contract law.

   b. Negotiating order instruments — An order instrument is negotiated by a physical delivery and a necessary indorsement by the transferor (who may be the payee or a prior indorsee to whom the instrument was specially indorsed) [UCC 3-201(b)].

   c. Negotiating bearer instruments — A bearer instrument is negotiated by a
       physical delivery; an indorsement is not necessary [UCC 3-201(b)].

   d. Converting order instruments to bearer instruments and vice versa
       [UCC 3-205].
       1) An instrument payable to an identified (named) payee and indorsed to
           bearer or indorsed in blank becomes bearer paper.
       2) An instrument that is bearer paper on its face, or, because of an
           indorsement is bearer paper, becomes order paper if it is specially
           indorsed to an identified, named person.
       3) Indorsements are discussed in the following section [VII.].

VII. Indorsements.

   A. An indorsement consists of a signature with or without additional words or
       statements; usually, an indorsement is written on the back of the instrument.

       1. When there is no space for an indorsement, an indorsement is effective if the
           indorsement is written on an *allonge*, a separate piece of paper that is firmly
           affixed to the original instrument [UCC 3-204(a)].

       2. An indorser is a transferor of the paper (such as a payee) who signs his or
           her name on the back and delivers the paper to another person.

       3. An indorsee is a transferee to whom or to whose order the paper is payable
           after the paper is indorsed.

       4. Order instruments — If an instrument is order paper, because the instrument
           is payable to the order of a named payee or to a specified indorsee, the payee
           or indorsee must indorse the instrument in order for the negotiation of the
           instrument to be effective so as to transfer the rights of the payee or indorsee
           to a transferee who will have the rights of a holder.

       5. Bearer instruments — If an instrument is bearer paper, an indorsement is not
           necessary for negotiation, but the transferee may request that his or her
           transferor indorse the instrument.

       6. An indorser can change the method required in order to transfer or negotiate
           an instrument by the indorsement that the indorser uses, but cannot change
           the negotiable character of the paper with an indorsement.

       7. A person who indorses an instrument usually becomes secondarily liable to
           subsequent holders.

           a. In general, an indorser is liable to pay a subsequent holder, if a primarily
               liable party does not pay.

           b. A person who indorses without indicating that he or she is indorsing in a
               representative capacity is liable in his or her individual capacity.

B. Types of indorsements — The indorsement determines the manner in which paper is transferred or negotiated in the future (blank or special), what rights are transferred (restrictive or nonrestrictive), and limitations on the liability of the indorser (qualified or unqualified).

1. Blank indorsements [UCC 3-205(b)].

   a. A blank indorsement consists of the signature of the holder or person who has possession of the instrument.

   b. After an instrument is indorsed in blank, the instrument is bearer paper and may be further negotiated by delivery alone.

2. Special indorsements [UCC 3-205].

   a. A special indorsement indicates a specific person to whom the indorser intends to make the instrument payable.
      1) A special indorsement consists of words, such as "Pay to the order of" the specified person, or "Pay to" the specified person, followed by the signature of the indorser [UCC 3-205(a)].
      2) After an instrument is specially indorsed, the instrument is order paper and further negotiation is by delivery and indorsement of the specified indorsee [UCC 3-205(b)].

   b. Bearer paper can be changed to order paper by using a special indorsement, and order paper can be changed to bearer paper by using a blank indorsement.

   c. If order paper is transferred for value without an indorsement, the transferee is treated as an assignee, but has the right to have the indorsement of the transferor [UCC 3-203(c)].

3. Qualified indorsements [UCC 3-415(b)].

   a. Indorser writes "without recourse" above his or her signature so that the indorser has limited liability to subsequent holders.
      1) A qualified indorser transfers title to the instrument, but does not guarantee payment of the instrument.
      2) A qualified indorsement is accompanied by a special or blank indorsement.

   b. Usually, an indorsement is unqualified; the indorser makes a blank or special indorsement without using qualifying words, signs his or her signature, and is secondarily liable to subsequent holders.

4. Restrictive indorsements [UCC 3-206].

a. A restrictive indorsement restricts, or conditions, the rights of the indorsee, but does not prevent further transfer of the instrument or change the obligations of the party who created the paper.

b. A restrictive indorsement does not destroy the negotiable character of an instrument. (Notice that, if the issuer of the paper imposes similar restrictions or conditions on the face of the instrument, the paper is not a negotiable instrument.)

c. A transferee from an indorsee, whose rights are restricted by a restrictive indorsement, must comply with the direction in the indorsement.

d. An indorsement prohibiting further transfer (e.g., "Pay Ace only") is interpreted as a special indorsement [UCC 3-206(a)].

e. Conditional indorsement [UCC 3-206(b)] — The rights of the indorsee are subject to the happening of some event; for example, "Pay Ace only if Ace (the indorsee) delivers the merchandise."

f. Indorsement for deposit or collection [UCC 3-206(c)] results in the indorsee (usually a bank) being an agent for purposes of obtaining payment for the indorser.

g. Trust indorsement [UCC 3-206(d)] — Payment to the indorsee must be consistent with the restriction.

h. If no conditions or restrictions are imposed upon the indorsee, the indorsement is nonrestrictive.

C. Miscellaneous indorsement problems.

1. Correction of name — If the name of the indorsee is misspelled, the indorsee may negotiate the instrument by indorsing in the misspelled name, the correctly spelled name, or both [UCC 3-204(d)].

2. Multiple payees [UCC 3-110(d)].

a. If an instrument is payable to multiple persons in the alternative (e.g., "Payable to order of A or B"), all that is necessary is that one of the payees indorse.

b. If an instrument is payable jointly (e.g., "Pay to order of A and B"), all of the payees must indorse.

4. Agents and officers [UCC 3-110(c)].

a. An instrument that is drawn or indorsed payable to an estate, partnership, unincorporated association, etc., may be indorsed by an authorized representative of the organization.

b. An instrument that is payable to a public officer by his or her title can be negotiated by the person who currently is holding the office.

Note: Letters of credit, which are covered in UCC Article 5, frequently are used in financing international sales transactions [See Chapter 23 at V.] and also are used in domestic transactions in order to assure performance of contractual obligations.

KEY WORDS AND PHRASES IN TEXT

revised Article 3 of the UCC
negotiable instrument
nonnegotiable commercial paper
functions of instruments
      (substitute for money or credit)
order to pay (draft or check)
demand instrument
demand deposit
issue (first delivery of instrument)
drawer, drawee and payee of draft
      or check
time drafts and sight drafts
acceptance
trade acceptance
banker's acceptance
cashier's check
teller's check
traveler's check
promises to pay (promissory notes and
      certificates of deposit (CDs))
maker and payee of note or CD
mortgage note
collateral note
installment note
transfer of nonnegotiable paper
      by assignment
transfer of negotiable instruments
      by negotiation
transferor
transferee
holder
holder in due course (HDC)
requirements for a negotiable
      instrument
writing that has permanence and
      portability
signature of the maker or drawer

unconditional promise or order
references to other agreements
payment out of a particular fund
statement that instrument is secured
fixed amount of money
variable rate of interest
payable on demand or at a definite time
presentment
acceleration clause
holder
extension clause
payable to order
order instrument
payable to bearer
bearer instrument
transfer by assignment
negotiation of negotiable instrument
negotiating order paper by
      indorsement and delivery
negotiating bearer paper by delivery
converting order paper to bearer paper
converting bearer paper to order paper
indorsement
allonge
indorser and indorsee
blank indorsement
special indorsement
qualified indorsement (without recourse)
restrictive indorsement
indorsement prohibiting further
      indorsement or transfer
conditional indorsement
indorsement for deposit or for collection
trust indorsement
instrument payable in the alternative
instrument payable jointly

FILL-IN QUESTIONS

1.   A draft is commercial paper that contains a written _____ to pay money.
      A check is a special form of draft that is payable on _____ and is drawn
      on a drawee that is a _____.

2.   Trade acceptances frequently are used in order to finance the purchase of goods. A
      trade acceptance is a draft that is accepted by the buyer, who is the _____ of
      the draft and who is referred to as the acceptor after the draft has been accepted. The
      seller of the goods is often both the _____ and the _____ of a
      trade acceptance.

3.   A promissory note is a written _____ to pay a sum of money. The person
      who issues the promissory note is the _____. The identified person to
      whom a promissory note is payable is referred to as the _____.

4.   Promissory notes and drafts may be payable _____ or at a future time.
      If promissory notes and drafts are payable in the future these writings are referred to
      as _____.

5.   You are given the following instrument:

> At sight I promise to pay to the order of
> John Jones the sum of $300.
>
> *Mary Smith*

      The instrument is a promissory _____. Mary Smith is the _____.
      The payee is _____. Because the instrument is not payable at a future
      time, the instrument is a _____ instrument.

6.   You are given the following instrument:

> January 6, 1998
>
> Pay to the order of bearer the sum of Two Hundred
> Dollars ($200.00) on January 6, 2001.
>
> To: Ben Beier
>   2002 Pine Street
>   Oil Town, OK
>
> *David DeVito*
> David DeVito

The instrument is a _____. The drawer is _____ and the drawee is _____. Because the instrument is not payable to an identified, named person, the instrument is _____ paper. The instrument is _____ paper because the instrument is payable on a fixed date in the future.

7.　Section 3-104(a) of the UCC provides that in order for an instrument to be negotiable the instrument must be in writing, signed by the _____ (if the instrument is a promissory note or certificate of deposit) or the _____ (if the instrument is a draft or a check), contain an unconditional promise (if the instrument is a promissory note) or _____ (if the instrument is a draft or check) to pay a fixed amount of _____ on demand or at a _____, and be payable to order of a named payee or to _____. A draft and a check must indicate the name of the _____, to whom the order to pay is directed.

8.　You are given the following instrument:

> Theodore Peters
> Atlanta, Georgia
>
> Pay to John Jonry the sum of fifty-four dollars ($54.00).
> *Sarah Peters*

The instrument satisfies the following requirements for negotiability: The instrument is in writing, _____ , contains an _____ to pay a _____ of money on _____. The instrument, however, is not negotiable because _____.

9.　You are given the following instrument:

> On June 3, 2000, I promise to pay to the order of N. Barnes five hundred dollars ($500.00), this note being payable out of the proceeds of the sale of my 1928 antique Ford automobile.
>
> *Thomas Edsel*
> Thomas Edsel

The instrument satisfies the following requirements for negotiability: _____
_____
_____

_____; but it is

not negotiable under the provisions of **unrevised** Article 3 because the commercial paper does not contain _____
_____. In states that have adopted the revised Article 3 of the UCC, the instrument is negotiable.

10.   You are given the following instrument:

> August 18, 1998
>
> I, *Suzanna Smart*, of Nenna, Alaska promise
> to pay to the order of Lucy Loring the sum of
> Three Thousand Dollars ($3,000.00) four months
> after ten or more inches of snow falls again in
> Fairbanks, Alaska.

This instrument satisfies the following requirements for negotiability: _____
_____
_____
_____; but it is not negotiable because
_____
_____
_____.

11.   A negotiable instrument is transferred by _____. An instrument that is payable on its face to the order of an identified payee is order paper and is negotiated by the identified payee by delivery of the instrument with an _____. In order to negotiate the instrument, the payee must place his, her, or its _____ on the instrument.

12.   A _____ is a person who is in possession of a negotiable instrument that has been issued to his, her, or its order, or to bearer, or specially indorsed to his, her, or its order, or to him, her, or it, or to bearer, or in blank.

13.   A blank indorsement consists of merely the _____ of the payee or indorser. In order to negotiate the instrument to another person, all that is necessary is a _____ of the instrument.

14.   A _____ indorsement indicates the person to whom the indorser intends to make a negotiable instrument payable. In order for the indorsee further to negotiate the instrument, he, she, or it must place his, her, or its _____ on the instrument. If the indorser merely signs the instrument, the paper is then considered to be bearer paper and may be negotiated by _____ alone. If the indorser specifies to whom the instrument is to be paid, the paper is then considered to be order paper and may be negotiated by _____
_____.

16.   You are given the following instrument:

```
┌──────────────────────────────────────────────┐
│                                                │
│   Pay to the order of Lori Low ------- $43.00  │
│   Forty-three and 00/100 ------------- dollars │
│                                                │
│   Amalgamated Bank                             │
│   New Woking, MD      Howard L. Low            │
│                       ────────────────         │
│                       Howard L. Low            │
│                                                │
└──────────────────────────────────────────────┘
```

Write the appropriate indorsement in order to transfer the instrument to Tom Trustee for the benefit of Benny Fishiary: _____ _____. Write the appropriate indorsement in order to transfer the instrument from Tom Trustee to Henry Hunt so that the instrument becomes bearer paper: _____ _____. Write the appropriate indorsement so that Henry Hunt can deposit or cash the check at his bank: _____.

MULTIPLE CHOICE QUESTIONS

1.   A draft is:
     A. a collateral note.
     B. a time instrument.
     C. payable to bearer.
     D. a three party instrument.

2.   The drawee of a check is:
     A. the one who writes the check.
     B. the person cashing the check.
     C. a bank.
     D. a bank or other person.

3.   An essential difference between a draft and a promissory note is:
     A. a promissory note is payable on a specific date.
     B. a draft is payable to a specific person.
     C. the drawer and drawee of a draft have a debtor-creditor relationship.
     D. two or more persons are required to sign a promissory note.

4.   Little owes Adams money. Instead of Adams being paid the money, the money is to be paid to Brown. The draft will be signed on its face by:
     A. Adams.
     B. Little.
     C. Brown.
     D. Little and Adams.

5. Smith made a contract to purchase a washing machine on credit from the Acme Appliance Co. He signed a paper in which he stated that he promised to pay $350, the purchase price, in six months from the date of the writing. This paper also stated that the paper was secured by the washing machine. Acme Appliance Co. transferred the paper to Easy Finance Corp., which paid Acme eighty percent of the face value. Smith was notified that Easy Finance Corp. was now in possession of the paper.
    A. The instrument was discounted by Easy Finance Corp.
    B. The instrument was a mortgage draft.
    C. The drawer of the instrument was Acme Appliance Co.
    D. The drawee of the instrument was Easy Finance Corp.

6. The following writing is given to you:

    > To Jessica Petry:
    >
    > Pay to Sherry Rider fifty dollars ($50.00)
    >
    > *Chris Petry*

    A. It is an example of a negotiable demand draft.
    B. It is an example of a negotiable bill of exchange.
    C. It is an example of a nonnegotiable promissory note.
    D. It is an example of a nonnegotiable sight draft.

Questions 7 and 8 are based on the following fact situation: Betty Barnes ordered merchandise for her art supply store located in Baltimore from Sam's Best Paints, Inc. in New York City. The merchandise was shipped by Sam's Best Paints, Inc. Sam's Best Paints, Inc.'s bank has sent a bill of lading covering the shipment and the following document to Betty Barnes' bank.

February 2, 19xx

Betty Barnes
Betty's Art Shop
Baltimore, Maryland

Sixty days from date pay to the order of Sam's Paints, Inc. Five Thousand and 00/100 Dollars ($5,000).

Accepted at Baltimore, Maryland
on February *9*, 19xx   Sam's Best Paints, Inc.

by _____*Betty Barnes*_____   by____*Sam Evans*____.
Payable at Second National Bank of Baltimore   Sam Evans, President

---

Betty Barnes' bank notified her of the bank's receipt of the document and asked her to come to the bank's main office in order to sign the document, which she did.

7. The document is:
   A. a sight draft.
   B. a trade acceptance.
   C. a time check.
   D. a banker's acceptance.

8. Sam's Best Paints, Inc. is:
   A. the drawer and drawee. Betty Barnes is the payee and became the acceptor when she signed the instrument.
   B. the payee. Sam Evans, a natural person, is the drawer and Betty Barnes is the drawee.
   C. the drawer and payee. Betty Barnes' bank is the drawee and Betty Barnes became the acceptor when she signed the draft.
   D. the drawer and payee. Betty Barnes was the drawee and became the acceptor when she signed the draft.

9. The signature of the maker of a negotiable promissory note must appear:
   A. on the instrument.
   B. in ink.
   C. as a subscription.
   D. in the lower right hand corner.

10. When no time of payment is specified in a promissory note, the note is payable:
    A. on demand.
    B. within a reasonable period of time.
    C. within one year.
    D. thirty days after issue.

11. The following paper is given to you:

Pay to the order of Peter Squires or bearer $33.00

To: Ricardo Carey
      5487 Main Street

Thomas O'Toole

   A. It is an example of a negotiable check.
   B. It is an example of a nonnegotiable check.
   C. It is an example of a nonnegotiable time draft.
   D. It is an example of a negotiable sight draft.

12.   The negotiability of an instrument is destroyed if the instrument contains the terms:
      A. this note is secured by a chattel mortgage dated June 4, 1997.
      B. this note is subject to the terms of a mortgage dated September 22, 1997.
      C. this check is given in payment of rent for June.
      D. this instrument is given as per agreement entered on the date of issue.

13.   A so-called "I.O.U." is:
      A. a draft.
      B. a promissory note.
      C. order paper.
      D. an acknowledgment of an obligation.

14.   The following words in a promissory note would destroy negotiability:
      A. subject to our agreement of October 2, 1997.
      B. payment for five crates of oranges.
      C. payable in three monthly installments.
      D. together with interest at the legal rate.

15.   A check that is payable "to the order of U.S. Treasurer" is:
      A. **not** negotiable because the check is not payable to an identified person's order or to bearer.
      B. a negotiable order check.
      C. a negotiable bearer check.
      D. treated as time paper.

16.   The negotiability of an otherwise negotiable promissory note is affected by:
      A. post-dating the note.
      B. a clause authorizing payment in silver.
      C. a clause authorizing payment in Mexican pesos.
      D. a clause providing for acceleration of payment.

17.   An order instrument;
      A. is merely an assignment.
      B. may be changed to bearer paper by indorsement.
      C. may be negotiated without an indorsement.
      D. is payable to bearer.

18.   An indorsement that specifies the person to whom the instrument is payable:
      A. changes order paper to bearer paper.
      B. is a restrictive indorsement.
      C. is a special indorsement.
      D. cannot be transferred subsequently to another person.

19.   Delivery and indorsement are the two elements of a valid negotiation for:
      A. negotiable instruments.
      B. commercial paper.
      C. order instruments.
      D. bearer instruments.

20. A qualified indorsement is best epitomized by the words:
    A. For deposit only.
    B. Without recourse.
    C. Pay to the order of an identified person.
    D. Any of the above.

21. The payee of a check signed his name on the back and wrote, "Pay to Richard Roe." This indorsement is:
    A. a qualified, nonrestrictive, blank indorsement.
    B. an unqualified, nonrestrictive, special indorsement.
    C. an unqualified, restrictive, special indorsement.
    D. an unqualified, nonrestrictive, blank indorsement.

22. The last indorsement on the back of a check reads, "Arthur's Annex, for collection only." This indorsement is:
    A. a qualified, nonrestrictive, blank indorsement.
    B. a qualified, restrictive, blank indorsement.
    C. an unqualified, restrictive, special indorsement.
    D. an unqualified, restrictive, blank indorsement.

23. "John Doe, without recourse" is written on the back of a promissory note. This indorsement is:
    A. a qualified, nonrestrictive, blank indorsement.
    B. a qualified, restrictive, blank indorsement.
    C. an unqualified, restrictive, blank indorsement.
    D. an indorsement that will prevent the further negotiation of the note.

MATCHING QUESTIONS

A. You are given the following instrument:

Front		Back

To: Pure Bank
      Upton, VT

                        April 5, 19xx

Pay to the order of Monroe West --------- $1,500.00
One Thousand Five Hundred and 00/100 - - Dollars
on May 1, 19xx.

                  Woodrow Fields
                  Woodrow Fields

Monroe West

Pay to Carrie Larr
T. Keaton

Without Recourse
Carrie Larr

For each item in the left hand column, select the correct answer from the list in the right hand column. An answer may be selected once, more than once, or not at all.

1.	The instrument is a (type of instrument) _____	A. Bearer paper
2.	The instrument is (negotiability) _____	B. Blank
3.	West's indorsement makes the instrument (type of instrument) _____	C. Check
4.	Keaton's indorsement makes the instrument (type of instrument) _____	D. Draft
5.	Larr's indorsement makes the instrument (type of instrument) _____	E. Negotiable
6.	West's indorsement would be (type of indorsement) _____	F. Nonnegotiable
7.	Keaton's indorsement would be (type of indorsement) _____	G. Note
8.	Larr's indorsement would be (type of indorsement) _____	H. Order paper

1. The instrument is a (type of instrument) _____
2. The instrument is (negotiability) _____
3. West's indorsement makes the instrument (type of instrument) _____
4. Keaton's indorsement makes the instrument (type of instrument) _____
5. Larr's indorsement makes the instrument (type of instrument) _____
6. West's indorsement would be (type of indorsement) _____
7. Keaton's indorsement would be (type of indorsement) _____
8. Larr's indorsement would be (type of indorsement) _____

A. Bearer paper
B. Blank
C. Check
D. Draft
E. Negotiable
F. Nonnegotiable
G. Note
H. Order paper
I. Qualified
J. Special
K. Restrictive

(These questions are adapted from objective question # 81 through # 88 on the Uniform CPA Examination, November 1994.)

B. John Adams has possession of an instrument. The face looks like this:

```
                                              9/5/98
   To:    Simone Burns
          18 Oak Street
          Peru, Indiana

   Three years from date, pay to the order of
   Peter Hanks Five Hundred Dollars ($500.00)


                           Jeffrey Smith
                           Jeffrey Smith
```

Select from the list in the right hand column the title that is most appropriate for each person who is named in questions 9 through 12.

9. Simone Burns _____
10. Peter Hanks _____
11. Jeffrey Smith _____
12. John Adams _____

A. Maker
B. Drawer
C. Drawee
D. Payee
E. Holder
F. Assignee

C.   The back of the instrument that John Adams has in his possession looks like this:

```
┌─────────────────────────────┐
│                             │
│     Peter Hanks             │
│                             │
│     Pay to Henry Hue        │
│     Julie Jones             │
│                             │
│     Henry Hue               │
│     without recourse        │
│                             │
│ /\/\/\/\/\/\/\/\/\/\/\/\/\  │
└─────────────────────────────┘
```

Select from the list in the right hand column the type of indorsement that each of the persons named in questions 13 through 15 has made.

13.   Peter Hanks   _____   A.   Special, restrictive indorsement
14.   Julie Jones   _____   B.   Qualified, blank indorsement
15.   Henry Hue   _____   C.   Qualified, special indorsement
                              D.   Nonrestrictive, blank indorsement
                              E.   Unqualified special indorsement

Chapter 27
Holder in Due Course and Defenses

Because a holder in due course of a negotiable instrument has greater rights than a person who is simply a holder, it is important that you be able to recognize whether or not a particular holder of an instrument is a holder in due course. As explained in the first part of the chapter, a holder in due course (an HDC) is a holder who takes a negotiable instrument for value, in good faith, and without notice that the instrument is overdue, has been dishonored, or that there are defenses or claims that may be asserted against the instrument.

A party to commercial paper who is obligated to pay may have one or more defenses that can be raised against a holder seeking payment of the instrument. If the holder is a holder in due course, certain defenses, which are called personal (or limited) defenses, cannot be successfully asserted against the holder in due course. Other defenses that are referred to as universal (or real) defenses, are available against all holders, including holders in due course. These defenses are the subject matter of the final portion of the chapter.

THINGS TO KEEP IN MIND

Before a determination can be made that a person in a holder in due course, it is necessary to ascertain whether or not the commercial paper is a negotiable instrument. If the paper is not negotiable, the person who has possession of the paper cannot be a holder. If the paper is a negotiable instrument, the next question to be asked is whether or not the person having possession of the negotiable instrument is a holder? A holder is a person who has possession of a negotiable instrument that either (1) is a bearer instrument or (2) is an order instrument payable to an identified person, and the person who has possession of the instrument is the identified person.

A person who is not a holder cannot be a holder in due course. If commercial paper is nonnegotiable, the payee or indorsee is not a holder. Even if commercial paper is negotiable, a person who possesses the paper, gave value for it, took it in good faith, and had no notice of any defects, may not be a holder. For example, a note may be payable to the order of an identified, named payee but may not have been indorsed by the payee, or the last indorsement may be a special indorsement, but the indorsee to whom the instrument was made payable may not have indorsed the instrument. A person, other than the identified payee or the identified person to whom the instrument was specially indorsed, is not a holder and, therefore, cannot be a holder in due course.

OUTLINE

I. Holder versus holder in due course.

    A. Holder — A person in possession of a negotiable instrument that is payable to bearer or payable to the identified person who possesses the instrument [UCC 1-201(20)] so that the person is entitled to enforce the instrument (e.g., receive payment) [UCC 3-301].

        1. If there are no indorsements, the person who has possession of a negotiable instrument that is payable to bearer or to whose order the instrument is drawn is a holder. (An original party to the issuance of an instrument, such as the payee, therefore, may be a holder.)

        2. If the instrument has been indorsed, the person who has possession of the instrument, which is indorsed to bearer or in blank or which is specially indorsed to that person or to that person's order, is a holder.

        3. A holder has the right to:

            a. Transfer or negotiate the instrument.

            b. Receive payment when it is due or, if the instrument is demand paper, when it is presented for payment.

            c. Assert any rights that his or her transferor might have asserted. (This is so because a holder has the status of an assignee.)

    B. Holder in due course (HDC).

        1. An HDC is a holder of a negotiable instrument who takes the instrument for value, in good faith, and without notice that the instrument is overdue or that it has been dishonored, or that any person has a defense against the instrument or a claim to it [UCC 3-302(a)].

        2. The instrument must be a negotiable instrument and the person who is seeking HDC status must be a holder.

        3. An HDC acquires a higher level of immunity to defenses against payment of the instrument or claims of ownership by other parties than does a person who is merely a holder.

II. Requirements for HDC status [UCC 3-302].

    A. A person who is asserting that he or she is an HDC must first be a holder.

    B. Taking for value [UCC 3-303].

1. Value must actually be given at the time that the instrument is acquired, rather than promised, unlike consideration for an informal contract.

2. A donee who receives an instrument as a gift does not give value.

3. Value is given by performing (executing) the promise for which the instrument was issued or transferred.

   a. A holder takes an instrument for value to the extent the agreed-upon consideration has been performed.

   b. Consideration may be services rendered, property sold, or money (not necessarily the face amount of the instrument).

   c. The adequacy of the consideration is immaterial. (The question of adequacy may, however, go to the issue of whether or not the holder took the instrument in good faith.)

4. A holder takes an instrument for value to the extent that he or she acquired a security interest in or a lien on the instrument (other than a lien obtained in a judicial proceeding).

5. Antecedent claim — Value is given if an instrument is given in payment of an antecedent (preexisting) debt or claim.

6. Negotiable instrument as value — Value is given if an instrument is exchanged for a negotiable instrument or if an irrevocable commitment is made to a third person.

7. Check deposits and withdrawals.

   a. A bank gives value to the extent that the bank has a security interest in an instrument [UCC 4-211].

   b. A depositary bank may be an HDC because the bank has a security interest as a result of the following transactions:
      1) A holder deposits a check drawn on another bank (the drawee) in the holder's account at a depositary bank, which credits the holder's account for the amount of the check.
      2) The holder then issues a check for an amount that is greater than the amount in the holder's account if the check [referred to above in 1)] was not included.
      3) The check [referred to above in 1)] is returned by the drawee bank to the holder's depositary bank rather than "paid" or "credited" by the drawee bank.
      4) To the extent that the holder has withdrawn funds relating to the deposited (and later returned) check, the depositary bank has given value because the bank has a security interest.

5) In determining the amount of value given by the depositary bank, UCC 4-210(b) prescribes that the "first-in, first-out" (FIFO) rule applies, so that the "first-money-in" is presumed to be the "first-money-out."

6) The depositary bank gives value for an amount equal to the amount in the holder's account before the check in question [referred to above in 1)] was deposited, less the amount of the returned check.

8. Special situations [UCC 3-302(c)] — Sufficient value is **not** given if a holder acquired the instrument:

a. At a judicial sale or under legal process;

b. In taking over an estate (as an executor or administrator); or

c. As part of a bulk transfer which was not in the ordinary course of business.

C. Taking in good faith.

1. Good faith is "honesty in fact and the observance of reasonable commercial standards of fair dealing" [UCC 3-103(a)(4)].

2. A holder takes the instrument in good faith (and, therefore, may be an HDC) if at the time that the holder acquires the instrument, the holder acts honestly and subjectively believes that the instrument is regular, even if a more prudent person would have been suspicious or put on notice that something was wrong [UCC 1-201(19)].

3. If the consideration given by the holder is "inadequate" relative to the purported value of the instrument, the holder does not take the instrument in good faith.

D. Taking without notice (of certain defects) [UCC 1-201(25), 3-302] — The holder must have taken the instrument without notice that the instrument was overdue, that the instrument had been dishonored, or that there was an uncured (uncorrected) default with respect to another instrument issued as part of the series, that the instrument contained an unauthorized signature or had been altered, or that there was a defense against the instrument or a claim to it.

1. What constitutes notice?

a. A holder cannot be an HDC if, at the time when the holder acquired the instrument, the holder had notice of certain specified defects.

b. Notice includes actual knowledge, receipt of notification, or having knowledge of available facts or circumstances, such that the holder should have known certain things. (Knowledge, therefore, may be imputed or implied.)

2. Overdue instruments — Holder must have taken the instrument without notice that the instrument was overdue.

    a. Demand instruments [UCC 3-304(a)] — A demand instrument becomes overdue:
        1) On the day after the day upon which a demand for payment was made;
        2) If the instrument is a check:
            a) Ninety days after the date of the check [UCC 3-304(a)(2)].
            b) In states that have not adopted the revised Article 3, 30 days after the date of the check   [UCC 3-304(3)(c))].
        3) If the instrument is not a check, when the instrument has been outstanding for an unreasonable period of time "in light of the nature of the instrument and usage of the trade" [UCC 3-304(a)(3)].
            a) Period is longer for interest bearing instruments than for instruments payable without interest.
            b) Business usage for demand drafts and notes has been approximately 60 days.

    b. Time instruments [UCC 3-304(b)].
        1) A time instrument is considered overdue on the day after the specified maturity date.
        2) The presence of an acceleration clause in installment paper is not notice that the instrument may be overdue.

3. Dishonored instruments — Holder must have taken the instrument without notice that it was presented for payment or acceptance which was refused.

4. Notice of claims or defenses — Holder must have taken the instrument without notice that somebody could assert defenses or had a claim to the instrument.

    a. Incomplete instruments [UCC 3-302(a)(2), 3-113(b), 3-115(b)].
        1) Defects that are apparent from examination of the instrument because the instrument is materially incomplete include omissions of the name of the payee of order paper, the name of the transferee on a special indorsement, and the amount to be paid when the author of the paper did not authorize its completion.
        2) Minor omissions, such as missing connective words, do not give a holder notice of defenses.

    b. Irregular instruments [UCC 3-302(a)(1)].
        1) An instrument may be irregular because there is visible evidence on the instrument of forgery of a signature or a material alteration that calls into question the instrument's validity or terms of ownership, or creates an ambiguity as to the party who is to pay.
        2) An instrument is not irregular because of differences in handwriting, postdating, antedating, or minor erasures or changes.

      c. Voidable obligations — A purchaser has notice of a defense or claim if the purchaser has information about facts that are apparent regarding the issuance or prior transfer of the paper, including a breach of contract by the drawer, maker, or indorser; a wrongful negotiation of the instrument by a fiduciary; discharge of parties; defective title of transferor because of illegality, fraud, theft, etc.; or other voidable transaction.

  E. A payee who was not an actual party to the issuance of the instrument may be an HDC [UCC 3-302(2)].

III. Holder through an HDC [UCC 3-203(b)] — The shelter principle.

  A. A holder, who derives his or her interest or title from an HDC, may acquire the rights of an HDC, because the holder is an assignee and, therefore, acquires the rights that the holder's assignor possessed.

  B. Limitations on the shelter principle.

    1. The shelter provision does not apply when the holder was a party to an irregularity, such as fraud or illegality.

    2. A holder who reacquires an instrument is entitled to the status that the holder previously had. (If an HDC reacquires an instrument from a person who is merely a holder, he or she reacquires his or her prior status as an HDC.)

    3. A holder (who was not an HDC) cannot improve his or her status by reacquiring an instrument from an HDC.

IV. Defenses — May be raised by a party who is liable to pay on an instrument.

  A. Universal (real) defenses [UCC 3-305] — Universal defenses, if proven, are effective against all holders, including HDCs and holders through HDCs.

    1. Forgery [UCC 3-401(a), 3-403] — A forged or unauthorized signature is not treated as the signature of the person whose name is signed, unless that person ratified the signature or is estopped from denying the forgery or lack of authority because of his or her negligence.

    2. Fraud in the execution [UCC 3-305(a)(1)(iii)].

      a. Fraud in the execution occurs when a person signs an instrument, without knowledge or a reasonable opportunity to obtain knowledge of its character or terms, and believes that he or she is doing something other than signing an instrument.

      b. Fraud in the execution (in the inception) is distinguishable from fraud in the inducement which is a personal defense.

    3. Material alteration [UCC 3-407].

a. If the holder is an HDC, the material alteration of a completed instrument is a universal defense to the extent of the alteration, unless the defendant is precluded from asserting the defense because of carelessness (e.g., issuing an incomplete instrument or an instrument with blank spaces).

b. Examples include changes in the number or relationship of the parties, completion of an instrument in an unauthorized manner, and an addition to or removal of part of the signed writing.

4. Discharge in bankruptcy is an absolute defense and can be asserted against all holders [UCC 3-305(a)(1)(iv)].

5. Minority (infancy), is a real defense to the extent that, under state law, infancy is a defense to a simple contract [UCC 3-305(a)(1)(i)].

6. Illegality is a real defense when a state statute provides that an illegal transaction is void or a nullity [UCC 3-305(a)(1)(ii)].

7. Mental incapacity — If state law provides that a contract of a person who is mentally incompetent is void, mental incapacity is a real defense [UCC 3-305(a)(1)(ii)].

8. Extreme duress [UCC 3-305(a)(1)(ii)].

B. Personal defenses [UCC 3-306].

1. All defenses that are not universal (real) defenses are personal (limited) defenses; personal defenses can be raised against holders but not against HDCs or holders through HDCs.

2. Breach of contract and breach of warranty — See Chapter 25 regarding contracts for sales and leases of goods.

4. Lack or failure of consideration [UCC 3-303(b), 3-305(a)(2)].

5. Fraud in the inducement (ordinary fraud), ordinary duress, or undue influence. (See Chapter 16.)

6. Illegality which causes a contract to be voidable rather than void. (See Chapter 17.)

7. Mental incapacity which results in a voidable, rather than void, contract. (See Chapter 15.)

8. Discharge by payment (or other satisfaction) or cancellation of an instrument which is permitted to circulate [UCC 3-601(b), 3-602(a), 3-603, 3-604].

9. Unauthorized completion of an incomplete instrument [UCC 3-115, 3-302, 3-407, 4-401(d)(2)].

10. Nondelivery or conditional delivery of an instrument [UCC 3-105(b), 3-305(a)(2)].

V. Federal limitations on HDC rights.

    A. Requirements of Federal Trade Commission (FTC) Rule 433.

        1. The FTC Rule is meant to protect a consumer who obtains goods, services, or a loan in a consumer credit transaction in which the consumer issues an instrument (e.g., a promissory note) evidencing the debt.

        2. Installment sales contracts and sales contracts that include promissory notes issued in order to finance consumer credit transactions must contain a notice preserving the right of the debtor to assert any defenses, which the debtor could have asserted against the creditor with whom the debtor dealt, against a subsequent transferee or holder.

    B. Effect of the Rule.

        1. An instrument containing the required notice, or a similar statement required by law, may be negotiable, but the instrument's holder does not possess all of the benefits that a holder normally would have as an HDC.

        2. When an instrument is issued in conjunction with a consumer credit transaction, the consumer (issuer) can assert personal defenses against any holder, including a person who is an HDC.

KEY WORDS AND PHRASES IN TEXT

holder in due course (HDC)
holder
requirements for HDC status
taking for value
antecedent claim
negotiable instrument as value
first-money-in, first-money-out rule
taking an instrument in good faith
takingan instrument without notice
overdue instrument
dishonored instrument
defenses against or claims to an
    instrument
incomplete instrument
irregular instrument
voidable obligation
holder through an HDC
shelter principle

universal (real) defense
forgery
fraud in the execution (inception)
discharge in bankruptcy
minority (infancy) and mental incapacity
illegality
extreme duress
personal defense
breach of contract and warranty
lack or failure of consideration
fraud in the inducement
ordinary duress and undue influence
discharge by payment or cancellation
unauthorized completion of
    an incomplete instrument
nondelivery of instrument
Federal Trade Commission (FTC) Rule 433

FILL-IN QUESTIONS

1. A person is considered to be a holder of an instrument that is not payable to an identified person when he or she has possession of the instrument and the instrument is drawn or issued to _____ or indorsed to _____ or indorsed in _____.

2. A holder in due course of a negotiable instrument is one who took the instrument _____ and without notice that it was _____ or that it had been _____ or without notice of _____ _____, or claims to it on the part of any person.

3. Giving value, as a requisite for being a holder in due course, differs from consideration necessary to support a contract, because value must be _____ _____, whereas consideration may be something promised. A person is not considered as having given value if nothing is given, or if something, such as performance of services, delivery or sale of _____, or payment of _____ is promised but not given, or if an instrument is acquired at a judicial sale or under legal process, in taking over an estate, or as part of a bulk transfer _____.

4. If you are in possession of a note, payable to the order of John Doe, and indorsed in blank by John Doe, you are a _____. If you paid $10 to your transferor in exchange for the note, and taken the note in good faith and without notice that _____ _____, you are also a holder in due course.

MULTIPLE CHOICE QUESTIONS

1. Henry Hunt needed $100 in a hurry. He asked Frank Franklin, an acquaintance, if Frank would give him $100 for a piece of paper that looked like this on its face:

> To: Earl Early
>
> Pay to Paula Paul or order the sum of $120.00.
>
> *Roberto Roberts*

The only writing on the back of the paper was Paula Paul's signature.
A. Earl Early was a holder but **not** a holder in due course.
B. Paula Paul could **not** have been a holder because she was the payee.
C. Henry Hunt will have to indorse the instrument in order for Frank Franklin to have the status of a holder in due course.
D. Frank Franklin will be a holder in due course if he has no notice of any defects in the paper or defenses available against the paper.

2. In exchange for $800, Peter Pill offers you a piece of paper. One side looks like this:

> I promise to pay to Barney Beaker or order the sum of
> One Thousand and   dollars
> on November 30, 2001.
>
> *Arthur Aspirin*

The back looks like this:

> *Barney Beaker*
>
> *Pay to L. Laughbaugh*
>
> *L. Laughbaugh*

You will not be a holder in due course because:
A. there is a blank on the face of the instrument.
B. the date upon which the instrument was issued has been omitted.
C. the consideration you give will not be adequate value.
D. the name of your transferor, Peter Pill, does not appear on the back.

3. Quoit paid Ridge for services performed by Ridge with a check payable to Ridge's order. Ridge indorsed the check in blank and gave the check to Strata as a gift.
A. Strata is neither a holder nor a holder in due course.
B. Strata is a holder but **not** a holder in due course.
C. Strata is a holder and a holder in due course.
D. If Strata transfers the check for value to Tracer, Tracer will be a holder through a holder in due course.

4. Viper induced Walsh to write a check payable to Viper's order by making a misrepresentation of a material fact upon which Walsh reasonably relied. The next day Viper gave the check to Houlder, who took the check in good faith, for value, and without notice of any defects in the paper or defenses against the check or claims to it. Two days later, Houlder indorsed the check payable to Ingram's order. Ingram, who knew of the original transaction between Viper and Walsh, gave value to Houlder and is the present holder of the check.
A. Houlder was a holder in due course.
B. Houlder was **not** a holder in due course but had the rights of a holder through a holder in due course.
C. Ingram is a holder in due course.
D. Ingram is **not** a holder in due course but had the rights of a holder through a holder in due course.

5. On April 1, Macon sold Norris defective goods for which Norris paid with a check. On April 3, Norris discovered that the goods were defective and stopped payment on the check. On April 8, Macon learned of the stop payment order. On July 4, Macon specially indorsed the check to Loring for value. Loring knew neither of the defective goods nor the stoppage of payment.
    A. Macon was a holder in due course.
    B. Loring was a holder in due course.
    C. Loring was **not** a holder in due course because the instrument was overdue when he acquired it.
    D. Loring was **not** a holder in due course because he acquired the instrument on a national holiday.

6. Henderson sold an $800 negotiable promissory note, which was payable in one month to her order, to Dumas for $790. When she delivered the note to Dumas, Henderson neglected to sign her name on the back.
    A. Dumas qualifies as a holder in due course.
    B. Dumas qualifies as a holder.
    C. Dumas has an enforceable right to obtain Henderson's unqualified indorsement.
    D. Dumas has a better right to receive payment of the note than Henderson had.
    (This question has been adapted from objective question #42 on the Uniform CPA Examination, May 1982.)

7. In order to be a holder of a bearer negotiable promissory note, the transferee must:
    A. give value for the note.
    B. take the note in good faith.
    C. acquire the note before receiving notice that another person has a claim to the instrument.
    D. have physical possession of the instrument.
    (This question has been adapted from objective question #42 on the Uniform CPA Examination, May 1984.)

8. Which of the following will **not** constitute giving value in determining whether or not a person is a holder in due course?
    A. The exchange of a check for goods to be delivered in one month.
    B. The taking of a negotiable note as security for a one year loan of money.
    C. The giving of a check in exchange for a negotiable time draft.
    D. The performance of services rendered to the payee of a negotiable draft, which the payee indorses.

9. Signing a note when it is believed that only an autograph is requested gives rise to:
    A. no defense.
    B. the defense of illegality.
    C. a personal defense.
    D. a universal or real defense.

10. With regard to a negotiable instrument, the following usually is considered to be a personal (limited) defense:
    A. the statute of limitations.
    B. breach of contract.

C. fraud in the execution.

D. discharge in bankruptcy.

11. With regard to a negotiable instrument, the following usually is considered to be a real (universal) defense:

    A. fraud in the execution.

    B. fraudulent concealment.

    C. failure of consideration.

    D. All of the answers above are correct.

12. Martin entered into a contract to purchase a television set for use in her business from TV City, Inc. Because credit was being extended, Martin signed a negotiable promissory note for the purchase price. TV City, Inc. transferred the paper to the Careful Credit Co., which paid TV City, Inc. ninety percent of the face value of the note. Martin, who was notified that Careful Credit Co. was now in possession of the note, has failed to pay Careful Credit Co. although the note is now due. Careful Credit Co., therefore, is suing Martin, who claims (1) she has been discharged in a state insolvency proceeding and (2) the television set had not been delivered by TV City, Inc. Careful Credit Co. had no notice of the existence of these defenses when it purchased the instrument.

    A. Both defenses can be raised against Careful Credit Co.

    B. Martin can raise the defense of discharge in an insolvency proceeding against Careful Credit Co. but **not** the defense of breach of contract.

    C. Martin can raise the defense of failure of consideration against Careful Credit Co., but **not** the defense of discharge in an insolvency proceeding.

    D. Martin **cannot** raise either defense against Careful Credit Co.

13. Cohen entered into a contract to purchase a television set for use in her home from TV City, Inc. Because credit was being extended, Cohen signed a negotiable installment promissory note for the purchase price. TV City, Inc. transferred the paper to the Careful Credit Co., which paid TV City, Inc. ninety percent of the face value of the note. Cohen, who was notified that Careful Credit Co. was now in possession of the note, has failed to pay Careful Credit Co. although the note is now due. Careful Credit Co., therefore, is suing Cohen, who claims (1) she has been discharged in a state insolvency proceeding and (2) the television set had not been delivered by TV City, Inc. Careful Credit Co. had no notice of the existence of these defenses when it purchased the instrument.

    A. Both defenses can be raised against Careful Credit Co.

    B. Cohen can raise the defense of discharge in an insolvency proceeding against Careful Credit Co., but **not** the defense of breach of contract.

    C. Cohen can raise the defense of failure of consideration against Careful Credit Co., but **not** the defense of discharge in an insolvency proceeding.

    D. Cohen **cannot** raise either defense against Careful Credit Co.

Chapter 28
Liability and Discharge

Parties who issue or transfer commercial paper have obligations and, therefore, acquire liability to subsequent holders of such instruments. Because commercial paper is a special form of contract, any person whose signature appears on the instrument is liable in contract. The contract liability of a party who makes an unconditional promise to pay, such as a maker of a note or an acceptor of a draft, is absolute and primary liability. Other parties, who place their signatures on an instrument, such as drawers of drafts and unqualified indorsers, also acquire contract liability. These parties are secondarily liable because their liability is conditioned upon (1) the proper and timely presentment of the instrument to the person who is required to pay or required, in the case of a draft, to accept; (2) dishonor (a refusal to pay or accept); and (3) notification of the dishonor.

Holders of instruments who transfer or present negotiable instruments also are treated as having made certain implied warranties, the effects of which are to cut off defenses that ordinarily might be raised. As a result, additional, unconditional liability may be imposed upon parties to instruments.

The liability of parties to pay the face amount of an instrument may be terminated or discharged. Normally, commercial paper is discharged by proper payment. In addition, parties may be discharged by giving other satisfaction (consideration), by cancelling or renouncing their rights, or by making a tender of payment. A party may also be discharged because of impairment of a right of recourse (the right to obtain reimbursement) against a party or collateral security; reacquisition of an instrument; a fraudulent, material alteration; certification of a check; a draft varying acceptance; an unexcused delay in presentment and/or giving notice of dishonor; or any act that would discharge a simple contract for the payment of money. No discharge, however, will be effective against a holder in due course (HDC) who lacked notice of the discharge when the instrument was negotiated to the HDC.

THINGS TO KEEP IN MIND

An underlying transaction gives rise to the issuance of negotiable instruments. The parties to the underlying transaction have contractual rights and obligations that are merely suspended by the issuance of an instrument. The same is true when instruments are transferred. For example, if R (a drawer) draws a check payable to P (a payee) on R's bank in order to pay for goods purchased from P, R remains contractually obligated to pay P for the goods should the drawee bank refuse to honor the check. Similarly, had P negotiated the check to H (a holder), in exchange for the performance of some services, P's liability to pay H for the services is merely suspended until H receives payment of the instrument.

OUTLINE

I. Signature liability.

   A. A person whose signature is on a negotiable instrument is liable for payment of the amount of money that is promised or ordered to be paid on the face of an instrument.

      1. A person, who signs an instrument himself, herself, or itself or whose authorized agent or representative places the signature of such a person (a principal) on an instrument, acquires either primary liability or secondary liability based upon the contract that is inherent in a negotiable instrument.

      2. A person is not liable on a negotiable instrument unless his or her signature appears thereon [UCC 3-401(a)].

      3. A signature may be handwritten, typed or printed, or some mark, such as a thumb print or a stamp, and may be placed upon an instrument by an agent or representative [UCC 3-401(b)].

      4. A signature indicates a "present intention to authenticate a writing" [UCC 1-201(39)].

   B. Primary liability.

      1. A person who is primarily liable on a negotiable instrument is absolutely required to pay, subject to being able to raise real defenses, until the period of time provided for in the applicable statute of limitations has run.

      2. The maker of a promissory note has primary liability.

         a. A maker promises to pay according to the original tenor of the note or certificate of deposit (CD) or according to the terms as completed, if the note or CD was not complete when issued [UCC 3-412].

         b   The underlying obligation for which the note or CD is given is suspended until payment of the note. Upon dishonor, the maker can be sued either on the note or the underlying obligation or both [UCC 3-310(b)].

         c   An accommodation party who cosigns along with the maker also is primarily liable on the instrument [UCC 3-419].

      3. The drawee-acceptor of a draft has primary liability [UCC 3-409, 3-413].

         a. No one is primarily liable on a draft when a draft is issued.

         b. If a draft is presented for acceptance to a drawee by a holder, the drawee becomes an acceptor upon acceptance of the draft and is making a primary promise to pay according to the tenor of the instrument at the time of acceptance.

   c. A drawee (who is not an acceptor) is not liable to a presenter if the drawee fails to pay or accept a draft.
     1) A drawee's contractual liability is only to the drawer.
     2) The refusal of a drawee to accept a draft is a dishonor of the instrument; as a result, the drawee retains his or her original status and is neither primarily nor secondarily liable on the instrument.

   d. An issuer of a cashier's check or other draft drawn on the drawer is primarily liable [UCC 3-412].

   e. Certification of a check is treated as an acceptance [UCC 3-409(d)].

C. Secondary liability — Secondary liability is contingent or conditional liability that arises when certain contingencies or conditioning event occurs.

   1. The secondary liability of drawers, unqualified indorsers, and accommodation parties (other than accommodation makers) is conditioned upon (or triggered by):

     a. Proper, timely presentment of the instrument for payment or acceptance;

     b. Dishonor of the instrument (refusal of payment or acceptance); and

     c. Timely notice of dishonor to the party who is secondarily liable or notice of protest (if the instrument is drawn or payable outside the U.S.).

   2. Rights against a secondarily liable party are preserved by complying with the conditions of making a presentment and giving notice of dishonor or protest.

   3. Presentment and notice of dishonor (or protest), a delay in presentment, or giving notice may be excused or waived [UCC 3-504].

   4. Proper presentment [UCC 3-414(f), 3-415(e), 3-501, 3-502].

     a. Presentment must be made by a holder to the proper person.
       1) A promissory note or CD must be presented to the maker for payment.
       2) A check is presented to the drawee-bank for payment.
       3) A draft is presented to the drawee for acceptance or payment, or both.

     b. Manner of presentment.
       1) By any commercially reasonable means (oral, written, or electronic communication) and may be through a clearinghouse.
       2) Presentment is effective upon receipt at the place specified in the instrument for acceptance or payment or, if no place is specified, at

the place of business or residence of the person required to accept or pay.

  c. Time of presentment.
    1) A time instrument must be presented for acceptance on or before due date; a time instrument must be presented for payment on due date.
    2) A demand instrument (other than a check) must be presented for acceptance or negotiated within a reasonable period of time after date or issue (whichever is later); reasonable time is determined by the nature of the instrument, trade or banking usage, and facts of the particular case.
    3) A domestic, uncertified check:
      a) Must be presented for payment within 30 after its date in order to trigger secondary liability of drawer. In states that have not adopted the revisions, the period is 30 days after its date or issue, whichever is later [UCC 3-503(2)].
      b) Must be presented for payment within 30 days after indorsement in order to trigger the secondary liability of an indorser. In states that have not adopted the revisions, the period is seven days [UCC 3-503(2)].
    4) Presentment must be made at a reasonable hour and, if being made at a bank, during its banking day.

  d. Delay in presentment is excused when:
    1) A person does not know that instrument is due (e.g., holder does not know that an acceleration clause in instrument became operative).
    2) The delay is caused by circumstances beyond the party's control, and the party used due diligence after the cause of the delay ceased.

  e. Presentment is excused when:
    1) The party entitled to presentment waived presentment.
    2) The holder has no reason to expect that instrument will be accepted or paid (e.g., party to whom presentment is to be made is dead or in insolvency proceedings).
    3) Even though due diligence is used, a presentment cannot be made.

5. Dishonor [UCC 3-501, 3-502].

  a. An instrument is dishonored if, after proper presentment, acceptance or payment is refused or cannot be obtained within the prescribed time; or if presentment is excused, the instrument is not accepted or paid.

  b. In order to determine if the instrument is properly payable, payment can be postponed to no later than the close of business on the date of presentment.

6. Proper notice of dishonor must be given by holder or a representative of the holder to any person who may be liable on the instrument [UCC 3-503].

a. Notice may be given orally, in writing, or electronically, in any terms which identify the instrument and state that the instrument is dishonored; written notice is effective when sent, rather than when received.

b. Notice being given by a bank must be given before midnight of the next banking day after the bank receives dishonor or notice of dishonor.

c. Notice being given by a person other than a bank must be given within 30 days. In states that have not adopted the revisions to Article 3, notice must be given before midnight of the third business day after dishonor or receipt of notice of dishonor [UCC 3-508(2)].

d. Notice operates for the benefit of all parties who have rights on an instrument against the notified party.

e. Notice of dishonor may be excused or waived; a delay in giving notice may be excused.

f. When a party to whom notice is to be given is dead, incompetent, or in insolvency proceedings instituted after the issuance of the instrument, notice may be given to the party's representative.

g. If a dishonored draft appears on its face to be drawn or payable outside the U.S. or its territories, protest is required, unless excused or waived; protest is a certificate of dishonor "made under the hand and seal of" a U.S. consul, vice consul, or person authorized to certify dishonor in the place where dishonor occurred [UCC 3-505(b)].

7. Parties who are secondarily liable.

   a. Drawers [UCC 3-414].
      1) The drawer engages that he or she will pay if a draft or check is dishonored and notice of dishonor is given.
      2) If a draft or check is payable at a bank, an unexcused failure to present or to give notice of dishonor (or an unexcused delay in making presentment or giving notice) does not discharge a drawer of secondary liability unless the drawee bank has become insolvent so that the drawer is thereby deprived of obtaining funds, which would have covered the instrument, from the bank [UCC 3-414(f)].

   b. Indorsers [UCC 3-415].
      1) An unqualified indorser engages that the indorser will pay according to the tenor of the instrument at the time of indorsement if the instrument is presented and dishonored and notice of dishonor is given.
      2) A qualified indorser is relieved of contractual liability on an instrument.

D. Accommodation parties [UCC 3-419].

1. An accommodation party signs an instrument for purposes of lending his or her name and credit to a party to the instrument.

2. The obligation of an accommodation party depends upon the capacity in which the accommodation party signed. (An accommodation maker is primarily liable and an accommodation indorser is secondarily liable.)

3. An accommodation party is not liable to the accommodated party and may obtain reimbursement for amounts paid on an instrument from the accommodated party.

E. Authorized agents' signatures — See also Chapters 33 and 34.

1. A signature may be provided by an authorized representative, such as an agent [UCC 3-401(a)(ii), 3-402].

2. Liability of the principal — If an agent indicates that he or she is signing the instrument on behalf of a clearly named principal, gives the appropriate signature of the principal, and signs the agent's name, indicating that the agent is signing in a representative capacity, only the principal is liable as a party to the instrument.

3. Liability of the agent — An agent, who signs in his or her own name only, is personally liable on the instrument.

4. If an agent signs for a principal and provides his or her own signature without indicating that he or she is acting in a representative capacity, both the principal and agent are liable on the instrument. Parol evidence is admissible between the original parties in order to establish the agency relationship.

5. If an agent signs his or her own name and indicates that he or she is signing in a representative capacity, but fails to indicate the name of the principal, parol evidence is admissible between the original parties in order to establish the agency relationship.

6. An authorized agent is not personally liable if the agent signs his or her name on a check payable from the principal's account and the check identifies the principal.

F. Unauthorized signatures.

1. A person who signs (forges) the name of another person without authority is liable on a negotiable instrument [UCC 3-403(a)].

2. A person (including a principal) whose signature has been used without authorization is not liable on a negotiable instrument unless that person has ratified its use on the instrument or is estopped from denying that the signature was his or her signature because of his or her negligence [UCC 3-403(a)].

3. Losses incurred because of negligence may be allocated among the negligent parties based upon comparative negligence in states that have adopted the revised Articles 3 and 4 [3-406(b)].

G. Special rules for unauthorized indorsements [UCC 3-403].

1. If a signature in an indorsement is forged or not authorized, the forger or unauthorized indorser is personally liable.

   a. The signature is not considered to be the signature of the person by whom it appears to have been written.

   b. If the signature was necessary for negotiation of order paper (i.e., the signature of the payee or an indorser to whom the instrument was specially indorsed), the transferee is not a holder.

   c. The rightful owner of the paper is entitled to payment; the loss falls on the person who received the paper from the forger.

2. Impostors.

   a. An impostor represents that he or she is another person and persuades a person to issue a negotiable instrument (as maker or drawer) payable to the order of the person whom the impostor is impersonating; the impostor indorses the instrument in the name of the impersonated payee.

   b. The impostor rule [UCC 3-404(a)] — The indorsement is effective so that the person who takes the instrument from the impostor qualifies as a holder and may be an HDC.
      1) The loss will fall on the issuer of the paper because the issuer dealt with the impostor and, therefore, was in the best position to prevent the loss.
      2) Losses incurred because of negligence may be allocated among the negligent parties based upon comparative negligence [3-404(d)].

3. Fictitious payees.

   a. An instrument is made payable to a named payee, who may or may not be fictitious, with the intention that the payee have no interest in the instrument.

   b. A dishonest employee or agent who has authority to issue the instrument may sign the instrument on behalf of his or her employer or principal (the maker or drawer) or may supply the payee's name to his or her employer or principal, who then issues the instrument payable to the order of "the fictitious payee."

   c. The instrument is indorsed in the name of "the fictitious payee."

    d. The "fictitious payee" rule [UCC 3-404(b), 3-405] — The indorsement is effective so that the person who takes the instrument from the fictitious payee qualifies as a holder and may be an HDC.
        1) The loss will fall on the issuer of the paper because the issuer was in the best position to prevent the loss.
        2) Losses incurred because of negligence may be allocated among the negligent parties based upon comparative negligence [3-404(d)].

II. Warranty liability.

   A. Liability may be imposed upon transferors and presenters of instruments because such transferors and presenters are considered to have made certain implied warranties; warranty liability is unconditional and is **not** subject to the conditions of proper presentment, dishonor, and notice of dishonor.

   B. Transfer warranties [UCC 3-416] — Implied warranties are made upon the transfer of an instrument by a person who negotiates the instrument and receives consideration.

     1. Transferor is entitled to enforce the instrument.

     2. All signatures are authentic (genuine) or authorized.

     3. The instrument has not been altered.

     4. The instrument is not subject to a defense or claim of any party that can be asserted against the transferor. (In states that have not adopted the Article 3 revisions, a qualified indorser merely warrants that he or she has no knowledge of any such defenses [UCC 3-417(3)]).

     5. The transferor has no knowledge of insolvency proceedings instituted against the maker, acceptor, or drawer of an unaccepted draft.

     6. Parties to whom warranty liability extends.

        a. If transfer has been by indorsement and delivery, warranties apply to immediate transferee and subsequent holders who take an instrument in good faith.

        b. If transfer was by delivery alone, warranties run only to immediate transferee.

     7. Recovery for breach of warranty.

        a. The transferee (holder) can sue for breach of warranty following giving notice to the transferor (warrantor) within thirty days after the transferee has reason to know of the breach of warranty [UCC 3-416(c) and (d)].

      b. Warranties can be disclaimed by writing "without warranties" in an indorsement for instruments other than checks [UCC 3-416(c)].

  C. Presentment warranties [UCC3-417(a) and (d)] — Warranties that are made upon presentment by a person presenting an instrument for acceptance or payment to a drawee or acceptor.

      1. The person making the presentment is entitled to enforce the instrument or is authorized to obtain payment or acceptance on behalf of a person who is entitled to enforce the instrument.

      2. The instrument has not been altered; this warranty is not made by an HDC.

      3. The person making the presentment has no knowledge that the signature of the maker or the drawer is unauthorized; this warranty is not made by an HDC.

III.   Discharge.

  A. A discharge is not effective against an HDC who lacks notice of the discharge when the instrument is negotiated to the HDC [UCC 3-602].

  B. Discharge by payment or tender of payment [UCC 3-602, 3-603].

      1. All parties to a negotiable instrument will be discharged when a primarily liable party (maker or acceptor) or a drawee of a draft or check pays the amount due in full, or other satisfaction is accepted by the holder.

      2. A party is not discharged if payment was made in bad faith or in a manner inconsistent with a restrictive indorsement.

      3. Payment by an indorser discharges that indorser and subsequent indorsers.

      4. Tender of payment does not discharge the obligation to pay the face amount but discharges liability for interest, costs, and attorney fees [UCC 3-603(c)].

  C. Discharge by cancellation or surrender [UCC 3-604(a)] — A party who has the right to enforce an instrument (the holder) may discharge the obligation of a party to pay the instrument by:

      1. A voluntary, intentional act, such as destruction, mutilation, or cancellation of the instrument, or striking out that party's indorsement.

      2. Surrender of the instrument to the party or renouncing rights against the party in a signed writing.

  D. Discharge by reacquisition — When a prior holder reacquires an instrument, prior indorsers are discharged [UCC 3-207].

E. Discharge by impairment of the right of recourse (a source of reimbursement) against a party or collateral security occurs when the holder (1) releases or agrees not to sue a party from whom an indorser can obtain reimbursement, (2) agrees to suspend the right to enforce an instrument against a party, (3) discharges prior indorsers by cancellation, or (4) without justification, impairs collateral which had been given as security that the instrument would be paid [UCC 3-605].

F. Discharge because of material, fraudulent alteration [UCC 3-407].

   1. An alteration is material if it changes the obligations of a party.

   2. Parties are discharged to the extent of the alteration.

G. Discharge by any act or agreement that would discharge a simple contract for the payment of money, such as a release or accord and satisfaction [UCC 3-601].

KEY WORDS AND PHRASES IN TEXT

signature liability
primary liability
acceptance of draft
certification of check
secondary liability of drawer
secondary liability of indorser
proper presentment
dishonor
notice of dishonor (or protest)
accommodation party
authorized agent's signature
unauthorized signature

forged indorsement
impostor
fictitious payee
warranty liability
transfer warranties
presentment warranties
discharge by payment or tender of
    payment
discharge by cancellation or surrender
discharge by reacquisition
discharge by impairment of right of
    recourse to collateral

FILL-IN QUESTIONS

1. A party to a negotiable instrument may be liable if the instrument is not paid when the instrument is due because that party's _____ appears on the instrument. He or she may be liable based upon the underlying obligation, the contract that is implied in the _____, or an implied warranty.

2. Parties who are primarily liable based on contract include _____ _____.
Parties who are secondarily liable include _____ _____ _____.

3. One of the purposes of giving a _____ to indorsers following a proper presentment and dishonor of a promissory note is to inform the indorsers

(who are the secondarily liable parties) that the maker of the note has failed to meet the maker's obligation to pay.

4. If a draft is presented by a holder for acceptance, the presenter warrants to the drawee/acceptor that (1) the holder is entitled to enforce the instrument, (2) _____ _____, and (3) _____ _____.

MULTIPLE CHOICE QUESTIONS

1. For breach of any of the transfer warranties imposed by the Uniform Commercial Code upon both qualified and unqualified indorsers, the transferor is:
    A. liable to the transferor's transferee and subsequent holders.
    B. never liable for unintentional acts.
    C. liable only to the transferor's immediate transferee.
    D. liable only to subsequent holders.

2. A payee who indorses a negotiable instrument with the words "without recourse" avoids:
    A. all liability if the instrument is not paid when due.
    B. liability based upon warranty if the instrument is not paid when due.
    C. liability based upon the contract that is implied in the instrument, but **not** liability based upon an underlying contract that gave rise to issuance of the instrument.
    D. liability based on the contract that is implied in the instrument, as well as liability based upon an underlying contract that gave rise to issuance of the instrument.

3. A principal is liable on a negotiable instrument that is signed by the principal's agent in the name of the agent:
    A. if the agent has authority to issue negotiable instruments on behalf of his or her principal.
    B. if the agent has signed only the agent's own name.
    C. and in the name of the principal.
    D. only if the agent indicates that the agent is signing in the agent's representative capacity.

4. Carson executed a promissory note in the amount of $400 payable to Donaldson. On the due date Donaldson went to Carson's place of business and told Carson: "Your note is due today, but I wish to renounce all my rights in connection with it."
    A. The note is effectively discharged by renunciation and cancellation.
    B. The note is effectively discharged by payment or other satisfaction.
    C. The note is **not** effectively discharged because Carson has not given value to Donaldson.
    D. The note is **not** effectively discharged unless the note is surrendered or Donaldson's statement is contained in a signed writing.

5. In order to borrow $15,000 from a local bank, Ink asked Pencil to sign a promissory note as an accommodation maker. Pencil agreed, and both Pencil and Ink executed the note as makers by signing their names on the face of the instrument.
    A. Pencil is liable as an accommodation indorser.

B. Pencil is **not** liable to pay, if Ink tendered the $15,000 plus the interest that was due to the bank when the note became due.

C. Ink may recover from Pencil, if Ink tendered the $15,000 plus the interest that was due to the bank when the note became due.

D. Ink and Pencil are completely discharged, if Ink tendered the $15,000 plus the interest that was due to the bank when the note became due, and the bank refused to accept the payment.

6. While visiting a friend, Fred, in Fresno, California, Bill's wallet was stolen. Bill was in need of funds and wished to cash a personal check drawn on the Mellon Bank in Pittsburgh, Pennsylvania. A bank in Fresno was willing to cash the check if Fred signed the check on the back, which Fred did. With regard to the check:

A. Bill is the drawee, the Mellon Bank is the drawer, and Fred is an indorser.

B. Bill is the drawer, the Mellon Bank is the drawee, and Fred is an accommodation maker.

C. Bill is the drawer, the Mellon Bank is the drawee, and Fred is an accommodation drawer.

D. Bill is the drawer, the Mellon Bank is the drawee, and Fred is an accommodation indorser.

7. The "impostor rule" may be described as:

A. a restatement of the general rule that liability is imposed upon the person who is in the best position to prevent a loss.

B. a restatement of the general rule that a payor is **not** liable to one whose signature has been forged.

C. a restatement of the general rule that a payor is liable to a true payee if the payor pays a forger rather than the payee.

D. None of the answers above is correct.

8. Zack wrote a check payable to the order of Vera, who claimed that she was collecting money for the United Fund. Vera was not really collecting for the United Fund, but she cashed the check at Zack's bank. The most probable result is that:

A. Zack will incur the loss.

B. Vera had good title to the check.

C. the bank will incur the loss because the bank paid out on a forged signature.

D. the bank will incur the loss even though there was no forgery.

9. Mary Munroe, the assistant to the treasurer of the XYZ Corporation, prepared the monthly payroll and the checks for the corporation. Munroe added the name of Jane Joker, a fictitious person, to the payroll and prepared a check payable to Jane Joker's order. The treasurer, who did not know the true facts, signed the check in good faith. Munroe then indorsed the check with the name of Jane Joker, negotiated the check to Kevin Kansas, obtained the money, and disappeared. Kevin Kansas cashed the check at the corporation's bank.

A. XYZ Corporation can recover the amount of the check from the bank.

B. Kevin Kansas was a holder in due course.

C. Jane Joker was a holder in due course.

D. Mary Munroe was a holder in due course.

Chapter 29
Checks and Electronic Fund Transfers

The most frequently used form of commercial paper is the check, a negotiable demand draft that is drawn on a financial institution. The provisions of Article 3 of the Uniform Commercial Code (UCC) that have been discussed in the preceding chapters apply to checks. In addition, Article 4 of the UCC contains rules pertaining to the bank deposit and collection systems and the relationship between a bank customer and the customer's bank, as well as other banks that may be involved in the collection process for checks and other types of commercial paper. These rules are meant to expedite the smooth flow of money, credit, and business transactions.

Federal statutes and regulations impose certain obligations upon banks. The Expedited Funds Availability Act (EFAA) and Regulation CC, adopted by the Board of Governors of the Federal Reserve System to implement this federal statute, provide for limitations on the amount of time during which banks can restrict withdrawal of deposited funds by depositors and for improvements in the check collection and return process. In some instances, EFAA preempts provisions in the UCC. The Truth in Savings Act and Regulation DD require that banks pay interest and make certain disclosures to customers.

Today, funds may be transferred electronically. When an electronic fund transfer (EFT) is used, the transaction is completed instantaneously without a physical movement of cash or other paper documentation in the form of a deposit slip and/or a negotiable instrument, such as a check. As discussed in the final portion of this chapter, the federal Electronic Fund Transfer Act (EFTA) applies to consumer electronic funds transactions and Article 4A of the Uniform Commercial Code (UCC) applies to commercial electronic transfers of funds.

THINGS TO KEEP IN MIND

1. A check is an order (a demand draft), issued by a drawer (a depositor at a depository bank, a bank that accepts deposits of fund), directing the drawer's bank (the drawee, depository bank) to pay out funds that the depositor had previously placed, or deposited, with the bank (demand deposits).

2. Often, a holder of a check who wishes to obtain cash for the check or to deposit the check in the holder's own bank account does not use the bank upon which the check is drawn. It is, therefore, necessary that the check be forwarded though a network of intermediary banks by the holder's bank (the depositary bank) for collection and payment purposes.

3. Electronic banking dispenses with the use of checks and eliminates "float" time, the period between the time that a check is issued and the time that the check is charged to the drawer's account by his or her bank.

OUTLINE

I.   Checks.

    A. A check is a draft that is drawn on a bank ordering or directing the bank to pay a stated, fixed amount of money on demand [UCC 3-104(f)].

        1. Drawer — The person who writes the check and who usually is a depositor in the bank on which the check is drawn.

        2. Drawee — The bank ("person engaged in the business of banking, including a savings bank, savings and loan association, credit union, or trust company" [UCC 4-105(1)]) upon which the check is drawn.

        3. Payee — The person to whom the check is drawn; a check also may be payable to bearer.

    B. Usually, a check is negotiable because it is signed by the drawer, contains a single, unconditional order to pay a fixed amount of money on demand to the order of bearer or an identified named payee [UCC 3-104(a)].

        1. The payee is a holder because the payee is in rightful possession of an instrument that is drawn to the payee's order; the person to whom the drawer gives bearer paper is a holder because that person is in possession of an instrument payable to bearer [UCC 1-201(20)].

        2. The payee or the person who received a bearer check from the drawer can demand payment of the check.

        3. The payee can negotiate the check by indorsing the check and delivering the check to another person, who will be a holder in possession of a check indorsed to that person's order or in blank; the person who received a bearer check from the drawer can negotiate the check by delivering the unindorsed check to another person, who also will be a holder.

        4. Any subsequent holder has the right to negotiate the check or present the check for payment.

        5. A check is not an assignment of funds [UCC 3-408]. Until final payment is made, there is no effect on the depositor's account, and the underlying obligation for which the check is given is not discharged.

    C. Checks and instruments issued by banks or other financial institutions.

        1. Cashier's check.

            a. A check drawn by a bank upon itself so that the bank is the drawer and drawee [UCC 3-104(g)]. (The bank lends its credit to the remitter, the purchaser of the check.)

b. A cashier's check is treated as being accepted in advance and is an independent, unconditional, primary obligation of the issuing bank.

2. Teller's check — A check drawn by a bank on another bank or financial institution or payable at or through a bank [UCC 3-104(h)].

3. Traveler's check — A check that is drawn on or payable through a financial institution and which requires a countersignature by the person whose signature appears on the instrument in order to be transferred [UCC 3-104(i)].

4. Certified check — A personal check that is drawn by a depositor on the depositor's bank and is "accepted" by the drawee bank [UCC 3-409(d)].

   a. The certifying bank unconditionally promises that the check will be paid when it is presented and the bank immediately charges the depositor's (drawer's) account.

   b. Effect of certification.
      1) Certification of a check discharges the drawer and prior indorsers [UCC 3-414(c)].
      2) In states that have not adopted revisions to Article 3 [UCC 3-411]:
         a) If certification is obtained by the drawer, the drawer remains secondarily liable, but prior indorsers are discharged.
         b) If certification is obtained by a holder, the drawer and prior indorsers are discharged.

5. If a bank wrongfully dishonors a cashier's check, teller's check, or certified check, the bank is liable to a holder for expenses incurred, interest, and consequential damages [UCC 3-411].

6. Lost, destroyed, or stolen cashier's, teller's, and certified checks [UCC 3-312].

   a. The payee of a cashier's or teller's check or drawer of a certified check can get a "refund" before the check is presented for payment and, if no one who is entitled to payment has presented the check, the bank is discharged.

   b. If a person who is entitled to enforce payment of the check presents the check within 90 days of its issue and drawee bank pays, the drawee bank is discharged.

II. The bank-customer relationship.

A. A customer is a person having an account with a bank or for whom a bank has agreed to collect items (negotiable instruments and other nonnegotiable promises to pay money and orders to pay money) [UCC 4-104(a)(5)].

B. A depositor is a creditor of his or her bank and a principal. The bank is a debtor and agent of its depositor [UCC 4-201(a)].

C. Banks serve their customers.

1. A bank is a depository bank because the bank agree to honor checks for the withdrawal of funds on deposit in the accounts of its customers and agree to accept deposits in U.S. currency.

2. A bank is a depositary bank when the bank collect checks (or other items) that are drawn on other banks, written to or indorsed to the bank's customer and deposited by the bank's customer.

III. Honoring checks.

A. A bank agrees to honor checks drawn by those of its customers who have sufficient funds in their accounts with the bank.

1. A bank is liable to a customer for a wrongful dishonor if the bank refused to pay when there were sufficient funds in the customer's account [UCC 4-402].

2. A customer is obligated to keep sufficient funds on deposit to cover all checks that the customer issues; if the customer does not have sufficient funds in his or her account and a check is dishonored, the customer is liable to the holder.

B. Overdrafts [UCC 4-401(a) and (b)].

1. A bank that has agreed to honor overdrafts is obligated to honor checks although there are insufficient funds in the customer's account with the bank.

2. When a bank receives a check drawn on a customer's account in which there are insufficient funds, the bank may:

a. Honor and pay the check — The bank charges the customer's account creating an overdraft; the bank is entitled to reimbursement from its customer and to subtract the difference from the customer's next deposit.

b. Dishonor and refuse to pay the check — the check "bounces."
   1) Holder must give notice of the dishonor to secondarily liable parties in order to avoid their discharge.
   2) Holder can resubmit the check.

C. Postdated checks.

1. A bank may charge a postdated check against a customer's account unless the customer has given the bank adequate notice not to pay the check until the issue date [UCC 4-401(c)].

2. In some states that have not adopted the revisions to Articles 3 and 4, a postdated check is treated as a negotiable time draft.

D. Stale checks [UCC 4-404].

1. A stale check is an uncertified check that is presented more than six months after the date of the check.

2. A bank is not required to, but may in good faith, honor and pay a stale check.

E. Death or incompetency of a customer [UCC 4-405].

1. A bank may honor checks of a deceased or legally incompetent depositor until the bank knows of the death or incompetency of the depositor.

2. Even if a bank receives knowledge of the death of a customer, the bank may pay or certify checks that were issued by the deceased depositor for ten days after the date of death, or earlier, if a person claiming an interest in the account orders the bank to stop all payment.

F. Stop-payment orders — A bank is required to follow an order from a customer to stop payment on a check [UCC 4-403].

1. Only the customer may give a stop-payment order.

2. The bank must receive the stop-payment order at such time and in such a manner that the bank has a reasonable opportunity to comply.

3. Duration — Fourteen days if oral; six months if written; a stop-payment order may be renewed.

4. Bank's liability for wrongful payment — If a bank fails to comply with a stop-payment order, the bank is liable to its customer for the amount of actual loss incurred.

5. Customer's liability for wrongful stop-payment order.

   a. A drawer who does not have a legal ground to issue a stop-payment order will be liable to the payee for the amount of the check and for consequential damages incurred by the payee.

   b. A drawer, who has a legal basis for issuing a stop-payment order because of a transaction with the payee, may not be able to raise personal (limited) defenses against a subsequent holder in due course. (See Chapter 27 in *Study Guide* at IV. B.)

6. Cashier's checks and teller's checks — Normally, payment cannot be stopped on a cashier's check or a teller's check [UCC 3-411].

G. Checks bearing forged signatures of drawers.

1. Banks maintain signature cards of their customers and are required to check the genuineness of signatures of drawers on checks.

2. The general rule [UCC 3-403(a)].

   a. A bank that pays an item on which the signature of its customer (the drawer) is forged is liable to its customer and cannot recover from the holder who presented the item without knowledge of the forged drawer's signature. [See Chapter 28 at II. C. regarding presentment warranties.]

   b. A bank that pays an item on which the signature of its customer (the drawer) is forged must recredit the customer's account unless the drawer's negligence contributed to the forgery or the customer failed to notify the bank promptly after the receipt of the canceled check and periodic bank statement.

3. Customer negligence (e.g., failure to secure check writing and/or signing equipment or stamp).

   a. A bank does not have to recredit a customer's account if the customer's negligence substantially contributed to the forgery [UCC 3-406(a)].

   b. Under the UCC revisions, when both the customer and the bank are negligent, the loss is allocated between the customer and the bank.

   c. Timely examination of bank statements by customer is required [UCC 4-406(c) and (d)].
      1) A customer has a duty to examine statements and canceled checks (or copies) and report forged (or unauthorized) signatures and alterations to bank.
      2) If a customer fails to so examine and report forgeries to bank and the bank incurred a loss because of the failure, the customer cannot require that the bank recredit the customer's account.

   d. Consequences of failing to detect forgeries — When there is a series of forgeries by the same wrongdoer, the failure to notify bank within 30 days (in states that have not adopted the revisions, 14 days) of the receipt of the statement and checks that contain the first forged item absolves (or discharges) the bank of liability, unless the customer can establish that the bank failed to exercise ordinary care in paying the item or items [UCC 4-406(d)].

   e. When the bank is also negligent.
      1) When the bank is also negligent, the loss is allocated between the customer and the bank based upon their respective comparative negligence in states that have adopted the revisions to Articles 3 and 4 [UCC 4-406(e)].

2) Ordinary care means "observance of reasonable commercial standards, prevailing in the area in which the person is located, with respect to the business in which that person is engaged" [UCC 3-103(a)(7)].

3) In the case of a bank that uses an automated means for processing checks, as long as the bank's procedures conform to general banking usage, the bank is not liable if the bank fails to examine a signature on a particular check [UCC 3-103(a)(7)].

4) Without regard to exercise of care (or lack of care) by the customer or the bank, the bank will not be liable to a customer who failed to discover and report a forgery or an alteration within one year [UCC 4-406(f)].

4. Other parties from whom the bank may recover.

   a. A bank may recover from a forger because the forged signature of the drawer is effective as the signature of the unauthorized signer [UCC 3-403(a)].

   b. The bank may recover from the holder who presented the check bearing the forged drawer's signature or a collecting bank based upon the warranty that "all signatures on the item are authentic and authorized" [UCC 4-207(a)(2)]; the drawee bank, however, cannot recover from "a person who took the instrument in good faith and for value or in good faith changed [his or her] position in reliance on the payment or acceptance" [UCC 3-418(c)].

H. Checks bearing forged indorsements.

   1. If a bank pays on a forged indorsement, the bank cannot rightfully charge the drawer's account because the item is not "properly payable" [UCC 4-401(a)].

   2. A bank that pays on a forged indorsement must credit the customer's account, but may recover from the person who presented the item for payment because of breach of presentment warranties [UCC 4-207(a)(2)].

   3. Usually, the eventual loss will fall on the first person who took the instrument bearing the forged indorsement because a forged indorsement does not effectively transfer title so that a transferee of the instrument cannot be a holder. (See Chapter 28 at II. C. regarding warranty liability.)

   4. Failure of a customer to examine statements and canceled checks and report discovered forged indorsement within three years relieves the bank of liability [UCC 4-111].

I. Altered checks.

1. A drawee bank is required to pay in accordance with its customer's order and is liable, therefore, if it pays a check that was altered after issuance (e.g., the amount of the check was raised).

2. The bank may charge the drawer's account for the amount of the check as originally issued [UCC 4-401(d)(1)].

3. Customer's negligence — A customer's negligence that contributes to the instrument being altered materially may shift the risk of loss to the customer.

   a. A customer left gaps around the numbers and words.

   b. A customer signed the check leaving the dollar amount blank so that the amount could be filled in by another person.

   c. When there are successive alterations, a customer failed to discover the initial alteration.

   d. A customer failed to examine statements and canceled checks and to notify the bank of alteration. [See above at III. G. 3. regarding forged signature of drawer.]

4. Other parties from whom the bank may recover — The drawee bank bears the loss to the extent of a raised amount, but may recover from the person who presented the check for payment based upon breach of the warranty that the instrument had not been altered [UCC 3-417(a)(2), 4-208(a)(2)].

IV. Accepting deposits.

A. Availability schedule for deposited checks — The Expedited Funds Availability Act of 1987 (EFAA) and supplemental Federal Reserve Board Regulation CC.

   1. Limitations are imposed upon banks' "hold" periods — the periods between the time bank customers deposit funds and the time the funds are to be made available for withdrawal by customers.

   2. When funds are to be made available at the start of a business day, the funds can be withdrawn at the later of 9:00 a.m. or the time that the depository bank's teller facilities, including automated teller machines (ATMs), are available for customers' withdrawals.

   3. Next business day availability for certain deposits.

      a. Cash deposits, wire transfers, electronic payments, and U.S. Treasury checks when deposited in accounts of the payees.

      b. Certain other checks when deposited in accounts of the payees and deposited in person to bank employees.
      1) U.S. Postal Service money orders.

       2) Federal Reserve Bank and Federal Home Loan Bank checks.

       3) State or local government checks when depositary banks are in the same state.

       4) Cashier's, certified, or teller's checks.

       5) On-us checks.

    c. The first one hundred dollars deposited by check or checks.

4. Local checks.

    a. A local check is a check drawn on a bank that is located in the same check processing region as the branch or proprietary ATM of the depositary bank at which the check was deposited.

    b. Funds are to be made available by 5:00 p.m. on the second business day following the banking day on which the deposit is made.

5. Nonlocal checks.

    a. A nonlocal check is a check drawn on a bank that is in a different check processing region.

    b. In general, funds are to be made available on the fifth business day following the banking day on which the deposit is made.

6. A five day hold is permitted on a deposit made at a nonproprietary ATM (an ATM that is not owned or operated by the bank in which the deposit is being made).

7. An eight day hold is permitted on deposits in accounts opened for less than thirty days (new accounts).

8. An extra four day hold is permitted on deposits over $5,000 (except deposits of government and cashier's checks), on accounts with repeated overdrafts, and on checks of questionable collectibility.

B. Interest-bearing accounts — The Truth-in-Savings Act (TISA) of 1991 and Federal Reserve Board Regulation DD.

    1. Banks must pay interest on the full balance of a customer's account each day.

    2. Disclosure requirements.

        a. A new customer must be given information relating to the minimum balance required to open an account and the interest to be paid, with the interest stated in terms of the annual percentage yield on the account, and the manner in which interest is calculated, and any fees, charges, and penalties, and the manner in which these are calculated.

    b. A customer's monthly statement must show the interest earned, any fees that were charged, how the fees were calculated, and the number of days covered by the statement.

E. The collection process.

  1. Designations of banks involved in the collection process [UCC 4-105].

    a. Depositary bank.
      1) The first bank to receive a check or other item for purposes of collection.
      2) The depositary bank is the only bank that is required to pay in a manner consistent with a restrictive indorsement [UCC 3-206(c)].

    b. Payor bank — The drawee bank, upon which a check is drawn, that is required to pay an item. (In the Federal Reserve System regulations, the payor bank is referred to as the "paying bank.")

    c. Collecting bank — Any bank, other than a payor bank, handling an item during the collection process.

    d. Intermediary bank — Any bank, other than the depositary bank or the payor bank, handling an item.

    e. Clearinghouse — An association of banks which exchange checks and other items drawn on each other.

    f. A bank may have one or more roles during the collection process.

  2. Check collection between customers of the same bank — When the holder, who is depositing the check or other item, and the drawer are customers of the same bank, the bank is the depositary and the payor bank, and the check is referred to as an "on-us" item.

    a. The bank charges (credits) the drawer's account and debits the depositor's account.

    b. The check is considered to be paid on the opening of the second banking day after the check was deposited [UCC 4-215(e)(2)].

  3. Check collection between customers of different banks.

    a. Depositary banks arrange for presentment of checks to drawee banks directly or through intermediary banks in the Federal Reserve System or a clearinghouse.

    b. Each intermediary bank must pass the check on before midnight of the next banking day following the bank's receipt of the check [UCC 4-202(b)].

     c. The depositor remains the owner of item until the check clears. The intermediary banks are subagents of the depositor.

  4. How the Federal Reserve System clears checks.

     a. When a check is deposited, the depositary bank makes a provisional credit for the amount of the check; the provisional credit can be revoked if the check is not collected.

     b. If the depositary bank sends the check to an intermediary bank (or a clearinghouse, such as the Federal Reserve Bank System), each collecting bank will provisionally credit the account of its transferor.

     c. When the check is received by the drawee (payor) bank, the check is examined; if the check contains no forgeries, alterations, etc., and there are sufficient funds in the account to cover the amount of the check, and there are no stop-payment orders, the check is posted to the drawer's account.

     d. Usually, a final settlement is made when, after a certain period of time, a provisional settlement is not revoked.

  5. Electronic check presentment.

     a. Most checks are processed electronically and information is encoded in the magnetic ink character recognition (MICR) strips on the bottom of checks by depositary banks so that the MICR strips can be read and processed by other banks' computers.

     b. Checks may be retained or stored under a Federal Reserve or other truncation agreement and only the images of the checks or descriptive information on the checks are transmitted for purposes of making presentments for payment [UCC 4-110].

     c. The bank that encodes information on a check or transmits the check's image or information warrants to subsequent collecting banks and the payor bank that the encoded or transmitted image or information is correct [UCC 4-209].

V.   Electronic fund transfers.

  A. Electronic funds transfers (EFTs) are transmissions of money, or funds, that are accomplished through the facilities of electronic funds transfer systems (EFTSs) using computers, terminals, telephones, magnetic tapes, etc.

    1. Commercial electronic funds transfers are governed by Article 4A of the UCC).

2. The federal Electronic Fund Transfer Act (EFTA) applies to consumer electronic funds transactions.

B. Types of EFT systems.

1. Automated teller machines (ATMs).

a. The ATM terminal is connected to a bank's computer and enables bank customers to make deposits and payments to an account, to perform other account transactions, such as withdrawing and transferring funds, and to obtain credit card advances.

b. Access to an ATM requires inserting a plastic access or debit card containing encoded data and entering a personal identification number (PIN).

2. Point-of-sales systems.

a. On-line terminals at checkout counters in stores connect to computers at customers' banks, or other financial institutions, which have issued access cards to customers.

b. After insertion of a customer's access card, a computer verifies customer's account balance and debits account for amount of purchases.

3. Direct deposits and withdrawals.

a. Bank customers may authorize direct deposits of payments of social security benefits, employers' wages or salaries, pension benefits, etc.

b. Customers may authorize their banks or other financial institutions to make automatic payments from accounts (in which customers have made deposits) at regular, recurrent intervals to third parties (e.g., insurance premiums, utility bills, home mortgages, automobile or other installment loan payments, and taxes due to Internal Revenue Service).

4. Pay-by-telephone systems — A customer may access a financial institution's computer system by telephone in order to direct a transfer of funds from one account to another or from the customer's account to another person (e.g., an entity, such as utility company).

C. Consumer fund transfers.

1. The Electronic Fund Transfer Act (EFTA) is a disclosure statute that is administered by the Federal Reserve Board which has adopted Regulation E in order to implement EFTA.

2. The EFTA governs financial institutions (including banks, savings and loan associations, credit unions, and other entities that directly or indirectly hold

accounts) that offer electronic funds transfers services to consumer account holders.

3. Electronic funds transfers (EFTs) to and from demand, savings, and other asset accounts established for personal, family, or household purposes, pursuant to a written prearranged plan under which periodic or recurring transfers are contemplated, are covered by the EFTA.

4. Disclosure requirements — Financial institution must make disclosures to consumers informing them of their rights and responsibilities.

   a. Liability when debit card or other device is lost, stolen, or misplaced.
      1) If a customer notifies the bank within two business days of learning of the loss or theft, the customer's liability for any unauthorized transfer is limited to $50.
      2) If a customer notifies the bank more than two business days after learning of the loss or theft, the customer's liability for any unauthorized transfers is limited to $500.
      3) If a customer fails to notify the bank of the loss or theft within 60 days after receipt of periodic statement reflecting an unauthorized transfer, the customer may be liable for the unauthorized transfers.

   b. A customer must notify the bank of any errors in the monthly statement within 60 days.
      1) The bank must make a good faith investigation and give a written report to the customer within ten business days.
      2) If more time is needed for investigation and resolution of the problem, the bank must recredit customer's account after ten days.
      3) If the bank finds that an error occurred, the bank must adjust the customer's account within one business day.
      4) If the bank finds that no mistake was made, the customer must return the money to the bank.

   c. The bank must give a receipt for each transfer made from an electronic terminal. (A receipt is not required for telephone transfers.)

   d. Periodic statements must be furnished.
      1) Contents of statement — Dates, types, and amounts of transfers; identity of any third parties involved in the transactions; fees charged; locations or identification of terminals that were used; and address and phone number for inquiries and error notices.
      2) The bank must provide a monthly statement for every month in which there is an electronic transfer and a quarterly statement if there are no electronic transactions.

   e. A customer may stop payment of a future preauthorized transfer by giving the bank three days notice but cannot reverse an EFT transaction after the transaction has occurred.

5. Unauthorized transfers — A transfer is unauthorized if:

   a. The transfer is initiated by a person (other than the consumer) who lacks authority to initiate the transfer;

   b. The consumer received no benefit from the transfer; and

   c. The consumer did not furnish the person with the card, PIN, code, or other means of access to the customer's account.

   d. The unauthorized use of an EFTS access device is a felony for which the penalties are imprisonment for up to ten years and a fine of $10,000.

6. Violations and damages.

   a. A bank is liable civilly for all damages that are proximately caused by the bank's failure to make an EFT (or bank's failure to comply with a direction to stop payment of a preauthorized transfer) in accordance with the terms and conditions of its agreement with its customer in the correct amount and in a timely manner when the customer properly instructs the bank to do so.

   b. Customer may recover actual damages and, if bad faith is shown, punitive damages of not less than $100 nor more than $1,000.

   c. In specific situations, class actions can be brought, in which case punitive damages are limited to the lesser of $500,000 or one percent of the institution's net worth.

   d. Certain violations of the EFTA are federal misdemeanors for which the penalty may be a fine of up to $5,000 and/or imprisonment for up to one year.

D. Commercial electronic funds transfers.

   1. Commercial EFTs are governed by private agreements, customary courses of dealings, and contract and tort case law as well as some Federal Reserve Board regulations.

   2. Contracts and customary courses of dealings provide for allocating risk of error, fraud, and loss among users of commercial EFT systems.

   3. Article 4A of the UCC is intended to cover commercial wholesale wire transfers and other types of transfers, including payments by mail.

   4. Wire transfers are unconditional orders to financial institutions to transfer funds to beneficiaries that are transmitted by electronic or other means over networks, which primarily are used to transfer funds between commercial accounts, such as Society for Worldwide Interbank Financial Telecommuni-

cations (SWIFT), Federal Reserve Fedwire, and New York Clearing House
Interbank Payments System (CHIPS).

KEY WORDS AND PHRASES IN TEXT

check
bank
cashier's check
remitter
teller's check
traveler's check
certified check
bank-customer relationship
honoring checks
overdraft
postdated check
stale check
missing indorsement
death or incompetence of a customer
stop-payment order
payment on a forged signature
customer negligence
altered check
depositary bank
payor (drawee or paying) bank
collecting bank

intermediary bank
bank collection process
"on-us" check
clearinghouse
provisional credit
Federal Reserve System
Expedited Funds Availability Act
Regulation E
hold on a deposited check
Truth-in-Savings Act
electronic fund transfer (EFT)
personal identification number (PIN)
automated teller machine (ATM)
point-of-sale system
direct deposit and withdrawal
pay-by-telephone system
consumer electronic transfer
Electronic Fund Transfer Act (EFTA)
preauthorized transfer
commercial electronic fund transfers

FILL-IN QUESTIONS

1. A check is a demand draft drawn on a bank or other financial institution. The bank is the drawee. The drawer of a check is termed the bank's _____. The bank is referred to as the _____ when the bank pays out on the check.

2. Often, particularly when a person is making a large purchase, a seller is concerned that the buyer's personal check will be dishonored. In order to ensure against a dishonor, the buyer will use a cashier's check or a certified check. A _____ check is a check drawn by a bank upon itself. A _____ check is a personal check drawn by the buyer on the buyer's own bank and is treated as being "accepted" by the drawee bank.

3. In states that have adopted the revisions of Articles 3 and 4 of the UCC, if certification of a check is obtained by a drawer or a _____, the drawer and the _____ are relieved of secondary liability based upon their signatures.

4. There is a contractual relationship between a depositor and the depositor's bank. The bank, therefore, is required to honor checks drawn on the depositor's account unless

(1) there are insufficient funds in the account and the bank has not agreed to honor overdrafts; (2) _____;
(3) _____;
(4) _____; or
(5) _____.

5. _____ refers to the period of time between the issuance of a check and the check's final payment, during which the drawer retains the use of funds. This period is eliminated when an electronic fund _____ is used.

6. At an _____ (ATM), a customer of a bank or other financial institution who is provided with access to an electronic fund transfer system initiates an electronic transfer by inserting the customer's _____ and typing in the customer's _____ (PIN).

7. The Electronic Fund Transfer Act applies to consumer electronic transfers and, therefore, demand, savings, and other asset accounts that are established for _____ purposes. The Act, however, does not apply to _____ electronic transfers that are electronic transactions between business firms or between business firms and financial institutions.

8. In addition to disclosing information to customers at the time of an agreement, with regard to each electronic fund transfer, a bank or financial institution must provide a customer with a _____ indicating the amount, date, and type of transfer, the customer's account number, the identity of any third party involved, and the _____ of the terminal that was used. The financial institution must also provide a _____ statement for every month in which there is an electronic transfer of funds.

9. The Electronic Fund Transfer Act provides that a bank customer's liability for unauthorized electronic fund transfers when the customer's access card is lost or stolen will be limited to $50 if the loss or theft is reported within _____ business days after the customer learns of the loss or theft. If such notification is given to the bank later, the liability of the customer is limited to $_____ as long as the notification is given within _____ _____ days after the customer has received a bank statement reflecting unauthorized transfers.

MULTIPLE CHOICE QUESTIONS

1. The status of a bank is such that:
    A. the bank is an agent of its depositor.
    B. the bank's status varies so that sometimes it is classified as an agent and other times as a holder of instruments in its own right.
    C. the bank acquires its status based on the classification given to the bank by its depositor.
    D. the bank is a holder.

2. In theory, a bank is liable for making a payment in all but one of the following situations. That situation is:
    A. The bank pays an altered instrument, such alteration being the result of the drawer's negligence.
    B. The bank pays a check on which the drawer's signature is missing.
    C. The bank pays after receipt of a valid stop-payment order given by the drawer, the bank's depositor.
    D. The bank pays a check on which the signature of the drawer is forged in such a way that the forgery cannot be detected.

3. A written stop-payment order is effective for:
    A. fourteen days.
    B. one month.
    C. six months.
    D. one year.

4. In general, a drawee bank is not obligated to pay a stale check. A stale check is a check that is presented for payment more than:
    A. three months after the date of the check.
    B. six months after the date of the check.
    C. a reasonable period after the issue of the check.
    D. one year after the issue of the check.

5. Under Article 4 of the UCC, if a check is presented to a drawee bank for payment, the drawee bank is under a duty to pay or dishonor such check:
    A. before the opening of business on the second banking day following the day of presentment.
    B. before the close of banking business on the day upon which the check is presented to the drawee bank.
    C. within three business days after presentment of the check.
    D. immediately upon presentment and agreement to pay the check.

6. On a Monday morning, McColgin deposits a $30,000 check in his account at a bank in Dallas, Texas. The check is drawn on another bank in Dallas. McColgin wishes to withdraw the funds as soon as possible. McColgin's bank has adopted a "hold schedule" that complies with the Expedited Funds Availability Act. McColgin may withdraw:
    A. the entire $30,000 on Tuesday (the next day).
    B. $100 on Tuesday (the next day) and the remaining $29,900 on the following day, Wednesday.
    C. $100 on Tuesday (the next day) and the remaining $29,900 two days later on Thursday.
    D. The entire $30,000 on the following Monday.

7. Assume that on the tenth day of a month, a Monday, McDevitt deposits a $40,000 check in her account at a bank in Newark, New Jersey. The check is drawn on a bank located in Seattle, Washington. McDevitt wishes to withdraw the funds by check as soon as possible. McDivitt's bank has adopted a "hold schedule" that complies with the Expedited Funds Availability Act. McDivitt may withdraw:

    A. the entire $40,000 on Tuesday, the eleventh of the month.

    B. $100 on Tuesday, the eleventh of the month, and the remaining $39,900 on Wednesday, the twelfth.

    C. $100 on Tuesday, the eleventh of the month, and the remaining $39,900 on Monday, the seventeenth.

    D. $10,000 on Tuesday, the eleventh of the month, and the remaining $30,000 on Wednesday, the nineteenth.

8. Lori has a checking account at the Sun City Bank. She also has borrowed $10,000 from the bank and has agreed that the monthly loan payments of $500 will be automatically withdrawn from her checking account and transferred to the bank on the fifteenth day of each month. Which of the following statement is correct?

    A. Lori has agreed to a preauthorized transfer for which the Sun City Bank need **not** furnish a receipt.

    B. The Sun City Bank must provide Lori with a monthly statement of her checking account transactions.

    C. Lori will be unable to stop the transfer of next month's loan installment payment to Sun City Bank.

    D. If Sun City Bank makes a mistake by transferring $900 from Lori's account on the fifteenth day of this month, Lori is entitled to an immediate credit of $500.

9. Elmco, Inc. has an account at the Bank of Elm County, as do its twenty employees. Rather than issue paychecks, Elmco, Inc. has agreed to make weekly payroll payments directly to the accounts of its employees at the bank.

    A. Even if Elmco, Inc. notifies its employees that the weekly payroll deposits are being made, the Bank of Elm County is required to notify the employees, who also are the bank's customers, of the deposits.

    B. Because Elmco, Inc.'s account at the Bank of Elm County is **not** established for personal, family, or household use, the transactions covering the direct payroll deposits are **not** within the purview of the Electronic Fund Transfer Act.

    C. If the Bank of Elm County fails to make payroll transfers this week because there are insufficient funds in Elmco, Inc.'s account, the bank will be liable to Elmco, Inc. for all damages proximately caused by the bank's failure to make electronic fund transfers.

    D. If the Bank of Elm County fails to make payroll transfers this week because severe storms have resulted in lack of electric service to the bank for four days, the bank will be liable to Elmco, Inc.'s employees for all damages proximately caused by the bank's failure to make the electronic fund transfers.

10. Jo's bank maintains an automated teller machine (ATM) for the use of the bank's customers. The bank has complied with the Electronic Fund Transfer Act. The bank, therefore, has made disclosures to its customers including a disclosure that the maximum amount that can be withdrawn from an ATM on any one day is $300. On May 2, Jo deposited checks totaling $872 at the ATM. She also withdrew $300 in cash on May 5 at the ATM. She received a bank statement on June 1 that listed the May 2 deposit as being for $800 and the May 5 withdrawal as being for $3,000. On Monday, June 2, Jo notified the bank of the errors.

    A. The bank need **not** do anything for ten business days, at which point the bank must begin a good faith investigation.

B. After 45 days, during which the bank must conduct a good faith investigation, the bank must credit $2,772 to Jo's account, if the bank cannot find the cause of the error.

C. The bank must conduct a good faith investigation and report the results thereof to Jo before June 13 and, if the bank is unable to find the error, credit $2,772 to Jo's account.

D. After ten business days, the bank must credit Jo's account for $72. Thereafter, the bank must conduct a good faith investigation and report the results to Jo before June 13 and, if the bank is unable to find the error, credit $2,700 to Jo's account.

Questions 11, 12, 13, and 14,are based upon the following fact situation: The Second Massachusetts Bank had properly notified its customers of its policy of permitting a maximum withdrawal of $300 per day from one of the bank's ATMs. Harold, who is a customer of the Second Massachusetts Bank, lost his access card on July 5. The card was found by Lucky who used the card in order to make five successive withdrawals of $300 on July 6, 7, 8, 9, and 10. Neither Harold nor the Bank knew that the access card was found by Lucky on July 5.

11. Assume that Harold notified the bank on July 6 that his access card was lost. Harold will be liable for:
    A. no more than $50.
    B. no more than $500.
    C. the entire $1,500.
    D. nothing.

12. Assume that Harold notified the Second Massachusetts Bank of the loss of his access card on July 8. Harold will be liable for:
    A. no more than $50.
    B. no more than $500.
    C. the entire $1,500.
    D. nothing.

13. Assume that Harold had difficulty remembering his personal identification number (PIN) and, therefore, wrote his PIN on his access card. If Harold notified the bank on July 6 that his access card was lost, Harold will be liable for:
    A. no more than $50.
    B. no more than $500.
    C. the entire $1,500.
    D. nothing.

14. Assume that Harold notified the Second Massachusetts Bank of the loss of his access card in September after receiving two bank statements on which the withdrawals by Lucky were included. Harold will be liable for:
    A. no more than $50.
    B. no more than $500.
    C. the entire $1,500.
    D. nothing.

UNIT FIVE:
CREDITORS' RIGHTS AND BANKRUPTCY

The material in this unit deals with the rights of debtors and creditors. Some of the methods available to creditors for ensuring that legally owed obligations will be paid and the protections afforded to borrowers and purchasers before and after they enter credit transactions are discussed in Chapters 30 and 31. The subject matter of Chapter 32 is the federal bankruptcy law, the purpose of which is to provide orderly procedures for discharging and rehabilitating or reorganizing debtors who are unable to pay their debts while providing for the equitable distribution of their assets among their creditors.

CHAPTER 30
SECURED TRANSACTIONS

Secured transactions are credit transactions that are coupled with security interests in personal property. The personal property that secures an obligation is called the collateral. In a secured transaction, the buyer or borrower (referred to as the debtor) gives rights in personal property to a seller or lender (referred to as the secured party) as security that an obligation will be paid or otherwise performed. If the debtor defaults by failing to carry out the underlying obligation (which often is for the payment of money), the secured party can reach the collateral as a substitute for the debtor's performance. Such devices are used to finance purchases made by manufacturers, retailers, other enterprises, and consumers. Article 9 of the Uniform Commercial Code (UCC or the Code) sets forth the legal rules that govern secured transactions.

The material in the latter part of the chapter deals with the priorities that secured parties have if they have perfected their security interests in collateral and the rights and duties of secured parties before and after a default by a debtor.

THINGS TO KEEP IN MIND

1. In order for a secured transaction to be effective between the parties to the transaction (the debtor and the secured party), the security interest must "attach" to the collateral; in order for the secured transaction to be effective against third parties, the security interest must be "perfected."

2. The objective of secured transaction devices is to protect creditors who have extended credit by giving them security interests in personal property that typically is in the possession of their debtors. Under the Code, lesser protection is afforded to debtors and to other people who may also have extended credit or otherwise dealt with the same debtors.

OUTLINE

I. The terminology of secured transactions.

    A. Definitions.

        1. Security interest — An interest in personal property or fixtures (personal property affixed to real property) that secures payment or performance of an obligation [UCC 1-201(37)].

        2. Secured party — A lender or seller who obtains a security interest in personal property [UCC 9-105(1)(m)].

3. Debtor — The party owing the obligation to pay money or otherwise perform [UCC 9-105(1)(d)].

4. Security agreement — An agreement which creates or provides for a security interest in personal property [UCC 9-105(1)(l)].

5. Collateral — Personal property that is subject to a security interest [UCC 9-105(1)(c)].

6. Financing statement — A document that is filed with a government office in order to give notice that a security interest exists in particular collateral [UCC 9-402].

B. Classification of collateral.

1. Tangible, physical, personal property (referred to as "goods" in Article 9) — Things that are moveable at the time that the security interest attaches or goods which are affixed to real property and referred to as fixtures [UCC 9-105(1)(h)].

   a. Includes standing timber, which is to be cut and removed, growing crops, and unborn young of animals.

   b. Goods are classified in accordance with their primary use [UCC 9-109]. They may be:
      1) Consumer goods — Used or bought primarily for personal, family, or household use.
      2) Equipment — Used or bought primarily for business use.
      3) Farm products — Crops, livestock, or supplies used or produced in farming operations, or products of crops or livestock in their manufactured state and in the possession of the debtor, who engages in farming or ranching.
      4) Inventory — Goods held for sale or lease, materials used or consumed in business, and work in progress.

2. Intangible personal property.

   a. Intangible personal property that is evidenced by a writing evidencing rights and sometimes referred to as "semi-intangible" property.
      1) Chattel paper — A writing (or a group of writings) evidencing a monetary obligation and a security interest in or lease of specific goods [UCC 9-105(1)(b)].
      2) Documents of title — Bills of lading, dock warrants or receipts, warehouse receipts, or other documents which, in the regular course of business or financing, are treated as evidence that the person in possession is entitled to receive, hold, and dispose of the document and the goods covered by the document [UCC 1-201(15), 7-201, 9-105(1)(f)].

3) Instruments — Writings that, in the ordinary course of business, are transferred by delivery with any necessary indorsement or by assignment [UCC 9-105(1)(i)].
   a) Negotiable instruments [UCC 3-104].
   b) Certificated investment securities, such as stocks and bonds [UCC 8-102(1)(a)].
   c) Writings that are not themselves security agreements or leases (e.g., nonnegotiable commercial paper).
4) Uncertificated investment securities [UCC 8-102(1)(b)].

b. Other intangible personal property [UCC 9-106].
   1) Accounts — Rights to payment for goods sold or leased or services performed that are not evidenced by an instrument or chattel paper (e.g., accounts receivable and contract rights).
   2) General intangible — Personal property other than goods, accounts, chattel paper, documents, instruments, and money (e.g., patents and copyrights).

II. Creating security interests.

   A. Attachment — Once attachment occurs, a security interest is enforceable between the debtor and the secured party so that the secured party is assured that certain predesignated property will be available to satisfy a debt should the debtor default [UCC 9-203].

   B. Requisites for the attachment:

      1. Written agreement — A statement that the parties have entered into a secured transaction signed by the debtor and containing a description of collateral.

         a. A writing is not necessary if the secured party is given possession of the collateral (a pledge).

         b. If a security interest is to cover after-acquired property, this must be specified in the security agreement [UCC 9-204(1)]. [See below at V.]

      2. Secured party must give value [UCC 1-201(44)]. A secured party gives value if the secured party acquires a security interest:

         a. In return for any consideration sufficient to support a simple contract;

         b. In return for a commitment to extend credit; or

         c. In satisfaction of or as security for a preexisting (antecedent) obligation.

      3. Debtor must have rights in collateral — The debtor must have an ownership interest in the collateral or a right to obtain possession of the collateral.

4. If the collateral is uncertificated investment securities, attachment occurs when the parties have entered into a security agreement, the secured party has given value, the debtor has rights in the uncertificated securities, and the security interest is registered with the issuer of the securities [UCC 8-320, 8-321, 8-408].

III. Purchase-money security interest — A purchase-money security interest (PMSI) is a security interest in specific collateral taken by the seller of the collateral or a creditor, who advances funds or incurs an obligation, enabling the debtor to acquire the collateral [UCC 9-107].

IV. Perfecting a security interest — The process whereby a secured party obtains priority over other third parties having claims against the debtor who may wish to have their debts satisfied out of the same collateral.

   A. The method used for perfection is determined by the classification of the collateral that is the subject of the security interest. [See above at I. B.]

   B. Perfection by filing.

      1. The filing of a financing statement with the appropriate public office gives constructive notice of the secured party's security interest to other creditors of the debtor.

      2. Required method of perfecting unless the secured party is given possession of the collateral or perfection is automatic when attachment occurs.

      3. The financing statement [UCC 9-402(1)] — Contents:

         a. Signature of the debtor;

         b. Names and addresses of the debtor and the secured party; and

         c. Description of the collateral — There must be a statement specifically indicating the type of collateral or describing the collateral.
            1) The description should be the same as the description in the security agreement.
            2) The security agreement itself may be filed as the financing statement.

      4. The financing statement is filed under the debtor's name; if a debtor's name is changed, it is necessary to file a new financing statement (which may be signed by the secured party [UCC 9-402(2)]) within four months.

      5. Where to file — The UCC gives three alternatives [UCC 9-401].

         a. Central filing with a state official, such as the secretary of state.

         b. Local filing with an official of the county.

c. Combination of local filing for consumer and/or farm goods and central filing for other types of collateral.

C. Perfection without filing.

1. Perfection by possession [UCC 9-305].

   a. The secured party can perfect a security interest by taking physical possession of tangible or semi-intangible collateral (a pledge).

   b. It is the method of perfection required for instruments, other than instruments that constitute part of chattel paper [UCC 9-304(1)].
      1) Instruments include negotiable instruments, certificated investment securities, and writings evidencing rights to receive payments of money, other than chattel paper, that are transferred in the ordinary course of business by negotiation or assignment.
      2) If the collateral, other than goods covered by a document of title, is in the possession of a bailee, the secured party is deemed to have possession of the collateral for purposes of perfection [UCC 9-305].

2. Perfection may be by attachment in the following cases [UCC 9-302(1)].

   a. Purchase-money security interest in consumer goods — A PMSI in consumer goods, other than motor vehicles and fixtures, is perfected when attachment occurs.

   b. An assignment of a small portion of accounts receivable to an assignee [UCC 9-302(1)(e)].

   c. Attachment of security interest in uncertificated investment securities by registration with the issuer [UCC 8-320, 8-321, 8-408].

D. Perfection of security interests in motor vehicles — In most states, perfection of a security interest is obtained when there is a notation of such interest on the certificate of title (registered with the state) for a motor vehicle, boat, or motor home.

E. Collateral moved to another jurisdiction.

1. A perfected security interest covers collateral that subsequently is moved to another state for the remaining perfection period or four months, whichever is shorter [UCC 9-103(1)(d) and (e)].

2. Automobiles — UCC 9-103(2).

   a. If the state in which an automobile is originally registered does not require a notation on a certification of title as part of the state's perfection process, perfection of a security interest ends at the expiration of four months after the vehicle is moved into another jurisdiction.

b. If the state in which an automobile is originally registered requires a notation on a certificate of title as part of the state's perfection process, perfection of a security interest continues after the vehicle is moved into another jurisdiction until the auto is registered in the new state.

E. Effective time of perfection.

1. Filing of a financing statement is effective for five years [UCC 9-403(2)].

2. Renewal of perfection is effected by filing a continuation statement within six months of expiration of prior filing [UCC 9-403(3)].

V.   The scope of a security interest — A security agreement may cover the proceeds of the sale of the collateral, property subsequently acquired by the debtor, and future advances made by the secured party.

A. Proceeds.

1. A secured party has an interest in the proceeds received from the sale, exchange, or other disposition of the collateral [UCC 9-203(3), 9-306(2)].

2. This security interest continues for ten days after the receipt of proceeds by the debtor, or a longer period if:

a. The filed financing statement covers the original collateral, and the proceeds are a form of collateral in which a security interest may be perfected by filing in the office in which the original financing statement was filed [UCC 9-306(3)(a)];

b. The filed financing statement covers the original collateral, and cash proceeds are used by the debtor to acquire other property that falls within the description of collateral in the original financing statement [UCC 9-306(3)(a)];

c. The filed financing statement covers the original collateral and the proceeds are identifiable cash proceeds [UCC 9-306(3)(b)]; or

d. The security interest in the proceeds is perfected before the ten-day period expires [UCC 9-306(3)(c)].

B. After-acquired property.

1. A security agreement may cover personal property, such as inventory, that is purchased or otherwise acquired by the debtor after the execution of the security agreement [UCC 9-204(1)].

2. If there is an after-acquired property clause in the security agreement, the security interest does not attach to consumer goods unless the debtor

acquired the goods within ten days after the secured party gave value [UCC 9-204(2)].

C. Future advances — A security agreement may cover advances to be made by a secured party in the future (a continuing line of credit) [UCC 9-204(3)].

D. The floating lien concept.

1. The security agreement may provide that the secured party will have a security interest in the proceeds of the sale, exchange, or other disposition of the collateral and specified after-acquired property of the debtor and that the same collateral will cover future advances to be made by the secured party [UCC 9-203, 9-204, 9-306].

2. The security interest may cover changing, or "floating," collateral; the obligation that is secured by the collateral may also change or "float."

3. Floating liens may be used in order to finance purchases of inventory and may apply to a stock of goods as the goods are processed, sold, and turned into cash, accounts receivable, or chattel paper [UCC 9-205].

VI. Resolving priority disputes.

A. Secured versus unsecured parties — A secured party whose security interest has attached to the collateral has priority over unsecured and judgment creditors [UCC 9-301].

B. Secured party versus lien creditor.

1. A lien creditor is a creditor who has acquired a lien by attachment, levy, or other judicial process, or is an assignee for the benefit of creditors, a trustee in bankruptcy, or a receiver in equity [UCC 9-301(4)]. [See also Chapters 31 and 32.]

2. A secured party whose security interest has attached to the collateral and been perfected prevails over a lien creditor who has acquired a lien on the same property.

3. A secured party whose security interest has attached, but has not been perfected, does not prevail over a lien creditor [UCC 9-301(1)(b)].

4. A secured party who has a PMSI and files a financing statement within ten (or, in some states, twenty) days after the debtor receives possession of the collateral prevails over a lien creditor whose rights arose after the secured party's interest attached to the collateral, but before perfection [UCC 9-301(2)].

C. When more than one party is secured [UCC 9-312].

1. The general rule.

    a. A secured party whose security interest has attached and been perfected prevails over those who have not perfected their security interests.

    b. If two or more parties have perfected security interests in the same collateral, the first in time to perfect has priority [UCC 9-312(5)(a)].

    c. If two or more parties have unperfected security interests in the same collateral, the party whose security interest first attached has priority [UCC 9-312(5)(b)].

2. An exception: The purchase-money security interest (PMSI).

    a. A perfected PMSI in inventory has priority over an earlier perfected nonpurchase-money security interest if the secured party having the PMSI gives the nonpurchase-money secured party written notice of his or her interest before the debtor takes possession of the inventory [UCC 9-312(3)].

    b. A perfected PMSI in collateral, other than inventory, has priority over a perfected nonpurchase-money security interest if the perfected PMSI is perfected either before or within ten days after the debtor takes possession of the collateral; notice need not be given [UCC 9-312(4)].

D. Secured party versus buyer.

1. The general rule is that a security interest in collateral is continuous even when the collateral is sold, unless the secured party has authorized the sale [UCC 9-306(2)].

2. Exceptions:

    a. Buyers in the ordinary course of business.
        1) A buyer in the ordinary course of business is a person who, in good faith and without knowledge that the sale is in violation of the ownership rights or security interest of a third party in the goods, buys the goods from a person who is in the business of selling goods of that kind [UCC 1-201(9)].
        2) Buyers of inventory and equipment in the ordinary course of business take the goods free of any security interest given by the seller, even if the security interest is perfected and the buyer knows of its existence [UCC 9-307(1)].

    b. Buyers of farm products.
        1) A buyer of farm products from a person engaging in farming operations takes the products subject to a security interest, even if the buyer does not know of its existence [UCC 9-307(1)].
        2) Such a buyer takes free of the security interest unless the buyer:

a) Received a detailed notice of the security interest within one year before the purchase; or

b) Failed to register with the secretary of state before the purchase and the secured party perfected his or her security interest by centrally filing; or

c) Received notice from the secretary of state that the farm products being sold are subject to an effective financing statement (EFS) [Food Security Act of 1985, a federal statute].

c. Buyers of consumer goods from consumers.

1) A PMSI in consumer goods (which are sold to a buyer for personal, family, or household use) is perfected by attachment [UCC 9-302(1)(d)]; the secured party also may file a financing statement.

2) A buyer (e.g., a second hand buyer) of consumer goods from the debtor takes free of the PMSI if the buyer does not have knowledge of the security interest, gives value, and purchases the goods for personal, family, or household use, unless the secured party had filed a financing statement [UCC 9-307(2)].

d. Buyers of chattel paper.

1) Chattel paper is a writing evidencing an obligation and a security interest or lease [UCC 9-105(1)(b)].

2) A security interest in chattel paper is perfected by taking possession or filing a financing statement.

3) The secured party who takes possession of chattel paper has priority over subsequent lien creditors, buyers, and secured parties [UCC 9-312(5), 9-301(1)(b) and (c)].

4) The secured party who takes possession of chattel paper may assign his or her rights to an assignee.

a) If the secured party gives possession of the chattel paper to an assignee (i.e., "repledges" the paper), the assignee then collects the debt directly from the debtor.

b) If the secured party retains possession of the chattel paper, the secured party (assignor) collects the debt from the debtor and remits payments to the assignee.

5) The secured party who perfects a security interest in chattel paper by filing a financing statement may assign his or her rights to an assignee.

6) The secured party who perfects a security interest in chattel paper by filing a financing statement loses priority when, in the ordinary course of business, a subsequent purchaser (a second secured party) of chattel paper from the debtor (who has retained possession of the paper) gives value and takes possession of the chattel paper without knowledge that the paper is subject to a prior security interest [UCC 1-201(32) and (33), 9-308(a)].

a) To avoid losing priority, the first secured party can put a notation on the chattel paper to the effect that he or she has a security interest.

b) If a negotiable promissory note is separated from a security agreement, the holder in due course of the note takes free of the security interest [UCC 9-309].

  e. Buyers of instruments.
    1) An instrument is a negotiable note, CD, draft, or check; a certificated investment security; or other writing evidencing a right to the payment of money, but which is not chattel paper [UCC 9-105(1)(i)].
    2) A security interest in an instrument is perfected by taking possession (although UCC 8-321(2) and (4) and 9-304(4) and (5) provide for limited exceptions) so that the first secured party who takes possession of an instrument has priority [UCC 9-301(1)(b) and (c), 9-304(1), 9-312(5), 8-317].

VII. Other rights and duties under Article 9.

  A. Unless the parties otherwise agree in the security agreement, their rights and duties prior to default or termination are determined by Article 9 of the UCC.

  B. Information requests by creditors.

    1. A secured party making a filing may ask that a note of the file number and the date and hour of the original filing be made on a copy of the financing statement [UCC 9-407(1)].

    2. A filing officer must give a certificate containing information regarding filed financing statements to others, such as potential secured parties, upon request and payment of a fee [UCC 9-407(2)].

  C. Assignment, amendment, and release.

    1. A secured party may release all or a part of the security interest by having an appropriate notation made on the financing statement or filing a written statement of release or assignment [UCC 9-405(2)].

    2. The parties may amend a security agreement and financing statement; the debtor must sign an amendment [UCC 9-402(4)].

  D. Reasonable care of collateral (when secured party has possession of the collateral).

    1. A secured party must use reasonable care in order to preserve the collateral [UCC 9-207(1) and (3)].

    2. If the collateral increases in value, the secured party can hold the increased value or profit as additional security, unless it is in the form of money which must be remitted to the debtor or applied toward reducing the secured debt [UCC 9-207(2)(c)].

3. Collateral, other than fungible goods, must be kept in identifiable form [UCC 9-207(2)(d)].

4. The debtor must pay reasonable charges incurred by the secured party in preserving, operating, and caring for the collateral, and bears the risk of loss or damage [UCC 9-207(2)(a) and (b)].

E. The status of the debt — The debtor may request information as to the status of the debt by signing a statement indicating the aggregate amount of the unpaid debt and requesting that the statement be approved or corrected and returned by the secured party within two weeks [UCC 9-208(1) and (2)].

F. Termination statement [UCC 9-404].

1. A termination statement is a written statement to the effect that the secured party no longer has a security interest in the collateral.

2. Collateral other than consumer goods — When the debt is paid, or other obligation satisfied, the secured party must send a termination statement to the debtor within ten days after a written request for such a statement from the debtor.

3. Consumer goods — If a financing statement had been filed, the secured party must file a termination statement in the filing office within one month after there is no outstanding secured obligation (or within ten days after a written request from the debtor).

4. If the secured party fails to send or file a termination statement within the prescribed time, the secured party is liable to the debtor for any loss caused by the failure to the debtor plus $100.

VIII. Default.

A. What constitutes a default by the debtor usually is stated in the security agreement, subject to the UCC good faith requirement and unconscionability doctrine.

B. Default occurs because of a breach of the terms of the security agreement, such as:

1. Failure of debtor to meet scheduled payments.

2. Bankruptcy of the debtor.

3. Breach of warranty of good title with regard to equipment or warranty that the equipment is free of liens, encumbrances, or other security interests.

C. Basic remedies — The rights and remedies provided for in UCC 9-501(1) are cumulative.

1. A secured party can relinquish a security interest and then sue the debtor based upon the underlying obligation of the debtor, obtain a judgment, and have the judgment enforced by execution and levy. [See Chapter 31.]

2. A secured party can take possession of the collateral and retain the collateral in satisfaction of the obligation or sell the collateral applying the proceeds toward the debt.

3. The Soldiers' and Sailors' Relief Act of 1940 provides that, if a security interest was created prior to the time a person in the military is assigned to active duty, the secured party cannot take possession and dispose of the collateral while the person is on active duty and for six months after the active duty ends.

D. Secured party's right to take possession — A secured party may take possession of collateral covered by a security agreement [UCC 9-503].

    1. The secured party must do so without breach of the peace.

    2. The secured party must use reasonable care in the custody and preservation of collateral [UCC 9-207].

    3. The secured party may have the debtor assemble the collateral and have the collateral available at a mutually convenient location.

    4. If the collateral is difficult to remove, the secured party may have the collateral rendered unusable by the debtor and dispose of the collateral on the debtor's premises.

E. Disposition of collateral — A secured party who has obtained possession of the collateral can retain the collateral in satisfaction of the obligation [UCC 9-505(2)] or sell, lease, or otherwise dispose of the collateral in any commercially reasonable manner [UCC 9-504(1)].

    1. Retention of the collateral by the secured party [UCC 9-505].

        a. A secured party, who is retaining the collateral in satisfaction of the obligation, must give written notice to the debtor (if the debtor has not signed a statement renouncing or modifying his or her rights after default) and other secured parties from whom the secured party has received written notice of a claim of an interest in the collateral.

        b. If within twenty-one days after the notice is sent, the secured party receives a written objection from a party entitled to receive notification, the secured party must dispose of the collateral in accordance with UCC 9-504 [See below at VIII. E. 3.]; if no such objection is received, the secured party may retain the collateral in full satisfaction of the debtor's obligation [UCC 9-505(2)].

2. Consumer goods — A secured party who has a PMSI in consumer goods may not retain the goods if more than 60% of the price, or loan, has been paid by the debtor, unless (after default) the debtor signed a written statement renouncing or modifying the right to demand the sale of the goods [UCC 9-505(1)].

3. Disposition procedures [UCC 9-504].

   a. A secured party may dispose of the collateral by sale (private or public), lease, or any other commercially reasonable means.

   b. Notice must be given to the debtor and other secured parties who have given notice of claims so that the debtor and the other secured parties may exercise their rights of redemption, unless the goods are perishable [UCC 9-506].

   c. A purchaser or other transferee takes the property free of claims of the debtor and the secured party [UCC 9-504(4)].

4. Proceeds from disposition — The order of distribution of the proceeds [UCC 9-504(1)]:

   a. Expenses of sale, possessing, holding, and preparing for sale, including attorney fees.

   b. Satisfaction of debt.

   c. Subordinate security interest holders who gave written notification.

   d. Usually, a debtor is entitled to any surplus.

5. Deficiency judgment [UCC 9-504(2)].

   a. If after proper disposition of the collateral the entire amount of the obligation is not collected, the debtor is liable for the balance and the secured party can obtain a deficiency judgment.

   b. If the underlying transaction was a sale of accounts or chattel paper, the debtor is liable for the deficiency only if the security agreement so provides.

6. Redemption rights — The debtor or any other secured party (a person who has a "junior" security interest) can redeem the collateral by tendering performance of all obligations that were secured by the collateral and by paying certain expenses to the secured party before the secured party disposes of the collateral or enters into a contract for the collateral's disposition or before the debtor's obligation has been discharged through the secured party's retention of the collateral [UCC 9-506].

KEY WORDS AND PHRASES IN TEXT

secured transaction
security interest
Article 9 of the UCC
secured party
debtor
security agreement
collateral
tangible collateral
consumer goods
equipment
farm products
inventory
fixtures
intangible collateral
chattel paper
documents of title
instruments
accounts
general intangibles
attachment
value given to debtor by secured party
rights of debtor in the collateral
perfection of a security interest
perfection by filing
financing statement

continuation statement
perfection by possession (pledge)
automatic perfection (by attachment)
purchase-money security interest (PMSI)
after-acquired property
future advances
line of credit
floating lien
lien creditor
buyer of collateral in the ordinary
      course of business
buyer of consumer goods from
      consumer
assignment or release of security interest
amendment to financing statement
termination statement
default by debtor
secured party's right to take
      possession of collateral
disposing of collateral following default
retention of the collateral
proceeds from disposition of collateral
deficiency judgment
redemption rights

FILL-IN QUESTIONS

1.   A secured transaction is one in which a debtor, who has an obligation (usually to pay a sum of money), gives a _____ in personal property or fixtures to a lender or seller. The personal property in a secured transaction is referred to as the _____. The lender or seller is known as the _____.

2.   Goods that may be the subject matter of a secured transaction are classified in accordance with the primary purpose for which the goods are purchased and used. If the goods are used primarily by the debtor for personal, family, or household use, such goods are termed _____ goods. If the goods are used or consumed by a business firm in the manufacturing process, these goods are part of _____.

3.   A security interest is enforceable by a secured party against a debtor who has defaulted if the security interest has _____ to the collateral. The secured party, however, will only have priority over other creditors if the secured party has _____ his or her security interest.

4. A security interest attaches when (1) a debtor has _____ _____ , (2) the secured party has _____ , and (3) the parties have entered into an agreement which is required to be in writing if the secured party does not have possession of the collateral.

5. A security agreement is referred to as a floating lien if the agreement provides that a security interest will attach to the proceeds of the sale or other disposition of specified collateral, _____ , or _____ .

6. If two secured parties have security interests in the same collateral and neither of them has perfected, the party _____ _____ will have priority over the other.

7. Upon default by a debtor, a secured party may take possession of the collateral, to which his or her security interest attached, and retain the collateral, or _____ _____ _____ .

MULTIPLE CHOICE QUESTIONS

1. Article 9 of the Uniform Commercial Code, dealing with secured transactions, does **not** apply to the creation of a security interest in:
   A. personal property that has a value of $500 or less.
   B. personal property in which the debtor has no rights.
   C. personal property that is in the possession of a debtor.
   D. personal property that is in the possession of secured party.

2. An automobile purchased by Landau and secured by a purchase-money security interest will be classified as inventory if:
   A. Landau is in the business of selling automobiles and the automobile in question was purchased for resale.
   B. Landau is a salesman and uses the automobile in order to call on customers.
   C. Landau purchased the automobile for his mother.
   D. Two of the answers above are correct.

3. Boyne borrowed $500 from Rater and signed a writing. The writing provided that Boyne promised to repay the $500 to Rater on March 1 and gave Rater the right to take possession of and sell her fully described television set if she failed to repay the money.
   A. The writing is **not** a security agreement because the words "security interest" are not included in the writing.
   B. A security interest has been created in the television set only if the money borrowed was used to purchase the television set.
   C. Rater is the secured party and has a security interest in the television set.
   D. A security interest did **not** attach to the television set because Rater did **not** sign the writing.

4. A document that evidences both an obligation to pay money and a security interest in specified collateral is referred to as:
   A. a negotiable instrument.
   B. a financing statement.
   C. a chattel mortgage.
   D. chattel paper.

5. Usually, a negotiable draft:
   A. may **not** be used as collateral for a secured transaction.
   B. is considered to be goods if used for a secured transaction.
   C. may be used as collateral for a secured transaction that is perfected by possession.
   D. may be used as collateral for a secured transaction that is perfected by filing.

6. Public notice of a security interest in personal property is provided by filing a:
   A. security of agreement.
   B. chattel mortgage.
   C. bill of sale.
   D. financing statement.

7. Brennan, a manufacturer of clothing, and Carver, a producer of fabric, signed an agreement whereby Carver agreed to sell Brennan $10,000 worth of fabric, to be paid for in six months. The agreement provided that the transaction would be secured by a security interest in Brennan's present and future inventory and that Carver agreed to provide Brennan with a continuing line of credit for a period of 18 months.
   A. In order for the agreement to be binding on both Brennan and Carver, a financing statement must be filed with an appropriate government official.
   B. The agreement is ineffective to give Carver a security interest in additions to Brennan's inventory, after the expiration of the six-month period.
   C. The agreement provides for a valid floating lien and it is binding on Brennan and Carver.
   D. If Carver advances $30,000 to Brennan eleven months later, Carver is an unsecured creditor to the extent of the $30,000.

8. TV Town, Inc., a seller of television sets, maintains a large inventory of television sets which TV Town, Inc. obtains from manufacturers on credit. The manufacturers (creditors) have all taken security interests in the television sets and the proceeds therefrom and have made the necessary filings in order to perfect their security interests. TV Town, Inc. sells to many consumers. Some of TV Town, Inc.'s customers pay cash and others buy on credit. TV Town, Inc., takes a security interest in each customer's television set when it makes a credit sale, but TV Town, Inc. does **not** file a financing statement.
   A. The television sets in TV Town, Inc.'s hands are consumer goods.
   B. Because TV Town, Inc. takes purchase money security interests in the goods that TV Town, Inc. sells to customers, TV Town, Inc.'s security interests are perfected upon attachment.
   C. The manufacturers can enforce their security interests against the television sets in the hands of the purchasers who paid cash for them.
   D. A subsequent sale by one of TV Town, Inc.'s customers to a purchaser for value will be subject to TV Town, Inc.'s security interest.

9. Cooper was an appliance dealer. Cooper financed her inventory with her local bank and signed a security agreement using the inventory as security. Burkett purchased a freezer for $500 from Cooper. Cooper defaulted on her payments to the bank.
   A. A security agreement of this kind is illegal.
   B. The bank may reclaim the freezer from Burkett because the bank's security interest never attached to the freezer.
   C. The bank may reclaim the freezer from Burkett because the bank's security interest has been perfected.
   D. Burkett takes the freezer free of any security interests of Cooper or the bank.

10. Nestler owned a candy store and was the holder of a warehouse receipt that provided that the goods stored were to be delivered to the order of Nestler. Nestler borrowed money from Hirshy and gave Hirshy the warehouse receipt as security.
    A. This is **not** a secured transaction because a warehouse receipt **cannot** be collateral in which a creditor may have a security interest.
    B. Hirshy has **not** perfected his security interest unless a financing statement was properly filed.
    C. Goodbard, who lent Nestler money before the transaction between Nestler and Hirshy, has priority over Hirshy with regard to the warehouse receipt.
    D. Hirshy has perfected his security interest and has priority over other creditors of Nestler with regard to the warehouse receipt.

11. Epsilon sold Delta a CB radio for $180. Delta paid $50 immediately and agreed to pay $10 a month for thirteen months. The agreement of Epsilon and Delta was reduced to writing and signed by both Epsilon and Delta. Their agreement included a provision under which Epsilon has the right to repossess the radio if Delta defaulted in her payments. Nothing else was signed, recorded, or filed. A few days later, Epsilon and Delta had an argument. Since that time, Delta has continued to use the CB, but has **not** made any of the agreed payments.
    A. Epsilon, the debtor, and Delta, the secured party, have entered into an effective secured transaction.
    B. The security interest has attached to the CB radio and Epsilon has the right to repossess the CB and either retain the CB in satisfaction of the unpaid purchase price or sell the CB applying the proceeds of the sale to the unpaid balance.
    C. If Delta's car is wrecked in an accident, in which the CB is totally destroyed, Epsilon has priority over other unsecured creditors of Delta with regard to Delta's remaining personal property.
    D. The security interest has attached to the CB radio and Epsilon has the right to repossess the CB but will be required to sell the CB and apply the proceeds of the sale to the unpaid balance.

12. At a properly conducted public sale of property that was collateral for a secured transaction:
    A. the debtor is liable for any deficiency if the sale does not produce enough to satisfy all of the incurred charges and the debt.
    B. the debtor may **not** purchase the collateral being sold.
    C. the secured party may **not** purchase the collateral being sold.
    D. junior secured parties may **not** participate in any excess proceeds.

Questions 13 through 18 have been adapted from objective question #3(b) on the Uniform CPA Examination, May 1995. The questions are based upon the following fact situation: On January 2, Gray Interiors Corp., a retail seller of sofas, entered into a contract with Shore Furniture Co. for the purchase of 150 sofas for its inventory. The purchase price was $250,000. Gray paid $50,000 in cash and gave Shore a negotiable promissory note and a signed security agreement for the balance. On March 1, the sofas were delivered to Gray. On March 10, Shore filed a financing statement.

On February 1, Gray negotiated a $1,000,000 line of credit with Float Bank. Gray gave Float a signed security agreement that provided that Gray gave Float a security interest in Gray's present and future inventory. On February 20, Gray borrowed $100,000 from the line of credit. On March 5, Float filed a financing statement.

On April 1, Dove, a consumer purchaser, bought a sofa from Gray in the ordinary course of business. Dove was aware of both security interests.

13. Shore's security interest in the sofas attached on:
    A. January 2.
    B. March 1.
    C. March 10.

14. Shore's security interest in the sofas was perfected on:
    A. January 2.
    B. March 1.
    C. March 10.

15. Float's security interest in Gray's inventory attached on:
    A. February 1.
    B. March 1.
    C. March 5.

16. Float's security interest in Gray's inventory was perfected on:
    A. February 1.
    B. March 1.
    C. March 5.

17. A. Shore's security interest has priority because it was a purchase-money security interest.
    B. Float's security interest has priority because Float's financing statement was filed before Shore's.
    C. Float's security interest has priority because Float's security interest attached before Shore's.

18. A. Dove purchased the sofa subject to Shore's security interest.
    B. Dove purchased the sofa subject to both the Shore and Float security interests.
    C. Dove purchased the sofa free of either the Shore or Float security interest.

Chapter 31
Other Creditors' Remedies and Suretyship

The law dealing with the rights of creditors to be paid obligations that legally are owed to them has undergone considerable change. In part, this is due to the expansion of consumer oriented legislation. In this chapter, the authors review some of the means available to creditors to ensure payment of debts owed to them. The focus is on statutory liens, the remedies afforded by courts, and contractual agreements, including those providing for sureties and guarantors.

THINGS TO KEEP IN MIND

A creditor who has lent money or extended credit to another person has a contractual right to be paid (or to receive some other specified, promised performance) when the obligation is due. You are already familiar with some methods available to a creditor to ensure payment, such as the use of commercial paper, which was discussed in Unit Four, and secured transactions, the subject matter of Chapter 30. In order to feel more secure that an obligation will be carried out by a debtor, a creditor may require that the debtor obtain a surety or guarantor who will also promise to render some performance to the creditor. In addition, a creditor may obtain a lien on property, owned by a debtor, which can be sold in order to satisfy the obligation.

OUTLINE

I. Laws assisting creditor.

    A. Liens — A lien is a claim, charge, or encumbrance on a debtor's property.

        1. If the debtor (the property owner) fails to satisfy (discharge) a debt owed to a creditor, the creditor may foreclose on the lien so that the property can be sold and the proceeds of its sale (or other disposition) used to satisfy the claim of the creditor (lienholder).

            a. A consensual lien is based upon an agreement of the parties.

            b. A lien creditor has priority over other creditors to the extent of the value of the collateral that is covered by the lien and the amount of the debt that is owed to the creditor.

        2. Some liens enabling creditors to reach their debtors' property were recognized at common law; today, many liens are provided for by statute so

that encumbered property can be sold and the proceeds of the sales used to pay the debts owed to the lienholders.

    a. Statutes provide for recording, giving notice to the debtors, foreclosures, the sales of property subject to such liens, and payments of the debts, costs, and any surpluses to the property owners out of the proceeds of sales.

    b. Mechanic's (or materialman's) lien on real property — If a debt arises because an owner of real property fails to pay for labor, services, or materials furnished for purposes of making improvements on real property, the party to whom the obligation is owed may obtain a lien on the improved property.
       1) Written notice of the foreclosure (enforcement) of the lien must be given to the property owner and filed within a specified time period.
       2) The lien may be enforced, and the proceeds of the sale of the real property used in order to satisfy the debt owed to the lienholder.

    c. Artisan's lien on personal property — A bailee, who has possession and improved or stored another person's property and has not been paid for services and/or the value added to the property, may enforce a possessory lien on the property.

    d. Innkeeper's or hotelkeeper's lien — A hotel (or other facility offering similar accommodations to the public) that has possession of a guest's property has a possessory lien for the value of unpaid hotel charges.

    e. A warehouse may have a possessory lien for unpaid storage charges.

B. Judicial liens.

    1. When a creditor has not been paid, the creditor may institute a lawsuit against the debtor which, in the typical case, will result in the creditor getting a judgment against the debtor for the amount of the debt plus interest and costs.

    2. After a legal action is commenced, the debtor's property may be seized.

       a. If the property is seized before the trial, the seizure is referred to as attachment.

       b. If the property is seized after a judgment is entered against the debtor, frequently, the court's order is referred to as a writ of execution.

    3. Attachment — A prejudgment, court-ordered seizure of specific property of a debtor provided for by statute.

       a. Some state statutes providing for prejudgment attachment have been held to be unconstitutional because these statutes conflict with the due process clause of the Fourteenth Amendment.

b. The typical statute requires that the creditor file an affidavit stating that the debtor is in default and the statutory basis for attaching the specified property and post a bond to cover court costs, the value of the loss of the use of the property, and the value of the property being attached.

c. The court issues a writ of attachment directing the sheriff or other appropriate official to seize the property; after the trial and entry of a judgment in the creditor's favor, the property can be sold.

4. Writ of execution.

a. An order of the court issued after the award of a judgment to a creditor directing the seizure of (levy on) the debtor's nonexempt property that is within the geographic jurisdiction of the court and the subsequent sale of the property.

b. The proceeds of the sale are used in order to pay the judgment, interest, and the costs of the sale; any excess is paid to the debtor.

c. The debtor can redeem the property by satisfying (paying) the judgment before the property is sold.

5. Garnishment — A legal process that can be used by a judgment creditor to reach property belonging to the debtor when the property is held by a third person (e.g., wages or funds in a bank account) .

a. The court issues an order directed to the sheriff or other appropriate official to attach or levy on property, credits, or funds under the control of a third person, such as an employer or bank.

b. If the third person is an employer, the employer is then required to pay a portion of the wages to the official for the benefit of the judgment creditor.
   1) Federal and state statutes ensure that a specified minimum amount (or percentage) of wages cannot be reached by garnishment.
   2) Some states do not permit garnishment of wages in order to collect debts.
   3) An employer cannot discharge an employee because his or her wages are subject to garnishment unless (in some states) wages are subject to multiple garnishments.

C. Creditors' composition (and/or extension) agreement — An enforceable agreement between a debtor and two or more of the debtor's creditors who agree to accept reduced payments in satisfaction of the debts that are owed to each of them and/or to extend the dates upon which the debts will be paid.

1. Each creditor's promise to accept the smaller sum and/or extend time for payment, instead of full, timely payment, is consideration for the other creditors' similar promises. (Other creditors are not bound by the agreement.)

2. The debtor and two or more of the debtor's creditors may agree that each creditor will:

   a. Accept a sum less than the amount owed by the debtor (a composition);

   b   Extend the period of time within which the debtor will pay the full amount owed (an extension); or

   c   Accept a partial cash payment and a scaling down of the amount owed and payable over a stated period of time (a composition and extension).

D. Mortgage foreclosure [See also Chapter 50].

   1. A creditor who lends money secured by real property enters into a mortgage agreement with the debtor. (The creditor is the mortgagee and the debtor is the mortgagor.)

   2. If the mortgagor defaults, foreclosure procedures may be instituted by the mortgagee.

      a. If, after payment of the cost of foreclosure and the debt, there is a surplus, the surplus is paid to the debtor (mortgagor).

      b. If the proceeds are insufficient to pay the obligation that was secured by the mortgage, the creditor (mortgagee) can obtain a deficiency judgment in order to attempt to reach other nonexempt property belonging to the debtor.

      c. Equity of redemption.
         1) Before the sale, the debtor (mortgagor) has the right to redeem the property by paying the full amount of the debt, accrued interest, and costs.
         2) In some states, the mortgagor may redeem the property after the sale within a statutory period of redemption.

E. Assignment for the benefit of creditors — Debtor transfers all of his or her assets to an assignee or trustee who liquidates the assets and distributes the proceeds *pro rata* (proportionately) among the creditors of the debtor.

II. Suretyship and guaranty.

A. Suretyship.

   1. A surety is a third party who promises a creditor that he or she will be liable for an obligation along with the primary debtor. (A surety is a joint obligor.)

   2. A surety is primarily liable to a creditor; a surety's promise need not be in writing unless required by statute to be written.

3. If the principal debtor defaults, the creditor may make an immediate demand upon the surety for payment.

B. Guaranty.

1. A guarantor makes a separate, collateral, secondary, conditional promise to the creditor that he, she or it will pay or otherwise perform in the event that the debtor does not carry out the primary obligation as promised.

2. The guarantor is promising to answer for the debt, default, or miscarriage of another person (the principal debtor).

a. The guarantor's liability is, therefore, secondary, and the guarantor's promise to pay (or otherwise perform) must be in a signed writing in order to comply with the statute of frauds, unless the "main purpose" exception applies. [See Chapter 17.]

b. If the debtor defaults, the creditor must first make a demand on the debtor before making a demand for payment on the guarantor.

3. Classifications of guaranty contracts.

a. Absolute — The guarantor is liable absolutely upon the default of the primary, principal obligor.

b. Conditional — The guarantor is liable only if a specified event occurs.

c. Continuing — The guarantor is liable for a series of transactions rather than a single transaction.

d. Unlimited — The guarantor is liable for an unlimited amount of money or for an unlimited period of time.

e. Limited — The guarantor is liable for a limited, specified amount of money or period of time.

C. Defenses of the surety and guarantor — If the surety or guarantor is sued for enforcement of his or her promise, the surety or guarantor may assert defenses. (Because the defenses of the surety and guarantor are similar, usually, these defenses are referred to as suretyship defenses.)

1. Material modification of the obligation owed by the principal debtor without the assent of the surety or guarantor.

2. Release of the principal debtor without the consent of the surety or guarantor and without an express reservation by the creditor of the creditor's rights against the surety or guarantor.

3. Discharge of the debtor because of payment by the debtor or another person on behalf of the debtor.

4. Tender of proper payment by the primary debtor or another person on behalf on the debtor.

5. A surety or guarantor may raise any defense that could be asserted by the debtor except lack of capacity or discharge in bankruptcy.

6. A surrender or impairment of any collateral by the creditor without the consent of the surety or guarantor (of whose existence the creditor knows) will release the surety/guarantor to the extent that the surety/guarantor incurs a loss.

D. Rights of the surety and guarantor.

1. Right of subrogation — When a surety or guarantor carries out the promise to pay, the surety or guarantor has all the rights that the creditor had against the debtor, such as the creditor's rights in bankruptcy, or rights to collateral or judgments that the creditor had (i.e., the surety or guarantor "stands in the shoes" of the creditor).

2. Right of reimbursement.

a. The surety or guarantor has a right to receive from the debtor payment for all outlays of funds that the surety or guarantor made, including the amount of the debt that was paid to the creditor and expenses.

b. A surety or guarantor is entitled to reimbursement from any sub-guarantors if there were any sub-guarantors.

3. Right of contribution — A surety or guarantor who pays more than his or her proportionate share upon a debtor's default is entitled to recover that excess amount from co-sureties or co-guarantors; each co-surety's or co-guarantor's share of the payment is in proportion to the maximum amount of liability that each agreed to cover.

III. Protection for debtors.

A. Exemptions — Certain property belonging to a debtor cannot be reached by creditors.

1. The homestead exemption — The family home is either exempt (and, therefore, cannot be sold) or, if the home is sold in order to satisfy a judgment, a specific amount of the sale price must be reserved for the debtor so that the debtor can provide shelter for the debtor and the debtor's family.

2. Exempt personal property — Typically, state statutes provide that a specified dollar amount of household furnishings, clothing, personal possessions,

vehicles used for transportation, certain classified animals, equipment that the debtor uses in a trade, profession, or business, pensions received from the government based upon military service, and a proportion of disposable income are exempt from satisfactions for debts.

B. Special protection for consumer debtors — Federal statutes protect consumers.

    1. Because of a Federal Trade Commission rule, a statement notifying any potential holders of a negotiable instrument or installment contract issued by a consumer that the consumer can raise personal defenses must be printed on the instrument. [See Chapter 27.]

    2. Consumer protection legislation is discussed in Chapter 45.

KEY WORDS AND PHRASES IN TEXT

lien
consensual lien
statutory lien
mechanic's lien on real property
artisan's lien on personal property
possessory lien
innkeeper's lien
judicial lien
attachment (prejudgment remedy)
affidavit
writ of execution and writ of attachment
garnishment
creditors' composition agreement
mortgage foreclosure on real property
mortgagee and mortgagor
deficiency judgment
equity of redemption

statutory period of redemption
assignment for benefit of creditors
suretyship and surety
guaranty and guarantor
secondarily liable party
absolute or conditional guarantor
continuing guarantor
limited or unlimited guarantor
defenses of the surety and the guarantor
rights of the surety and the guarantor
right of subrogation
right of reimbursement
co-sureties
right of contribution
exempt property
homestead exemption

FILL-IN QUESTIONS

1. If a debt is incurred (but not paid) by the owner of real property for services rendered or materials furnished in order to improve the property, the creditor who furnished the services or supplied the materials may obtain a _____ lien, which will be enforceable by the sale of the real property.

2. A bailee in possession of personal property that the bailee has stored, cared for, and/or repaired has an _____ lien, if the charges for storage and/or improvements are not paid.

3. If a judgment creditor has not been paid the amount of a judgment, the judgment creditor may apply for a writ of execution which is an order of a court

_____
_____.

4. _____ is a procedure enabling a judgment creditor to obtain a court order directing the sheriff to reach specified property (such as money) of a debtor that is in the hands of a third person so that it can be applied to reduce the amount of a judgment.

5. Following the foreclosure of a real property mortgage, if the proceeds of the judicial sale are inadequate to satisfy the cost of foreclosure and the debt, the _____ is liable for any deficiency.

6. Statutes provide that certain property of a debtor cannot be reached in order to satisfy his or her debts. Usually such property includes a specific amount of the sale price realized on the sale of _____ as well as clothing and personal possessions. Certain income is also exempt because a creditor cannot reach _____
_____.

7. A _____ is a person who is primarily liable because he or she joins an obligor in promising to pay a debt to a creditor. A _____ is secondarily liable because his or her promise to pay an obligation is conditioned on the failure of the primary obligor to pay a debt to a creditor.

MULTIPLE CHOICE QUESTIONS

1. Certain creditors may have common law and/or statutory liens on the real property owned by their debtors. Such liens are referred to as:
   A. mechanics' liens.
   B. artisans' liens.
   C. prejudgment writs of execution.
   D. homestead exemptions.

2. Pine supplied lumber to Holmes for the construction of a barn on Holmes' land. Carpenter was employed by Holmes to build the barn. Neither Pine nor Carpenter has been paid by Holmes. By complying with state statutes, requiring recording and notice to a debtor, Pine and Carpenter may obtain and enforce:
   A. mechanic's liens on Holmes' real property.
   B. mechanic's liens on Holmes' personal property.
   C. artisan's liens on Holmes' real property.
   D. artisan's liens on Holmes' personal property.

3. Wage garnishment statutes enable a creditor of a debtor who is employed to obtain a portion of the wages due to the employed debtor from the debtor's employer. There are, however, statutory provisions that protect the debtor when the remedy of garnishment is used. For example:
   A. some minimum amount of wages cannot be used in order to satisfy a garnishment.

    B. usually, the creditor must first obtain a judgment against the debtor.

    C. the employer is prohibited from discharging the employee because the employee's wages are subject to the garnishment.

    D. All of the answers above are correct.

Questions 4 and 5 are based on the following fact situation: Dunstone owns no real property, but she owns an automobile worth $4,000, a television set worth $300, and miscellaneous personal property worth $5,000. She is employed at a salary of $900 per week. Dunstone also owes a local bank $2,000 for a loan that is past due.

4.   The bank can obtain:

    A. a writ of execution for the immediate seizure of Dunstone's automobile.

    B. an order for immediate garnishment of a proportion of Dunstone's salary.

    C. a lien on Dunstone's television set and/or her automobile by recording this lien and notifying Dunstone.

    D. a writ of execution for the seizure of Dunstone's television set after obtaining a judgment against Dunstone.

5.   If the bank obtains a judgment against Dunstone and an appropriate court order:

    A. a proportion of Dunstone's salary **cannot** be reached through garnishment.

    B for the seizure and sale of Dunstone's property, a specific amount of the sale price must be set aside so that Dunstone can provide shelter for her family.

    C. the bank will have liens on Dunstone's property that may then be foreclosed.

    D. the bank will **not** be able to recover from any of Dunstone's assets because of statutory exemptions.

6.   An agreement that provides that a creditor/lender will have a security interest in real property which is owned by a debtor/borrower, who retains title to and possession of the real property, is called a mortgage.

    A. The debtor/borrower is the mortgagee and the creditor/lender is the mortgagor. If the mortgagee defaults in making payments on the loan, the mortgagor may bring an action for foreclosure.

    B. The debtor/borrower is the mortgagor and the creditor/lender is the mortgagee. If the mortgagor defaults in making payments on the loan, the mortgagee may bring an action for foreclosure.

    C. The debtor/borrower is the mortgagor and the creditor/lender is the mortgagee. If the mortgagor defaults in making payments on the loan, the mortgagee may obtain a deed of trust in a court procedure.

    D. The debtor/borrower is the mortgagee and the creditor/lender is the mortgagor. If the mortgagee defaults in making payments on the loan, the mortgagor may bring an action for foreclosure subject to the mortgagee's right of redemption.

7.   Swann has assets worth $248,000 and liabilities of $310,000 all owed to unsecured creditors, Duck, Quail, and Partridge, each of whom is owed $100,000, and Pheasant, who is owed $10,000. Duck, Quail, and Partridge agree with Swann and each other to accept 80¢ on the dollar in immediate satisfaction of their debts.

    A. The agreement is void and unenforceable because of lack of consideration.

    B. The agreement is a composition with creditors.

    C. The agreement is an assignment for the benefit of creditors.

   D. Pheasant is also bound by the agreement.

8.   David owed Goliath a $10,000 debt, due November 1. On October 15, for
     consideration, Rocke promised in writing that he would pay Goliath the $10,000 in
     the event that David failed to pay the debt. On November 1, David failed to pay
     Goliath.
     A. Rocke is a surety and, therefore, is primarily liable to Goliath.
     B. Rocke is a guarantor and, therefore, is primarily liable to Goliath.
     C. Rocke is a surety and, therefore, is secondarily liable to Goliath.
     D. Rocke is a guarantor and, therefore, is secondarily liable to Goliath.

9.   Beta owed Kappa a $400 debt due December 1. On November 15, Xi, for
     consideration, promised Kappa orally that he would pay the $400 in the event that
     Beta did not pay the debt. On December 1, Beta failed to pay Kappa. Kappa
     demanded that Xi pay the $400 but Xi refused saying that his promise was **not**
     legally enforceable.
     A. Xi's promise to act as surety is unenforceable because this promise is **not** in
        writing.
     B. Xi's promise to act as a guarantor is unenforceable because this promise is **not** in
        writing.
     C. Xi is a surety and Kappa, therefore, must proceed against Beta before demanding
        payment from Xi.
     D. Xi is a guarantor and Kappa, therefore, need **not** proceed against Beta before
        demanding payment from Xi.

10. Deb loaned Molly $10,000 for one year. Molly obtained a bond from the Sue-Us
     Bonding Company which guaranteed payment of the $10,000 to Deb. Molly did not
     pay Deb, and Deb is suing the bonding company for payment.
     A. The guaranty made by Sue-Us Bonding Company did **not** have to be in writing
        in order to be enforceable.
     B. If Molly was a minor, spent the money, and disaffirmed her promise to repay the
        loan, Deb may **not** recover from the bonding company.
     C. If Molly had given Deb a promissory note for $20,000 in exchange for the
        $10,000 loan, the defense of usury can be successfully raised by the Sue-Us
        Bonding Company.
     D. Sue-Us Bonding Company can successfully raise the defense of bankruptcy if
        Molly has been discharged in bankruptcy.

11. Salt has agreed in writing to act as guarantor of payment of a debt owed by Pepper to
     Sugar, Inc. The debt is evidenced by a promissory note. If Pepper defaults, Sugar,
     Inc. will be entitled to recover from Salt, **unless**:
     A. Salt is in the process of exercising her rights against Pepper.
     B. Salt proves that Pepper was insolvent at the time that the note was signed.
     C. Pepper dies before the promissory note is due.
     D. Sugar, Inc. has **not** attempted to enforce the promissory note against Pepper.
     (This question is adapted from objective question #26 on the Uniform CPA
     Examination, November 1990.)

Chapter 32
Bankruptcy and Reorganization

Article 1, Section 8 of the United States Constitution empowers Congress to enact uniform bankruptcy laws. In accordance with this authorization, Congress first passed a bankruptcy act in 1898. The current federal bankruptcy statute is the Bankruptcy Reform Act of 1978, as amended, which substantially changed and modernized the law relating to bankruptcy. Important changes in the bankruptcy law were made as a result of the Bankruptcy Reform Act of 1994. The bankruptcy law is codified in Title 11 of the United States Code and is referred to as the Bankruptcy Code. Today, bankruptcy proceedings dealing with the administration of estates of debtors are held in federal bankruptcy courts. Bankruptcy court rulings may be appealed to the federal district court or to a tribunal composed of bankruptcy court judges in the applicable circuit.

The goals of the bankruptcy law are to provide relief for honest debtors from the oppressive burden of indebtedness and for the fair, ratable distribution of debtors' assets among creditors. Alternative debtor rehabilitation solutions in the form of reorganization and adjustments of debts are also provided for in the Bankruptcy Code.

THINGS TO KEEP IN MIND:

In addition to the federal bankruptcy law, other means are available for assuring a fair distribution of the assets of an insolvent debtor among the debtor's creditors so that the debtor has an opportunity to rehabilitate himself, herself, or itself financially. State insolvency statutes, which do not conflict with the U.S. Constitution (by impairing the obligations of contracts) or the federal bankruptcy statutes and affect only property within the state, may be utilized. Other solutions based upon principles of contracts, trusts and/or equity, such as compositions and/or extensions, assignments for the benefit of creditors, and equitable receivership, also may be used.

In this chapter of the *Study Guide* (Bankruptcy and Reorganization), all references to Chapters are references to Chapters in the Bankruptcy Code.

OUTLINE

I.   Types of bankruptcy relief.

  A. The Bankruptcy Code provides procedures for:

     1. Voluntary and involuntary liquidation of the bankruptcy estates of natural persons, firms, partnerships, and corporations (including unincorporated companies and associations) [Chapter 7].

   2. Adjustment of debts of municipalities [Chapter 9].

   3. Reorganizations of individuals, firms, and corporations [Chapter 11].

   4. Adjustments of debts of family farmers [Chapter 12].

   5. Adjustments of debts of individuals with regular income [Chapter 13].

B. The clerk of the court is required to give a consumer-debtor (an individual whose debts are primarily consumer debts) written notice of each chapter under which the debtor may proceed before the commencement of a bankruptcy proceeding.

II.   Liquidation proceedings [Chapter 7].

A. In a Chapter 7 liquidation (ordinary or straight bankruptcy), the debtor states his or her debts and turns assets over to a trustee who sells nonexempt assets and distributes the proceeds to creditors.

   1. Applies to individuals, partnerships, and corporations (including unincorporated companies and associations, and labor unions), except railroads, insurance companies, municipal corporations, banks, savings and loan associations, investment companies licensed by the Small Business Administration, and credit unions (to which other laws or chapters of the Code apply).

   2. After completion of a bankruptcy liquidation, with some exceptions, the balance of debts owed by the debtor are discharged (extinguished) so that the debtor no longer has an obligation to pay creditors to whom the debts are owed.

B. Filing the petition — A liquidation proceeding is commenced by the filing of a voluntary or involuntary petition in bankruptcy.

   1. Voluntary bankruptcy.

      a. Debtor must file in the bankruptcy court an accurately completed, signed, and sworn to official form (petition in bankruptcy) with the following schedules:
         1) A list of secured and unsecured creditors with their addresses and the amounts owed to each creditor.
         2) A statement of the financial affairs of the debtor.
         3) A schedule of all property that is owned by the debtor including exempt property.
         4) A list of current income and expenses.

      b. The petitioning debtor need not be insolvent — Under the Code, an equitable insolvency (inability to pay debts as they become due) test, rather than a balance sheet insolvency (liabilities exceed assets) test, is used for determining whether or not a debtor is insolvent.

    c. A consumer-debtor must state that he or she understands the alternative relief available under other chapters or, if the debtor is represented by an attorney, the attorney must file an affidavit stating that the debtor was informed of the relief available under each of the chapters.

    d. A debtor will be granted an order for relief (which is the beginning of the liquidation procedure that leads to the ultimate discharge of the debtor) if the petition is proper and debtor had not been discharged in bankruptcy within the past six years as long as the granting of relief would not constitute a substantial abuse of Chapter 7.

    e. Any notice that a debtor is required to give to creditors must include the debtor's name, address, and taxpayer identification number.

2. Involuntary bankruptcy.

    a. An involuntary bankruptcy proceeding may not be commenced against any person other than a charitable institution, a farmer, or a rancher.

    b. Creditors who have noncontingent, unsecured claims amounting to $10,000 or more file a petition with a bankruptcy court.
       1) If there are twelve or more creditors, three creditors must join in the petition; if there are less than twelve creditors, one or two creditors having claims exceeding $10,000 may sign the petition.
       2) If a party so requests, a temporary trustee may be appointed to take possession of the debtor's property in order to prevent loss.
       3) Beginning in 1998, the threshold amount will be adjusted every three years to reflect changes in the Consumer Price Index.

    c. The court will grant an order for relief if the debtor fails to file an answer or, if the debtor files an answer, the creditors prove that:
       1) The debtor is not paying debts as the debts become due; or
       2) A general receiver, assignee, or other custodian was appointed or took possession of the debtor's property within 120 days preceding the filing of the petition.

    d. If an order for relief is granted, the debtor must supply the same information as is required in a voluntary proceeding. [See above at II. B. 1. a.]

C. Automatic stay.

1. The filing of a voluntary or involuntary petition stays or suspends most litigation or other actions that might be taken by creditors against the debtor or the debtor's property, such as commencing or continuing actions in order to enforce judgments, liens, or security interests.

2. Secured creditors may apply for relief from an automatic stay, however, if they are not adequately protected, and the bankruptcy court may require that the debtor make periodic payments or provide additional collateral.

3. Secured parties may perfect purchase money security interests and file financing and continuation statements within twenty days of the filing of a petition.

4. Paternity, alimony, maintenance, and support obligations are not subject to the automatic stay.

5. Exceptions to the automatic stay are provided for tax audits, demands for tax returns, assessments of taxes, demands for payments of assessed taxes, and creation of statutory liens for property taxes that become due after the filing of the petition.

6. If a creditor knowingly violates the automatic stay, the creditor will be liable to any injured party including the debtor, for actual damages, costs, attorneys' fees, and possibly punitive damages.

D. Property of the estate.

1. The estate in property consists of all tangible and intangible property (wherever located) in which the debtor had legal and/or equitable interests at the time that the petition was filed.

2. The estate includes:

   a. Property that may be exempt.

   b. Community property; property that the debtor transferred, but which trustee can reach because the transfer is voidable; causes of action; and proceeds, rents, and profits generated by property in the estate.

   c. Property that was received by the debtor as a gift and/or inheritance and property acquired in a settlement with a spouse or as a beneficiary of life insurance within 180 days after the filing of the petition.

E. Creditors' meeting and claims.

1. The court calls a meeting of the creditors within ten to thirty days after the order for relief is granted.

   a. The debtor attends the meeting; at the meeting, the trustee is elected or the interim trustee becomes the permanent trustee.

   b. A debtor may be denied a discharge if the debtor fails to appear (unless excused by the court) or makes false statements under oath.

   c. The trustee must inform the debtor of the effect of a bankruptcy filing on the debtor's credit history, the availability of other chapters of the bankruptcy law, and the effect of reaffirming a debt.

2. Claims of creditors.

    a. Proofs of claims are filed within ninety days after the meeting of creditors.

    b. Claims that arose before the filing of the petition are allowed (unless the claims are objected to or unenforceable or excluded):
       1) Claims for interest accruing after petition was filed.
       2) Claims of landlords or employees (based upon breaches of leases or contracts) for no more than one year's rent or wages.

F. Exemptions.

1. The debtor has the option of taking exemptions provided for by either the law of the state in which the debtor resides (or a husband and wife who file jointly reside) or the Bankruptcy Code, as long as the state law does not preclude the use of the federal exemptions. (The federal exemptions are available only in approximately one-third of the states.)

2. Exemptions provided for in the federal Bankruptcy Code — Note that the dollar amounts are doubled for married debtors filing jointly and that, beginning April 1, 1998, the following dollar amounts will be adjusted every three years based upon changes in the Consumer Price Index.

    a. Equity in home and burial plot, not exceeding $15,000 (or $30,000 for married debtors filing jointly).

    b. Interest in one motor vehicle (up to $2,400).

    c. Interest in personal household goods, clothing, books, animals, etc. (up to $400 for any single item but not exceeding a total of $8,000).

    d. Interest in jewelry (up to $1,000).

    e. Other property worth up to $800, plus up to $7,500 of the unused part of the $15,000 exemption for equity in a home and/or burial plot.

    f. Items used in a trade or business (up to $1,500).

    g. Certain interests in accrued dividends or interest under life insurance policies owned by the debtor.

    h. Professionally prescribed health aids.

    i. Federal and state benefits, such as social security, veterans' disability, and unemployment benefits.

    j. Alimony and child support, pensions, and annuities.

k. Rights to receive certain personal injury and other awards (up to $15,000).

G. The trustee.

1. After the order for relief is granted, the U.S. Trustee appoints an interim (or provisional) trustee who serves until the first meeting of the creditors at which a permanent trustee is elected or the interim trustee becomes the permanent trustee.

2. The trustee is required to inform the debtor of the effect of a bankruptcy filing on the debtor's credit history, the availability of other chapters in the Bankruptcy Code, and the effect of reaffirmation of debts owed to creditors.

3. The trustee takes title to property that is included in the debtor's estate and administers the estate by collecting the assets, reducing such assets to cash for distribution, approving claims, and preserving the interests of the debtor and the unsecured creditors.

4. Trustee's powers.

   a. The trustee may assume or reject executory contracts.

   b. The trustee occupies a position equivalent to that of other parties.
      1) The trustee has the same rights as a lien creditor (who could have obtained a judicial lien on the debtor's property) and has priority over an unperfected secured party with respect to the debtor's property.
      2) The trustee has power equivalent to that of a bona fide purchaser of real property from the debtor.

   c. The trustee's powers must be exercised within two years of the filing of the petition even if a trustee has not been appointed.

5. Voidable rights.

   a. The trustee may bring actions to avoid transfers of the debtor's assets that the debtor or a judgment, lien or unsecured creditor would have had a right to avoid under state law or the Bankruptcy Code.

   b. The trustee may disaffirm contracts that were entered into by the debtor because of fraud, duress, incapacity, mutual mistake, etc.

   c. The trustee is empowered to avoid transfers to secured parties of security interests that were not perfected when the petition was filed.

6. Preferences.

   a. The trustee may avoid preferential transfers of property or payments that favor one creditor over other creditors.

b. With some exceptions, a preferential transfer includes a transfer made:
 1) By an insolvent debtor to or for the benefit of a creditor for or on account of an antecedent debt;
 2) Within ninety days prior to the filing of the petition during which the debtor is presumed to be insolvent; and
 3) Which results in the receipt by the creditor of a greater percentage of payment than would be made under the provisions of the Bankruptcy Code.

c. If the recipient of the preference is an insider (an individual, partner, partnership, officer or director of a corporation, or a relative of one of these, and the recipient has a close relationship with the debtor), the trustee can avoid the transfer if it was made within one year before the filing; the presumption of insolvency is, however, limited to the ninety-day period.

d. In general, a payment made in the ordinary course of business for services rendered within a ten to fifteen day period prior to the payment is considered to be made for current consideration and is not, therefore, an antecedent debt.

e. If the preferred creditor has sold the property to an innocent third person, the preferred creditor is accountable for the value of the property.

f. A transfer that is made by a consumer-debtor of property having a value of up to $600 to one creditor and the payment of paternity, alimony, maintenance, and/or support debts do not constitute preferences.

7. Liens on debtor's property — The trustee can avoid the fixing of certain statutory liens, liens that first become effective upon the insolvency or bankruptcy of the debtor, and liens that are unperfected or unenforceable against a bona fide purchaser on the date upon which the petition was filed.

8. Fraudulent transfers.

 a. A fraudulent transfer is one that is made in order to hinder, delay, or defraud creditors or for less than reasonable consideration when the debtor was insolvent or, as a result of the transfer, becomes insolvent.

 b. The trustee has the power to avoid conveyances and other transfers that were made within one year before the filing of the petition or within the state statutory period that often is two to five years.

H. Distribution of property.

1. Secured creditors having valid liens or security interests in property are entitled to exercise their security interests.

 a. A secured creditor can accept the collateral in full satisfaction of the debt.

b. A secured creditor has the option of foreclosing on the collateral and using the proceeds in order to "pay off" the debt.
   1) If the proceeds exceed the amount of the debt:
      a) Excess may be used to cover reasonable costs incurred by the secured creditor because of debtor's default.
      b) Any remaining balance is payable to the trustee.
   2) If there is a deficiency, the secured creditor becomes an unsecured creditor as to the balance.

2. Priorities for payment of claims of unsecured creditors.

   a. Each class of debts must be fully paid before the next class of creditors is entitled to share in the remaining proceeds; if there are insufficient proceeds to pay a particular class of creditors fully, the proceeds are distributed pro rata and remaining classes receive nothing.

   b. For purposes of priority of payment, the classes are:
      1) Costs and expenses of preserving and administering the debtor's estate.
      2) In an involuntary proceeding, claims arising in the ordinary course of business after the commencement of the action but before the election of the trustee.
      3) Claims for unpaid wages, salaries, and commissions (not exceeding $4,000 per claim) earned within ninety days of the filing of the petition.
      4) Claims (not exceeding $4,000 per employee) for employee benefit plan contributions arising within 180 days before filing of the petition.
      5) Claims (not exceeding $4,000) of farm producers and fishers against debtors who own or operate grain storage facilities or fish storage or processing facilities.
      6) Claims for deposits made for consumer purchases, up to $1,800 per claim.
      7) Claims for alimony or spousal or child support.
      8) Taxes and penalties legally due and owing within three years before the filing of the petition.
      9) Claims of general creditors (including any unpaid balances owed to creditors who had limited priorities) on a pro rata basis.

   c. Beginning April 1, 1998, the priority dollar amounts for wage, benefit, consumer deposit, etc., claims will be adjusted every three years based upon changes in the Consumer Price Index.

I. Discharge.

   1. Exceptions to discharge — Claims that are not dischargeable:

      a. Claims for back taxes accruing within three years prior to bankruptcy.

b. Claims for debts incurred in order to pay nondischargeable federal taxes.

c. Claim against property or money obtained by the debtor under false pretenses or because of false representations.

d. Claims by creditors who were not notified of the bankruptcy proceedings because their names did not appear on the schedules filed by the debtor.

e. Claims based upon fraud, embezzlement, misappropriation, or defalcation by the debtor while the debtor was acting in a fiduciary capacity.

f. Alimony, child support, and with some exceptions, property settlements.

g. Intentional tort claims.

h. Certain fines and penalties imposed by governmental units.

i. Certain student loans unless payment imposes undue hardship on the debtor and the debtor's dependents.

j. Consumer debts of more than $1,000 for luxury goods or services owed to a single creditor within sixty days of the order for relief.

k. Cash advances aggregating more than $1,000 as extensions of open-end consumer credit obtained by the debtor within sixty days of the order for relief.

l. Judgments or consent decrees entered against the debtor for liability incurred as a result of the debtor's operation of a motor vehicle while intoxicated.

m. Payment of court orders for criminal restitution.

2. Objections to discharge.

a. Upon an objection to discharge by a creditor, a debtor may be denied a discharge in which case the debtor's assets are distributed; the debtor, however, remains liable for unpaid portions of the claims.

b. A discharge will not be granted if the debtor:
   1) Concealed or destroyed property with the intention of hindering, delaying, or defrauding a creditor.
   2) Fraudulently concealed or destroyed financial records.
   3) Had been granted a discharge in bankruptcy within six years before the filing of the current petition.

3. Effect of discharge.

  a. The debtor is released from all of his or her obligations to pay debts, other than those which are nondischargeable. [See above at II. I. 1.]

  b. Judgments entered against the debtor and unperformed promises by the debtor to pay money based upon contract are unenforceable.

 4. Revocation of discharge.

  a. Upon petition by a creditor or the trustee filed within one year of the debtor's discharge, the bankruptcy court may revoke the discharge if it is established that the debtor acted fraudulently or dishonestly during the bankruptcy proceeding.

  b. If the discharge is revoked, unpaid creditors can enforce unsatisfied claims, judgments, and contracts against the debtor.

J. Reaffirmation of debt — A debtor's voluntary reaffirmation agreement to pay a debt that otherwise is dischargeable in bankruptcy is effective if the agreement is made before the bankruptcy court grants a discharge and is filed with the court.

 1. Bankruptcy court approval is given when the debtor is not represented by an attorney and the court finds that there is no undue hardship and the agreement is in the best interest of the debtor.

 2. Debtor may rescind within sixty days of the filing of the agreement. (Rescission period must be clearly and conspicuously stated in the agreement.)

III. Reorganizations [Chapter 11].

A. After the filing of a Chapter 11 petition, the creditors and the debtor formulate a plan for payment of some debts and discharge of others; the plan is submitted for court approval.

 1. A voluntary or involuntary petition may be filed if the debtor is an individual, firm, or corporation, which is eligible for a Chapter 7 liquidation (with the exception of a stockbroker or commodities broker, and the inclusion of a railroad).

 2. Chapter 7 principles relating to the filing of the petition, the automatic stay, the entry of an order for relief, and adequate protection also govern a Chapter 11 reorganization.

 3. Workouts as an alternative to bankruptcy proceedings.

  a. Privately negotiated adjustments of creditor-debtor relationships may be more flexible and conducive to speedy settlement than Chapter 11 reorganization.

b. Creditor compositions and extensions are discussed in Chapter 31 of this *Study Guide* at I.C.

4. A Chapter 11 proceeding may be dismissed or suspended after notice and a hearing if to do so would best serve the interests of the creditors.

5. A Chapter 11 proceeding may also be dismissed after notice and a hearing for cause in the following situations:

   a. The absence of a reasonable likelihood of rehabilitation.

   b. The inability to effectuate a plan.

   c. An unreasonable delay by the debtor that is prejudicial to the creditors.

6. A Chapter 11 proceeding may be converted into a Chapter 7 liquidation proceeding.

B. Debtor in possession.

1. Usually, the debtor continues to operate his, her, or its business as a debtor in possession (DIP) after entry of the order for relief.

2. The court may appoint a trustee to operate the debtor's business if it is in the best interests of the estate.

3. The role of the DIP or trustee is similar to that of a trustee in a liquidation proceeding — The DIP or trustee may avoid:

   a. Preferential payments, fraudulent transfers, and executory contracts made before the petition was filed.

   b. Obligations or transfers of property that could have been avoided by certain creditors or bona fide purchasers of real property.

C. Collective bargaining agreements — A trustee or debtor in possession can reject an existing collective bargaining agreement if the debtor has proposed modifications, conferred with the labor union in good faith, and the union has rejected the modifications without good cause.

D. Creditors' committees.

1. After entry of the order for relief, the creditors' committee composed of unsecured creditors is appointed; the committee may consult with the trustee or debtor in possession regarding administration and the formulation of the plan for reorganization.

2. Upon request, a bankruptcy court may order that a creditors' committee not be appointed for a "small business" debtor (a person engaged in business

activities, other than owning or managing real estate, and having debts of less than two million dollars) for whom a "fast track" procedure is available.

E. The reorganization plan.

1. A fair and equitable rehabilitation plan for conserving and administering the debtor's assets must designate classes of claims and interests; specify the treatment to be afforded to the classes with equal treatment for each claim within a class; and provide an adequate means for the plan's execution.

2. The debtor may file a plan within 120 days after entry of the order for relief; a small business debtor has 100 days within which to file a plan.

3. If the debtor does not file a plan or if the plan is not approved, the trustee or creditors' or other committee appointed by the court, or any party in interest may file a plan within 180 (160 in the case of a small business) days after the date of the order for relief.

4. The plan must be approved by a majority in number and two-thirds in amount of each class of creditors (and, in the case of a corporation, shareholders) whose interests will be impaired or adversely affected.

5. Confirmation of the plan.

   a. The "cram down" provision of the Code — Although not accepted by a class of creditors (or shareholders or others having interests), if the court finds that the plan is fair and confirms it, the plan is binding on all parties.

   b. Upon confirmation, the debtor is given a Chapter 11 discharge from all claims not protected under the plan; this does not apply to a claim that would be denied discharge under Chapter 7.

IV. Additional forms of relief.

A. Individuals' repayment plans [Chapter 13 Adjustment of Debts of an Individual with Regular Income].

1. An individual debtor who is a wage earner or is engaged in business may voluntarily file a petition for adjustment of his or her debts if the debtor's noncontingent, liquidated, unsecured debts amount to less than $250,000 and secured debts to less than $750,000. (Beginning in 1998, the dollar amounts will be adjusted every three years based upon changes in the Consumer Price Index.)

2. Filing the petition — The proceeding is initiated by the filing of a voluntary petition by the debtor.

   a. A trustee is appointed.

b. Certain Chapter 7 and Chapter 11 proceedings may be converted to Chapter 13 proceedings with the debtors' consent.

c. A Chapter 13 proceeding can be converted to a Chapter 7 liquidation at the request of the debtor or a creditor (for cause); and, after a hearing, a Chapter 13 proceeding can be converted to a Chapter 11 reorganization.

3. The automatic stay provisions apply to actions relating to consumer debts but not to business debts.

   a. The stay prevents creditors from taking action against co-obligors of the debtor.

   b. A creditor can request that a stay be vacated (removed) against a co-obligor of the debtor. If there are no written objections filed within twenty days after the request, the stay against the co-obligor is terminated without a hearing.

4. The repayment plan.

   a. A rehabilitation plan must provide for:
      1) The turnover to the trustee of such future earnings or income of the debtor as is necessary for execution of the plan.
      2) Full payment in deferred cash payments of all claims entitled to priority.
      3) Equal treatment of each claim within a particular class; co-debtors, such as guarantors and sureties, may be listed as a separate class.

   b. Filing the plan.
      1) The plan filed by the debtor may provide for payment in full or lesser amounts during a three year period; the period may be extended for up to five years with court approval.
      2) The debtor must make timely payments to the trustee beginning within thirty days of the filing of the plan.
      3) Until the plan is confirmed, the trustee retains the payments for later distribution.
      4) If the plan is denied, the trustee returns the payments less costs to the debtor.
      5) If the debtor fails to commence payments within the thirty-day period or to make timely payments, the court may convert the Chapter 13 proceeding to a Chapter 7 liquidation or dismiss the proceeding.

   c. Confirmation of the plan — After a confirmation hearing at which interested parties may object, the court will confirm a plan if:
      1) The secured creditors have accepted the plan.
      2) The plan provides that creditors retain their liens and the value of the property to be distributed to the creditors is not less than the secured portion of their claims.

          3) The debtor surrenders the property securing the claims to the creditors.

    d. Objection to the plan.
       1) Unsecured creditors do not have a vote in order to approve a plan, but these creditors or the trustee may object to the plan.
       2) The court can approve a plan over such objections if:
          a) The value of the property to be distributed is at least equal to the amount of the claims; or
          b) All of the debtor's projected three years disposable income (equal to all income less amounts necessary to support the debtor and dependents and/or necessary to meet ordinary expenses in continuing the operation of a business) will be applied to making payments.

    e. Modification of the plan — The plan may be modified upon the request of the debtor, the trustee, or an unsecured creditor.

  5. Discharge.

    a. A discharge is granted after completion of all payments under the plan.

    b. All debts are dischargeable (including fraudulently incurred debts and claims resulting from intentional torts) except claims not provided for by the plan and claims for alimony and child support.

    c. A hardship discharge may be granted without completion of the plan because of circumstances beyond the debtor's control if the value of the distributed property is greater than would have been paid in a Chapter 7 liquidation.

    d. Discharge may be revoked within one year if the discharge was obtained by fraud.

B. Family-farmer plans [Chapter 12, The Family Farmer Bankruptcy Act].

  1. Provisions of Chapter 12 are similar to Chapter 13.

  2. Petition may be filed by a family farmer who is an individual, partnership, or closely held corporation, whose gross income is at least 50 percent dependent upon farming and whose debts are at least 80 percent farm-related and less than $1,500,000.

  3. The farmer-debtor files a plan (providing for payment of debts) within ninety days after the order for relief.

  4. The filing of the petition acts as an automatic stay which prevents creditors and co-obligors from commencing actions against the debtor.

5. Usually, the farmer-debtor remains in possession of the farm, a trustee is appointed, and the debtor files a plan within ninety days after the order for relief.

6. The provisions relating to confirmation of the plan and discharge are similar to those in Chapter 13.

7. A Chapter 11 or 13 proceeding may be converted to a Chapter 12 proceeding; a Chapter 12 proceeding may be converted to a Chapter 7 liquidation.

KEY WORDS AND PHRASES IN TEXT

Bankruptcy Reform Act of 1978
Bankruptcy Code
consumer-debtor
Chapter 7 liquidation
trustee
petition in bankruptcy
voluntary bankruptcy
order for relief
involuntary bankruptcy
automatic stay
adequate protection doctrine
estate in property
creditors' meeting
proof of claim
exempt property
U.S. Trustee
trustee's powers
powers of avoidance
preferences

insider as recipient of a preference
fraudulent transfers
distribution of property
discharge in bankruptcy
revocation of discharge
reaffirmation agreement
Chapter 11 reorganization
workouts
debtor in possession (DIP)
rejection of collective bargaining
    agreement
creditors' committees
reorganization plan
cram-down provision
Chapter 13 adjustment of debts of an
    individual with regular income
Chapter 12 (Family Farmer
    Bankruptcy Act)

FILL-IN QUESTIONS

1. There is a uniform bankruptcy law in the United States because Article I, Section 8 of the _____ provides that _____ is empowered to enact "uniform Laws on the subject of Bankruptcies throughout the United States."

2. The goals of the bankruptcy law are to provide relief and protection to debtors and to provide a fair method of distributing a debtor's assets among the _____.

3. When voluntary or involuntary petitions are filed for liquidations or _____ or voluntary petitions are filed for adjustments of debts of individuals with regular income or family farmers, most litigation against a debtor is suspended. This is called an _____ which bars creditors from commencing or continuing actions against a debtor.

4.   In a liquidation proceeding instituted under the federal bankruptcy law, usually the creditors elect the trustee for the debtor's estate at the first meeting of the creditors. This meeting is called by _____. Creditors have _____ days from the date of the meeting within which to file their claims.

5.   The trustee in bankruptcy may avoid transfers of the debtor's property if _____ or a judgment, lien, or unsecured creditor would have had the right to avoid the transfer under state law or the federal bankruptcy law.

6.   A preferential transfer by a debtor is one in which the debtor transferred money or property to one creditor which resulted in _____ _____ and may be avoided by _____ _____.

7.   Either debtors or their creditors may commence liquidation proceedings (under Chapter 7) or _____ proceedings (under Chapter 11) but only a debtor may apply for _____ (under Chapter 13).

MULTIPLE CHOICE QUESTIONS

1.   A debtor who is in financial difficulty and transfers all of his property to another person, in trust, for distribution among his creditors has:
     A. entered into a composition.
     B. agreed to an extension.
     C. made an assignment for the benefit of creditors.
     D. made a voidable fraudulent conveyance.

2.   An insolvent debtor owes money to many creditors and has filed a petition for voluntary liquidation. If the debtor had transferred title to his $15,000 automobile to one creditor a month before filing the petition, he has made a voidable:
     A. fraudulent conveyance.
     B. assignment for the benefit of creditor.
     C. admission of debt.
     D. preferential transfer.

3.   Although Paul has assets valued at $500,000, he has many unpaid current debts totaling $300,000. Paul has not been paying his debts as they become due and appears to have been in financial difficulty for some time. A month ago, Paul transferred title to his $18,000 automobile to Charles and, two weeks later, Paul transferred all of his remaining property to Thomas in trust for purposes of distributing the proceeds of their sale among Paul's creditors. Yesterday, a group of almost all of his creditors filed a petition with the bankruptcy court for involuntary liquidation of Paul's property. Which of the following statements is correct?
     A. The transfers of the automobile to Charles and all of Paul's property to Thomas were fraudulent conveyances that may be voided by the trustee in bankruptcy.
     B. The transfer of the automobile to Charles was a voidable transfer because Charles received a preference, but a trustee in bankruptcy will be unable to avoid the transfer.

C. The petition will be dismissed and no order for relief granted because Paul is not insolvent.

D. An order for relief may be granted because Paul transferred all of his property to Thomas, who was a custodian or general receiver of Paul's assets.

4. Organizations that may be subjected to involuntary liquidation under Chapter 7 of the federal Bankruptcy Code include:
A. manufacturing corporations.
B. banking corporations.
C. insurance companies.
D. charitable associations.

5. Spendthrift is in financial difficulty. She is insolvent in the bankruptcy sense but has not filed a petition for voluntary liquidation. A few of Spendthrift's creditors are threatening to force Spendthrift into liquidation.
A. If Spendthrift makes an assignment of her property to a third person, as custodian, for the benefit of her creditors, the bankruptcy court will grant an order for relief following the filing of a petition for involuntary liquidation.
B. If Spendthrift has ten creditors, whose claims are not contingent as to liability and amount to more than $10,000, a petition for involuntary liquidation must be signed by a least three of the creditors.
C. As long as Spendthrift is able to meet her current obligations, there is no basis for her creditors to file a petition for involuntary liquidation.
D. Spendthrift **cannot** file a voluntary petition for liquidation without the approval of her creditors.

6. Environment Heat, Inc. is a medium sized corporation that has been having some difficulty paying current bills. For example, checks issued by the corporation have not been honored by its bank because of insufficient funds. The corporation's principal creditors have held a meeting in order to consider possible alternative courses of action. At the meeting, these creditors have learned that Environmental Heat, Inc. has sufficient assets to meet liabilities in the event of liquidation and that the corporation has the potential to be profitable in the next five years.
A. The best action that the creditors can take is to file a petition for involuntary liquidation.
B. A bankruptcy court will **not** grant an order for relief if the creditors file a petition for involuntary liquidation because Environmental Heat, Inc. is **not** insolvent in the bankruptcy sense.
C. If the creditors file a petition for involuntary reorganization, Environmental Heat, Inc. will have to submit a plan for reorganization and all creditors will have an opportunity to vote on the plan.
D. If the creditors file a petition for involuntary reorganization, a bankruptcy court may confirm a plan for reorganization submitted by the shareholders of the corporation even if the plan was not accepted by two-thirds of one class of creditors.

Questions 7, 8, 9, and 10 (which have been adapted from objective questions #30 and #31 on the May 1987 Uniform CPA Examination) are based on the following fact situation: On March 10 last year, the creditors of Stowe, a sole proprietor engaging in the business of selling hardware, filed an involuntary petition in a bankruptcy court for liquidation of Stowe's property in accordance with Chapter 7 of the Bankruptcy Code. Stowe's nonexempt property has been converted to cash which is available to satisfy the following expenses and unsecured claims as may be appropriate:

Expenses

Administration costs necessary to preserve the property of Stowe's bankruptcy estate	$ 20,000
Salary to Stowe for services rendered in operating the hardware business after the commencement of the bankruptcy action	30,000

Unsecured Claims

Claims by two of Stowe's employees for wages earned within 90 days of the filing of the bankruptcy petition in the amounts of $4,000 and $7,000, respectively	$ 11,000
Claim by Hammond Hammer Co. for delivery of merchandise to Stowe on February 20 that was prior to the filing of the petition	10,000

7. What amount will be distributed to Stowe for Stowe's services if the cash available for distribution is $25,000?
    A. $0.
    B. $5,000.
    C. $15,000.
    D. $25,000.

8. What amount will be distributed as salary to Stowe if the cash available for distribution is $55,000?
    A. $0.
    B. $2,000.
    C. $22,000.
    D. $30,000.

9. What amount will be distributed to the two employees if the cash available for distribution is $25,000?
    A. $0.
    B. $4,000.
    C. $8,000.
    D. $11,000.

10. What amount will be distributed to the two employees if the cash available for distribution is $70,000?
    A. $0.
    B. $4,000.
    C. $8,000.
    D. $11,000.

OTHER OBJECTIVE QUESTIONS: (These questions are based upon question #3(a) on the Uniform CPA Examination, November 1995.)

On June 1, Rusk Corp. was petitioned involuntarily into bankruptcy. At the time of the filing, Rusk had the following creditors:

- Safe Bank, for the balance due on the secured note and mortgage on Rusk's warehouse.
- Employees salary claims.
- Federal income taxes due for the current year.
- Accountant's fees outstanding.
- Utility bills outstanding.

Before the bankruptcy filing, but while Rusk was insolvent, Rusk engaged in the following transactions:

- On February 1, Rusk repaid all corporate directors' loans made to the corporation.
- On May 1, Rusk purchased raw materials for use in its manufacturing business and paid cash to the supplier.

Questions 1 through 5 relate to Rusk's creditors and the February 1 and May 1 transactions. For each question, select from the list whether only statement I is correct, whether only statement II is correct, whether both statements I and II are correct, or whether neither statement I nor statement II is correct.

<u>List</u>

A.   I only.
B.   II only.
C.   Both I and II.
D.   Neither I nor II.

1.   I. Safe Bank's claim will be the first paid on the listed claims because Safe is a secured creditor.
      II. Safe Bank will receive the entire amount of the balance due as a secured creditor regardless of the amount received from the sale of the warehouse.

2.   I. The employee salary claims will be paid in full after the payment of any secured party.
      II. The employee salary claims up to $4,000 per claimant will be paid before payment of any general creditors' claims.

3.   I. The claim for current federal income taxes due will be paid as a secured creditor claim.
      II. The claim for current federal income taxes due will be paid prior to the general creditors claims.

4.   I.   The February 1 repayments of the directors' loans were preferential transfers even though the payments were made more than ninety (90) days before the filing of the petition.

      II.   The February 1 repayments of the directors' loans were preferential transfers because the payments were made to insiders.

5.   I.   The May 1 purchase and payment were **not** a preferential transfer because they were part of a transaction in the ordinary course of business.

      II.   The May 1 purchase and payment was a preferential transfer because it occurred within ninety (90) days of the filing of the petition.

UNIT SIX:
AGENCY

Whether a business enterprise is a sole proprietorship, partnership, corporation, or limited liability company, the efficient operation of the business depends upon employing other people, some of whom are considered to be agents. How agency relationships are created is discussed in Chapter 33. If an agency relationship exists, the agent and the person employing the agent, the principal, owe certain duties to each other. This topic also is covered in Chapter 33

Because an agent acts on behalf of and instead of the principal, the actions of an authorized agent are treated as being the acts of the principal. As a result, a principal will be liable in contract to third parties with whom the agent has dealt and in tort to those who have been injured by an agent while the agent was acting within the scope of his or her authority. The extent of contractual and tort liability is explored in Chapter 34. Chapter 34 concludes with a discussion of the manner in which agency relationships are terminated.

Chapter 33
Agency Formation and Duties

An agency is a representative relationship that arises when one person, the agent, represents or acts for the benefit and in the place of another person, the principal. An agency is a consensual relationship. In most cases, consent of the parties to the creation (and the termination) of an agency relationship is, in fact, given. In other instances, the parties may be treated as having consented because of their conduct. In either case, by using a representative or agent, one person may conduct multiple business operations. For example, a corporation can function only by using agents.

If an agency relationship exists, the principal and agent owe each other those duties that are specified in their agreement and other duties that are implicit because of the agency relationship. Some of these duties are based on the fact that an agency relationship is a fiduciary one founded upon trust and confidence. As a result, agents and principals are required to act with good faith, honesty, and loyalty toward each other.

In this chapter, the authors first discuss the nature of the agency relationship and the ways in which agencies are created. Next, there is a section devoted to the duties that are owed by the principal and agent to each other.

THINGS TO KEEP IN MIND

1. It is sometimes necessary to distinguish agency relationships from those of employment or independent contractors. Although there are no hard and fast rules for doing so, usually the issue is resolved by examining the relative amount of independent discretion given to the agent/employee and the amount of control exercised by the principal/employer. Note that, at the minimum, an agent is considered to be an employee.

2. Duties that are owed by principals and agents may arise out of the fact that the agency relationship is usually a contractual relationship. A law suit or action based upon a failure of either party to perform, an agent to account, or a principal to compensate an agent, therefore, are founded on contract. On the other hand, a suit or action based upon a breach of the fiduciary duty (competing with one's principal, acting for a third person's benefit, failing to reveal material information, or making a secret profit) are founded on tort and do not require a showing of fraud or actual, measurable damages.

OUTLINE

I.   Agency relationships — For many reasons, it is necessary to distinguish agency relationships from other relationships in which services are rendered; courts examine a number of factors in distinguishing among the various relationships.

A. Principal-agent relationship — An agency relationship (which is a form of employment relationship) is a fiduciary relationship based upon trust and confidence because:

    1. An agent acts on behalf of and instead of a principal in engaging in business transactions.

    2. An agent may bind his or her principal in contract with a third person.

    3. An agent has some independent discretion.

B. Employer-employee relationship.

    1. To some extent, the rights and duties of an employee differ from those of an agent.

    2. Today, the distinction is important for purposes of applicability of legislation, such as tax, social security, unemployment, workplace safety, and workers' compensation statutes. [See Unit Seven.]

C. Employer-Independent contractor relationships.

    1. An independent contractor engages to bring about some specified end result and is normally paid at the completion of performance in accordance with a contract with the person for whom services are rendered.

    2. The person employing an independent contractor does not exercise control over the details of the performance.

    3. An independent contractor cannot bind the person employing him or her in a contract with a third party, unless the independent contractor also is an agent.

    4. Usually, an independent contractor engages in an occupation or business which is distinct from that of the person employing the independent contractor and an independent contractor furnishes his or her own materials, equipment, and employees.

D. Criteria for establishing employee status — In order to determine if a relationship is one of employment, a court will examine surrounding circumstances.

    1. The employer controls or has the right to control the employee in the performance of physical tasks. (This is the most important factor.)

    2. The employee has little or no independent discretion and is supervised under the direction of the employer or a representative of the employer.

    3. The employer supplies equipment, tools, etc. that are necessary in order to carry out the employee's tasks and the work is performed at the employer's place of business.

4. The employee engages in an occupation or business that is not distinct from that of the employer; factors that are examined are length of time for which a person is employed and the level of skill that is necessary.

5. The employer has the right to discharge the employee, pays employment taxes, etc.

6. The employee is paid on a periodic basis for time rather than results.

II. Formation of the agency relationship.

A. An agency is a consensual relationship but not necessarily a contractual one.

1. Consideration need not be given by the principal to the agent.

2. In general, no special formality, such as a writing, is necessary in order to create an agency. [See Chapter 34 at I. C. 2.]

3. Contractual capacity.

a. `A principal must have legal (contractual) capacity because contracts entered into by the principal's agent are treated as contracts of the principal. If a principal lacks capacity, such contracts are voidable by the principal but not by the third party.

b. A person does not need to have legal capacity in order to act as agent. The contract of agency may be avoided by the agent who lacks capacity but not by the principal.

4. An agency may be formed for any legal purpose.

a. If the purpose of the agency is illegal or against public policy, the agency agreement is void and unenforceable.

b. A person who engages in certain specified professions for which a license is required may not employ an unlicensed agent to perform professional acts.

B. Agency by agreement.

1. When the agency is created by agreement, the agent and principal affirmatively manifest that they consent to the formation of the agency.

2. The agreement may be an express oral or written agreement or may be implied from the conduct of the parties. (If authority is conferred by the principal in writing, it is referred to as a power of attorney.)

C. Agency by ratification — An agency may be created by express or implied ratification.

1. The principal's consent to the agency may be given after a purported agent acted on behalf of the principal.

2. Ratification relates back to the time that the agent acted without authorization. [See Chapter 34 at I. G.]

D. Agency created because of estoppel — A person (a principal) may be estopped to deny the existence of an agency if he or she caused a third party reasonably to believe that another person was his or her agent because there is an appearance that an agency relationship existed. [See Chapter 34 at I. E.]

E. Agency created by operation of law.

1. A court may find that an agency exists in order to carry out a social policy when credit has been extended for the purchases of necessaries by a family member or in emergency situations.

2. Statutes provide that a state official will be treated as having been appointed as an agent to receive service of process under certain circumstances. [For example, see Chapter 40 at III. A. 2.]

III. Duties of agents and principals.

A. Agency relationships are fiduciary ones that are based upon trust; many of the duties that are owed by one of the parties (e.g., the agent) correspond to duties owed by the other party (e.g., the principal).

B. Agent's duties to principal.

1. Some of the duties of an agent are specified in the agency agreement; other duties are implied from the agency relationship.

2. A subagent appointed or employed by an agent owes the same duties to the principal as any other agent owes to the principal.

3. Performance.

a. An agent is required to follow instructions, to use reasonable diligence and skill in carrying out agency obligations, and to use special skills which the agent possesses if such skills are applicable.

b. An agent who fails to perform properly may be liable for breach of contract and for the tort of negligence.

c. A gratuitous agent (an agent who is not paid for his or her services) who fails to perform properly is not liable for breach of contract, but may be liable for negligence.

4. Notification — An agent has a duty to notify the principal of material information that relates to the subject matter of the agency.

5. Loyalty — The fiduciary duty.

   a. An agent may neither compete with the agent's principal nor act for another principal unless full disclosure is made to the principal and the principal consents.

   b. During and after termination of an agency, the agent may not disclose trade secrets, confidential information, customer lists, etc., acquired in the course of the agent's employment.

   c. Any secret profits or benefits received by an agent while acting adversely to the interests of the principal belong to the principal who may recover such profits or benefits from the agent.

6. Obedience.

   a. An agent must follow all lawful and clearly stated instructions of the principal.

   b. In emergencies, an agent who is unable to contact his or her principal may deviate from instructions if the situation so warrants.

7. Accounting.

   a. An agent must account to his or her principal for any money or property that rightfully belongs to the principal and that has come into the agent's hands.

   b. An agent should not commingle property or money of the principal with the agent's own property or funds or the property or funds of other persons.

C. Principal's duties to agent — Some of the duties of a principal are specified in the agency agreement; other duties are implied from the agency relationship.

   1. A principal has an obligation to perform in accordance with his or her contract with an agent.

   2. Compensation.

      a. A principal is required to pay any agreed compensation to an agent.

      b. If no compensation is specified, a principal is required to pay expenses, losses, and reasonable compensation for services rendered by the agent unless the agency is a gratuitous one or there are circumstances, such as a family relationship, indicating that compensation had not been intended.

c.   There is no duty to pay compensation to an agent who has failed to perform his or her duties properly.

3.   Reimbursement and indemnification.

   a.   A principal has a duty to reimburse the agent for disbursements of money made at the principal's request and disbursements made for necessary expenses in the course of the agent's performance of his or her duties.

   b.   A principal has a duty to indemnify an agent for liabilities incurred while the agent was acting within the scope of the agent's authority and for losses incurred because of the principal's failure to perform his or her duties.

4.   Cooperation — A principal is required to assist an agent in performing the agent's duties and to do nothing to prevent such performance.

5.   Safe working conditions — A principal has a duty to provide a safe working environment. [See Chapter 35.]

IV.   Remedies and rights of agents and principals.

   A.   Agent's rights and remedies against principal.

      1.   An agent has the right to be compensated, reimbursed, and indemnified, and to work in a safe environment.

      2.   The remedies available to the agent include those generally available in breach of contract and tort cases.

         a.   An agent may sue for damages because of a breach of contract or commission of a tort or counterclaim if sued by the principal.

         b.   If there are appropriate circumstances, an agent may bring an action for an accounting by the principal and may withhold further performance.

      3.   An agent can recover for unpaid past performance and future damage but the agent cannot force the principal to continue to employ him or her as agent.

   B.   Principal's rights and remedies against agent.

      1.   A principal can recover from an agent for breach of contract, breach of fiduciary duties, or commission of a tort and, when appropriate, may terminate the agency.

      2.   Constructive trust — A court will impose a constructive trust on property received by an agent who has used his or her agency position in conflict with those of his or her principal so that the property (or proceeds of its sale) is treated as held for the benefit of the principal.

3. Avoidance — Transactions engaged in by an agent in violation of the agency agreement or the agent's duties are voidable at the election of the principal.

4. Indemnification — If a principal is required to pay damages to an injured party for an agent's tortious conduct or incurs a loss as a result of an agent's violation of the principal's instructions, the principal may recover the amount of resulting damages from the agent.

KEY WORDS AND PHRASES IN TEXT

agency relationship
agent
principal
fiduciary relationship
employer-employee relationship
employer-independent contractor
    relationship
formation of the agency relationship
agency agreement
agency created by ratification
agency created by estoppel
agency created by operation of law
agent's duty of performance

agent's duty of notification
agent's fiduciary duty of loyalty
agent's duty of obedience
agent's duty of accounting
principal's duty to pay compensation
principal's duties of reimbursement,
    indemnification, and cooperation
principal's duty to provide safe
    working conditions
constructive trust
avoidance of contracts
principal's remedy of indemnification

FILL-IN QUESTIONS

1. A person who agrees to work for another person subject to his or her control and directions for an agreed hourly rate would most likely be considered an _____ rather than an _____.

2. A person who agrees to construct a house for another, furnishes the materials, supplies, and employees, and is to be paid a lump sum upon completion of the house would most likely be considered to be an _____.

3. An agency may be created by agreement of the parties, _____ _____, or _____.

4. An agent is contractually obligated to his or her principal to perform in accordance with their agency agreement. This means that an agent is required to _____ _____ _____ _____, and to use special skills that the agent possesses and which are relevant to the principal's business.

5. An agent is a fiduciary. As a result, an agent must act _____ _____ _____

_____. The agent must reveal information relating to the subject matter of the agency to his or her principal and will have to account to his or her principal for any secret profit or benefit obtained while acting for the principal. If an agent violates the fiduciary duties, the contract of agency is _____ by the principal.

6. A principal is obligated to pay his or her agent _____
    _____ unless the agency agreement or other circumstances clearly indicate that such services were to be rendered gratuitously.

7. A principal has a right to _____ if the principal incurs a loss as a result of the failure of his or her agent to carry out lawful instructions. An agent has a similar right of _____ for payments made or liabilities incurred in executing his or her agency duties.

MULTIPLE CHOICE QUESTIONS

1. Creation of an agency relationship does **not** require:
    A. consent of the agent.
    B. contractual capacity on the part of the principal.
    C. consideration.
    D. Any of the above.

2. An agency relationship:
    A. must be evidenced by a writing.
    B. creates a constructive trust.
    C. may be terminated only by the principal.
    D. may be created by estoppel.

3. Parmer sent Anders a letter requesting that Anders act as his agent to sell an acre of land which Parmer owns. Anders accepted by signing a carbon copy of the letter and returning the copy to Parmer. This is an example of:
    A. an agency created by express agreement of the parties.
    B. an agency created by implied agreement of the parties.
    C. a formal contract of ratification.
    D. an illegal power of attorney.

4. As to third parties, an agency by estoppel:
    A. is the same thing as an agency created by operation of law.
    B. is the same thing as an agency created by ratification.
    C. can be imposed upon the principal even though there is, in fact, no agency relationship created by an agency agreement.
    D. will be found to exist if a third party sold goods to a minor or did not pay for them even though they were necessaries.

5. Pearson, a minor, entered into a contract of agency with Argyle, an adult. Argyle made a contract with Yeager, while acting as agent for Pearson. The contract:
    A. of agency is voidable by Argyle.

B. of agency is voidable by Pearson.

C. with Yeager is voidable by Argyle.

D. with Yeager is voidable by Yeager.

6. Prince, an adult, enters into a contract of agency with Queen, a minor. Queen made a contract with Zephir, while acting as agent for Prince.

A. The contract of agency is **not** binding on Prince.

B. The contract of agency is **not** binding on Queen.

C. The contract with Zephir is **not** binding on Prince.

D. The contract with Zephir is **not** binding on Zephir.

7. An agent owes a duty of loyalty to his or her principal:

A. because the agent occupies a fiduciary relation with the principal.

B. that is violated if the agent acts in a negligent manner.

C. and if this duty is violated, the agent is liable only for actual losses incurred by the principal as a result of the breach of the duty.

D. but this duty prohibits an agent from making a secret profit while representing the principal only if the interests of the principal are adversely affected.

8. An agent employed by both the buyer and seller of certain personal property will be considered as violating his fiduciary duty:

A. although both the buyer and seller know of her dual position and consent thereto.

B. although no actual monetary damage can be shown.

C. but is entitled to retain compensation paid for her services by the seller.

D. but neither the buyer nor the seller can rescind an executory contract made on her behalf by the agent.

9. J.P. Metty hired Leopard as his agent for purposes of finding a building contractor and supervising the construction of a new mansion for Metty. It was anticipated that the cost would be at least $500,000. For his services, Leopard would receive a fee of $30,000. Leopard contacted Castle Construction Co., which agreed to construct the stately manor house for Metty for $500,000 and an addition to Leopard's house at no charge. The Metty mansion and the addition to Leopard's house have been completed and Metty has paid the $500,000 to Castle Construction Co. Leopard is liable to Metty because:

A. Leopard failed to inform Metty that the mansion could be constructed for less than $500,000.

B. Leopard acted disloyally by failing to obtain the most favorable terms for Metty.

C. Leopard failed to account for a benefit Leopard received as a result of the agency.

D. All of the answers above are correct.

10. Paul appointed Fred as his agent to purchase 500 shares of ETT Co. stock for $18 per share. Unknown to Paul, Fred owned 500 shares of ETT Co. stock. Fred sold his own shares to Paul at $18 per share.

A. Paul must carry out his duty of compensating Fred for the services performed.

B. A court will impose a constructive trust on the 500 shares of ETT Co. stock now held by Paul.

C. The contract of sale is voidable by Paul so that Paul can return the 500 shares of stock to Fred and recover the $9,000 paid therefor.

D. If the value of the stock increases to $24 per share, Paul has no basis for suing Fred.

11. A principal engages an agent for three months as the principal's exclusive agent to sell the principal's products in a three-state area.
    A. The contract creating the agency must be in writing.
    B. If the principal sells its products in the same three-state area through another agent, the principal will be liable for damages to the first agent.
    C. If there was no provision for payment of compensation to the agent in the agency agreement, the agent has no right to receive compensation and reimbursement for expenses.
    D. The principal can disaffirm contracts made by the agent when it is discovered that the agent is a minor.

12. Markell's agent, Quincy, had access to a secret formula which Markell developed and used for the manufacture of a substance that absorbs snow causing the snow to disappear. Quincy sold the trade secret to Soto.
    A. Markell **cannot** discharge Quincy without liability.
    B. Markell can recover the consideration paid by Soto to Quincy, even though the sale of the trade secret occurred after Quincy left Markell's employment.
    C. Markell can recover the consideration paid by Soto to Quincy or recover in tort for the breach of Quincy's fiduciary duty, but **not** both.
    D. There is no basis for a suit by Markell against Soto.

13. Austin was the purchasing agent for the Paragon Store. Austin purchased goods from Simple Sales Corp. for the Paragon Store. Without the store's knowledge, Austin accepted a $3,000 commission from Simple Sales Corp.
    A. Austin is **not** liable to the Paragon Store because Austin did **not** violate any duties that were owed by Austin to Paragon.
    B. Simple Sales Corp. is entitled to the return of the $3,000 because Austin violated the fiduciary duty of loyalty that was owed to Paragon.
    C. Austin violated duties that Austin owed to the Paragon Store and, therefore, forfeits the right to receive compensation from Paragon, but Austin may keep the $3,000 because it was paid by a third party and not by the principal.
    D. The Paragon Store is entitled to recover the $3,000 from Austin, and Austin forfeits her right to compensation from Paragon for her services rendered in making the purchases from Simple Sales.

Chapter 34
Liability to Third Parties and Termination

A named principal is liable as a party to an act or transaction engaged in or conducted by his or her agent. As a result, a principal may be liable in contract or tort to a third party. In such case, the third party will have to establish that there was an agency relationship and that the agent was acting within the scope of his or her actual or apparent authority or that the act of the agent was later ratified by the principal. In this chapter, the authors discuss the nature of the rights and liabilities of principals and agents with regard to third parties and, in the final section, the manner in which agency relationships are terminated.

THINGS TO KEEP IN MIND

An agent's authority to do a particular thing may have been expressly or impliedly conferred by his or her principal. If so, the agent has actual authority. An agent may lack the actual power to perform a particular act but may possess apparent authority if, because of his or her principal's words or conduct, a third party reasonably and justifiably believed that the agent had the necessary authority.

OUTLINE

I. Scope of agent's authority.

    A. A principal is liable as a party to a lawful contract made for and on behalf of the principal by his or her agent and for torts committed by his or her agent while the agent is acting within the scope of his or her actual or apparent authority or subsequently ratified by the principal. In order to recover from a principal, the third party, therefore, must show that:

        1. The agency relationship existed [covered in Chapter 33]; and

        2. The agent acted within the scope of his or her actual or apparent authority, or the principal ratified the actions of the agent.

    B. Actual authority — Expressly or impliedly conferred by the principal upon the agent in order to accomplish the purpose of the agency.

    C. Express actual authority.

        1. Express authority may be given orally or in writing.

2. Unless required by the statute of frauds or other statute, a writing is not necessary.

    a. The equal dignity rule.
       1) In most states, when an agent is empowered to enter into contracts that are required to be evidenced by a signed writing because of the statute of frauds, the agent's authority to do so must be granted in a writing signed by the principal.
       2) Exception — When corporate executives are acting for corporations in the ordinary course of business, written authorization is not required.

    b. If the appointment of an agent is in a writing, the writing is called a "power of attorney" which may be notarized by a notary public (a public official authorized to attest to the authenticity of signatures and who signs his or her name, dates, and imprints his or her seal on the document).

3. An agent has special authority if the agent is empowered only to do specified acts; an agent has general authority when the agent is empowered to engage in all types of business transactions on behalf of a principal.

D. Implied authority — Implied actual authority may be:

1. Inferred because of the conduct of the principal;

2. Conferred on the agent because of custom; or

3. Reasonably necessary in order to carry out the purpose and express authority of the agent.

E. Apparent authority and estoppel.

1. Apparent authority exists when a principal manifests (or "holds out") to a third person that his or her agent has authority, and the third person reasonably relies upon the principal's statement or conduct, deals with the agent, and incurs a loss or is otherwise injured.

2. The principal is estopped from asserting that the agent lacked authority.

3. Apparent authority may arise if a principal gives an agent possession of the principal's property or evidence of ownership of property (e.g., a deed to land).

4. Apparent authority cannot be based upon declarations or conduct of the agent alone.

5. An agency relationship may be created by estoppel. [See Chapter 33.]

   a. An ostensible agency (an agency by estoppel) exists when communications or conduct of a person (who, in fact, has not appointed another person to act as his or her agent) causes a third person reasonably to believe that the purported (ostensible) agent is the appointing person's agent and has authority to act on the appointing person's behalf, the appointing person is estopped from denying the existence of the agency.

   b. The ostensible agent has apparent authority to do those things which a similar agent customarily has the implied actual authority to do; the principal is estopped from denying that the agent had authority.

F. Emergency powers — In an unforeseen emergency situation, when an agent is unable to communicate with the principal, it is inferred that the agent has power to take necessary, appropriate action in order to protect or preserve the property or other interests of the principal.

G. Ratification — The affirmation by a principal of a previously unauthorized contract or act.

   1. The effect of ratification is to bind the principal as if the act or contract had been authorized originally.

   2. Express ratification — Principal clearly approves and actually expresses an intent to be bound to the terms of a contract that the agent entered into without authorization.

   3. Implied ratification — Principal indicates an intention to be bound to the terms of a contract that the agent entered into without authorization by accepting the benefits or by failing to repudiate the contract promptly.

   4. Requirements for effective ratification.

      a. The principal must have knowledge of all material facts surrounding the transaction.
        1) If the principal lacks complete knowledge, the principal may rescind or repudiate the ratification unless the third person has changed his or her position in reasonable reliance on the principal' ratification.
        2) It does not matter that the lack of knowledge results from the agent's wrongful conduct or a mistake.

      b. The entire transaction must be ratified by the principal.

      c. The agent must have held himself or herself out as acting for the person (the principal) who subsequently ratifies.

      d. The principal must have had capacity at the time the act was performed by the agent and at the time the act was ratified by the principal.

e. Death, incapacity, or withdrawal of the third party before ratification prevent the principal from effectively ratifying.

II. Liability for contracts.

A. A disclosed principal is a principal whose identity is known by the third party with whom the agent enters into a contract on behalf of the named principal.

B. A partially disclosed principal is a principal whose existence, but not identity, is known by the third party.

C. An undisclosed principal is a principal whose existence and identity are completely unknown by the third party.

D. Authorized acts.

1. When a contract is made in the disclosed principal's name and authorized by the principal, the parties to the contract are the principal and the third party.

   a. If there is a breach of the contract by the principal, the principal is liable to the third party.

   b. If there is a breach of the contract by the third party, the third party is liable to the principal.

   c. The agent is not a party to the contract and, therefore, does not incur contract liability unless the agent expressly obligates himself or herself or guarantees performance by the principal.

2. In most states, when the agent is acting within the scope of the agent's authority for a partially disclosed principal, both the principal and agent are treated as parties to the contract and the third party can enforce the contract against either the principal or the agent.

3. When the agent is acting for an undisclosed principal, the agent is a party to the contract and is liable as such to the third party.

   a. If the agent was acting within the scope of the agent's authority, the agent is entitled to indemnification from the undisclosed principal.

   b. The third party also is liable to the agent (who is a party to the contract) in the event of a breach of contract by the third party.

   c. If the agent was acting within the scope of the agent's authority, the third party can enforce the contract against the principal following the disclosure of the principal's existence and identity unless:
      1) The undisclosed principal was expressly excluded as a party to the contract;

2) The contract is a negotiable instrument (because the instrument neither names the principal nor shows that the agent signed in a representative capacity);

3) The performance of the agent is personal to the contract; or

4) The agent or principal knew that the third party would not have entered into a contract with the principal had the third party known the principal's identity, and the third party rescinds the contract.

d. The third party has a right to elect to hold either the principal or the agent liable.

e. The undisclosed principal can enforce the contract against the third party if the contract was entered into on the principal's behalf by an authorized agent unless:

1) Liability is based upon a negotiable instrument and the principal did not acquire rights to the instrument.

2) The third party was being defrauded by the principal.

3) The contract was for the performance of personal services by the agent.

E. Unauthorized acts.

1. When a contract is made in the name of a disclosed principal by an agent who lacks authority and the contract is not ratified by the principal:

a. The principal is not liable to the third party and the third party is not liable to the principal.

b. The agent is not liable as a party to the contract (but may be liable to the third party because of a breach of warranty).

2. An agent impliedly warrants that the principal is in existence and that the agent has authority to enter into the contract with the third party.

a. An agent, who lacks authority or exceeds the scope of his or her authority, may be liable to the third party for breach of the implied warranty of authority (but is not liable to the third party for a breach of contract).

b. The agent is liable for the breach of warranty of authority even if the breach was unintentional or made because of a good faith mistake.

c. The agent is not liable for breach of the warranty of authority if the third party knew that the agent made a mistake about the extent of the agent's authority or the agent indicated uncertainty as to the extent of the agent's authority.

III. Liability for agent's torts.

A. An agent is personally and primarily liable for his or her own torts, even if the torts were authorized by the agent's principal.

B. A principal may be liable to an injured third person for a tort committed by an agent because of the principal's own tortious conduct, the principal's authorization of a tortious act, or the agent's tortious misrepresentation, or because of the application of the doctrine of *respondeat superior*. [See below at II. F.]

C. Principal's tortious conduct — A principal may be liable for negligence if the principal gives improper instructions; authorizes the use of improper material, tools or equipment; establishes improper rules; or fails to prevent an agent's tortious conduct while the agent is on the principal's property or using the principal's equipment, materials, or tools.

D. Principal's authorization of tortious conduct — If a principal authorizes the agent to commit a tortious act, the principal is liable because the act is considered to be the act of the principal.

E. Misrepresentation — A principal is liable for a misrepresentation made by an agent who has actual or apparent authority to make representations, and the particular misrepresentation was made while the agent was acting within the scope of such authority.

   1. Fraudulent misrepresentation — A principal who places an agent in a position is liable for the agent's misrepresentations when:

      a. The agent's position conveys to third parties the impression that the agent has authority to make statements and perform acts consistent with the ordinary duties that are within the scope of the position; and

      b. The agent appears to be acting within the scope of authority that the position of agency confers.

   2. Innocent misrepresentation — A principal is liable for an agent's innocent misrepresentation that is made when the agent is acting within the scope of authority.

F. The doctrine of *respondeat superior* — A person in a superior position (such as an employer or principal) is liable vicariously for torts committed by a subordinate (such as an employee or agent) if the subordinate is acting within the scope of his or her employment or authority in furtherance of the superior's business.

   1. Vicarious, secondary, strict liability is imposed upon employers, who have duties to manage their affairs (including those accomplished by employees and agents) so as not to injure other people, and who are in better positions than injured parties to control their own agents and employees to prevent the injury and to bear the financial loss.

2. Scope of employment [Restatement (Second) of Agency, Section 229] — The factors used in determining whether or not a particular act occurred within the course of employment or scope of authority include:

   a. Whether or not the act was authorized by the employer.

   b. The time, place, and purpose of the act.

   c. Whether the act was one commonly performed by employees.

   d. The extent to which the employer's interest was advanced by the act.

   e. Whether the employer furnished the means or instrumentality by which an injury was inflicted.

   f. Whether the employer had reason to know that the employee would do the act in question and whether the employee had done the act before.

   g. Whether the act involved the commission of a crime.

3. Liability for employee's negligence.

   a. The principal/employer is liable if a negligent act of an agent/employee causes an injury to a third party and the negligence occurs when the agent/employee is acting within the scope of employment even if the act is not authorized and is contrary to the instructions of the principal/ employer.

   b. The principal/employer cannot contractually disclaim vicarious liability for a subordinate's torts.

   c. In general, traveling to and from the place of employment is considered to be outside the scope of employment; travel time of a traveling salesperson (including the return trip home) is considered to be within the scope of employment.

   d. Departure from the employer's business — A substantial departure or deviation from the employer's business and the employee's required duties (such that the employee is on "a frolic of his or her own") is outside the scope of employment.

   e. Borrowed servants — An employer who has the primary right to control a "borrowed" employee is liable for the torts of the borrowed employee.

   f. Notice of dangerous conditions — Notice of material facts relating to a principal's or an employer's business received by an agent or employee will be imputed to the principal or employer.

4. Liability for employee's intentional torts.

a. Because of the doctrine of *respondeat superior*, an employer is liable (secondarily and vicariously) for intentional torts (such as assault, battery, and false imprisonment) committed by an employee (the tortfeasor) during the course of the employee's employment.

b. If an employee commits a tort at the direction of the employer, both the employer and employee are liable even though the employee was unaware of the wrongfulness of the act.

c. An employer has the right to control the activities of his or her employees, is liable for employees' intentional torts, and has a duty to restrain employees from engaging in reckless acts.

IV. Liability for independent contractor's torts.

A. An employer is not liable for harm to a third party caused by the intentional or negligent acts of an independent contractor in the performance of the contract because the employer does not have the right to control the manner of performance by the independent contractor.

B. Strict liability, however, is imposed upon both the employer and the independent contractor if the independent contractor is engaging in exceptionally hazardous activities, such as blasting, transportation of highly volatile chemicals, or the use of poisonous gases; in some states, strict liability is imposed on employers because of case law or because of statutes.

V. Liability for crimes.

A. An agent or employee is liable for his or her own crimes even if the agent or employee is acting within the scope of his or her authority or employment.

B. A principal or employer is not liable for the criminal actions of an agent or employee even if the agent or employee was acting within the scope of his or her authority or employment unless:

1. The principal or employer participated in the crime or expressly directed or authorized the crime's commission.

2. A specific statute imposes liability on the principal or employer.

VI. Liability for subagent's acts.

A. An agent who is so authorized by a principal can hire a subagent or an employee when the duties are simple and definite, when it is a business custom, or when there is an unforeseen emergency.

B. If an agent is authorized to employ subagents for a disclosed principal, the principal is responsible for compensating the subagent and is liable for the acts of the subagent.

C. If an agent is not authorized to employ subagents for a principal, the principal is not responsible for compensating the subagent and is not liable for the acts of the subagent.

D. If an agent is authorized to employ subagents for an undisclosed principal, the agent is responsible for compensating the subagent, but the undisclosed principal is liable for the tortious acts of the subagent.

VII. Termination of an agency.

    A. Termination by act of the parties.

        1. Lapse of time.

           a. Agency expires at the end of a specified time if one is stated.

           b. Agency terminates after the expiration of a reasonable period of time if no term has been specified.

        2. Purpose achieved — An agency is terminated when the objective for which the agency was created has been accomplished.

        3. Occurrence of a specific event — An agency ends upon the happening of a particular event if the agency's formation had been so conditioned.

        4. Mutual agreement — The parties mutually may consent to the termination of an agency.

        5. Termination by one party.

           a. A principal may revoke the authority of an agent or an agent may renounce his or her appointment as an agent.

           b. Either party (the principal or the agent) may have the power, but not necessarily the right, to terminate an agency.
              1) If an agency is an agency at will (not for a stated term or for a particular purpose), either party has the power and right to terminate the agency.
              2) If an agency is not an agency at will, a party may have the power but not the right to terminate the agency, and that party is, therefore, liable to the other party for the wrongful termination; a wrongful termination is a breach of contract.

           c. An agency may be terminated for cause.

           d. Agency coupled with an interest — An agency that is created for the benefit of the agent who has a beneficial interest in the subject matter cannot be revoked by the principal.

1) An agency coupled with an interest is also referred to as a power given as security.
2) Usually, an agency coupled with an interest is irrevocable by the principal and is not terminated by death of the principal.
3) This agency is distinguishable from situations in which agents merely derive proceeds or profits from transactions.
4) Even though the principal lacks the power to terminate the agency coupled with an interest, the agent may renounce the authority to act as an agent.

6. Notice of termination.

   a. If termination is by act of a party, the agency continues between the principal and the agent until notice is given by the principal who is revoking or the agent who is renouncing his or her authority.

   b. Notice must be given to third persons.
      1) Actual notice must be given to third persons who dealt with the agent.
      2) Constructive notice must be given to those who knew of the agency by publication in a newspaper, posting of a sign, etc.
      3) The party terminating the agency or another person (e.g., a new agent who is employed by the principal) may give the notice.

   c. Ordinarily, notice is not required if the agency is terminated by operation of law.

B. Termination by operation of law.

   1. Death or mental incompetency — If either the principal or agent dies or is adjudicated to be incompetent, an agency is terminated.

      a. Knowledge of the death or adjudication of incompetency is not required.

      b. Statutory exceptions exist. [See Chapter 29 at III. E. regarding checks.]

      c. An agency coupled with an interest is not terminated by the death or incompetency of the principal.

   2. Impossibility — An agency is terminated if the subject matter of the agency is lost or destroyed or if a change in law makes further conduct of the agency illegal.

   3. Changed circumstances — An agency is terminated if there is an unforeseen occurrence that has an unusual effect on the subject matter of the agency, such that the agent reasonably can infer that the principal does not want the agency to continue.

   4. Bankruptcy.

a. Usually, the bankruptcy of the principal terminates the agency.

b. The bankruptcy of the agent does not necessarily terminate the agency.

c. Insolvency is distinguishable from bankruptcy and does not necessarily terminate the agency.

5. Outbreak of war — When the countries of which the principal and agent are citizens are at war the agency is terminated.

KEY WORDS AND PHRASES IN TEXT

scope of agent's authority
express actual authority
power of attorney
equal dignity rule
notary public
implied actual authority
apparent authority based upon estoppel
emergency powers of agent
ratification
express or implied ratification
contract liability
disclosed principal
partially disclosed principal
undisclosed principal
agent's implied warranty of authority
misrepresentation made by an agent
vicarious liability
doctrine of *respondeat superior*
liability for agent's intentional torts
     and negligence
principal's authorization of
     tortious conduct

liability for torts of borrowed servants
notice of dangerous conditions
scope (or course) of employment
independent contractor's torts
criminal liability
liability for subagent's acts
termination of agency by acts of the
     parties (lapse of time, purpose
     achieved, occurrence of a specific
     event, or mutual agreement)
termination by an act of one party
     (agent's renunciation or
     principal's revocation)
power to terminate agency
right to terminate agency
agency coupled with an interest
notice of termination
termination of agency by operation of law
     (death or incompetency,
     impossibility, war, changed
     circumstances, and bankruptcy)

FILL-IN QUESTIONS

1. The extent of an agent's power to engage in transactions on behalf of his or her principal is referred to as the agent's _____.

2. Actual authority may be _____, if a principal uses words to confer authority upon an agent, or implied because such authority is incidental to and clearly necessary or logically inferred from the express powers granted or based upon _____, or necessitated by an emergency situation.

3. When a third party deals with an agent (who in fact lacks express or implied actual authority) reasonably believes that the agent has authority to act on behalf of the

agent's principal and the third party changes his or her position in reliance on the principal's words or conduct, the principal may be _____ from denying that the agent lacked actual authority. In such a case, the agent is said to be acting within the scope of his or her _____ authority.

4.   A principal is liable on a contract made in the principal's name by an agent acting within the scope of the agent's authority or subsequently _____ by the principal. In such case, the agent is _____ liable to the other contracting party as a party to the contract. If, however, an agent lacked authority, the agent is liable to the other contracting party based upon the theory of an i m p l i e d _____.

5.   A disclosed principal is a principal whose existence and identity are known by a third party at the time that the third party is dealing with the principal's agent. A partially disclosed principal is a principal whose existence is known, but whose _____ is not known by a third party at the time that the third party is dealing with the principal's agent. An _____ is a principal whose existence and identity are not known by a third party at the time that the third party is dealing with the principal's agent.

6.   The doctrine of *respondeat superior* results in an employer or principal (who is in a superior position) being liable vicariously without actual fault for _____ committed by his or her subordinates while the subordinates are acting within _____ in furtherance of the business of the employer or principal.

7.   A principal may terminate an agency by _____ the authority of his or her agent, without liability to the agent for cause or if _____ _____.

8.   Most agencies are created for the benefit of the principal. An agency _____, however, is created for the benefit of the agent, and is irrevocable by the _____.

9.   An agency is terminated by operation of law upon the death or adjudication of incompetency of either the principal or agent, the bankruptcy of the principal, impossibility, such as _____ _____, or unforeseen difficulties.

MULTIPLE CHOICE QUESTIONS

1.   Pace gives Ace a power of attorney. The power of attorney:
      A. may be oral.
      B. is valid and effective only if Ace is a licensed attorney at law.
      C. may limit Ace's authority to enter into specific types on transactions.
      D. must be signed by both Pace and Ace.
      (This question is adapted from objective question #13 on the Uniform CPA Examination, November 1991.)

2. An agent is liable to the third party, with whom the agent deals, for breach of a contract that the agent has entered into on behalf of the agent's principal in the event that the contracted performances is not given:
    A. whenever the agent exceeds the agent's authority.
    B. whenever the agent is acting as an agent for a nonexistent principal.
    C. whenever the agent acts for the benefit of a principal who did not have contractual capacity at the time of the transaction.
    D. only if the agent expressly assumes liability and, thus, becomes a party to the contract.

3. An agent is thought of as possessing the same authority as is possessed by other agents in similar positions. Such authority is normally:
    A. express actual authority.
    B. express apparent authority.
    C. implied actual authority.
    D. implied express authority.

4. If a principal leads a third party to believe that the principal has conferred authority on an agent, although the principal, in fact, has **not** conferred such authority on the agent, the agent will be considered as having:
    A. express actual authority.
    B. implied actual authority.
    C. apparent authority.
    D. **no** authority.

5. Arnold is the manager of a snow clearing service. Although not expressly authorized to do so, Arnold would have:
    A. implied authority to discharge an employee who has refused to lift a shovel and has thrown snowballs at customers.
    B. implied authority to borrow money to purchase twenty snowblowers.
    C. apparent authority to borrow money to purchase twenty snowblowers.
    D. actual authority to cancel an order for snow plows that was placed by the purchasing agent of the snow clearing service.

6. Cramer, chief clerk for Morris, is asked by Morris to assume management of his store while Morris is on special undercover assignment for the CIB. If Morris cannot be reached for advice, Cramer is justified in:
    A. discharging an incompetent employee.
    B. borrowing money in Morris' name for purposes of enlarging the store.
    C. lending Egger, an employee in the store, $12,000.
    D. All of the answers above are correct.

7. If a principal accepts the benefits of a contract entered into by his agent who was acting outside the scope of his authority, the principal will be considered to have ratified the contract:
    A. in the contract's entirety.
    B. although the principal lacked actual knowledge of some of the material terms of the agreement.
    C. although the other party to the contract has withdrawn.

D. retroactive to the date upon which the contract was entered although at that time the principal was incompetent.

8. Paul has authorized Arthur to purchase a television set from Exeter on his (Paul's) behalf. Instead of purchasing a television set, Arthur, fully disclosing the agency relationship, purchased a CB radio. Paul used the CB radio for one month, but neither he nor Arthur paid Exeter for the CB radio.
   A. Only Arthur is liable for the purchase price of the CB radio.
   B. Paul is liable for the purchase price of the radio because Paul ratified the transaction by accepting the benefits.
   C. Paul is liable for the purchase price of the radio because Arthur had actual authority to purchase the radio.
   D. Paul is **not** liable for the purchase price of the radio because he made no implied warranty as to his capacity.

9. Auten is an agent for a disclosed principal, Pine. On May 1, Auten entered into an agreement with Taupte Corp. on behalf of Pine although she lacked authority to do so. On May 5, Taupte Corp. learned of Auten's lack of authority and immediately notified Auten and Pine that it was withdrawing from the May 1 contract. On May 7, with full knowledge of all the material facts, Pine ratified the May 1 contract in its entirety. If Taupte Corp. refuses to honor the agreement, and Pine brings an action for breach of contract, Pine will:
   A. prevail, because the May 1 contract was ratified by Pine in its entirety.
   B. prevail, because Pine's capacity to act as a principal was known to Auten.
   C. lose, because the May 1 contract was void due to Auten's lack of authority.
   D. lose, because Taupte Corp. notified Auten and Pine of its withdrawal before Pine's ratification.
   (This question has been adapted from objective question #6 on the Uniform CPA Examination, May 1987.)

10. Bauten is an agent for a disclosed principal, Plane. On May 1, Bauten entered into an agreement with Teme Corp. on behalf of Plane, although she lacked authority to do so. On May 5, with full knowledge of all the material facts, Plane ratified the May 1 contract in its entirety. On May 7, Teme Corp. learned of Bauten's lack of authority and immediately notified Bauten and Plane that it was withdrawing from the May 1 contract. If Teme Corp. refuses to honor the agreement, and Plane brings an action for breach of contract, Plane will:
    A. prevail because the May 1 contract was ratified by Plane in its entirety.
    B. prevail because Plane's capacity to act as a principal was known to Bauten.
    C. lose because the May 1 contract was void due to Bauten's lack of authority.
    D. lose because Teme Corp. notified Bauten and Plane of its withdrawal within a reasonable time.

11. Archer is an agent for Penguin. In the past, Archer has purchased equipment from ZYX Machine Co. for use in Penguin's business. Last month, Archer entered into a contract with ZYX Machine Co. for the purchase of equipment on Penguin's behalf and in Penguin's name. The equipment has not been paid for even though it was delivered and is being used in Penguin's business. ZYX Machine Co. can recover:
    A. the contract price from Penguin.

B. the contract price from Archer.

C. the contract price from either Archer or Penguin.

D. for breach of an implied warranty of authority from Archer.

12. Peach is the principal and Apple is the agent in an agency coupled with an interest. In the absence of a contractual provision relating to the duration of the agency, who has the power and the right to terminate the agency before the interest has expired?

	Peach	Apple
A.	Yes	Yes
B.	No	Yes
C.	Yes	No
D.	No	No

13. An agent, who has been appointed by a principal to move lumber that is obstructing a road which the principal is required to keep clear, is:

A. liable to a third person who is injured while trying to climb over the lumber that the agent failed to remove.

B. **not** liable to a third person who is injured by a falling two-by-four because the agent has moved the lumber, but stacked the lumber in a negligent manner.

C. liable to a third person with whom she gets into a dispute while in the process of moving the wood and hits the third person with a two-by-four.

D. **not** liable to a third person if, under the doctrine of *respondeat superior*, her principal is liable for the tort committed by the agent.

14. If an employee (while acting within the scope of employment) has committed both negligent and intentional acts that resulted in injuries to third parties, the employer:

A. may be liable to the third parties even if the employee's acts were unauthorized.

B. may effectively limit its liability to the injured third parties if the agent has signed a disclaimer absolving the employer from liability.

C. will be liable under the doctrine of *respondeat superior* only for the intentional acts.

D. will never be criminally liable unless the employer actively participated in the acts with its employee.

(This question has been adapted from objective question #5 on the Uniform CPA Examination, May 1987.)

15. Watson was an employee of the HM Contracting Corp. Watson was specially trained in procedures to be used in blasting operations with particular emphasis on safety precautions. HM Contracting Corp. contracted to construct a factory. In order to put in the foundation for the factory, it was necessary to do some blasting and Watson's services were used. Watson disregarded a number of safety precautions. As a result, neighboring buildings were damaged, and Watson incurred personal injuries.

A. HM Contracting Corp. is liable to the owners of the damaged buildings, despite the fact that Watson disregarded the precautions and the fact that the corporation exercised reasonable care.

B. HM Contracting Corp. is **not** liable to the owners of the damaged buildings because Watson disregarded safety precautions and the corporation exercised reasonable care.

C. HM Contracting Corp. is **not** liable to Watson under the workers' compensation statutes.

D. Watson is **not** liable for the damage to the neighboring buildings because he was acting on behalf of his employer.

16. A lender is given authority to collect rents due to a borrower as security and to apply these rents to the payment of a debt owed to the lender.
    A. This does **not** create an agency.
    B. The agency is created by operation of law.
    C. This is an agency coupled with an interest.
    D. The agency is terminated by the death of the borrower.

17. April was an agent of Primmer. April died last month. The agency is, therefore, terminated by:
    A. mutual assent.
    B. revocation of authority.
    C. implied agreement of the parties.
    D. operation of law.

18. Marple has been authorized to act as Christie's agent until December 31 of the current year. The agency will be terminated without liability to either Marple or Christie:
    A. only when the agency expires on December 31 of the current year.
    B. upon the insolvency of Christie before December 31 of the current year.
    C. upon the death of Marple before December 31 of the current year.
    D. upon the dismissal of Marple by Christie without cause.

19. In order to terminate the authority of an agent to bind his or her principal, actual notice to creditors who dealt with the agent or to creditors who extended credit to the principal through the agent must be given:
    A. if the principal is bankrupt.
    B. to the attorney general of the state in which the principal resides.
    C. if a change in law makes the further continuation of the agency illegal.
    D. if the principal revokes the authority of the agent.

UNIT SEVEN:
EMPLOYMENT AND LABOR RELATIONS

Traditionally, the rights and obligations of parties in an employment relationship were governed by common law principles derived from the law of contracts and torts. Many of these principles became inappropriate and difficult to apply as the United States became increasingly industrialized. Early in this century, the states began to enact statutes in order to protect workers who were employed in unsafe and unhealthy environments. During the depression in the 1930s, the federal Congress also adopted laws relating to employment.

Today, the objectives of government regulatory legislation affecting the employment relationship are to protect the health, safety, and general welfare of the nation's workforce and to promote an environment that is relatively free from inequalities in bargaining power and industrial strife (as discussed in Chapter 35) as well as discriminatory practices (the subject matter of Chapter 36).

Chapter 35
Employment and Labor Law

In this chapter, the focus is upon areas of employment law that are of concern to both employers and employees. The topics covered include the labor management relationship, employees' working conditions, compensation, income security, privacy, and wrongful discharge. To a great extent today, these are areas of law that are based upon statutes. These statutes have been enacted in order to protect employees and correct perceived imbalances in the bargaining power between employers and people who are employed or who are seeking employment.

THINGS TO KEEP IN MIND

1. In addition to the federal government, states also have enacted statutes dealing with employment. For example, workers' compensation laws, providing for payments in case of deaths, injuries, and diseases related to employment, are state statutes. In some cases, such as the regulation of minimum wages and maximum hours of work, state laws often duplicate the federal statutes and apply to employees who may not be covered by the federal Fair Labor Standards Act.

2. Many of the laws referred to in this chapter only apply to people who are classified as employees. You may, therefore, wish to refer to Chapter 33, in which the criteria for distinguishing agency relationships from those of employment are discussed.

OUTLINE

I.   Wage-hour laws.

    A. Employees working on government construction projects are required to be paid at the wage rate prevailing in the geographic area (Davis-Bacon Act of 1931).

    B. Manufacturers or suppliers that enter into contracts with agencies of the federal government are required to pay employees a minimum wage and "time and a half" for overtime (Walsh-Healy Public Contract Act of 1936).

    C. Fair Labor Standards Act of 1938 (FLSA).

        1. Child labor.

            a. With some exceptions, children under the age of 14 may not be employed.

b. Children between the ages of 14 and 16 may be employed only during non-school hours and only in non-hazardous occupations.

c. Children who are less than 18 may not be employed in hazardous occupations.

2. Hours and wages.

a. Maximum hours provisions — Employees who work more than 40 hours per week are required to be paid one and a half times their regular pay for all time over 40 hours, except for employees:
    1) Whose duties necessitate irregular working hours;
    2) Who are employed pursuant to *bona fide* individual contracts or collective bargaining agreements;
    3) Whose contracts specify a regular rate of pay for up to 40 hours per week and one and a half times that rate for hours in excess of 40; and
    4) Whose contracts provide a weekly guarantee for not more than 60 hours.

b. Minimum wage provision — The minimum wage rate to be paid by covered employers is periodically established by Congress; as of September 1997, it is $5.15 per hour.

c. Exempt employees include executives, administrators, professionals, and outside sales personnel.

II. Labor unions.

A. Federal laws recognize that employees have the right to form and join labor organizations (unions).

1. Norris-La Guardia Act (1932) — Recognition was given to the rights of employees to organize and engage in peaceful strikes, picketing, and boycotts.

2. National Labor Relations Act (1935) — The NLRA (which often is referred to as the Wagner Act) established the rights of employees to engage in collective bargaining and to strike.

a. The NLRA sets forth certain employer practices that are treated as unfair to labor.
    1) Refusing to bargain in good faith with representatives of employees (NLRB certified unions).
    2) Interfering with efforts of employees to form, join, or assist labor organizations (unions).
    3) Dominating or contributing to labor unions.
    4) Discriminating against employees because of their union activities.
    5) Discriminating against employees who file charges or give testimony to the National Labor Relations Board (NLRB).

b. The NLRA provided for the creation of the National Labor Relations Board (NLRB) to oversee union elections and to enforce provisions of the Act relating to unfair practices.
1) Investigation of charges of unfair labor practices are conducted at the regional level.
2) If a charge is found to have merit and no settlement is reached, a complaint is issued and a fact finding hearing is held before an Administrative Law Judge who makes a recommendation to the NLRB.
3) The NLRB may issue a cease and desist order and give other appropriate relief in order to put employees in the position that they would have been in if the unfair labor practice had not occurred.
4) Appeal from an NLRB decision is to a U.S. Court of Appeals.

3. Labor-Management Relations Act (1947) — The LMRA also is referred to as the Taft-Hartley Act.

   a. The LMRA prohibits closed shops.
   1) Union membership may not be required by an employer in order for an employee to obtain employment.
   2) Union shops are permitted so that employees may be required to become union members within a specified period of time after obtaining employment unless prohibited in states with "right to work" laws.

   b. The LMRA empowers the President to obtain an injunction against a strike for an 80 day cooling-off period if the strike would result in a national emergency.

   c. The LMRA sets forth certain union practices that are treated as unfair to employers.
   1) Refusing to bargain in good faith with an employer.
   2) Charging excessive or discriminatory initiation fees or dues.
   3) Causing an employer to pay for work that was not performed (featherbedding).
   4) Coercing or restraining employees from exercising their rights to join a union.
   5) Causing or attempting to cause an employer to discriminate against employees or to encourage (or discourage) membership in a particular union.
   6) Engaging in a strike, picketing, or boycott directed at a secondary employer (a firm that does business with the primary employer) for an illegal purpose.

4. Labor-Management Reporting and Disclosure Act (1959) — The LMRDA also is referred to as the Landrum-Griffin Act.

   a. The LMRDA establishes a bill of rights for employees.

b. The LMRDA regulates internal operations of labor organizations and union elections in order to assure union democracy.

c. The LMRDA requires that reports be filed with the Secretary of Labor and that officers be bonded; in addition, certain loans to officers and members are prohibited.

d. The LMRDA prohibits hot cargo contracts (agreements between unions and employers providing that employers will not handle, use, sell, etc., goods of other employers).

B. The purpose of much of the federal legislation (and similar state laws) relating to the employment relationship is to protect workers' rights to organize and to engage in collective bargaining with employers.

1. Union organization.

a. A union may solicit authorization from employees authorizing the union to act as the collective bargaining representative of the employees with their employer.

b. If a majority of the workers sign authorization cards, the union asks the employer to recognize the union as the representative of the workers. If the employer refuses to recognize the union, the union may petition the NLRB for an election.

c. Union elections.
   1) When a union can show that at least 30% of the employees support the union or support an election on unionization, the NLRB supervises a secret election.
   2) The NLRB certifies the union as the exclusive bargaining representative of the workers if a majority of the employees voted for the union.

2. Collective bargaining — Employers and legally recognized unions are required to engage in collective bargaining in good faith when negotiating wages, benefits, working conditions, and other terms of employment contracts (collective bargaining agreements).

3. Strikes — If the collective bargaining process breaks down, a strike may be called by the union.

a. A strike occurs when the workers leave their jobs and refuse to work; the workers also may picket by standing outside the employer's premises with signs.

b. The right to strike is provided for in the NLRA and certain strike activities are protected by the free speech guarantee in the First Amendment to the U.S. Constitution.

c. Certain strikes, such as wildcat strikes by a minority of the employees, violent strikes, and sitdown strikes in which workers refuse to leave the place of employment, are illegal.

d. With limitations, an employer may hire replacement workers during a strike and, after a settlement, is not required to employ strikers (unless the employer engaged in unfair labor practices).

III. Worker health and safety — Statutes are meant to protect employees and their families from the risks of job-related accidental injuries, illnesses, and deaths.

A. The Occupational Safety and Health Act (1970).

1. The Act requires that places of employment be "free from recognized hazards" which may result in death or serious harm and that employees comply with safety and health rules.

2. Enforcement agencies.

a. The Occupational Safety and Health Administration (OSHA) in the Department of Labor enforces the Act and is authorized to promulgate rules, establish safety and health standards, and conduct investigations and inspections.

b. The National Institute for Occupational Safety and Health in the Department of Health and Human Services conducts research and makes recommendations to OSHA.

c. The Occupational Safety and Health Review Commission, an independent agency, handles appeals from actions taken by OSHA administrators.

3. Procedures and violations.

a. Employees can file complaints of violations with OSHA; an employer cannot discharge an employee who files a complaint or who, in good faith, refuses to work in a high-risk area.

b. Employers having more than eleven employees must keep and update five-year occupational injury and illness records for each employee; the records must be available for inspection by an OSHA inspector.

c. Work-related injuries and diseases must be reported to OSHA; if an employee is killed or five or more employees are hospitalized as a result of a work-related accident, the Department of Labor must be notified within 48 hours and a complete inspection of the premises is mandatory.

d. Inspections (including surprise inspections, but not warrantless inspections) can be conducted by OSHA; a citation directing an employer to correct any violations may be issued and civil penalties may be assessed by OSHA.

   e. Employers who willfully violate the Occupational Safety and Health Act may be criminally prosecuted; employers also may be prosecuted under state criminal laws because state laws are not preempted by the federal Act.

B. State statutes dealing with working conditions also protect the health and safety of employees.

C. State workers' compensation acts.

   1. Employers are strictly liable to employees for accidental deaths, injuries, and diseases arising out of or during the course of their employment.

      a. Some employees (e.g., temporary, agricultural, and domestic workers) may not be covered.

      b. The amount of compensation is limited to statutorily-scheduled benefits that vary from state to state; employers may carry workers' compensation insurance or be self-insurers. [See Chapter 53.]

   2. Common law defenses, such as the fellow servant rule, assumption of the risk, and comparative (or contributory) negligence, are eliminated.

   3. Rulings made by state agencies that administer workers' compensation laws are subject to judicial review.

   4. In order to recover workers' compensation, a worker must establish that:

      a. The worker was an employee and not an independent contractor. [See Chapter 33.]

      b. The worker incurred an injury or illness that was accidental and arose out of or in the course of employment (occurred on the job). [See Chapter 34.]

      c. The employee must notify the employer of the injury or illness promptly and file a workers' compensation claim with the appropriate state agency within a specified period of time.

   5. In some states, workers' compensation remedies (benefits) are the only relief in cases involving negligence, but employees may not be barred from bringing civil actions for intentional torts or gross negligence.

IV. Income security.

A. Social Security and Medicare.

1. The Social Security Act of 1935, as amended, provides for old-age, retirement, survivors, and disability insurance (OASDI).

2. Benefits are paid when families' incomes cease or are reduced because of death, disability, or retirement; the amount of the payments increase with increases in the cost of living.

B. Medicare.

1. Medicare is a health insurance program which is administered in part by the Social Security Administration for people who are 65 years of age or older and other people who are disabled.

2. Medicare hospital insurance (Part A) benefits are premium-free for people who receive Social Security benefits and cover some costs of inpatient hospital and skilled nursing home care, home health care, and hospice care.

3. Additional Medicare medical insurance (Part B) is available to people who pay premiums and covers some services, supplies, and equipment that are not covered by Medicare hospital insurance.

C. The Federal Insurance Contribution Act (FICA) requires that employers deduct specified percentages (currently, 6.2% for Social Security and 2.9% for Medicare) of employees' wages, and pay a matching sum on all earnings up to a statutory maximum amount (the wage base) for Social Security.

1. The current wage base for Social Security is $65,400.

2. There is no cap on the amount of wages subject to the Medicare contribution.

D. Private pension plans.

1. The Employee Retirement Income Security Act of 1974 (ERISA) protects private pension plans that are provided by employers and unions.

   a. Standards requiring that pension plans be adequately funded are established by ERISA.

   b. In general, contributions made by employees vest immediately, and employees' rights to contributions made by employers vest after five years.

2. The legislation is administered by the Labor Management Service Administration of the Department of Labor. Important regulations also have been promulgated by the Internal Revenue Service.

3. Tax deferred individual retirement income accounts may also be established by employees and those who are self-employed.

E. Unemployment compensation.

1. The Federal Unemployment Tax Act (FUTA) of 1935, as amended, provides for a joint federal-state program.

2. A tax is imposed upon covered employers and paid quarterly to the states, which then make deposits into the federal Unemployment Insurance Fund, in which each state has an account.

3. An employee who has been discharged without cause is entitled to draw payments for a specified period of time (which varies from state to state), if the employee:

   a. Is ready, willing, and able to accept another position;

   a. Had been employed in a covered industry; and

   c. Had worked for at least a specified minimum period of time or earned at least a specified minimum amount of wages. (The time periods and minimum earned wages vary from state to state.)

V. The Consolidated Omnibus Budget Reconciliation Act of 1985 (COBRA).

A. An employer cannot eliminate medical, optical, or dental insurance coverage for an employee whose employment is terminated (voluntarily or involuntarily) or whose hours have been reduced so that the worker is no longer eligible for coverage under the employer's health plan.

B. Application of COBRA — The employee has 60 days within which to choose either to discontinue coverage or to continue coverage (in which case the employee may be required to pay premiums and a 2% administrative charge).

C. Employers' obligations under COBRA.

1. Employers having more than 20 employees that have benefits plans must give information about COBRA provisions to their workers.

2. Employers do not have to provide benefit coverage if they eliminate group health plans or when workers become eligible for Medicare, are covered by spouses' plans, become insured under different plans, or fail to pay premiums.

VI. Family and medical leave.

A. The Family and Medical Leave Act (FMLA) of 1993.

1. Coverage and applicability of the FMLA.

a. An employer having more than 50 employees is required by FMLA to give a worker up to 12 weeks of family or medical leave during any 12 month period, continue health-care coverage during the leave, and guarantee employment in the same or a comparable position when the employee returns to work (unless the employee is a key employee).

b. Employees who have worked less than one year or less than 25 hours a week during the year are not covered by COBRA.

c. Employees may take family leaves to care for newborn, newly adopted, and foster children.

d. An employee may take a medical leave when the employee, or the employee's spouse, child or parent has a "serious health problem."

2. Remedies for violations of the FMLA.

a. Damages for unpaid wages or salary, lost benefits, denied compensation, and actual monetary losses up to an amount equivalent to the employee's compensation for 12 weeks.

b. Job reinstatement and, if relevant, promotion.

c. Court costs and attorney's fees, and double damages if the employer exercised bad faith.

B. Many states also have laws covering leave from employment for medical and family reasons and many firms have family-leave plans for their employees.

VII. Employee privacy rights.

A. The U.S. Constitution does not expressly guarantee a right of privacy, but the First, Third, Fourth, Fifth, and Ninth Amendments have been interpreted as inferring that there is a right to privacy. [See also Chapters 5 and 6.]

B. Lie detector (polygraph) tests.

1. The federal Employee Polygraph Protection Act (1988) prohibits certain employers from:

a. Requiring, causing, suggesting, or requesting that employees or applicants for jobs take lie detector tests;

b. Using, accepting, referring to, or asking about the results of lie detector tests taken by employees or applicants; and

c. Taking or threatening negative action related to employment based upon results of or refusals to take lie detector tests.

2. Exempt employers include federal, state, and local governments, certain security service firms, and companies manufacturing and distributing controlled substances.

3. Employers may use polygraph tests when investigating losses attributable to thefts.

C. Drug testing.

1. Constitutional limitations may not apply to private employers; state constitutions and statutes (as well as collective bargaining agreements), however, may protect employees' rights of privacy, including protection against mandatory drug testing.

2. Testing of government employees has been held to be constitutional when there is a reasonable basis for suspecting use of drugs by a person who was employed in a position that could threaten public safety.

D. Acquired immune deficiency syndrome (AIDS) testing — The federal Americans With Disabilities Act may prohibit discharging employees who test positive for the HIV virus. [See Chapter 36.]

E. Electronic performance monitoring.

1. The federal Electronic Communications Privacy Act (1986) prohibits intentional interception of wire and electronic communications as well as disclosure or use of the information subject to a "business-extension exception."

2. Few statutes restrict the use in the workplace of electronic eavesdropping, video, or similar surveillance equipment, or other intrusive activities, such as searches of employees' offices, desks, lockers, etc., by employers.

3. An employee may bring a tort action based upon an unreasonable intrusion of privacy against an employer, in which case a court will balance the offensiveness of the intrusion against the employer's purpose in conducting surveillance or a search and the possible consent given by an employee.

F. Screening procedures — Preemployment tests must serve a job-related purpose and have a close connection to the potential employer's interest.

VIII. Employment-related immigration law.

A. The Immigration Reform and Control Act (IRCA) of 1986 is administered by the Immigration and Naturalization Service and prohibits the employment of illegal aliens. (Employers must verify that each employee who is not a U.S. citizen is entitled to work in the U.S.)

B. The Immigration Act of 1990 — Employers employing aliens must establish that there is a shortage of qualified, non-alien, skilled workers and that bringing immigrants into the U.S. will not adversely affect the labor market in the particular geographic area.

IX.   Wrongful discharge.

A.   The common law at-will employment doctrine — An at-will employee (a person who is not hired for a specified term or period of time) may be discharged by his or her employer for a good reason, no reason, or even a bad reason.

B.   In many states today, this traditional employment at-will doctrine has been eroded by statutory and case law exceptions so that an employer may be liable for the wrongful discharge of an at-will employee; the theories used in recognizing exceptions to the at-will doctrine vary from state to state.

C.   Exceptions based upon contract theory.

1.   Statements of employers' policies in handbooks or other oral or written communications to the effect that employees will be discharged only for good and sufficient cause are part of the contracts of employment. Some courts will award damages, therefore, if there are breaches of these implied contractual promises not to discharge employees without cause.

2.   In a few states, courts have held that there is an implied covenant of good faith in all employment contracts which is violated when employers arbitrarily and without justification discharge employees.

D.   Exceptions based on tort theory.

1.   In extreme cases, courts in some states recognize a tort cause of action for intentional infliction of emotional distress or defamation because of abusive discharge procedures of employers.

2.   Some courts have held that an employer is liable for fraud if the employer made representations to a prospective employee upon which the prospective employee relied in accepting a position with the employer, and the employer subsequently discharged the employee.

E.   Exceptions based on public policy.

1.   Employers may be liable for discharging employees for reasons that violate public policies which are pronounced in statutes, such as serving on juries or refusing to commit illegal acts.

2.   Whistleblowers who have pressured employers to comply with consumer credit laws or informed law enforcement authorities of violations of criminal statutes, unsafe practices, or interferences with the civil rights of other people have recovered for wrongful discharge in some states. [See below at X.]

X.   Statutory protection for whistleblowers.

A. Whistleblowing — An employee informs the government or representatives of the press or other media that his or her employer is engaged in an illegal or unsafe activity and, in retaliation, the employee may be discharged, disciplined, or otherwise injured by his or her employer.

B. Federal statutes protect whistleblowers employed by defense contractors from retaliation for revealing overcharges and protect other people from retaliatory discharge as well as provide monetary incentives to whistleblowers (e.g., the False Claims Reform Act of 1986 and Whistleblower Protection Act of 1989).

C. State statutes also protect whistleblowers from retaliation by employers.

KEY WORDS AND PHRASES IN TEXT

wage-hour law
Fair Labor Standards Act (FLSA)
child labor
minimum wage
labor unions (labor organizations)
strikes, picketing, and boycotts
National Labor Relations Act
National Labor Relations Board (NLRB)
unfair labor practice
cease and desist order
Labor-Management Relations Act
closed shop and union shop
right-to-work laws
Labor-Management Reporting and
        Disclosure Act
hot-cargo agreement
secondary boycott
union election and certification
collective bargaining
Occupational Safety and Health Act
Occupational Safety and Health
        Administration (OSHA)
state workers' compensation laws
death, injury, or illness arising out of or
        in the course of employment
Social Security Act

Old Age, Survivors, and Disability
        Insurance (OASDI)
Federal Insurance Contributions Act
        (FICA)
Medicare
Employee Retirement Income Security
        Act (ERISA)
vesting of employees' rights to receive
        pension benefits
unemployment compensation
Consolidated Omnibus Budget
        Reconciliation Act (COBRA)
Family and Medical Leave Act (FMLA)
Employee Polygraph Protection Act
electronic employee performance
        monitoring
Immigration Reform and Control Act
Immigration Act of 1990
wrongful discharge
employment at will
exceptions to employment-at-will
        doctrine based on contract,
        tort, and public policy
whistleblowing
False Claims Reform Act
Whistleblower Protection Act

FILL-IN QUESTIONS

1. Prohibitions against employing children are established in state statutes and in the federal _____ Act. The general rule is that children who are younger than eighteen cannot be employed in _____ occupations.

2. Recognition of the rights of employees to organize was first accorded in the _____ Act of 1932. The public policy encouraging collective bargaining is supported by provisions in federal labor relations laws, such as the _____ Act of 1935, which provides that the refusal to bargain collectively with designated representatives of labor organizations is an unfair labor practice, and the _____ Act of 1947, which provides that the refusal to bargain collectively with representatives of employers is an unfair labor practice.

3. Today, _____ shops (requiring that union membership be a prerequisite to employment) are prohibited. _____ shops are, however, legal in states that do not have _____ laws. In order to have continued employment, employees may, therefore, be required to become members of a labor organization within a specified period of time.

4. In general, employees who incur accidental injuries or diseases or die as result of or in the course of their employment have a right to recover under the terms of state _____ laws and the federal _____ Act, which provides for survivors and disability insurance.

5. _____ is a joint federal-state plan, which requires that _____ pay a tax on their payrolls to the _____ Insurance Fund, and provides that eligible employees, who have been discharged without cause, may receive periodic payments from the _____ Insurance Fund while the eligible former employees are unemployed.

6. Because of common law principles, employers are required to provide their employees with a safe place of employment. This common law principle has been reinforced by state statutes and by the federal _____ _____ Act.

7. If an employee is not hired for a specified term, an employee is considered to be an _____ employee. The common law rule has been that an _____ employee can be discharged at any time by an employer without liability. The employer, therefore, can discharge the employee with "good cause, no cause, or even bad cause." The trend has been to recognize exceptions to this rule. Some states rely upon _____ theories, others upon _____ theories, and a few upon tort theories in order to provide remedies to _____ employees who have been wrongfully discharged.

MULTIPLE CHOICE QUESTIONS

Questions 1 and 2 are based on the following fact situation: The ABC Co. is a manufacturing firm. ABC's only factory is located in Pennsylvania, where it employs 158 people including 67 women above the age of 16 and five children who are 15 years of age. All employees work a minimum of 38 hours per week and are paid a minimum of ten dollars per hour. Sales of its product in Pennsylvania account for 90% of ABC Co.'s business.

1. Under the general rules of the federal Fair Labors Standards Act, ABC Co.:

A. has violated the statute because ABC Co. employs children under the age of sixteen and does not fall under an exemption.

B. has violated the statute because ABC Co.'s employees work less than 40 hours a week.

C. does **not** violate the statute by employing children if the work that the children engage in is not hazardous.

D. does **not** violate the statute because ABC Co. pays its workers more than the minimum wage.

2. ABC Co.:
   A. is exempt from the federal Occupational Safety and Health Act because all of ABC Co.'s employees are working in the state of Pennsylvania.
   B. is exempt from the federal Occupational Safety and Health Act only if Pennsylvania has equivalent legislation.
   C. is subject to the federal Family and Medical Leave Act because ABC Co. employs more than 50 workers and engages in interstate commerce.
   D. is **not** subject to the Pennsylvania Workers' Compensation Act because ABC Co. pays its employee more than the federal minimum wage.

3. The employees at the PQ Manufacturing Company plant have elected the LMW Union as their representative for collective bargaining purposes. The president of the local chapter of the LMW Union is Smith.
   A. If PQ Manufacturing Company demotes Smith because she filed a complaint with the NLRB, the company has committed an unfair labor practice.
   B. If PQ Manufacturing Company gives Smith $3,000 to be used for union purposes, the company has committed an unfair labor practice.
   C. If PQ Manufacturing Company agrees with the LMW Union that Smith will continue to be paid her regular wages, but will not be expected to work for PQ Manufacturing Company for more than four hours a week, the company has committed an unfair labor practice.
   D. If PQ Manufacturing Company engages in any of these activities, the company has committed an unfair labor practice.

4. Workers' compensation laws are:
   A. governed by federal regulation.
   B. designed to eliminate some common law defenses, such as the fellow servant rule, when an employee is injured.
   C. **not** applicable if an employee's negligence contributed to his or her own injury.
   D. applicable to all employees and agents.

5. While driving an automobile, Davidson was injured in an automobile accident. Davidson will **not** be able to recover workers' compensation if it is proven that at the time of the accident:
   A. Davidson was on his employer's business, but was negligent in the operation of the vehicle.
   B. Davidson was driving from home to his place of employment.
   C. Davidson was using his personal automobile in order to call on a client of his employer.
   D. All of the answers above are correct.

6. Kroll, an employee of Acorn, Inc., was injured in the course of his employment while operating a forklift. The forklift was manufactured and sold to Acorn by Buffalo Corp. The forklift was designed in a defective manner by Buffalo Corp. Under the state's mandatory workers' compensation statute, Kroll will be successful in:

	obtaining workers' compensation benefits.	a negligence action against Acorn.
A.	Yes	Yes
B.	Yes	No
C.	No	Yes
D.	No	No

   (This question has been adapted from objective question #13 on the Uniform CPA Examination, May 1993)

7. Emeree, an at-will employee, worked for Rogue for five years but was discharged yesterday. Emeree probably will be successful in a lawsuit against Rogue for wrongful discharge if Rogue fired Emeree for the following reason:
   A. After notifying Rogue that he had been called for jury duty, Emeree served on a jury for one week.
   B. Emeree refused to follow Rogue's instructions to make repairs at the place of employment.
   C. Emeree assaulted one of Rogue's customers.
   D. Rogue's business has not been profitable for the past year, and she has made a business decision to reduce the staff.

MATCHING QUESTIONS

Snowey Shovel Co. manufactures shovels at its plant in Ohio. All of Snowey's 687 workers at the plant are paid at the rate of ten dollars per hour. One worker, Alpha, worked 40 hours last week and another worker, Beta, worked 50 hours last week.

Select the title of the applicable federal statute from the list in the right hand column for each of the following statements.

1. _____ Snowey Shovel Co. may not require Beta to take a lie detector test.

2. _____ Snowey Shovel Co. must pay Beta $550.

3. _____ Snowey Shovel Co. must engage in good-faith bargaining with the duly elected representative (union) of its employees.

4. _____ Snowey Shovel Co. must deduct $24.80 and $11.60 from Alpha's weekly wages.

A. Fair Labor Standards Act.
B. National Labor Relations Act
C. Unemployment Compensation Act
D. Employee Polygraph Protection Act
E. Labor Management Relations Act
F. Federal Insurance Contribution Act
G. Unemployment Compensation Act

Chapter 36
Employment Discrimination

The objective of laws prohibiting discriminatory practices in employment is to ensure that all people have unrestricted opportunities to be employed and to advance in their chosen fields. Before the civil rights movement of the 1960s, employers were able to exclude entire classes of job-seekers from their work forces. Similarly, labor organizations excluded members of minority groups from their ranks. Today, however, employers and labor unions are legally obligated not to discriminate against prospective and current employees who are members of protected classes on the basis of race, skin color, religion, national origin, gender, age, or disability.

THINGS TO KEEP IN MIND

In the United States, the Civil Rights Act of 1964 is the primary federal statute dealing with discrimination against certain groups of people (referred to as protected classes). One portion of the Civil Rights Act (Title VII) applies to discrimination in employment. Since the enactment of Title VII, amendments to Title VII, other legislation (such as the Age Discrimination in Employment Act and the Americans With Disabilities Act), and Equal Employment Opportunity Commission (EEOC) regulations have supplemented the federal law in this area. In addition, state anti-discrimination statutes and local ordinances have been enacted.

OUTLINE

I. Title VII of the Civil Rights Act of 1964 — Title VII prohibits discrimination in employment based upon race, skin color, national origin, religion, and gender.

    A. Title VII applies to firms employing 15 or more people, labor unions having 15 or more members, employment agencies, federal, state, and local governments, and governmental agencies.

    B. Prohibited acts and protected classes — Title VII prohibits discrimination in hiring, discharging, terms of employment, compensation, promotion, and granting of privileges based upon religion, gender, race, skin color, or national origin unless there is a *bona fide* occupational qualification for employment.

    C. Procedures under Title VII — The Equal Employment Opportunity Commission (EEOC) administers Title VII.

        1. A person who is a member of a protected class and believes that he or she has been injured because of discrimination may file a claim with the EEOC.

2. The EEOC investigates and seeks a voluntary conciliation (a settlement) between the employer and the claimant.

3. The EEOC may sue the employer. If the EEOC determines that the case has little merit or otherwise chooses not to pursue the claim, the claimant may sue the employer.

D. Intentional and unintentional discrimination.

   1. Intentional discrimination often is referred to as disparate-treatment discrimination because an employer imposes rules, standards, or policies that result in people being treated differently based upon physical attributes (e.g., skin tone or color).

      a. A *prima facie* case of discrimination is established by showing that:
         1) Plaintiff is a member of a protected class;
         2) Plaintiff applied for and was qualified for the position in question;
         3) Plaintiff was rejected by the employer; and
         4) Employer continued to seek applicants for the position and filled the position with a person who was not a member of a protected class.

      b. Once a *prima facie* case is established, there is a presumption of discrimination that can be rebutted by the employer (defendant) showing that a legitimate nondiscriminatory reason existed for the employer's employment decision. (The plaintiff then has an opportunity to show that the reason given was not the true reason for the employer's decision.)

      c. See V. below for discussion of the defenses that may be raised by an employer who allegedly discriminated.

   2. Unintended or disparate-impact discrimination.

      a. An apparently neutral and fair employment practice may have a discriminatory effect.

      b. A plaintiff can establish a *prima facie* case and, therefore, does not have to prove the existence of discriminatory intent by showing:
         1) The employer employs a smaller percentage of people who are members of a protected class than would be expected when the employee group is compared to the number of applicants or the percentage of members of the protected class in the local population.
         2) The low percentage of such employees is the result of an employer practice that has the effect of excluding large numbers of members of the protected class.

   3. An employer policy requiring testing or imposing educational standards may result in discrimination and is not an acceptable policy unless the policy or standards bears a substantial, demonstrable relationship to job performance.

E. Discrimination based upon race, color, and national origin.

   1. Intentional and unintentional discrimination in employment selection, promotion, benefits, and working conditions based upon race, skin color, or country of national origin is prohibited.

   2. The Civil Rights Act of 1866 [42 U.S.C. Section 1981] prohibits discrimination in forming or enforcing contracts based upon race or ethnicity; and, unlike Title VII, does not limit the amount of damages a successful plaintiff can recover.

   3. An employer English-only policy is permissible if the policy does not apply during employees' non-working breaks and is justified because of business necessity.

F. Discrimination based upon religion — Employers must make reasonable accommodations for employees' religious practices and sincere beliefs.

G. Discrimination based upon gender.

   1. The prohibition against gender discrimination does not apply when gender is essential criteria for a particular position or job.

   2. The Pregnancy Discrimination Act of 1978 — Women affected by pregnancy, childbirth, or related medical conditions must be treated in the same manner as are other persons who are temporarily disabled for all employment related purposes.

H. Sexual harassment.

   1. *Quid pro quo* harassment occurs when hiring, promotion. or other employment conditions or opportunities are dependent upon giving sexual favors.

   2. "Hostile environment" harassment occurs when continual conduct or comments have the purpose or effect of creating an offensive, hostile, abusive, demeaning, or disconcerting work environment, unreasonably interferes with a person's performance in the work place, or adversely affects a person's employment opportunities.

   3. The sexually offensive conduct must be abusive both objectively (as perceived by a reasonable person) and subjectively (as perceived by the victim).

   4. Harassment by supervisors and co-workers — An employer is liable for sexual harassment engaged in by a supervisory employee, but not for harassment engaged in by a lower-level employee, unless the employer knew or should have known about the harassment and failed to take corrective action.

   5. Liability may be imposed for harassment of employees by nonemployees on employers who are able to take action to prevent the harassment.

6. Same-gender harassment — In a 1998 decision, the U.S. Supreme Court held that same-gender harassment is a form of sexual harassment and may be a violation of Title VII.

I. Remedies under Title VII.

1. Reinstatement, retroactive promotion, and back pay.

2. Injunction (prohibiting future discrimination) and other corrective relief.

3. Compensatory damages for intentional discrimination and punitive damages if the employer acted with malice or reckless indifference.

4. Caps on damages range from a maximum of $50,000 against employers with 100 or fewer employees to a maximum of $300,000 against employers having more than 500 employees.

II. Equal Pay Act of 1963 [an amendment to the Fair Labor Standards Act which is discussed in Chapter 35] — Employers are prohibited from discriminating on the basis of gender in the payment of wages for equal work.

III. Discrimination based on age.

A. The Age Discrimination in Employment Act of 1967 (ADEA) prohibits employers having 20 or more employees from discriminating against people who are 40 years of age or older and prohibits mandatory retirement for non-managerial employees.

B. An employee (who is more than 40 years of age) alleging that he or she was discriminated against because of age must show that he or she was qualified for the position from which the employee was discharged under circumstances that give rise to an inference of discrimination.

C. An employer may be liable for age discrimination, unless the alleged discriminatory practice was justified because of a legitimate, nondiscriminatory business reason (e.g., the employee can no longer perform the necessary skills).

IV. Discrimination based on disability — The Americans with Disabilities Act of 1990 (ADA).

A. The ADA applies to firms with 15 or more employees and prohibits discrimination against a person with a disability.

B. The federal Rehabilitation Act of 1973 protects employees of the federal government and workers employed by employers who receive federal funds from discrimination based upon their disabilities.

C. Procedures and remedies under the ADA — The procedure (e.g., a claim is first filed with the EEOC) and remedies are the same as those provided for in Title VII of the Civil Rights Act. [See above at I. C. and I.]

D. What is a disability? A disability is "(1) a physical or mental impairment that substantially limits one or more of the major life activities of such individuals; (2) a record of such impairment; or (3) being regarded as having such an impairment."

E. Reasonable accommodations — An employer cannot arbitrarily exclude a qualified person who, with reasonable accommodation (modifications or adjustments) by the employer, can perform the essential functions of the particular job.

   1. Reasonable accommodation includes a more flexible working situation or adapting the employee's work requirements.

   2. An employer is not required to make an accommodation that causes undue hardship to the employer's business.

F. Job applications and preemployment physical examinations.

   1. The process for job applicants must be such that people with disabilities can compete with those who do not have disabilities.

   2. Employers may neither inquire about applicants' disabilities nor require pre-employment physical examinations unless this requirement is imposed upon all applicants.

G. Dangerous workers and substance abusers — Employers are not required to employ workers who, because of their disabilities, pose a "direct threat to the health and safety" of other people or illegal substance abusers (or casual users); the ADA, however, covers persons with alcoholism or those that test positive for the HIV virus (the disease that causes AIDS).

H. Health-insurance plans.

   1. Employees who have disabilities must be given the same access to health insurance as are other employees, but there may be some exclusions from coverage and limitations on the amount of health care payments.

   2. A disability-based distinction in benefits may be made only if required to maintain the financial soundness of the plan, or providing the coverage would cause a significant increase in premiums, or the disparate treatment is justified because of the risks and costs associated with the particular disability.

I. Undue hardship — An employer cannot deny an employment opportunity to a qualified person because of the requirement of providing a reasonable accommodation unless it would cause the employer an undue hardship.

    1. An undue hardship is "an action requiring significant difficulty or expense."

    2. Among the factors to be considered are the nature and the cost (which may be reduced by tax credits) of the accommodation and the financial resources of the employer.

V. Defenses to employment discrimination.

    A. Business necessity defense.

        1. There must be a valid business reason for educational standards or tests and a relationship between any such requirements and performance in the position as described by the employer.

        2. If an employer asserts that a business reason justifies a particular practice, the person alleging discrimination has the burden of proving that the practice is not justified by business necessity.

    B. *Bona fide* occupational qualification (BFOQ) defense.

        1. The BFOQ defense has been restricted by the courts to instances in which religion or gender is an essential requisite for a position.

        2. Employers may impose relevant skill and educational standards.

    C. Seniority system defense — An employer has a good defense if no present intent to discriminate is shown, and promotions or other employment benefits are distributed according to a fair seniority system.

    D. After-acquired evidence of employee misconduct.

        1. Following a discriminatory discharge, an employer may obtain evidence relating to some wrongful action of the employee, which would have been a valid basis for discharging (firing or dismissing) the employee.

        2. The after-acquired evidence of an employee's job-related misconduct may be used in order to limit the liability of the employer for the discriminatory discharge of the employee (who is a member of a protected class), despite the fact that the misconduct is not the actual cause of the discharge.

VI. Affirmative action.

    A. Executive orders issued by Presidents and regulations of the Department of Labor have required that government contractors undertake affirmative recruitment efforts (actively seeking employees who are members of protected classes) and ensure nondiscriminatory treatment of employees and applicants for positions.

B. Title VII does not prohibit an employer or union from adopting a voluntary affirmative action hiring or promotion plan in an attempt to remedy racial, gender, or other imbalances.

C. The issue of whether or not affirmative action programs violate the equal protection clause of the Fourteenth Amendment.

    1. The *Bakke* Case — In *Regents of the University of California v. Bakke* (1978), the U.S. Supreme Court held that affirmative action programs that result in "reverse discrimination" (discrimination against groups other than protected classes), but are designed to correct existing imbalances, will be upheld if factors, other than gender or race, are considered in making decisions.

    2. The *Adrand* Case and subsequent developments — In *Adrand Constructors, Inc. v. Peña* (1995), the U.S. Supreme Court held that a governmental affirmative action program violates the equal protection clause of the Fourteenth Amendment, unless the goal of the program is to remedy past discrimination, the program does not use quotas or preferences, and the affirmative action program is changed or discontinued after the remedial goal is achieved.

VII. State antidiscrimination laws.

A. States must give their citizens at least the same degree of protection as is guaranteed under the federal Constitution and may offer greater protection than does the federal Constitution.

B. Some states prohibit discrimination based upon homosexuality, which is not included under Title VII of the Civil Rights Act; some states imposed sexual harassment rules before the courts interpreted Title VII as covering gender.

KEY WORDS AND PHRASES IN TEXT

protected class
employment discrimination based upon
    race, skin color, national origin,
    religion, and sex (gender)
Title VII of the Civil Rights Act of 1964
Equal Employment Opportunity
    Commission (EEOC)
intentional (disparate treatment)
    discrimination
unintentional (disparate impact)
    discrimination
prima facie case of discrimination

sexual harassment
quid pro quo discrimination
hostile environment harassment
Equal Pay Act of 1963
Age Discrimination in Employment Act
    (ADEA)
Americans with Disabilities Act (ADA)
Rehabilitation Act of 1973
reasonable accommodation
preemployment physical examinations
undue hardship to employer
business necessity defense

bona fide occupational qualification
  (BFOQ) defense
seniority system defense

after-acquired evidence of misconduct
affirmative action programs
reverse discrimination

FILL-IN QUESTIONS

1. Title VII of the Civil Rights Act, as amended, prohibits discrimination in employment based upon race, skin color, _____. The statute is administered by the _____ Commission.

2. A person who believes that she has been discriminated against because of her race in violation of Title VII of the Civil Rights Act of 1964, as amended, must first file a claim with the _____.

3. In order to prove disparate-treatment or intentional discrimination, a complainant must show: (1) that the complainant is a member of a protected class; (2) that the complainant _____ for a particular job and was qualified; (3) that he or she was _____ by the employer; and (4) that the employer continued to seek applicants or filled the position with a person who was not a member of a _____.

4. The Age Discrimination in Employment Act prohibits an employer from imposing a _____ retirement age on non-managerial workers.

5. Under the Americans with Disabilities Act, a person with a disability is a person with a physical or mental impairment that substantially limits major _____.

6. A prospective employer can require a _____ physical examination only if such examination is required of all applicants.

7. Federal employees and employees of firms and other persons that receive federal funds have been protected against discrimination based upon disabilities since 1973 under the _____.

MULTIPLE CHOICE QUESTIONS

1. Title VII of the Civil Rights Act of 1964 prohibits certain employers that engage in interstate commerce from discriminating against potential and existing employees because of their race, skin color, gender, religion, or national origin. Title VII:
   A. is administered by the Department of Labor.
   B. has been interpreted as prohibiting discrimination based upon the sexual preference of an applicant for a job.
   C. prohibits unions and employment agencies from discriminating because of gender (sex), race, skin color, religion, or national origin.
   D. also prohibits employment discrimination based upon age.

2. Title VII of the Civil Rights Act of 1964 prohibits certain employers that engage in interstate commerce from discriminating against potential and existing employees because of their race, skin color, gender, religion, or national origin. Title VII:
    A. prohibits employers from establishing educational criteria for different jobs.
    B. does **not** prohibit such discrimination if the employer can show that the discrimination is based upon a *bona fide* occupational qualification for a position.
    C. requires that every covered employer adopt an affirmative action plan.
    D. provides that a person who believes that he or she is a victim of discrimination may directly and immediately sue the employer and, if successful, recover treble damages.

3. It is a violation under Title VII of the Civil Rights Act of 1964 to discriminate against a potential employee because of his or her:
    A. sexual preference.
    B. religious beliefs.
    C. use of illegal substances.
    D. inability to communicate orally.

4. Which of the following fact scenarios is most likely to be considered sexual harassment by a modern court?
    A. Jack, Marisa's secretary, asks her to have dinner with him on two occasions.
    B. Loretta, president of Bambell Company, tells her limo driver that if he does not sleep with her, he will lose his job.
    C. Peter, Cathleen's co-worker, parks his car outside Cathleen's house for four hours last Tuesday night.
    D. Ivan, manager of Igor's studio, does not know that Joanne is repeatedly asking customers for dates.

5. Which of the following is a *bona fide* occupational qualification that may be imposed by an employer on prospective workers?
    A. All applicants for positions in a hair styling salon must have certificates from beauty schools.
    B. The Berrytown elementary school librarian must be able to speak English.
    C. Applicants for telephone repair work that requires climbing telephone polls must not have fear of heights.
    D. All of the answers above are correct.
    E. None of the answers above is correct.

6. Title VII of the Civil Rights Act is violated in which of the following situations?
    A. Shirley, a librarian, is 82 years of age and no longer can read the titles of books. Shirley also screams at invisible visitors. Shirley is discharged by the library.
    B. The Grubb accounting firm demotes all employees who refuse to take off their hats at work. The only people demoted are three Hindu men who wear turbans.
    C. Mike, a restaurant employee, claiming a religious belief, refuses to wash his hands when he leaves the rest room. Mike is fired by the restaurant.
    D. Clarissa, a clerk, asks all patrons of the donut shop where she works to marry her. Clarissa's employer discharges her because many of the patrons never come back.

7. Which of the following is a violation of the Age Discrimination in Employment Act?
    A. Kiki is **not** hired for a position for which she applied at the local library. The chief librarian claims this occurred because Kiki is 13 years old.
    B. Daniel, a stripper, is discharged when he reaches his ninety-second birthday. The employer claims that Daniel no longer can dance as well as he did in the past.
    C. Louise, who is 52 years of age and has 27 years of experience at an accounting firm, is **not** given a promised raise in salary. The firm gives raises to three younger and less qualified employees.
    D. Larry, a 55 years old dog catcher, no longer can run fast enough to catch dogs. Larry's employer gives him the option of being discharged or taking a desk job.

8. Pfieffer works at the information desk in the state motor vehicle department. During the past three years, Pfieffer has become increasingly hard of hearing. The motor vehicle department does **not** violate the Americans with Disabilities Act if the department:
    A. reassigns Pfieffer at the same pay level to a different position that does not require answering questions.
    B. requires that Pfieffer continue answering questions at the information desk and "docks" Pfieffer's pay for improper responses.
    C. reassigns Pfieffer to a lower-paying position that does not require that Pfieffer answer questions.
    D. All of the answers above are correct.

9. Four people apply for a job selling vacuum cleaners door-to-door. Tyrone, a male, who is 25 years old, white, and has no visible disabilities, is hired. The employer may have violated Title VII of the Civil Rights Act because one of the applicants is:
    A. blind.
    B. fifty-six years old.
    C. Vietnamese.
    D. an alcoholic.

UNIT EIGHT:
BUSINESS ORGANIZATIONS

Various forms of organizations may be adopted in order to engage in a business enterprise, the most common of which are the sole proprietorship, the partnership, and the corporation. The formation, termination, management, and rights and liabilities of partnerships and corporations and those associated with these forms of organizations are explored in the chapters in this unit. Each of these common forms of business organization has both advantages and drawbacks, which are discussed particularly in the introductory chapter (Chapter 37). As explained in that chapter, other methods of associating together in order to engage in commercial ventures have been developed with the objective of ameliorating some of the disadvantages of the traditional types of business organizations. For example, many states have enacted legislation permitting the formation of limited liability companies and partnerships, which foreseeably will assume greater importance in tomorrow's business world.

Note that the law of contracts and agency form a foundation for your understanding of the material in this unit.

Chapter 37
Forms of Business Organizations
and Private Franchises

In the first portion of this chapter, the basic forms of business organizations (about which, no doubt, you have learned in other courses) — the sole proprietorship, the partnership, and the corporation — are briefly explained and compared. Some important, newer types of business organizations, such as limited liability companies and limited liability partnerships, also are introduced.

The chapter concludes with a discussion of private franchises. The relationship between the franchisee and the franchisor may be one of agency, especially if the franchisor may exercise considerable control over the activities of the franchisee and derives substantial benefit from these activities. In other instances, the franchisee has a great deal of discretion and is subject to little control by the franchisor, in which case the franchisee will be treated as an independent contractor. As pointed out in Unit Six (Agency), the nature of a relationship determines the respective liability of the parties.

THINGS TO KEEP IN MIND

1. When a business firm is required to file documents in a central state agency, typically that agency is the office of the secretary of state of the particular state.

2. There is considerable disparity in bargaining power in many franchise relationships. For this reason, a number of states have enacted statutes protecting franchisees, and courts have refused to enforce grossly unfair termination provisions in franchise agreements and have prevented franchisors from unconscionably refusing to renew franchise licenses without good cause.

OUTLINE

I.   Sole proprietorships — A sole proprietorship is the simplest form of business organization and exists when an enterprise is owned by an individual who is liable personally for business obligations.

    A. Advantages of sole proprietorships.

        1. The proprietor receives all profits, business operations are flexible, and the owner is the sole decision maker (i.e., the sole proprietor is his or her "own boss").

2. It is easier and less costly to start a sole proprietorship than other forms of business organizations.

3. Possible tax benefits — The owner pays only personal income taxes and may be subject to a lower tax rate than that imposed on corporations.

4. The proprietor may establish a tax-exempt retirement account (Keogh plan).

B. Disadvantages of sole proprietorships.

1. A sole proprietor has unlimited liability (legal responsibility) for all obligations incurred in conducting business.

2. It may be difficult to raise large amounts of capital.

3. Lack of continuity upon the death of the proprietor.

II. Partnerships.

A. A general partnership is an association based upon the agreement of two or more persons to control and carry on a business jointly as co-owners for the purpose of making a profit.

1. A partnership is a legal entity only for limited purposes.

2. Each partner has unlimited liability for partnership obligations.

3. A partnership can be organized simply, with no particular form of agreement being necessary to create the partnership. (It is suggested that the agreement be in writing.)

4. A partnership is not subject to federal income tax, but a partnership is required to file an information return; each partner's distributed and undistributed share of profits is taxed as individual income.

B. Partnerships are discussed in Chapters 38 and 39 — Partnerships are governed by the Uniform Partnership Act or the Revised Uniform Partnership Act. [See Appendices E and F of the textbook.]

III. Limited partnerships.

A. A limited partnership is a partnership in which at least one partner is a general partner and at least one other partner is a limited partner who does not participate in management and has limited liability.

B. A limited partnership is created by agreement and comes into existence when a certificate (or other prescribed document) is filed in the prescribed manner.

C. Limited partnerships are subject to state statutes that are discussed in Chapter 39. [See also Appendix G.]

IV. Corporations.

A. A business corporation is a legal entity created by the state upon compliance with the appropriate statute. [Excerpts from the Revised Model Business Corporation Act are found in Appendix H.]

B. The owners (shareholders) have limited liability and elect the board of directors that manages the business and normally appoints officers to oversee the corporation's day-to-day operations.

C. Corporate income that is distributed to shareholders is taxed twice.

1. The corporation pays taxes on its income; when income is distributed to shareholders, the shareholders pay taxes on the distributed corporate income.

2. Some small corporations may avoid double taxation. (See discussion of S corporations in Chapter 40.)

D. The formation, management and operation, liability, and termination of corporations are discussed in Chapters 40 through 43.

V. Limited liability companies (LLCs).

A. State statutes permit formation of LLCs whose owners (called members) have limited liability and whose income (in most states) is passed through the company so that only the shareholders pay taxes, thus avoiding double taxation of income that is generated by the entity.

B. State statutes regarding formation of LLCs are not uniform, but the statutes do provide that articles of organization must be filed with a state agency (e.g., the secretary of state) and the LLC's name must include the words, limited liability company or the initials, L.L.C.

C. Characteristics that are required by some statutes governing LLCs (the "four-factors test"):

1. Firm members have limited liability.

2. Continuity of the life of the company.

3. Interests of members are freely transferable.

4. Centralization of management of the company.

D. In addition to LLCs, limited liability partnerships (discussed below at VI.), limited partnerships (discussed in Chapter 39), and S corporations (discussed in

Chapter 40) also have the pass-through tax advantages of partnerships and the limited liability features of corporations.

E. Internal Revenue Service (IRS) 1997 rules, relating to partnership (pass-through) treatment of income for tax purposes, apply to business organizations, with the exceptions of corporations, whose shares are publicly traded or which are incorporated under state incorporation laws, and to firms choosing to be taxed as corporations.

   1. The "four-factors test" does not apply; a business firm simply indicates that it chooses to be taxed as a partnership on its filed tax form.

   2. A firm with only one owner (including a LLC) is taxed as a sole proprietorship unless the firm chooses to be taxed as a corporation.

   3. State LLC statutes are being revised to conform to the IRS rules.

VI. Limited liability partnerships (LLPs).

A. Many states have enacted statutes that provide for the formation of LLPs, whose "innocent partners" may avoid personal liability for the wrongful acts of copartners. [See Chapter 39.]

B. State statutes regarding formation of LLPs are not uniform, but the statutes do provide that an appropriate form must be filed with a state agency (e.g., the secretary of state) and the LLP's name must include the words, limited liability partnership or the initials, L.L.P. [See Chapter 38.]

VII. Major business forms (of organization) compared. [See also Exhibit 37-2.]

A. Ease of creation.

   1. Sole proprietorship — No formality is necessary in order to organize.

   2. General partnership — Simple and inexpensive to organize.

   3. Limited partnership — Compliance with formalities prescribed by statute and payment of fees and other costs are necessary in order to organize.

   4. Corporation — Compliance with formalities prescribed by statute and payment of fees and other costs are necessary in order to organize.

B. Liability of owners.

   1. Sole proprietors and general partners have personal liability.

   2. Limited partners' and shareholders' liability theoretically is limited to the amount of their investments.

3. Frequently, shareholders in small corporations voluntarily assume additional liability.

C. Tax consideration — See Exhibit 37-2 in the textbook.

D. Need for capital.

1. A sole proprietor may find it difficult to raise capital for expansion.

2. A partnership may be able to borrow from lenders and raise capital by increasing the number of partners; this, however, may reduce effective operations.

3. A corporation can raise capital by issuing shares of stock.

E. The appropriate organizational form — Selecting the appropriate organizational form for a business enterprise depends upon a number of considerations, some of which, such as capital needs, liability of participants, and tax advantages, are referred to in the text. (The type of organization selected in each case is a matter for sound business judgment based in part upon knowledge of legal implications.)

V. Other organizational forms.

A. Joint venture — An association that is formed to carry out a single transaction or a series of similar transactions; for most purposes (including tax purposes), a joint venture is treated in the same manner as a partnership.

1. Characteristics of joint ventures.

a. Because the activities of a joint venture may be more limited that those of a partnership, the joint venturers may have less implied actual and apparent authority than partners.

b. Ordinarily, the death of a joint venturer does not terminate the joint venture.

c. Joint venturers agree (usually in a contract) to combine their skills, resources, and capital in order to carry out a business enterprise for profit.

2. Duration — If the duration is not precisely specified, the joint venture terminates when the venturers' purposes are accomplished or at the will of a member.

3. Duties, rights, and liabilities among joint venturers — As is true in a partnership, joint venturers are agents for one another, owe duties to each other, have rights to participate in management, and are jointly liable to third parties. [See Chapter 47 regarding potential violations of antitrust laws when competitors form joint ventures.]

B. Syndicate or investment group — A number of persons agree to pool their resources in order to finance a business venture.

C. Joint stock company — An association that structurally resembles a corporation but often is treated as a partnership.

D. Business trust — Arises if a number of people turn over management and legal title to property to one or more trustees who distribute the profits to the participants (the beneficiaries of the trust).

E. Cooperative — An association (that may be incorporated) organized in order to provide an economic service to its members (or shareholders).

VI. Private franchises.

A. A franchise is an agreement or arrangement in which the franchisor (the owner of a trademark, trade name, copyright, or similar interest) grants the right to use the mark, name, or other interest to another person (the franchisee) in connection with selling, marketing, or supplying goods and/or services.

B. Types of franchises.

1. Distributorship — A manufacturer licenses a dealer to sell its product.

2. Chain-style business operation — A franchisee operates under a franchisor's name and is identified as a member of the group engaged in the franchisor's business.

3. Manufacturing or processing-plant arrangement —The franchisor furnishes ingredients or a formula for making or processing a particular product and marketing the product in accordance with the franchisor's standards.

C. Laws governing franchising.

1. The courts apply appropriate statutory and general common law principles in cases involving franchising.

2. Federal protection for franchisees.

a. Automobile Dealers' Franchise Act (Automobile Dealers' Day in Court Act) — If a manufacturer-franchisor terminates a franchise because a dealer-franchisee failed to comply with unreasonable demands, the franchisor is liable for damages.

b. Petroleum Marketing Practices Act — Prescribes conditions under which a gasoline franchisor may terminate or refuse to renew a gasoline station franchise.

c. Federal antitrust laws apply if there is an illegal price-fixing agreement. [See Chapter 47.]

d. A Federal Trade Commission (FTC) rule requires disclosure by franchisors of material facts necessary to a prospective franchisee in making a decision concerning purchasing a franchise.
   1) FTC Rule 436 (1979) requires that franchisors and franchise brokers furnish prospective franchisees with detailed information about the franchisor and its business in a Basic Disclosure Document.
   2) Failure to comply with FTC Rule 436 is an unfair or deceptive act or practice under Section 5 of the Federal Trade Commission Act.

e. Franchise agreements have been held not to be investment securities subject to regulation under the Securities Act of 1933. [See Chapter 43.]

3. State protection for franchisees — State statutes provide for disclosure of material information by franchisors and prohibit franchisors from terminating franchises without good cause.

   a. Franchise agreements that primarily cover the sale of products manufactured by franchisors are governed by Article 2 of the UCC. [See Unit Three.]

   b. There has been little interest in state adoption of the model law drafted by the National Conference of Commissioners on Uniform State Laws.

D. The franchise contract — Usually, the contract embodying the agreement of the franchisor and franchisee is prepared by the franchisor.

   1. Prospective franchisees should decide upon the types of businesses they wish to undertake, should obtain information from the franchisors, and may rely on the franchisors in setting up the business organization.

   2. Payment for the franchise — Ordinarily, the franchisee pays an initial fee or lump-sum price for the franchise license, fees for products provided or sold by the franchisor, a percentage of sales or profits, and (sometimes) payments of a proportion of the franchisor's costs and expenses.

   3. Location and business organization of the franchise — Often, the franchisor exercises control over the franchisee's business location, organization, and decisions.

      a. A franchisee may be required to lease or own the premises and/or supply equipment. In some cases, the franchisor supplies equipment and leases the premises.

      b. The franchisor may impose standards for the form of business organization, its capital structure, the operations, training of personnel, and the price and quality of products or services.

    c. Usually the agreement contains exclusive dealings provisions and "territorial rights" within a certain geographic area. [See Chapter 14.]

  4. Price and quantity controls of the franchisor — The franchisor may require that the franchisee purchase supplies and products at a price established by the franchisor, but the franchisor may only suggest retail prices.

  5. Termination of the franchise.

    a. The initial duration may be limited to one year.

    b. A franchise arrangement may be terminated by the franchisor for cause or because of death, disability, or insolvency of the franchisee, breach of the agreement, or failure to meet sales quota.

    c. Notice of termination is generally necessary.

    d. Courts have read good faith and commercial reasonableness into franchise contracts and will not enforce unconscionable provisions.

KEY WORDS AND PHRASES IN TEXT

entrepreneur
sole proprietorship
general partnership
federal income tax information return
limited partnership
corporation
limited liability
S corporation
limited liability company (LLC)
limited liability partnership (LLP)
forms of organization compared based
    upon ease of creation, liability
    of owners, tax considerations,
    and need for capital
joint venture
syndicate

joint stock company
business trust
cooperative
private franchises
franchisee and franchisor
distributorship franchise
chain-style business operation
manufacturing or processing-plant
    arrangement
franchise contract
payment for the franchise
location and business organization of the
    franchise (control by franchisor)
price and quality controls of the franchise
termination of the franchise

FILL-IN QUESTIONS

1. A major disadvantage of the sole proprietorship form of business organization is that the sole proprietor has _____ or legal responsibility for all obligations incurred in doing business. In addition, the sole proprietor may have limited opportunities to raise _____ and, upon the death of the proprietor, the continuity of the business ceases.

2. A limited partnership is distinguishable from a general partnership. All partners in a general partnership are co-owners of a business enterprise and share in its management, operations, and _____. General partners, however, also have _____ for obligations incurred in doing business. In a limited partnership, there must be at least one general partner who will have _____ liability and manage the partnership's business operations. The limited partners do not have "a voice" in the business operations, but have limited liability because the limited partners are not responsible for partnership losses that exceed the amounts of their "capital" _____.

3. A corporation is "owned" by its shareholders, but managed by the board of directors, the members of which are elected by the _____, and the officers who are appointed by the board of directors. Shareholders receive shares of corporate _____ in the event that the board of directors declare dividends, but are not liable for obligations of the corporation unless the shareholders voluntarily assume personal _____. The liability of shareholders is, therefore, limited to their original _____ which the shareholders made when the shareholders purchased shares of stock in the corporation.

4. _____ are structured in the same way as partnerships but, unlike partners in a general partnership, innocent partners are not personally liable for the negligence of misconduct of other partners.

5. A _____ exists when two or more persons engage in a business activity or a series of similar activities and agree to share decision making and profits (or losses) jointly or in proportion to their contributions. In general, the members of the _____ are treated as partners. If the participants engage in continuing activities and expand the nature of those activities, their relationship may be considered to be a _____.

6. Six years ago, Fern and Burn agreed to build a sailboat together. If they each contributed equal time and money in order to purchase material and agreed to sell the finished boat as well as to divide the purchase price equally, Fern and Burn formed a _____. Having been successful in this venture, Fern and Burn agreed to continue their arrangement with one another and to continue building sail boats together. They have been financially very successful in doing so and have expanded their enterprise to the extent that they now employ more than a hundred employees and manufacture a variety of boats, and the enterprise produces annual profits of $5,000,000. Fern and Burn, the co-venturers may be treated, as _____ because they are co-owners of property used in a business enterprise and share in its management, operations, and profits. Fern and Burn, therefore, should file an _____ with the Internal Revenue Service (IRS).

7. A franchise arrangement is based upon a contract which provides that one party, the _____, who is the owner of a trademark, trade name, or copyright gives a license to another person, the _____, to use the trademark, trade name, or copyright in selling goods or services.

8.   State and federal statutes dealing with franchising require that the _____ make disclosures of material information so that a potential _____ can make an informed decision regarding the purchase of a franchise and place restrictions upon the ability of the _____ to terminate the franchise without good cause.

9.   Franchise arrangements can take different forms. A manufacturer may license a dealer to sell its product in a specified geographic area, in which case a _____ is created. This type of arrangement is used in the automobile industry. A franchisor may license a franchisee to operate under the franchisor's name and, thus, identify the franchisee as a member of a select group of franchisees that engage in the franchisor's business. In such a _____ business franchise (which is typical in the fast-food industry), the franchisee may be required to follow certain defined methods of operations and may be obligated to obtain its materials and supplies from the franchisor. In the soft-drink bottling industry, the typical _____ franchise agreement provides that the franchisee is licensed to use essential ingredients or a formula in order to make or produce a particular product.

10.   Because a franchisor wishes to protect itself and assure the successfulness and, therefore, profitability, of ventures engaged in by its franchisees, frequently franchisors include provisions in the contract embodying a franchise agreement which give the franchisor the right to specify the geographic _____ of the franchisee's establishment, whether the premises are to be leased or constructed, the form of _____ to be adopted by the franchisee, and specify certain standards of quality, operations, and record keeping that the _____ must maintain.

11.   When a franchise agreement provides that the franchisor has the right to require that the franchisee sell certain products and not sell other products, and the franchisor is to receive a percentage of the sales price, it is likely that the franchisee will be treated as the _____ of the franchisor. When the franchisee is required to make a lump sum payment to the franchisor for a license to use a trademark, trade name, or copyright, but is given considerable discretion as to what products he or she wishes to sell, the franchisee most likely will be treated as an _____.

MULTIPLE CHOICE QUESTIONS

1.   The form in which a business is organized will determine the liability of the owners of the business and may have tax implications. Usually, the shareholders of a corporation are **not** personally liable for the debts of the corporation, and the dividends that the shareholders receive from the corporation are subject to taxation even though the corporation also is taxed on its profits. A sole proprietor or a partner in a partnership is personally liable for the obligations incurred by the enterprise or partnership. A sole proprietor pays individual income taxes on profits derived from the enterprise, and a partner:
      A. pays individual income taxes on distributed and undistributed profits of the partnership.

B. pays individual income taxes on distributed, but **not** on undistributed profits of the partnership.

C. pays individual income taxes on distributed, but **not** on undistributed profits of the partnership if the partnership has paid income taxes on the undistributed profits of the partnership.

D. does **not** pay individual income taxes because the partnership is required to pay income taxes on partnership profits.

2. Simon Proper is the sole owner of SP Enterprises. He has filed the necessary forms with a government official in order to conduct his business under the trade name SP Enterprises. After paying taxes last year, Simon had profits of $182,000, $100,000 of which was used to make improvements in the plant and equipment of SP Enterprises. The balance of $82,000 initially was retained personally by Simon but later spent by Simon on consumer goods and services. AAA Advertising, Inc. asserts that its bill for $90,000 for services rendered has not been paid. AAA has, therefore, sued Simon, doing business as SP Enterprises.

A. Simon Proper is personally liable for payment of the $90,000 obligation because Simon engaged in business as a sole proprietor.

B. SP Enterprises is a corporation and it alone is liable for the $90,000 obligation.

C. Simon Proper and SP Enterprises are engaging in business as a general partnership and Simon, therefore, is individually liable as a partner for the $90,000 obligation.

D. Simon Proper and SP Enterprises are engaging in business as a limited partnership in which SP Enterprises is a general partner and Simon is a limited partner. Simon, therefore, is **not** individually liable for the $90,000 obligation.

3. Warm and Tepid agree to pool their business property and talents in order to form and jointly operate a firm that will engage in the business of supplying computer services. They foresee that in the first two years the business will not be profitable. Warm and Tepid, therefore, agree to make equal additional contributions of capital during that period. They expect that after the two years "start up" period, the business will generate profits which they agree to share equally. Warm and Tepid have formed:

A. a general partnership.

B. a limited partnership.

C. a business corporation.

D. a joint venture.

4. Hot and Cold agree to pool their computer programming talents in order to create a computer billing program for the Tri-County Water Company. Hot and Cold agree that they will divide profits earned in the endeavor equally. Hot and Cold have formed:

A. a limited partnership.

B. a business corporation.

C. a joint venture.

D. a joint stock company.

5. In most states today, a business corporation may be a member of:

A. a general partnership.

B. a limited partnership.

C. a joint venture.
D. All of the answers above are correct.

6. A typical franchise agreement may provide that a franchisee pay the franchisor:
    A   a one-time flat fee for the franchise.
    B. a percentage of the franchisee's gross or net sales or profits.
    C. a proportion of the franchisor's costs and expenses.
    D. All of the answers above are correct.

7. Usually, a franchise agreement provides that it may be terminated by the franchisor because:
    A. the franchisee has died or become insolvent.
    B. the franchisee has failed to meet a specified sales quota.
    C. the initial duration of the franchise arrangement has expired, and there was no provision in the franchise agreement for renewal of the arrangement.
    D. All of the answers above are correct.

8. Usually, a franchise agreement provides that it may be terminated by the franchisee because:
    A. the franchisor has died or become insolvent.
    B. another franchisee has failed to meet a specified sales quota.
    C. the initial duration of the franchise arrangement has expired, and there was no provision for renewal.
    D. All of the answers above are correct.

9. Federal Trade Commission Rule 436 requires that franchisors and franchise brokers furnish prospective franchisees with detailed information regarding:
    A. the franchisor and the franchisor's business.
    B. the premises that the prospective franchisee is required to lease.
    C. the equipment that the prospective franchisee is required to purchase from the franchisor.
    D. All of the answers above are correct.

10. States have enacted statutes requiring disclosure of certain information by franchisors to prospective franchisors in order to:
    A. ensure that state statutes and case law concerning franchising arrangements are uniform.
    B. afford some protection to potential franchisees given the considerable disparity in bargaining power in many franchise relationships.
    C. extend common law remedies to potential franchisees who have incurred losses but are unable to prove that the franchisor used fraud.
    D. comply with Federal Trade Commission rules.

Chapter 38
Partnerships: Nature, Formation, and Operation

When two or more people pool their efforts, labor, and skills, and make contributions of funds (capital) to a business enterprise of which they are co-owners, and share common control over the business operations with the intention of also sharing profits (and losses), they probably have formed a general partnership. Much of the law relating to general partnerships is codified in the Uniform Partnership Act (UPA). The UPA defines a partnership as "an association of two or more persons to carry on as co-owners a business for profit" [UPA 6(1)]. For purposes of the UPA, a "person" means a natural person, other partnership, association, or corporation, and "business" includes trades, occupations, and professions [UPA 2].

The UPA has been adopted in all of the states (except Louisiana) and the District of Columbia, Guam, and the Virgin Islands. It is reproduced in Appendix E of the textbook. In 1992, the Conference of Commissioners on Uniform State Laws proposed a Revised Uniform Partnership Act (RUPA) that gradually is being adopted by the states. Portions of the RUPA that changed the law are highlighted in the text and reproduced in Appendix F.

Normally, partners have rights and duties to participate in the management of the affairs and business of the partnership and to share in the profits thereof. Because each partner is an agent for his or her co-partners, a partner owes fiduciary duties to his or her partners as well as a duty to account to other partners. In addition, each partner may incur liability as a principal for contracts entered into and torts committed by co-partners acting within the scope of their authority or which subsequently are ratified. Knowledge received by one partner is imputed to the other members of the partnership and representations made by a partner are treated as having been made by all the partners.

THINGS TO KEEP IN MIND

1. The provisions of the UPA do not explicitly provide the manner in which partnerships are required to be formed. If the parties expressly or impliedly have created a partnership, the UPA provisions (relating to the rights and duties among the partners, the partners' liability to third parties, and the manner in which the partnership is terminated) govern.

2. Partnership law (as stated in the UPA) is based upon the law of agency that is covered in Unit Six. As a result, each partner is treated as an agent of his, her, or its co-partner, and each partner may be liable as a principal to third parties for partnership obligations. A partnership, however, is distinguishable from an agency relationship because, unlike an agent, a partner has an ownership interest in the partnership business and may be obligated to bear responsibility for ordinary partnership business expenses and losses.

3. Normally, partners include explicit terms relating to their respective rights and duties in the partnership agreement. These provisions will be enforced as long as they are lawful. If the partners have not included express terms, the provisions of the UPA will be controlling in those states that have adopted that Act.

OUTLINE

I.   Definition of partnership — "An association of two or more persons to carry on as co-owners a business for profit" [UPA 6(1)].

   A. The elements (characteristics) of a partnership include a sharing of profits or losses of the business, joint ownership interests in an ongoing business, and an equal right to participate in the management of the operation of the business.

   B. A partnership may be created expressly by the partners.

   C. A partnership may exist (or be impliedly created) if the elements of a partnership are present — A problem may arise when there is insufficient evidence to establish all three factors.

   1. The sharing of profits of a business is *prima facie* evidence that a person is a partner, but no such inference is to be drawn merely because a person receives a share of the profits in payment of:

      a. A debt.

      b. Wages of an employee or rent to a landlord.

      c. An annuity to a widow, widower, or representative of a deceased partner.

      d. Interest on a loan (even though the amounts of the payments vary with the profits of the business).

      e. Consideration for the sale of goodwill or other property [UPA 7(4)].

   2. If a group of people are co-owners of property, whether or not they share the profits derived from the property's use or gross returns, this does not necessarily mean that they have formed a partnership [UPA 7(2) and (3)].

II.   The nature of partnerships — At common law, a partnership was never treated as an entity, separate and apart from its members; today, for limited purposes, the partnership may be treated as an independent entity.

   A. Partnership as an entity.

   1. Legal capacity.

    a. The capacity of a partnership to sue and to be sued in the name of the partnership varies from state to state; in many states, plaintiffs sue both the partnership and the individual partners.

    b. When a federal question is involved in a case being heard by a federal court, the suit may be brought by or against the partnership in the name of the partnership.

2. Judgments.

    a. Judgments entered against a partnership in its firm (partnership) name may be collected from partnership property.

    b. If partnership property is insufficient to satisfy the judgment and individual partners were also sued, assets of the partners can be reached in order to satisfy the judgment.

3. Marshaling assets — An equitable doctrine used in many states for ranking assets and claims of creditors.

    a. Partnership creditors have priority with respect to partnership assets; creditors of individual partners have priority with respect to personal assets of each partner.

    b. If partnership assets are insufficient in order to pay a partnership creditor, the creditor cannot reach assets of an individual partner until the claims of the creditors of that partner have been satisfied.

4. Bankruptcy.

    a. Marshaling of assets doctrine is modified by Chapter 7 (Liquidation) of the Bankruptcy Code. [See Chapter 32.]

    b. When a partnership is given an order for relief by a bankruptcy court, but partnership assets are insufficient to satisfy claims of the firm's creditors, each general partner becomes personally liable to the trustee in bankruptcy for the amount of the deficiency.

5. Conveyance of property.

    a. The partnership can own (hold title to) real and personal property in the firm name and can convey or transfer property in the firm name [UPA 8].

    b. At common law, title to real property could not be held in the partnership's name, but was owned by the co-partners as tenants in partnership; all partners, therefore, had to join in a conveyance of real property.

B. Aggregate theory of partnership.

1. A partnership is treated for some purposes as an aggregate of the individual partners.

2. Under the federal income tax laws, although a partnership is required to file an information return, a partnership is treated as an aggregate so that each partner is taxed according to his or her share of partnership profits or losses.

III. Partnership formation — The formation of a partnership is based upon the assent and agreement of all the partners.

A. Formalities — Ordinarily, no special formality is necessary in order to form a partnership; a partnership may be created expressly or impliedly.

1. Usually, a partnership agreement (articles of partnership) is written.

a. Because of the Statute of Frauds, a partnership agreement must be in a signed writing in order to be enforceable, if, by its terms, a partnership is to continue for more than one year or the agreement authorizes partners to deal in transfers of real property. [See Chapter 17.]

b. The agreement may contain any terms the partners wish as long as the terms are not illegal or against public policy.

c. Usual contents of partnership agreement.
   1) Name — State law may restrict use of certain names and/or words.
   2) Nature of business and duration.
   3) Contributions to be made by individual partners.
   4) Manner of dividing profits and losses — Unless otherwise specified, partners share profits equally; if no provision is made for the manner of sharing losses, losses are shared in the same proportion as are profits.
   5) Salaries and drawing accounts, if any.
   6) Restrictions on the authority of any partners.
   7) Conditions for withdrawal from partnership and provisions for the continuation of the business if the partnership is dissolved (partnership buy-sell agreement).

2. A partnership may be implied because of the conduct of the parties who indicated their intentions to operate a business as co-owners and to share profits. [See above at I.C.]

3. The mutual assent of all partners is necessary to form a partnership.

B. Duration of partnership — If a partnership is formed for a term of more than one year, but the agreement is oral, the partnership will be treated as a partnership at will which may be terminated by any party without liability, unlike a partnership for a term which requires the assent of all the partners for dissolution.

C. Capacity — Any person who has capacity to enter into a contract can become a partner.

    1. Minors — A partnership agreement is voidable by a partner who is a minor, but, if rights of creditors are involved, the minor cannot withdraw his or her original investment in the partnership.

    2. If a partner is adjudicated to be mentally incompetent after the partnership is formed, the partnership is not automatically dissolved.

D. The corporation as partner.

    1. Traditionally, a corporation could not be a partner.

    2. Restrictions on the ability of corporations to be partners have become less common and courts in some states having such limitations have treated what would otherwise be partnerships with corporate partners as joint ventures.

    3. The Model Business Corporation Act, the Revised Model Corporation Act [excerpts of which are in Appendix H of the textbook], and Section 2 of the UPA provide that a corporation may be a partner.

E. Partnership by estoppel [UPA 16].

    1. A person, who is not in fact a partner, may be estopped from denying that he or she is a partner; if so, that person will be held liable as a partner to a third party who reasonably relied and dealt with or advanced credit to the partnership because that person held himself or herself out as being a member of a partnership; or consented to a misrepresentation of an alleged partnership relationship by another person (e.g., a member of the partnership).

    2. The purported partner does not become a partner although he or she may be liable as a partner to third persons.

    3. Only if all of the partners consent to the representation, can a partnership act or obligation result.

IV. Partnership operation.

A. Rights among partners — Unless otherwise specifically provided for in the partnership agreement, the UPA governs the partners' rights and duties.

    1. Management — Each partner has a right (and duty) to participate in the management of the partnership [UPA 18(e) and (h)].

        a. Each partner has one vote regardless of the size of his or her interest in the firm.

b. In connection with ordinary business decisions, majority vote controls; partners may delegate daily management responsibilities to a committee.

c. Unanimous consent is required in matters that significantly affect the nature of the partnership [UPA 9 and 18(g) and (h)], including:
   1) Altering the essential nature of the business or the capital structure of the partnership.
   2) Admitting new partners.
   3) Making an assignment in trust or for the benefit of creditors.
   4) Disposing of the partnership's goodwill.
   5) Making a confession of judgment against the partnership or submitting partnership claims to arbitration.
   6) Amending the partnership agreement.
   7) Undertaking any act that would make further conduct of partnership business impossible.

2. Interest in the partnership.

   a. Each partner shares profits and losses in accordance with the proportion designated in the partnership agreement.

   b. If the agreement does not provide for such an apportionment, profits are shared equally, and losses are shared in the same ratio as profits [UPA 18(a)].

3. Compensation [UPA 18(f) and 21].

   a. Each partner is expected to devote full time and exclusive service to the partnership (absent a contrary agreement).

   b. Unless otherwise agreed, partners do not receive remuneration for their partnership services, except that surviving partners are entitled to reasonable compensation for services rendered in winding up the affairs of a dissolved partnership.

4. Inspection of books — Each partner has the right to examine the books and records of the partnership that should be maintained at the place of business of the firm and has the right to information concerning the partnership's business from his or her co-partners [UPA 19 and 20].

5. Accounting [UPA 22] — The purpose of an accounting is to determine the value of each partner's proportionate share in the partnership.

   a. An accounting may be rendered voluntarily.

   b. A partner may bring an equitable action for an accounting.
      1) Usually, an accounting occurs in connection with dissolution proceedings.
      2) An accounting is available if:

      a) The partnership agreement so provides.

      b) A partner has been excluded from the business wrongfully.

      c) A partner is wrongfully withholding profits.

      d) Other circumstances "render it just and reasonable."

6. Property rights.

    a. Partner's interest in the firm.

      1) Each partner has a right to his or her share of the profits and surplus which is considered to be personal property [UPA 26].

      2) A partner's interest in the partnership is subject to assignment, attachment, and other charging orders. An assignment does not dissolve the partnership or permit an assignee to interfere with management [UPA 27 and 28].

    b. Partnership property.

      1) Partnership property consists of:

        a) Real and personal property contributed by the individual partners at the time of the partnership's formation, and later, for the permanent use of the partnership.

        b) Property subsequently acquired with partnership funds on account of the partnership [UPA 8].

      2) Partners' rights with respect to specific partnership property [UPA 25].

        a) Partners are tenants in partnership — Co-owners of partnership property with the right to possession for partnership purposes.

        b) Upon the death of a partner, that partner's rights in specific partnership property vest in the remaining partners.

        c) A partner may neither assign rights to specific partnership property nor subject such property to marital rights, attachment, or execution by his or her individual creditors, etc.

B. Duties and powers of partners.

  1. Fiduciary duty — Each partner is an agent for his or her co-partners and, therefore, is accountable as a fiduciary [UPA 21].

    a. A partner must act in good faith with loyalty and honesty for the benefit of the partnership and make full disclosure to his or her co-partners of matters relating to the partnership.

    b. A partner will be liable for any personal gain or profits derived from using the partnership property or the exercise of power as a partner.

  2. General agency powers.

    a. In dealing with third parties on behalf of the partnership, each partner acts as a principal for himself or herself and as an agent for the partnership and his or her co-partners [UPA 9(1)].

b. Authority of partners — A partner's authority to bind the partnership (and his or her co-partners) contractually may be based upon the express actual authority provided for in the partnership agreement or upon implied actual authority.

c. The scope of implied powers.
   1) A partner's implied actual authority extends to doing things that are necessary for the conduct or the ordinary business of the partnership.
   2) Usually, partners have broad implied authority which will vary with the nature of the particular business of each partnership unless limited by agreement.
   3) A partner in a trading partnership has authority to buy and sell goods of the type in which the firm regularly deals, to give warranties, to borrow money, and to issue and indorse a negotiable instrument.
   4) A partner has the power to pay and collect debts, hire and discharge employees, give a security interest in personal property, and lease or purchase property that is needed in the usual operation of the firm's business.
   5) Restrictions on partners' implied authority — Unanimous consent is required in order to:
      a) Convey or mortgage real property other than in the ordinary course of the partnership's business.
      b) Make an assignment of property rights.
      c) Dispose of the firm's goodwill.
      d) Confess judgment or submit a controversy to arbitration.
      e) Do any act which would make it impossible to continue the business of the partnership [UPA 9].

d. A partner's authority to bind the partnership (and his or her co-partners) contractually may be based upon the partner's apparent authority.
   1) A third person who deals with a partner may assume that the partner has authority to bind the firm in a transaction relating to the usual business of the firm.
   2) Unless the third person knows that the partner lacks authority, the partnership and co-partners will be liable to the third person for any damage.

e Partners may ratify unauthorized acts of a partner.

f. Admissions and representations concerning partnership affairs made by an authorized partner bind the partnership when such admissions and representations are made by the partner while the partner is conducting the ordinary business of the partnership [UPA 11].

g. Actual knowledge of a partner, or notice to a partner, of facts concerning matters relevant to the partnership's affairs will be imputed to the partnership and other partners [UPA 12].

h. The partnership and the co-partners are liable for breaches of trust and torts committed by a partner or employee while acting within the scope of his or her authority in the ordinary course of the business of the partnership.

3. Joint liability — A third party seeking to recover for a partnership obligation should sue all of the partners together.

   a. If one partner is sued, that partner can require that the other partners be sued with him or her.

   b. If all of the partners are not sued jointly, the third party who gets a judgment cannot look to the partners who were not sued or to partnership assets for satisfaction of the judgment.

   c. In most states, actions based upon contract must be brought against all the partners jointly [UPA 15(b)].

   d. In some states, statutes provide that a partnership may be sued in its partnership name and that a judgment against the partnership is enforceable against partnership assets and the assets of one or more of the partners.

   e. A partner who pays the entire amount of a partnership debt is entitled to indemnification from the partnership [UPA 18(b)] or, if the partnership is unable to pay the money, from co-partners.

4. Joint and several liability.

   a. Partners are jointly and severally liable for torts and breaches of trust [UPA 15(a)].

   b. In some states, joint and several liability is imposed upon partners for partnership contracts and debts.

   c. An injured third party may sue all the partners together or any one or more of the partners separately.

   d. The third party who obtains a judgment can enforce the judgment only against assets of partners who were defendants in the lawsuit.

   e. The partner who personally committed a tort is required to indemnify the partnership for damages that the partnership pays in order to satisfy a judgment.

5. Liability of incoming partner — A newly admitted partner to an existing partnership is liable for existing partnership obligations, but only to the extent of his or her capital contribution [UPA 17].

KEY WORDS AND PHRASES IN TEXT

general partnership
sharing of profits and losses as *prima facie* evidence of partnership
joint ownership of property
partnership as an entity
capacity of partnership to sue and be sued
judgments against partnership
marshaling assets
adjudication of bankruptcy in the partnership name
conveyance of partnership property
tenants in partnership
aggregate theory of partnership
articles of partnership (partnership agreement)
partnership for term
partnership at will
capacity of partners
the corporation as a partner
partner by estoppel

rights among partners regarding management
partnership decisions that require unanimous consent and majority vote
apportionment of losses among partners
confession of judgment
compensation of partners
right to inspect books and records
accounting
partnership property
partners' interests in the firm
charging order
duties and powers of partners
fiduciary duty
scope of express and implied actual authority of partners
joint liability of partners
joint and several liability of partners
liability of incoming partner

FILL-IN QUESTIONS

1. A partnership is created by an express _____ based upon the mutual assent of those participating in the partnership to engage in business as co-owners. Frequently, the partners' _____ is entitled articles of partnership. A partnership may also be formed based upon the implied consent of its members who: (1) agree to be co-owner of a business enterprise for profit, to contribute their skills and capital (making joint investments); (2) are _____ of property that is used for partnership purposes; and (3) agree to _____ of the partnership business.

2. A partnership may be treated by state law as having the capacity to sue and be sued and to transfer property in its firm name in which case the partnership is considered to be an _____. In other instances, such as application of the federal income tax laws, the partnership is treated as an _____ of the partners.

3. Unless the partnership agreement provides otherwise, partners are presumed to have equal rights to possess partnership property for partnership purposes, to share in partnership profits, and to _____.

4. Majority vote will be effective in connection with ordinary business decisions of a partnership. Unanimity is necessary, however, in order to _____ _____ _____ _____.

5. In a partnership, each partner has the right to _____ _____, to have an interest in the partnership, and to participate in management.

6. Partners' ownership rights with regard to specific partnership property are those of _____.

7. If a partner makes a contract on behalf of the partnership, the co-partners will be liable if the partner who made the contract acted within the scope of the partner's _____ or if the other partners ratify the contract.

8. In addition to the usual implied actual authority of a partner, a partner in a trading partnership, has power: (1) to buy and sell goods of the kind in which the partnership regularly deals; (2) to _____; (3) to _____; and (4) to issue and negotiate commercial paper on behalf of the other partners.

9. Partners are _____ liable for a contract of the partnership entered into by an authorized partner. In most states, therefore, partners must all be included in a lawsuit based upon the contract. Partners are _____ liable for torts and may, therefore, be sued separately or together.

MULTIPLE CHOICE QUESTIONS

1. Able and Baker, doing business as Aber Co., a partnership, hold out to the public that Charlie is also a partner. In his relations with third persons, Charlie acts as though he is a partner. Frank enters into a contract with the firm through Charlie. Aber Co. now denies that Charlie is a partner.
   A. Charlie is **not** personally liable as a partner on the contract with Frank.
   B. Charlie is liable as a partner by estoppel on the contract with Frank.
   C. Charlie is, in fact, a partner of Aber Co.
   D. Charlie is, in fact, **not** a partner of Aber Co. but has some of the rights of a partner.

2. Unanimous consent is **not** required in order to:
   A. enlarge the scope of the business of a partnership.
   B. admit new partners.
   C. sell equipment of the partnership used in the ordinary operation of its business.
   D. purchase personal property needed in the ordinary operation of the business of the partnership.

3. Murray and Norton conducted a business in the name of Norton and Murray Associates. Their relationship was informal and neither one considered himself to be a partner of the other. Stationery printed with the name of Norton and Murray Associates was used for business purposes. Loon loaned Murray $10,000 for and on behalf of the business. Murray informed Norton of this, but Norton stated to Murray: "That's your responsibility. I've had nothing to do with it." Murray failed to pay the loan back and Loon seeks to hold both Murray and Norton liable on the debt. Under these circumstances:

A. Loon **cannot** recover from Norton because Norton's statement to Murray was effective against Loon.

B. Norton and Murray are partners by estoppel.

C. because there was no signed, written partnership agreement, Loon **cannot** recover from Norton.

D. the fact that neither Murray nor Norton considered their relationship to be a partnership precludes recovery against Norton.

Questions 4 and 5 are based on the following fact situation: M, N, and O operated a pizza restaurant as a partnership. All three partners worked in the restaurant. The partnership agreement provided that only M had authority to order beverages.

4.   O ordered 200 cases of soda from the salesman for a bottling company. The salesman knew that O was a partner, but did not know that O was not the soda purchaser for the partnership.
A. Only O is liable for the 200 cases of soda.
B. O had apparent authority to make the purchase of soda.
C. O had actual and apparent authority to make the purchase of soda.
D. M and N and are jointly and severally liable for the purchaser of soda.

5.   One day N was mopping the floor, but N failed to clean up some anchovies that had fallen on the floor. H, a customer, slipped on the anchovies and broke a leg. H's damages total $11,000.
A. H may sue each of the partners in separate actions for tort.
B. H must sue the partnership in order to recover for his injury.
C. H may sue and recover only from N.
D. H may sue M, N, and O in separate actions and recover $11,000 from each of them.

6.   Orange, Plum, and Quince were general partners in the marmalade manufacturing business. Orange managed the partnership, Plum contributed her name, and Quince contributed his capital. Absent an agreement to the contrary:
A. Quince has the majority vote in respect to new business.
B. Quince has assumed the responsibility of paying Plum's debts upon the insolvency of the partnership.
C. Orange, Plum, and Quince share profits and losses equally.
D. Orange is entitled to a reasonable salary for his services.

7.   D, E, and F are partners in the DEF partnership that engages in the retail grocery business. D, one of the partners, gave X, a personal creditor (of D), a security interest in the inventory owned by the partnership. E, another partner, gave Y, a wholesaler who supplied the firm with canned goods, a similar security interest in the inventory to secure the payment of the purchase price of canned goods delivered to the store.
A. Y has **no** rights with respect to his security interest in the inventory.
B. X has **no** rights with respect to his security interest in the inventory.
C. E, but neither D nor F, will be personally liable for the purchase price of the canned goods purchased from Y.
D. D, E, and F are jointly and severally liable for the debt owed to X.

Chapter 39
Partnerships: Termination, Limited Partnerships, and Limited Liability Partnerships

The first portion of the chapter is devoted to the ways in which a partnership may be dissolved (by acts of the parties, operation of law, or judicial decree) and the process of winding up the firm's affairs so that its assets are liquidated or otherwise distributed. Following its winding up, the partnership ceases to exist.

Limited partnerships are the subject of the next portion of this chapter. A limited partnership is formed by complying with state statutory requirements. A limited partnership consists of at least one general partner (who potentially has personal liability for all debts of the partnership) and one or more limited partners. A limited partner contributes capital in the form of money or other property, owns an interest in the firm, and shares in the profits of the partnership, but does not participate in management and is not personally liable for partnership obligations beyond the amount of the limited partner's investment. This form of organization enables an investor to limit his or her liability and, in some instances, take advantage of certain tax benefits available to high risk enterprises. [The Revised Uniform Limited Partnership Act (RULPA) that is applicable to limited partnerships in most states is reproduced in Appendix G in the textbook.]

The remainder of the chapter relates to limited liability partnerships, as well as limited liability limited partnerships, which also are formed pursuant to state statues. These are partnerships in which innocent partners are not liable for other partners' wrongful acts, negligence, or other misconduct.

THINGS TO KEEP IN MIND

1. If a limited partnership fails to comply with the statutory requirements or if a limited partner participates in management, the partnership will be treated as a general partnership, and the limited partner will be liable as a general partner.

2. For a comparison between the provisions of the Uniform Partnership Act (UPA) which governs general partnerships and the Revised Uniform Limited Partnership Act (RULPA), see Exhibit 39-1 in the textbook.

OUTLINE

I.   Partnership termination — Following completion of the processes of dissolution and winding up, the partnership's legal existence ends.

A. Dissolution — Dissolution occurs when there is a change in the relations of the partners because a partner ceases to be associated with the partnership business [UPA 29].

1. Dissolution by acts of the partners [UPA 31(1) and (2)].

   a. Dissolution by agreement.
     1) The partnership is dissolved when the term has elapsed (if the partnership agreement provided for a partnership for term) or the purpose for which the partnership was formed has been accomplished.
     2) Partners mutually may agree to dissolve the partnership relationship.

   b. Partner's power to withdraw.
     1) If the partnership is a partnership at will, a partner's good faith withdrawal or expulsion dissolves the partnership without liability.
     2) If the partnership was established for a specified term, withdrawal of a partner (without cause) will subject the withdrawing partner to liability; expulsion (without cause) subjects other partners to liability.

   c. Admission of a new partner — The admission of a new partner results in the dissolution of the former partnership (without liquidation) and the creation of a new partnership that is liable for the obligations of the old partnership [UPA 41(1) and (7)].

   d. Transfer of a partner's interest — The voluntary or involuntary transfer of a partner's interest for the benefit of personal creditors does not dissolve a partnership automatically [UPA 27 and 28].
     1) The transferee acquires the right to receive the transferring partner's share of profits.
     2) The trransferee does not have the right to interfere with the management or to inspect the books of the partnership.
     3) A partner's interest in the partnership is subject to assignment, attachment, or other charging orders.

2. Dissolution by operation of law [UPA 31(3), (4) and (5)].

   a. Death of a partner.

   b. Bankruptcy of the partnership or a partner (in most cases).

   c. Illegality which makes it unlawful to continue the business or to do so with one of the partners.

3. Dissolution by judicial decree [UPA 32].

   a. Upon application of a partner for one of the following reasons:
     1) Insanity (mental incompetency) — A partner has been declared by a court as being mentally incompetent (insane or of unsound mind).

          2) Incapacity — A partner is permanently incapable of participating in management.

          3) Business impracticality — The partnership business can be operated only at a loss.

          4) Improper conduct of a partner.

          5) Other circumstances (such as serious personal dissension among partners) when the court finds it equitable to dissolve the partnership.

      b. Upon application of a third party.

          1) Assignee of a partner if partnership was a partnership at will.

          2) Judgment creditor of a partner who obtained a charge on the interest of his or her debtor (the partner) in the partnership.

   4. Notice of dissolution — Failure to give required notice results in liability [UPA 35].

      a. Notice to partners — A withdrawing partner must give actual or constructive notice to each of the other partners.

      b. Notice to third parties — Personal notice must be given to those persons who extended credit to the partnership and public (constructive) notice must be given to persons who dealt with the firm on a cash basis if dissolution occurs because of acts of the parties or by operation of law (other than because of illegality or bankruptcy) [UPA 35].

B. Winding up [UPA 37].

   1. Dissolution terminates all the authority of the partners except the authority to complete unfinished business and that which is necessary for winding up. (This includes collecting, preserving, and selling partnership assets, discharging liabilities, collecting debts owed to the partnership, allocating current income, and accounting to each other for the value of their interests in the partnership.

   2. When dissolution is caused by a partner's act in violation of the partnership agreement, the other innocent partners may sue for damages resulting from the dissolution and have the right to buy out the offending partner and the right to continue the business without winding up and liquidating assets [UPA 38].

   3. When dissolution is caused by the death of a partner, all partnership property vests in the surviving partners who act as fiduciaries in winding up the partnership business and are entitled to compensation for their services and reimbursement for their expenses incurred in the process [UPA 18(f)].

C. Distribution of assets [UPA 40].

1. Distribution is made out of partnership assets and any additional "contributions" made by partners that are necessary in order to pay liabilities of the partnership.

2. Order of payment.

   a. Payment to third party (outside) creditors.

   b. Payment to partners who have made advances or incurred liabilities on behalf of the partnership.

   c. Return of capital contributions to partners.

   d. Payment of any surplus to partners in accordance with the ratio fixed by the partnership agreement or equally if no ratio was fixed.

3. Concept of marshaling of assets arises when the partnership and/or an individual partner is insolvent.

   a. When the partnership is insolvent, third-party creditors of the partnership have priority over individual partners' creditors with respect to partnership assets and may then look to personal assets of the partners.

   b. If a partner is insolvent, the order of payment is:
      1) The insolvent partner's individual creditors.
      2) Partnership creditors.
      3) Other partners who may be entitled to contribution (reimbursement).

D. Partnership buy-sell (or buy-out) agreements.

   1. Partners may provide in the original partnership agreement that, under certain future conditions, one or more partners may purchase the interest of another partner at a specified price or will be given the opportunity to buy the interest at a price determined by one or more of the partners.

   2. Partners may also agree that, upon the death of one partner, the surviving partners can purchase the deceased partner's interest from his or her representative; frequently, the purchase price is funded by life insurance obtained by the partnership or partners. [See Chapter 52.]

II. Limited partnerships.

A. Rules governing limited partnerships are found in the Revised Uniform Limited Partnership Act (RULPA) that has been adopted in most of the states or the Uniform Limited Partnership Act (ULPA) that has been adopted in other states.

B. Formation of a limited partnership.

1. The statute requires compliance with a public and formal procedure in order to form a limited partnership.

2. A limited partnership must have two or more partners one of whom is a general partner; general partners have management responsibilities and unlimited liability.

3. A certificate (setting forth the firm name, nature and duration of business, location of principal place of business, names and addresses of members, capital contributions of limited partners, share of profits or other compensation that limited partners are entitled to receive, and methods for changes in membership and subsequent continuation of the business) is signed by partners and filed with a designated state official, such as the secretary of state [RULPA 201].

C. Rights and liabilities of limited partners.

1. General partners are personally liable to partnership creditors; in those states that permit a corporation to be a general partner, the shareholders of the corporation have limited liability because of the corporation laws.

2. Rights of limited partner [RULPA 305, 503, 504, 702 and 1001].

   a. A limited partner has the same rights as do partners in a general partnership with respect to suing, examining books, accounting, the return of his or her capital contribution, the assignments of rights to his or her interest, etc.

   b. A limited partner has the right to sue or bring an action on behalf of the firm if the general partners with authority to do so have refused to bring an action [RULPA 1001].

   c. Protection is also given to limited partners under the securities laws. [See Chapter 43.]

3. Liabilities of limited partners.

   a. A limited partner is liable to partnership creditors only to the extent of the limited partner's capital contribution or promised contribution [RULPA 303 and 502].

   b. If a certificate filed by the partnership contains a false statement, a person who incurred a loss because he or she relied on the statement can recover for the loss from a general partner (who knew or should have known that the statement was false) or any person who executed the certificate and knew that the statement was false [RULPA 207].

   c. A limited partner who discovers a defect in the formation of the limited partnership can avoid liability by causing an appropriate certificate or amendment to be filed or by renouncing an interest in the profits of the firm [ULPA 304].

4. Limited partners and management — A limited partner will be liable as a general partner if:

   a. The surname of the limited partner is included in the partnership name [RULPA 102].

   b. The limited partner participates in management [RULPA 303]. (Note that a limited partner will not be treated as participating in control of the business if that limited partner acts as an agent of the firm, attends meetings of partners, or votes on certain matters, such as a transfer of all of the assets of the firm or the admission or removal of a partner.)

   c. The limited partner learns that the firm is defectively formed and fails to withdraw from the partnership [RULPA 304].

D. Dissolution of a limited partnership.

   1. A limited partnership is dissolved at the time specified in the certificate of limited partnership, upon the happening of events specified in the written partnership agreement, the unanimous written consent of all partners, or the withdrawal, retirement, death, or mental incompetency of a general partner if the business cannot be continued by one or more of the general partners [RULPA 801].

   2. Upon application to a specified court by a partner, a limited partnership may be dissolved by court decree when it is not reasonably practicable to carry on the business [RULPA 802].

   3. A limited partner's withdrawal, death, assignment of his or her interest, or bankruptcy (unless it causes the bankruptcy of the firm) does not result in the dissolution of the limited partnership.

E. The winding up and liquidation procedure (following dissolution) is the same as that for a general partnership except for the priorities in distribution of assets [RULPA 804].

   1. Creditors, including partners who have made advances or incurred liabilities on behalf of the partnership.

   2. Unpaid distributions of partnership assets to general and limited partners (unless otherwise provided in the partnership agreement).

   3. Return of capital contributions to general and limited partners (unless otherwise provided in the partnership agreement).

4. General and limited partners' shares of profit (unless otherwise provided in the partnership agreement).

III. Limited liability partnerships (LLPs) — See also Chapter 37.

A. Limited liability partnerships are a newer form of business organization that enable partners to enjoy both the tax advantages of partnerships and the limited liability of corporations. (Family-owned businesses and professional service firms may be formed as LLPs.)

B. Family limited liability partnerships (FLLPs).

1. In a FLLP, a majority of the partners are family members and all partners are natural persons who act in a fiduciary capacity for the benefit of natural persons.

2. In addition to having the same advantages of other LLPs, FLLPs also may be exempt from real estate transfer taxes when partnership real property is transferred among partners.

C. Liability in a LLP.

1. A disadvantage of professional service firms (such as law and accounting firms) organized as partnerships is that partners have unlimited liability; firms organized as LLPs, however, allow professional partners to avoid personal liability for malpractice committed by their other partners, subject to certain limitations.

2. Liability outside the state of formation.

a. While most states have adopted LLP statutes, courts in states that have not yet adopted LLP statutes and do not recognize foreign LLPs expressly may not recognize the LLP's limitations on the liability of the LLP's partners and, instead, may treat the LLP-organized firm as a general partnership.

b. When a LLP conducts business in another state that has a LLP statute, but the statute provides different liability protection, usually, the applicable law is the law of the state in which the LLP was formed.

3. Supervising partner's liability.

a. As is true for partners in all types of partnerships, a partner in a LLP who commits a wrongful or negligent act is personally liable as is the partner who supervises the partner who committed the wrongful act.

b. State LLP statutes differ with regard to assessing liability when more than one partner of an LLP is negligent.
1) Statutes in some states provide for joint and several liability.

2) Statutes in other states provide for proportionate liability, in which case separate determinations are made as to the relative negligence of the partners. (This is supported by the American Institute of Certified Public Accountants.)

IV. Limited liability limited partnerships (LLLPs) — The liability of a general partner in a LLLP is the same as the liability of a limited partner; the liability of all partners in a LLLP, therefore, is limited to the amount of their investments in the firm. (Currently, only a few states have statutes providing for formation of LLLPs.)

KEY WORDS AND PHRASES IN TEXT

partnership termination (including
    dissolution and winding up)
dissolution by acts of the partners
agreement to dissolve
partnership for term
partnership at will
partner's power to withdraw
admission of new partner
transfer of a partner's interest
dissolution by operation of law because
    of death, bankruptcy, illegality
dissolution by judicial decree
    because of insanity, incapacity,
    impracticability, improper
    conduct, or other circumstances
notice of dissolution to partners and
    to third parties
actual and constructive notice
winding up
distribution of assets
right of contribution

partnership buy-sell agreements
limited partnership
general partner
limited partner
certificate of limited partnership
rights and liabilities of limited partners
corporation as limited and general partner
defect in formation of limited partnership
restriction on limited partner's
    participation in management
dissolution of limited partnership
withdrawal of limited partner
winding up and distribution of assets
    of limited partnership
limited liability partnership (LLP)
family limited liability partnership (FLLP)
supervising partner's liability
joint and several liability
proportionate liability
limited liability limited partnership
    (LLLP)

FILL-IN QUESTIONS

1. A partnership is dissolved by _____ if the partners mutually agree to its dissolution or if the partnership agreement provides that the partnership will exist for a limited period of time, and the period has expired.

2. A partnership is dissolved by operation of law if continuation of the business is illegal or if continuation of the business with one or more of the partners is unlawful. A partnership is also dissolved by operation of law upon the _____ _____.

3. A partnership will be terminated following dissolution and the completion of _____ _____.

4.   In order to form a limited partnership, compliance with certain statutory requirements is necessary. A certificate, stating the partnership name (which cannot include the name of a _____ partner), its duration, the nature of its business, the location of its business, the names and addresses of the partners (specifying the general partners and the _____ partners separately), the _____ made by the partners, the partners' shares of profits and other compensation, methods for changes in membership and subsequent continuation of the business, and other matters the partners wish to include, must be signed by the _____.
The certificate must be filed with the appropriate governmental office, which typically is the office of the _____.

5.   If the state limited partnership statute is complied with in all respects, a limited partner is not liable to creditors of the firm except to the extent of the limited partner's
_____.

6.   A limited partner will be liable to a creditor if the firm was defectively organized and the limited partner failed to withdraw after receiving knowledge of the defect or if
_____
_____.

7.   Assume that a limited partnership was formed for a term of ten years. Prior to the expiration of the ten-year period, the partnership may be dissolved if a general partner
_____
_____, or if the continuation of the firm will be illegal, or if the firm is bankrupt. The _____
or bankruptcy (unless it results in the bankruptcy of the partnership) of a limited partner does not result in the dissolution of the firm.

8.   The _____ partnership form of organization enables partners to enjoy both the benefit of _____ that is accorded to share-holders in a corporation and the tax advantages afforded to partnerships.

9.   _____ are LLPs in which a majority of the _____ are related to each other and all partners are natural persons or persons that act as fiduciaries for the benefit of natural persons. Such a LLP may be exempt from real estate transfer taxes when there is a transfer of partnership real estate among
_____.

MULTIPLE CHOICE QUESTIONS

1.   A general partnership is dissolved by operation of law when:
     A. one of the partners is bankrupt.
     B. one of the partners is imprisoned for a year.
     C. the purpose for which it was formed has been accomplished.
     D. a court enters a decree of dissolution.

Questions 2, 3, and 4 are based on the following fact situation: The partnership of Parnell and Quincy is being dissolved. The firm has assets of $100,000 and liabilities of $145,000, all owed to outside creditors. Parnell's total capital contribution was $10,000 and Quincy's was $5,000. The partnership agreement did not provide for sharing of profits or losses. The partnership and the two general partners have all filed for voluntary liquidation under Chapter 7 of the federal Bankruptcy Act. Parnell has personal assets of $200,000 and personal liabilities of $150,000. Quincy has personal assets of $85,000 and personal liabilities of $80,000. Neither Parnell nor Quincy is entitled to any exemptions.

2. The total amount due to be distributed by the partnership is:
   A. $100,000.
   B. $145,000.
   C. $160,000.
   D. None of the above is the correct amount.

3. The total amount that the outside creditors of the partnership will receive is:
   A. $145,000.
   B. $135,000.
   C. $130,000.
   D. $100,000.

4. Parnell's share of the total firm deficiency is:
   A. $30,000, but the actual amount to be paid to creditors of the partnership from his personal assets is $40,000.
   B. $30,000, but the actual amount to be paid to creditors of the partnership from his personal assets is $20,000.
   C. $30,000, but the actual amount to be paid to creditors of the partnership from his personal assets is $10,000.
   D. $40,000, but the partnership creditors **cannot** obtain anything from his personal assets.

5. R, S, and T were equal general partners in a partnership that engaged in the business of buying and selling real property for profit. Title to all property purchased with partnership funds was taken in the name of R. R died with partnership real estate (valued at $100,000) and personal property (valued at $10,000) standing in his name. The partnership had no debts. R's wife claims a marital right in the real property. R's children (to whom he had bequeathed all his personal property) claim a statutory right to one-third of the personal property. Under the circumstances:
   A. R's wife has a valid marital right to all the real property held in her deceased husband's name.
   B. R's children are entitled to one-third of the personal property standing in their deceased father's name.
   C. R's wife is entitled to R's share of undistributed partnership profits.
   D. R's estate is entitled to settlement for the value of R's partnership interest that is considered to be personal property.

6. Y and Z formed a partnership. Y contributed $10,000 and Z contributed $5,000. The firm has been dissolved and its creditors have been paid. There is $21,000 left.
   A. Y gets $13,000, and Z gets $8,000.

B. Y gets $10,500, and Z gets $10,500.

C. If Y had lent the firm an additional $10,000, Y would get $20,000, and Z would get $1,000.

D. Unless one of the partners died or became bankrupt, the partnership **cannot** be dissolved.

7. A, B, and C, partners, have decided to dissolve their partnership. The partnership has assets of $50,000 (all cash) and owes outside creditors $75,000. A had made a $5,000 loan to the partnership (which has not been repaid) and owns personal property worth $10,000. B has no assets but is a member of another partnership. The value of his interest in that partnership is $3,000. C has no personal assets. The capital balance of A, B, and C in the partnership is $10,000 each.

A. Partnership creditors can receive no more than $50,000 of the partnership property and $10,000 from A.

B. Partnership creditors can receive only $50,000 of the partnership property.

C. Partnership creditors can receive no more than $50,000 of the partnership property, $10,000 from A and $3,000 from B.

D. Partnership creditors can receive no more than $45,000 of the partnership property, and A can receive $5,000 of partnership property.

8. Kincaid, a member of the Joker Co., a partnership, wishes to retire as a partner. Kincaid, therefore, transfers his interest in the partnership to Lensing for $50,000 by assigning all his rights, title, and interest in the partnership to Lensing who Kincaid names as his successor partner in Joker Co.

A. Absent any limitation regarding the assignment of a partner's interest in the partnership agreement, Kincaid is free to assign his partnership interest at his will.

B. Lensing is entitled to an equal voice in the management of the partnership.

C. The assignment to Lensing effectively dissolves the partnership.

D. Although Lensing does not have the status of a partner, she can inspect the partnership books upon making a proper demand.

9. Angus is a limited partner in the partnership of Digby, Ernst, and Friendly, Ltd. Angus' existence and name are not disclosed to the public. Angus' liability to creditors of the partnership will **not** be limited to the amount of her contribution of capital because:

A. her surname is **not** included in the name of the firm.

B. her capital contribution is less than that of the general partners.

C. she participates in decisions concerning the day-to-day operation of the business.

D. the government official with whom the partnership certificate was file is **not** notified of Angus' change of address.

10. Pipe, Quarry, and Rayne are active members of the PQR Plumbing Co., a partnership. Lake is a limited partner in the firm. Pipe installed the plumbing system in Gardner's new $150,000 home. Gardner moved in and turned on the water, only to learn that the water lines had been installed in a negligent manner. The pipes burst, and the entire house was flooded. Damage has been extensive.

A. If Gardner bases an action on tort, Gardner must sue all the partners jointly.

B. If Gardner bases an action on contract, Gardner may sue all the partners separately.

C. Gardner will **not** be able to recover from Lake if Gardner's action is based on contract.

D. Gardner will **not** be able to recover from Pipe, Quarry, or Rayne if Gardner sues them jointly but does **not** include Lake as a party.

11. The partnership agreement of the GH Limited Partnership provides for sharing of profits equally. The partnership is insolvent. Lyon is a limited partner and is solvent. Gnu and Hippo are general partners. Gnu is insolvent, but has no non-exempt property. Gnu owes $20,000 to personal creditors. Hippo has a truck worth $10,000 and an interest in Hippo and Rhino Co., another partnership, valued at $20,000. Hippo has no individual debts. Lyon's net worth is $500,000. The liabilities of the GH Limited Partnership amount to $30,000 all owed to Vicuna. No financial adjustments among the partners are necessary.

A. Assume that Lyon participated in management. Vicuna may collect only from Lyon.

B. Assume that Lyon did **not** participate in management. Vicuna may collect only from Hippo by attaching Hippo's truck and Hippo's interest in the Hippo and Rhino partnership.

C. Assume that Lyon did **not** participate in management. Vicuna may collect only from Lyon.

D. Assume that Lyon did **not** participate in management. Vicuna may collect $15,000 from Lyon and $15,000 from Hippo.

Questions 12 and 13 are based on the following fact situation: A certificate of limited partnership has been properly filed by a partnership, the books of which indicate the following:

The partnership consists of three partners, Manfred, Norstad, and Oops, who share profits equally. The partnership agreement is silent as to the manner of sharing losses.

Manfred loaned the partnership $10,000, without interest, and made a capital contribution of $20,000. Norstad made a capital contribution of $10,000. Oops made no capital contribution, but has devoted all his time to the partnership's busness. Manfred, a general partner, and Norstad, a limited partner, have devoted no time to the management of the partnership.

12. Which of the following statements is **false**?

A. Norstad will be liable as a general partner if the name of the partnership is Manfred, Norstad and Oops, Ltd.

B. Norstad will be liable as a general partner for willful, intentional torts committed by Oops while Oops was acting within the scope of his authority.

C. The partnership will not be dissolved upon Norstad's death.

D. The partnership will be dissolved upon the bankruptcy of Oops.

13. The partners have agreed to dissolve the partnership. The firm has $180,000 in assets. Outside creditors are owed $50,000. Each of the partners is solvent. Under the Revised Uniform Limited Partnership Act, the order of distribution is:
    A. First: Outside creditors ($50,000) and Manfred ($10,000) in repayment of his loan. Second: Manfred ($20,000) and Norstad ($10,000) for their capital contributions. Third: Manfred, Norstad, and Oops each receive $10,000 as their respective share in the profits.
    B. First: Outside creditors ($50,000). Second: Norstad for his $10,000 share of the profits and his capital contribution of $10,000. Third: Manfred $10,000 for his loan. Fourth: Manfred and Oops each receive $10,000 as their respective share in the profits, and Manfred receives $20,000 for his capital contribution.
    C. First: Outside creditors ($50,000). Second: Manfred $10,000 in repayment for his loan. Third: Norstad $10,000 for his capital contribution. Fourth: Manfred $20,000 for his capital contribution. Fifth: Manfred, Norstad, and Oops each receives $10,000 as their respective share in the profits.
    D. the same as that of a general partnership.

14. A firm that is organized as a limited liability partnership:
    A. must be a law or accounting firm whose partners have unlimited personal liability.
    B. must permit its professional partners to avoid personal liability for malpractice committed by their other partners.
    C. must be incorporated in order to provide limited liability for its partners.
    D. must be a family-owned business.

Chapter 40
Corporations: Formation and Financing

A corporation is a legal entity created by the state in accordance with the terms of a general corporation law. Important characteristics of a corporation include perpetual existence, centralized management, ease of transferability of ownership interests, and limited liability for owners (the shareholders). The formation, operation, and rights and duties of corporations and those associated with corporations are regulated by state statutes that, with varying degrees, closely resemble the Model Business Corporation Act (MBCA) and the Revised Model Business Corporation Act (RMBCA). The RMBCA is an internally consistent model for legislation. Excerpts from the RMBCA are found in Appendix H.

After first discussing the nature, powers, and classifications of corporations, the authors examine the process for forming corporations. Usually, the preparatory groundwork for organizing a corporation is done by promoters prior to formal organization. During the preincorporation period, arrangements are made for assembling personnel, property, and capital; and subscriptions for shares of stock (to be issued by the corporation after its formation) are solicited. In addition, the necessary steps are taken in order to comply with the state statutory requisites for incorporation. The legal status of agreements made during the promotional period and the procedures for formal incorporation are subjects covered in this chapter.

Once a corporation comes into existence, the corporation issues securities in order to finance its operations. All corporations issue shares of stock (equity securities) representing ownership interests and many corporations issue debt securities, such as bonds and debentures, which are evidences of obligations to pay money. Corporate financing and the various types of securities are topics covered in the concluding section of the chapter.

THINGS TO KEEP IN MIND

1. The document prepared for purposes of incorporation may be referred to as a charter or articles of incorporation. These terms are used interchangeably in this book.

2. Usually, corporations are empowered to do almost anything unless the action is criminal, tortious, or contrary to public policy. As a result, it is rare today that a corporation is found to have exceeded its powers.

OUTLINE

I. The nature of the corporation.

A. A corporation is an artificial person (in contrast to a natural person), whose creation and operations are governed by state statutes. Because it is a legal entity, a corporation can conduct business and incur liability in its own name.

B. Corporate personnel — The corporation is separate and apart from the shareholders (who own the corporation), the board of directors (which is elected by the shareholders and is responsible for the corporation's overall management), and the corporation's officers (who are employed by the board of directors and who run the corporation's daily business operations).

C. Corporate taxation — Distributed and retained profits of corporations are taxed by the state and the federal government.

  1. Double taxation of corporate income.

    a. Income taxes are paid by a corporation on profits.

    b. When a corporation distributes profits as dividends, the individual shareholders who receive the dividends also pay income taxes (unless the dividends represent distributions of capital).

  2. Earnings that are retained and invested by the corporation may yield higher future corporate profits; this will cause the market value of the stock to rise; when the shareholders later sell their shares of stock, the shareholders will receive the benefit of the corporation's having retained earnings (capital gains).

D. A corporation is regarded as a "person" separate and apart from the shareholders (the owners of interests in the corporation) for most purposes under federal and state constitutions and laws, unless application of a law is restricted to natural persons.

E. Constitutional rights of corporations. [See also Chapter 5.]

  1. A corporation is treated as a person under the due process clause of the Fifth and Fourteenth Amendments and the equal protection clause of the Fourteenth Amendment to the U.S. Constitution.

    a. A corporation may sue and be sued; a corporation is protected against unreasonable searches and seizures and double jeopardy.

    b. A corporation is not protected against self-incrimination.

  2. A corporation is regarded as a citizen of the state in which it is incorporated for purposes of jurisdiction.

  3. A corporation is not necessarily considered to be a citizen entitled to all the privileges and immunities of citizens in the several states as provided for in Article IV, Section 2. (For example, one state may impose burdens on a

corporation that is incorporated in another state if the corporation wishes to engage in intrastate, as distinguished from interstate, business within its boundaries and the burdens are comparable to those imposed upon domestic corporations.)

4. Corporations are excluded from some professions which require personal qualifications.

F. Torts and criminal acts.

1. Liability for torts — A corporation is liable vicariously for torts that are committed by its employees and agents when the employees and agents are acting in the scope or course of their employment because of the doctrine of *respondeat superior*. [See Chapter 34.]

2. Criminal liability of corporation.

   a. A corporation may be convicted of a crime if the criminal law expressly so provides.
      1) A criminal act may have been committed by an agent or employee of the corporation (while the agent or employee was acting within the scope of his or her employment) and the purpose of the statute defining the crime is to impose liability on corporations.
      2) The crime consists of a failure to perform a specific affirmative duty that is imposed upon corporations by law.

   b. Even if a criminal statute does not specify that it applies to corporations, a corporation may be convicted of a crime for which the penalty imposed is a fine when:
      1) Intent is not an element of the crime.
      2) Intent is an element of the crime, but the criminal intent of a corporate agent or employee may be imputed to the corporation.

3. Corporate sentencing guidelines apply when federal crimes are committed. [See also Chapter 10.]

   a. The federal corporate sentencing guidelines cover 32 levels of offenses and require federal judges to use a formula (the culpability score) when penalties are imposed for corporate crimes.

   b. The factors that are to be considered when penalties are imposed include:
      1) The seriousness of the offense.
      2) The degree of the company's guilt.
      3) The role played in the wrongdoing by senior managerial personnel.
      4) The company's history of past violations.
      5) The extent of the company's cooperation with investigators.

   c. If a company takes substantial internal steps to prevent, investigate, and punish wrongdoing and cooperates with the government, a federal judge may impose a less severe penalty (by giving credits) when the company has adopted and complies with internal controls that:

1) Establish and communicate written crime-prevention standards and procedures for all agents and employees (e.g., training programs).
2) Require that high-level managers or officers enforce the compliance standards.
3) Prevent an employee who has demonstrated a propensity to engage in criminal activity from exercising discretionary authority.
4) Implement methods of detection and prevention of crime.
5) Protect whistleblowers from reprisals.

II. Corporate powers — Certain powers are necessary to accomplish the purpose for which the corporation is formed.

A. Express powers.

1. Order of priority in case of conflict.

   a. U.S. Constitution and federal statutes.

   b. State constitutions.

   c. State statutes.

   d. Certificate of incorporation (charter).

   e. Bylaws (the rules adopted for management of the corporation).

   f. Resolutions of the board of directors.

2. General, statutory powers apply to all corporations organized under a state business corporation law and, usually, include the power to have perpetual existence, to enter into contracts, to sue and be sued, to lend and borrow money, to buy, hold, lease, receive, dispose of, and sell real and personal property, etc. [RMBCA 3.02].

3. Express powers of a corporation may be specifically enumerated in the corporate charter.

B. Implied powers — Corporations also have implied (or incidental) powers to do those things that are necessary in order to execute their purposes and express powers.

1. Today, with some limitations, a corporation has implied power to borrow money, to lend money or to extend credit to those with whom the corporation has a legal or contractual relationship, and to make charitable contributions.

2. Corporate officers have the implied power to bind the corporation in matters directly connected with the corporation's ordinary business affairs.

C. *Ultra vires* doctrine — An *ultra vires* act occurs when a corporation exercises power that the corporation does not possess.

1. If, while acting as an agent of the corporation, a corporate board of directors or officer does something that the corporation is not authorized to do, because the act is not in furtherance of the corporation's purpose, an *ultra vires* act has been committed.

2. Illegal acts are *ultra vires* and may not be ratified by the shareholders.

3. Some *ultra vires* acts may be ratified by the shareholders.

    a. The act was one that could have been authorized by the shareholders when it was originally done.

    b. Unanimous ratification is necessary if there has been a gift or wasting of corporate assets.

4. Judicial treatment of *ultra vires* in the past (and in a few states today).

    a. The corporation has no capacity to perform the *ultra vires* act. An *ultra vires* contract that is completely executory (not performed by either party) or partially or completely executed, therefore, is void.

    b. An agent (corporate officer) acting without authority does not bind his or her principal (the corporation).

    c. The defense of *ultra vires* can be raised in order to prevent enforcement of an executory contract; not all courts, however, recognize the defense if the contract has been executed.

5. Modern judicial and statutory approach [RMBCA 3.04].

    a. The defense of *ultra vires* may not be raised in an action to enforce a contract (even if the contract is executory) by the corporation or by the party with whom the corporation entered into the contract.

    b. The issue of *ultra vires* may be asserted only in an action brought by:
        1) Shareholders in order to enjoin the carrying out of the act.
        2) The corporation (or shareholders in a derivative action) in order to recover from officers or directors who entered into an *ultra vires* contract or carried out the unauthorized act.
        3) The state attorney general in order to enjoin the *ultra vires* act or to dissolve the corporation.

III. Classification of corporations.

A. Domestic, foreign, and alien corporations — Corporations are classified based upon the geographic locations in which the corporations are formed.

1. Domestic corporation — A corporation is a domestic corporation in the state in which it is incorporated and with whose statute it must comply with regard to formation and internal operations.

2. Foreign corporation — A corporation is a foreign corporation in a state (other than the state of incorporation) in which it is conducting business.

   a. If a foreign corporation does intrastate (as contrasted with interstate) business in a state, the foreign corporation must comply with the laws of that state.
      1) Normally, the foreign corporation must apply for and obtain a certificate to do business from a state official (such as the secretary of state) [RMBCA 15.01 and 15.03] and, thereafter, will enjoy the same rights as domestic corporations [RMBCA 15.05].
      2) The foreign corporation must maintain a registered office and agent within the state [RMBCA 15.07] upon whom legal process may be served. If such service cannot be effected, the secretary of state will be an agent for this purpose [RMBCA 15.01]. (See also Chapter 33 at II. E. relating to agencies created by operation of law.)

   b. A foreign corporation is doing business within a state, such that a state court can obtain jurisdiction over the corporation, if the corporation has some minimum contact with the state.
      1) The minimum contacts requirement is met if the corporation conducts systematic commerce or maintains a plant, factory, or principal office in the state.
      2) Minimum contact does not include holding meetings, maintaining or defending legal action, maintaining bank accounts or transfer agents, soliciting orders that are accepted outside the state, etc. [RMBCA 15.01].

3. An alien corporation is a corporation that is incorporated in a country other than the United States but is doing business in this country.

B. Public and private corporations — Corporations may be classified based upon their sources of funds (or revenues), function, and ownership arrangements.

   1. Public corporations — Corporations that are formed by legislative bodies for governmental purposes.

      a. Cities, towns, and other municipalities.

      b. Federal government organizations, such as the U.S. Postal Service, the Tennessee Valley Authority, AMTRAK, and the Federal Deposit Insurance Corporation (FDIC).

   2. Private corporations — Corporations created for private benefit that issue shares of stock, including business corporations and public benefit corporations, such as utility companies.

C. Nonprofit (not-for-profit or eleemosynary) corporations are organized for charitable, religious, educational, social, etc., purposes and governed by special state statutes.

D. Close corporations — A close (closely-held, family, or privately-held) corporation whose shares of stock are held by one individual or by a small group.

   1. Close corporation statutes.

      a. In some states, statutes (providing greater flexibility than general business corporation laws) apply to corporations that have limited numbers of shareholders (e.g., 30 or 50) and whose shares of stock are not publicly offered for sale and can be transferred only subject to certain restrictions.

      b. Some states have adopted provisions of the Statutory Close Corporation Supplement to the MBCA or RMBCA 7.32.

      c. Shareholders are not individually liable for corporate debts and torts.

   2. Management of close corporations.

      a. Management may resemble that of a sole proprietorship or partnership.

      b. In states having close corporation statutes, management formalities are relaxed; there may be no need for a board of directors, or shareholders may have unlimited power to restrict decisions of the board but, if so, shareholders will owe fiduciary duties to the corporation.

      c. Close corporation may require that action can be taken by the board only upon approval of more than a majority of the directors.

   3. Transfer of shares in close corporations.

      a. Statutes in a few states prohibit the transfer of shares unless certain persons are given the first opportunity to purchase the shares.

      b. The articles of incorporation and the share certificates, or a separate shareholder agreement, may specify restrictions on transferability.

      c. Reasonable restrictions on transfer in the event of the death of a shareholder or a desire by a shareholder to sell his or her shares are specifically enforceable by the courts.

E. S corporations.

   1. A corporation that meets certain qualifications provided for in Subchapter S of the Internal Revenue Code may elect to be treated in a manner similar to a partnership for federal income tax purposes, thus avoiding double taxation of

income (to which all other corporations, or C corporations, are subject); corporate income is not taxed, but corporate income is allocated among the shareholders for income tax purposes.

2. Disadvantage — Fringe benefit payments to employee-shareholders owning more than two percent of the shares are not deductible by the S corporation.

3. Qualification requirements for S corporations.

   a. Corporation must be incorporated in a state (rather than be an alien corporation).

   b. Corporation cannot be a member of an affiliated group of corporations.

   c. Shareholders of the corporation must be individuals, estates, or certain trusts and not corporations, partnerships, or nonqualifying trusts.

   d. The corporation must have 75 or fewer shareholders.

   e. The corporation can issue only one class of stock; shareholders, however, may have different voting rights.

   f. No shareholder of the corporation can be a nonresident alien.

4. Benefits of S corporations.

   a. When the S corporation has losses, the shareholders can use the losses to offset other income.

   b. When the shareholders are in a lower tax bracket than that applied to a non-S corporation, the S corporation's entire income is taxed at the shareholders' rate (whether or not the income is distributed).

   c. Corporate distributed and retained income is taxed only once.

F. Professional corporations.

1. A service corporation (S.C.), professional corporation (P.C.), incorporated firm (Inc.), or professional association (P.A.) is a private corporation or association, the members of which engage in a profession and organize in order to gain advantages relating to taxes, pensions, insurance plans, etc.

2. Statutes governing professional corporations are similar to general business corporation laws under which members of some professions cannot organize because of professional ethics codes.

3. Shareholders of a professional corporation have limited liability subject to certain exceptions.

        a. A typical statute provides that each shareholder of a professional corporation is personally liable for his or her own negligent acts and malpractice as well as for wrongful acts committed by other persons whom he or she supervises.

        b. Under general corporation laws, one member of a corporation is not liable for the malpractice of another member.

        c. A court may regard the corporation as a partnership in order to impose liability on all members for the malpractice of one member committed while he or she was acting within the scope of the firm's business.

        d. A shareholder in a professional corporation is protected from the liability imposed because of torts (unrelated to malpractice) committed by other members.

    4. State statutes provide for alternative forms of organization, such as limited liability companies (LLCs) and partnerships (LLPs), professional limited liability companies (PLLCs), and professional limited liability partnerships (PLLPs), so that professionals are able to enjoy both the limited liability benefits of the professional corporation and the advantages of the partnership. [See Chapter 37.]

IV. Corporate formation — Preliminary organizational and promotional undertakings and the legal process of incorporation.

  A. Promotional activities.

    1. Before a corporation comes into existence, promoters analyze economic feasibility, prepare the prospectus (the document required by securities laws containing material facts concerning the financial operations of the corporation so that a prospective investor can make an informed decision), find investors, assemble necessary personnel, property, and capital, as well as take the preliminary steps in order to organize the corporation.

    2. Promoter's liability — In general, promoters are personally liable as parties to preincorporation contracts.

        a. Liability during the promotion period.
           1) A promoter is a party to a contract and, therefore, is bound as a party.
           2) The corporation is not in existence and, therefore, is not liable as a party to a contract.

        b. Liability after incorporation.
           1) A promoter remains liable to other contracting parties, unless:
              a) The promoter is released by the other contracting parties.
              b) The contracting parties clearly indicated that the promoter would not be personally liable.

           c) Corporation is substituted as a party to the contract in a novation. [See Chapter 19.]

       2) The corporation becomes liable after incorporation, if:
           a) The corporation enters into a novation.
           b) The corporation adopts or becomes an assignee of the rights of the promoter who remains secondarily liable.

       3) A corporation cannot ratify a preincorporation contract because the corporation was not in existence (and, therefore, could not be a principal) at the time that the contract was made.

   3. Subscribers and subscriptions.

      a. A subscription is an agreement to purchase unissued shares of stock in a corporation that has not yet been formed.

      b. Subscription may be treated as:
       1) A continuing offer by the subscriber that may be accepted by the corporation following incorporation.
       2) A contract among subscribers and, therefore, irrevocable.
       3) An irrevocable offer for the period specified in the statute (which typically is six months) unless all subscribers consent to revocation [RMBCA 6.20].

B. Incorporation procedures.

   1. State chartering.

      a. The corporate laws vary among the states; some states have laws that are more advantageous regarding taxation, incorporation, or operation.

      b. Historically, Delaware had the least restrictive laws and, therefore, many business corporations were incorporated in that state.

      c. Most states permit domestic corporations to locate their headquarters and business operations in other states.

      d. Usually, close corporations and professional corporations incorporate in the state in which their principal shareholders reside and are employed.

   2. Articles of incorporation — Contents [RMBCA 2.02].

      a. Corporate name [RMBCA 4.01].
       1) The word, "corporation," "company," "incorporated," or "limited" or an abbreviation (e.g., "corp.," "co.," "inc.," or "ltd.") must be used.
       2) The name cannot be misleading or subject to confusion with the name of another organization.
       3) Before incorporation, a name can be reserved [RMBCA 4.02].

      b. Nature and purpose [RMBCA 3.01].

      1) In most states, the corporate purpose may be to engage in any legal business.

      2) Some states prohibit those engaging in professions or activities, such as banking, insurance, or public utilities, from incorporating under the general corporation laws because they are governed by other statutes.

  c. Duration [RMBCA 3.02] — Unless otherwise provided in the articles of incorporation, a corporation has perpetual existence.

  d. Capital structure — The number, classes, and par value of shares of stock that the corporation will be authorized to issue, as well as other relevant information concerning equity, capital, and credit.

  e. Internal organization.

      1) Internal management structure should be described in the articles but may be described in bylaws.

      2) Bylaws contain internal rules for governing and regulating the conduct of corporate affairs and cannot conflict with state or federal statutes or the articles of incorporation [RMBCA 2.06].

        a) A corporation may provide that bylaws may be amended or repealed by the board of directors [RMBCA 10.20].

        b) Bylaws prescribe voting rights, quorums for meetings, the manner and time of scheduling shareholders' and directors' meetings, etc.

  f. Registered office and agent — The location of the registered office and the name of the registered agent (at that address) who is authorized to receive service of process and other notices [RMBCA 5.01 and 5.04].

  g. Incorporators — Names, addresses, and signatures of incorporators are necessary.

      1) Usually, incorporators need not have any interest in the corporation or be subscribers to shares of stock.

      2) The number varies from one to three; state statute may provide that incorporators need not be natural persons [RMBCA 2.01].

3. Certificate of incorporation — The articles of incorporation are filed with the appropriate state official (e.g.,, the secretary of state), necessary fees are paid, and notice of the filing is given by the state official; usually, the official issues a certificate of incorporation or the corporate charter [RMBCA 2.06].

4. First organizational meeting [RMBCA 2.05].

  a. The incorporators elect the board of directors, adopt bylaws, authorize the board to issue stock, etc.

b. The board of directors adopts minutes of meeting of incorporators (if such a meeting was required), adopts preincorporation contracts, seal, form for stock certificates, accepts subscriptions, etc. [RMBCA 2.05].

V. Improper incorporation.

A. A *de jure* corporation is a corporation organized in accordance with required, mandatory conditions precedent to incorporation so that the corporate status and existence cannot be attacked.

B. A *de facto* corporation is a corporation that operates as a corporation but failed to comply with some statutory mandate so that the state may challenge the corporation's existence. Element:

1. A statute under which the corporation could be validly incorporated exists.

2. Good faith attempt to comply with the statute.

3. Some exercise of the functions of a corporation.

C. Corporation by estoppel.

1. Corporation has neither *de jure* nor *de facto* status.

2. Associates (alleged shareholders and/or directors) who participated in holding the association out as a corporation are precluded from denying that it was a corporation against third parties who, in reliance upon the holding out, changed their positions and were, therefore, injured.

3. Parties who dealt with the association and entered into contracts with the association in the belief that only the corporation would be liable may be estopped from denying that the association was a corporation.

4. If a corporation by estoppel cannot be established, the associates who actively participated in management will be liable as partners.

VI. Disregarding the corporate entity.

A. In unusual situations, a court may ignore the legal fiction of the corporation as an entity (pierce the corporate veil) when it is used to perpetrate fraud, circumvent law, accomplish an illegal purpose, or otherwise evade law.

B. Courts will disregard the corporate entity (even though technically a corporation exists) and hold directors, officers, or shareholders personally liable for the transactions conducted in the corporate name.

C. Courts will disregard corporate entity if a corporation is not maintained as an entity, separate from its shareholders, in order to prevent abuse of corporate privilege for personal benefit.

1. Records and funds have been commingled, and the enterprise has not been established on an adequate financial basis (e.g., "thin capitalization").

2. This arises occasionally in the case of a close corporation with only one or a few shareholders or in the case of parent-subsidiary corporations.

VII. Corporate financing.

A. Corporations issue securities that are sold to investors.

B. Bonds (debentures) or debt securities are evidences of obligations to pay money; issuance of bonds is a method of splitting up debt so that it can be more easily marketed and is used for long-term corporate financing.

1. Bonds are issued by business firms and governments to investors from whom the firms or governments are borrowing funds.

2. A bond usually has a designated maturity date (at which time the principal or face amount is repaid to the investor) and provides for periodic payment of interest prior to maturity.

3. Technically, a bond is a debt security that is secured by collateral and a debenture is a debt security that is not secured by any specific property of the corporation.

4. Debt securities may be sold for less than their face value at a discount or for more than their face value at a premium.

5. The bond indenture is the written agreement for the sale of debt securities; in general, bondholders do not have rights to participate in corporate affairs.

6. Types of corporate bonds.

   a. Debenture bonds represent unsecured obligations backed by the general credit of the issuing corporation; if the corporation defaults, holders of debentures can look only to corporate assets in which other creditors and bondholders have no security interests. [See Chapter 30.]

   b. Mortgage bonds are secured by property that can be reached by the bondholders upon default by the corporation.

   c. Convertible bonds are bonds that can be exchanged at a specified rate for shares of common stock if the bondholders so desire.

   d. Callable bonds provide that the issuing corporation has the right to repay the principal prior to maturity in accordance with specified conditions.

   e. "Junk bonds" are bonds that credit rating agencies rate as below investment grade because these bonds are risky investments.

        1) Junk bonds pay higher yields than investment-grade bonds.

        2) Junk bonds have been used to finance corporate takeovers, mergers, and acquisitions.

C. Stocks (equity securities) are evidences of the right to participate in earnings and corporate distributions; issuance of stocks is the principal method of initial corporate financing.

   1. Stocks represent ownership in a firm.

   2. Characteristics.

      a. The shareholder has no right to repayment.

      b. The shareholder receives dividends after dividends are declared by the board of directors.

      c. Shareholders are the last investors to be paid upon the dissolution of the corporation.

      d. Shareholders vote for members of the board of directors and on major issues.

   3. Every corporation issues common stock and may be authorized to issue preferred stock.

   4. Common stock.

      a. The owners of common stock are entitled to a pro rata share of properly declared dividends paid out of corporate profits, without any preferences and after payment of taxes, interest to lenders and bondholders, etc., and any specified dividends required to be paid to preferred shareholders if any preferred stock has been issued.

      b. Common stock shareholders have right to vote.

      c. Common stock shareholders have rights to the ultimate distribution of the assets of the corporation upon dissolution.

   5. Preferred stock.

      a. Holders of preferred stock have a preference that usually is in rights to receive dividends or distributions upon the liquidation of the corporation.

      b. Preferred stock may have voting rights; often, preferred stock is issued as nonvoting stock.

      c. A corporation may issue different classes and/or series of preferred stock.

d. Cumulative preferred — If the corporation fails to pay a dividend, the dividend is carried over and paid in a subsequent year before the holders of common stock receive dividends.

e. Participating preferred — Preferred shareholders share in distribution of additional dividends after payment of dividends to holders of preferred and common stock if there are additional distributions of corporate profits.

f. Convertible preferred — Preferred shares may be exchanged for common stock or other preferred stock at a specified rate.

g. Redeemable (callable) preferred — Corporation has the right to purchase, reacquire, and cancel shares at a specified price.

h. Position of preferred stockholder.
    1) Preferred shareholders have priority over common stockholders with respect to dividends and claims on assets in case of liquidation.
    2) Usually, preferred stockholders receive periodic fixed dividends.
    3) Based upon the returns on a preferred shareholder's investment and the associated risk, the preferred stockholder's position is between that of a common stock shareholder and a bondholder.

6. Terminology.

    a. Authorized shares — Stock that the corporation is empowered by its charter to issue.

    b. Issued shares — Authorized shares that have been sold.
        1) Outstanding shares — Shares that have been issued and are in the hands of shareholders.
        2) Treasury shares — Issued shares that have been reacquired by the corporation.

    c. Par value shares — Shares that have been assigned a stated, fixed dollar value.
        1) May be issued originally for an amount greater than par (premium).
        2) In most states, par value shares cannot be issued originally for less than par value (discounted).

    d. No par shares — Shares that are not assigned any specific fixed price. No par shares are usually issued for a price that is fixed by the board of directors.

    e. Stated capital.
        1) The sum of the par value of all issued par value shares and the consideration received for all no par value shares.
        2) Includes outstanding and treasury shares.

D. Corporations also finance operations with short-term borrowing in the form of accounts payable and commercial paper (covered in Unit Four) and with long-term leaseback arrangements.

KEY WORDS AND PHRASES IN TEXT

Model Business Corporation Act (MBCA)
Revised Model Business Corporation Act (RMBCA)
the corporation as a legal person
the corporation as an entity
retained earnings
charter or articles of incorporation
bylaws
federal sentencing guidelines
express powers
implied powers
ultra vires doctrine
domestic corporation
foreign corporation
alien corporation
certificate of authority to do business
minimum-contacts requirement for jurisdiction over a corporation
public corporation
private corporation
nonprofit (not-for-profit) corporation
close corporation
S corporation
professional corporation
incorporation
promotional activities
promoter
prospectus
subscribers
subscription for shares of stock
incorporators

corporate name
nature and purpose of corporation
duration of corporation
capital structure
internal organization
registered office and registered agent
certificate of incorporation
first organizational meeting
improper incorporation
de jure corporation
de facto corporation
corporation by estoppel
disregarding the corporate entity (piercing the corporate veil)
inadequate capitalization
commingling personal and corporate property and interests
securities
bond (debt or fixed income security)
maturity date of bonds
sale of bonds at a discount or premium
bond indenture
debenture, mortgage, convertible, callable, and junk bonds
stock (equity security)
common stock
preferred stock
cumulative, participating, convertible, and/or redeemable (callable) preferred stock

FILL-IN QUESTIONS

1. A corporation is an artificial being that is treated as a legal entity. It may conduct business, own property, and sue and be sued in its own _____.

2. The _____ of a corporation are the owners of the corporation who elect the _____ that oversees the general management of the corporation and appoints the corporate _____ who run the daily operations of the corporation.

3. Shareholders of a corporation may be distinguished from partners in a general partnership because, unlike partners, shareholders are not personally liable for obligations of the corporation, shareholders do not have the right to possess corporate property (shareholders are not tenants in partnership, tenants in common, or joint tenants with respect to corporate property), and the death of a _____ does not dissolve the corporation. In addition, shareholders are neither representatives nor _____ of the corporation, and do not owe fiduciary duties to the _____ or to the _____.

4. A municipality (city) may have a charter and be created by statute for governmental purposes. It is a _____ rather than a _____ corporation.

5. A corporation, incorporated in one state but desiring to engage in business in another state, is required to obtain a _____ in the other state and will have to maintain a _____ in that state. The purpose of this requirement is to protect residents of the state so that a state court can obtain jurisdiction over the corporation.

6. If a foreign corporation has complied with statutes relating to qualifying to do business and has received a _____ from the appropriate state official, the corporation is empowered to do anything that a domestic corporation may do and those things that the corporation is authorized to do in the state of its incorporation.

7. A corporation that has complied with all statutory requirements relating to incorporation is considered to be a _____ corporation. A _____ corporation is one, which believed that it was properly organized, but whose organization was defective. Normally, the existence of such a corporation may be challenged only by _____.

8. _____ powers are those possessed by all corporations formed within a particular state. Examples of such powers would be _____
    _____
    _____
    _____
    _____.

9. Corporations are empowered by corporation statutes to purchase real property, but if a corporation is not organized for the purpose of purchasing and selling real estate, the corporation commits an _____ act if it buys land purely for speculative purposes. In most states today, however, the corporation _____ the defense that it lacked the power or capacity to make such a purchase in a lawsuit brought by the seller of the land for the unpaid purchase price.

10. Corporations obtain funds for their operations by issuing equity securities, or _____, and debt securities, such as _____ _____, and by retaining some of their corporate earnings and profits rather than distributing such earnings and profits in the form of _____ to shareholders.

11. Debt securities include _____ which are secured by liens or other security interests in the assets of a corporation and _____ which are backed only by the general credit of a borrowing corporation.

12. Preferred stock refers to shares having some measure of preference in respect to priority rights associated with _____ or _____ _____ or, in some instances, voting.

MULTIPLE CHOICE QUESTIONS

1. The United States Supreme Court has ruled that the protection afforded by the Fourth Amendment to the U.S. Constitution against unreasonable searches and seizures and by the Fifth Amendment against double jeopardy extends to:
   A. natural persons.
   B. corporate officers and employees.
   C. corporations.
   D. All of the answers above are correct.

2. The United States Supreme Court has ruled that the privilege against self-incrimination which is protected by the Fifth Amendment may be invoked by:
   A. natural persons.
   B. the Internal Revenue Service.
   C. corporations and other legal entities.
   D. All of the answers above are correct.

3. The Federal Organizational Corporate Sentencing Guidelines prescribe specific sentences for "white-collar crimes" committed by corporate personnel. The penalties for corporate offenses under these guidelines depend upon:
   A. whether or not the company has established and enforced written crime-prevention standards and procedures that apply to all employees.
   B. whether or not the company has taken substantial steps to prevent, investigate, and punish wrongdoing internally.
   C. the seriousness of the offense, the amount of money involved, and the extent to which the company's executives were involved.
   D. whether or not the company cooperates with the government.
   E. All of the answers above are correct.

4. The concept of double taxation means that:
   A. the federal and state governments tax both the salaries of corporate officers and any dividends that have been paid to them.
   B. the federal and state governments tax both corporate earnings and dividends that are paid to corporate shareholders.
   C. the tax rate for corporations is double that for individuals.
   D. taxes are imposed upon corporations by both the federal and state governments.

5. A California corporation sells goods to residents of Illinois by mail but has no employees or offices in Illinois.
   A. The California corporation is required to register or qualify as a foreign corporation in Illinois.

B. The California corporation will **not** be able to sue an Illinois resident in Illinois if the resident fails to pay for merchandise purchased from the California corporation.

C. The California corporation will be required to qualify to do business in Illinois if the corporation establishes a shipping office in Chicago where it employs 40 people and solicits and enters into contracts from that office.

D. An Illinois resident who has been injured by merchandise purchased from the California corporation can sue the corporation in Illinois by serving the corporation with a complaint in California.

6. The certificate of incorporation of the Green and Red Corp., a New York corporation, states that the corporation is formed for the purpose of manufacturing Christmas decorations in Rhode Island where the corporation maintains a plant and office.
   A. The corporation must qualify to do business in New York.
   B. The corporation must qualify to do business in Rhode Island.
   C. The corporation must qualify to do business in Utah if the corporation sends a traveling salesperson to Utah in order to solicit orders.
   D. The corporation must qualify to do business in Delaware if the corporation maintains a transfer agent there.
   E. All of the answers above are correct.

7. Piper, the promoter of the Atlas Corporation, made a contract (for and on behalf of the Atlas Corporation) with World Copy, Inc. for the purchase of a copying machine. Piper failed to disclose that the corporation had **not** been created. Thereafter, the corporation was duly organized.
   A. Piper will **not** be liable on the contract if Atlas Corporation (after coming into existence) rejects the contract.
   B. Piper will **not** be liable on the contract if Atlas Corporation (after coming into existence) adopts the contract.
   C. Piper will **not** be liable on the contract if Atlas Corporation, World Copy, Inc., and Piper enter into a novation regarding the contract.
   D. Piper will **not** be liable on the contract if Atlas Corporation was improperly organized.

8. A written subscription that is signed by a subscriber to purchase shares of stock in a corporation to be formed in a state that has adopted the Revised Model Business Corporation Act, is:
   A. unenforceable by the corporation when the corporation comes into existence.
   B. revocable until the corporation comes into existence.
   C. irrevocable for six months after the corporation comes into existence.
   D. irrevocable for six months after the subscription is signed by the subscriber.

9. Martin has determined that there is a large market for copper widgets. She, therefore, engaged in promotion activities for the purpose of organizing the Winking Widget Co. Before filing articles of incorporation, she ordered a large quantity of copper from Koper Co. and leased office space in the name of the corporation. The copper was shipped to and used by Winking Widget Co. after its organization, but payment for the copper has not been made. If, at the first meeting of the board of directors, the board:

A. refused to accept the contract with Koper Co., the corporation will be required to pay for the copper.

B. declined to accept the lease of office space, the corporation will be liable for breach of contract.

C. accepted all the subscriptions for stock that Martin had obtained, the corporation may later revoke some of its acceptances.

D. refused to accept some of the subscriptions that Martin had obtained, the corporation will be obligated to all the subscribers.

10. Under the Model Business Corporation Act and the Revised Model Business Corporation Act, incorporators must:
    A. be natural persons.
    B. be residents of the state of incorporation.
    C. subscribe to at least one share of stock.
    D. None of the answers above is correct.

11. U, V, and W did business as Z Corporation but made no effort to incorporate. They never filed any documents with any state official. Arcus entered into a contract with Z Corporation to supply stationery to the corporation but did not know that Z Corporation had not been formally incorporated. U, V, and W breached the contract with Arcus by failing to pay for the stationery. Arcus is now suing Z Corporation and U, V, and W jointly.
    A. U, V, and W are liable to Arcus as general partners unless they are estopped from denying the existence of Z Corporation.
    B. Z Corporation is a *de facto* corporation and, therefore, Arcus cannot dispute its existence.
    C. U, V, and W are liable to Arcus because the Z Corporation is a *de jure* corporation.
    D. U, V, and W are liable to Arcus because they are principals with relation to each other.

12. A, B, and C represented to F that they are shareholders and directors of a corporation and persuade F to purchase stock in the corporation. There is, in fact, no corporation but A, B, and C have been engaging in a business together. A, B, and C manage the business. F does **not** participate in any way in running the business.
    A. F will **not** be liable to a third party on a contract entered into by B in the name of the corporation.
    B. A, B, and C will be estopped to deny the existence of the corporation.
    C. A third party, with whom the purported corporation contracted, will be estopped to deny the corporate existence because, when the third party contracted with the "association," the third party's expectation was that only the corporation would have liability.
    D. All of the answers above are correct.

13. The articles of incorporation of the Careful Chew Corporation state that the corporation is formed for the purpose of manufacturing chewing gum. Even if there is no express authorization in the articles of incorporation to do so, the corporation has the implied power to:
    A. purchase gum base, sugar, and artificial flavoring.

B. purchase 50 acres of land that the board of directors, in good faith, believes will triple in value in one year.

C. manufacture razor blades.

D. purchase and use a factory in a state in which the corporation is **not** incorporated without qualifying to do business in that state.

14. Jones paid $900 for a document that provided that ten years from the date of its issue the ABC Corporation promised to pay the holder $1,000 and until that date the corporation promised to pay the holder $40 on the first day of every March and September.

A. Jones is a shareholder of the ABC Corporation.

B. Jones has purchased a bond at a discount.

C. Jones has a right to cumulative dividends.

D. Jones has the right to vote at the annual shareholders' meeting.

Questions 15, 16, and 17 are based on the following fact situation: A corporation has issued 20,000 shares of common stock and 10,000 shares of nonparticipating, nonconvertible, redeemable, cumulative preferred stock.

15. Which of the following statements is correct?

A. A preferred shareholder has a right to exchange his or her shares of preferred stock for common stock.

B. A shareholder holding common stock has a right to exchange his or her shares for preferred stock.

C. The corporation has the right to purchase, reacquire, and cancel the preferred shares at a specified price.

d. The corporation has the right to purchase and reacquire the preferred shares at a specified price and to reissue the shares.

16. An owner of:

A. common stock is entitled to vote at the annual meeting of the shareholders.

B. common stock is entitled to receive a pro rata share of dividends before payment of dividends to preferred shareholders.

C. either common or preferred stock is entitled to vote at the annual meeting of the shareholders even though this right is **not** indicated on his or her share certificate.

D. preferred stock has a right to share in the distribution of additional dividends after payment of dividends to common shareholders.

17. If the corporation is dissolved and all taxes and other obligations are paid:

A. the preferred shareholders must be paid the face amount of their respective shares before any distribution is made to common stock shareholders.

B. each preferred and common shareholder shares pro rata in the distribution of remaining assets.

C. the common shareholders must be paid the face amount of their respective shares before any distribution is made to the preferred shareholders.

D. only the common shareholders share in the distribution of the corporate assets.

Chapter 41
Corporations: Directors, Officers, and Shareholders

In a corporation, the overall managerial responsibility rests with the board of directors that is elected by the shareholders. The actual operation of a corporation is conducted by officers (who are elected or appointed and supervised by the board) and other managers, agents, and employees. The rights and duties of directors and officers and their potential liability to the corporation are discussed in the first part of this chapter.

Ultimately, the risks and benefits of incorporation inure to the shareholders, the investors who provide the funds that initially finance the corporate operations. As a rule, after shareholders participate at the meetings at which the board of directors is elected, the shareholders exercise no control over policies adopted by the corporation. The rights and liabilities of shareholders are treated in the last two sections of the chapter.

THINGS TO KEEP IN MIND

1.   In theory, a corporation is owned by and for the benefit of its shareholders. Managerial policies, however, are determined by the board of directors elected by the shareholders. Normally, the actual operations of a corporation are conducted by officers who are appointed and supervised by the directors.

2.   Directors and officers are fiduciaries and have obligations to act in good faith with care, honesty, and loyalty in the best interests of their corporation. The trend has been to expand the nature and the extent of directors' and officers' responsibilities to the corporation.

OUTLINE

I.   Role of directors.

    A. Directors manage the corporation and establish general policies and the scope of the business within the purposes and powers stated in the corporation's articles of incorporation and bylaws [Revised Model Business Corporation Act (hereinafter RMBCA) 8.01].

        1. The directors must act convened as a board. (Directors act collectively for and on behalf of the corporation; an individual director, therefore, cannot act as an agent in order to bind the corporation.)

2. Directors are fiduciaries because their relationship with the corporation is one that is based upon trust and confidence. Directors are similar to trustees because directors occupy positions of trust and control over the corporation, but, unlike trustees, the directors do not own or hold title to property for the use and benefits of others.

3. There are few statutory requirements for qualification as a director [RMBCA 8.02].

B. Election of directors.

1. The number of directors is specified in the charter or bylaws; in some states, the minimum is one and, if there are fewer than 50 shareholders, there need not be a board of directors [RMBCA 8.01 and 8.03].

2. The initial board of directors is named in the charter or elected by the incorporators, and subsequent directors are elected by the shareholders [RMBCA 2.05 and 8.05].

3. The term of a director is usually one year but may be longer; directors may be divided into classes with staggered terms [RMBCA 8.06].

4. Provisions in the charter and/or the corporation statute determine the method of filling vacancies [RMBCA 8.10].

5. Shareholders have the power to remove directors, with or without cause, in accordance with the charter or bylaws. Directors may have power to remove a director for cause [RMBCA 8.08].

C. Board of directors' meetings [RMBCA 8.20 through 8.24].

1. The board acts as a body at a meeting; provisions are made in the state statutes for signed written unanimous consent in lieu of meetings and for directors' participation at meetings through conference telephone communications [RMBCA 8.20 and 8.21].

2. Regular meetings are provided for in bylaws or articles; notice of a regular meeting is not necessary [RMBCA 8.22].

3. Special meeting may be called, but usually notice is required.

4. Quorum requirements vary from state to state; usually, a quorum is a majority and is specified in the bylaws [RMBCA 8.24].

5. Ordinarily, a majority vote is necessary for board action.

D. Rights of directors.

1. Participation and inspection.

  a. In order to function properly as a director, a director has the responsibility and right to participate in meetings of the board of directors.

  b. Directors have the necessary right to inspect books and records of the corporation.

 2. Compensation and indemnification.

  a. Compensation of directors may be fixed and, ordinarily, is specified in the corporate articles of incorporation or the bylaws; the articles or bylaws may provide that directors' compensation be fixed by the board. (If there is no express provision or an agreement providing for directors' compensation, directors serve without compensation.) [RMBCA 8.11].

  b. Today, a director has the right to be indemnified for judgments, fines, costs, etc., incurred in corporate related criminal or civil actions, other than actions brought by or on behalf of the corporation (even if the director is not absolved of liability), as long as the director's acts were done in good faith and based upon a reasonable belief that the acts were in the best interests of the corporation [RMBCA 8.50 through 8.58].

  c. Corporations may purchase liability insurance to cover indemnification of directors and officers.

 E. Directors' management responsibilities — Corporate powers are exercised by the board of directors which makes policy decisions related to the management of corporate affairs [RMBCA 8.20]. The board of directors:

 1. Makes policy decisions concerning the scope of the corporation's business, oversees major contract (including labor-management) negotiations, and initiates major changes in corporate structure, finance, etc.

 2. Appoints, supervises, and removes officers and other managerial employees, and fixes their compensation.

 3. Makes financial decisions including declarations of dividends.

 4. Functions relating to ordinary, interim managerial decisions may be delegated to an executive committee [RMBCA 8.25].

II. Role of corporate officers and executives [RMBCA 8.40].

 A. Normally, functions relating to daily operations are delegated to officers who act as agents in carrying out transactions on behalf of the corporation and who owe duties to the corporation. [See Chapters 33 and 34.]

 B. Usually, officers include a president, one or more vice presidents, a secretary, and a treasurer; officers are selected and may be removed by the board of directors [RMBCA 8.43].

C. In most states, one person can hold more than one office; officers also may be members of the board of directors.

III. Duties of directors and officers [RMBCA 8.30, 8.41, and 8.42].

A. Corporate officers and managers deal with third persons as agents of and on behalf of the corporation [RMBCA 8.40 and 8.41]. — Agency law applies. [See Chapters 33 and 34.]

   1. The authority of officers, other agents, and employees may be express (in the charter, bylaws, or resolutions of the board of directors) or implied (customary and incidental power of such officers) actual authority, or apparent authority (because the corporation holds out that its officers have the usual power of similar officers of other corporations); in addition, the board may ratify unauthorized acts of its officers.

   2. Officers have fiduciary duties similar to those of directors. [Standards of conduct for officers are set forth in RMBCA 8.42.]

B. Because directors and officers are considered to be agents of the corporation, they owed duties of exercising care and fiduciary duties to the corporation.

   1. Duty of care.

      a. Directors and officers must exercise the same degree of care that reasonably prudent people in similar positions use in conducting business affairs and must carry out their responsibilities in an informed, businesslike manner.

      b. Duty to make informed and reasonable decisions — Directors may make decisions based upon information furnished by competent officers, employees, professionals, or an executive committee of the board even if the information turns out to be inaccurate, incomplete, faulty, or even false [RMBCA 8.30(a)(3)].

      c. Duty to exercise reasonable supervision — Directors may be liable for negligence or mismanagement if the directors fail to supervise officers and employees to whom the directors have delegated work; officers also are expected to exercise reasonable care in supervising corporate personnel.

      d. Dissenting directors — Directors are expected to be informed and attend meetings.
         1) If a director is present at a meeting, a director is presumed to assent to action taken, unless the director files a written dissent or has his or her dissent entered in the minutes.
         2) A director having a personal interest in a matter being considered by the board should not vote on the matter.

2. Duty of loyalty.

    a. Directors should not use corporate funds or confidential information in order to secure personal advantages and must fully disclose corporate opportunities and possible conflicts of interest in transactions involving the directors and the corporation. [RMBCA 8.31 and proposed substitute Subchapter F composed of 8.60 through 8.63.]

    b. Cases have dealt with directors and officers:
       1) Competing with the corporation or usurping a corporate opportunity.
       2) Having (or failing to disclose) an interest that conflicts with an interest of the corporation.
       3) Engaging in insider trading in buying or selling shares by using confidential information that the directors or officers possess because of their positions. [See Chapter 43 regarding liability to shareholder to whom they sold or from whom the directors or officers purchased stock and other potential liability under the securities laws.]
       4) Authorizing a corporate transaction that is detrimental to minority shareholders.
       5) Selling control over the corporation.

3. Conflicts of interest — Directors may serve on boards of more than one corporation but must disclose any potential conflicts of interest that might arise in a corporate transaction.

    a. Contracts between director and corporation.
       1) A director (or officer) must fully disclose any personal material interest in a corporate transaction and must abstain from voting on the proposed contract or transaction.
       2) A contract will be valid and enforceable if the contract was fair and reasonable to the corporation at the time the contract was made, there was full disclosure of the director's or officer's interest, and the contract was approved by a majority of the disinterested directors or shareholders.

    b. Contracts between corporations having common directors.
       1) Contracts between corporations having one or more common directors are closely scrutinized by the courts.
       2) Section 8 of the Clayton Antitrust Act [discussed in Chapter 47] prohibits interlocking directorates if one of the corporations has capital surplus and undivided profits of more than specified threshold amounts.

IV. Liability of directors and officers.

    A. Directors and officers are liable to the corporation for breaches of duties that are owed to the corporation. — The corporation may sue in its own name or a derivative suit may be brought by a shareholder or a representative, such as a trustee in bankruptcy, on behalf of the corporation.

B. The business judgment rule.

   1. Directors, officers, and other agents normally are not liable for poor business judgment or honest mistakes if the directors, officers, or agents act in good faith in what the directors, officers, or agents consider to be the best interests of the corporation and with the care that an ordinarily prudent person would exercise under similar circumstances.

   2. The directors and officers are not insurers of business success.

C. Liability for torts and crimes. — See also Chapters 6, 7, 8, 10, 34, and 40.

   1. Corporate directors, officers, and other agents can be held liable personally for torts and crimes of the corporation or its employees (when they act within the scope of their employment) if the directors, officers, or agents participate in, direct, or permit the commission of the torts or crimes, or if, because they are negligent, they fail to supervise employees properly.

   2. Supervision and the "responsible person" doctrine — Criminal liability may be imposed upon a corporate officer who is in a responsible relationship to a corporation and has the power to prevent the commission of illegal acts without regard to whether or not the officer has knowledge of the criminal violations.

   3. Pervasiveness of control — A corporate officer or director whose control over corporate operations is "so pervasive and total that the officer or director is in fact the corporation" may be liable for crimes committed by the corporation.

V. The role of shareholders.

A. Shareholders' powers — Shareholders have limited power.

   1. The shareholders' approval is necessary in order to make fundamental changes affecting the corporation, such as amending the charter, merging with another corporation, or dissolving the corporation.

   2. The shareholders have power to elect and remove members of the board of directors for cause.

   3. The shareholders do not participate in the management of the corporation.

B. Shareholders' meetings.

   1. An annual meeting of the shareholders is held on the date and at the place fixed in the bylaws [RMBCA 7.01]; special meetings may be called [RMBCA 7.02].

2. Notice of meetings — Written notice must be given within the specified statutory periods of time, but may be waived [RMBCA 7.05].

3. Conduct of meetings — Usually, the corporate president or chairperson of the board of directors presides, and the secretary records the minutes.

4. Proxies.

    a. Proxy voting is regulated by Section 7.22 of the RMBCA, Section 14(a) of the Securities Exchange Act of 1934, and Securities and Exchange Commission (SEC) Rule 14a-8.

    b. Shareholders may vote in person or by proxy.

    c. A proxy is a written, revocable authorization to an agent to cast the vote of the shareholder and typically is solicited by management.

    d. A proxy generally is effective for eleven months under state law.

5. Proxy material and shareholder proposals — Persons who solicit proxies from shareholders for voting at meetings must make full and accurate disclosures of facts relating to matters that are to be voted on at shareholders' meetings.

    a. A shareholder who owns at least $1,000 worth of stock may submit proposals for inclusion in proxy material [SEC Rule 14a-8].

    b. Proposals dealing with significant policy issues must be included in proxy material, but proposals relating to "ordinary business operations" may be excluded.

C. Shareholder voting.

1. Quorum requirements — A quorum (minimum number of shares that must be represented at a meeting) is fixed in the charter and usually is a majority of issued outstanding shares.

2. Unless otherwise specified by statute or the charter [RMBCA 7.21], the usual vote required for shareholder action:

    a. Election of members of the board of directors — Plurality of those shares represented at meeting.

    b Other non-extraordinary matters — Majority of those shares represented at meeting.

    c Extraordinary matters.
        1) Statute or charter may require a specified proportion of all shares.
        2) Usually, a greater than majority vote is required.

3. Voting lists — List of record owners of shares as of a cutoff date is prepared by corporation [RMBCA 7.07 and 7.20].

4. Voting methods.

   a. Straight voting — One vote per share standing in the name of a record holder.

   b. Cumulative voting for election directors.
      1) May be provided for in the corporate charter [RMBCA 7.28].
      2) In some states, cumulative voting is mandatory.
      3) A shareholder's vote is equal to the number of shares which the shareholder owns multiplied by the number of directors to be elected and may be cast for one or more nominees for directors (i.e., the votes may be distributed among more than one nominee).

   c. Other voting techniques (other methods that may be provided for regarding shareholders' voting).
      1) Shareholders' voting agreements — Shareholders may enter into voting agreements to pool votes by casting their votes in a prescribed manner [RMBCA 7.31].
      2) Voting trusts — Legal title to shares is transferred to a trustee who then votes the shares for the benefit of shareholders; shareholders retain the rights to receive dividends and to receive voting trust certificates [RMBCA 7.30].

5. Normally, common and preferred shareholders have the right to vote unless denied in the charter [RMBCA 7.21].

   a. Often, preferred shareholders are denied the right to vote.

   b. Treasury shares cannot be voted.

VI. Rights of shareholders.

   A. Stock certificates — A shareholder has the right to receive a stock certificate, which is a document issued by a corporation that evidences ownership of a specified number of shares in the corporation [RMBCA 6.25].

   1. Stock is intangible personal property.

   2. A shareholder has the right to have his or her ownership interest recorded in the stock record books; today, many corporations have computerized these records.

   3. If the corporation issues certificated shares, an owner has the right to receive a stock certificate that states the number of fully paid and nonassessable shares which the shareholder owns.

4. In many states, uncertificated shares of stock may be issued, in which case the corporation sends the owner a transaction memorandum containing the same information that is required to be included on a stock certificate [RMBCA 6.26]. (See also Uniform Commercial Code (UCC) 8-408.)

5. A shareholder whose ownership interest is recorded has rights to receive:

   a. Notice of meetings and participate in meetings.

   b. Dividends when declared and to participate in distribution of assets upon dissolution.

   c. Operational and financial reports and a new stock certificate in accordance with UCC 8-405 if the shareholder's certificate is lost or stolen.

B. Preemptive rights.

1. Preemptive rights are the rights of current shareholders to purchase or subscribe to newly-issued stock in proportion to the amount of stock currently owned before the stock is offered to the public in order to preserve the prior relative power of each shareholder.

2. The state statutes vary.

   a. Right is denied unless provided for in charter [RMBCA 6.30].

   b Right is granted unless denied in charter, but does not apply to certain issues [MBCA Alternate Section 26].

C. Stock warrants — Stock warrants are issued to the shareholders of record so that these shareholders can purchase the shares in accordance with their preemptive rights.

D. Dividends [RMBCA 6.40].

1. Dividends are distributions of cash or other property (including shares of stock in the corporation or in other corporation in which the corporation owns stock) to shareholders in proportion to the shareholders' respective number of shares or interests in the corporation.

2. Dividends are payable to record holders on a specified record date.

3. Shareholders do not have rights to dividends (distributions of profits) until the dividends are declared by the board of directors.

   a. Cash dividends — Cash dividends are corporate debts and cannot be rescinded after the dividends are declared.

b. Stock dividends — Stock dividends may be revoked before the dividends actually are issued to shareholders.

4. Statutes impose restrictions on issuance of dividends which will result in the corporation's insolvency or in impairment of the corporation's capital.

   a. Dividends may be paid only out of legally available funds of a corporation in accordance with state law.

   b. Statutory prescribed sources:
      1) Retained earnings — All states allow dividends to be paid out of undistributed net earned profits (earned surplus or retained earnings), including capital gains from the sale of fixed assets.
      2) Net profits — A few states allow dividends to be paid from current net profits without regard to prior deficits.
      3) Surplus — Some states permit payment of dividends out of any kind of surplus.

5. Illegal dividends.

   a. Dividends cannot be declared if the result will be the insolvency of the corporation or the impairment of the corporation's capital.

   b. Shareholders must return illegal dividends only if the shareholders knew that the dividends were illegal when the dividends were received.

   c. Directors may be liable to the corporation for improper issuance of dividends, especially if the directors acted in bad faith.

   d. Directors must act diligently, prudently, and in good faith and may be civilly and criminally liable for improperly or illegally declaring dividends.

6. Directors' failure to declare a dividend — Ordinarily, directors are not required to declare dividends, unless the director's refusal to do so is an abuse of discretion.

E. Inspection rights [RMBCA 16.02 and 16.03].

1. A shareholder has a right to obtain information and may examine and copy relevant books, records, and minutes for proper purposes in person or by an agent, attorney, etc.

2. A shareholder for more than six months or a holder of more than five percent of the outstanding shares may so inspect.

3. Written demand stating the purpose must be given and the shareholder must act in good faith and for a proper purpose.

F. Transfer of shares. — Shareholders have the right to transfer shares of stock in the corporation. [See UCC Article 8.]

    1. Usually, a stock certificate is transferred by negotiation.

        a. A negotiation is a physical delivery and indorsement on the certificate itself so that a good faith purchaser for value is the owner of the shares represented by the certificate free of adverse claims and is entitled to be registered as a shareholder and to receive a new certificate.

        b Until the corporation is notified of the transfer, the corporation recognizes the holder of record (the transferor) as the person entitled to all shareholder rights.

    2. Restrictions on transferability are enforceable if noted on the certificate. Such limitations are usually provided for in the case of a small closely-held corporation in order to maintain ownership within the group.

        a. The rights of first refusal — Shares being offered for resale must first be offered to the corporation or the other shareholders.

        b. The consent of a specified group of people may be necessary in order to transfer shares.

    3. Article 8 of the UCC provides for transfers of uncertificated securities.

    4. When shares (in certificated or uncertificated form) are transferred, an entry is made in the corporate stock book. [See above at VI. A. 2.]

G. Rights on dissolution. [See also Chapter 42.]

    1. Some classes of shareholders may have priority when assets of the corporation are distributed upon liquidation of the corporation. [See Chapter 40 at VII C.]

    2. Shareholders have certain rights upon dissolution or an extraordinary change in the corporation. [See Chapter 42.]

H. Shareholder's derivative suit — A shareholder may bring an action on behalf of the corporation against another person (such as a corporate officer or director) in order to enforce a claim, which the shareholder believes the corporation has against the other person and, therefore, to redress a wrong incurred by the corporation.

VII. Liability of shareholders — Usually, shareholders are not personally liable to creditors of the corporation; liability may, however, be imposed upon shareholders in the following situations:

A. In cases involving fraud, undercapitalization, or careless observation of corporate formalities, a court may "pierce the corporate veil" and hold shareholders liable. [See Chapter 40 at VII.]

B. A shareholder is liable for illegally or improperly paid dividends if the shareholder had knowledge that payment was improper. [See above at VI. D.]

C. Stock-subscription agreement — A shareholder is liable for any unpaid stock subscriptions.

D. Watered stock — A shareholder may be liable if shares of stock are issued in exchange for less than full consideration.

   1. Shares of stock may be issued for money, property, or services actually performed [MBCA 19 and RMBCA 6.21].

   2. The RMBCA provides that the consideration for shares may also be promissory notes, contracts for services to be performed, or other securities of the corporation [RMBCA 6.21].

   3. Directors are liable for an improper stock issue (watered stock) if the directors overvalue the consideration (property or services) received by the corporation for shares; shareholders also may be liable to the corporation and ultimately to creditors of the corporation.

   4. Many states have requirements that:

      a. Par-value shares cannot be issued for less than par value (except in states whose statutes permit bonus or discount issues).

      b. No-par shares cannot be issued for less than the consideration fixed by the board of directors or the shareholders (if the shareholders are so empowered by the corporation's charter).

   5. When shares are issued for less than their stated values, the shares may be referred to as watered stock.

      a. The directors may be liable for the improper issue; and

      b. The shareholder may be liable for the difference between the consideration the shareholder gave for the stock and the par value or stated value of no-par shares.

   6. A shareholder who gave no consideration or gave overvalued consideration or gave consideration that did not satisfy the statutory requirements for the shares may be liable, because of the watered stock, to the corporation (which received assets that were overvalued) and to creditors of the corporation in some states.

VIII. Duties of majority shareholder — In some cases, a majority shareholder is treated as owing fiduciary duties to the corporation and minority shareholders.

KEY WORDS AND PHRASES IN TEXT

the role of directors and officers
directors and officers as fiduciaries
directors' election and terms of office
board of directors' meetings
quorum
directors' rights of participation, inspection,
     compensation, and indemnification
directors' management responsibilities
dissenting directors
corporate officers and executives
duties of directors and officers
duties of care and loyalty
directors' conflicts of interests
liability of directors and officers
business judgment rule
supervision and the responsible
     person doctrine
pervasiveness of control
the role of shareholders
shareholders' meetings
proxy
contents of proxy materials
shareholder voting

voting lists
cumulative voting
voting agreements and voting trusts
rights of shareholders
stock certificate
uncertificated shares of stock
preemptive rights
treasury shares
stock warrant
dividend
illegal (improper) dividend
directors' failure to declare dividend
inspection rights of shareholders
right of shareholder to transfer shares
right of first refusal
rights of shareholders on dissolution
shareholder's derivative suit
liability of shareholders
stock-subscription agreement
liability for unpaid stock subscription
watered stock
par-value shares and no-par shares
duties of a majority shareholder

FILL-IN QUESTIONS

1. Directors are not necessarily agents of a corporation, but are fiduciaries and as a result owe certain duties relating to trust and loyalty to the _____.

2. The directors of a corporation establish general policy for the corporation. In order to participate in meetings at which the board takes action, a director has a right to _____. Action taken by the board of directors must be taken by the _____ convened as a board.

3. A director is not liable to the corporation for action taken by the board of directors if the director's _____ or _____. In addition, a director is not liable for losses caused by honest mistakes or _____. A director may have a right of _____ for costs, expenses, and judgments incurred as a result of defending in a lawsuit in an action relating to the corporation when the action is not brought by the corporation or on behalf of the corporation.

4. Although a corporation may not be found guilty of a particular crime, the corporate officers who knowingly commit criminal acts in pursuit of personal gain may be criminally liable because of the " _____ " doctrine.

5. Under the " _____ " doctrine, a corporate officer may be held liable as an employer if the control that the officer exercises over the workplace and corporate operations is so _____ that the officer, in effect, is more than merely an agent of the corporation.

6. A voting trustee is given _____ title to the shares of shareholders who are participating in a voting trust. The shareholders are considered to be the owners of the _____ interests in the shares.

7. The _____ but not the _____ may vote by proxy at their respective meetings.

8. In general, shareholders of a corporation are not liable for corporate indebtedness. They are, however, liable to creditors for the amounts of _____
_____
_____
_____ .

9. Payment for stock subscriptions may be made in money, _____ , or
_____ .

10. Shareholders' _____ refer to the right to subscribe to newly issued stock in a corporation in proportion to the amount of stock currently owned before it is offered to the public.

MULTIPLE CHOICE QUESTIONS

1. Gleason was the president and a director of the M Company, a manufacturing corporation. Gleason learned that the corporation probably could obtain adequate, inexpensive electric power in the town of Electra, located near a nuclear power plant that was due to be completed and operational in two years. Gleason represented this information to the board of directors and recommended moving the corporation's operations to Electra. The board agreed, and a new factory was constructed in Electra. Before operations were begun, the Electra Power Co., a public utility, advised M Company that Electra Power Co. would be unable to provide electricity to the factory because its plant was denied a license to begin its operations by the Nuclear Regulatory Commission. As a result, the corporation has sustained a considerable loss.
   A. Because Gleason was a director of the corporation, Gleason could **not** also serve as an officer.
   B. Gleason owed a fiduciary duty to the corporation. Gleason breached this duty when he recommended the move.
   C. The directors are liable to the shareholders for the loss.
   D. Gleason is **not** liable for any loss sustained by the corporation.

2. An officer of a corporation may be held liable personally by a court:
   A. for the torts and crimes committed by personnel under the officer's direct supervision.
   B. for the wrongful actions that were committed by corporate employees at the officer's direction or with the officer's permission.
   C. when the officer either failed to supervise corporate employees adequately or exercised extensive control over corporate affairs.
   D. All of the answers above are correct.

3. Which of the following acts is a crime?
   A. Telling your brother to invest in the company of which you are a vice president because you know that the company is developing a "dynamite" new video game.
   B. Jonah Jones, the CEO of company C, tells his secretary, Smith, to shoot the president of company D because company D produces better products.
   C. Janet Jones, a CEO, knows that the firm's treasurer, who also is her husband, has been diverting funds to their personal Swiss bank account but ignores his activities.
   D. All of the answers above are correct.

4. If a crime for which the statutory penalty is payment of a fine has been committed in the corporation's name by an officer of a corporation, the state may prosecute:

	the corporation.	the corporate officer.
A.	Yes	Yes
B.	Yes	No
C.	No	Yes
D.	No	No

5. On March 2, an explosion and fire destroyed the Rubber Products Co. plant. The corporation promptly filed an insurance claim with its insurer. On April 15, the corporation, the president, and two other people were charged with arson (the intentional burning of any structure, punishable by imprisonment for up to 50 years) in connection with the March 2 fire. It was alleged and later proven that the president of the corporation paid $50,000 out of corporate funds to an "arson squad" that started the fire. Which of the following statements is **false**?
   A. The corporation can escape criminal liability for the fire.
   B. The president is liable for breach of duties owed to the shareholders of the corporation.
   C. The shareholders may bring a derivative action against the president for the *ultra vires* act.
   D. The defense of *ultra vires* cannot be raised in a lawsuit instituted by the corporation against the insurer that refused to pay the claim.

6. The shareholders of the Unispol Corp. are to elect five directors at the shareholders' meeting. If there is cumulative voting, a shareholder with 100 shares may cast a maximum of:
   A. five votes for one person.
   B. 100 votes for one nominee.

C. 500 votes for one person.

D. 500 votes for one nominee and 500 in connection with other matters that are voted on at the meeting.

7. At a meeting of shareholders of a corporation:

A. in order to amend the articles of incorporation, notice of the meeting must be given to the shareholders, and a majority of the shareholders present must approve the amendment.

B. shares of a deceased shareholder may be voted only if the shares are transferred to and registered in the name of the representative of the decedent.

C. shareholders have the right to elect directors and to vote on any other business that may properly come before the meeting by cumulative voting.

D. a shareholder may vote by proxy only if the shareholder gives an irrevocable proxy.

8. The following is prohibited by statute:

A. A voting pool.

B. A voting trust.

C. The sale of a proxy.

D. The sale of property by a shareholder to the corporation in which the shareholder owns stock.

9. MNO Co. is incorporated in a state that has adopted the Revised Model Business Corporation Act. MNO Co. has a board of directors composed of nine people. The corporate articles of incorporation and the bylaws contain no provisions relating to quorum requirements for meetings of the board of directors or the conduct of such meetings. The charter provides for cumulative voting by shareholders. Six members of the board of directors attended a meeting that had been called after due notice to ratify an important contract. Prior to the annual shareholders' meeting, P, a holder of 200 shares, gave A a proxy to vote her shares.

A. The board can ratify the contract by a vote of four to two.

B. The board can unanimously ratify the contract if two directors leave the meeting before the board acts on the contract.

C. A may **not** cast 1,800 votes for a single director.

D. A may vote P's shares if, on the day before the meeting, P gives her proxy to Z.

10. Shares of stock may be issued without par value for such consideration as may be fixed by:

A. a corporation's board of directors.

B. a corporation's officers.

C. the bylaws of the corporation.

D. the statutes of the state of incorporation.

11. The Sell Wrong Corp. issued 1,000 shares of its $10 par value common stock to Rite, its vice president, for a price of $10,000. In consideration for the stock, Rite gave the corporation $1,000 in cash, a promissory note for $2,000, canceled the $4,000 salary that was owed to him for services rendered to the corporation in the past month, and promised to render $3,000 worth of services in the following month.

If the Sell Wrong Corp. was incorporated in a state that has **not** adopted the Revised Model Business Corporation Act, Rite's shares are:
A. paid in full.
B. 70% paid for.
C. 50% paid for.
D. completely unpaid for.

12. The Bell Wring Corp. issued 1,000 shares of its $10 par value common stock to Lite, its vice president, for a price of $10,000. In consideration for the stock, Lite gave the corporation $1,000 in cash, a promissory note for $2,000, canceled the $4,000 salary that was owed to him for services rendered to the corporation in the past month, and promised to render $3,000 worth of services in the following month. If the Bell Wring Corp. was incorporated in a state that has adopted the Revised Model Business Corporation Act, Lite's shares are:
A. paid in full.
B. 70% paid for.
C. 50% paid for.
D. completely unpaid for.

13. An owner of common stock in a corporation that is incorporated in a state in which the Model Business Corporation Act has been adopted will **not** have liability beyond the shareholder's actual investment, even though the shareholder:
A. purchased treasury shares for less than par value.
B. paid less than par value for stock purchased in connection with an original issue of shares.
C. failed to pay the full amount owed on a subscription contract.
D. was the sole shareholder and treated the corporation as a personally owned proprietorship.

14. DEF Corporation is authorized to issue 1,000 shares of $10 par-value common stock and 1,000 shares of no par preferred stock. DEF Corporation has issued 1,200 shares of the common stock and 300 shares of the preferred stock at $10 per share. The Uniform Commercial Code (Section 8-104) provides that:
A. the recipients of the 200 shares representing an overissue are entitled to receive 200 shares of the preferred stock.
B. the recipients of the 200 shares representing an overissue are entitled to the same rights of shareholders as the recipients of the 1,000 shares of properly issued common shares.
C. with regard to the preferred stock, stated capital would only include the 300 authorized and issued shares.
D. the preferred shares are considered to be a form of debt security.

15. A dividend that has been declared by a corporation, but not actually been distributed, may be revoked by the corporation if the dividend is:
A. a cash dividend.
B. a stock dividend.
C. a liquidating dividend.
D. All of the answers above are correct.

Chapter 42
Corporations:
Merger, Consolidation, and Termination

As discussed in this chapter, a corporation making a fundamental change in its structure or the nature of the corporation's business or terminating its existence must comply with the laws of the state of its incorporation. (For example, see the Revised Model Coporation Act, RMCA.) These fundamental or extraordinary changes may be accomplished by a merger or consolidation with another corporation, the sale of all or substantially all of the assets or stock of the corporation to another corporation, amendment of the articles of incorporation, or the dissolution and termination of the corporation.

THINGS TO KEEP IN MIND

Any fundamental change in the corporation and extraordinary corporate matters (which will destroy the means for accomplishing the purposes for which the corporation was formed and actually performs) must be consented to by the shareholders. The corporate laws, therefore, give voting and dissenting shareholders rights in the event of the corporation's merger or consolidation, the sale or exchange of all or substantially all of the corporation's assets (other than in the ordinary course of business), and the dissolution of the corporation as well as proposals for certain amendments to the corporation's charter or articles of incorporation.

A corporation cannot avoid compliance with statutory procedures that are meant to safeguard the rights of corporate shareholders and creditors by camouflaging an extraordinary, fundamental corporate change as something else.

OUTLINE

I.   Merger and consolidation — Exchange of shares of stock in one corporation for stock in another corporation.

A. Merger — One corporation (the surviving corporation) acquires the assets of one or more other corporations (the merged corporations).

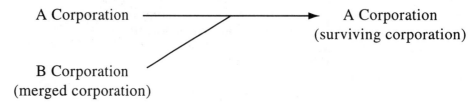

1. The surviving corporation assumes the obligations and debts of the merged corporation, and the existence of the merged corporation ceases.

2. The shareholders of the merged corporation become the shareholders of the surviving corporation.

   a. The surviving corporation exchanges its stock for the assets of the merged corporation, which distributes the stock to its shareholders; or

   b. The surviving corporation exchanges its stock directly with the shareholders of the merged corporation.

B. Consolidation (exchange of shares of stock) — Two or more corporations combine so that each corporation ceases to exist, and a new successor corporation comes into existence. The new corporation acquires the assets and assumes the obligations and debts of the consolidated corporations.

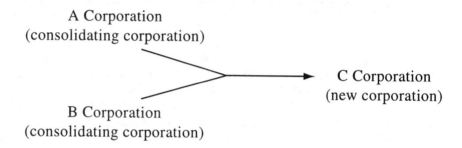

A Corporation
(consolidating corporation)

C Corporation
(new corporation)

B Corporation
(consolidating corporation)

C. The applicable legal principles, effect, and procedure are basically the same for either merger or consolidation.

D. Merger and consolidation (share exchange) procedures [RMBCA Chapter 11].

   1. General procedure.

      a. The board of directors of each corporation adopts a plan. Contents of plan:
         1) Names of constituent merging or consolidating corporations and name of the surviving or new corporation.
         2) Terms of the merger or consolidation.
         3) Manner of converting shares of stock of constituent corporations into securities of the surviving or new corporation.
         4) In the case of a merger, the changes in the charter of the surviving corporation or, in the case of a consolidation, the appropriate provisions for the articles of incorporation of the new corporation [RMBCA 11.01].

      b. Shareholder approval after notice to all (voting and nonvoting) shareholders of all corporations.

              1) The RMBCA [11.03] requires a majority vote.
              2) In some states a two-thirds vote of shares is required [MBCA 73].

      c. Filing of Articles of Merger or Consolidation (containing the plan) with the appropriate state official (Secretary of State) who issues a certificate and any local officials as required by law [RMBCA 11.05].

  2. Short-form (parent-subsidiary) merger — Formal shareholder consent is not required when the surviving (parent) corporation owns more than a stated proportion, such as 90% or 95%, of the outstanding shares of each class of stock of the subsidiary (merged) corporation [RMBCA 11.04].

  3. If one or more of the corporations is a foreign corporation and the laws of each state permit merger or consolidation, each corporation complies with the laws of the state of its incorporation [RMBCA 11.07].

  4. The surviving corporation (in the case of merger) or new corporation (in the case of consolidation) acquires the assets, rights, liabilities, and debts of the constituent corporations [RMBCA 11.06].

  5. Appraisal rights — Dissenting shareholders' rights to the fair value of shares [RMBCA Chapter 13].

      a. Normally, if a shareholder disagrees with corporate policy or decisions, the shareholder's recourse is to sell the stock.

      b. A dissenting shareholder may have appraisal rights in cases of:
              1) Merger and consolidation, including short-form merger in some states.
              2) Disposition of all or substantially all of the assets of the corporation.
              3) In some states only:
                  a) Amendments of charter, affecting classifications of shares, when shareholders are adversely affected and not otherwise protected by preemptive rights.
                  b) Acquisition of securities to be distributed to shareholders when disposing of the assets of a dissolving corporation [RMBCA 13.02].

      c. Dissenting shareholders must strictly adhere to statutory procedure [RMBCA 13.20-13.28].
              1) Vote against the particular corporate action.
              2) Give notice to the corporation which then makes an offer to buy the shares.
              3) Apply for appraisal of the fair value of shares by an appropriate court if the offer of the corporation is not accepted.

      d. Appraisal rights and shareholder status.
              1) In some states, a dissenting shareholder loses his or her shareholder status and, therefore, the rights to vote, receive dividends, and to

bring an action for an injunction to enjoin the action that prompted the shareholder's dissent.

   2) In other states, shareholder's rights may be reinstated during the appraisal process or after the appraisal process is concluded.

   e. Valuation of shares — When the corporation makes a written offer to purchase a dissenting shareholder's shares at the fair value of the shares on the day prior to the date on which the applicable vote was taken, the offer must be accompanied by a current balance sheet and income statement of the corporation [RMBCA 13.01].

II. Purchase of assets.

A. The sale of all or substantially all of the assets of a (selling) corporation to another (acquiring or purchasing) corporation, other than in the regular course of business, is a fundamental change in the nature of the selling corporation [RMBCA 12.02].

   1. Transaction may be a sale, lease, exchange, or other disposition of assets.

   2. Acquiring corporation may pay for the assets in cash, property, or stock.

   3. Each corporation remains in existence, but the character of each corporation's assets and business change.

B. The procedure for a corporation disposing of assets includes giving notice to all shareholders and a vote of some prescribed proportion of the shareholders.

C. Approval of shareholders of the acquiring corporation is not necessary unless payment is to be made in shares that are unauthorized or unavailable or if required by a stock exchange upon which one or more of the corporations are listed.

D. Purchasing corporation is not liable for obligations of selling corporation unless:

   1. The purchasing corporation expressly or impliedly assumes selling corporation's liabilities;

   2. The sale of assets, in effect, is a merger or consolidation;

   3. The purchasing corporation continues operating the business of the selling corporation and retains the officers of the selling corporation; or

   4. The sale of assets is executed fraudulently in order to avoid the selling corporation's liabilities.

E. U.S. Department of Justice Guidelines constrain some mergers that could result from a purchase and sale of assets. [See Chapter 47.]

III. Purchase of stock — An acquiring (or aggressor) corporation may begin with a proposal for a merger or an anonymous purchase of shares on a stock exchange, followed by a public offer to purchase stock directly from the shareholders of another (the target) corporation in order to acquire voting control of the target company. (This process is referred to as a takeover.)

    A. Tender offers — The acquiring corporation makes a public offer to the shareholders of the target corporation to buy their shares at a specified price within a stated period of time.

        1. Usually, the tender offer price is higher than the market price of the stock.

        2. The tender offer may be conditioned upon the receipt of a specified number of offers from the target company's shareholders to sell their shares by a certain date.

        3. The acquiring corporation may make a tender offer to exchange cash or securities of the acquiring corporation or a combination of cash and securities for the shares.

        4. Today, this method of gaining control is regulated by federal and state takeover laws.

    B. Takeover tactics — In a case of a "hostile" takeover, there may be a "war".

        1. When the target's management opposed a takeover, the "raider" may use a variety of tactics to prevent the target's management learning of the hostile takeover.

        2. Beachhead acquisitions and proxy fights.

            a. A raider establishes a "beachhead" by acquiring a bloc of shares and then "launches" a proxy fight in order to acquire a sufficient number of proxies so that the raider will be able to elect a board of directors that supports the raider's views and thus gain control of the target corporation.

            b. Takeovers are costly and often result in litigation.

            c. Factors that favor incumbent management in proxy contests:
               1) Expenses for the solicitations of the shareholders' proxies by the target's management may be charged to the corporation if the solicitations are justified because of corporate policy.
               2) The solicitation process can be lengthy and expensive, especially for an aggressor if the target's management resists turning over list of shareholders.

            d. Factors that favor an aggressor in a proxy contest.

1) An aggressor may not need to contact a majority of individual shareholders of a target corporation if the aggressor obtains the support of institutional investors.

2) A successful aggressor may recoup its takeover expenses by having the acquired (target) corporation reimburse the aggressor.

3. Leveraged buyouts (LBOs) — Arrangements for "going private."

   a. A group of people, such as a company's existing management group, purchases the outstanding publicly-held stock of the corporation.

   b. An LBO is financed by borrowing funds to be secured by the corporation's assets; bonds may be issued or a loan obtained from an investment or other bank.

   c. Often, the heavy debt load and burdensome interest payments result in the ultimate demise of the corporation.

C. Takeover responses.

1. The board of directors of the target corporation must disclose all material facts — Material facts are facts that it is likely reasonable shareholders will consider important in deciding whether to accept or reject the tender offer.

2. The board of directors of the target corporation in the exercise of the board's fiduciary duty makes a recommendation to shareholders in good faith.

   a. A board of directors may consider a tender offer to be favorable and recommend acceptance by shareholders.

   b. A board of directors may recommend rejection of a tender offer and adopt a strategy directed at avoiding the takeover, such as:
   1) A corporate offer to buy stock from shareholders in order to retain control (a self-tender).
   2) Solicit a merger with a different corporation (a white knight).
   3) Attempt to take over the acquiring corporation (Pac-Man).
   4) A target corporation that adopts these defensive tactics is subject to the same federal and state statutes as an acquiring corporation that makes a tender offer.

3. Tactics of target corporations that are used in order to resist takeover.

   a. Scorched earth — Make the target corporation less attractive by selling off assets or divisions (the crown jewels) or taking out loans that are to be repaid if a takeover occurs.

   b. Shark repellent — Change articles of incorporation or bylaws of target corporation to require a greater shareholder vote for merger or other fundamental changes.

c. Poison pill — Issue shares of target corporation that are to be redeemed for cash in the event of a takeover.

d. Commence an action for an injunction against the acquiring corporation asserting that the acquiring corporation is violating a statute (e.g., antitrust laws).

e. Golden parachutes — Provide for payments to executive officers in the event that these officers are discharged or demoted.

f. Greenmail — Purchase shares of target corporation's stock that was acquired by the acquiring corporation at a higher-than-market (or premium) price.

g. Lobster traps — Convertible securities holders are prohibited from converting the securities into shares of common stock if holders own or will own more than a specified percent of the company's voting shares.

D. Insider trading — See Chapter 43.

IV. Termination — Dissolution and liquidation.

A. Dissolution.

1. Voluntary (nonjudicial) dissolution.

a. By incorporators [RMBCA 14.01].

b. By unanimous action of all the shareholders [RMBCA 7.04].

c. By act of the corporation after adoption of a resolution by the board of directors and the resolution's approval by shareholders [RMBCA 14.02].

2. Involuntary dissolution.

a. Administrative dissolution by the secretary of state in the state of incorporation if the corporation fails to pay franchise taxes, deliver annual reports, or give notification of change in registered office or agent, or if period of duration of corporation expires [RMBCA 14.21].

b. Judicial dissolution [RMBCA 14.30] — Proceedings are instituted by:
   1) Attorney general if the articles of incorporation were obtained through fraud or if the corporation has exceeded or abused its authority.
   2) Shareholders.
      a) Deadlock in board of directors that shareholders cannot break, and irreparable injury is threatened or is being suffered by the corporation, or the business of the corporation cannot be conducted to the advantage of the shareholders.

      b) Actions of directors or those in control of the corporation are illegal, fraudulent, or oppressive (i.e., *ultra vires* acts that are abuses of corporate powers).

      c) Shareholders are deadlocked and have failed to elect directors for two years.

      d) Corporate assets are being misapplied or wasted.

  3) Creditor when corporation is insolvent.

      a) A judgment creditor's execution on a judgment was returned unsatisfied; or

      b) The corporation admitted in writing that the creditor's claim is due and owing.

  4) The corporation in order to have a voluntary dissolution continued under court supervision.

B. Liquidation.

  1. The procedure for liquidation and winding up is set forth in RMBCA, Chapter 14; usually, the liquidation and winding up procedure is conducted by the members of the board of directors who act as trustees.

  2. The corporation is required to:

    a. Cease conducting new business, notify creditors, pay debts and liabilities, including taxes, fulfill existing contracts, and collect and sell assets.

    b. Distribute remaining assets among shareholders according to their respective interests and preferences.

    c. Make any filings required by state law.

  3. A receiver will be appointed by the court to wind up the affairs of the corporation and liquidate the corporation's assets if there is an involuntary dissolution, if members of the board do not wish to conduct the winding up, or if shareholders or creditors show cause why the board should not be permitted to assume the function of a trustee.

KEY WORDS AND PHRASES

merger	target corporation
surviving corporation	tender offer
consolidation	takeover
procedure for merger or consolidation	beachhead acquisitions of shares
short-form merger	proxy fight
dissenting shareholders' rights	leveraged buyouts (LBOs)
appraisal rights of shareholders	target responses to hostile takeover
valuation of fair value of shares	self-tender
purchase of corporate assets	white knight
purchase of stock in target corporation	Pac-Man and scorched earth tactics
aggressor corporation (raider)	crown jewels

shark repellent, golden parachute,   deadlock in board of directors
    greenmail, and lobster trap   winding up corporate affairs
termination of a corporation   liquidation
voluntary and involuntary dissolution   receiver

FILL-IN QUESTIONS

1.   A, B, and C Corporations are planning to merge. Upon completion of the statutory requirements, C Corporation will continue to exist. A and B Corporations will _____ and C Corporation will acquire the _____ of A and B Corporations and assume the _____ of A and B Corporations. The shareholders of A and B Corporations will receive _____.

2.   E and F Corporations are planning to consolidate. Upon completion of the statutory requirements, E and F Corporations will _____. Their assets will be acquired and their liabilities assumed by G Corporation, _____.

3.   State corporation laws require _____ if a corporation is selling, leasing, or otherwise disposing of all or substantially all of its assets, other than in the ordinary course of its business, even though the corporation's existence will not cease, because it results in a fundamental change in _____ _____.

4.   The objectives of statutory provisions requiring shareholder approval for plans resulting in fundamental changes in the nature and structure of a corporation and filing with a state official are to protect the rights of _____ and _____ of the corporation. A corporation _____ avoid compliance with the statutory procedures by characterizing or disguising a transaction in such a way as not to require such approval or filing.

5.   A shareholder who has voted against a merger, consolidation, or disposition of all or substantially all of the assets of a corporation is a dissenting shareholder. The dissenting shareholder has a right to be paid the _____ of his or her shares by the corporation. If the statutory provisions are adhered to, an appropriate court will determine the _____ of the dissenting shareholder's stock.

6.   In a takeover attempt, an aggressor corporation may begin by gradually _____ shares of stock in a target corporation in order to establish a beachhead, and then launch a full-blown _____ for control of the target by trying to secure the _____ of enough shareholders in order to elect a board of directors that supports its views.

MULTIPLE CHOICE QUESTIONS

1.   Which of the following statements is **not** correct:
    A. The surviving corporation in a merger assumes the liabilities of the corporation that merged into the surviving corporation.

B. Assets of all consolidating corporations are acquired by the surviving corporation after consolidation.
C. A shareholder, who dissents from a lease of all the assets of a corporation in the ordinary course of business, is entitled to the fair value of her shares.
D. Bondholders have rights to corporate assets upon dissolution and these bondholders' rights are superior to those of common shareholders.

2. C Co. was merged into D Co. C Co. had issued only common stock. Under the terms of the plan of merger, each share of common stock of C Co. received one share of 8% cumulative, nonvoting D Co. preferred stock. The directors and the required proportion of shareholders of both corporations voted in favor of the merger. The holders of 10% of the common stock of C Co. voted against the plan and have demanded that the corporation purchase their share rather than give them D Co. stock.
A. Creditors of C Co. are **not** entitled to payment from D Co. if D Co. did not agree to assume C Co.'s obligations.
B. The merger is ineffective because the shareholders of C Co. are to receive nonvoting shares in exchange for these shareholders' voting shares.
C. Dissenting shareholders of C Co. are entitled to the fair value of these shareholders' shares.
D. If the corporation refuses to pay the dissenting shareholders a price that these shareholders believe is adequate, a court will **not** substitute its judgment for that of the directors.

3. When a corporation acquires all or substantially all of the assets of another corporation (other than in the regular course of business):
A. the selling corporation must have the approval of its shareholders, but the acquiring corporation need **not** obtain shareholder approval.
B. the acquiring corporation must have the approval of its shareholders, but the selling corporation need **not** obtain shareholder approval.
C. both the selling corporation and the acquiring corporation must have the approval of their shareholders.
D. neither the selling corporation nor the acquiring corporation must have the approval of their shareholders.

Questions 4 and 5 are based on the following fact situation: The ABD Land Corp. has sold 98.3% of its assets, all of which is real property, to the FGH Land Corp.

4. Which of the following statements is correct?
A. The board of directors of ABD may authorize the sale without the approval of shareholders of ABD if this sale is in the regular course of business.
B. The sale must be approved by the shareholders of ABD if this sale is in the regular course of business.
C. The sale must be approved by the shareholders of FGH if this sale is **not** in the regular course of business.
D. The ABD Corp. will be dissolved by operation of law following the transfer of ABD Corp.'s asset to FGH.

5. If the sale is **not** in the regular course of business of ABD Land Corp.:

    A. the sale must be approved by all the shareholders of ABD, including those shareholders without voting rights.

    B. the sale need **not** be approved by the shareholders of ABD if the directors unanimously approved the sale.

    C. a dissenting shareholder of ABD has a right to be paid the fair value of her shares if she promptly notified and made a demand on the corporation.

    D. a dissenting shareholder of FGH has a right to be paid the fair value of his shares if he promptly notified and made a demand on the corporation.

6.   When a dissenting shareholder of a corporation elects appraisal rights, the corporation:

    A. has the option of offering to purchase the dissenting shareholder's shares.

    B. must offer to purchase the dissenting shareholder's shares, but has discretion as to how to value the shares.

    C. must offer to purchase the dissenting shareholder's shares at the fair value of the shares.

    D. None of the answers above is correct.

7.   In a hostile takeover attempt, the management of a target corporation:

    A. may resist providing a list of shareholders of the target corporation to the aggressor, but may be required by a court to supply the list of shareholders.

    B. is never required to provide a list of shareholders in the target corporation upon the request of the aggressor.

    C. must pay the costs incurred by the aggressor in contacting and mailing requests for proxies to the shareholders of the target corporation if the aggressor fails to win control over the target corporation.

    D. may **not** contact and solicit proxies from the target's shareholders.

8.   A majority of the shareholders of a corporation may petition for dissolution if the:

    A. assets of the corporation are insufficient to meet the corporation's liabilities.

    B. directors of the corporation have failed to declare a dividend.

    C. directors of the corporation are deadlocked in the management of the corporation.

    D. never.

9.   A corporation's existence terminates when:

    A. the sole owner/shareholder dies.

    B. the corporation becomes insolvent.

    C. all of the corporation's shares are purchased by another corporation.

    D. the corporation legally consolidates with another corporation.

10.   Under the provisions of the Revised Model Business Corporation Act, a business corporation may be dissolved administratively if:

    A. the corporation's sole shareholder has died.

    B. the corporation has failed to notify the appropriate Secretary of State of the change of address of its registered office.

    C. the articles of incorporation of the corporation have been obtained through fraud, or the corporation has entered into *ultra vires* transactions.

    D. all of the shareholders of the corporation consent to the corporation's dissolution in writing.

Chapter 43
Corporations: Securities Regulation and
Investor Protection

The issuance and sale of corporate securities are regulated extensively by the Securities and Exchange Commission (the SEC), a federal agency that administers the Securities Act of 1933 (the 1933 Act), the Securities Exchange Act of 1934 (the 1934 Act), and other federal statutes. Relevant provisions of these federal laws are explained in this chapter and reproduced in appendices J and K of the textbook. In addition, the states also regulate the offer and sale of securities.

A major objective of securities regulation is to protect the investing public by requiring full and correct disclosure of relevant information. The federal securities laws, therefore, impose certain registration requirements and set forth various antifraud provisions designed, in part, to prevent manipulative and deceptive trading practices and the misuse of material nonpublic information by officers, directors, and other insiders. Both criminal and civil liability for securities law violations are imposed by the statutes.

THINGS TO KEEP IN MIND

The area of law relating to the issuance, resale, and trading of investment securities is most complex. Should the occasion arise, you are advised to consult an expert.

OUTLINE

I.   The Securities and Exchange Commission (SEC).

   A. Following enactment of the Securities Act of 1933, Congress passed the Securities Exchange Act of 1934 that provided for the creation of the SEC, an independent regulatory commission, and empowered the SEC to administer the federal securities laws.

   B. The basic functions of the SEC.

      1. Administer the requirements of disclosure of material facts concerning offerings of securities listed on national securities exchanges and certain securities traded in the over the counter (OTC) market.

      2. Regulate the trading in securities on the thirteen national and regional securities exchanges and in the OTC market.

      3. Investigate securities frauds.

4. Regulate the activities of securities brokers, dealers, and investment advisers.

5. Supervise activities of mutual funds and insurance products.

6. Recommend administrative sanctions, injunctive remedies, and criminal prosecution of violators of the securities laws by the Fraud Section of the Criminal Division of the Department of Justice.

C. The expanding powers of the SEC.

1. The Securities Enforcement Remedies and Penny Stock Reform Act of 1990 expanded the types of securities violations cases that SEC administrative judges can hear and the SEC's enforcement options as well as gave courts the power to bar people who have engaged in securities frauds from serving as officers and directors of publicly held corporations.

2. The Securities Act Amendments of 1990 authorized the SEC to seek sanctions against people who violate foreign securities laws.

3. The Market Reform Act of 1990 authorized the SEC to suspend trading in securities when prices rise and fall excessively in a short period of time.

4. The National Securities Markets Improvement Act of 1996 expanded the SEC's power to exempt persons, securities, and transactions from the requirements of the securities laws and limited the authority of the states to regulate certain securities transactions and certain investment advisers.

5. Currently, Congress and the SEC are revising some rules and eliminating other rules governing securities regulations in order to streamline and increase the efficiency of the regulatory process.

II. The Securities Act of 1933.

A. The 1933 Act requires full disclosure of material information that is relevant to investment decisions and prohibits fraud and misstatements when securities are offered for sale to the public through the mail and/or interstate commerce ("going public").

B. Definition of a security — The term "security" is defined broadly.

1. "[A]ny note, stock, treasury stock, bond, debenture, evidence of indebtedness, certificate of interest or participation in any profit-sharing agreement ... investment contract ... or, in general, any interest or instrument commonly known as a 'security' or any certificate of interest or participation in, ... receipt for, ... or right to subscribe to or purchase, any of the foregoing" [1933 Act, Section 2].

2. Courts have determined that a security exists in any transaction when:

      a. A person invests money or property in a common enterprise or venture; and

      b. The investor reasonably expects to make a profit primarily or substantially as a result of the managerial efforts of others.

C. Registration statement.

  1. An issuer of nonexempt securities to be offered to the public must file a registration statement with the SEC.

  2. The principal document in the registration statement is the prospectus that is required by the 1933 Act to be furnished to an investor prior to any purchase.

  3. Contents of the registration statement:

      a. Thorough description of the securities (including the relationship between the securities and other securities of the issuer) and the manner in which the proceeds of the sale of the securities are to be used.

      b. Description of the issuer's property and business.

      c. Description of the financial structure of the issuer and audited financial statements (i.e., balance sheets at the end of the last two fiscal years, income statements, and statements of changes in financial positions for the last three fiscal years) certified by an independent public accountant.

      d. Description of the management personnel, their securities holdings, remunerations and other benefits, including pensions and stock options (i.e., contractual rights to buy shares of stock in the issuing corporation during a specified period of time), and any interests which directors or officers have in transactions with the corporation.

      e. Description of significant pending litigation against the issuer.

  3. The registration statement must be signed by the issuer, a majority of the board of directors, and the chief executive, financial, and accounting officers.

  4. Other requirements.

      a. During the prefiling period, the issuer prepares a prospectus (containing most of the information that is in the registration statement), may obtain an underwriter (i.e., a company that agrees to sell securities and may even agree to a firm commitment to purchase securities that subsequently are not sold), and may publish a very limited notice concerning the prospective issue of securities; the issuer, however, may not sell, offer for sale, accept offers to purchase, etc., any securities.

b. After the registration statement is filed, there is a waiting period of 20 days that may be reduced (unusual) or extended (usual) by the SEC; during this period, the issuer may not sell any securities, but may:
   1) Distribute red herring (preliminary) prospectus which states in red that the registration statement has been filed but has not yet become effective.
   2) Solicit and receive oral, revocable offers for the purchase of the securities.
   3) Place tombstone advertisements that state that the advertisements are not offers.

c. After the waiting period, when the SEC states that the registration is effective, the registered securities can be offered for sale, bought, and sold, but each prospective buyer must be given a copy of the final prospectus; advertisements can also be placed in newspapers and other publications.

D. Exempt securities — Securities that are exempt from the registration requirement [1933 Act, Section 3(a)].

1. Issuer is a governmental body or nonprofit organization.

2. Issuer is a bank, savings institution, common carrier, or farmers' cooperative and subject to other regulatory legislation.

3. Commercial paper having a maturity date of less than nine months.

4. Stock dividends, stock splits, and securities issued in connection with corporate reorganizations (unless a corporate reorganization represents a new investment decision on the part of the shareholders).

5. Insurance, endowment, and annuity contracts issued by state-regulated insurance companies.

6. Issuer's offer of up to $5 million in securities in any twelve-month period (often issued in order to "test the waters" for potential interest).

E. Exempt transactions — Transactions that are exempt from registration requirement under the 1933 Act typically are "private" or "small" offerings.

1. Small offerings [SEC Regulation D].

   a. Private, noninvestment company offerings of less than $1 million worth of securities in a twelve-month period [SEC Regulation D, Rule 504].

   b. Offerings of less than $500,000 by companies, whose only plans are to locate business opportunities, in a twelve-month period to investors who will not resell the securities [SEC Regulation D, Rule 504a].

1) No general solicitation or advertising can be used, except if the offering is made solely in states that provide for registration and disclosure, and the issuer complies with the state requirements.
2) SEC is notified by the filing of a notice (on Form D) of sales and precautions are taken against nonexempt, unregistered resales.

c. Private, offerings by companies, other than investment companies, of less than $5 million worth of securities in a twelve-month period to:
1) Accredited investors (An accredited investor is a natural person with annual income of more than $200,000 and whose net worth exceeds $1,000,000); or
2) Investors who are represented by purchaser representatives and who are knowledgeable and experienced regarding finance and business; or
3) Up to 35 unaccredited investors having financial and business knowledge and experience and who are furnished with the same information as would be contained in a full registration statement prospectus [SEC Regulation D, Rule 505].

2. Private placements — Private offerings of any amount of securities to any number of accredited investors and/or to no more than 35 unaccredited investors who have sufficient knowledge or experience in financial matters to be capable of evaluating the merits and risk of the investments and who are furnished with material information [SEC Regulation D, Rule 506].

3. Small offerings (Section 4(6) of the 1933 Act) — Offerings of not more than $5 million made solely to accredited investors, provided that no general, public solicitations or advertising are used, the SEC is notified of sales, and precautions are taken against non-exempt, unregistered resales (because these are restricted securities and, thus, may be sold only by registration or in an exempt transaction).

4. Intrastate issues (Rule 147) — All offerees are residents of the state in which the issuer is incorporated and performs substantially all of its operations [1933 Act, Section 3(a)(11)].

a. Eighty percent of the issuer's assets must be located in the state, 80% of the issuer's gross revenue must be derived from business in the state, and 80% of the issuer's net income from the sale of the securities must be spent in the state [SEC Rule 147].

b. No resale of the securities can take place for nine months after the last sale.

c. These offerings remain subject to applicable state statutes.

6. Less demanding disclosure and registration are required for small issues of less than $1.5 million [SEC Regulation A, Rule 254].

F. Resales — Resales of securities by most persons, other than issuers and under-writers, are exempt from registration requirements.

1. Securities purchased under SEC Rule 504(a), SEC Rule 505, or Section 4(6) of the 1933 Act, however, are subject to restrictions; resales of such securities must be registered, unless the seller complies with the safe harbor provisions of SEC Rule 144 or Rule 144A.

2. Rule 144 exempts restricted securities from registration upon resale if adequate public information about the issuer has been reported in periodic filings to the SEC, the seller has owned the securities for at least two years, the securities are sold in certain limited amounts in unsolicited brokers' transactions, and the SEC is given notice of the resale.

3. Rule 144A exempts from registration upon resale those securities that are not listed on a national securities exchange or quoted in a U.S. automated interdealer quotation system and are sold only to qualified institutional buyers (i.e., insurance companies, investment companies, or banks with capitalization exceeding $100 million) which buyers are aware that the seller is relying on the exemption under Rule 144A.

G. Violations of the 1933 Act [Section 11].

1. Liability is imposed for:

   a. Intentional fraud because of material misstatements and omissions in a registration statement or prospectus.

   b. Negligence because of a failure to discover fraud.

   c. Failure to register an issue, selling securities before the effective date of a registration statement, or selling securities under a exemption for which the securities do not qualify.

2. Liability is imposed upon the issuing corporation, the corporation's directors, anyone else who signed or provided information that was incorporated into the registration statement, and the underwriters.

3. Defenses.

   a. Even if a statement was not true or was omitted, the statement or omission was not material.

   b. The plaintiff (purchaser of the securities) bought the securities with knowledge of the misrepresentation.

   c. Due diligence — The defendant (other than the issuer) used due diligence and reasonably believed (at the time that the registration became effective) that representations in the registration statement were true and that there were no omissions of material facts. [See Chapter 54 regarding exercise of due diligence by accountants.]

4. Criminal penalties — If the U.S. Department of Justice is successful in prosecutions for willful violations, violators may be imprisoned for up to five years and/or fined a maximum of $10,000.

5. Civil sanctions.

   a. The SEC may seek an injunction to prevent further sales of the securities and other relief, such as a court order directing a willful violator to refund profits.

   b. An injured purchaser of the securities may sue in a federal district court for damages, including any losses resulting from a material misstatement or omission.

III. The Securities Exchange Act of 1934.

A. The 1934 Act deals with the resale of securities ("being public") and provides for regulation of securities exchanges (i.e., the markets in which securities are traded), corporations having assets of more than a threshold amount (fixed by the SEC) and more than 500 shareholders, and proxy solicitations for shareholder voting.

B. Section 12 of the 1934 Act provides that an issuer of publicly-traded securities must register and file periodic reports with the SEC if:

1. The securities are traded on an exchange; or

2. The issuer engages in interstate commerce or its securities are traded through the mails or an instrumentality of interstate commerce, and the issuer has assets exceeding $10 million and more than 500 shareholders. [SEC Rule 12g-1]

C. Section 10(b) of the 1934 Act and SEC Rule 10b-5.

1. Section 10(b) and Rule 10b-5 make it "unlawful for any person to use the facilities of a securities exchange, the mails or any instrumentality of interstate commerce to defraud or to make any misstatements or omissions of a material fact in connection with the purchase or sale of any security."

2. Insider trading — Corporate insiders are required either to disclose information (which may be a breach of the fiduciary duty owed to the corporation) or to refrain from trading in securities of the corporation (for a "reasonable waiting period" after the information is available to the public).

3. The SEC, a purchaser, or seller of the securities who has been damaged may bring an action based upon a violation.

4. Disclosure requirements under SEC Rule 10b-5.

   a. Liability is imposed when there has been a misleading or deceptive misrepresentation or omission of material facts in connection with the purchase or sale of securities.

   b. A fact is material if there is a substantial likelihood that a reasonable shareholder would consider the fact important in making a decision to "buy, sell, or hold" the securities.

   c. Courts use a "balancing test" to determine if undisclosed facts are material under Rule 10b-5 — With respect to a particular fact, a court will balance the indicated probability that the event will occur against the anticipated magnitude of the event in light of the totality of the company activity should the event occur.

5. Applicability of SEC Rule 10b-5.

   a. The rule applies to transactions in securities without regard to whether or not the securities are registered by the issuer under the securities laws.

   b. The rule applies when the facilities of a securities exchange, the mails, or instrumentalities of interstate commerce are used; as a result, most transactions are within the purview of the rule and those transactions that are not so covered may be covered by state regulations.

   c. Criminal and/or civil liability may be imposed upon corporate officers, directors, some shareholders, and certain "outsiders" (tippees), who have access to or have received information that is not available to the public and which may affect the future market value of the corporation's securities.

6. Outsiders and SEC Rule 10b-5 — Liability is imposed upon some "outsiders" who trade on indirectly-acquired nonpublic inside information.

   a. Tipper/tippee theory.
      1) A tippee (or a tippee from a tippee) who trades in securities after receiving inside information from a corporate insider (who breaches his or her fiduciary duty) violates Rule 10b-5 if the tippee knew or should have known of the insider's breach of the fiduciary duty.
      2) A breach of the insider's fiduciary duty depends upon whether the insider personally will gain directly or indirectly from the insider's disclosure; if there is no personal benefit to the insider, there is no breach of the fiduciary duty and, therefore, no derivative breach of Rule 10b-5 by the tippee.

   b. Misappropriation theory — An outsider who uses (misappropriates) material nonpublic information in breach of a fiduciary duty of confidentiality owed to an employer (other than the corporation that issued the securities) and who trades in securities based upon the misappropriated information violates Rule 10b-5 if other (defrauded) persons are harmed.

D. Insider reporting and trading — Section 16(b) of the 1934 Act.

1. Officers, directors, and holders of more than 10% of a class of equity securities that are registered under the 1934 Act are required to file reports with the SEC [Section 16(a)] and are liable to the corporation for "short-swing" (i.e., within a six month period) gains made in trading in (buying and selling, or selling and buying) the securities [Section 16(b)].

2. It is irrelevant whether or not the insider actually uses inside information.

3. In determining whether or not a person is an officer, courts examine the responsibilities and the functions that the person performs rather than just the person's title.

E. Proxy statements — Section 14(a) of the 1934 Act.

1. Persons who are soliciting proxies from shareholders for voting at meetings must make full and accurate disclosure of facts relating to the matters to be voted upon.

2. Remedies include damages and injunctive relief to prevent a vote being taken.

F. Violations of the 1934 Act — Insider-trading sanctions.

1. Criminal penalties — The Insider Trading and Securities Fraud Enforcement Act of 1988:

a. Enlarged the class of persons who may be subject to civil liability for insider-trading violations.

b. Authorized the SEC to award bounty payments to persons providing information leading to prosecutions of insider trading violations and enlarged the SEC's rule-making authority.

c. Increased criminal penalties to up to ten years imprisonment and fines of $1 million for individuals and $2.5 million for partnerships and corporations.

2. Civil sanctions — The Insider Trading Sanctions Act of 1984 authorizes the SEC to bring a civil suit against a person who, while in possession of material nonpublic information, violates or aids in the violation of the 1934 Act or SEC rules through the facilities of a national securities exchange or from or through a broker or dealer; treble damages may be awarded for three times the profits gained or the loss avoided.

IV.   Regulation of investment companies [Investment Company Act of 1940, as amended].

A. An investment company sells ownership interests to the public or to special, separate accounts of insurance companies and invests in large blocks of securities of many issuers by maintaining and managing a portfolio of securities for the benefit of shareholder-owners who have pooled their funds for investment purposes. Investment companies often give smaller investors opportunities to enjoy many of the advantages afforded to larger, institutional investors (e.g., lower commissions and fees).

B. Classes of investment companies:

1. Face-amount certificate companies which issue face-amount certificates of the installment type.

2. Unit investment trusts which are organized as trusts with no boards of directors and issue only redeemable securities.

3. Management companies which are corporate entities with boards of directors.

a. An open-end investment company, commonly known as a mutual fund, that continually offers for sale or has outstanding redeemable securities of which the company is the issuer.

b. A closed-end investment company that usually is not required to redeem (buy back) company shares from shareholders, who generally must look to the marketplace in order to sell their closed-end company shares.

C. Investment companies must register with the SEC by filing a notification of registration and an initial registration statement.

D. After it is registered, an investment company must file periodic reports and statements with the SEC, including annual post-effective amendments to the company's registration statement, in order to update financial statements, increase the number or amounts of registered securities, or to register an indefinite amount of securities.

E. The operation and investment activities of investment companies are strictly regulated.

1. An investment company cannot pay dividends from sources other than accumulated undistributed net income and, subject to limited exceptions, cannot make short sales of portfolio securities, purchase any portfolio securities on margin, sell short, or participate in joint trading accounts.

2. In order to safeguard company assets, all investment company portfolio securities must be held in the custody of a bank or stock exchange member that must follow strict procedures established by the SEC.

V. State securities law.

A. Article 8 of the Uniform Commercial Code deals with the transfer of investment securities.

B. Blue Sky Laws — State securities laws also regulate, and typically require registration or qualification in connection with, the offering and sale of securities in intrastate commerce.

1. Anti-fraud provisions are similar to those in federal laws.

2. Regulation of brokers and dealers in securities and investment advisers.

3. Registration and disclosure are required before securities can be offered for sale.

4. Some state statutes impose standards of "fairness."

C. The National Securities Markets Improvement Act of 1996 eliminated some of the duplicate regulations of securities markets by federal and state agencies and limited the authority of the states to regulate securities offerings and investment advisers.

VI. Technology and securities law — Electronic securities offerings and delivery of information.

A. The SEC permits a company to conduct an initial public offering over the Internet and to trade its shares through its Web site without registering as a broker-dealer provided that the company has program controls designed to protect the interests of investors.

B. Regulations of the SEC permit the electronic delivery of prospectuses and other information.

C. Securities firms now routinely maintain Web sites that offer the opportunity for investors to invest and trade online at reduced costs.

KEY WORDS AND PHRASES IN TEXT

Securities and Exchange Commission
    (SEC)
national securities exchanges
over the counter (OTC) market
Securities Act of 1933 (covering issues
    of securities)
definition of security
registration requirements of 1933 Act
registration statement
audited financial statements

prospectus
underwriter
red herring prospectus
tombstone ad
liability under Section 11 of 1933 Act
material misstatements and omissions
exempt securities under the 1933 Act
exempt transactions under the 1933 Act
SEC Regulation D
accredited investor

private placement
intrastate transaction
SEC Regulation A
Section 4(6) offering
restricted securities
resales under 1933 Act
Securities Exchange Act of 1934
insider trading
Section 10(b) of 1934 Act and SEC
        Rule 10b-5
nonpublic inside information
trading by outsiders
tipper-tippee theory
misappropriation theory

insider reporting and trading (Section 16)
short-swing profits
proxy statements
Insider Trading Sanctions Act of 1984
Insider Trading and Securities Fraud
        Enforcement Act of 1988
bounty payment
investment company
mutual fund
state securities laws (blue sky laws)
National Securities Markets
        Improvement Act of 1996
electronic securities offerings

FILL-IN QUESTIONS

1. The regulation of securities is covered concurrently by state statutes, often termed _____, and federal legislation under the _____ _____ and _____, administered by the _____. The basis for federal regulation is the power of Congress to regulate _____ and the use of the U.S. _____.

2. The Securities Act of 1933 relates to new issues of securities. It requires that an issuer of non-exempt securities register with _____. The registration statement must contain information such as _____ _____ _____ _____ _____, and a copy of the prospectus that will be furnished to investors.

3. Private offerings under Rule 506 of SEC Regulation D of any amount of securities may be made to any number of _____ investors and/or to no more than 35 _____ investors who have sufficient knowledge or _____ to be capable of evaluating the merits and risk of the investments and who are furnished with material information.

4. Acme Corp. conducts most of its business in New Jersey. Acme Corp. wishes to issue preferred stock in an intrastate offering that will be exempt from registration under the Securities Act of 1933 and SEC Rule 147. The corporation will be able to issue the stock in an intrastate offering if _____ percent of the Acme Corp.'s assets are located in New Jersey, _____ percent of its _____ revenue is derived from business conducted in New Jersey and _____ percent of Acme Corp.'s net income from the sale of the preferred stock will be spent in _____.

5. Rule 144 (under the 1933 Act) exempts restricted securities from registration upon resale if adequate public information about the issuer has been reported in periodic

filings to the SEC, the seller has owned the securities for a minimum of _____, the securities are sold in certain limited amounts in _____, and the _____ is given notice of the resale.

6. The _____ regulates the security markets in which securities are traded after the securities have been issued. Section 12 companies are those that have assets in excess of a threshold amount (which currently is $10,000,000) and _____ or more shareholders. Section 12 corporations are required to register their securities with _____.

7. Liability for insider trading may be imposed under Section 10(b) of the 1934 Securities Exchange Act and SEC Rule 10b-5 upon corporate insiders and also may be imposed upon "_____" based upon either the "tipper-tippee" theory or the "_____" theory.

8. An investment company must register with the SEC by filing notification of registration and an initial _____. After an investment company is registered, the investment company must file periodic reports and statement with the SEC giving information relating to subsequent amendments to the company's registration statement and updated _____.

MULTIPLE CHOICE QUESTIONS

1. The Securities Act of 1933 requires that the following securities be registered with the SEC:
   A. Securities issued by the XYZ Benevolent Society, a charitable organization.
   B. Securities issued by United Transportation Lines, Inc., a common carrier.
   C. A stock dividend issued by General Motors Corporation.
   D. All of the answers above are correct.
   E. None of the answers above is correct.

2. The Securities Act of 1933 provides that firms that sell securities to the public furnish certain financial information to the SEC:
   A. after the sale of the securities.
   B. prior to the sale of the securities.
   C. before and after the sale of securities.
   D. if the purchasers of the securities are all financially sophisticated and are the three partners in a partnership that is changing its form of organization to a corporation.

3. Acme Canning Corporation has filed a registration statement with the SEC because Acme Canning Corporation is planning to issue 600,000 shares of $10 par value preferred stock to the public.
   A. Acme Canning Corporation may not sell any of the stock, but Acme may receive revocable offers from prospective investors who are furnished with a prospectus during the 20-day waiting period after the filing of the registration statement.
   B. Acme Canning Corporation may neither sell nor receive revocable or irrevocable offers for the purchase of securities during the 20-day waiting period after the filing of the registration statement.

C. Acme Canning Corporation may sell shares of the stock to the public immediately after filing the registration statement only if Acme furnishes prospective investors with a prospectus.

D. Acme Canning Corporation may sell shares of the stock to the public immediately after filing the registration statement because the stock issue is exempt from the requirements of the 1933 Act.

4. Which of the following is exempt from registration under the Securities Act of 1933?
    A. Interests in a limited partnership.
    B. Convertible preferred corporate stock.
    C. Corporate bonds secured by real property.
    D. An annuity contract issued by an insurer.

5. Which of the following is exempt from registration under the Securities Act of 1933?
    A. The JKL Company, a private noninvestment company, sells less than $6,000,000 worth of securities in a 14 month period to accredited investors and to 40 unaccredited investors.
    B. The DEF Company makes a private offering of $6,000,000 worth of corporate bonds to accredited investors and to 25 unaccredited investors who are highly knowledgeable and experienced in financial matters.
    C. The PQR Company, a Delaware corporation, offers to sell $1,000,000 of common stock only to residents of the Commonwealth of Virginia.
    D. All of the answers above are correct.
    E. None of the answers above is correct.

6. Section 10(b) 1934 Act empowers the SEC to adopt rules and regulations in order to protect the investing public. Rule 10b-5 adopted by the SEC prohibits:
    A. short swing transactions by directors, officers, and holders of more than 10% of any class of stock.
    B. trading on inside information by directors, officers, and holders of more than 10% of any class of stock.
    C. trading on inside information by directors, officers, holders of more than 10% of any class of stock, and those who receive "tips" from insiders.
    D. All of the answers above are correct.

7. The tipper-tippee theory is applied in a case involving insider trading. Liability is imposed when an insider violates the fiduciary duty and depends, in part, upon whether or not:
    A. the tippee personally will benefit directly or indirectly from the tipper's disclosure.
    B. the tippee knew or should have known of the insider's breach of the fiduciary duty by the insider.
    C. the tipper has misappropriated significant and material information.
    D. All of the answers above are correct.
    E. None of the answers above is correct.

8. The Zebra Corporation is planning to sell $200,000 worth of corporate debentures that will mature in 25 years from the date of issue to the public in the United States. The issue need **not** be registered with the SEC because:

A. the federal securities acts apply only to the issuance of equity securities.
B. bonds of this nature are not considered to be securities.
C. Zebra Corporation is a municipal corporation.
D. the Zebra Corporation's securities are listed on a national exchange.

9. A corporation that desires to issue $2,000,000 worth of preferred shares has complied with the appropriate state Blue Sky Law and filed a registration statement with the SEC. The corporation, however, has omitted a material fact regarding the corporation's financing.
A. An accountant who certified a financial statement made in conjunction with the registration statement is liable to a purchaser of the new issue.
B. The underwriter of the new issue is liable to a purchaser of the shares.
C. A director of the corporation issuing the shares is liable to any person who acquires the shares of the new issue.
D. All of the answers above are correct.

10. Which of the following statements is or are currently true regarding SEC policy affecting online, electronic activities by corporations?

	Companies are permitted to conduct initial offerings over the Internet.	Companies are permitted to deliver prospectuses over the Internet.
A.	Yes	Yes
B.	Yes	No
C.	No	Yes
D.	No	No

OBJECTIVE (YES-NO) QUESTIONS

The following questions are based upon Question Number 2 that appeared on the Uniform CPA Examination in November 1992.

Butler Manufacturing Corp. planned to raise capital for a plant expansion by making several stock offerings. Butler engaged a certified public accountant to audit its financial statements. The financial statements were to be included in the corporation's prospectus for the stock offering. In performing the audit, the accountant failed to discover overstatements regarding the value of Butler's assets. In addition, although the accountant was aware of a pending product liability lawsuit that would result in substantial losses to Butler, this information was not disclosed in Butler's financial statements.

Butler raised $16,450,000 through the following stock offerings, all of which offered shares of stock were completely sold:

March: Butler made a $450,000 unregistered offering of Class B nonvoting stock under Rule 504 of SEC Regulation D. This offering was sold over a two year period to 30 nonaccredited investors and 20 accredited investors by general solicitation. The SEC was notified eight days after the first sale of this offering.

June: Butler made a $10,000,000 unregistered offering of Class A voting stock under SEC Rule 506 of Regulation D. This securities' offering was sold during a two-year period to 300 accredited investors and 30 nonaccredited investors through a private placement. The SEC was notified 14 days after the first sale of this offering.

August: Butler made a $6,000,000 unregistered offering of preferred stock under Rule 505 of Regulation D. This offering was offered during a one-year period to 40 nonaccredited investors by private placement. The SEC was notified 18 days after the first sale of this offering.

The SEC claims that all three of Butlers' securities offerings were improperly made because these offerings were not exempt from registration with the SEC.

The following questions require a yes or no answer:

A.   The following questions relate to the March offering made under Rule 504 of SEC Regulation D:

  1.   Did the offering comply with the dollar limitation of Rule 504?
  2.   Did the offering comply with the method of sale restrictions?
  3.   Was the offering sold during the applicable time limit?
  4.   Was there timely notification of the first sale of the securities to the SEC?
  5.   Was this offering exempt from registration under Rule 504?

B.   The following questions relate to the June offering made under Rule 506 of SEC Regulation D:

  6.   Did the offering comply with the dollar limitation of Rule 506?
  7.   Did the offering comply with the method of sale restrictions?
  8.   Was the offering sold during the applicable time limit?
  9.   Was there timely notification of the first sale of the securities to the SEC?
  10. Was this offering exempt from registration under Rule 506?

C.   The following questions relate to the August offering made under Rule 505 of SEC Regulation D:

  11. Did the offering comply with the dollar limitation of Rule 505?
  12. Did the offering comply with the method of sale restrictions?
  13. Was the offering sold during the applicable time limit?
  14. Was there timely notification of the first sale of the securities to the SEC?
  15. Was this offering exempt from registration under Rule 505?

UNIT NINE:
GOVERNMENT REGULATION

The federal, state, and local governments have played increasing roles in regulating activities of individuals and businesses. The power to do so and to legislate in this area is derived from the government's general power to protect and provide for the common defense, safety, health, and welfare ("the police power") and, in the case of the federal government, Congress's authority to pass laws regulating interstate and foreign commerce [U.S. Constitution, Article I, Section 8]. Evidence of regulation is referred to in the preceding and subsequent units of the text in addition to the material in this Unit.

Chapter 44 provides a survey of such regulation by administrative agencies of government. Chapters 45 and 46 focus on consumer and environmental protection, areas about which each student, because of his or her own individual concerns, will have varying personal interest. Chapter 47 deals with antitrust law and governmental efforts to regulate the economy in order to maintain fair competition and the private enterprise system.

Chapter 44
Administrative Law

The objective of this chapter is to familiarize you with the federal regulatory process and the general scope of activities that are regulated by governmental administrative agencies. In the United States, rulings, orders, decisions, rules, and regulations promulgated by such agencies affect business firms. For example, the Federal Trade Commission influences how firms market their products and services; the Securities and Exchange Commission regulates the financial capital markets; and the National Labor Relations Board, the Occupational Safety and Health Administration, and the Equal Employment Opportunity Commission affect the relationship between firms and their employees.

Government agencies are created by legislative bodies and may be given legislative, judicial, and/or executive authority. Federal agencies are established by the United States Congress and empowered to administer certain laws. These bodies exercise their functions in accordance with the Administrative Procedure Act (APA). Some federal agencies are part of the executive branch and others are independent bodies. Today, the myriad of administrative agencies constitutes what is considered to be the governmental bureaucracy.

THINGS TO KEEP IN MIND

The emphasis in the chapter is on federal agencies and their powers. Regulatory agencies (sometimes termed boards, departments, commissions, or authorities) also exist in the states and at local levels of government.

OUTLINE

I.   Agency creation and powers.

    A. Enabling legislation — Congress passes a statute in order to create an administrative agency and in which it sets forth its name, composition, purpose, and powers.

    B. The Federal Trade Commission (FTC) — An example.

        1. The FTC was created in 1914 when the Federal Trade Commission Act (prohibiting certain unfair trade or business practices) was enacted.

        2. The Act describes the procedures that must be followed by the FTC when there are violations of the statutes administered by the FTC and provides for judicial review of the agency's orders.

        3. The statute grants the power to the FTC to make rules and regulations, to obtain reports from companies engaging in interstate commerce concerning

their business practices, to conduct investigations concerning possible violations, to publish findings, to recommend new legislation, to conduct trial-like hearings, and to adjudicate certain disputes.

4. The functions of the FTC include those associated with the three branches of government, the legislature (rulemaking and, to a lesser extent, investigatory), the courts (adjudication), and the executive branch (investigation and enforcement of the law).

C.   Types of agencies.

1. Executive agencies.

   a. All cabinet level departments have executive branch agencies and subagencies; for example, the Department of Labor includes the Occupational Safety and Health Administration (OSHA).

   b. Executive agencies are subject to the control of the President.

2. Independent regulatory agencies.

   a. These agencies are non-cabinet level governmental bodies; examples include the Federal Trade Commission and the Securities and Exchange Commission (discussed in Chapter 43).

   b. Independent agencies are intended to be controlled through appointed officials who serve for a specified term and, in theory, only can be removed for just cause.

D. Agency powers and the United States Constitution.

1. Some of the formal functions of the three branches of government defined in the U.S. Constitution have been delegated to administrative agencies.

   a. Some agencies have legislative authority because they can make rules and regulations that are substantive in nature and implement federal statutes.

   b. Agencies that are empowered to enforce laws are exercising executive functions.

   c. Agencies that hold adjudicatory hearings have authority associated with the judicial function of dispute resolution.

2. Article I, Section 8 of the Constitution grants to Congress the implied power to make all laws that are necessary in order to carry out Congress' enumerated powers — This has been interpreted to mean that Congress has the power to create administrative agencies and may grant such agencies extensive rulemaking, enforcement, adjudicatory, and investigatory powers (the delegation doctrine).

II.   Administrative process — The administrative process consists of the three basic operations of administrative agencies (rulemaking, enforcement, and adjudication) and investigation.

A. Procedural requirements that must be followed by administrative agencies in carrying out functions are set forth in the Administrative Procedure Act (APA).

B   Rulemaking.

1. A rule is a statement made by an agency that establishes future general or specific policy.

2. The notice-and-comment rulemaking process.

a. Notice of the proposed rule is published in the *Federal Register*.

b. Comment period.
   1) Public comments may be submitted in writing within a specified period of time (e.g., 60 days).
   2) Public hearings may be held at which oral comments may be made and evidence examined.
   3) The agency prepares a written statement.
   4) The agency may accept comments after the comment period is closed and summarize these *ex parte* (private, off-the-record) comments in the record.

c. The final rule is published first in the *Federal Register* and later in the *Code of Federal Regulations (CFR)*.

C. Investigation.

1. Investigatory powers are necessary in order to obtain information concerning the activities that an agency is charged with overseeing so that the agency can adopt appropriate rules and ascertain whether or not the statute or its regulation are being violated.

2. Inspections.

a. An agency may request to make an on-site inspection of facilities or an inspection of business records; if a request is denied, the agency may obtain a subpoena or search warrant.

b   Subpoenas may be used in order to compel disclosure of information.
   1) Types of subpoenas.
      a) Subpoena *ad testificandum* — An order directing a person to appear at a hearing in order to testify.
      b) Subpoena *duces tecum* — An order compelling an individual or organization to produce specific books, records, or documents.

      2) In determining if an agency is abusing its discretion, a court considers certain factors, such as:

        a) The purpose of the investigation — An investigation must relate to a legitimate purpose and the power of the agency as conferred in the enabling statute.

        b) The relevance of the information being sought.

        c) The specificity of the demand for information.

        d) The burden of the demand on the party from whom information is being sought.

  c. Search warrants.

    1) The Fourth Amendment to the Constitution (protecting the right of people to be free from unreasonable searches and seizures and to be free from the issuance of warrants without probable cause) applies to administrative agencies.

    2) Warrantless searches may be made only in limited situations (e.g., searches relating to highly regulated or hazardous activities or during emergency circumstances).

D. Adjudication.

1. Agencies may have adjudicative powers relating to civil violations, may make decisions regarding certain defined "unfair practices," and may "recommend" criminal prosecutions by the United States.

2. Administrative adjudicative proceedings may be initiated by private parties, but usually are initiated by the agency following an investigation during which sworn testimony may be taken and evidence obtained.

3. Negotiated settlements — Often, the need for a formal adjudication is avoided because agencies conduct informal conferences that result in negotiated settlements with the parties.

4. Formal complaints — If no settlement is reached, a formal complaint may be issued by the agency, and an answer is filed by the person to whom the complaint is directed.

5. The role of the administrative law judge (ALJ).

  a. Hearings in non-criminal disputes are held before ALJs who are agency employees but are required to be unbiased adjudicators.

  b. The ALJ presides over a hearing, administers oaths, takes evidence, and decides questions of law and fact without a jury.

6. Hearing procedures.

  a. Hearing procedures vary from agency to agency and may be informal or formal, in which case the process is similar to that used by courts.

b. In a formal proceeding, pre-hearing discovery may be conducted, the parties are represented by counsel, testimony is taken, evidence presented, and adverse witnesses may be cross-examined; the rules for admission of relevant evidence, however, are more liberal than those used by courts.

7. Agency orders.

a. The ALJ renders an initial order that may be appealed by either side; usually, appeal is taken to the Court of Appeals for the Federal Circuit but, in some cases, appeal is taken to the appropriate District Court.

b. In some agencies, the commissions that govern the agencies may review cases.

c. In some agencies, the ALJs make findings of facts (and may make recommendations), and the commissions or boards then make their determinations based upon the ALJs' findings.

d. If there is no appeal or review by the agency or commission, the ALJ's initial order becomes the final order of the agency.

e. If there is an appeal, the final order comes from the court; if there is review by the commission, the final order comes from the commission.

f. The final order may provide a remedy, such as payment of damages and/or a direction that the party not carry on a specified activity (a cease-and-desist order that is the equivalent of an injunction issued by a court).

III. Limitations on agency powers.

A. Judicial controls.

1. The APA provides for judicial review of most agency decisions, but a party who is challenging an agency's action must meet certain conditions.

a. There must be an actual, present controversy.

b. The party bringing the action must have "standing to sue" and, therefore, be able to show that interests of the party have been substantially affected by the agency's action.

c. The party must exhaust all possible alternative means of resolving the controversy with the agency.

2. Ordinarily, courts accept the findings of facts by administrative agencies; a court may review whether or not:

    a. The agency exceeded its authority as conferred by the enabling legislation;

    b. The agency properly interpreted laws applicable to the agency action being reviewed;

    c. The agency violated a provision of the Constitution or a procedural requirement of the law;

    d. The agency's actions were arbitrary, capricious, or an abuse of discretion; or

    e. Conclusions drawn by the agency were supported by substantial evidence.

B. Executive controls — The President indirectly influences the policies of agencies, because the President:

    1. Appoints and may remove federal officers.

    2. May exercise veto power over enabling legislation or subsequent legislation which modifies an agency's authority and provides budget recommendations to Congress.

C. Legislative controls — Congress has the power to pass subsequent legislation and, therefore, can:

    1. Reduce the power of an agency, abolish an agency, or revise appropriations to an agency.

    2. Investigate the implementation of laws that it has passed.

    3. Individual members of Congress may engage in "casework" in helping to ensure that constituents are treated fairly by federal agencies.

    4. "Freeze" enforcement of federal regulations as provided for in the Small Business Regulatory Enforcement Fairness Act of 1996.

IV.   Public accountability.

A. Freedom of Information Act (FOIA).

    1. Any persons may request disclosures of certain records of the federal government (provided that the information is not exempted from the FOIA) without giving the reason for the request by complying with the FOIA procedures.

    2. Federal agencies are required to make their records available electronically and to provide a clear index of their documents.

B. Government-in-the-Sunshine Act (the Sunshine Act or open meeting law).

   1. Meetings that are held by a group of agency officials for purposes of conducting deliberations or taking actions must be open to public observations.

   2. An agency must give notice of a planned meeting and its agenda.

   3. There are certain exceptions, and meeting may be closed when the following matters are under discussion:

      a. Accusation of commission of a crime.

      b. Information that would frustrate implementation of a future agency action.

      c. Information that involves agency participation in future rulemaking or litigation.

C. Regulatory Flexibility Act.

   1. Purpose — Reduce the burden of regulation on small business firms.

   2. An agency must conduct a regulatory flexibility analysis when a new rule will have a "significant impact upon a substantial number of small entities."

   3. In some cases, small business record keeping requirements are reduced.

D. Small Business Regulatory Enforcement Fairness Act.

   1. Federal agencies are required to prepare guides that explain in "plain English" how small business firms can comply with federal regulations.

   2. The National Enforcement Ombudsman in the Small Business Administration is authorized to rate agencies and publicize its findings based upon comments received from small businesses.

   3. If a court finds that an agency's demands for fines or penalties are excessive, small business firms may recover their expenses and legal fees from the government.

V. State administrative agencies.

A. Parallel agencies — Often, a state agency serves the same purpose as a parallel federal agency, provides similar services, and imposes similar rules on a local level.

B. Conflicts between parallel agencies — Because of the supremacy clause in Article V of the U.S. Constitution, although a state agency may provide rules that are similar to a parallel federal agency, if the state agency promulgates a rule that is inconsistent with the federal agency rule, federal law is supreme.

KEY WORDS AND PHRASES IN TEXT

administrative agencies
administrative law
enabling legislation
executive regulatory agencies
independent regulatory agencies
delegation doctrine
administrative bureaucracy
substantive, legislative rule
administrative process
Administrative Procedure Act (APA)
rulemaking
notice of proposed rulemaking
comment period
notice-and-comment rulemaking
ex parte comment
final rule
Federal Register
Code of Federal Regulations
investigation by agency
inspection

subpoenas *ad testificandum* and
    duces tecum
search warrant
judicial process
negotiated settlement
formal complaint
adjudication
administrative law judge (ALJ)
adjudicatory hearing
initial and final order
judicial, executive, and legislative control
    over administrative agencies
standing to sue
exhaustion of remedies
Small Business Regulatory Enforcement
    Fairness Act
Freedom of Information Act (FOIA)
Government-in-the-Sunshine Act
Regulatory Flexibility Act
parallel state agencies

FILL-IN QUESTIONS

1. The Treasury Department and the Department of Justice are agencies that are part of the _____ branch of the federal government. Many administrative agencies, such as the Securities and Exchange Commission and the Federal Trade Commission, are not part of the executive branch. They are _____ _____ agencies.

2. Congress can create an administrative agency by enacting an _____ statute in which it delegates power to the agency within defined limits. The grant of power to an administrative agency may incorporate functions associated with the legislative branch if the agency is authorized to engage in _____, or those associated with the judicial branch if the agency is authorized to engage in _____. Many agencies are given investigative functions that may be necessary for rulemaking or for enforcement of laws that typically is a function of the _____ branch.

3. In order to carry out its enforcement function, an administrative agency collects facts during an investigation. If it wishes to have a person appear at a hearing before an _____ (ALJ), a subpoena *ad testificandum* may be issued directing the person to so appear. A subpoena *duces tecum* is used in order to

compel a person to produce and hand over _____
_____.

4. A person may challenge the investigative powers of an agency by establishing that the power being exercised by the agency has not been conferred upon it or that the agency did not have a legitimate purpose in conducting its investigation. A person may also challenge the agency's investigatory actions based upon protections afforded by the Constitution. For example, the Fourth Amendment prohibits unreasonable and warrantless _____. For this reason, the information sought by the agency must be _____ and its demands must be _____ and not unreasonably burdensome.

5. The privilege against self-incrimination afforded by the Fifth Amendment may be asserted by an _____ in a case in which the sanction being sought by the government is a _____ penalty. A corporation _____ assert the privilege against self-incrimination. The Fifth Amendment protection is available in criminal prosecutions but not in cases that are _____ in nature or in which the remedy being sought is monetary damages or a _____ penalty.

6. The power to formulate regulations is conferred upon federal administrative agencies that engage in rulemaking. When an agency promulgates a _____ rule, it must do so in accordance with the Administrative Procedure Act (APA). The APA requires that notice of the proposed rulemaking be published in the *Federal Register*, that an opportunity be given to members of the public to _____ on the proposal, and that the agency publish the final version of the regulation with its statement describing the _____ of the rule.

7. When an agency is exercising its adjudicative powers, after a complaint is issued, an administrative hearing is held before an administrative law judge (ALJ). At the hearing, the ALJ acts as both the trier of the _____. If the ALJ renders an initial order, either party may appeal. Usually, the appeal would be to the _____. In some cases, the decision can be appealed to a federal district court.

8. The courts may review action taken by an administrative agency. The party requesting review must show that he or she has _____, and has exhausted all other available remedies, and that the issue is an actual controversy.

MULTIPLE CHOICE QUESTIONS

1. Both at the federal and state level, enabling statutes providing for the creation of administrative agencies. These government agencies may be authorized to exercise:
   A. judicial powers
   B. executive powers.
   C. legislative powers.
   D. All of the answers above are correct.

2.   Control over the administrative process exists because of:

	the doctrine of judicial review.	the power possessed by the Congress.	provisions in the Administrative Procedure Act.
A.	Yes	Yes	Yes
B.	Yes	No	Yes
C.	No	Yes	Yes
D.	Yes	No	No

3.   A warrantless search of the premises of a business firm is constitutional if it is conducted:
    A. by the police but not by an administrative agency.
    B. by an administrative agency or the police, if it is necessary in order to gain the advantage of surprise.
    C. by an administrative agency or the police in an area that is open to plain view so that there is no expectation that the right of privacy will be violated.
    D. by the police at the request of an administrative agency when the premises to be searched are a commercial establishment or a private residence at which it is believed corporate records have been hidden.

4.   A federal administrative agency must comply with the procedural and substantive requirements of the United States Constitution and:
    A. the Administrative Procedure Act.
    B. the appropriate state rules of evidence.
    C. the National Labor Relations Board's rulings.
    D. the Association of Administrative Judges' rulings.

5.   When a court reviews a decision made by an administrative law judge, the court:
    A. ordinarily, will accept the factual conclusions reached by the administrative law judge.
    B. is guided by the "substantive evidence rule."
    C. usually, will defer to the expertise of the administrative law judge.
    D. All of the answers above are correct.

6.   Arrow Corporation was charged with having violated a provision of the Consumer Product Safety Act. Widger, an examiner for the Consumer Product Safety Commission, concluded that Arrow Corporation had violated the statute and made adverse determinations on several issues. Arrow believes that Widger had not based his decision upon substantial evidence and that Widger's determinations were made in an arbitrary manner. Widger has made his decision and submitted his opinion. Arrow Corporation does not wish to accept the determination. The corporation:
    A. is bound by the decision under all circumstances.
    B. should proceed in a state court in order to obtain injunctive relief ordering Widger to reopen the case and make a new determination.
    C. should appeal to a federal district court that may overturn Widger's determination if the determination was not based upon substantial evidence or was arbitrary.
    D. should not bother appealing to a court because a court will not substitute its judgment for that of the administrator.

(This question has been adapted from objective question #31 on Uniform CPA Examination, November 1983.)

OBJECTIVE (YES-NO) QUESTION

There have been substantiated complaints about five deaths among employees of Healthy Foods, Inc. and ten buyers of a new product manufactured by Healthy Foods, Inc. The federal Occupational Safety and Health Administration and the state Department of Health wish to make inspections of the facilities of Healthy Foods at which the new product is manufactured.

The following questions require a yes or no answer.

A.   The following questions relate to the power of the federal Occupational Safety and Health Commission (OSHA).

    1. An inspection cannot be made of Healthy Foods' premises by representatives of OSHA without the consent of Healthy Foods.

    2. An inspection cannot be made of Healthy Foods' premises by representatives of OSHA without the consent of employees of Healthy Foods.

    3. Healthy Foods has standing to bring an action in order to prevent an inspection of Healthy Foods' premises.

    4. In order to make an inspection of Healthy Foods' premises, OSHA first must make an attempt to obtain a search warrant from a state court.

    5. In order to make an inspection of Healthy Foods' premises, OSHA first must make an attempt to obtain a search warrant from a U.S. District Court.

    6. Before representatives of OSHA may make an inspection of Healthy Foods' premises, OSHA must complete the notice-and-comment rulemaking process as prescribed in the federal Administrative Procedure Act.

B.   The following questions relate to the power of the state Department of Health.

    7. An inspection can be made of Healthy Foods' premises by representatives of the Department of Health without the consent of Healthy Foods.

    8. An inspection can be made of Healthy Foods' premises by representatives of the Department of Health without the consent of employees of Healthy Foods.

    9. Healthy Foods has standing to bring an action in order to prevent an inspection of Healthy Foods' premises by representatives of the Department of Health.

    10. In order to make an inspection of Healthy Foods' premises, the Department of Health first must make an attempt to obtain a search warrant from a state court.

    11. In order to make an inspection of Healthy Foods' premises, the Department of Health first must make an attempt to obtain a search warrant from a federal District Court.

    12. Before representatives of the state Department of Health may make an inspection of Healthy Foods' premises, the Department of Health must complete the notice-and-comment rulemaking process as prescribed in state statutes.

Chapter 45
Consumer Law

The distinct trend away from the *caveat emptor* (let the buyer beware) philosophy can be observed in judicial decisions, statutes, and regulations issued by administrative agencies. The focus of this chapter is upon the protection afforded to consumers engaging in sales and credit transactions. The emphasis of protective legislation and regulation has been upon preventing deceptive practices and assuring full disclosure of material information relating to sales of personal property, real property, and services, and to credit transactions.

Federal statutes relating to advertising, labeling, packaging, sales, credit, debt collection, health, and safety and the ways in which federal administrative agencies carry on consumer protection activities are discussed in this chapter. A section dealing with state consumer protection laws is found in the last portion of the chapter.

The concept of consumer protection overlaps other areas of the law with which you are already familiar. Recall, for example, discussions dealing with torts [Chapters 6 and 7], illegal bargains [Chapter 17], fraud and misrepresentation [Chapter 16], written agreements [Chapter 17], product liability based upon tort law and warranties [Chapters 8 and 25], secured transactions [Chapter 30], and securities regulation [Chapter 43]. See also material dealing with environmental protection [Chapter 46], the Federal Trade Commission [Chapter 44], and real property transactions [Chapter 50].

THINGS TO KEEP IN MIND

1. A consumer usually is considered to be a natural person who obtains or tries to obtain personal property, real property, services, money, or credit for personal, family, or household use. In some cases, small business firms and farmers or farm units are also afforded protection under legislation and regulations dealing with consumers.

2. Public policy considerations arise when balancing the potential benefits and costs of consumer protection. Frequently, the argument is raised that the existing and potential costs of compliance with consumer laws result in increases in the prices charged for consumer goods and services and fewer firms engaging in the production and distribution of those goods and services.

OUTLINE

I.   Deceptive advertising.

    A. The Federal Trade Commission (FTC), an independent regulatory agency, administers a number of federal consumer protection statutes and is authorized to prevent "unfair or deceptive acts or practices in commerce," such as deceptive advertising.

B. Deceptive advertising defined.

1. Deceptive advertising refers to intentional misrepresentations of facts which are material factors in inducing purchasers' decisions to buy advertised products or services.

2. Statements made in an advertisement are deceptive if they are scientifically untrue or contain false product differentiation.

3. An advertisement is deceptive if a reasonable consumer would be misled by the advertisement. In general, puffing is not considered to be deceptive.

C. Bait-and-switch advertising.

1. An advertisement refers to one item that is offered for sale at a low price. When a consumer tries to purchase the advertised item, a salesperson tries to get the consumer to buy a more expensive item.

2. Guidelines issued by the FTC are designed to prevent practices, such as refusal to sell an advertised item, failure to have an adequate quantity of an advertised item available, failure to supply the advertised item within a reasonable time, and discouraging employees from selling an advertised item.

D. FTC actions against deceptive advertising.

1. The procedures that are followed when the FTC believes that a deceptive advertisement is being used by a business firm are described in Chapter 44.

    a. An investigation is conducted by the FTC on its own initiative or following a consumer's or competitor's complaint.

    b. If negotiations do not lead to a settlement, a hearing is held before an administrative law judge (ALJ).

2. Remedies.

    a. Cease and desist order — The offender is directed to discontinue and not resume the advertising.

    b. In some cases, civil penalties may be imposed.

    c. Counteradvertising or corrective advertising — The offender must admit in a new advertisement that prior claims about its product were not true.

        d. Multiple product order — The offender must cease and desist from false advertising regarding both the product that was the subject of the action and its other products.

   E. Telemarketing and electronic advertising.

      1. The Telephone Consumer Protection Act of 1991 prohibits the use of pre-recorded telecommunication messages and unauthorized use of fax machines.

      2. The Telemarketing and Consumer Fraud and Abuse Prevention Act of 1994 empowered the FTC to establish rules covering telemarketing and to bring actions against telemarketers engaging in fraudulent activities.

      3. The FTC Telemarketing Sales Rule.

         a. Telemarketers must inform recipients that calls are sales calls and identify the sellers and products before beginning sales pitches.

         b. Misrepresentations regarding the goods or services, earnings' potential, profitability, risk, or nature of a prize are prohibited.

         c. Telemarketers must inform recipients of the total cost of goods, restrictions on obtaining or using goods, and if sales are final and nonrefundable.

II. Labeling and packaging laws.

   A. The Fair Packaging and Labeling Act — Labels on consumer goods must identify the product, the manufacturer, packer or distributor, and its place of business, as well as the net quantity of contents and the quantity of each serving if the number of servings is stated.

   B. Labeling and packaging of specific products, such as cigarettes, tobacco, drugs, cosmetics, food products, and fabrics, are also regulated by federal statutes.

III. Sales.

   A. The FTC and other agencies are empowered to enforce federal laws regarding certain disclosures and unfair trade practices; states have also enacted laws regarding unfair sales practices.

   B. Regulation Z of the Federal Reserve Board covers credit provisions in sales contracts.

   C. Door-to-door sales.

      1. States have enacted "cooling-off" legislation permitting buyers to rescind a door-to-door purchase within a specified period of time.

2. The FTC regulations provide for a three day "cooling-off" period during which purchasers may cancel sales contracts that were solicited in the home and require that sellers notify buyers of the right to cancel.

D. Telephone and mail-order sales.

1. Telephone sales are regulated by two FTC rules, the Mail Order Rule of 1975 and the Mail or Telephone Order Merchandising Rule of 1993. The 1993 rule updated restrictions against the misuse of the mails and extended protection to sales in which orders are transmitted using computers, fax machines, or other means involving use of telephone lines.

2. State consumer protection statutes parallel and supplement the federal laws against mail fraud.

3. The Postal Reorganization Act provides that unsolicited merchandise sent through the U.S. mail may be retained, used, discarded, or disposed of without the recipient incurring any obligation to the sender.

E. FTC regulation of specific industries — The FTC has issued regulations requiring truthful disclosures and prohibiting unfair sales practices engaged in by people in specific industries (e.g., funeral homes and used car dealers).

F. Real estate sales.

1. Interstate Land Sales Full Disclosure Act — The Act is administered by the Department of Housing and Urban Development (HUD) and requires that there be full disclosure of facts to assure that potential purchasers are able to make informed judgments concerning land purchases.

2. Real Estate Settlement Procedures Act — Requires disclosure of necessary information about the settlement process and the residential property buyer's costs.

IV. Credit protection.

A. The Truth-in-Lending Act.

1. Title I of the Consumer Credit Protection Act (CCPA) which is referred to as the Truth-in-Lending Act (TILA) is administered by the Federal Reserve Board, an independent agency.

2. The Act applies when a debtor is a natural person; the creditor in the ordinary course of its business is a lender, seller of goods, or provider of services; the amount being financed is less than $25,000; and payments are to be made by the debtor in more than four installments.

3. Disclosure requirements — Regulation Z.

a. The purpose of uniform disclosure requirements is to provide consumers with a means of comparing the terms and costs of credit.

b. Financing charges must be stated in an annual percentage rate (APR); financing charges include:
    1) Interest;
    2) Charges for loans and insurance premiums; and
    3) Credit report, appraisal, financing, and service fees.

c. A consumer must be informed of the number of payments, dollar amount of each payment, dates upon which payments are due, and prepayment provisions including any prepayment penalties.

d. Credit arrangements must be clearly noted in a noticeable, conspicuous location on credit documents. (It must be separated from other information so that it is obvious.)

4. If a creditor fails to provide a disclosure statement or fails to discover an error in a disclosure statement, an injured consumer can bring a civil action for rescission or an action to recover damages of not less than $100 or more than $1,000. (If a suit is brought within one year of the violation, the creditor is liable for twice the amount of finance charges plus attorney's fees.)

5. The Equal Credit Opportunity Act prohibits discrimination based upon race, religion, national origin, color, gender, marital status, age, or receipt of certain types of income.

6. Credit card rules.

    a. Credit cardholder will not be liable for more than $50 if there was an unauthorized use of his or her card and notice thereof was given to the card issuer.

    b. Credit card issuer may not bill a cardholder for unauthorized charges if a credit card is improperly issued.

    c. A credit cardholder is given limited right to withhold payment if there is a dispute concerning goods that were purchased with a credit card. (If a credit cardholder believes that an error has been made by issuer of the credit card, the cardholder may suspend payment but must notify and give an explanation to the card issuer concerning an error within 60 days of receipt of the bill.)

7. Consumer leases — The Consumer Leasing Act of 1988 amended the TILA to cover the leasing of consumer goods for less than $25,000.

    a. This Act covers leases that are for more than a four month period.

    b. All material terms of the lease must be disclosed.

    c. Disclosures must be clear and conspicuous and cannot be hidden among non-related information.

B. The Fair Credit Reporting Act.

    1. Upon request, a person who is refused credit or employment because of information in a credit bureau report must be supplied with a summary of the information in the report, the sources and recipients of the information, and given an opportunity to correct errors.

    2. Consumers have the right to be informed of the nature and scope of a credit investigation, the kind of information that is being compiled, and the names of people who will receive a credit report.

    3. A compiler of a credit report must exercise reasonable care in preparing the credit report.

    4. Inaccurate or misleading data must be removed from a credit report, and the consumer has the right to add a statement regarding a disputed matter.

    5. Remedies for improper or negligent disclosure of consumer credit information include actual damages, additional damages of no more than $1,000, and attorneys fees.

C. The Fair Debt Collection Practices Act.

    1. The Act is enforced by the FTC and prohibits debt collection agencies from engaging in certain practices.

        a. Contacting a debtor at the debtor's place of employment, if the employer objects.

        b. Contacting a debtor at unusual or inconvenient times or, if the debtor is represented by an attorney, at any time.

        c. Contacting third parties about the payment of the debt without court authorization.

        d. Harassing or intimidating a debtor or using false and misleading approaches.

        e. Communicating with the debtor after receipt of notice that the debtor is refusing to pay the debt, except to advise the debtor of action to be taken by the collection agency.

2. A collection agency must include a validation notice informing the debtor that the debtor has 30 days in which to dispute the claim and also has a right to written information about the debtor's credit reports.

D. Garnishment of wages.

1. Rights and remedies of unpaid creditors are discussed in Chapter 31.

2. A state court may issue an order for garnishment of a portion of a debtor's wages in order to satisfy a judgment that was obtained by a creditor.

3. The TILA provides that a certain minimum income and no more than 25% of a judgment debtor's after-tax earnings can be garnished.

V. Consumer health and safety.

A. The Federal Food, Drug, and Cosmetic Act (FFDCA) and amendments thereto.

1. The Food and Drug Administration (FDA) is authorized to establish standards and conduct inspections.

2. Adulteration and misbranding of food are prohibited and standards for food and cosmetic products, including the levels of potentially dangerous additives, have been established.

3. Safety standards for automobiles, children's toys, and fabric flammability have also been established.

4. Medical devices and equipment are regulated under an amendment to the FFDCA. Faulty and mislabeled medical objects must be removed from the market.

B. The Consumer Product Safety Act (CPSA).

1. The Consumer Product Safety Commission (CPSC) is authorized to regulate potentially hazardous consumer products; the CPSC conducts research on product safety and maintains a clearinghouse of information.

2. The CPSC may ban products that present an "unreasonable risk" to the user.

VI. State consumer protections laws.

A. Uniform Commercial Code (UCC) — See chapters in Units 3, 4, and 5 dealing with the sale and leases of goods, commercial paper, and secured transactions.

B. Uniform Consumer Credit Code (UCCC).

1. The UCCC, which is similar to the federal TILA, has been adopted in some states, in some cases with variations; similar legislation has been enacted in other states.

2. The UCCC is a comprehensive body of rules that apply to consumer credit. Provisions of the UCCC cover maximum credit ceilings and interest rates; home solicitation and referral sales, required disclosure statements; and the form and contents of sales agreements.

KEY WORDS AND PHRASES IN TEXT

caveat emptor
Federal Trade Commission (FTC)
unfair and deceptive advertising
puffing
bait-and-switch advertising
cease and desist order
counteradvertising (corrective advertising)
multiple product orders
telemarketing and electronic advertising
Fair Packaging and Labeling Act
door-to-door sales
"cooling off" period
telephone and mail-order sales
"used-car rule"
Interstate Land Sales Full Disclosure Act
Department of Housing and Urban
      Development (HUD)

Real Estate Settlement Procedures Act
Truth-in-Lending Act (TILA — Title I,
      Consumer Credit Protection Act)
Federal Reserve Board Regulation Z
Equal Credit Opportunity Act
credit card rules
Consumer Leasing Act
Fair Credit Reporting Act
Fair Debt Collection Practices Act
validation notice
garnishment of wages
Federal Food, Drug, and Cosmetic Act
Consumer Product Safety Act
Consumer Product Safety Commission
Uniform Consumer Credit Code (UCCC)
state consumer protection statutes

FILL-IN QUESTIONS

1. The federal administrative agency that regulates deceptive acts and practices, including advertising, is the _____, an independent administrative agency. Federal consumer protection regulations relating to construction and safety standards for mobile homes and interstate land sales are enforced by the _____, an administrative agency that is part of the executive branch of the federal government.

2. Advertisements may be considered to be _____ if they include false statements or claims about the quality, effects, origins or availability of products or services, or omit important material information. In order to prevent the use of such advertisements, cease and desist orders (which have the same effect as injunctive relief granted by courts) can be issued by the _____.

3. Misuse of the _____ and _____ by advertisers can harm a business firm because, today, many companies rely upon these two machines, and useless advertisement can obstruct legitimate transactions and inquiries.

4.   The regulation of the misuse and deceptive use of the telephone is governed by the "_____ Rule" of 1975 and the "_____ Order Merchandising Rule" of 1993. The more recent rule was needed because of the recent advances in _____ technology.

5.   The _____, which is enforced by the Federal Trade Commission and the Department of Health and Human Services, requires that consumer goods have labels that identify the product, the manufacturer, and the net quantity or weight of the contents.

6.   The Federal Reserve Board administers the Consumer Credit Protection Act, which is commonly known as the _____ Act. The Consumer Credit Protection Act is a disclosure law. It requires that credit or loan terms be disclosed by a seller of _____ goods or services, or a lender of money to be used in order to purchase _____ goods and services, to a debtor when the debtor is a natural person. The Act requires that the debtor be informed about the _____. The annual percentage rate of certain charges, including interest and finance, loan, appraisal, insurance, etc., fees must be stated. (The Act, however, does not regulate the rate of these charges.)

7.   State statutes and the Postal Reorganization Act provide that recipients of _____ will not be liable to senders for the purchase price of the goods if they do not return the merchandise.

MULTIPLE CHOICE QUESTIONS

1.   A store that sells compact discs (CDs) has advertised that it is selling a line of CDs whose sounds are "as clear as bells."
     A. Because the advertisement is deceptive and misleading, the FTC may begin the process for issuing a cease and desist order.
     B. Because the advertisement is deceptive and misleading, the FTC probably will prosecute the advertiser for a violation of an FTC regulation prohibiting false and deceptive advertising.
     C. Because the advertisement is deceptive and misleading, the state, in which the advertisement appeared, probably will prosecute the advertiser for a violation of a state statute prohibiting false and deceptive advertising.
     D. Even though some purchasers of the CDs were misled by the advertisement, the claim made in the advertisement was puffing, which usually is not a violation of a federal or state statute.

2.   A store that sells compact discs (CDs) has advertised in a magazine that is distributed throughout the U.S. that it is selling a line of CDs whose sounds have been tested by more than 50 bell ringers, all of whom agreed that the CDs sounds are "as clear as bells."
     A. Because the advertisement is deceptive and misleading, the FTC may begin the process for issuing a cease and desist order.
     B. Because the advertisement is deceptive and misleading, the FTC probably will prosecute the advertiser for a violation of an FTC regulation prohibiting false and deceptive advertising.

C. Because the advertisement is deceptive and misleading, a state, in which the advertisement appeared, probably will prosecute the advertiser for the crime of larceny.
D. Even though some purchasers of the CDs were misled by the advertisement, the claim made in the advertisement was puffing, which usually is not a violation of a federal or state statute.

3. A chain of stores that sells eyeglasses has advertised on television that any customer who purchases a pair of eyeglasses will receive a second pair of glasses free. In each of the stores in the chain, the prices of eyeglasses are approximately 90% higher than those sold by competitors in the same geographic area. This is an example of:
A. deceptive advertising.
B. bait-and-switch advertising.
C. affirmative advertising.
D. counteradvertising.

4. A salesperson selling small appliances visited the Smiths in their home. During the visit, the Smiths agreed to buy two appliances and signed a preprinted form that contained a notice to purchasers that they had the right to cancel the contract for the sale of the appliances within three days. The Smiths can exercise the right to cancel:
A. within two days, rather than three days, if a state statute provides for a two-day cooling-off period.
B. within five days, rather than three days, if a state statute provides for a five-day cooling-off period.
C. within three days, rather than five days, even if a state statute provides for a five-day cooling-off period.
D. within a reasonable period of time.

5. Many of the federal statutes in the area of consumer protection provide for full and accurate disclosures to consumers and confer authority upon federal administrative agencies to enforce the statutes and to adopt appropriate regulations. For example, the Truth-in-Lending Act (TILA) requires that creditors who, in the ordinary course of business, lend money or sell goods or services on credit or arrange for the extension of credit to natural persons must make certain disclosures regarding the loan or credit terms. The TILA is administered by:
A. The Federal Trade Commission, which promulgated Regulation Z.
B. The Federal Reserve Board, which promulgated Regulation Z.
C. The Securities and Exchange Commission, which promulgated Regulation Z.
D. The Securities and Exchange Commission, which promulgated Regulation C.

6. The Truth-in-Lending Act:
A. requires creditors to disclose all finance charges, including interest, in terms of annual percentage rates.
B. establishes a maximum amount that may be charged by a lender or seller in a loan or credit transaction.
C. is regarded as the federal usury law.
D. applies to credit transactions between creditors and debtors without regard to the fact that they are natural persons or corporations.

7.   Ordinary expenses incurred by a lender in a loan situation, which will be allowed in addition to the maximum contract rate of interest, are costs of:
      A. examining title to property that is being given as collateral security.
      B. investigating the financial character of the borrower.
      C. drawing necessary documents.
      D. All of the answers above are correct.

8.   The Truth-in-Lending Act:
      A. applies to any lender or seller who, in the ordinary course of business, lends money or extends credit to others, if the amount lent or the amount of credit given is less than $25,000.
      B. applies to any lender or seller who, in the ordinary course of business, lends money or extends credit to natural persons for purchases, not exceeding $25,000, for personal, household, or business use.
      C. establishes a maximum percentage amount that can be charged for extending credit.
      D. is a disclosure statute requiring lenders and sellers to disclose the cost of credit.

Chapter 46
Environmental Law

Increased urbanization, economic growth, and advanced methods of production have accentuated the conflict between freedom of contracting and the right to use one's own property, on one hand, and the needs of society to be protected against harm caused by pollution to the environment, on the other.

The United States Congress and the state legislatures have responded to the increased awareness of the presence and harmful effects of pollution by enacting statutes aimed at reducing contamination and improving the quality of the air, water, and land.

OUTLINE

I. Common law actions — See also Chapters 6.

   A. Nuisance — Liability is imposed upon an owner of property who uses his or her own property in a manner that unreasonably interferes with the rights of other people to use and enjoy their property.

      1. Nuisance may include effusions, or pollution, in the form of dirt, smoke, noxious odors, toxic substances, and noise.

      2. In a case based upon the common law tort of nuisance, a court weighs the harm to the plaintiff caused by the pollution, the defendant's cost for stopping the pollution, and the interests of the community.

      3. A person who incurs an injury because of a private nuisance (which is distinct from the harm incurred by the general public) has standing to sue and may seek compensatory damages and/or injunctive relief.

      4. If there is a public nuisance that affects the public at large, a governmental body may seek an injunction and/or a criminal prosecution.

   B. Negligence and strict liability.

      1. Liability, based upon the tort of negligence, may be imposed upon a polluter who failed to exercise reasonable care causing a foreseeable injury to the plaintiff.

      2. Strict tort liability will be imposed upon a firm that engaged in an abnormally dangerous activity that normally is not conducted in the geographic area, and as a result of which there is a high degree of serious risk of harm to other

people or their property. (In an action based upon strict liability, a plaintiff does not have to establish that the defendant was negligent.)

3. Toxic torts — During much of this century, the development of new products, with insufficient study of the effects of those products on both producers and users, has led to litigation brought by people who have been injured by these products. (Examples include nuclear energy and its by-products, the transportation and disposal of radioactive materials, and the use of asbestos.)

II. Federal regulation.

A. Environmental regulatory agencies.

1. Many of the environmental protection statutes are administered by the Environmental Protection Agency (EPA) that has been empowered to promulgate rules in order to control the emissions of pollutants.

2. The Departments of Defense, Labor, and the Interior as well as the Food and Drug Administration and the Nuclear Regulatory Commission regulate certain specified environmental matters.

B. Assessment of the impact of agencies' actions on the environment.

1. The National Environmental Policy Act (NEPA) requires than an environmental impact statement (EIS), analyzing the environmental effects of proposed federal action (including legislation and action taken by an agency), or a statement explaining why an impact statement is not required, must be prepared.

2. The EIS indicates the social benefits, risks, and costs of the proposed action.

3. Environmental impact statements are prepared by the agencies responsible for carrying out proposed actions and, in some cases, private companies which enter into contracts for major federal actions.

4. Other federal laws that require consideration of environmental effects.

   a. The Fish and Wildlife Coordination Act requires that federal agencies proposing approval of the impounding or diverting waters of a stream consult with the Fish and Wildlife Service.

   b. The Endangered Species Act requires that all federal agencies take steps to ensure that their actions "do not jeopardize the continued existence of endangered species" or their habitat.

III. Air pollution.

A. The Clean Air Act of 1963 (as amended) delegates the establishment of air quality standards to the EPA.

B. Mobile sources.

1. Regulations issued by EPA governing air pollution from automobiles and other mobile sources specify pollution standards and time schedules.

2. Service stations are also subject to environmental regulations.

C. Stationary sources.

1. The primary responsibility for preventing and controlling air pollution by stationary sources, such as utilities and industrial plants, rests with state and local governments.

2. The EPA sets primary and secondary levels of ambient standards and the states formulate plans to achieve these standards within certain time periods.

3. Firms in certain industries are required to use the maximum achievable control technologies (MACTs) in order to limit specified emissions.

D. Hazardous air pollutants.

1. Industries that use air pollutants that are likely to result in death or irreversible or incapacitating illness are required to use the MACTs.

2. Landfills that emit hazardous air pollutants are subject to federal and state controls.

E. Violations of the Clean Air Act..

1. Civil penalties of up to $25,000 per day may be assessed by the EPA, or the EPA may impose a penalty equal to the violator's economic benefits from noncompliance.

2. Criminal fines may be imposed upon those who knowingly violate the Clean Air Act.

3. Private citizens can also sue violators and receive up to $10,000 if they provide information about violations of the Act.

IV. Water pollution.

A. Navigable waters.

1. The earliest statute, the Rivers and Harbors Act of 1899 (as amended), required permits for discharging or depositing refuse in navigable waters.

2. The objectives of the Federal Water Pollution Control Act (FWPCA), as amended by the Clean Water Act and the Water Quality Act, are to make water safe for swimming, to protect fish and wildlife, and to eliminate the discharge of pollutants into the water.

   a. Time schedules are set forth, and the EPA establishes limitations for discharges of pollutants based upon the best available technology for controlling them.

   b. Municipal and industrial polluters must apply for permits before discharging waste into navigable waters.

3. Navigable waters include coastal waters, lakes, streams, wetlands, and swamps.

4. Wetlands — Recognition of the importance of wetlands (marshy areas, saturated by water) to local and migratory animals, fish and birds, and to local environments (because wetlands act to filter natural and man-made impurities) has led to controversy regarding enforcement of wetland regulations.

5. Violations of the Clear Water Act.

   a. Civil remedies available — A person violating the Act may have to pay a maximum of from $10,000 to $25,000 per day for a violation, and be required to clean up the pollution or pay for the cost of cleaning up the pollution. (The Act also encourages injured parties to bring civil suits.)

   b. Criminal penalties for "knowing endangerment" — Imprisonment for a maximum of 15 years and fines of a maximum of $250,000 for natural persons and $1 million for corporate offenders.

B. Drinking water.

1. The Safe Drinking Water Act required that the EPA set maximum levels for pollutants in public water systems; operators of public water systems must use the best available technology that is economically feasible in attempting to meet the EPA standards.

2. Suppliers of water must send an annual statement describing the source of its water, the level of any contaminants in the water, and health concerns that might be associated with the contaminants to its customers.

C. Ocean dumping.

1. The Marine Protection, Research, and Sanctuaries Act of 1972 (Ocean Dumping Act) as amended, regulates the transportation and dumping of materials into ocean waters.

2. Ocean dumping of radiological, chemical, and biological warfare agents, and high-level radioactive waste is prohibited and those who are transporting or dumping nonexempt materials must obtain permits.

3. Criminal and civil penalties may be imposed and injunctions obtained.

D. Oil pollution.

1. Much of the world's production of crude oil is carried by ships over the oceans. (As demonstrated by the *Exxon Valdez* oil spill in Alaska's Prince William Sound, environmental clean-up costs can be substantial.)

2. The Oil Pollution Act of 1990.

   a. Penalties, damages, and liability for clean-up costs are imposed upon oil facilities, oil shippers, vessel owners, and operators that discharge oil into navigable waters or onto adjoining shores.

   b. The Act creates a one billion dollar oil clean-up and compensation fund and requires that oil tankers using U.S. ports be double hulled by the year 2011.

V. Noise pollution — The Noise Control Act of 1972 provides for the establishment of noise emission standards that are achievable by using the best available and economically reasonable technology.

VI. Toxic chemicals.

A. Pesticides and herbicides.

1. The Federal Insecticide, Fungicide, and Rodenticide Act of 1947 (FIFRA) provides that pesticides and herbicides be:

   a. Registered before they can be sold;

   b. Certified and used only for approved applications; and

   c. Used in limited quantities when applied to food crops.

2. Registration of a substance may be canceled if it is identified as harmful.

3. The EPA may inspect plants in which chemicals are manufactured.

4. A pesticide can remain on the market only if there is "reasonable certainty of no harm" to people from exposure to the pesticide.

5. Violations of FIFRA.

a. The sale of a pesticide or herbicide is prohibited if the pesticide or herbicide:
  1) Is not registered or if the registration has been canceled or suspended.
  2) The label is false or misleading or the label does not comply with the labeling requirements of FIFRA.

b. Criminal penalties may be imposed for knowing violations of FIFRA.
  1) Fines of up to $50,000 may be imposed upon producers
  2) Fines of up to $25,000 may be imposed upon dealers.
  3) Fines of up to $1,000 may be imposed on users.
  4) Officials of producers and dealers are subject to imprisonment for up to one year, and individual users may be imprisoned for up to 30 days.

c. Civil penalties include a maximum of up to $5,000 for a violation by a registrant, wholesaler, distributor, or retailer and a maximum of up to $1,000 for a violation by a user.

B. Toxic substances — Toxic Substances Control Act of 1976.

1. Before manufacturers, processors, and others use chemicals, a determination must be made of the effect upon human health and the environment.

2. The EPA is authorized to regulate substances that pose an imminent hazard or an unreasonable risk of injury to health or to the environment.

3. The EPA may require special labeling, limit the use of a substance, set production quotas, and prohibit the use of toxic substances.

C. Hazardous wastes.

1. The Resource Conservation and Recovery Act of 1976 (RCRA), as amended, provides for the establishment of regulations by the EPA for monitoring and controlling hazardous waste disposal.

   a. Hazardous waste being transported must be packaged and labeled properly.

   b. There are provisions for civil and criminal penalties.

2. Superfund — Comprehensive Environmental Response, Compensation, and Liability Act (CERCLA) establishes a federal fund to be used by the EPA for cleaning up hazardous waste disposal sites.

   a. Potentially responsible parties — Clean-up costs may be recovered from potentially responsible parties (PRPs), who generated or transported the waste, or were owners or operators of the site when the waste was disposed of, and/or are currently owners or operators of the site.

    b. Liability under Superfund.

       1) In general, a PRP is jointly and severally liable for all of the clean-up costs, but a PRP may obtain contribution from other persons who also are liable.

       2) Parent corporations, corporate officers who exercise control over a corporate owner, and successor corporations of corporate owners or operators have been found liable for clean-up costs.

       3) Liability of lending institutions and fiduciaries.

           a) A lending institution can be held liable for violations of CERCLA on property the institution holds as collateral for a loan if the institution actually participates in the management or operations of the borrower.

           b) A fiduciary (e.g., a trustee who manages or holds property in trust for another person) may be liable as a PRP under limited circumstances.

VII. Radiation.

A. The Atomic Energy Act provides for regulation of the private nuclear industry by the Nuclear Regulatory Commission (NRC), which reviews plans for proposed nuclear plants, issues construction permits after preparation of environmental impact statements, and licenses the operation of plants.

B. Standards for radioactivity in the environment and for the disposal of some radioactive waste are set by EPA.

C. The Low Level Radioactive Waste Policy Act of 1980 (as amended) provides for state responsibility for control of low-level radioactive waste generated by private facilities; the use and disposal of other radioactive waste is regulated by the NRC.

D. Liability for injuries resulting from exposure to radioactive material has been imposed in suits based upon common law tort theories, such as strict liability, and based upon violations of state and federal statutes (e.g., the Clean Water Act, RCRA, and CERCLA).

VIII. State and local regulation.

A. State statutes and regulations of state administrative agencies may require alterations in proposals for development of land in order to reduce the negative impact on the environment, as well as restrict discharges of chemicals and other substances into the air and water (including motor vehicle emissions), and regulate the disposal and recycling of toxic and nontoxic wastes.

B. Aspects of the environment that often are controlled by city, county, and other local governments.

    1. Land use — Zoning is used to inhibit or direct growth of communities and to protect the environment.

2. Waste removal and disposal.

3. Construction and appearance of buildings and other structures.

4. Emissions of substances, odors, and noise.

5. Location and conditions of land used for public purposes.

KEY WORDS AND PHRASES IN TEXT

private and public nuisances
injunctive relief
negligence and strict tort liability
business polluter
ultrahazardous activities
toxic tort
National Environmental Policy Act
      (NEPA)
environmental impact statement (EIS)
Fish and Wildlife Coordination Act
Endangered Species Act
Environmental Protection Agency
      (EPA)
Clean Air Act
mobile sources of air pollution
stationary sources of air pollution
maximum achievable control
      technology (MACT)
navigable waters
Federal Water Pollution Control Act
      (Clean Water Act)
wetlands

Safe Drinking Water Act
Marine Protection, Research, and
      Sanctuaries Act (Ocean
      Dumping Act)
Oil Pollution Act of 1990
Noise Control Act
Federal Insecticide, Fungicide, and
      Rodenticide Act (FIFRA)
Toxic Substances Control Act
Resource Conservation and Recovery
      Act (RCRA)
Superfund — Comprehensive Environ-
      mental Response, Compensation,
      and Liability Act (CERCLA)
potentially responsible party (PRP)
liability of lending institutions and
      fiduciaries under CERCLA
Nuclear Regulatory Commission (NRC)
Low-Level Radioactive Waste Policy Act
Nuclear Waste Policy Act
state and local zoning laws

FILL-IN QUESTIONS

1. Common law remedies may be sought by individual plaintiffs who have been harmed as a result of pollution because of torts committed by other persons. Such remedies include _____ and injunctions.

2. If a plaintiff was harmed because of pollution caused by the owner of a factory, the plaintiff may bring an action based upon the tort of _____ but will have to show that the injury that the plaintiff incurred was separate and distinct from the harm to the general public. A plaintiff also may have a cause of action based upon the tort of negligence, but will have to establish that the defendant's (the factory owner's) failure to exercise _____ caused a foreseeable injury to the plaintiff. Strict tort liability will be imposed upon the factory owner if the factory owner engaged in an _____, as a result of which there was a high degree of risk of harm to other people or their property.

3.   During the twentieth century, the development of new products without adequately studying the effects of these products has led to a new field of litigation referred to as _____. Plaintiffs in these cases rely upon theories of law, such as _____ and _____, as well as upon statutes.

4.   The National Environmental Policy Act (NEPA) prescribes that an _____ _____ statement (EIS) must be prepared if a major federal action will affect the quality of the environment. The statement must contain an analysis of the impact that the federal action will have on the environment, including any adverse effects and alternative actions that might be taken, as well as any _____ effects that the action might generate.

5.   The federal agency which is empowered to oversee and monitor many of the federal environmental statutes is the _____.

6.   In addition to state regulation aimed at reducing air pollution, federal legislation has been enacted to improve the air quality. One such federal statute is the Clean Air Act that provides for regulation of air pollution generated by _____ sources, such as motor vehicle emissions, and _____ sources, such as pollution created by manufacturing plants, processing facilities, and utilities that generate power.

7.   The area of environmental protection that first was addressed by the United States Congress was pollution of navigable waters. The scheme of regulation that has been used in order to reduce water pollution is to require municipalities and industrial firms that are discharging or depositing waste in bodies of water to obtain _____. The Marine Protection, Research, and Sanctuaries Act, which is known as the _____ Act, requires that _____ be obtained by municipalities and industrial firms that are transporting or depositing waste materials in _____ waters.

8.   State, county, city, and other local governments directly regulate the use of land that is _____ when these governments pass zoning statutes and ordinances and indirectly can affect business firms because of the control that these governments may exercise over _____ land, such as parks, streets, and highways.

MULTIPLE CHOICE QUESTIONS

Questions 1, 2, and 3 are based upon the following fact situation: The Zeta Chemical Corp. uses toxic substances in order to produce chemicals at its plant in Anytown. Thirty percent of the local population is employed by Zeta Chemical Corp. at the Anytown plant. Zeta Chemical Corp. stores the toxic material in a building on its property. Some of the toxins have seeped into the ground and into the Anytown water system. Five residents of the municipality were hospitalized as a result of nervous system disorders caused by drinking the toxic water. Six hundred other residents were treated for headaches and nerve impairment, but they were not hospitalized.

1.   The 605 residents, who are ill, have brought a tort action against Zeta Chemical Corp.

A. Only the five residents who were hospitalized have a cause of action based upon common law nuisance.
B. Only the 605 residents who actually had symptoms of illnesses caused by toxin seepage can recover damages in a common law nuisance action.
C. The 605 residents who actually had symptoms of illnesses caused by the toxin seepage can recover damages and injunctive relief in a common law nuisance action.
D. The only remedy that can be recovered by the 605 residents who were harmed is an injunction in order to prevent future harm.

2. Which of the following statements is **false**?
A. If the municipality of Anytown commences an action against Zeta Chemical Corp. based upon a common law public nuisance, the municipality of Anytown may recover damages for the costs of trucking in unpolluted water and installing new equipment that will filter out the toxins in the water in addition to an injunction.
B. Residents of Anytown who have **not** had any symptoms of illness have standing to sue Zeta Chemical Corp.
C. In tort actions based upon private and public nuisance, Zeta Chemical Corp. will be liable for damages that already have been incurred by residents and the municipality of Anytown.
D. In a public nuisance suit, Zeta Chemical Corp. will **not** be liable for damages for the cost to Anytown of installing new filtering equipment for the municipality's water system if the company can prove that the cost of establishing a new storage facility for the toxic substances is equal to the cost to the municipality of installing new equipment that will filter out the toxins in the water.

3. In addition to basing their actions on the tort of nuisance, the five hospitalizedresidents of Anytown are also basing their actions against Zeta Chemical Corp. on negligence and strict liability. In order to recover for their injuries based upon the strict liability theory, the five plaintiffs will have to prove that (1) their injuries were directly caused by the seepage of the toxins; (2) the storing of toxic substances in Anytown is an unusually dangerous activity that normally is not conducted in the municipality of Anytown; (3) the activity has a high degree of serious risk of harm to residents in the municipality; and that (4):
A. the risk of harm could **not** be eliminated even if the chemical company exercised reasonable care.
B. the risk of harm could have been eliminated if the chemical company exercised reasonable care.
C. the chemical company's failure to have the storage facility constructed in a more careful manner was the proximate cause of their injuries.
D. their injuries were **not** caused by their contributory negligence.

4. The National Environmental Policy Act requires that an environmental impact statement (EIS) must be filed whenever:
A. any person is going to construct a building that will affect the environment.
B. a state is going to take action that will affect the environment.
C. any federal governmental activity that will affect the environment is to be conducted.
D. All of the answers above are correct.

5. The Clean Air Act, as amended:
   A. establishes a national standard for air pollutants that are emitted by industrial plants.
   B. provides that each state is to develop a state implementation plan.
   C. requires that the Environmental Protection Agency develop emission standards for hazardous air pollutants, such as sulfur dioxide and lead.
   D. All of the answers above are correct.

6. The major purpose of the Resource Conservation and Recovery Act's manifest (tracking) system is to:
   A. provide a framework for documenting cases in which natural persons have been injured by dangerous chemical wastes.
   B. provide a regulatory framework for the tracking of hazardous chemical wastes from the generator to the storage or disposal site.
   C. provide for a recording system in order to document the natural resources that have been adversely affected by hazardous wastes.
   D. provide a systematic record of the effect of pollutants on endangered species in the United States.

7. Mikhail managed the Magnum Manufacturing Plant (MMP), a producer of photographic chemicals, for Oily Co., the owner of the MMP. Upon Mikhail's return from a seminar on known toxic pollutants, which include MMP's products, Mikhail learned that MMP has been leaking waste chemicals into the local stream. Mikhail reported the leakage to Oily Co., handed in his resignation from his managerial position to Oily, and departed for Europe. Oily Co. hired Depo to replace Mikhail as manager of the MMP. Upon discovery of the leaking waste chemicals, Depo reported the leakage to the state pollution commission. Liability will be imposed upon:

	Mikhail.	Depo.	Oily Co..
A.	Yes	Yes	Yes
B.	Yes	No	Yes
C.	No	No	Yes
D.	No	No	No

8. The Pollu-No Company manufactures a much needed, low-cost measles vaccine. Recently, it was discovered that the local plant in the town of Melting was leaking deadly by-products of the vaccine production process into the local river. The Melting Town Council is seeking relief from the courts. Which relief is the town of Melting most likely to obtain?
   A. An order directing Pollu-No Company to close down the plant.
   B. An order directing Pollu-No Company to move the manufacturing plant to the neighboring town of Seepington.
   C. An order directing Pollu-No Company to filter all discharges from the plant in order to prevent leakage of the pollutants into the river.
   D. No relief will be given to the town of Melting, but the Pollu-No Company will have to pay a fine to the state for the past pollution.

Chapter 47
Antitrust Law

In the United States, strong public policies, which are predicated upon the premise that economic concentration is harmful, favor the maintenance of business competition. For this reason, restraints of trade and other unfair methods of competition have been discouraged and, in some cases, prohibited by judicial decisions and statutes.

Late in the nineteenth century, the trust device was used in order to amass market power and monopolize certain industries. (A trust is an arrangement in which a trustee holds legal title to property for the benefit of another person or group of people.) Shareholders transferred their stock in corporations to trustees in exchange for trust certificates. The trustees made decisions fixing prices, controlling output, and allocating geographic markets in which the firms in an industry could engage in business without competing with one another. In 1887, in order to deal with anticompetitive practices and monopolization, Congress enacted the Interstate Commerce Act that provided for the creation of the Interstate Commerce Commission (ICC) and empowered the Commission to regulate the railroad industry. The Interstate Commerce Act was followed, in 1890, by the Sherman Act, a broadly worded statute that prohibits certain agreements between competitors that restrain trade and monopolization or attempts to monopolize. In 1914, Congress passed the Clayton Act and the Federal Trade Commission Act creating the Federal Trade Commission (FTC) which was given enforcement powers.

The Sherman Act prohibits contracts, combinations, conspiracies, and other joint actions to restrain or limit trade as well as monopolization and attempts to monopolize trade or commerce. The Clayton Act and subsequent legislation have been directed at particular types of business behavior that have the effect of reducing competition. The prohibitions that are set forth in the Clayton Act (as amended) are directed at price discrimination, exclusionary practices, and certain mergers and acquisitions "when their effect might be to substantially lessen competition or increase monopoly."

THINGS TO KEEP IN MIND

The common law rule is that general restraints of trade (agreements or promises not to compete) are against public policy and will not be enforced but that reasonable ancillary, partial restraints that are necessary to protect a property interest (such as goodwill) may be enforced. [See Chapter 17.]

OUTLINE

I.   The Sherman Antitrust Act.

    A. Major provisions of the Sherman Act.

1. Section 1 prohibits concerted action among firms to restrain trade; a restraint of trade is an agreement or other group action that has the effect of reducing competition in the marketplace.

2. Section 2 prohibits unilateral and joint misuses of monopoly power.

B. Jurisdictional requirements.

   1. The Sherman Act applies to restraints of trade that have a significant impact on interstate or foreign commerce.

   2. The states can regulate restraints of trade that affect intrastate commerce.

   3. Today, courts construe the meaning of "interstate commerce" broadly so that a seemingly local activity that touches or has an impact on interstate commerce or business is within the purview of the Sherman Act.

II. Section 1 of the Sherman Act.

A. "Every contract, combination in the form of trust or otherwise, or conspiracy, in restraint of trade or commerce among the several states or with foreign nations is declared to be illegal."

B. The rule of reason.

   1. Anticompetitive agreements providing for unreasonable restraints of trade are violations of the Act.

   2. In determining whether or not agreements are reasonable, courts weigh the potential benefits against the potential harm and consider the purpose that the parties had in effecting the agreement, the capability of the parties to implement the agreement, the potential effect of the agreement, and, occasionally, the availability to the parties of less restrictive means of achieving their goals.

C. *Per se* violations — As a matter of law, certain conduct violates the Sherman Act without regard to proof of injury to the public, the reasonableness of the action, or worthiness of motives, even if the benefits to society outweigh the anticompetitive effect.

D. The distinction between the *per se* rule and the rule of reason is clearer in theory than it is in application.

E. Horizontal restraints — Agreements and other concerted activities among rival firms (firms that directly compete in the same market) the objectives of which are to restrict competition.

   1. Price fixing — Agreements to establish or fix prices (directly or indirectly) by limiting supply are *per se* violations of Section 1.

2. Group boycotts — A group boycott is a concerted refusal to deal or do business with another person or organization who is the object of the boycott.

   a. An objective of a boycott may be to eliminate or discipline a competitor and, therefore, to enforce an anticompetitive arrangement among firms; a group boycott may also be used in order to promote economic efficiency, moral or social causes, or the general well-being of the group without intending to injure competition.

   b. In the past, group boycotts were treated as *per se* violations of Section 1; more recently, the Supreme Court has indicated that the rule of reason is to be applied to group boycotts.

3. Horizontal market division — Geographical or functional allocations or divisions of the markets (in which products are sold) among rival firms have been held to be *per se* violations of Section 1.

4. Trade associations — Trade associations are organizations that promote the common interests of groups of competitors.

   a. Activities, such as collecting and distributing information among members, enhancement of the public images of industries, trades or professions, setting industrial or professional standards, and the pooling of resources to represent the members' interests to governmental bodies and thus benefit the economic well-being of the members, are not necessarily anticompetitive activities.

   b. A trade association in a concentrated industry (one in which a single firm or a small number of firms control a large portion of sales) may engage in activities that are viewed as being anticompetitive.

   c. The rule of reason is applied to trade association activities; activities that may result in fixing prices or limiting supplies but which are beneficial to the public and do not substantially harm competition are not Section 1 violation.

5. Joint ventures.

   a. A joint venture is an undertaking by two or more firms or individuals who pool their resources, participate together, and share risks in order to achieve a specific goal. [See Chapter 37.]

   b. A joint venture that does not involve price fixing or market divisions will be analyzed using the rule of reason.

F. Vertical restraints — The *per se* rule applies to some vertical restraints of trade; the rule of reason is applied to other vertical restraints.

1. A vertical restraint may exist when firms in different industries at successive stages (or levels) in the chain of production and/or distribution make an agreement or when a single vertically integrated firm engages in business at different functional levels.

2. Territorial (locational) or customer restrictions — Distributional arrangements between a manufacturer and its dealers or retailers restricting the sale of products in specific markets or to certain classes of customers do not violate Section 1 if these arrangements are reasonable and used in order to compete more effectively with other manufacturers.

3. Resale price maintenance (fair trade) agreements.

   a. An agreement between a seller (manufacturer) and buyer (a retailer who sells to the public) establishing a minimum or maximum price for a product is illegal *per se*.

   b. A seller, however, may suggest a price at which the seller's products may be sold by a retailer.

   c. A seller who makes a consignment of goods to a consignee retains title to goods, bears the risks associated with ownership, and may specify the price at which the goods are to be sold by the consignee.

4. Refusals to deal.

   a. The concept of freedom of contract has been held to support the rule that a manufacturer, which is acting unilaterally, is free to deal or not to deal with whomever the manufacturer chooses.

   b. A unilateral refusal to deal may violate Section 2 if the firm has or will acquire monopoly power, and the refusal to deal is likely to have an anticompetitive effect in a particular market.

III. Section 2 of the Sherman Act.

A. "Every person who shall monopolize or attempt to monopolize, or combine or conspire with any other person or persons to monopolize any part of the trade or commerce among the several States, or with foreign nations, shall be deemed guilty of a felony. . . "

B. Monopolization.

1. In order to establish that a defendant has violated Section 2 the following elements must be proven:

   a. Possession of monopoly power in the relevant product or service market.

b. Intentional, willful, purposeful acquisition or maintenance of monopoly power.

2. Monopoly power.

   a. For purposes of Section 2, a monopoly or monopolization exists when one firm (regardless of size) controls such a high proportion of the market for a product or service that the firm is able to dictate the price and exclude competition.

   b. Courts use the market share test based upon the firm's percentage share of the relevant market; in general, a 70% or greater share constitutes market power.

   c. Relevant market is defined in terms of the product market and the geographic market.
      1) A relevant product market is a market in which the same product or substitute (interchangeable) products are sold.
      2) A relevant geographic market generally is that section of the country within which a firm can increase its price without attracting new sellers or without losing many customers to alternative suppliers outside the area.

3. The intent requirement — The acquisition or maintenance of dominant market share (monopoly power) must be a result of intentional, willful, purposeful anticompetitive conduct rather than the result of legitimate competitive behavior, business acumen, or development of a superior product.

C. Attempts to monopolize.

   1. Section 2 provides that a unilateral or concerted attempt to monopolize violates the Sherman Act.

   2. An attempt to monopolize is a violation of the Sherman Act when there is a high probability of its success, particularly if the alleged offender possesses some degree of market power.

IV. The Clayton Act.

A. The Clayton Act prohibits certain anticompetitive practices "where the effect" of the practice "may be to substantially lessen competition or tend to create a monopoly in any line of commerce."

B. Price discrimination [Section 2, as amended by the Robinson-Patman Act].

   1. It is unlawful for a seller to discriminate in price for goods or other commodities between different purchasers when the effect would be to lessen competition or tend toward monopoly, except when the difference is due to grade, quality, quantity, or cost of transportation or if done, in good faith, to

meet competition; price discrimination occurs when a seller performs services for purchasers that are not available on equal terms to all customers.

2. It is unlawful for any person "knowingly" to induce or receive a discriminatory price for goods.

C. Exclusionary practices [Section 3].

1. It is unlawful to sell, lease, or fix the price of commodities on condition that the purchaser or lessee agrees not to deal in the goods of a competitor of the seller or lessor when the effect would be to reduce competition or tend to create a monopoly.

2. Exclusive-dealing contracts.

a. A seller promises to supply a buyer with certain goods (and services, such as advertising) and the buyer agrees to buy products only from the seller. [See Chapter 37 regarding franchising.]

b. Courts apply a modified rule of reason in cases involving exclusive-dealings arrangements.

3. Tying (tie-in sales agreements or bundling) arrangements.

a. A seller who has substantial market power requires that a buyer of one product also agrees to buy a second, different commodity.

b. A tying arrangement violates the Clayton Act if the arrangement will have a significant effect in the market for either product.

4. Exclusionary practices that are agreements in restraint of trade also may be violations of Section 1 of the Sherman Act in which case a different test is applied.

a. The Supreme Court has stated that the *per se* test applies to tying arrangements, but the Court has shown a willingness to look at factors that are used in a rule of reason analysis.

b. Clayton Act violations relate to tying the sale of one product with the sale of another product but not to tying the sale of a commodity with services.

c. In judging the legality of tying arrangements, courts examine the firm's market power in the tying-product market and the amount of commerce affected in the tied-product or service market; a tying arrangement violates the antitrust laws if:
   1) The firm has sufficient market power in the tying product because the firm is able to coerce the purchase of the tied product or service; and
   2) The tying arrangement affects a substantial amount of commerce in the market for the tied product or service.

5. Requirements (and output) contracts.

   a. In a requirements contract, the seller agrees to furnish and the buyer promises to purchase all of a particular product that the buyer might need over a specified period of time. [See Chapter 14.]

   b. Requirements contracts violate the Clayton Act only if the contracts substantially lessen competition in the relevant markets for the goods.

D. Mergers (and other acquisitions).

1. Section 7 of the Clayton Act, as amended by the Celler-Kefauver Act, prohibits acquisitions of stock or assets of another corporation when the effect might be to substantially lessen competition or tend to create a monopoly in any line of business in any geographic area of the country.

2. The purpose of Section 7 is to preserve competition; the provisions of Section 7 are enforced by the Federal Trade Commission (FTC) and the Department of Justice (DOJ).

3. In merger cases, courts consider market concentration and barriers to entry.

   a. Market concentration is measured by the market shares (percentages) of the various competitors in the relevant market.

   b. Barriers to entry affect the ability of firms to enter a market and may exist because of the necessity of high capital investment or other factors.

4. Horizontal mergers.

   a. Horizontal combinations involve competitors in the same market.

   b. In determining whether or not a merger will tend to result in anti-competitive effects, the FTC has relied upon the degree of existing and potential concentration (market shares) of the merging firms as well as the capital requirements and economies of scale in the industry.

   c. Factors that are considered by the courts in determining the legality of a proposed horizontal merger include:
      1) The size of the market share of the entity that results from the merger.
      2) The overall concentration in the relevant market.
      3) The increased concentration in the relevant market.
      4) The relevant market's history of tending toward concentration.
      5) Whether or not the apparent design of the merger is to establish market power or restrain competition.

   d. The DOJ Guidelines indicate that the DOJ will oppose mergers which result in the creation or expansion of market power ("the ability of one or more firms profitably to maintain prices above competitive levels for a significant period of time").

1) Quantitative tests that are based upon the Herfindahl-Hirshman Index (HHI) of market concentration are set forth in the Guidelines.
2) The HHI is calculated by adding the sum of the squares of the market shares of all the firms in a particular industry or market.
3) HHI $= \Sigma$ [(market share of firm A)^2 + (market share of firm B)^2 + (market share of firm C)^2 + . . . (market share of firm N)^2].
   a) If the HHI is below 1,000, the industry is unconcentrated, and the DOJ will not object to a merger.
   b) If the HHI is between 1,000 and 1,800, the industry is moderately concentrated. The merger may be challenged if the HHI will increase by more than 100 and if other factors are present.
   c) If the HHI exceeds 1,800, the industry is highly concentrated. If, as a result of the merger, the HHI will increase by less than 50, the merger will not be challenged. If, as a result of the merger, the HHI will increase by 50 to 100, the merger may be challenged if other factors are present. If, as a result of the merger, the HHI will increase by more than 100, it is likely that the merger will be challenged.

5. Vertical mergers.

   a. Vertical combinations involve control over firms in industries at successive stages of production and/or distribution.

   b. Vertical mergers may result in restrictions in supply of resources to competitors (backward acquisitions) or blocking (foreclosing) competitors from part of a market for the sales of their products.
      1) Such vertical combinations result in barriers to entry into the industry itself or the market in which a product is sold
      2) Factors considered by the FTC and courts include definitions of the relevant product (and the amount of product differentiation), the degree of concentration, and the market for the product.

6. The DOJ Guidelines appear to deemphasize the distinction between horizontal and vertical mergers.

7. Conglomerate mergers.

   a. Types:
      1) Market extension — A firm seeks to sell its product in a new market by merging with a firm that already exists in that market.
      2) Product extension — A firm seeks to add a closely related product to the firm's existing line of products by merging with a firm which already produces the product.

3) Diversification — A firm seeks to merge with a firm that offers a product that is unrelated to its existing activities; usually, such a merger does not affect individual market concentration.

b. The legality of a market extension or product extension merger is determined based upon the firm's effect as a potential competitor ("potential competition doctrine").

1) Because the firm may itself enter a market in the future, there is a favorable competitive effect that is similar to the effect which the firm would have had if the firm entered the market or merged with a small firm that already was in the market.

2) This procompetitive effect is lost or eliminated if the firm merges with a dominant firm in the industry.

c. Factors that a court considers include whether or not:
1) The pre-merger market is concentrated.
2) There are barriers to entry in the market.
3) The firm would be able to enter the market without the merger.
4) There are other firms in the market after the merger.
5) The merger will increase competition in the relevant market.

E. Interlocking directorates — An interlocking directorate exists when one person serves as a director of two or more corporations.

1. Section 8 prohibits interlocking directorates if one of the corporations has capital, surplus, and undistributed profits over a threshold amount when elimination of competition between the corporations would violate the antitrust laws.

2. No person may be a director of two or more corporations if either of the corporations has capital, surplus or undistributed profits of more than $13,813,000 or if the competitive sales of the company exceed $1,321,300 [threshold amounts as adjusted by the FTC in 1997].

V. The Federal Trade Commission Act.

A. Section 5 provides that: "Unfair methods of competition in or affecting commerce, and unfair or deceptive acts or practices in or affecting commerce are hereby declared illegal."

B. The act provided for the creation of the FTC which enforces the antitrust laws and other statutes relating to consumer protection. [See Chapter 45.]

VI. Enforcement of the antitrust laws.

A. The federal antitrust laws are enforced by the antitrust division of the Department of Justice (DOJ) which is part of the executive branch and the Federal Trade Commission (FTC), an independent agency.

B. The DOJ can prosecute violators of the criminal provisions of the Sherman Act and can bring civil proceedings based upon civil violations of the Sherman Act and the Clayton Act seeking remedies such as an injunction or divestiture (an order to sell or give up stock, or an interest in a company or property).

C. The FTC has power to prevent "unfair methods of competition in commerce and unfair or deceptive acts or practices in commerce" [Section 5 of the Federal Trade Commission Act as amended] including:

1. Investigatory power relative to alleged antitrust violations.

2. Authority to make recommendations and report to Congress.

3. Power to promulgate rules, policy statements, and regulations defining particular acceptable or unacceptable acts or practices.

4. The FTC can commence administrative cease and desist proceedings and can seek court sanctions for violations of administrative orders of the FTC.

D. A private party who has been or who may be injured because of violations of the provisions of the antitrust laws (except for Section 5 of the Federal Trade Commission Act) may seek civil legal remedies (including treble damages and attorneys' fees) or equitable remedies (e.g., specific performance, injunction, and rescission).

E. A party suing under the Sherman Act must prove that:

1. The antitrust violation directly caused or was a substantial factor in causing the injury that was incurred; and

2. The unlawful action of the defendant affected business activities of the plaintiff that were intended to be protected by the Sherman Act.

VII. Exemptions from antitrust laws.

A. Exemptions based upon statutes or case law include: Labor organizations, agricultural and fishing associations and cooperatives, the insurance industry, firms engaged in foreign trade, professional baseball organizations, and oil marketing.

B. Other exemptions:

1. Activities that are approved by the President in furtherance of national defense.

2. Cooperative research ventures among small business firms.

3. Research consortiums of competitors that agree to cooperate in the development of new computer technology.

4. State actions, when the state policy is clearly and expressly articulated and actively supervised by the state or other governmental unit.

5. Activities of regulated industries (e.g., transportation, communications, and banking) when federal administrative agencies have primary regulatory authority.

6. Some joint efforts by businesspersons to obtain legislative or executive action that are not shams or solely aimed at injuring an economic rival.

KEY WORDS AND PHRASES IN TEXT

antitrust law
monopoly
market power
business trusts
Section 1 of the Sherman Act
restraint of trade
monopoly power
agreements that unreasonably
    restrain trade
per se violation of Sherman Act
rule of reason
horizontal restraint of trade
price-fixing agreement
group boycott
horizontal market division
trade association
concentrated industry
joint venture
vertical restraint of trade
vertically integrated firm
territorial restrictions
customer restrictions
resale price maintenance (fair trade)
    agreement
refusal to deal
Section 2 of the Sherman Act

monopolization
relevant-product and geographic markets
market share test
the intent requirement
attempted monopolization
price discrimination (Section 2 of the
      Clayton Act)
exclusionary practices (Section 3 of the
      Clayton Act)
exclusive-dealings contract
tying arrangement (tie-in sales agreement)
mergers (Section 7 of the Clayton Act)
market concentration
barriers to entry
horizontal merger
Herfindahl-Hirschman Index (HHI)
vertical merger
Department of Justice merger guidelines
conglomerate merger
market-extension merger
product-extension merger
diversification merger
potential competition doctrine
interlocking directorates
remedies of divestiture and dissolution
exemptions from antitrust laws

FILL-IN QUESTIONS

1. A voting trust is a legal arrangement whereby shareholders give the right to vote their shares to a trustee. Under Section 1 of the Sherman Act, it is not illegal to create a voting trust unless it is a _____.

2. As a matter of law, certain forms of restraints of trade are treated as violations of the Sherman Act, even if the restraints are reasonable and are not be shown to have been injurious. These restraints of trade are referred to as _____ violations or

illegal activities and include _____
_____
_____.

3. The Clayton Act declares that certain activities are unlawful. Section 2 prohibits
    _____. Section 3 prohibits certain tying and
    _____ contracts and Section 8 prohibits certain
    corporate purchases and acquisitions of stock or assets of other corporations when
    the effect is to _____ or tend to create a monopoly.

4. The term, monopolize, is not defined in the antitrust laws. Any person, however,
    who _____ violates
    Section 2 of the Sherman Act. The Clayton Act prohibits certain monopolistic
    practices, such as _____
    _____, when
    the effect might be to reduce competition or tend to create a monopoly. In addition,
    Section 8 of the Clayton Act prohibits certain interlocking _____.

5. A and B Corporations both manufacture the same product and are planning to merge.
    The merger will be a _____ merger or combination. If the effect
    of the merger will be _____, it is prohibited by the
    antitrust laws.

6. C Corporation manufactures a particular product that is sold by D Corporation in its
    chain of retail stores. C and D Corporations enter into a contract providing that C will
    supply all of D's requirements for 20 years and will not sell the product to stores with
    which D competes, and D agrees that it will sell the product at a price to be
    determined by C. This is _____ restraint of trade.

7. With regard to its authority to enforce the provisions of the antitrust laws, the Federal
    Trade Commission has power to issue _____ orders. The FTC also
    has power to initiate _____ and to promulgate policy statements,
    interpretative _____ and _____.

8. The United States, through the Department of Justice, can bring a
    _____ action against a person or corporation that violates the Sherman
    Act. An individual or corporation that has been injured as a result of a violation of the
    Sherman Act may recover _____ damages in a _____ action against
    the violator.

9. Most labor and agricultural organizations are _____ from the federal anti-
    trust laws. Unlike other professional sports, _____ is _____
    from the antitrust laws.

MULTIPLE CHOICE QUESTIONS

1. Strawberry, Coffee, and Vanilla are operators of ice cream manufacturing plants in a
    metropolitan area. They meet informally to compare prices and production and have

agreed to divide the market into three equal shares. Strawberry, Coffee, and Vanilla have **not**, however, agreed to sell their comparable ice cream at the same prices.
   A. Because they are **not** fixing prices, the arrangement is **not** illegal *per se*.
   B. The arrangement is an illegal vertical restraint of trade.
   C. The arrangement is an illegal tying agreement under the Clayton Act.
   D. The division of the market is an illegal restraint of trade.

2.   Resale price maintenance is:
   A. a form of vertical price fixing.
   B. a form of horizontal price fixing.
   C. a means of territorial allocation.
   D. never a *per se* violation of the antitrust laws.

3.   Seller Manufacturing Company produced widgets and contracted to sell 2,000 widgets to Buyer Retail Store. Buyer agreed that it would sell the widgets at a price of at least seven dollars each.
   A. Although the agreement is contrary to public policy, Buyer's promise is enforceable if the quantity being sold is insufficient to give Buyer a monopoly on such goods in its trading area.
   B. Although the agreement is contrary to public policy, Buyer's promise is enforceable because the federal antitrust laws so provide.
   C. The agreement will be treated as a restraint of trade today because the agreement provides for resale price maintenance.
   D. The provision of the agreement is legal and Buyer, therefore, may be sued for breach of contract if Buyer sells the widgets for six dollars each.

4.   A trade association engages in compiling data about a manufacturing industry and supplying the firms participating in the industry with the collected information. The trade association:
   A. is engaging in an activity that is a *per se* violation of the Sherman Act.
   B. and its members are engaging in an activity that is a *per se* violation of the Sherman Act.
   C. violates the Sherman Act if the association's activities go beyond information gathering and supplying and are a facade for price fixing or dividing the market.
   D. does **not** violate the Sherman Act if the association's activities go beyond information gathering and supplying when the members of the association represent a small group in the industry with a total market share of 15%.

5.   P Corp., a large national manufacturer of paper products, acquires more than 50% of the outstanding shares of common stock of L Co., a national producer of paper. P Corp. previously had purchased its paper needs from competitors of L Co. but now P Corp. obtains all of its requirements from L Co. alone.
   A. The acquisition of the stock of L Co. does **not** violate the Clayton Act because the acquisition was **not** a purchase of the assets of L Co.
   B. Competitors of L Co. have standing to sue P Corp. under the Clayton Act and may recover damages for the actual harm incurred.
   C. Competitors of P Corp. have standing to sue P Corp. under the Clayton Act and may recover treble damages.

D. This is an example of a horizontal combination that is prohibited by the Clayton Act.

Questions 6, 7, and 8 are based on the following data:

	Alpha Industry				Beta Industry		
Firm	% of sales revenue	Minimum efficient scale as a % of the total market	Capital required for minimum efficient scale, in millions	Firm	% of sales revenue	Minimum efficient scale as a % of the total market	Capital required for minimum efficient scale, in millions
1	40	20	$ 100	1	15	2.5	$ 2
2	20	5	70	2	15	2.5	2
3	20	5	70	3	15	2.0	3
4	10	2	50	4	15	2.0	3
5	10	2	55	5	10	1.0	2
				6	10	1.0	2
				7	10	1.0	2
				8	10	0.5	2
5	100%	34%	$345	8	100%	12.5%	$ 18

6. A consolidation is being considered by firms 4 and 5 in Alpha industry.
   A. A consolidation is different from a merger and is **not** within the purview of the Clayton Act.
   B. Firm 3 cannot bring an action in order to obtain an injunction.
   C. The FTC will issue a cease-and-desist order because the consolidation will reduce competition in the industry, despite the fact that, if firms 3 and 4 do **not** consolidate, these two firms will be forced out of the industry.
   D. The FTC may **not** issue a cease-and-desist order, even though the consolidation will result in fewer firms in the industry, because it is established that, if firms 3 and 4 do **not** consolidate, these two firms will be forced out of the industry.

7. Which of the following statements is **incorrect**?
   A. The opportunity for collusion is greater in Alpha industry than it is in Beta industry.
   B. The degree of concentration is higher in Beta industry than it is in Alpha industry.
   C. A new firm will be more likely to enter Beta industry than Alpha industry.
   D. Firm 1 in Alpha industry has a more dominant position than firms 1 and 2 combined in Beta industry.

8. Assume that there is no evidence of direct agreement among the firms in Beta industry, but there is evidence that the firms in Beta industry all charge the same

price. The firms in the industry are being prosecuted for violation of the antitrust laws by the U.S. Department of Justice. The prosecution will:
A. **not** be successful because there is no evidence of a conspiracy.
B. be successful because the fact that these firms will charge a uniform price is sufficient evidence of a conspiracy.
C. be successful because proof of evidence of a conspiracy may be implied from the fact that the firms simultaneously had changed their previously varying prices to the uniform price.
D. None of the answers above is correct.

9.   An agreement between a manufacturer of gidgets and a wholesaler dealer which agrees not to sell any parts used in order to repair the gidgets to a particular retail seller is an illegal:
A. joint boycott or tying contract.
B. exclusive-dealings and tying contract.
C. vertical price-fixing agreement.
D. monopolization.

10.   An agreement between a manufacturer of photocopy machines and a lessee, to whom the manufacturer leases a machine, whereby the lessee agrees not to purchase its copy paper from any supplier other than the machine lessor, is an example of:
A. a joint boycott and price-fixing contract.
B. price-fixing and an exclusive-dealings contract.
C. exclusive-dealings or tying contract.
D. a fair trade agreement.

11.   The following organization is **not** exempt from the provisions of the antitrust laws:
A. an American manufacturing firm that sells its products in three states.
B. an American firm that engages in exporting goods to foreign countries.
C. a labor union that represents workers in three states.
D. an agricultural cooperative that sells the products of farmers in twenty states.

12.   The impact of antitrust legislation is felt directly and most heavily by:
A. sellers of a commodity in a market in which many firms compete.
B. sellers of a commodity in a market in which few firms compete.
C. consumers who purchase a commodity that is produced by only a few manufacturers.
D. the U.S. government to which fines imposed for violations of the antitrust laws are payable.

UNIT TEN:
PROPERTY

Property refers to the collection of rights and interests associated with the ownership of things. Traditionally, real property (rights and interests relating to land and those things growing on the land or affixed to the land or contained above or below the land) has been accorded special status by the law. All other things that are capable of being owned and possessed are treated as personal property. Note that contracts (the topic of Unit Two) frequently affect the rights of owners of property and that, if the property is tangible personal property, it may be the subject matter of a transaction involving a sale or lease of goods (covered in Unit Three).

Real property and personal property may be owned by the government. If so, it is public property. For example, the White House in Washington, DC is publicly owned real property because it is owned by the United States government, and highways, roads, and streets that are owned by states and local governments are public, real property. Similarly, military vehicles used by the armed forces, state and local police vehicles, the paper and paper clips purchased and used by governments, etc., are all publicly owned personal property.

Real and personal property that is not publicly owned is private property. A home that is owned by a person is the owner's private, real property. The clothes that you wear and the paper and paper clips you buy are your private, personal property.

The nature of personal property, how personal property may be acquired and transferred, and the bailment relationship (which is created when one person who has possession of personal property transfers possession of it to another person) are discussed in Chapters 48 and 49.

The nature of real property, the various forms of interests that may exist in real property, the manner of its transfer, and restrictions on its use are presented in Chapter 50. The subject matter of Chapter 51 is the landlord-tenant relationship which exists when a tenant is given possessory rights in real property by a landlord.

Chapter 48
Personal Property

Property consists of the legally protected rights and interests a person has in anything that is capable of being owned. The importance of property is reflected in the Fifth Amendment of the United States Constitution which provides that "no person shall be deprived of life, liberty, or **property**, without due process of law; nor shall private **property** be taken for public use, without just compensation." (Emphasis added.)

Traditionally, property has been classified as being either real property or personal property. Real property includes land and things, such as structures, that are permanently attached to the land, as well as things beneath the surface of the land, such as oil, gas, water, and minerals and things growing on the land, such as trees and crops. The terms, realty and real estate, are synonyms for real property. Personal property, or personalty, includes rights and interests in tangible and intangible things, other than real property, that have ascertainable values and are capable of being possessed. Items of personal property are sometimes referred to as chattels.

In this chapter, the focus is on the ways in which ownership rights in property can be held and the manners in which ownership interests in personal property can be acquired and transferred.

THINGS TO KEEP IN MIND

Property is not an object itself. Rather, property is the collection of rights and interests, associated with ownership, that are protected by law.

OUTLINE

I.   Personal property and real property.

   A. Real property — Rights in land and things associated with or attached to land.

   B. Personal property — Rights in things, other than real property, that have ascertainable value and can be possessed.

      1. Tangible personal property — Rights in moveable property that has physical substance and can be physically possessed.

      2. Intangible personal property — Rights in a thing that lacks physical existence, such as contract rights, stocks, bonds, patents, trademarks, copyrights, goodwill, and computer programs.

II. Fixtures.

   A. Fixtures are things that are affixed or permanently attached to real property; fixtures are included in the sale of real property unless the contract of sale provides otherwise.

   B. The role of intent — The objective intention of the party who placed the item on the real property determines whether or not the item is a fixture.

   C. Trade fixtures.

      1. Items attached to rented premises by a tenant (who pursues a trade or business) in connection with the tenant's business are treated as personal property of the tenant and usually are intended to be removed by the tenant. If their removal causes harm to the premises, the tenant is required to reimburse the landlord.

      2. If fixtures are not trade fixtures, usually, they are treated as parts of the real property and are not removable by a tenant.

III. Property ownership.

   A. Ownership rights include the right to possession of the property and the right to transfer or dispose of the property.

   B. Fee simple — The entire collection of ownership interests in property that can be transferred during the lifetime of the owner by sale or gift and by inheritance. [See Chapters 50 and 53.]

   C. Concurrent ownership.

      1. Property can be owned by two or more persons at the same time.

      2. Tenancy in common — Two or more persons own undivided shares (which may be unequal) in property that are transferable during their lifetimes and transferable by inheritance without rights of survivorship among the co-tenants.

      3. Joint tenancy (with right of survivorship).

         a. Two or more persons own equal undivided interests (which were acquired simultaneously) and have equal rights to use, enjoy, etc., the property and equal rights of survivorship.

         b. The transferor must have clearly indicated an intention to create a joint tenancy.

         c. A joint tenant may sever and transfer his or her interest during the joint tenant's lifetime (partition).

      d. Today in most states, there is a presumption that a cotenancy is a tenancy in common, unless there is a clear expressed intention to establish a joint tenancy.

    4. Tenancy by the entirety — A joint tenancy existing between spouses that cannot be transferred by either spouse without the consent of the other.

    5. Community property — Undivided interests held by spouses in property acquired during the course of marriage in Arizona, California, Idaho, Louisiana, Nevada, New Mexico, Texas, Washington, Wisconsin, and Puerto Rico.

IV. Acquiring ownership of personal property.

  A. Purchase.

    1. The most common method of acquiring and transferring ownership of personal property is by purchase based upon a contract between the buyer and seller.

    2. Sales of tangible personal property (goods) are covered by Article 2 of the Uniform Commercial Code. [See Unit 3, Chapters 21 through 25.]

  B. Possession.

    1. Possession with the intent to control and exclude others gives a person rights with respect to personal property.

    2. A person may take possession of unowned property, such as wild animals, fish in their native state, and personal property that has been voluntarily abandoned.

  C. Production — Property that is created through mental or physical labor belongs to the producer or creator. [See Chapter 9.]

    1. Patents — A federal statute gives inventors monopolies or exclusive right to use their inventions for specified periods of time in exchange for full disclosure.

    2. Trademarks — A federal statute provides for perpetual protection from infringement to the person who first adopts and uses a distinctive symbol, design, or mark.

    3. Copyright — A federal statute prohibits reproduction of literary or other creative works, without permission, for the life of the creator plus fifty years. This is subject to some exceptions, such as "fair use," library reproduction, and works created prior to 1978.

  D. Gift.

1. A gift is a voluntary transfer of ownership rights without the exchange of consideration; a gift can be made during the lifetime of the donor (the person making the gift) or in a last will and testament (a testamentary gift).

2. The requirements for an effective gift are delivery, donative intent, and acceptance by the donee (the person receiving the gift).

3. Delivery — The donor must give up complete dominion and control over the property.

   a. Actual physical transfer of possession to the donee.

   b. Constructive delivery by transferring symbol, such as a key to a safe deposit box or a stock certificate, to donee without retention of control or dominion.

   c. Constructive delivery to a third person with unconditional and absolute instructions to deliver to donee. (Gifts to minors by delivery to a custodian are governed by a Uniform Act; trusts are covered in Chapter 53.)
      1) If the third person is an agent of the donor, delivery occurs when the agent delivers the property to the donee.
      2) If the third person is an agent of the donee, delivery occurs when the donor delivers the property to the donee's agent.

4. Donative intent — Donor has the present intention to transfer the rights of ownership to the donee and relinquishes control over the property.

5. Acceptance by donee.

6. *Inter vivos* gifts and gifts *causa mortis.*

   a. *Inter vivos* gift — Absolute, present, irrevocable transfer of property during the donor's lifetime.

   b. Gift *causa mortis* — A transfer given in contemplation of imminent death as a result of illness or peril is revocable:
      1) Expressly by the donor while living.
      2) If and when the donor recovers or survives the peril.
      3) Upon the death of the donee before the donor.

E. Will or inheritance — See Chapter 53.

F. Accession — Annexation or addition of new value to an existing item of personal property by use of labor or materials.

   1. Without consent of owner.

a. When the accession is done innocently and is not severable, if the identity of the original object is changed, or the value added exceeds the prior value of the property, the improver has ownership rights, but the original owner can recover the value of the property before the accession.

b. If accession is willful, usually, the original owner is entitled to the property with the improvements.

2. Annexation pursuant to contract with the owner's consent.

a. Owner retains rights to property with the improvements.

b. If the owner fails to pay for contracted improvements, the improver may exercise a possessory artisan's or mechanic's lien by selling the property and retaining part of the price to reimburse himself or herself and giving the balance to the owner. [These liens are discussed in Chapter 31.]

G. Confusion.

1. Goods that are owned by a number of people may be commingled so that the goods of individual owners cannot be identified.

2. Fungible goods — Every unit is the same as every other unit (e.g., grain, oil, livestock, steel, logs, and money).

3. When confusion occurs because of an agreement, an innocent mistake, or an act of a third person:

a. If proportionate ownership shares are known, all the parties have rights to their proportionate shares.

b. If amounts owned are unknown, each party shares equally in ownership.

4. If confusion is caused intentionally or because of negligence of a party:

a. If there has been no loss, each party shares as in 3 above.

b. If there has been a loss, only the innocent parties share in the manner set forth in 3 above.

V. Mislaid, lost, or abandoned property.

A. Mislaid property.

1. Property is mislaid or misplaced if the owner intentionally left the property at a location that was inadvertently forgotten.

2. The owner of the premises where the property has been found is entrusted with holding the property as a bailee for the owner. [See Chapter 49.]

B. Lost property — Property is left by the owner involuntarily or accidentally.

1. A finder's right of possession is good against all but the true owner.

2. In many states, if the lost property is found on private real property by a person who is trespassing, the owner of the premises holds the lost property as a bailee for the true owner.

3. If the lost property is found by an employee, the employer holds lost property as a bailee.

4. Estray statutes — Statutes provide that the finder of lost property becomes the owner of the property (after publication of notice) if the property is not reclaimed by the true owner within a specified period of time.

C. Abandoned property.

1. Property that has been discarded by the owner who has no intention of reclaiming the property.

2. The property belongs to the first person who takes possession of the item with the intention of owning the item.

3. Treasure trove — A nontrespassing finder has right to possession of money that has been hidden so long in the past that it is unlikely the owner will return.

KEY WORDS AND PHRASES IN TEXT

property
real property (realty or real estate)
personal property (personalty)
chattel
tangible property
intangible property
fixture
trade fixture
fee simple ownership
concurrent ownership by cotenants
tenancy in common
joint tenancy
tenancy by the entirety
community property
purchase of personal property
acquisition of property by possession
acquisition of property by production

acquisition of property by gift
delivery of gift by donor
testamentary gift
constructive delivery
donative intent
acceptance of gift by donee
inter vivos gift
gift *causa mortis*
acquisition of property by will or
    inheritance
acquisition of property by accession
confusion of goods
mislaid property
lost property
estray statutes
abandoned property
treasure trove

FILL-IN QUESTIONS

1. Property is a concept that deals with _____ in things. Those things that are not part of real property, but which are moveable and _____, are considered to be personal property.

2. Fixtures are items that are personal property until such items are _____ _____. If such items are affixed to business premises by tenants with the understanding that these items may be removed, these items are referred to as _____.

3. Usually, personal property is acquired by purchase. Personal property, however, also may be acquired by _____ _____.

4. In order to transfer ownership of personal property by gift, there are three requisites. These requisites for a gift are _____, _____ and _____.

5. Personal property is mislaid if the owner _____ _____, but personal property is considered to be lost if the owner _____.

MULTIPLE CHOICE QUESTIONS

1. When a judge refers to personal property, the judge means:
    A. rights associated with ownership of things other than real property.
    B. rights associated with ownership of physical objects.
    C. tangible physical things that are not part of real property.
    D. property that is privately owned.

2. A United States Treasury Bond is considered to be:
    A. intangible personal property.
    B. intangible real property.
    C. tangible personal property.
    D. public property.

3. Which of the following things is classified as intangible personal property?
    A. A truck manufactured by Ford Motor Company.
    B. One hundred shares of stock issued by Ford Motor Company.
    C. Trees growing on property owned by Ford Motor Company.
    D. Computer chips that are installed by Ford Motor Company in trucks that Ford manufactures.

4. Which of the following things is classified as tangible personal property?
    A. An automobile manufactured by General Motors Corp.
    B. One hundred shares of stock issued by General Motors Corp.
    C. Trees growing on property owned by General Motors Corp.
    D. Goodwill that is possessed by General Motors Corp.

5.   Peg will acquire ownership of a rabbit by possession if:
      A.   the rabbit was previously wild and Peg took possession of the rabbit when Peg
           went to visit a wildlife preserve owned by the state.
      B.   the rabbit was previously wild and Peg took possession of the rabbit when it
           came on Peg's land.
      C.   the rabbit ran away two years before from its owner who had not been able to
           find it.
      D.   All of the answers above are correct.

6.   Sarah never flew in a plane because of her fear of flying. She had a great desire to
      see Disneyland and, despite her fear, she decided to fly there. Before leaving, Sarah
      signed over title to her automobile and gave the car keys to Fred, her dear friend,
      saying, "I'll probably never make it back alive and I don't want my relatives to have
      my car, so it's yours." Fred drove off. Later, he opened the glove compartment and
      found a box. Inside the box were a ring and a note to Gloria, Fred's ex-girlfriend, in
      which Sarah stated that the ring was for Gloria.
      A.   Gloria becomes the owner of the ring by accession.
      B.   When Sarah safely returns, Sarah may not reclaim the car from Fred because she
           made an irrevocable *inter vivos* gift.
      C.   When Sara returns safely, she may reclaim the car from Fred because she made a
           revocable gift *causa mortis.*
      D.   Sarah has made a valid *inter vivos* gift of the ring to Gloria by constructive
           delivery.

7.   Pat has received a gift of the contents of a safe deposit box by constructive delivery if
      Pat's father put the key to the box in an envelope with Pat's name on the envelope
      and:
      A.   placed the key in a drawer in his own desk.
      B.   left the key in Pat's desk with instructions to Pat to keep the key for her father.
      C.   gave the key to his attorney with instructions to give the key to Pat in three years
           if Pat's father did not reclaim the key within the three years.
      D.   mailed the key to Pat who received the key in the mail.

8.   R, S, and T stored varying quantities of grain in M's silo. Half of the grain and M
      have disappeared. R can prove the he stored 100 bushels of grain in the silo, and S
      and T are able to prove that each of them stored 200 bushels in the silo. M had stored
      100 bushels of his own grain in the silo.
      A.   R is entitled to 60 bushels, S is entitled to 120 bushels, and T is entitled to 120
           bushels.
      B.   R is entitled to 50 bushels, S is entitled to 100 bushels, and T is entitled to 100
           bushels.
      C.   R is entitled to 50 bushels, S is entitled to 100 bushels, and T is entitled to 100
           bushels. R, S, and T then share equally in M's share.
      D.   R, S, and T share equally in the grain.

9.   Lorelli has invented a device that enables the user of the device to produce gasoline
      from walnut shells. If Lorelli obtains a patent, Lorelli can prevent other people from
      using his idea:
      A.   for as long as Lorelli uses the idea.

B. for his lifetime even if Lorelli does not use the idea.
C. for a statutory period of 20 years from the date of Lorelli's patent application even if Lorelli does not use the idea.
D. for a statutory period of 28 years if the patent was obtained before 1978.

10. Harry deposited ("dumped") an old painting that he no longer wanted in a street waste container. Tom found the painting and kept it.
A. Tom will be treated as a bailee of the painting that was mislaid property.
B. Tom's right to possession of the painting is good against all but Harry who is the true owner.
C. The painting is now Tom's property because Tom found the painting after the painting was abandoned.
D. If Tom paints over the picture, Harry still is entitled to reclaim the painting.

Chapter 49
Bailments

A bailment is a legal relationship that is created when one person, the bailor, delivers temporary possession of personal property to another person, the bailee. The bailee has a duty to return the property to the bailor or to deliver the property or dispose of the property as directed by the bailor. In a bailment, possession of property, but not ownership interests in or title to the property, is given to the bailee.

THINGS TO KEEP IN MIND

1. Usually, but not always, bailments are created by contract.

2. In most instances, problems involving bailment relate to the contract or tort liability of a bailee who has not carried out his, her, or its duty of returning or correctly disposing of the bailed property.

OUTLINE

I. Elements of a bailment.

    A. The subject matter of a bailment is personal property, possession of which is delivered by the bailor to the bailee in accordance with an agreement that the bailee is to return the property to the bailor or otherwise dispose of or deliver the property as directed by the bailor.

    B. Personal property requirement.

        1. The subject matter of a bailment is personal property in which the bailor has a possessory interest.

        2. The subject matter of a bailment cannot be natural persons or real property; possession of real property is given by a landlord, or lessor, to a tenant, or lessee, in accordance with a lease. [See Chapter 51.]

        3. Usually, the property that is bailed is tangible personal property; the indicia of ownership of intangible personal property (e.g., a promissory note or stock certificate) also may be the subject matter of a bailment.

    C. Delivery of possession.

1. There must be an actual or constructive delivery of the property to the bailee so that the bailee has exclusive possession of the property and knowingly accepts possession intending to exercise control over the property.

2. Actual delivery — A physical delivery to the bailee will create a bailment.

3. Constructive delivery.

   a. Bailee may be given some symbol that evidences right to possession.

   b. Bailee may have possession of property belonging to another person under circumstances which obligate the bailee to deliver the property to the rightful owner (involuntary bailment).
      1) Finder of lost property.
      2) Bailee to whom stolen property was delivered or bailee who has knowledge of an adverse claim to the property.
      3) A person who has absolute control over area in which property is deposited.
      4) A person to whom a container is delivered has sufficient control over its contents to be considered a bailee of objects which normally would be expected to be in the container.

D. The bailment agreement.

1. The bailment agreement may be express or implied; in general, the agreement need not be embodied in a writing.

2. The agreement provides that the bailee is to return the specific, identical property to the bailor or to dispose of the property in the manner which the bailor directs.

3. If the property consists of fungible goods, only the same quantity of goods is to be returned or disposed of by the bailee.

4. In a bailment with an option to purchase (e.g., a sale on approval), the prospective buyer (the bailee) must either return the property at the termination of the agreed period of time or buy the goods.

II. Ordinary bailments.

A. Bailments may be classified based upon which party receives a benefit from the bailment; to some extent, the liability of the bailee is determined by the type of bailment.

B. The bailee must exercise reasonable care — The general rule is that what is reasonable care depends upon the surrounding circumstances and the nature of a transaction and, in the case of a bailment, is determined by the nature of the bailment.

C. Types of ordinary bailments.

1. A bailment for the sole benefit of the bailor is a gratuitous bailment because no consideration is given to the bailee; the bailee must exercise reasonable care, which in this case is slight care, and is liable only for gross negligence.

2. A bailment for the sole benefit of the bailee is a gratuitous bailment because no consideration is given to the bailor; the bailee must exercise reasonable care, which in this case is great or extraordinary care, so that the bailee is liable for negligence even if the bailee has exercised ordinary care.

3. Most bailments are bailments for the mutual benefit of the parties and based upon a contract.

    a. Each of the parties gives consideration — A fee or compensation is given.

    b. The bailee must exercise the degree of care that a reasonably prudent person would use under the circumstances and is liable for ordinary negligence.

III.   Rights and duties of the bailee.

A. Rights of the bailee.

1. Right of possession — A bailee who has temporary control and possession of bailed property can recover from a third party who interferes with the bailee's possessory rights.

2. Right to use bailed property — A bailee may use the property in accomplishing the purpose of the bailment.

3. Right of compensation.

    a. Mutual benefit bailment — The bailee (or bailor in a rental bailment) has a right to receive compensation in accordance with the agreement of the parties.

    b. Gratuitous bailment — The bailee has a right to be reimbursed for costs incurred in keeping the bailed property.

    c. A bailee who has a right to compensation, but who is not paid, has a right to place a possessory (artisan's) lien on the bailed property that is in the bailee's possession. [See also Chapter 31.]

4. Right to limit liability — A limitation on the type of risk and/or the amount of liability is enforceable if:

    a. The limitation is called to the attention of the bailor; and

    b. The limitation, or disclaimer in an exculpatory clause, is not illegal or against public policy. [See also Chapter 17.]

B. Duties of the bailee — A bailee's duties are based upon tort and contract law.

    1. Duty of care — A bailee has a duty to exercise reasonable care of property in the bailee's possession [See also Chapter 6.]. What is proper care depends upon:

        a. The time and place of the bailment.

        b. The facilities of the bailee.

        c. The nature of the property and the bailee's knowledge of the property's nature.

        d. The type of bailment:
            1) For benefit of bailor — Slight care.
            2) For benefit of bailee — Great or extraordinary care.
            3) Mutual benefit — Ordinary care.

    2. Duty to return bailed property — The (ordinary) bailee has a contractual duty to relinquish the property at the end of a bailment in the same condition in which the property was received, unless the property has been lost, stolen, or damaged through no fault of the bailee.

        a. A bailee who fails to properly return bailed property may be liable for breach of contract and/or the tort of conversion.

        b. Allowance is made for normal wear, depreciation, and deterioration.

        c. A bailee who is to perform services in order to repair or improve the property has a duty to complete the services.

        d. Delivery of goods to the wrong person — A bailee who delivers the property to the bailor or an agent of the bailor knowing that the property was stolen property or that another person has a legitimate claim of ownership to the property may be liable for conversion because of the misdelivery.

        e. Presumption of negligence — There is a rebuttable presumption that a bailee was negligent if the property is not returned or the property is not in the correct condition when it is returned.

IV. Rights and duties of the bailor — The bailor's rights are a complement to the bailee's duties and the bailor's duties are a complement to the bailee's rights.

A. Rights of bailor — Bailor has a right to expect that the bailee will:

1. Use reasonable care to protect the property that is bailed.

2. Correctly relinquish the property at the end of the bailment.

3. Perform in accordance with the contract of bailment.

    a. If the bailee has the right to use the property, bailee does so in the agreed manner.

    b. If bailee is to compensate bailor, bailee makes the agreed-upon payment.

    c. If bailee is to render services on the property, the bailee correctly does so.

4. The bailor will not be bound by any limitations of the liability of the bailee unless the limitations are known to the bailor, or the bailor's attention is called to the limitations and the limitations are enforceable by law; often, absolute disclaimers and exculpatory clauses are not enforceable.

B. Duties of the bailor.

1. Tort liability — A bailor has a duty to furnish property that is free from certain defects.

    a. Mutual benefit bailment — The bailor must notify bailee of known and latent (hidden and not ordinarily discoverable) defects.

    b. Bailment for sole benefit of bailee — The bailor must inform the bailee of defects of which the bailor has actual knowledge.

2. Contract liability.

    a. A bailor may be liable for breach of an implied warranty that goods that are the subject matter of a bailment (or lease) are fit for the intended purpose of the bailment.

    b. Article 2A of the UCC extends implied warranties of merchantability and fitness for a particular purpose to bailments that include the rights to use the bailed goods.

V. Termination of bailments.

A. If a bailment is for a specified term, the bailment ends at expiration of the term.

B. If a bailment is not for a specified period, the bailment may be terminated by demand of either party or completion of the purpose of the bailment.

C. A bailment also may be terminated by:

1. Mutual agreement;

2. Act of a party that is inconsistent with the terms of the bailment; or

3. Operation of law.

VI. Special features of specific bailments.

   A. Documents of title and Article 7 of the Uniform Commercial Code (UCC) — A document of title "must purport to be issued by or addressed to a bailee and purport to cover goods in the bailee's possession which are either identified or are fungible portions of an identified mass" [UCC 1-201(15)].

      1. Types of documents of title.

         a. A bill of lading is "a document evidencing the receipt of goods for shipment issued by a person engaged in the business of transporting or forwarding goods, and includes an airbill" [UCC 1-201(6)].

         b. A warehouse receipt is "a receipt issued by a person engaged in the business of storing goods for hire" [UCC 201(45)].

         c. A delivery order is "a written order to deliver goods directed to a warehouseman, carrier or other person who in the ordinary course of business issues warehouse receipts or bills of lading" [UCC 7-102(d)].

      2. Functions of a document of title.

         a. Receipt for property that is bailed.

         b. Represents the goods so that the person holding the document of title has the right to the property represented by the document of title.

         c. Contains the contract for shipment or storage.

   B. Negotiability of documents of title.

      1. Negotiable documents of title.

         a. A document of title is negotiable if the document provides that "goods are to be delivered to bearer or to the order of a named person" [UCC 7-104(1)(a)].

         b. A holder is a person who purchases a document of title for value, in good faith, and without notice of any defenses against or claim to it [UCC 7-501(4)].

         c. The holder of a negotiable document of title has the right to receive, hold, and dispose of the document and the goods covered by the negotiable document of title, and may acquire greater rights to the document of title and the goods than the holder's transferor.

2. Transfer of documents of title.

    a. Negotiable document of title is "duly negotiated:"
        1) By indorsement and delivery if the document of title runs to the order of a named person or has been indorsed to a specified person.
        2) By delivery alone if the document of title runs to bearer or is indorsed in blank or to bearer. [UCC 7-501]

    b. Nonnegotiable document of title may be transferred by assignment.

C. Common carriers.

    1. Common carriers are publicly licensed and are distinguishable from contract carriers (which provide transportation services under individual contracts to selected users) and private carriers (which maintain transportation facilities that are privately owned and operated for the sole benefit of the owner and not for hire).

    2. A common carrier holds itself out to furnish transportation to the public, without discrimination, as long as the carrier has available facilities, and often has a definite route and/or schedule.

    3. The contract for transportation by a common carrier creates a mutual benefit bailment; the carrier's liability, however, approaches that of an insurer.

    4. A common carrier is absolutely liable for loss, destruction, or damage to property which the carrier transports, without regard to fault, unless the loss or damage is due to:

        a. Act of God.

        b. Act of war or public enemy.

        c. Order of public authority.

        d. Act of the shipper.

        e. Inherent nature of the goods.

    5. Shipper's loss.

        a. The shipper bears a loss that occurs through the shipper's own fault.

        b. In order to be relieved of liability (so that a loss will fall on the shipper), the carrier has the burden of proof in establishing that the carrier was not negligent and that the loss was due to one of the causes (listed above) that absolves the carrier of liability.

6. Carriers issue documents of title (bills of lading and airbills).

7. Connecting carriers.

   a. Carriers to whom goods are delivered issue "through bills of lading" when goods are to be delivered to other (connecting) carriers so that the goods can reach their ultimate destinations.

   b. In case of damage or loss, the issuer of the bill of lading is liable to the holder of the document of title but can recover reimbursement from a connecting carrier or other person who had possession of the goods when the breach of an obligation occurred [UCC 7-302].

8. A carrier may limit its liability by contract to:

   a. Stated losses but may not relieve itself of liability based on intentional wrongful acts or negligence.

   b. Some maximum dollar amount, but must afford a shipper an opportunity to obtain a higher limit by paying a higher charge.

D. Warehouse companies.

   1. Warehouse companies engage in the business of storing personal property of other people for compensation without discrimination.

   2. The rights and duties of warehouse companies are those of bailees for mutual benefit as modified by statutes.

      a. A public warehouse is liable for its failure to exercise reasonable care.

      b. If property is lost, damaged, or destroyed while in the possession of the warehouse, the warehouse has the burden of proving its nonliability.

      c. Warehouses issue documents of title, known as warehouse receipts.

E. Innkeepers, hotels, motels, etc.

   1. At common law, a person who offered living accommodations to transients, was practically an insurer with respect to the personal property of the guests.

   2. Statutes limit liability or provide methods by which liability may be limited by a hotel, motel, etc.

a. Typically, a hotel will not be liable for valuables unless the property is deposited in a safe provided by the hotel, notice of which is given to guests.

b. A hotel will be liable for ordinary negligence resulting in the loss of property of a guest, which is not put in the safe that is provided by the hotel, if the nature of the property is such that it normally is not put in a safe (e.g., part of usual wearing apparel).

KEY WORDS AND PHRASES IN TEXT

bailment
bailor
bailee
actual delivery of possession
constructive delivery of possession
bailment agreement
ordinary bailment
gratuitous bailment
bailment for the sole benefit of bailor
bailment for the sole benefit of bailee
mutual benefit bailment
rights of the bailee to take possession
       of and to use the property,
       and to receive compensation
artisan's (possessory) lien
limitations on liability of bailee
exculpatory clause
duties of the bailee to take care of and sur-
       render or dispose of the property
       at the end of the bailment

bailee's duty of care
bailee's duty to return bailed property
rights of bailor
duty of bailor (to provide the bailee with
       property that is free from defects
       that can injure the bailee)
termination of bailment
Uniform Commercial Code, Article 7
documents of title
bill of lading
warehouse receipt
delivery order
negotiable document of title
due negotiation of document of title
common carriers
liability of a common carrier
connecting carrier
through bill of lading
warehouse company
innkeeper

FILL-IN QUESTIONS

1. A bailment arises when one person, called the _____, delivers temporary possession of _____ property to another person, called the _____. The person to whom possession of the property is delivered is obligated to _____ the property to the person who delivered the property or dispose of the property in the manner in which that person directed.

2. Personal property may be actually or _____ delivered to a bailee. If the bailee is given some symbol evidencing a right to possession or has possession of the property involuntarily, under circumstances that obligate the bailee to deliver the property to the rightful owner, there has been a _____ delivery of the personal property.

3. A bailee owes a duty of exercising reasonable care with respect to bailed property. A bailment may be for the sole benefit of the bailee, in which case the bailee must

exercise _____ care. If a bailment is for the sole benefit of the bailor, the bailee will be liable if the bailee fails to exercise _____ care. Most bailments are _____, in which case the bailees owe a duty of exercising _____ reasonable care.

MULTIPLE CHOICE QUESTIONS

1. In a bailment relationship:
    A. the bailee has temporary title to the bailed personal property.
    B. consideration is necessary to form the relationship.
    C. the bailee has temporary possession of the bailed property.
    D. the property is returned to the bailor or a person who the bailee believes has valid title to the property.

2. Which of the following statements is **false**?
    A. A person who is **not** an owner of personal property may be a bailor of the property.
    B. A person who has possession of, but **not** title to, personal property and sells the property to another person may never avoid liability to the owner of the property.
    C. A person need **not** be given actual physical possession of personal property in order to be considered a bailee.
    D. A person who has possession of personal property is **not** a bailee of the property unless the owner of the property entered into an express bailment agreement.

3. Jackson brought his car to a local garage for a tune-up and a number of repairs. The garage will be liable to Jackson:
    A. for the value of the car if the car was stolen because the mechanic left the keys in the ignition.
    B. for the value of the golf clubs that had been in the truck of the car but now are missing.
    C. if the garage refuses to deliver the car to Jackson because Jackson has not paid for the repairs to the car.
    D. for damage done to the car while on the garage's premises a month after the garage notified Jackson that the work on the car was completed.

4. The owner of a parking lot is liable to the owner of an automobile:
    A. who had parked and locked his own car and retained the keys if the car is stolen.
    B. who had parked and locked his own car and delivered the keys to an attendant if the car is stolen.
    C. whose car was parked by an attendant, even if there is a large sign stating that the parking lot will not be liable for cars that are damaged by persons other than its employees, when the car is damaged by another user of the parking lot.
    D. whose car was parked by an attendant if his briefcase containing business papers and securities worth $10,000 was stolen from the car while the car was parked in the lot.

5. Lukins placed a suitcase containing clothing in a self-service locker at an airport. Lukins put one dollar in the slot, locked the door, and took the key. Marlin checked his suitcase containing clothing in a checkroom at the same airport. In this case, an

attendant took the case from Marlin and put the suitcase on a rack in full view of all the attendants in the checkroom. The attendant charged three dollars for the storage and gave Marlin a claim check with nothing but a number printed on the claim check. Both the lockers and the checkroom were owned and maintained by the airport.

A. The airport will be liable to Lukins if Lukins' suitcase is missing when Lukins returns to reclaim the suitcase.

B. The airport will be liable to Marlin if Marlin's suitcase is missing when Marlin returns to reclaim the suitcase.

C. The airport will be liable to Marlin if Marlin's suitcase cannot be returned because an explosion wrecked the checkroom, the explosion having been caused by a bomb left by terrorists and in no way due to the fault of the airport.

D. The airport will be liable to Lukins if Lukins' suitcase cannot be returned because an explosion wrecked the lockers, the explosion having been caused by terrorists and in no way due to the fault of the airport.

E. All of the answers above are correct.

6. Martina left her watch with a jeweler in order for the watch to be cleaned and repaired. The charges were $29.

A. The jeweler may sell the watch and retain the proceeds because Martina failed to reclaim the watch within one year.

B. The jeweler may retain possession of the watch and use the watch because Martina failed to pay the $29.

C. The jeweler acquires ownership rights in the watch by occupation.

D. The jeweler may sell the watch, retain the $29, and hold the balance for Martina if Martina fails to pay the $29.

7. A common carrier is:

A. liable for damage caused to food carried by the carrier when the food is harmed by unseasonably warm temperatures.

B. **not** liable for livestock destroyed by a mentally deranged railroad engineer.

C. **not** a contract carrier.

D. **not** liable for injuries to its passengers.

8. A common carrier is **not** liable for damage to property being shipped if the damage is caused by:

A. theft.

B. a tornado.

C. rioters.

D. negligence of a trespasser.

9. A public warehouse may contractually limit its liability to the owner of goods for loss, destruction, or damage to goods which the warehouse stores for the owner of the goods:

A. but the warehouse is required to offer the owner higher limits of liability at increased rates.

B. by using exculpatory clauses.

C. but the warehouse must obtain a release from the owner in the warehouse receipt that functions as the contract of bailment.

D. by calling the owner's attention to the limitations on the warehouse's liability after the delivery of the goods by the owner to the warehouse.

10. The common law liability of hotels has been changed by statute so that, if a hotel provides a safe and posts notices of the safe's availability and a guest has been robbed, the hotel:
    A. will be liable for a $600 gold watch even if the watch is not deposited in the safe by a guest.
    B. will **not** be liable for a $700 gold watch if the watch is not deposited in the safe by the guest.
    C. will be liable for $10,000 worth of uncut diamonds if the diamonds were not deposited in the safe by the guest.
    D. will never be liable for the property of guest.

11. Traveler was staying at the Buena Vista Motel in a state that permits innkeepers to limit their liability by providing safes for valuables belonging to their guests and notifying the guests of the safe's availability. Traveler did not use the safe. Among Traveler's belongings were a rare 1882 inverted stamp worth $50,000, diamond cuff links that are worth $10,000 and which Traveler wears a few times a week, and dirty laundry of uncertain value. All of these items have disappeared from Traveler's motel room. The motel is:
    A. liable to Traveler for the loss of the rare 1882 stamp.
    B. **not** liable to Traveler for the dirty laundry.
    C. liable Traveler for the cuff links.
    D. liable to Traveler for the loss of the 1882 stamp, the dirty laundry, and the cuff links.

12. Which of the following is **not** a warranty made by the seller of a negotiable warehouse receipt or bill of lading to the purchaser of the document of title under the provisions in UCC Section 7-507?
    A. The negotiation or transfer of the document of title is fully effective with respect to the goods that the document of title represents.
    B. The issuer of the document of title will honor the document.
    C. The seller of the document of title has no knowledge of any facts that would impair the document's validity.
    D. The document of title is genuine.
    (This question has been adapted from objective question #42 on the Uniform CPA Examination, November 1988.)

Chapter 50
Real Property

Real property refers to rights associated with ownership or possessory interests in land, things of a permanent nature growing on or affixed to the land, and things contained above or below the surface of the land. Most of the material in this chapter relates to the nature of real property, the types of present ownership and present possessory interests in land, and the manner in which real property may be acquired or transferred.

Nonpossessory interests in land also may be created. For example, it is possible for owners of real property to grant rights in the form of easements to other people to go onto the land or rights (referred to as profits and licenses) to take things from the land. Easements, profits, and licenses may restrict the present and future rights of the owners of land.

As discussed in the last section of the chapter, additional limitations on the use of land may be imposed privately with restrictive covenants in conveyances and by state zoning statutes or local zoning ordinances.

THINGS TO KEEP IN MIND

The rights to possession and enjoyment of land are protected by law. Typically, if there is an interference with the use and enjoyment of real property, a tort action may be brought based upon trespass. If a person has acquired title to real property by conveyance and there is a defect in the title, the transferee may sue the grantor because of a breach of a covenant or a warranty contained in the deed.

OUTLINE

I.   The nature of real property.

    A. Land — Land includes the soil itself, bodies of water on or beneath the surface, natural plant life and vegetation growing on the land, and structures that are attached permanently to the land.

    B. Air space and subsurface rights.

        1. Air rights — Today, a property owner has rights to the air immediately above the land sufficient to have a cause of action based upon trespass for a direct interference with the use and enjoyment of the land.

        2. Subsurface rights.

a. A property owner has the exclusive right to minerals, oil, and other matter found beneath the surface and may transfer these rights to another person.

b. The right to subsurface real property may be transferred separately and apart from the surface real property, or the right to remove minerals, oil, natural gas, etc., may be given to another person in the form of profits.

c. If the person who has rights to the subsurface excavates, the common law rule is that the owner of the surface has the right to have the land supported in its natural condition by the owner of the interest in the subsurface who is absolutely liable to the owner of the surface rights for damage caused by subsidences; liability also may be imposed based upon statutes.

C. Plant life and vegetation.

1. When realty is sold, the sale includes crops that are growing on the land, unless otherwise specified in the contract of sale.

2. When crops or trees are sold separately, the sale is governed by Section 2-107 of the Uniform Commercial Code. [See Chapter 21.]

II. Ownership interests in real property.

A. Estates in land are collections of rights associated with ownership of real property; a "fee" is an estate in land that can be conveyed or transferred by sale, gift, or inheritance.

B. Fee simple — The owner of a fee simple absolute possesses all the rights, privileges, and power that a person may possess in land.

1. There are no limitations or conditions on the exclusive right to use and enjoy the land for whatever purposes the holder of the fee wishes, other than those activities that unreasonably interfere with the rights of other people to the quiet enjoyment of their land and those activities that are prohibited in applicable zoning laws.

2. A fee simple absolute is potentially infinite in duration and can be transferred by deed or by will; today, a fee simple absolute can be conveyed by using words such as "to A and his heirs" or "to A."

C. Life estates — A life estate is an ownership interest in land that exists until the death of a specified person or persons.

1. The duration of a life estate may be measured by the life of the person to whom the estate is given or the life of another person (an estate *pur autre vie*).

2. A life estate may not be inherited by another person but may be conveyed during the lifetime of the person by whose life the life estate is measured.

3. A life tenant has the right to possess, use, and convey his or her specific interest in the property, and has an obligation to pay taxes, make repairs, and not commit waste (cause an impairment in the value of the land).

4. Life estates may be created by voluntary acts of the parties or by operation of law (i.e., marital interests which are discussed in Chapter 53).

D. Leasehold estates — A leasehold estate is created when the owner of real property (the landlord or lessor) conveys the qualified right to possess and to use the property to the tenant (or lessee) for a determinable period of time. [Leases and the rights and duties of lessors and lessees are discussed in greater detail in Chapter 51.]

1. Leasehold estates are distinguishable from estates in fee or life estates, which are of indefinite duration.

2. A tenant's right to exclusive possession is qualified because the landlord has a right to enter upon the property to assure that waste is not being committed.

3. Tenancy for a specified term (which may be measured in one or more months or years).

  a. Most leases are created expressly for specified terms or periods of time; these tenancies end at the terminations of the terms that are specified unless the leases are extended or renewed.

  b. If the tenant dies, usually the rights under the lease are treated as part of the decedent's (the tenant's) personal property.

  c. Statutes may require that leases be in writing in order to be enforceable.

4. A periodic tenancy is created by contracting to pay rent periodically without stating the duration of the lease or is created as a result of a tenant holding over after the expiration of a lease for a specified term. [A periodic tenancy ends and is terminated after giving one period's notice or as provided for by statute.]

5. Tenancy at will — A tenancy at will is terminated upon death, or (at common law) the will of either party, or after giving such notice as is required by a statute.

6. Tenancy at sufferance — Wrongful possession of land without the right to so possess and occupy the property.

E. Nonpossessory interests.

1. Easements and profits.

    a. Easement — The limited right to make use of real property belonging to another person without taking anything from the property.

    b. Profit — The limited right to go onto the real property of another person and remove something from the property.

    c. Easement (or profit) appurtenant — The right to go onto and/or remove something from the land (the subservient parcel) of another person. The easement or profit is created for the benefit of the owner of an adjacent parcel of land (the dominant parcel).

    d. Easement (or profit) in gross — The right to use or remove something from the land of another person (which need not be adjacent to the land of the party given the right) for a specific personal or commercial purpose.

    e. Creation of an easement or profit may be by:
       1) Contract, deed, or will.
       2) Implication, when circumstances surrounding a division of property infer the creation of an easement or profit, and the use of the property is apparent, necessary, and continuous.
       3) Necessity, when circumstances, other than a division of property, are such that it is clearly necessary that one person use another person's real property.
       4) Prescription, when one person (without permission) adversely, openly, notoriously, and continually uses (a right-of-way) or takes something from the land of another person for the period of time specified in a statute.

    f. Effect of a sale of property.
       1) When a parcel of land that benefits from an easement or profit appurtenant (the dominant parcel) is sold, the easement or profit also may be transferred.
       2) When a parcel of land that is burdened by an easement or profit appurtenant (the subservient parcel) is sold, the subsequent owner of the subservient parcel must recognize the easement or profit if the new owner knew of the easement or profit or should have known of the easement or profit because it was recorded in the appropriate public office.

    g. Termination of an easement or profit may be by:
       1) Deed, expiration of agreed duration, or fulfillment of the purpose for which the easement or profit was created.
       2) Intentional abandonment.
       3) Merger of the dominant and subservient parcels.
       4) Destruction of the subservient property.

        5) Prescription, when the owner of the subservient property prevents the use of the easement or profit for a statutorily specified period of time.

    2. Licenses — A license is a revocable, nontransferable right or privilege to use another person's property with the owner's consent.

III. Transfer of ownership.

    A. Deeds — In order to transfer an interest in land (title and/or right to possession) by sale or gift (i.e., consideration is not necessary), a conveyance is made by delivery of a document called a deed.

        1. Contents of deed.

            a. The names of the grantor (seller or donor) and the grantee (buyer or donee);

            b. Description of the property and the interest conveyed;

            c. Words indicating the grantor's present intention to make a present transfer of title to real property; and

            d. Signature of the grantor (the person who is conveying the real property).

            e. If there are multiple owners of the property, all of the owners must be named and sign the deed. In many states, the spouse of a grantor must be named and sign the deed. [See also Chapter 53].

        2. A deed may be classified according to the interests that the deed conveys and the consequent degree of protection that the deed provides against defects in the title to the property because of clauses (covenants, warranties, or promises) included in the deed.

        3. Warranty deed — Contains the most extensive protection against defects in title including the following covenants or warranties:

            a. Good title — Grantor has all present rights of ownership and possession (seisin) and the right to convey the particular estate.

            b. Quiet enjoyment — No one has a superior title and no one will disturb possession.

            c. Against encumbrances — The property is not subject to any outstanding rights that would diminish the value of the land.

        4. Special warranty deed — Includes all covenants but warrants only against defects in title arising when the grantor had title.

5. Quitclaim deed — Transfers only that title which the grantor had and contains no warranties.

6. Grant deed — Includes implied warranty that the grantor owns the property and has not previously encumbered the property or conveyed the property to another person.

7. Sheriff's deed — Transfers ownership rights to buyer at a sale held in order to satisfy a judgment. [See Chapter 31.]

8. Recording statutes.

    a. After the grantor signs the deed before a notary public, the deed is recorded in a public office in the county in which the real property is located.

    b. Recording gives notice to the whole world that the grantee is the owner of the property.

    c. Types of recording statutes:
        1) Race statute — The first grantee to record a deed has a superior right to the property.
        2) Pure notice statute — A good faith purchaser who purchases the property for value in good faith and without notice has a superior right over other persons, including a person who may have first filed (recorded a deed) but who had knowledge of the prior transfer.
        3) Notice-race statute protects a purchaser who records first without knowing that another person had already bought the property.

B. Contracts for the sale of real estate.

1. Brokers — Real estate brokers usually are licensed by the state and act as agents in the sale of realty. [See also Unit Six.]

    a. In most instances, a broker is an agent for the seller who agrees to pay the broker a commission (a specified percentage of the sales price).

    b. Ordinarily, a broker cannot act as an agent for both parties unless consent is given by both parties to the dual agency.

2. Formation of the sales contract.

    a. The person wishing to purchase realty makes a written offer in which the offering price and appropriate conditions are stated.
        1) Frequently, the buyer will pay earnest money (a binder or deposit of money) indicating the buyer's serious intention and ability to carry out the contract; if the buyer (the offeror) withdraws the offer, the earnest money may be forfeited as liquidated damages.

2) The offer may be conditioned on the offeror's ability to obtain financing.

b. If the seller accepts the offer, a contract of sale is signed.
  1) Frequently, the buyer will make a deposit toward the purchase price that is held in an escrow account by an escrow agent which may be a title company, bank, or special escrow company.
  2) A potential buyer and seller may enter into an option contract that provides that the potential buyer will have the right to purchase the property within a specified period of time at a stated price; in order to be enforceable, the option contract must be evidenced by a signed writing and consideration given to the seller. [See Chapters 14 and 17.]

3. Title examination — The records at the recording office (containing the history of all past transfers, sales of the property, and liens on the property) are examined.

   a. The seller has an implied obligation to transfer marketable title (i.e., title that is free from encumbrances, defects in the chain of title, and other matters that affect title).

   b. An abstract prepared by an abstract company is examined by a title examiner who gives an opinion as to the validity of the title.

   c. A buyer may purchase title insurance; in case a defect in the title was not discovered, the title insurer will defend the owner's interest and pay legal expenses.

4. Financing.

   a. A mortgage loan is a long term loan made to the buyer (the mortgagor) by a financial institution or other person (the mortgagee) that is secured by the real property.

   b. A conventional mortgage loan provides for periodic payments at a fixed interest rate.
     1) Today, a mortgage loan may provide for a variable rate of interest that is pegged to a specified standard and adjusted at specified times.
     2) A seller may provide financing to the buyer who will make periodic payments to the seller until the purchase price is paid in full.

5. Closing (settlement or closing escrow) is coordinated with the recording of the deed, the obtaining of title insurance, and other activities, such as payments of costs. [See Chapter 45 regarding the notice which lending institutions are required by the Real Estate Settlement Procedures Act to give to applicants for loans.]

6. Warranty of habitability.

      a. In an increasing number of states, the courts have held that there is an implied warranty that a new house is fit for human habitation.

      b. In some states, the warranty of habitability has been created by statute.

    7. Seller's duty to disclose — Today in many states, a seller has a duty to disclose to the buyer any known defects that materially affect the value of the property and that the buyer reasonably could not discover.

C. Transfer by inheritance — See Chapter 53.

D. Adverse possession — A person in actual, open, exclusive, continuous, hostile possession of real property for a statutory period of time acquires title to the property.

IV. Limitations on the rights of property owners.

A. Owners of real property must comply with laws relating to nuisance, environmental protection, and taxes; real property can be seized in order to satisfy judgments obtained by creditors to whom the owner owed debts.

B. Eminent domain — The power of the government to acquire real property for public use or purpose in accordance with the Fifth Amendment of the U.S. Constitution requirement that "just compensation" be paid to the owner.

C. Zoning — Local regulations adopted for land use control.

    1. State and local governments can control the use of land by exercising their police powers in order to protect the public health, safety, morals, and general welfare (without payment of compensation).

    2. Limitations on the power of the states to restrict land use.

      a. If a regulation is confiscatory, compensation must be paid to the owner.

      b. If a restriction is arbitrary, unreasonable, discriminatory, or without a rational basis, the restriction will be deemed to be a taking of property without due process or a denial of the equal protection of the laws, both of which are prohibited by the Fourteenth Amendment.

    3. Variances — A variance may be granted to an owner, whose use of land is limited by existing zoning regulation, in order to use the land for an alternative purpose when the owner is able to show that:

      a. As zoned, the land will not produce a reasonable return.

      b. The adverse effect of zoning is peculiar to the applicant rather than all land owners in the zone.

c. The variance will not substantially alter the essential character of the zoned area.

4. Building permits.

a. Property owners may be required to obtain permits prior to construction.

b. Restrictions may be included in a permit if they "substantially advance legitimate state interests" and do not deny "an owner economically viable use of his land" (*Agins* v. *Tiburon*, U.S. Supreme Court, 1980).

D. Restrictive covenants.

1. A covenant running with the land is based upon an agreement made by an owner of land that binds subsequent owners of the land to a restriction or limitation on some ownership rights.

2. Requisites for enforceability:

a. Written agreement that usually is contained in a conveyance.

b. Clear intention that the covenant is to bind subsequent owners. (The use of words "successors, heirs, and assigns" usually is sufficient.)

c. The subject matter of the covenant has some connection with the land.

d. The successors to the original parties to the covenant must have notice of the covenant.

3. Illegal restrictive covenants — A restrictive covenant which provides for discrimination is not enforceable if it violates the U.S. Constitution, the state constitution, or a statute.

KEY WORDS AND PHRASES IN TEXT

air space and subsurface rights
plant life and vegetation
ownership interests in real property
conveyance
fee simple absolute
life estate
nonpossessory interest in real property
easement
profit
easement or profit appurtenant
easement or profit in gross
creation of easement or profit by contract,
      deed, will, necessity, or prescription
license

leasehold estate
landlord or lessor
tenant or lessee
tenancy for specific period of time
periodic tenancy
tenancy at will
tenancy at sufferance
deed
warranty deed
special warranty deed
quitclaim deed
grant deed
sheriff's deed
recording statutes (race, pure notice, and

notice-race statutes)	closing
real estate broker	implied warranty of habitability
sales contract	seller's duty to disclose
earnest money	transfer by inheritance
escrow account	adverse possession
title examination	eminent domain
marketable title	zoning
title insurance	zoning variance
mortgage	building permit
mortgagor (borrower)	restrictive covenant running with the land
mortgagee (lender)	

FILL-IN QUESTIONS   Some of the information that is necessary in order to answer the questions below is found in Chapter 48.

1. Real property includes rights associated with land and things of a permanent nature that are _____
    _____.

2. Ownership interests in land may be transferred or conveyed by _____, gift, or inheritance.

3. If A and B concurrently own equal undivided shares of an entire estate in real property, A and B will be considered to be _____ only if the grantor clearly indicated an intention to create such a tenancy. Upon A's death, his interest passes to _____. If A and B are spouses, in most states, they will be considered as having a _____.

4. A _____ is created when two or more persons own undivided shares of an entire estate in real property (which may not be equal) that may be transferred separately during the lifetimes of the co-tenants and, upon death of a co-tenant, by will or inheritance. A surviving co-tenant has no rights to a deceased co-tenant's interest in the property.

5. Real property may be transferred by the owner during his or her lifetime by _____. If the grantor is transferring merely the interest that he or she had, the document of conveyance is called a _____ deed. Frequently, it is used to remove clouds or _____ in the title to the property.

6. The right to use property of another person in a specified manner without removing anything from it is referred to as _____. The right to go onto the property of another person and remove something from the land is called _____. These rights are _____ interests in land and may be given to owners of adjacent property, in which case these rights are called _____.

7. A grantor may restrict the right to use or to further transfer land by making a conveyance containing _____.

MULTIPLE CHOICE QUESTIONS In answering these questions, unless otherwise indicated, assume that there are no relevant statutes and that common law rules are applicable.

1. On December 15, 1996, Tower, McClellan, and Oak were deeded a tract of land as tenants in common. The deed provided that Tower owned 1/2 of the property and McClellan and Oak owned 1/4 each. If Oak dies, the property will be owned as follows:
    A. Tower 1/3, McClellan 1/3, Oak's heirs 1/3.
    B. Tower 1/2, McClellan 1/4, Oak's heirs 1/4.
    C. Tower 1/2, McClellan 1/2.
    D. Tower 5/8, McClellan 3/8.
    (This question has been adapted from objective question #51 on the Uniform CPA Examination, May 1993 and May 1995.)

2. The greatest ownership interest a person may have in real property is a:
    A. fee simple absolute.
    B. life estate.
    C. tenancy for ten years.
    D. joint tenancy.

3. The least amount of protection is given to a grantee who receives:
    A. a warranty deed.
    B. a grant deed.
    C. a quitclaim deed.
    D. a special warranty deed.
    (This question has been adapted from objective question #58 on the Uniform CPA Examination, November 1988.)

4. The greatest amount of protection is given to a grantee who receives:
    A. a warranty deed.
    B. a special warranty deed.
    C. a grant deed.
    D. a quitclaim deed.
    (This question has been adapted from objective question #58 on the Uniform CPA Examination, November 1988.)

5. Jacobs' land was sold to pay his delinquent taxes. The purchaser at the sheriff's sale acquires title by:
    A. adverse possession.
    B. full warranty deed.
    C. right of eminent domain.
    D. None of the answers above is correct.

6. In order to be enforceable against the mortgagor, a mortgage must meet all of the following requirements **except**:
    A. be delivered to the mortgagee.

B. be in writing and signed by the mortgagor.
C. be recorded by the mortgagee.
D. include a description of the debt and the real property in which the mortgagee is given a security interest.
(This question has been adapted from objective question #55 on the Uniform CPA Examination, November 1990.)

7. A mortgage on real property must:
   A. be acknowledged by the mortgagee.
   B. state the exact amount of the debt to be paid by the mortgagor.
   C. state the consideration given for the mortgage.
   D. be delivered to the mortgagee.
   (This question has been adapted from objective question #55 on the Uniform CPA Examination, November 1991.)

8. On August 2, 1996, Chance bought a tract of land that was subject to an existing unrecorded mortgage held by Hauke. On April 2, 1997, Chance borrowed money from Link Finance Co. and gave Link Finance Co. a mortgage on the property. Link Finance Co. did not know about the Hauke mortgage and did not record its mortgage until July 8, 1997. On June 4, 1997, Chance borrowed money from Zone Bank and gave Zone Bank a mortgage on the same real property. Zone Bank knew about the Link Finance Co. mortgage, but did not know about the Hauke mortgage. Zone Bank recorded its mortgage on June 9, 1997. If these transactions took place in a notice-race jurisdiction, which mortgage would have priority?
   A. The Hauke mortgage because it was first in time.
   B. The Link Finance Co. mortgage because Zone Bank had notice of the Link Finance Co. mortgage.
   C. The Zone Bank mortgage because Zone Bank was the first recorded mortgage.
   D. The Zone Bank and Link Finance Co. mortgages share priority because neither the finance company nor the bank had notice of the Hauke mortgage.
   (This question has been adapted from objective question #57 on the Uniform CPA Examination, May 1993.)

9. Abrams owned 100 acres of land, only ten acres of which bordered on a road. Abrams sold and conveyed 25 acres to Bennett. Because the 25 acres did not border on any road, Abrams granted the right to Bennett (in the deed for the 25 acres) to go over a described strip of his (Abrams') land in order to reach Bennett's land.
   A. Bennett has an easement by prescription.
   B. If Bennett later conveys the land to Calahan, Calahan does **not** have the right to go over Abrams' land.
   C. Bennett has an easement in gross.
   D. Bennett has an appurtenant easement.

10. A municipal ordinance requiring that pet animals be restrained from leaving their owner's property is:
    A. unconstitutional because the ordinance interferes with an owner's rights with respect to his or her real property.
    B. **not** a valid exercise of governmental power because an owner of property has an absolute right to use his or her own property.

    C. a valid interference with owners' rights with respect to property.

    D. an invalid interference with the use of both personal and real property.

MATCHING QUESTIONS

Five years ago, when McCormick purchased real property, he obtained a mortgage from Aries Mortgage Co. The Aries mortgage was recorded. On March 1 last year, McCormick sold the property to Nesbett for $400,000. With Aries' agreement, Nesbett assumed the $300,000 Aries mortgage. Nesbett also borrowed $100,000 from Best Finance, Inc. and gave Best a $100,000 mortgage. The Best mortgage was not recorded. This year, on May 1, Nesbett sold the property to Owen for $420,000. Owen knew about the Aries mortgage but was unaware of the Best mortgage. In order to finance the purchase, Owen obtained a $300,000 loan from County Savings Bank that was secured by a mortgage. On May 2, when County Savings recorded its mortgage, County Savings knew about the recorded Aries mortgage, but had no knowledge of the unrecorded Best mortgage.

McCormick, Nesbett, and Owen have defaulted on their loans. Today the outstanding balances on the mortgages are as follows: Aries mortgage $250,000, Best mortgage $80,000, and County Savings mortgage $260,000. Assume that the state has a race-notice statute and that Aries, Best, and County Savings foreclose on their mortgages. The property is sold for $420,000 in accordance with the appropriate state statute.

A.   Select from List A the priority of each of the mortgagees. A priority may be selected only once.

                        List A

    1.   Aries Mortgage Co.   A. First Priority.

    2.   Best Finance, Inc.   B. Second Priority.

    3.   County Savings Bank.   C. Third Priority.

B.   Select from List B the reason for the priority of each mortgagees. A reason may be selected once, more than once, or not at all.

                        List B

    4.   Aries Mortgage Co.   A. An unrecorded mortgage has priority over all subsequent mortgages.

    5.   Best Finance, Inc.   B. A recorded mortgage has priority over a prior unrecorded mortgage if the subsequent mortgagee did not know about the unrecorded mortgage.

    6.   County Savings Bank.   C. The first recorded mortgage has priority over all subsequent mortgages.

                               D. An unrecorded mortgage has priority over a subsequently recorded mortgage if the subsequent mortgagee had knowledge of the unrecorded mortgage.

                               E. An unrecorded mortgage does not have priority over a subsequently recorded mortgage if the subsequent mortgagee did not know about the unrecorded mortgage.

C. For each mortgage select from List C the amount of the sale proceeds that each mortgagee would be able to receive. An amount may be selected once, more than once, or not at all.

		List C
7.	Aries Mortgage Co.	A. $0.00.
8.	Best Finance, Inc.	B. $80,000.
9.	County Savings Bank.	C. $90,000.
		D. $170,000.
		E. $250,000.
		F. $260,000.
		G. $420,000.

D. Assume that all the facts are the same **except** that, on May 2, when County Savings recorded its mortgage, County Savings **knew** about the recorded Aries mortgage and the **unrecorded Best mortgage**. Select from List D the priority of each of the mortgagees. A priority may be selected only once.

		List D
10.	Aries Mortgage Co.	A. First Priority.
11.	Best Finance, Inc.	B. Second Priority.
12.	County Savings Bank.	C. Third Priority.

E. Assume that all the facts are the same **except** that, on May 2, when County Savings recorded its mortgage, County Savings **knew** about the recorded Aries mortgage and the **unrecorded Best mortgage**. Select from List B the reason for the priority of each mortgagees. A reason may be selected once, more than once, or not at all.

List E

13. Aries Mortgage Co.
14. Best Finance, Inc.
15. County Savings Bank.

A. An unrecorded mortgage has priority over all subsequent mortgages.

B. A recorded mortgage has priority over a prior unrecorded mortgage if the subsequent mortgagee did not know about the unrecorded mortgage.

C. The first recorded mortgage has priority over all subsequent mortgages.

D. An unrecorded mortgage has priority over a subsequently recorded mortgage if the subsequent mortgagee had knowledge of the unrecorded mortgage.

E. An unrecorded mortgage does not have priority over a subsequently recorded mortgage if the subsequent mortgagee did not know about the unrecorded mortgage.

Chapter 51
Landlord-Tenant Relationships

A landlord-tenant relationship exists when the owner of real property transfers temporary, exclusive possession of the property to another person. The owner of the real property is referred to as the landlord or lessor. The person to whom possession is transferred is called the tenant or lessee. Their agreement is referred to as a lease and provides for the payment of rent by the tenant. Leases are contracts to which common law principles apply. In addition, state statutes, including in some states, the Uniform Residential Landlord and Tenant Act (URLTA), and local ordinances that relate to landlord-tenant relationships have been enacted.

THINGS TO KEEP IN MIND

1. Statutes relating to the landlord-tenant relationship vary from state to state.

2. Often, the form of the lease and the rights and duties of the landlord and tenant depend upon the use to be made of the leased property. It may, therefore, be necessary to distinguish commercial from residential property.

OUTLINE

I. Creation of the landlord-tenant relationship — The lease.

   A. Statutes provide that some leases (typically, those for more than one year) be written.

   B. A lessee, who acquires temporary possession of real property, is distinguishable from a purchaser, who acquires permanent possession and title to the property; a lessee, who acquires exclusive use of the property, also is distinguishable from a licensee, who acquires a right to the temporary, nonexclusive use of property.

   C. The lease form — Contents.

      1. Expression of intent to establish a landlord-tenant relationship.

      2. Provision for transfer of possession of the property to the tenant at the beginning of the term.

      3. Provision for the reversionary (a future) interest of the landlord entitling the landlord to retake possession at the end of the term.

      4. Description of the property.

5. Statements indicating the length of the term, the amount of the rent, and the manner and time for payment of the rent.

D. Illegality — Statutory and public policy prohibitions.

1. Statutes may prohibit a provision that tenant agrees to pay attorneys' fees in a suit to enforce lease.

2. Statutes and public policy prohibit leasing or using property for illegal purposes.

3. Local building codes and zoning ordinances may restrict leasing of property that is not in compliance with their provisions.

4. Discrimination based upon race, skin color, religion, gender, national origin, or disability is prohibited.

   a. Owners of real property cannot discriminate against prospective tenants who are members of protected classes.

   b. Commercial tenants cannot agree to discriminate against members of protected classes.

E. Unconscionability — A lease or clause in a lease may be found to be unconscionable and, therefore, unenforceable because of the circumstances surrounding the transaction and/or the relative bargaining power of the parties.

II. Parties' rights and duties.

A. Possession.

1. Landlord's duty to deliver possession — The lessor has the obligation to deliver possession of the property to the tenant at the beginning of the term.

   a. The English and URLTA rule — Lessor must give lessee actual physical possession, in which case the lessor has obligation to remove a previous tenant who has remained in possession.

   b. The American rule — Lessor gives lessee right to possession, in which case the lessee has the responsibility of removing a previous tenant who has remained in possession.

2. Tenant's right to retain possession — A tenant has the right to retain exclusive possession until the expiration of the lease term.

   a. This right is lost if the tenant defaults under the terms of the lease.

b. Usually, a landlord has the right to come onto the property in order to inspect, to make repairs, or to show property to prospective buyers or tenants.

3. Covenant of quiet enjoyment.

   a. Landlord will not evict or dispossess tenant from the premises.

   b. Landlord will not interfere with the tenant's right to use and possess the premises. The landlord's interference with the tenant's rights is a constructive eviction.

4. Eviction — A wrongful eviction occurs if a landlord deprives a tenant of possession or enjoyment of property.

   a. Partial eviction — If a tenant is deprived of the use of a portion of the premises, the tenant may cease paying rent and terminate the lease or sue for damages or possession.

   b. Constructive eviction — If a tenant's use and enjoyment of the premises is made difficult or impossible because of a landlord's failure to carry out obligations correctly, the tenant may vacate the premises and cease paying rent after notifying the landlord.

   c. Retaliatory eviction — If a landlord evicts or attempts to evict a tenant in retaliation for reporting violations of local codes to a government agency, the tenant may be able to stop the eviction or recover damages.

B. Using the premises — The tenant has a right to use the property for legal purposes that do not injure the landlord's interest and that are reasonably related to the purpose for which the property is adapted or ordinarily used.

1. A tenant should not create a nuisance by interfering with rights of others.

2. Tenant's duty not to commit waste — A tenant has a duty not to commit waste by abusive or destructive use of the property and is liable for such damage; a tenant, however, is not liable for ordinary wear and tear.

3. Altering the premises — Alterations made by a tenant include improvements and changes that substantially affect the property.

   a. In most states, tenants cannot make alteration without landlord's consent.

   b. Fixtures are items of personal property that are affixed to the real property. [See also Chapter 48.]
      1) In some states, fixtures in residential property become part of the landlord's property and may not be removed by tenant.
      2) In other states, residential tenants can remove fixtures if their removal can be accomplished without damage to the premises.

C. Maintaining the premises.

   1. Statutory requirements.

      a. A landlord must comply with statutory construction and maintenance standards.

      b. Common areas, such as halls, stairs, and elevators, must be maintained by the landlord, who is required to repair known defects and defects about which the landlord should reasonably know.

   2. Obligations under the lease.

      a. A lease, particularly a commercial lease, may expressly designate which party is to maintain the premises.

      b. A tenant has a duty to make repairs that are necessitated as a result of the tenant's intentional or negligent acts.

   3. Implied warranty of habitability.

      a. In most states, the landlord of residential property must furnish premises that are safe and suitable for people to live in at the time when the lease term begins and during its entire term.

      b. The warranty applies to substantial material physical defects about which the landlord knows, or should know, and which the landlord has had a reasonable time to repair.

      c. Factors used in determining if there is a breach of warranty of habitability.
         1) Whether the tenant caused or was responsible for the defect.
         2) The length of time during which the defect existed.
         3) The real and potential impact of the defect on the health, safety, and normal activities of occupants of the premises.
         4) Whether or not the defect violates applicable housing, building, or sanitation codes or regulations.

   4. Remedies of tenant for landlord's failure to maintain leased property.

      a. Withholding rent — A tenant may have a statutory right to withhold all or a portion of the rent or to pay rent into an escrow account or to an escrow agent.

      b. Repairing and deducting — A tenant who makes necessary repairs to correct a defect, about which the landlord has been notified, may deduct the cost of the repairs from the rent.

c. Canceling the lease — A tenant may terminate the lease when there has been a constructive eviction or a breach of the warranty of habitability.

d. Suing for damages — A tenant may institute a lawsuit for damages for breach of the lease when there has been a constructive eviction or a breach of the warranty of habitability.

D. Rent.

1. The tenant has an obligation to pay the agreed-upon rent, or, if none is provided for, reasonable rent, even if the tenant fails to occupy the premises or if the tenant moves out without justification while the lease is in force.

2. Security deposits.

a. The landlord may require a security deposit that will be subject to forfeiture in whole or part if the tenant fails to pay rent or damages the property.

b. At the end of the term, the deposit must be returned, less deductions for damages or unpaid rent; in some states, interest must be paid on the deposit.

3. Late charges may be imposed upon a tenant if the tenant fails to pay rent when it is due.

4. Rent escalation — Unless there is a rent escalation clause, the rent cannot be increased during the term of the lease.

5. Property taxes — Usually, the landlord has the duty to pay assessments and taxes on leased property.

6. Landlord's remedies for tenant's failure to pay rent.

a. If a tenant vacates the premises without justification, the tenant remains liable to pay the rent for the remainder of the term of the lease and may be sued for unpaid rent; the landlord, however, may be required to mitigate (reduce the amount of) damages by making a reasonable attempt to lease the property to another person.

b. Landlord's lien — Statutes in some states provide that a landlord may have a lien on a tenant's personal property if rent is not paid.

c. Lawsuit — A landlord may sue in order to recover unpaid rent.

d. Recovery of possession — If there is a breach of the lease by a tenant, the landlord has a legally enforceable right of entry in order to obtain possession peaceably.
   1) Common law action for ejectment.

2) Summary procedure for unlawful detainer.

III. Liability for injuries on the premises.

A. The party who controls an area of the property owes a duty to exercise reasonable care in order to avoid foreseeable risks that might cause injuries to other people. What is reasonable care depends upon the circumstances, including the status of an injured person. [See also Chapter 6.]

1. Invitee — A person, such as a guest or customer, who has been invited onto the premises by the tenant for the benefit of the tenant.

2. Licensee — A person, such as a salesperson, who is invited or allowed onto the premises by the tenant for the benefit of the licensee.

3. Trespasser — An uninvited person who has no right to be on the premises.

4. The attractive nuisance doctrine may apply if an injured trespasser was a young child.

B. Landlord's liability.

1. A landlord is liable for injuries occurring on part of the property over which the landlord has control; a landlord has the duty to inspect and maintain common areas properly.

2. A landlord is liable for injuries caused by the landlord's failure to make repairs or negligence in making repairs when the landlord has an obligation or has undertaken to make repairs.

3. Injuries caused by defects on the premises — Liability may be imposed on a landlord for injuries resulting from a dangerous condition about which the landlord knew, should have known, or failed to inform a tenant.

4. Commercial property.

a. Landlord has a duty to inspect and make repairs to commercial property before a tenant takes possession in order to prevent unreasonable risks to members of the public.

b. Unless otherwise provided, a landlord may be liable only for injuries resulting from latent, nonobvious defects that were known to the landlord at the time of leasing but which the landlord concealed from the tenant.

5. Common areas — A landlord is liable for injuries resulting from the condition of common areas where people reasonably could be expected to go and over which the landlord has control.

6. Repairs.

a. A landlord may be required to put and/or keep the premises in good repair because of codes, the warranty of habitability, or express provisions in the lease.

b. A landlord may be liable to an injured party for negligence for failure to make repairs within a reasonable period of time or if repairs are made in a negligent manner.

7. Injuries caused by crimes of third persons.

a. A landlord may be liable for injuries that were caused by criminal acts of third persons when the crimes are reasonably foreseeable and preventable, and the landlord has not taken steps to prevent the crimes.

b. Factors used in determining whether or not a crime is foreseeable include:
   1) Prior criminal activity in the geographic area of the rental property and the recentness of the prior criminal activity.
   2) The types of crimes that occurred in the past; a court may use the prior similar incidents rule or the totality of the circumstances rule.

8. Exculpatory clauses relieving a landlord of liability are unenforceable if these clauses relieve the landlord of liability for injury or damage caused by the landlord's failure to comply with a statute or caused by the landlord's own negligence or intentional acts.

C. Tenant's liability.

1. A tenant is liable for injuries occurring on part of the premises over which the tenant has control and which the tenant has a duty to reasonably maintain.

2. A commercial tenant owes a duty of exercising reasonable care, including warning invitees of any latent dangerous conditions on areas of approach to the tenant's premises and areas used in common with other tenants, as well as on the premises which are leased by the tenant; in some cases, both the landlord and the commercial tenant may be liable to an injured party.

IV. Transferring rights to leased property.

A. Transfer of the landlord's interest.

1. The landlord, as a property owner, can sell or otherwise transfer the interests in real property that the landlord owns including the reversionary interest (the right to retake possession at the end of the term).

2. When a landlord transfers title to the leased property, an existing tenant becomes the tenant of the transferee.

B. Transfer of the tenant's interest.

1. A lease may prohibit assignment and/or subleasing, or a statute or a clause in a lease may require the landlord's consent to the tenant's assignment of the tenant's interest in the lease or the subleasing of the premises.

2. Assignments.

   a. If a tenant makes an assignment of all the remaining rights under the terms of the lease, the assignee assumes the tenant's obligations.

   b. If the assignee fails to pay the rent, the original tenant (the assignor) is liable for payment of the rent to the landlord.

3. Subleases — If a tenant transfers less than all the remaining rights (a sublease), the transferee is liable to the tenant, and the tenant remains liable to the landlord for payment of the rent.

V. Termination or renewal of the lease.

A. Termination of lease.

1. A lease and the tenant's obligation to pay rent terminates at the expiration of the specified term of the lease or in accordance with a provision of the lease.

2. Termination by notice.

   a. A statute or a lease may provide that notice of termination is required to be given by the landlord.

   b. A periodic tenancy (e.g., from month to month) is renewed automatically; a periodic tenancy can be terminated by giving a single period's notice or as provided by statute.

3. Release and merger.

   a. If a landlord conveys the landlord's interest in the real property to a tenant, the transfer is a release and the tenant's interest in the property is merged into the title to the property.

   b. Usually, evidence of this is required to be in a signed writing. [See Chapter 17.]

4. Surrender by agreement — The tenant and landlord may agree to terminate a lease prior to the end of the term, in which case the tenant surrenders possession of the property.

5. Abandonment.

   a. A tenant may abandon the property by completely moving off the premises with no intention to return.

b. Abandonment may be treated as an offer to surrender the rights under the lease so that the obligation of the tenant to pay rent may cease if the landlord retakes possession.

6. Forfeiture — A statute or lease may provide that when the landlord or tenant fails to comply with a lease provision, there is a forfeiture, and the lease is terminated.

7. Destruction of the property — Destruction of the premises by a cause that was beyond the control of the landlord may terminate a residential lease; if there is no relevant provision in a commercial lease, the destruction of an entire building may relieve a commercial tenant of the responsibility for paying rent.

B. Renewal — A lease may provide for renewal in which case the tenant must comply with provision for timely notification, or the landlord and tenant may mutually agree to renew a lease.

KEY WORDS AND PHRASES IN TEXT

landlord-tenant relationship
Uniform Residential Landlord and
     Tenant Act (URLTA)
landlord (lessor)
tenant (lessee)
lease
rent
temporary exclusive possession
reversionary (future) interest of
     landlord
commercial or residential lease
prohibitions against discrimination
compliance with building codes
     and zoning ordinances
unconscionability of lease provisions
landlord's duty to deliver possession to
     tenant
tenant's right to retain possession
covenant of quiet enjoyment
eviction
partial, constructive, and retaliatory
     evictions
duty of tenant not to create nuisance
     or waste
alterations to leased premises
fixtures
maintaining the premises
common areas
implied warranty of habitability

substantial physical defect
remedies of tenant for landlord's failure
     to maintain leased premises
withholding of rent
deposit of withheld rent in escrow
     account or with escrow agent
repair-and-deduct statute
canceling the lease
security deposit
late charges
rent escalation clause
payment of property taxes
landlord's remedies for tenant's failure
     to pay rent
mitigation of damages
landlord's lien
recovery of possession by landlord
right of entry
remedy of ejectment
unlawful detainer procedure
liability for injuries on the premises
invitee
licensee
trespasser
attractive nuisance doctrine
duty of landlord to make repairs
liability for injuries caused by crimes of
     third persons
exculpatory clauses

tenant's liability for failure to maintain safe conditions
effect of transfer of landlord's interest
effect of transfer of tenant's interest
assignments and subleases
termination of lease by notice

termination of lease by release and merger
surrender of premises by agreement
abandonment of premises by tenant
forfeiture of lease
effect of destruction of the property
renewal of lease

FILL-IN QUESTIONS

1. A landlord-tenant relationship arises when an owner of real property transfers temporary exclusive _____ of the property to another person in exchange for the payment of _____. The owner of the real property is referred to as the _____ or lessor. The party who is given the right to assume temporary _____ of the property is called the tenant or lessee.

2. In order to create a landlord-tenant relationship, the parties enter into a contract, that is referred to as a _____, in which the parties' intent to agree to the transfer of possession of real property is expressed. The _____ is a document that contains a description of the property and indicates the period of time during which the tenant is entitled to have possession of the property and the amount of consideration, or _____, which the tenant will pay to the landlord. The lease also provides for the landlord's _____ interest, which entitles the landlord to regain possession of the property at the end of the term specified in the lease.

3. It is implied, if not expressed, that a landlord promises that the tenant's use and enjoyment of the leased property will not be disturbed or interfered with by the landlord or another person having superior title during the term of the lease because of the covenant of _____. In addition, today, the landlord makes an implied warranty of _____ to the effect that the premises are _____ and, therefore, fit for human occupancy.

4. Because of state statutes and local ordinances, a _____ is required to meet certain standards relating to construction and maintenance of a residential building. In addition, the landlord is required to maintain _____, such as hallways, stairways, and elevators that are used by tenants, so that these areas are free from defects of which the landlord has actual knowledge and those about which the landlord reasonably should know.

5. If a tenant makes an assignment of his or her rights under a lease, the assignee pays rent to the _____. If the tenant subleases his or her rights, the sublessee pays rent to the _____ from whom the sublease was obtained. In either event, if the assignee or sublessee fails to pay the rent, the _____ is liable for the unpaid rent to the landlord.

MULTIPLE CHOICE QUESTIONS

1. A tenant must exercise reasonable care in maintaining leased property over which the tenant has control. A landlord must exercise reasonable care in maintaining leased

property over which the landlord has control. If another person is injured because repairs have not been made to an area over which both the landlord and tenant have control:
- A. only the landlord will be liable to the injured person who may recover damages because of the landlord's negligence.
- B. only the tenant will be liable to the injured person who may recover damages because the tenant has created a nuisance.
- C. both the landlord and tenant will be liable to the injured person who may be awarded damages against both the landlord and the tenant.
- D. the injured person may **not** recover from the landlord if the landlord is able to prove that the repairs were not made to correct a latent condition.

2.   A tenant is required to exercise reasonable care in order to prevent harm to people who foreseeably may be in the area over which the tenant exercises control. Similarly, the landlord is required to exercise reasonable care in order to prevent harm to people who foreseeably may be in the area over which the landlord exercises control. What is reasonable care depends upon the circumstances, including whether an injured party was an invitee, licensee, or trespasser. Which of the following statements is true?
- A. An invitee is a person whom a tenant invites onto the premises for the tenant's benefit.
- B. A licensee is a person whom the tenant allows on the premises for the benefit of the landlord.
- C. An invitee is a person whom the tenant allows on the premises for the benefit of the invitee.
- D. Because a trespasser is a person who has no right to be on the premises, no duty to exercise care is owed to a trespasser by either a tenant or landlord.

3.   Luxor Realty Co. is the owner of an apartment house in which there are 88 units. Tucker has leased one of the apartments. Tucker, Friendley (a friend of Tucker's), Charity (who was soliciting contributions for the local United Fund), and Burgler (a thief) were injured when a cable for the elevator in which the four people were riding broke.
- A. Luxor Realty Co. owes a greater degree of care in order to prevent harm to Charity than the company owes to Tucker.
- B. Luxor Realty Co. owes a greater degree of care in order to prevent harm to Charity than the company owes to Friendley.
- C. Luxor Realty Co. owes a greater degree of care in order to prevent harm to Burgler than the company owes to Friendley.
- D. Luxor Realty Co. owes a greater degree of care in order to prevent harm to Friendley than the company owes to Burgler.

Questions 4 and 5 are based upon the following fact situation: Tennent leased a building under a five-year written lease at a monthly rental of $12,000. The premises were used as a restaurant and Tennent, therefore, installed an air conditioning system, a counter, and stools. Six months after the commencement of the lease, the landlord turned off the water and has since refused to reconnect the water pipes. Tennent moved out and wishes to remove the counter and stools without damage to the premises and the air conditioning system, which will inflict considerable damage to the premises.

4. By turning off the water, the landlord has:
   A. violated the implied terms of the year-to-year lease.
   B. actually evicted Tennent by breaching the covenant of possession.
   C. constructively evicted Tennent by breaching the covenant of quiet enjoyment.
   D. **not** terminated the lease and has a right to receive the monthly rent of $12,000 from Tennent.

5. The counter, stools, and air conditioning system are:
   A. part of the real property and their removal by Tennent is wrongful.
   B. fixtures. The counter, stools, and air conditioning system became part of the real property and can be removed only by the owner of the premises.
   C. trade fixtures. Tennent may remove the counter and stools because their removal does not damage the premises, but he may **not** remove the air conditioning system.
   D. trade fixtures. Tennent may remove the counter, stools, and air conditioning system, but will be required to reimburse the landlord for damage caused by the removal of the air conditioning.

6. In January, Great Records, Inc. rented a store in a building from Hamilton Realty Corp. under a three-year written lease. Great Records, Inc. operated a record store on the premises. In May, the structure was damaged badly when a helicopter lost one of its rotors and crashed into the building. The record store cannot be used without substantial repairs. If Great Records, Inc. leased:
   A. only the store, the lease is terminated and Great Records, Inc. need not continue to pay rent.
   B. only the store, the lease is **not** terminated until the expiration of the three-year period.
   C. the entire building, the lease is terminated and Great Records, Inc. need **not** continue to pay rent.
   D. the entire building, Great Records, Inc. will be required to make the necessary repairs, and Great Records, Inc., but **not** Hamilton Realty Corp., may recover damages from the operator of the helicopter.

7. A tenant, who has rented an apartment, has a one-year written lease that does **not** contain any restrictions specifying conditions under which the tenant may be evicted. The tenant may be evicted by the landlord for:
   A. maintaining a crack-cocaine operation in the apartment.
   B. keeping a pet cat in the apartment.
   C. making repairs to the windows in the apartment.
   D. keeping a cat in the apartment or maintaining a crack-cocaine operation in the apartment.
   E. none of the reasons stated above.
   (This question has been adapted from objective question #53 on the Uniform CPA Examination, May 1990.)

8. Larkspur leased a factory building to Tearose under a ten-year written lease that had no prohibitions against Tearose's transfer of her rights as a tenant to another person. Which of the following statements is correct?

A. Larkspur's death terminates the lease, and Tearose can recover compensatory damages from Larkspur's estate for actual losses which Tearose incurs as a result of the termination of the lease.
B. Larkspur's sale of the factory building terminates the lease, unless both Tearose and the purchaser consent to the assumption of the lease by the buyer of the real property.
C. Tearose does **not** need Larkspur's consent in order assign her rights under the lease to another person.
D. Tearose needs Larkspur's consent in order to sublease the factory building to another person.

(This question has been adapted from objective question #54 on the Uniform CPA Examination, May 1990.)

UNIT ELEVEN:
SPECIAL TOPICS

The five chapters in this unit, the final portion of the Seventh Edition of *West's Business Law: Alternate Edition*, deal with topics that will have significance to the readers, both in their future personal lives and in their business and professional endeavors.

Chapters 52 and 53 are corollaries to Unit Ten (Property). For example, the subject matter of Chapter 52 is insurance, a means of shifting risks that can have detrimental effects on people and business firms. Recognizing that they will incur financial or economic losses if their property is destroyed or damaged, property owners may obtain insurance in order to assure that, in such event, their property can be replaced or repaired. Other forms of insurance, such as life, liability, and automobile insurance (which typically combines property and liability coverage), are also presented in Chapter 52. Chapter 53 deals with transfers of ownership interests in property by forming trusts and, upon death, by will or in accordance with inheritance statutes.

As discussed in Chapter 54, accountants, attorneys, and other people who are members of professions owe responsibilities to those for whom they perform professional services. Liability is imposed upon professionals who fail to carry out their responsibilities properly. It is important, therefore, for professionals to appreciate the nature of their obligations — it also is important for those who employ professionals to understand the nature of their rights when they seek the services of professionals.

Chapter 54 includes information about the common law and statutory duties that accountants owe to their clients and, in some cases, third parties who foreseeably may rely upon statements and other documents that are prepared by accountants. For those of you preparing to sit for the Uniform Certified Public Accountant (CPA) Examination, there is a series of objective questions at the end of the chapter. The questions have been adapted from questions that have been on past Uniform CPA Examinations and will be helpful in your review. You may have noticed in previous chapters that some questions have been based upon those appearing on past CPA exams and that most of the other objective questions in the *Study Guide* are similar in format and content to those used on the CPA Examination. Note too, that, following this unit of the *Study Guide to Accompany West's Business Law*, there is a section containing information about the Uniform CPA Business Law and Professional Responsibilities Examination.

Chapter 55, covering the international environment of business, is illustrative of a theme in this book — the evolving nature of business and law that results from changes in the general environment in which both business and law exist and function — for both law and business have adapted to the gradual, and dynamic, changes that have occurred in society over time. Today, business people recognize that they must be sensitive to the law that is relevant when they engage in international business transactions. Chapter 55 contains information about the internationalization of business and some of the germane legal doctrines and problems that one may encounter when conducting business in the global economy.

The final chapter, Law for Entrepreneurs, highlights topics previously covered in the *West's Business Law* and this *Study Guide* that are particularly significant for people who contemplate beginning their own businesses.

Chapter 52
Insurance

Insurance plays an important role in risk management. The objective of insurance is to transfer and allocate risk — an existing contingency over which a person has little control but which, if the contingency occurs, will result in an economic or pecuniary loss. In order to obtain insurance, one enters into a particular kind of contract, called an insurance policy. In order for the insurance policy to be valid and enforceable, all the requisites of a contract must be present and, in addition, the person obtaining the insurance must have an insurable interest in the subject matter (e.g., life, health, or property) that is insured.

The first part of the chapter is devoted to general principles of insurance law. Characteristics of particular types of insurance are discussed in the last segment of the material.

THINGS TO KEEP IN MIND

Insurance companies, insurance agents and brokers, the contents of insurance policies, the rates charged as premiums, etc., are subject to regulation by the several states.

OUTLINE

I. Insurance concepts and terminology.

A. Insurance terminology.

1. Policy — The insurance contract.

2. Premium — The consideration paid to the insurer by the party obtaining insurance.

3. Parties to an insurance policy.

a. Insurer — The insurance company or underwriter that issues the policy.

b. Insured — The person who is covered by the policy (i.e., the person obtaining property or liability insurance or the person whose life is insured under the terms of a life insurance policy).

c. Insurance agent — A person who ordinarily is employed by the insurer for which that person is an agent. [See Chapters 33 and 34.]

d. Insurance broker — An independent contractor who is treated as an agent for the person for whom the broker is obtaining insurance (the applicant), except when otherwise provided by state statute.

B. The concept of risk pooling.

1. An insurance company is able to spread certain risks among a large group of people based upon the estimated amount of benefits that the company will have to pay in case certain contingencies occur.

2. An insurance company establishes premium rates, which the company will charge to each member in the group, based upon the company's predictions as to the total benefit payments that the company will have to pay and to assure that it will receive a profit.

C. Classifications of insurance.

1. Insurance is classified according to the nature of the risk and the persons and interests that are protected.

2. Three major categories are property, liability, and life insurance.

D. Insurable interest — A legal or equitable interest in the subject matter of insurance (a life or property), such that a person will benefit from the preservation of the subject matter or incur a direct, pecuniary, or monetary loss if the subject matter ceases to exist or is destroyed or damaged.

1. Life insurance.

a. Every person has an insurable interest in his or her own life.

b. A spouse, child, or parent has an insurable interest in the life of his or her spouse, parent, or child.

c. Partners have insurable interests in the lives of co-partners and shareholders in close corporations have insurable interests in the lives of the other shareholders.

d. Business units have insurable interests in the lives of "key" personnel.

e. A creditor has an insurable interest in the life of a debtor.

f. An insurable interest must exist at the time the policy is obtained, but the owner of the policy does not have to have an insurable interest at the time of the insured's death.

g. A beneficiary or assignee need not have an insurable interest in the life of the person whose life is insured.

2. Property (real or personal) insurance.

    a. An insurable interest must exist when the insured-against loss occurs.

    b. The following people have insurable interest in property: owners including life tenants, joint tenants, tenants in common, owners of remainders, lessees, mortgagees, bailees, pledgees, trustees, and buyers who have entered into executory contracts for the purchase of property.

II. The insurance contract.

A. General principles of contract law are applicable.

B. Application for insurance.

    1. Usually, an application form is completed, is attached to the policy, and is part of the contract of insurance.

    2. Insurers evaluate the risk factors based upon the information in the application; a policy may be canceled because of misrepresentations or misstatements made in the application.

C. Effective date.

    1. The effective date of the insurance contract determines when the applicant for insurance is protected (has "coverage").

    2. Application made to an insurance broker — Customer is not insured until the broker procures a policy.

        a. The applicant is a customer of the broker and the principal; the broker is an agent for the applicant.

        b. A broker who fails to obtain an insurance policy is liable to the applicant/principal if the applicant is damaged as a result of the broker's failure to obtain coverage.

    3. Application made to an agent of the insurer.

        a. Life insurance — Insurance is effective after the application is accepted and the first premium is paid. A written binder may result in earlier coverage upon payment of a premium.

        b. Property insurance is effective when an agreement is reached as to coverage. A written binder may be given.

D. Provisions and clauses in insurance policies.

    1. State statutes mandate inclusion of certain provisions.

2. Incontestability clause in life or health insurance policy.

    a. An insurance company may not contest or refuse payment after a stated period of time.

    b. An incontestability clause does not prevent an insurance company from refusing to pay benefits or reducing the amount of benefits because of lack of insurable interest, failure to pay premiums, or failure to file proof of loss within a specified period.

3. Coinsurance clause — The insured is required to insure property at a stated percentage of the property's full replacement value in order to recover the face amount of the policy in case of a total loss or the replacement cost when there has been a partial loss. The following formula is used:

$$\text{Amount of recovery} = \frac{\text{amount of insurance carried}}{\substack{\text{amount of insurance required} \\ (\% \ X \ \text{replacement value})}} \ X \ \text{amount of loss.}$$

4. Appraisal and arbitration clause — Value of property will be determined by appraisal or arbitration when the insured and the insurer disagree as to value of a loss.

5. Multiple insurance coverage (other insurance or *pro rata* clause) — If there are multiple policies covering the same property or health risk, the loss is apportioned among the several insurers.

6. Antilapse clause.

    a. Most life insurance policies contain provisions for grace periods during which delinquent payments can be made in order to prevent lapse of insurance coverage.

    b. Statutes often require that, if a premium is not paid, a smaller paid-up policy be issued or extended insurance coverage be given, or that the cash surrender value be paid to the owner of the policy.

E. Interpreting provisions of an insurance policy — When the terms of a policy are ambiguous:

1. Words are given their ordinary meaning unless it is clear that a technical or unusual meaning has been intended.

2. Provisions are interpreted most strongly against the insurer which prepared the contract.

F. Cancellation.

1. Written notice of cancellation must be given and unearned premiums that were paid in advance must be refunded by the insurance company.

2. Property and automobile insurance may be canceled by either party upon giving required notice.

3. Life and health insurance can be canceled by insurer prior to effective incontestability date.

4. Life insurance antilapse provisions are an alternative to cancellation.

G. Basic duties and rights.

1. Basic contractual duties apply. [See Unit Two dealing with contracts.]

2. An applicant must disclose all material facts that are necessary in order for the insurer to evaluate risk (i.e., those facts that would influence the insurance company's decision to refuse to insure against a risk or to charge a higher premium).

3. After a claim is filed, the insurer may conduct an investigation and is required to make reasonable efforts to settle third party claims and defend an insured in any suits that are brought against an insured who had a liability insurance policy.

4. Subrogation.

   a. If an insurer of property pays an insured for a loss caused by another person's intentional or negligent act, the insurer is subrogated to the rights (or "stands in the shoes") of the insured.

   b. An insurer has no right of subrogation against a third person who caused the death of a person covered by life insurance.

H. Defenses against payment — When the event giving rise to a claim for payment occurs, the insurer may refuse to pay. (Before the occurrence of such an event, an insurer, having a valid reason, may disaffirm or rescind a policy.)

1. Failure to comply with reasonable requirements as to notice and proof of loss.

2. Acts that are illegal or against public policy.

3. Lack of insurable interest.

4. Policy procured through use of fraud, misrepresentation, etc.

5. An insurance company may not contest or refuse payment after a stated period of time if the insurance policy contained an incontestability clause.

I. Because of a state statute or case law, an insurance company may be estopped (or prevented) from asserting a defense that normally would be available.

III. Types of insurance.

    A. Life insurance.

       1. Types of life insurance.

          a. Whole (straight, ordinary, or cash value) life insurance — Stated premiums are paid during the lifetime of the insured.
            1) Investment feature — Cash value increases over time and may be borrowed.
            2) The policy may provide for retirement income (annuity or living benefit program).

          b. Limited payment whole life insurance — Premiums are paid for a specified number of years after which the policy is paid up and fully effective.

          c. Term insurance — Provides temporary coverage during a stated period but may be renewable after the period or convertible into whole life insurance. Term insurance does not have savings features.
            1) Level term insurance.
            2) Decreasing term insurance.
            3) Mortgage term insurance.

          d. Endowment insurance — Premiums are paid for a specified term at the end of which fixed periodic payments are made to the insured (an annuity) or, upon the death of the insured, to a beneficiary.

          e. Universal life insurance.
            1) Permanent life insurance that provides for investment by insurer of premiums (less expenses) in interest bearing government securities and payment of the proceeds to policyholders.
            2) Proceeds (which are tax free) increase the cash value of the policy and may be used for payment of premiums or withdrawn.
            3) The amounts of death protection and premiums may be adjusted up or down.

       2. Features of life insurance policies.

          a. Liability — Common exclusions from insurers' liability include death due to suicide, service in military action during war, and execution for a crime as well as death while a passenger in a commercial vehicle.

          b. Adjustment due to misstatement of age — If the age of the insured was misstated, the premium payments and/or benefits are adjusted.

c. Assignment — The owner of the policy designates one or more beneficiaries to whom the death benefits are to be paid and, unless the beneficiaries' rights are vested, the policy owner may change the beneficiaries and assign the rights to the policy upon giving notice to the insurer.

d. Creditors' rights.
   1) Creditors can reach insurance proceeds that are payable to the estate of the insured or payable to a beneficiary if the payment of premiums constituted a fraud on creditors.
   2) Usually, creditors cannot reach the cash surrender value of a policy or compel changing the name of a beneficiary to that of a creditor.
   3) In most states, at least part of the proceeds of life insurance are exempt from creditors' claims.

e. Termination occurs upon default in premium payments, death of the insured and payments of benefits, expiration of the term of the policy, and cancellation by the policy owner.

B. Fire and homeowners' insurance.

1. Standard fire insurance policies.

   a. The insurer's liability extends to losses caused by hostile fires (but not by friendly fires) and to other casualty losses if there is extended coverage.

   b. Liability of insurer when there is a total loss.
      1) Valued policy — Insurer is liable for amount specified in policy.
      2) Open policy — Insurer is liable for the lesser of the fair market value of property or a maximum specified amount.

   c. When there is a partial loss, insurer is liable for the actual loss; the amount of the payment by the insurer may be reduced because of a coinsurance clause. [See above at II. D. 3.]

   d. Proof of loss must be filed by the insured within a specified period of time or immediately (which is interpreted as meaning within a reasonable period of time after a loss).

   e. Occupancy clause — Most policies provide that coverage is suspended if the premises are unoccupied for a stated period of time.

   f. Assignment — Property insurance is nonassignable without the consent of the insurer before there is a loss.

   g. Property insurance is treated as an indemnity contract because the insurer agrees to pay the amount of loss upon the occurrence of a contingency that may or may not happen.

2. Homeowner's policies — A homeowner's, renter's, or condominium owner's policy may include property and liability insurance.

    a. Property coverage.
       1) Perils insured against usually include fire, lightening, wind, hail, vandalism, and theft.
       2) Often, coverage for certain personal property is excluded (e.g., motor vehicles, farm equipment, airplanes, and boats) or limited to a specified maximum amount (e.g., jewelry and securities).
       3) An insured may obtain a floater policy on specific personal articles that are located at the insured property or on personal effects when the property is taken off the property.

    b. Liability coverage in case someone is injured on the insured property.
       1) Coverage includes injuries to persons and property because of unsafe conditions and negligence.
       2) Usually, liability arising from business or professional activities, operation of vehicles, and intentional wrongdoing are excluded.

C. Automobile insurance.

  1. Liability insurance.

    a. Insurance covers liability up to specified maximum amounts for bodily injuries and property damage to other persons.

    b. Umbrella policies have higher liability limits.

  2. Collision insurance covers damage to the insured's automobile.

  3. Comprehensive insurance covers loss, damage, and destruction caused by fire, hurricane, hail, and vandalism.

  4. Other automobile insurance.

    a. Uninsured motorist coverage insures the driver and passengers against injuries caused by a driver of another auto who does not have insurance.

    b. Accidental death benefits (double indemnity) provide for payments of lump sums to named beneficiaries if the policyholder dies in an automobile accident.

    c. Medical payment coverage provides for payment of hospital and medical expenses for passengers in the insured's car when the insured is driving.

    d. Other-driver coverage (omnibus clause) protects the owner of the vehicle and anyone else who is driving the vehicle with the owner's permission.

e. No-fault insurance — An insured's insurance company will pay for injuries or damage up to a specified amount without regard to the fault (or lack of fault) of the insured.

D. Marine insurance — A vessel owner and a shipper of goods may obtain ocean or inland marine insurance covering damage to or loss of the vessel or the vessel's cargo due to perils at sea or during a voyage.

1. Often, a marine insurance policy is a valued policy and may be a voyage policy or time policy.

2. The insured vessel owner or shipper warrants that the vessel is seaworthy.

E. Business liability insurance.

1. General liability — Comprehensive general liability insurance can cover a number of risks and special coverage may be obtained on a individualized basis.

2. Product liability insurance. [Product liability is discussed in Chapter 8.]

3. Professional malpractice insurance. [Liability of professionals is discussed in Chapter 54.]

4. Workers' compensation insurance. [Workers' compensation laws are discussed in Chapter 35.]

KEY WORDS AND PHRASES IN TEXT

insurance
risk
risk management
insurance policy (insurance contract)
premium
insurer (insurance company or
    underwriter)
the insured
insurance agents and brokers
risk pooling
insurable interest
life insurance
key-person insurance
property insurance
application for insurance
effective date of insurance coverage
binder
incontestability clause
coinsurance clause
appraisal and arbitration clauses

multiple insurance coverage
antilapse clauses
grace period
cash surrender value
cancellation of insurance policy
disclosure of material facts by applicant
defenses against payment by insurer
whole (straight, ordinary, cash value)
    life insurance
limited-payment life insurance
term life insurance
endowment insurance
annuity
universal life insurance
exclusions from liability
adjustments due to misstatement of age
assignment and change of beneficiary
creditors' rights to benefits
termination of life insurance
standard fire insurance policy

hostile as opposed to friendly fire	uninsured-motorist coverage
valued policy	accidental death benefits (double
open policy	indemnity)
proof of loss	medical payment coverage
occupancy clause	omnibus (other-driver) coverage
assignment (nonassignability of fire	no-fault insurance
insurance policy)	marine insurance
homeowners' policy with property	comprehensive general liability insurance
and liability coverage	product liability insurance
automobile liability insurance	professional malpractice insurance
collision insurance	workers' compensation insurance
comprehensive automobile insurance	

FILL-IN QUESTIONS

1.   In general, wagering bargains are illegal because these bargains are agreements based upon _____ risks and are distinguishable from contracts of insurance which provide for _____ existing risks.

2.   With regard to property insurance, any person who has a legal or equitable interest in real or personal property is treated as having an _____ interest because he or she will benefit if the property is not damaged or destroyed or will _____ _____ if the property is damaged or destroyed.

3.   In order to recover under a policy providing for property insurance, the insured must have an _____ interest at the time that _____.

4.   With regard to life insurance, the owner of a life insurance policy must have an _____ interest in the life of the person whose life is insured. One can obtain a life insurance policy covering his or her own life or the life of another person if he or she will benefit economically from the continued life of the person whose life is insured or will _____ if the person whose life is insured dies.

5.   In order to recover under a life insurance policy, the owner of the policy must have had an _____ interest at the time _____.

MULTIPLE CHOICE QUESTIONS

1.   John, an insured, is 50 years of age. In applying for life insurance, he misstates his age as being 47. The amount of insurance on his life will be adjusted to the sum that the premium paid by John would purchase:
     A. at age 47.
     B. at age 50.
     C. at a reasonable age.
     D. at no age because the policy is unenforceable.

2. Cortez and Douglas were business partners. Cortez and Douglas agreed that each would insure the life of the other for his own benefit. On the application for insurance on Douglas's life, it was stated that Douglas had never had a heart attack. In fact, Douglas had suffered a heart attack three years before. Cortez's policy on Douglas's life contained the usual two-year incontestability clause. Four years later, after the dissolution of the partnership, but while the policy on Douglas's life was still in force, Douglas was killed when he was struck by a car driven by Drover.
    A. Cortez **cannot** recover from the insurer because of the misrepresentation in the application for insurance on the life of Douglas.
    B. Cortez **cannot** recover from the insurer because the partnership has been dissolved, and Cortez, therefore, lacks an insurable interest.
    C. Cortez can recover from the insurer in a lawsuit if the insurance company refuses to pay the proceeds of the life insurance on Douglas's life to Cortez.
    D. If the insurance company has to pay the proceeds of the life insurance on Douglas's life to Cortez, the insurance company will be subrogated to Douglas's rights against Drover.

3. An insurance company paid Zandarski for a loss due to fire. The insurance company has a right to recover from Frazer, who caused the fire. Such right is known as:
    A. insurable interest.
    B. subrogation.
    C. assignment of rights.
    D. contribution.

4. The Smart Corp. obtained a fire insurance policy on its factory from the ABC Insurance Company. The policy was for $5,000,000 which was the value of the insured property. The policy was the standard fire insurance policy sold in the United States. A fire occurred and resulted in a $1,000,000 loss. Which of the following will prevent Smart Corp. from recovering the full amount of its loss from ABC Insurance Company?
    A. The coinsurance clause.
    B. Smart Corp. had a similar policy with another company for $3,000,000.
    C. Aprroximately $400,000 of the loss was caused by smoke and water damage.
    D. Smart Corp. did not notify ABC Insurance Company of the fire until the day after the fire.

Questions 5 and 6 are based on the following fact situation: Young was the owner of a warehouse that was insured by the Ivy Fire Insurance Co. The face value of the fire insurance policy was $600,000. The policy covered the warehouse itself and the contents and contained a 90% coinsurance clause. Careless, an employee of Young, negligently dropped a lighted cigarette on some packing material that caught fire. The fire spread to the contents of the warehouse and the building.

5. Assume that the fire totally destroyed the warehouse and the goods stored in the warehouse. After the fire, the loss was appraised at $1,000,000. Young is entitled to a payment of:
    A. $600,000, the face amount of the policy, from Ivy Fire Insurance Co. because there was a total loss.
    B. $900,000 from Ivy Fire Insurance Co. because of the coinsurance clause.

    C. $540,000 from Ivy Fire Insurance Co. because of the coinsurance clause.

    D. Nothing because the fire was caused by the negligence of an employee of Young.

6.   Assume that the fire damaged the warehouse and destroyed goods that were valued at $100,000. Repairs to the warehouse will cost $80,000. At the time of the fire loss, the replacement value of the warehouse was $900,000.

    A. Young is entitled to a payment of $120,000 from Ivy Fire Insurance Co. because of the coinsurance clause.

    B. Young is entitled to a payment of $162,000 from Ivy Fire Insurance Co. because of the coinsurance clause.

    C. Young is entitled to a payment of $20,000 from Ivy Fire Insurance Co., and the Ivy Fire Insurance Co. will be required to pay $100,000 to the people who had stored the goods that were destroyed in the fire.

    D. Young is entitled to a payment of $72,000 from Ivy Fire Insurance Co. The owners of the goods stored (and destroyed) in the warehouse are entitled to a payment of $90,000 from Ivy Fire Insurance Co. and $10,000 from Young.

7.   Orr was employed by Core who relied upon Orr's ability to supervise the operation of Core's restaurant. Core, therefore, obtained a $50,000 insurance policy on Orr's life and paid the annual premiums when they were due to the insurance company. The policy provided that, upon Orr's death, half of the face value was payable to Core and the other half was payable to Orr's spouse. Orr died three years after the policy was issued and a year after leaving Core's employ. Which of the following statements is correct?

    A. Orr's spouse did **not** have an insurable interest because the policy was owned by Core.

    B. Orr's spouse is entitled to all of the proceeds of the policy.

    C. Orr's spouse is entitled to half of the proceeds of the policy, but Core is **not** entitled to the other half of the proceeds of the policy.

    D. Core is entitled to half of the proceeds of the policy regardless of whether or not Orr was employed by Core at the time of Orr's death.

(This question has been adapted from objective question #60 on the May 1990 Uniform CPA Examination.)

8.   Beal occupies a building as a tenant under a 25-year lease. Beal also has a mortgagee's interest in an office building that is owned by Real Realty Corp. to which Beal had made an $800,000 loan. In which capacity does Beal have an insurable interest?

	Tenant	Mortgagee
A.	Yes	Yes
B.	Yes	No
C.	No	Yes
D.	No	No

(This question has been adapted from objective question #60 on the May 1988 Uniform CPA Examination.)

Chapter 53
Wills, Trusts, and Estates

As explained in Unit Ten, a person may transfer ownership rights with respect to personal and real property by sale or gift during his or her lifetime. A person also may provide for the disposition of his or her property upon his or her death. Compliance with certain formalities relating to wills, however, is required. If a person dies without having executed a valid will, state intestacy laws prescribe the manner in which the decedent's property is to be distributed among heirs and next of kin. The concept of private ownership of property, the effectuation of a natural person's testamentary intent, and the public policy of protecting the family underlie inheritance laws that exist in all states. These statutes regulate the disposition of decedents' estates by will and, in the case of intestacy, by descent and distribution.

Owners of property may establish trusts by transferring the legal title to property that they own to trustees who are obligated to use the property for the benefit of other people, the beneficiaries of the trusts.

Wills, trusts, and other techniques used in estate planning as well as planning for disabilities are discussed in this chapter.

THINGS TO KEEP IN MIND

Although the purposes of laws relating to inheritance, trusts, and methods of planning for possible disability are similar among the states, the manner in which these objectives are achieved varies.

OUTLINE

I. Wills.

A. A will (testamentary disposition of property) is a final, formal declaration by a person (the testator) concerning the manner in which his or her property is to be disposed of after his or her death; a testator may revoke and/or change his or her will during his or her lifetime.

1. The testator (male) or testatrix (female) is the person who has made a will.

2. A person who has made a valid will is said to have died testate. (A person who has died without leaving a will is said to have died intestate.)

3. A testator may appoint a guardian for minor children or incapacitated adults in a will.

4. A testator can appoint a personal representative (an executor) to carry out the testator's wishes regarding disposition of the testator's estate (property).

    a. Executor (male) or executrix (female) — A personal representative named in a will to settle the affairs of a decedent.

    b. Administrator (male) or administratrix (female) — Personal representative appointed by a court to settle the affairs of a decedent, who did not leave a will, or who left a will but failed to name an executor, or named an executor, who is unable or unwilling to serve.

B. Laws governing wills.

1. To probate ("prove") a will means to establish the will's validity and administer the execution of the will through a court.

2. Probate courts administer the law relating to wills and estates of decedents. (In some states, a different title, such as Surrogate Court, is used.)

3. Although most states have adopted all or portions of the Uniform Probate Code (UPC), there are variations among the states regarding probate laws and procedures.

C. Gifts by will.

1. Devise — A gift of real property provided for in a will; title to the real property vests in the devisee.

2. Bequest (legacy) — A gift of personal property provided for in a will; title to the personal property initially vests in the decedent's personal representative.

3. Types of gifts.

    a. Specific devise or bequest — A gift of identified, particular, described property.

    b. General devise or bequest — A gift of a quantity of real property or personal property (usually a sum of money) without a specific identification or description of the property.

    c. Residuary (residuum) — A residuary clause provides for the disposition of remaining property that is not otherwise effectively disposed of by devise and bequest, after payment of decedent's obligations.

4. Abatement — If, after payment of taxes, debts and administration expenses, the assets of the estate are insufficient to pay all the bequests in full, the bequests are reduced.

5. Lapsed legacy.

a. Common law rule — If a legatee (intended recipient of a bequest) died before the testator, or before the legacy is to be paid or delivered, the legacy fails.

b. Legacy does not lapse if the legatee was in a specified family relationship to the testator and left surviving heirs.

D. Requirements for a valid will.

1. Testamentary capacity and intent.

a. In most states, eighteen is the minimum age for executing a will.

b. The testator must have been of "sound mind" when executing a will.
   1) Testator must intend the document to be the testator's last will and testament.
   2) Testator must comprehend the kind and character of the property that is to be distributed.
   3) Testator must comprehend and remember the "natural objects of his or her affection or bounty."
   4) Testator must be able to formulate and comprehend a personal plan for the disposition of property.

c. Testamentary capacity is not necessarily the same as contractual capacity.

d. The validity of a will may be challenged if the will was executed because of undue influence (excessive, improper pressure by another person), fraud in the execution, fraud in the inducement, or duress.

e. Sometimes, courts engage in testamentary construction or interpretation in order to determine the intention of the testator who omitted or used ambiguous or unclear language in a will.

2. Writing requirements — A will must be in writing.

a. The writing may be informal; a handwritten will that is dated and signed by the testator is a holographic (or olographic) will.

b. Nuncupative, oral wills
   1) A few states permit oral wills that are made in expectation of imminent death before three witnesses in order to make gifts of personal property.
   2) Statutes permit people serving in the armed forces to make nuncupative wills when they are on active duty.

3. Signature requirements — A will must be signed by the testator.

4. Witness requirements — A will must be attested by two or more witnesses. Some statutes require that the witnesses be disinterested (not benefit from the

will), witness the signing of the will by the testator, and sign in each other's presence.

    5. Publication requirements — In some states, the testator is required to declare orally (publish) that the will is the testator's last will and testament.

E. Revocation of wills.

    1. Revocation by a physical act of the maker (the testator) — A will may be revoked by the intentional and deliberate burning, tearing, cancellation, obliteration, or destruction of the will by the testator or another person, in the presence of and at the direction of the testator, or in a manner that is provided for in a statute.

    2. Revocation by a subsequent writing — A codicil is a separate writing that revokes, amends, or supplements a prior will.

        a. A codicil is executed with the same formality as a will and must refer expressly to the testator's will.

        b. If a codicil or a later will does not expressly revoke a prior will, the codicil or later will controls when the codicil or subsequent will is inconsistent with a provision in an earlier will.

    3. Revocation by operation of law — Varies from state to state.

        a. Marriage — A subsequent marriage by the testator has the effect of a revocation to the extent that the spouse can receive the amount that the spouse would receive if the testator died intestate unless the omission was intentional.

        b. Divorce or annulment of marriage after execution of a will has the effect of a revocation of any disposition of property to the former spouse.

        c. In most states, a child born or adopted after a will has been executed is entitled to receive the portion of the estate that the child would receive under the intestacy laws. [See below at II.]

F. Rights under a will. [Note: Intestacy laws are discussed below at II.]

    1. A surviving spouse often has a right to take a statutory marital, intestate share (a forced, elective, dower, widow's, or widower's share), rather than take under the will of a deceased spouse.

    2. A beneficiary may renounce a devise or legacy and instead elect to take his or her intestate share.

G. Probate procedures.

1. Informal probate proceedings that may be used in order to save time and money.

    a. In many states, alternative procedures (involving transfer of a decedent's property by affidavit) may be used when most of the property is held in joint tenancy with right of survivorship or when there is only one heir.

    b. Family settlement agreements — Beneficiaries may enter into a private agreement to settle the distribution of the decedent's assets.

    c. Summary procedures.
       1) Simpler, less formal procedures may be used when there are no minors or incompetent devisees, legatees, or heirs.
       2) A person may establish *inter vivos* trusts and/or make investments with named beneficiaries or joint-tenancy arrangements during his or her lifetime so that probate is not necessary.

2. Formal probate procedures are conducted under court supervision — In instances when there are larger estates, contents of safe deposit boxes, other complications, etc., formal probate procedures are required and are more time consuming than informal procedures.

H. Property transfers outside the probate process.

1. Living trusts — See below at III. C. 1.

2. Joint ownership of property so that a survivor or survivors inherit deceased co-tenant's interest. [See Chapter 48.]

3. Gifts to children and other people during a person's lifetime and insurance.

II.   Intestacy laws.

A. Statutes of descent and distribution provide for inheritance and distribution of property of a decedent who failed to execute a valid will or omitted a provision for the disposition of some property, after the decedent's debts are paid.

1. The rules of descent and distribution vary from state to state.

2. Title to real property vests in heirs upon the death of the owner (decedent); title to personal property vests in the personal representative of a decedent (an administrator, appointed by the court) who makes distributions in accordance with the statute, after paying taxes and obligations of the decedent and the estate.

B. Surviving spouse and children — The general statutory pattern for distribution of decedent's property is as follows if decedent is survived by:

1. Spouse and no descendants (children, grandchildren, etc.) — The spouse inherits entire estate.

2. Spouse and one or more descendants — The spouse takes one-third (the elective, marital share) and children share remaining two-thirds equally.

    a. In some states, if there is only one child, the spouse takes one-half and the child one-half.

    b. If a child of the decedent predeceased (died before) the decedent, the child's children (the grandchildren of the decedent) share equally the share that their parent would have taken (*per stirpes*).

    c. A statute also may provide that a spouse is entitled to the homestead (in fee or as a life estate) and household and other allowances.

3. Surviving children or lineal descendants but no surviving spouse.

    a. Usually, children share equally and descendants of children who died before decedent (i.e., grandchildren of decedent) share *per stirpes*.

    b. Some state statutes provide for *per capita* distribution to all heirs in a certain class; if so, grandchildren inherit equally, rather than taking an equal portion of (or splitting) their parent's share.

C. Order of distribution when there is no spouse or lineal descendant:

1. Parents and/or siblings (and lineal descendants of deceased brothers and sisters *per stirpes*).

2. Grandparents.

3. Collateral heirs such as aunts, uncles, nieces, and nephews.

4. If no relatives survive decedent, property escheats to the state or county.

D. Stepchildren, adopted children, and illegitimate children.

1. Stepchildren are not considered to be children of deceased spouse of the children's parent, unless the stepchildren are adopted.

2. Adopted children are considered to be children of adopted parents.

3. Illegitimate children — In some states illegitimate children may inherit only if the children have been "legitimized" or "acknowledged" by the deceased parents.

E. Distribution to grandchildren — See above at II. B.

III. Trusts.

   A. A trust is created when one person (the settlor or grantor) transfers legal title to property to another person (the trustee), who is to administer the property (the *corpus* or *res*) for the benefit of another person or persons (beneficiaries).

   B. Essential elements of a trust.

      1. The settlor must have an interest in the specific, identified property that becomes the *corpus* of the trust and an intention to create the trust.

      2. The beneficiary must be an identified, existing natural person or entity.

      3. The trustee must be designated.

      4. The property must actually be delivered to the trustee with the intention of passing title.

   C. Express trusts — An express trust is created by the grantor/settlor.

      1. Living trusts — A living (*inter vivos*) trust is created during the lifetime of the grantor (settlor).

         a. Property that is in the trust is not included in the grantor's estate after the grantor's death.

         b. The trustee administers the property as directed by the grantor for the benefit of the beneficiaries. [Duties of trustees are discussed below at III. E.]

         c. An irrevocable living trust is created when a grantor executes a trust deed in which the grantor gives legal title to the trustee without reserving the right to amend, alter, or revoke the trust.

         d. A revocable trust exists when title to property is given to the trustee, but the grantor retains the right to change, amend, and revoke the trust during the grantor's lifetime.

      2. Testamentary trusts — A testamentary trust comes into existence upon the death of the settlor.

         a. The formalities required in order to execute a will must be complied with.

         b. Usually, the trustee is named in the grantor's (settlor's) will; if the trustee is not specified by the grantor, a trustee can be appointed by the court.

      3. Charitable trust — A trust that is created for charitable (eleemosynary or philanthropic), educational, religious, scientific, or general social purposes.

4. Spendthrift trust — A trust that provides for maintenance of the beneficiary and secures the corpus against the beneficiary's improvidence by bestowing periodic payments and prohibiting creditors from reaching the beneficiary's interest in future distributions.

5. Totten trust — A tentative, revocable trust that is created when a person deposits money in his or her own name as trustee for a beneficiary.

D. Implied trusts are created by operation of law.

   1. A constructive trust may be imposed as an equitable remedy without regard to the intentions of the parties in order to prevent unjust enrichment.

   2. A resulting trust is implied when a grantor makes a disposition of property under circumstances from which it can be inferred that the grantor's intention was to create a trust and not to transfer a beneficial interest in the property.

E. The trustee.

   1. Trustee's duties.

      a. A trustee must act with honesty, good faith, loyalty, and prudence in administering the trust for the exclusive benefit of the beneficiary.

      b. A trustee must maintain accurate accounts; keep trust assets separate from the trustee's own personal assets; furnish complete, accurate information to a beneficiary or beneficiaries; pay net income to an income beneficiary (or beneficiaries) at reasonable intervals; and distribute the risk of loss from investments by diversification and disposal of assets that do not represent prudent investments.

   2. Trustee's powers.

      a. The powers of the trustee may be prescribed by the settlor.

      b. State statutes typically restrict investments to conservative debt securities and apply if settlor has not otherwise defined trustee's investment power.

   3. Allocations between principal and income — To the extent that the trust instrument does not provide instructions, ordinary receipts and expenses are to be allocated to the income beneficiaries, and extraordinary receipts and expenses are allocated to the principal beneficiaries.

F. Trust termination.

   1. The trust instrument usually specifies a termination date or provides that the trust will end upon accomplishment of a specific purpose.

2. Unless otherwise provided in the trust instrument, a trust is not terminated by the death of the trustee or beneficiary.

3. A trust terminates if the purpose for which the trust was created becomes illegal or impossible to execute.

IV. Estate administration.

A. Locating the will — It is necessary to determine whether or not a decedent left a will and, if so, to find the will.

B. Duties of the personal representative — The executor or appointed administrator is a fiduciary, is supervised by the court, and has duties:

1. To collect, inventory, and preserve the decedent's property without waste and unnecessary depletion.

2. To receive and pay valid claims of creditors and federal and state income and estate or inheritance taxes.

3. To act as a fiduciary in the best interests of the estate.

4. The representative is required to post a bond to insure the honest and faithful performance of his or her duties, unless the will specifies that a bond need not be posted by the representative.

C. Estate taxes.

1. The federal estate tax is levied upon the total value of the estate after payment of debts and expenses and after allowance for exemptions.

2. Some states impose inheritance taxes on the recipient of a bequest; others impose an estate tax that is similar to the federal estate tax; typically, the tax rates are graduated based upon the relationship between the decedent and the beneficiary.

D. Distribution of assets — The personal representative distributes the remaining estate pursuant to court order and renders an accounting before the estate is closed.

V. Planning for disability — Techniques that can be used in planning for possible future disability.

A. A person can appoint an agent to handle legal affairs. [See Chapter 34.]

B. A durable power of attorney is a written authorization to act on behalf of a person if and when that person becomes incapacitated.

C. A health-care power of attorney designates a person who will be authorized to determine the type and amount of medical treatment to be given to a person who cannot make those decisions because of a disability.

D. A living will specifies what medical treatment may be given to a person in the event that that person has a serious accident of illness.

KEY WORDS AND PHRASES IN TEXT

decedent
intestate
intestacy laws (statutes of descent and
    distribution)
escheat
estate planning
will
testate
testamentary disposition of property
testator
personal representative of decedent
    (executor or administrator)
probate and probate court
devise of real property
bequest or legacy of personal property
specific devise or bequest (legacy)
general devise or bequest (legacy)
legatees
abatement of legacy
lapsed legacy
residuary (residuum)
testamentary capacity and intent
writing, signature, witness, and
    publication requirements
holographic (or olographic) will
nuncupative will
revocation of a will by physical act,
    codicil, or subsequent will

revocation of a will by operation of law
renunciation by a beneficiary
spouse's forced share (marital, elective,
    widow's, or widower's share)
Uniform Probate Code (UPC)
informal probate procedures
formal probate procedures
lineal descendants
collateral heirs
order of distribution
distributions *per stirpes* and *per capita*
trust
settlor or grantor of trust
trustee
beneficiary
living or *inter vivos* trust
testamentary trust
charitable, spendthrift, and Totten trusts
constructive and resulting trusts
trustee's duties and powers
allocations between principal and income
trust termination
federal estate tax
state inheritance and estate taxes
durable power of attorney
health-care power of attorney
living will

FILL-IN QUESTIONS

1. A personal representative of a decedent is referred to as an _____ if the representative has been named by the decedent in a properly executed and witnessed _____. If a personal representative is appointed by a _____ court to settle the affairs of a decedent, the representative is referred to as an _____.

2. In general, in order to be effective, the person who executes a last will and testament must have testamentary capacity. The will must be in _____, signed by the _____, and attested to by two or more _____ (who may be

required to be disinterested and who are required to _____ the signing of the will by the _____ and sign in the presence of each other). In some states, a will must be _____ and declared by the _____ to be the last will and testament of the _____.

3. Statutes of descent and distribution provide for inheritance of property if a decedent failed to execute a valid will or to provide for the disposition of some property in his or her will. Such statutes usually provide that, if a decedent died leaving a spouse and children, the _____ may take an elective one-third share and the remaining share is divided equally among _____. Grandchildren, whose parents died before the decedent, equally divide _____ and, therefore, share *per stirpes*.

4. A trust is created when a person (the _____) transfers title to real property or personal property to another person (the _____) for the benefit of another party or parties (the _____).

5. An *inter vivos* trust is a trust that comes into existence _____. A testamentary trust is one that comes into existence upon the _____ of the settlor and will be effective if the settlor has complied with statutes prescribing formalities for the execution of _____.

MULTIPLE CHOICE QUESTIONS

Questions 1 and 2 are based on the following fact situation: At the time of his death, John Doe, a widower, was the owner of a farm, $200,000 worth of General Motors Corporation stock, and $300,000 worth of miscellaneous personal property. John Doe's properly executed and witnessed will provided that the farm be left to his only son, the stock in General Motors to his only daughter, and the remaining personal property be divided equally between the son and daughter after payment of taxes and debts.

1. Upon John Doe's death:
   A. title to the farm vests in John Doe's son.
   B. title to the stock vests in John Doe's daughter.
   C. title to the miscellaneous personal property vests in an executor, who is appointed by a court to administer the estate if none was named in the will by John Doe.
   D. title to the miscellaneous personal property vests in the testator, who was named in the will by John Doe to administer the estate.

2. The gift:
   A. of the farm to the son is a general bequest.
   B. of the stock to the daughter is a general bequest.
   C. of the stock to the daughter is a specific devise.
   D. of the miscellaneous personal property is a general bequest.

Questions 3 and 4 are based on the following fact situation: In 1990, Mary executed a will which provided that, upon her death, her estate was to be equally divided among her children, August, April, and May. Mary died in 1998.

3.   If Mary:
   A. was declared by a court to be mentally incompetent in 1993, the will was revoked by operation by law.
   B. was divorced from her husband in 1986, the will was revoked by operation of law.
   C. crossed out May's name in the will in 1994, Mary has effectively amended the will.
   D. signed a writing in 1994, in the presence of two neighbors, who witnessed the writing, stating that her daughter, June, was to share in her estate with her other children, Mary has made an effective codicil.

4.   Mary's husband:
   A. is **not** entitled to any share in her estate if he married Mary in 1987.
   B. is **not** entitled to any share in her estate if they were separated in 1988.
   C. is entitled to take his statutory intestate (marital, forced, widower's) share.
   D. is entitled to share equally with the named children.

Questions 5, 6, and 7 are based on the following fact situation: H, the husband of W, and father of two living children, A and B, died without leaving a will. Before the death of H, H's son, S, who had two children, and H's daughter, D, who had four children, died.

5.   Under the statutes of descent and distribution in most states:
   A. W inherits the entire estate.
   B. W takes a life estate in all of H's property.
   C. W, A, and B share the entire estate equally.
   D. W may renounce her right to take any share in H's estate.

6.   After W has taken her elective share, the rest of the estate is divided:
   A. equally among A and B.
   B. A takes a one-quarter share, B takes a one-quarter share, and D's four children and S's two children share equally in the remaining one-half.
   C. A takes a one-quarter share, B takes a one-quarter share, D's children share D's one-quarter share equally, and S's children share S's one-quarter share equally.
   D. equally among A, B, and the six grandchildren.

7.   Assume that H left $18,000 worth of property that has all been reduced to cash. The distribution will be as follows:
   A. W receives $6,000; A receives $3,000; B receives $3,000; S's two children each receive $1,500; D's children each receive $750.
   B. W receives $6,000; A receives $3,000; B receives $3,000; S's children each receive $1,000; D's children each receive $1,000.
   C. W receives $6,000 and A, B, each of S's children, and each of D's children receive $1,500.
   D. W, A, B, S's children, and D's children each receive $2,000.

8.   In her will, Settling conveyed real property to the Orphans' Foundation, a charitable organization, for use in benefiting orphans.
   A. This is an *inter vivos* trust.
   B. The Orphans' Foundation holds legal and equitable title to the property.

C. A resulting trust arises for the benefit of orphans.

D. The Orphans' Foundation is a fiduciary and has power to sell the property in order to carry out the purposes of the trust.

9. A person has acquired property under circumstances which make it unjust for him to retain the property.

A. An implied resulting trust will arise by operation of law.

B. An implied constructive trust may be imposed by a court.

C. A probate court will administer the distribution of the property.

D. None of the answers above is correct.

Questions 10 and 11, which have been adapted from essay question #5 on the May 1987 Uniform CPA Examination, are based upon the following fact situation: Ralston established an inter vivos trust on January 1,1995. The written trust instrument was signed by Ralston and provided that income be paid to her son for his life with the remainder to her granddaughter. Ralston transferred rental property and securities to Central Bank, which was designated as the trustee. Assume that a calendar year has been selected as the accounting period and that the trust instrument is silent as to the allocation of trust receipts and disbursements to principal and income.

10. Which of the following allocations of annual receipts and disbursements would be proper?

A. The allocation of rental receipts of $35,000 to income and the payment of a fire insurance premium of $2,000 charged to principal.

B. The allocation of mortgage interest payments of $8,000 charged to income and the allocation of mortgage principal payments of $10,000 charged to principal.

C. The allocation to income of insurance proceeds of $16,000 for the destruction of two rental units as a result of a fire.

D. The allocation of a street assessment of $1,000 charged to principal and the allocation of half of forfeited rental security deposits of $1,000 to principal and half to income.

11. Which of the following allocations of receipts and disbursements would be improper?

A. The allocation to income of bond interest received.

B. The allocation to income of cash dividends on stock.

C. The allocation to income of dividends of additional shares of stock.

D. The allocation to principal of the proceeds of the sale of rights to receive additional shares of stock in the distributing corporation.

12. Kramer's will provided for the creation of a trust, to which all of Kramer's securities were to be transferred. The will named Kramer's wife as both the trustee of the trust and executrix of the estate and his children as beneficiaries of the trust.

A. Kramer has created an *inter vivos* trust.

B. Kramer has created a testamentary trust.

C. Kramer's wife may **not** serve both as the trustee and personal representative of Kramer's estate.

D. Because the trust is invalid, it will **not** become effective until Kramer's death.

(This question has been adapted from objective question #6 on the Uniform CPA Examination, November 1988.)

Chapter 54
Liability of Accountants and Other Professionals

Accountants, attorneys, physicians, and other people who are members of professions are expected to comply with standards of professional ethics and standards of performance that commonly are accepted within their professions. As discussed in the first section of this chapter, obligations are also imposed upon professionals because of past court decisions. Professionals who fail to carry out these common law duties may be civilly liable to clients for whom professionals have agreed to provide services. The chapter includes an examination of the relationship between professionals and their clients.

Materials that relate to accountants' potential liability to third persons, who may have relied upon financial statements, audits, etc., prepared by the accountants, and to potential civil and criminal liability that may be imposed upon accountants because of statutes, such as the federal securities laws, are presented in this chapter.

THINGS TO KEEP IN MIND

Much of the material in this chapter involves applications of principles of law that relate to contracts, torts, and the federal securities acts (topics covered in earlier chapters) to situations dealing with accountants and other professionals. Cross references to other relevant units and chapters in the textbook and the *Study Guide*, therefore, are supplied in the following chapter outline.

OUTLINE

I. Common law liability to clients.

   A. Liability for breach of contract. [See Chapter 20.]

      1. The failure to perform contractual duties is a breach of contract for which the breaching party is liable to the party to whom the performance was to be rendered.

      2. If a professional, who has agreed to perform certain services for a client, fails to carry out his or her contractual duties honestly, properly, and completely, the professional is civilly liable to the client for breach of contract.

      3. Ordinarily, if there has been a breach of contract by a professional, a court in a civil suit will award compensatory damages as a remedy to the client.

    a. The measure of damages will be equal to the foreseeable losses that the client incurred as a result of the breach.

    b. Damages may include expenses incurred by a client in order to secure the services of another member of the same profession and penalties imposed upon the client who failed to meet statutory deadlines.

4. In an action that is based upon breach of contract, liability is not imposed because of breach of a duty that exists as a result of tort law. It is, therefore, **not** a defense that the professional exercised reasonable care or that the client's own negligence contributed to the client's injury.

B. Liability for negligence. [See Chapter 6.]

1. In order to establish negligence, a plaintiff must show that:

    a. The professional (the defendant) owed a duty of exercising care;

    b. There was a breach of the duty of care by the professional;

    c. The plaintiff incurred a recognized injury; and

    d. The plaintiff's injury was proximately caused by the professional's breach of the duty of care.

2. Accountant's duty of care — An accountant has a duty to exercise the same standard of care that a reasonably prudent and skillful accountant in the community would exercise under the same or similar circumstances.

    a. Standard of care.
        1) A violation of generally accepted accounting principles (GAAP) and/ or generally accepted auditing standards (GAAS) is *prima facie* evidence of negligence.
        2) Although an accountant may have complied with GAAP and GAAS, the accountant may still be considered as not having acted with reasonable care.
        3) An accountant is not liable for errors of judgment.
        4) An accountant is liable for negligence in failing to discover fraud, improprieties, and defalcations (embezzlement).
        5) If an accountant is found to be liable for negligence, damages may be awarded in order to compensate the client for any reasonable, foreseeable injuries that were incurred by the client.

    b. Defenses to negligence — Possible defenses that an accountant may assert include:
        1) Lack of negligence.
        2) Lack of proximate cause between the breach of duty that was owed by the accountant and the injury that was incurred by the client.

        3) The client's own negligence (or intentional acts) contributed the client's loss. (Courts in most states apply the comparative negligence theory.)

    c. Qualified opinions and disclaimers — An accountant who gives a specific (as opposed to a general) opinion or disclaimer may be relieved of liability regarding matters that are specifically covered in the opinion or disclaimer.

    d. Unaudited financial statements — Liability based upon negligence may be imposed if an accountant fails to delineate a balance sheet as "unaudited" or to inform a client of information concerning possible misstatements.

  3. Attorney's duty of care.

    a. The conduct of attorneys is governed by rules established by each state and by the American Bar Association's Model Rules of Professional Conduct.

    b. An attorney has a duty to use the degree of skill, diligence, and competency that ordinarily is exercised by other attorneys practicing in the same or a similar geographic area.

    c. Standard of care — An attorney is required to be familiar with well-settled principles of law applicable to a case, to discover relevant law that can be found through a reasonable amount of research, and to investigate and discover material facts affecting a client's rights.

    d. Liability for malpractice — An attorney who breaches the duty of care, by allowing a statute of limitations to lapse on a client's claim or failing to inform a client of a settlement offer, may be liable for malpractice (professional misconduct).

C. Liability for fraud [See Chapter 16.] — In an action based upon fraud, the plaintiff (client) suing a professional must establish that:

  1. The professional (defendant) made a false representation of a material fact.

  2. The representation was made by the professional with knowledge that the representation was false (actual fraud) or with reckless disregard for the truth or falsity of the representation (constructive fraud).

  3. The professional intentionally made the misrepresentation in order to induce the client to rely on the misrepresentation and to act in a particular manner.

  4. As a result of the client's reasonable and justified reliance on the misrepresentation, the client was injured.

II.   Auditors' liability to third persons.

   A. Traditionally, an accountant (or other professional) did not owe a duty to a third person, who had knowledge of statements, audits, etc., that were prepared by the accountant, when the third person was not a client and had no direct contractual relationship with the accountant.

   B. Contract liability.

      1. The traditional common law rule is that an accountant does not owe contractual duties to another person unless that person is a direct party to, or a third party beneficiary of, a contract for the services of the accountant.

      2. This is so because there is lack of privity of contract between the accountant and the other (the third) person.

   C. Tort liability to third parties may be imposed based upon negligence in failing to exercise ordinary, reasonable care in preparing financial statements, audits, etc.

      1. The *Ultramares* rule (*Ultramares v. Touche*, N.Y. 1931) — The New York rule relates to tort liability of accountants for negligence to third parties and is followed in a minority of states.

         a. The strict *Ultramares* rule — An accountant is not liable for negligence to persons with whom the accountant is not in privity.

         b. Modifications of the *Ultramares* rule.
            1) An accountant's liability for negligence to third persons extends only to those for whose primary benefit accounting statements are prepared.
            2) An accountant may be liable to a third person when the accountant is aware of the existence of the third person, the purpose of the report, and that an "end and aim" of the preparation of a statement and/or audit also is to provide information to the third person. [*Credit Alliance Corp. v. Arthur Anderson and Co.* (N.Y. 1985).]

      2. The *Restatement of Torts (Second)* rule.

         a. An accountant may be liable to a third person with whom there is no privity of contract but who reasonably and foreseeably relies upon the statements, audits, etc., that were prepared by the accountant.

         b. Today, the *Restatement* position is followed in a majority of the states.

      3. Liability to reasonably foreseeable users — In a few states, an accountant is liable to a third party user whose reliance on reports or statements was reasonably foreseeable.

III.   Liability of attorneys to third parties — An attorney who issues an opinion containing misstatements or omissions of material facts may be liable under the *Restatement* rule to a non-client when the attorney knows the purpose of the opinion and knows or should know that the opinion will be relied upon by a non-client.

IV.   Liability of accountants under securities laws.

   A. Liability under the Securities Act of 1933. [See Chapter 43.]

      1. Liability under Section 11.

         a. The Securities Act of 1933 relates to new issues of investment securities (i.e., "going public").

         b. Registration statements (including financial statements) must be filed with the Securities and Exchange Commission (SEC) before investment securities can be offered for sale by issuer.

         c. An accountant who prepares a financial statement that is included in a registration statement is liable for misstatements and omissions of material facts in the registration statement.

         d. Liability to purchasers of securities — An accountant's liability extends to those who acquire the securities that are covered by a registration statement (i.e., purchasers of the securities who incur losses).
            1) Purchasers need not show that they relied upon the misrepresentations or omissions.
            2) Privity of contract between the accountant and a purchaser is not a requisite.

         e. The due diligence standard — An accountant has the burden of proving that the accountant exercised "due diligence" in preparation of financial statements.
            1) The failure to follow GAAP and GAAS is proof of lack of due diligence.
            2) An accountant must establish that, after reasonable investigation, the accountant had a reasonable basis to believe that the statements in the registration statement were true and that there was no omission of material facts which were required or necessary in order to prevent the statements from being misleading.

         f. Defenses to liability:
            1) There were no misstatements or omissions in the registration statement.
            2) If there were misrepresentations or omissions of facts, the particular facts that were misrepresented or omitted were not material.
            3) There was no causal connection between the misstatements or omissions and the purchaser's loss.

4) The purchaser bought the securities with knowledge of the misstatement or omission.

g. In a civil action, a purchaser of a security may recover the difference between the amount paid for the security and either:
   1) The value of the security at the time that the suit was brought;
   2) The price at which the security was disposed of in the market prior to commencing the suit; or
   3) The price at which the security was disposed of after the suit was commenced (but prior to judgment) if the amount is less than the difference between the amount paid for the security and the value of the security at the time the suit was commenced [Securities Act of 1933, Section 11(e)].

2. Liability under Section 12(2).

   a. Civil liability for fraud may be imposed upon a person who offers or sells a security and misrepresents or omits a material fact in a written or oral communication to an investor; civil liability had been imposed upon persons (e.g., accountants) who "aided or abetted" offerors or sellers who made misrepresentations or omissions, when such persons knew or should have known of the misstatements or omissions.

   b. It is unlikely in the future that liability will be imposed upon accountants for aiding or abetting a seller or offeror of securities who misstates or omits a material fact because of the 1994 U.S. Supreme Court decision in *Central Bank of Denver, N.A. v. First Interstate Bank of Denver, N.A.* [See below at IV. B. 3. e. and IV. C.]

3. Penalties and sanctions for violations — Purchasers of securities who have been harmed may bring civil actions (discussed above); violators may be prosecuted for willful fraud; and the SEC is authorized to bring actions against violators for injunctions and other civil remedies.

B. Liability under the Securities Exchange Act of 1934. [See Chapter 43.]

1. The Securities Exchange Act of 1934 relates to the purchase and sale of investment securities in the market (i.e., "being public").

2. Liability under Section 18 — An accountant is liable for false and/or misleading statements of material facts that are made in applications, reports, documents, and registrations statements that are prepared by the accountant and filed with the SEC.

   a. An accountant is liable to purchasers or sellers of securities when:
      1) False or misleading statements affected the price of the securities; and
      2) The purchasers or sellers of the securities relied upon the statements and were not aware of the inaccuracy of the statements.

b. An accountant who exercised "good faith" and did not have intent to deceive ("scienter") is not liable to purchasers or sellers of the securities.

3. Liability under Section 10(b) and SEC Rule 10b-5.

a. Liability is imposed upon those (including accountants) who, because of their "inside" positions, have access to material information (which is not available to the public and which may affect the value of securities) and trade in the securities without making disclosures of the information.

b. Section 10(b) provides that it is unlawful to use any manipulative or deceptive device in connection with the sale or purchase of securities.

c. Rule 10b-5 provides that, "in connection with the purchase or sale of any security," it is unlawful:
    1) To "employ any device, scheme, or artifice to defraud."
    2) To "make any untrue statement of a material fact or to omit to state a material fact necessary in order to make the statements made, in the light of the circumstances under which they were made, not misleading."
    3) To "engage in any act, practice, or course of business which operates or would operate as a fraud or deceit upon any person."

d. The requirement of scienter — An accountant may be liable to a person who purchased or sold securities when it can be established that:
    1) The fact that was misstated or omitted was material;
    2) The accountant had scienter (wrongful intention to deceive or defraud others); and
    3) As a result of the purchaser's or seller's reliance upon the misrepresentation, the purchaser or seller incurred a loss.

e. Liability of aiders and abettors.
    1) Before 1994, liability had been imposed upon accountants and other nonprivity parties for "aiding and abetting" violators of securities laws in civil actions brought by injured sellers or buyers of securities, in civil enforcement actions brought by the SEC, and in administrative proceedings heard by administrative law judges.
    2) In 1994, the U.S. Supreme Court held that a private plaintiff cannot maintain a suit for aiding and abetting under Section 10(b) and Rule 10b-5. [*Central Bank of Denver, N.A. v. First Interstate Bank of Denver, N.A.*]

C. The Private Securities Litigation Reform Act of 1995.

1. The 1995 Act added new Section 20(f) to the 1934 Act authorizing the SEC to bring civil actions against "any person that knowingly provides substantial assistance to [aids and abets] another person in violation of" the 1934 Act or an SEC rule or regulation. (No comparable provision, however, covers private civil actions.)

2. Obligations imposed upon auditors. [15 U.S.C.A. Section 78j-1.]

   a. Auditors are required to establish procedures to detect illegal acts and to determine if an issuer of securities has the financial ability to continue as a going concern during the next fiscal year. (Existing auditing standards provide for such procedures.)

   b. An auditor who has information indicating that an illegal act may have been committed, must determine if the illegal act occurred and the possible effect of the illegal act on the issuer's financial statements.

   c. The auditor then must inform the issuer's management and the board of director's audit committee (if there is one) or the board of the illegal act.

   d. If timely, remedial action is not taken, the illegal act will have a material effect on the financial statements, and the failure to take remedial action warrants a departure from a standard report or resignation from the engagement, the auditor must report the auditor's findings to the board.
      1) Within one day, the board of directors must notify the SEC and the auditor; if the auditor is not notified, the auditor must resign or furnish the auditor's report to the SEC.
      2) If the auditor resigns, the auditor must give a copy of the report to the SEC.

3. The 1995 Act provides for proportionate civil liability in some cases.

   a. In a private action, joint and several liability continues to be imposed on a defendant who knowingly violate securities laws.

   b. A defendant whose wrongdoing is less than knowing is "liable solely for the portion of the judgment" that corresponds to that defendant's percentage of responsibility; there are, however exceptions. [15 U.S.C.A. Section 78u-4(g)(2)(B)(i).]

V. Potential criminal liability.

A. Criminal liability for willful conduct is imposed by:

1. The Securities Act of 1933, in which case the maximum fine is $10,000 and/or imprisonment for not more than five years.

2. The Securities Exchange Act of 1934, in which case, usually, the maximum fine imposed on a natural person is $1,000,000 and/or imprisonment for up to ten years, and the maximum fine that may be imposed on a corporation or other entity is $2,500,000.

3. Other federal statutes and state criminal codes.

B. Criminal liability under the Internal Revenue Code — A tax preparer may be liable for:

    1. Aiding or assisting in the preparation of a false tax return.

    2. Negligent or willful understatement of a client's tax liability or intentional or reckless disregard of rules or regulations.

    3. Failure to furnish a taxpayer with a copy of the tax return, to sign a tax return, or to furnish an appropriate tax identification number.

    4. Aiding or abetting an individual's understatement of tax liability.

    5. The criminal penalties vary based upon the nature of the violation and whether or not the violation is committed by a natural person or an entity.

VI. Working papers — Documents used and developed during an audit.

A. Unless there is an agreement or statute that provides otherwise, working papers are the property of the accountant.

B. Information in working papers is confidential.

    1. The client has a right of access to working papers; contents of working papers cannot be disclosed without the consent of the client or in response to a subpoena.

    2. Working papers cannot be transferred to another accountant without the consent of the client.

VII. Confidentiality and privilege.

A. Ethical tenets of professions require professionals to keep communications with their clients confidential.

B. Because attorney-client communications are privileged, the general rule is that an attorney cannot make disclosures of confidential material obtained during the course of such communications.

C. Communications between the accountant and client.

    1. Under the AICPA Code of Professional Ethics, accountant-client communications are considered to be confidential and cannot be disclosed without the consent of the client, or in accordance with GAAP or GAAS, or in response to a subpoena.

    2. The majority of the states and the federal courts, however, do not treat accountant-client communications as privileged.

a. An accountant, therefore, cannot refuse to testify or reveal information in response to a subpoena.

b. The Internal Revenue Service has investigatory powers and can obtain subpoenas directing people to testify and/or produce relevant books, records, etc.

3. In those states that recognize the accountant-client relationship as privileged, an accountant may refuse to testify concerning the contents of communications with clients.

VIII. Limited professionals' liability.

A. Professionals, such as accountants, may limit their liability with disclaimers [See above at I. B. 2. c.]

B. Professionals may avoid liability for misconduct by their associates by forming professional corporations (PCs), limited liability partnerships (LLPs), and limited liability companies (LLCs). [See Chapters 37, 39, and 40.]

KEY WORDS AND PHRASES IN TEXT

professional's liability to clients for
    breach of contract and negligence
malpractice
generally accepted accounting principles
    (GAAP)
generally accepted auditing standards
    (GAAS)
defalcation
liability to third persons for negligence
due diligence
privity of contract
the *Ultramares* rule
Restatement rule regarding liability of
    accountants to third parties
Sections 11 and 12(2) of the Securities
    Act of 1933

misstatements and omissions of facts
accountant's liability to purchasers
    of securities
aiding and abetting
Sections 18 and 10(b) of the Securities
    Exchange Act of 1934
Securities Exchange Commission (SEC)
    Rule 10b-5
scienter
criminal liability of accountants under the
    securities laws and Internal
    Revenue Code
working papers
confidentiality of communications with
    professionals (privilege)
limitations of liability of professionals

MULTIPLE CHOICE QUESTIONS

1. Filipo, a CPA, was engaged by Alpha Corp. in order to audit Beta, Inc. Alpha Corp. purchased Beta, Inc. after receiving Beta, Inc.'s audited financial statements that included Filipo's unqualified auditor's opinion. Filipo was negligent in the performance of the Beta, Inc. audit. As a result of Filipo's negligence, Alpha Corp. incurred damages of $50,000. Alpha Corp. appears to have grounds to sue Filipo for:
A. breach of contract and negligence.

B. breach of contract but not negligence.
C. negligence but not breach of contract.
D. neither breach of contract nor negligence.
(This question has been adapted from objective question #1 on the Uniform CPA Examination, November 1983.)

2.   When a CPA fails to carry out his, her, or its duties in performing a contract for services, liability to a client may be based upon:

	breach of contract.	strict liability.
A.	Yes	Yes
B.	Yes	No
C.	No	Yes
D.	No	No

(This question has been adapted from objective question #6 on the Uniform CPA Examination, May 1989.)

3.   Which of the following statements best describes whether or not a CPA has met the required standard of care in conducting an audit of a client's financial statements?
A. The client's expectations with regard to the accuracy of the audited financial statements.
B. The accuracy of the financial statements and whether or not the statements conform to generally accepted accounting principles.
C. Whether or not the CPA conducted the audit with the same skill and care expected of an ordinary prudent CPA under the circumstances.
D. The audit was conducted in order to discover all acts of fraud.
(This question has been adapted from objective question #2 on the Uniform CPA Examination, November 1993.)

4.   Caesar and Napoleon, CPAs, rendered an unqualified opinion on the financial statements of a corporation. Based upon a false statement in the financial statements, Caesar and Napoleon are being sued for fraud by a shareholder. The following represents the best defense for Caesar and Napoleon:
A. Caesar and Napoleon did **not** benefit financially from the alleged fraud.
B. The shareholder's lack of privity bars the shareholder from suing Caesar and Napoleon.
C. Detection of the false statement by Caesar and Napoleon occurred after the date of their examination of the financial statements.
D. The false statement related to a fact that was immaterial.
(This question has been adapted from objective questions #2 on the Uniform CPA Examination, May 1989, and #5 on the Uniform CPA Examination, November 1983.)

5.   Which of the following is the best defense that a CPA firm can assert in a suit for common law fraud based on its unqualified opinion on materially false financial statements?
A. Contributory negligence on the part of the client.
B. A disclaimer contained in the engagement letter.
C. Lack of privity.

D. Lack of scienter.

(This question appeared as objective question #10 on the Uniform CPA Examination, November 1995.)

6. In which of the following situations concerning a CPA firm's action is scienter or its equivalent absent?
   A. The CPA firm has actual knowledge of fraud.
   B. The CPA firm has made a statement with reckless disregard for its truth or falsity.
   C. The CPA firm intended to gain a financial benefit by concealing fraud.
   D. The CPA firm failed to use generally accepted auditing procedures.
   (This question has been adapted from objective question #2 on the Uniform CPA Examination, November 1983.)

7. Gibson is suing Carter, Prito & Adams, CPAs, in order to recover losses that were incurred in connection with Gibson's transactions in Zebra Corporation securities. Zebra's Annual Form 10-K Report contained false and misleading statements relating to material facts in the financial statements that had been audited by Carter, Prito & Adams. In order to recover from Carter, Prito & Adams under the Securities and Exchange Act of 1934, Gibson, among other things, must establish that:
   A. all of Gibson's past transactions in Zebra Corporation securities, both before and after the date of the auditor's report, resulted in a net loss.
   B. the transaction in Zebra Corporation securities that resulted in a loss to Gibson occurred within 30 days of the date of the auditor's report.
   C. Gibson relied upon the financial statements in his decision to purchase or sell Zebra Corporation securities.
   D. the market price of the stock dropped significantly after corrected financial statements were issued by Zebra Corporation.
   (This question has been adapted from objective question #8 on the Uniform CPA Examination, November 1983.)

8. Alpha Corp.'s shareholders approved a plan of merger with Beta, Inc. One of the determining factors in approving the merger was the strong financial statements of Beta, Inc. that were audited by the CPA firm of Greco & Co. PC. Greco & Co. had been engaged by Alpha Corp. to audit Beta, Inc.'s financial statements. While performing the audit, Greco & Co. failed to discover certain irregularities that have subsequently caused Beta, Inc. to incur substantial losses. In order for Greco & Co. to be liable to Alpha Corp. under common law, at a minimum, Alpha must prove that Greco & Co.:
   A. acted recklessly or with a lack of reasonable belief in the information at Greco & Co.'s disposal.
   B. knew of the irregularities in the financial statements.
   C. failed to exercise reasonable care.
   D. was grossly negligent.
   (This question has been adapted from objective question #1 on the Uniform CPA Examination, November 1986 and May 1993.)

9. Ace, a CPA, was engaged by United Co. to audit United Co.'s financial statements so that the company could obtain a loan from a bank. Ace issued an unqualified opinion on May 20, but the loan was delayed. On August 8, the bank made an

inquiry to Ace. Ace relied upon a representation of the United Co.'s CEO to the effect that there were no material changes in the company's financial condition and assured the bank that United Co.'s financial status was unchanged after May 20. Late in June, however, there had been a significant change in United Co.'s financial status so that the representation made by United Co.'s CEO was not true. The bank, in reliance upon Ace's assurances, made the loan to United Co., which shortly thereafter became insolvent. If the bank sues Ace, the CPA, for negligent misrepresentation, Ace probably will be found to be:

A. liable, because Ace should have undertaken sufficient auditing procedures in order to verify the financial status of United Co.

B. liable, because Ace should have contacted the chief financial officer, rather than the chief executive officer, of United Co.

C. **not** liable, because United Co.'s chief executive officer misled Ace, and a CPA is not liable for a client's untrue representations.

D. **not** liable, because Ace's unqualified opinion covered only the period up to May 20.

(This question has been adapted from objective question #1 on the Uniform CPA Examination, May 1989.)

10. An accountant has prepared a tax return for a client in a fraudulent manner. With regard to the accountant's potential liability to various parties, which of the following actions would be dismissed?

A. A federal criminal action.

B. A federal action for civil penalties.

C. A federal action to revoke the accountant's CPA certificate.

D. A malpractice action brought by the client.

(This question has been adapted from objective question #7 on the Uniform CPA Examination, November 1983.)

11. A tax preparer who aids and abets federal tax evasion is subject to:

	an injunction prohibiting him, her or it from acting as a tax preparer.	federal criminal prosecution.
A.	No	No
B.	Yes	No
C.	No	Yes
D.	Yes	Yes

(This question has been adapted from objective question #3 on the Uniform CPA Examination, May 1989.)

12. Clark, a professional tax return preparer, prepared and signed a client's federal income tax return that resulted in a $600 refund. Which one of the following statements is correct with regard to an Internal Revenue Code penalty to which Clark may be subject if Clark indorses and cashes the client's refund check?

A. Clark will be subject to the penalty if Clark indorses and cashes the check.

B. Clark may indorse and cash the check without a penalty being imposed if Clark is enrolled to practice before the Internal Revenue Service.

C. Clark may **not** indorse and cash the check without a penalty being imposed because the check is for more than $500.

D. Clark may indorse and cash the check without a penalty being imposed if the amount of the check does **not** exceed Clark's fee for preparation of the federal income tax return.

(This question has been adapted from objective question #9 on the Uniform CPA Examination, November 1993.)

13. A CPA's working papers:

A. need **not** be disclosed under a federal district court subpoena.

B. must be disclosed under an Internal Revenue Service administrative subpoena.

C. must be disclosed to another accountant who is purchasing the CPA's practice even if the client has not given permission.

D. need **not** be disclosed to a state CPA society quality review team.

(This question has been adapted from objective question #10 on the Uniform CPA Examination, November 1993.)

14. A CPA is permitted to disclose confidential client information without the consent of the client to:

I. Another CPA who has purchased the CPA's tax practice.

II. A successor CPA firm if the information concerns suspected tax return irregularities.

III. A voluntary quality control board.

A. Only I and III.

B. Only II and III.

C. Only II.

D. Only III.

(This question has been adapted from objective questions #5 on the Uniform CPA Examination, May 1989 and #6 on the May 1993 Examination.)

15. Working papers that are prepared by a CPA in connection with an audit engagement are owned by the CPA, subject to certain limitations. The rationale of this rule is to:

A. protect the working papers from being subpoenaed.

B. provide the basis for excluding admission of the working papers as evidence because of the privileged communication rule.

C. provide the CPA with evidence and documentation that may be helpful in the event of a lawsuit.

D. establish a continuity of relationship with the client whereby indiscriminate replacement of a CPA is discouraged.

(This question has been adapted from objective question #10 on the Uniform CPA Examination, November 1983.)

16. Nardone, CPA, was engaged to audit Star Co.'s financial statements. During the audit, Nardone discovered that Star's inventory contained stolen goods. Star was indicted and Nardone was subpoenaed to testify at the criminal trial. Star claimed that the accountant-client privilege prevents Nardone from testifying. Which of the following statements is correct regarding Star's claim?

A. The accountant-client privilege can be claimed in a majority of the states because of common law.
B. The accountant-client privilege can be claimed only in states that have enacted statutes creating such a privilege.
C. The accountant-client privilege can be claimed only in federal courts.
D. The accountant-client privilege can be claimed only to limit testimony to work performed preparing the audit.
(This question has been adapted from objective questions #15 on the Uniform CPA Examination, November 1995, and #9 on the May 1993 Examination.)

OTHER OBJECTIVE QUESTIONS

Under Section 11 of the Securities Act of 1933 and Section 10(b) of the Securities Exchange Act of 1934 (and SEC Rule 10b-5), an accountant may be sued in a civil action by a purchaser of securities. For each of the following statements, determine whether the statement must be proven by the plaintiff in order to recover under Section 11 of the 1933 Act (Answer A), Section 10(b) (Answer B), both the 1933 Act and the 1934 Act (Answer C), or neither the 1933 or 1934 Act (Answer D).

	Only Section 11 of the 1933 Act	Only Section 10(b) of the 1934 Act	Both	Neither
The purchaser of a security must prove:	A	B	C	D

1. Material misstatements were included in a document filed with the SEC.
2. A measurable monetary loss was incurred.
3. The accountant did not exercise due diligence.
4. Privity of contract existed with the accountant.
5. The plaintiff relied upon the statement.
6. The accountant had scienter.
(This question is adapted from objective questions #61-66 on the Uniform CPA Examination, May 1994.)

Chapter 55
The International Legal Environment

Because of the increasing globalization of business, business people need to be aware of important principles and sources of international law. The international agreements, legal doctrines, and statutes of the United States that are relevant to international transactions and trade introduced in this chapter affect United States firms that engage in international business. This is particularly true when the firms export their products directly or through foreign firms; establish manufacturing facilities abroad themselves or through foreign subsidiary firms; or enter into joint ventures, licensing, or franchising agreements.

THINGS TO KEEP IN MIND

Unit Three (in which contracts for international sales of goods are highlighted) supplements this chapter. Excerpts from the United Nations Convention on Contracts for the International Sale of Goods (CISG), the General Agreement on Tariffs and Trade (GATT), and the North American Free Trade Agreement (NAFTA) are found in the textbook in Appendices D, P, and Q respectively.

OUTLINE

I.   The nature and sources of international law.

    A. International law is composed of written and unwritten laws that are observed by independent nations (or states) and that govern the acts of nations and their residents and citizens when engaging in international dealings.

    B. International law is the result of attempts by nations to reconcile the sovereignty (absolute supreme power) of each country with the desire of nations to benefit from trade and harmonious relations with one another.

    C. International customs — General practices among nations in their relations with one another that have evolved over time and are accepted as law [Article 38(1) of Statute of International Court of Justice].

    D. Treaties and international agreements — A treaty is an agreement, or contract, between two or more nations that is authorized and ratified by the supreme power of each nation.

        1. A treaty of the U.S. is entered into by the President with the advice and consent of the Senate provided that two-thirds of the Senate concurs [U.S. Constitution, Article II, Section 2].

2. A bilateral agreement is one to which two nations agree and which governs their commercial exchanges or other relationships.

3. A multilateral agreement is one to which a number of nations are parties; examples include the European Union (EU), North American Free Trade Agreement (NAFTA), Association of Southeast Asian Nations (ASEAN), and Andean Common Market (ANCOM).

E. International organizations and conferences.

1. International organizations refer to international bodies and groups, such as the United Nations (U.N.), composed mainly of nations and usually established by treaties.

2. Resolutions, declarations, and standards for behavior of nations have been adopted by such organizations; for example, the U.N. General Assembly has adopted numerous nonbinding resolutions and declarations that embody principles of international law.

3. Legal disputes between nations may be voluntarily submitted to and resolved by the International Court of Justice.

4. The U. N. Commission on International Trade Law (UNCITRAL) has made progress in establishing uniformity in law as it relates to international trade and commerce; for example, see the discussion of the Convention on Contracts for the International Sale of Goods (CISG) in Chapters 21-24.

II. Legal principles and doctrines — Over time, generally accepted legal principles and doctrines have evolved and been employed by the courts of various nations to resolve or reduce conflicts among nations.

A. Because some of these principles and doctrines tend to immunize foreign nations from the jurisdiction of U.S. courts, firms and individuals who own property or do business abroad may not have protection against certain actions of foreign governments.

B. The principle of comity — The courts in one nation will defer, give effect to, and enforce the laws and judicial decrees of another country because of mutual respect and courtesy when the other country's procedures and rules are consistent with those of the accommodating nation.

C. The act of state doctrine — The courts of one country will not examine the validity of acts engaged in by a foreign government when the acts take place within the territory of the foreign nation.

1. The doctrine is premised on the theory that a country's judicial branch should not pass on the validity of a foreign nation's acts when to do so would interfere with the harmony of international relations with that foreign nation.

2. The doctrine may be applied when a government seizes privately owned property.

    a. Expropriation — Seizure of property by a government for a proper public purpose with an award of compensation.

    b. Confiscation — Seizure of property by a government for an improper purpose without awarding just compensation.

3. A U.S. court does not apply the act of state doctrine when the act of a foreign nation consists of a commercial transaction or when the court would not have to determine the validity of an act of a foreign nation in deciding the case.

D. The doctrine of sovereign immunity — A foreign nation is not subject to the jurisdiction of courts of another country and, therefore, is immunized against lawsuits.

1. Foreign Sovereign Immunities Act of 1976 (FSIA) codifies the doctrine but also provides for exceptions to sovereign immunity of foreign countries.

    a. Actions (including attempts to attach a foreign nation's property) may be brought against a foreign government in a U.S. District Court.

    b. Courts, rather than the Department of State, determine claims of sovereign immunity in the U.S.

2. Under Section 1605 of FSIA, U.S. courts have jurisdiction and a foreign state is not immune when the foreign nation has either:

    a. Waived immunity explicitly or by implication; or

    b. Engaged in actions "based upon a commercial activity carried on in the United States by the foreign state that have a direct effect in the United States."
        1) A foreign state includes political subdivisions and instrumentalities of the foreign nation.
        2) Commercial activity means business (rather than governmental) transactions engaged in by a foreign nation.

3. The FSIA's "commercial activity" exception differentiates between a foreign state's public acts performed in the state's sovereign capacity and a state's private acts performed as a market participant.

III. Doing business internationally.

A. Exporting — Domestically produced goods and services of U.S. firms are exported and sold in foreign markets.

1. A U.S. company that sells its products to buyers located in other countries may engage in direct exporting by entering into sales contracts with foreign purchasers.

2. A U.S. firm may engage in indirect exporting by establishing marketing operations through a representative in a foreign country.

   a. Foreign agent.
      1) A U.S. company may establish an agency relationship with a foreign firm (the agent) which agrees to act on behalf of the U.S. firm (the principal). [See Chapter 33.]
      2) The foreign agent is given authority to enter into contract in its country on behalf of the U.S. company.

   b. Foreign distributor.
      1) A distribution agreement (a contract to which contract law applies) setting forth the terms and conditions of the distributorship may be entered into by a U.S. company (the seller) and a foreign distributor.
      2) In a distributorship, the foreign distributor takes title to goods when the goods are received and bears the risks that might arise in the sales transaction.
      3) Antitrust issues relating to exclusive distributorships are discussed in Chapter 47.

B. Manufacturing abroad.

   1. U.S. firms may establish foreign manufacturing facilities in order to reduce the costs of raw materials, labor, and shipping, and to gain the benefits of fewer trade restrictions and lower taxes; similarly, foreign companies may establish manufacturing facilities in the U.S.

   2. Licensing.

      a. Firms may engage in technology licensing of processes and/or product innovations as an alternative to establishing production facilities in a foreign country.

      b. Patent considerations include patent protection, acquisition of parallel patents, and international patent agreements are covered in Chapter 9.

      c. A licensing agreement usually provides for payment of royalties to the licensor.

      d. A firm may license the right to use "know-how" and unpatented trade secrets to a foreign firm that agrees to keep the information confidential and to pay royalties.

   3. Franchising — A franchise is an arrangement in which the owner of a trademark, trade name, or copyright (the franchisor) grants to a franchisee the

right to use the mark, name, or copyright, under certain conditions, in connection with selling, marketing, or supplying goods and/or services, in exchange for the payment of a fee. [See Chapter 37.]

4. Investing in a wholly owned subsidiary or a joint venture.

   a. A U.S. firm may establish a subsidiary firm in a foreign country — The parent company retains complete ownership of all of the facilities of the subsidiary in the foreign country and is able to control its operations.

   b. A U.S. company may engage in a joint venture, a joint commercial undertaking with a foreign firm (a separate entity in which the U.S. firm has no ownership interest).
      1) In a joint venture, the U.S. firm owns only part of the operation with the rest being owned by the foreign party involved in the venture.
      2) The joint venturers share responsibility, profits, and losses.
      3) Other countries may impose limitations to ensure that U.S. firms have only minority interests in joint ventures.

IV. The regulation of specific business activities.

   A. Investing — Investors in property or business firms in foreign countries risk losing their investments because of confiscation by the foreign government.

      1. In some cases, negotiations between the United States and the nations that have taken property have been resolved by lump-sum settlements.

      2. Protection of investments in foreign countries.

         a. Many nations make guarantees in national constitutions, statutes, or treaties that compensation will be paid if property is taken by the government.

         b. Insurance against losses incurred as a result of confiscation of assets, owned by U.S. citizens and firms, by foreign governments, war, or other causes may be obtained from the Overseas Private Investment Corporation (OPIC, a federal agency) or from private insurance companies.

   B. Export control.

      1. Article 1, Section 9 of the U.S. Constitution prohibits imposition of taxes on products being exported; Congress, however, may use a variety of devices to control and impose restrictions on exports.

         a. Congress may establish export quotas.

         b. The Export Administration Act (1979) authorizes certain restrictions on the flow of technologically advanced products and technical data.

2. Export incentives and subsidies may be used in order to assist domestic firms.

   a. The Revenue Act of 1971 gives tax benefits to firms that market products through certain foreign sales corporations by exempting from taxes income produced by the overseas sale of the exports.

   b. The Export Trading Company Act of 1982 encourages investment by U.S. banks in export trading companies.

   c. The Export-Import Bank provides credit guarantees to commercial banks that lend to U.S. exporting companies.

C. Import control — All nations impose trade barriers such as prohibitions, quotas, and tariffs in order to restrict imports and to raise revenue.

   1. Prohibitions include goods from nations which are designated as enemies of the U.S., illegal drugs, books urging insurrection against the United States, and agricultural products that pose dangers to domestic crops or animals.

   2. Quotas are limitations on the amount of goods that can be imported.

   3. Tariffs are taxes on imports and cause foreign goods to be more expensive in the domestic market.

   4. Antidumping laws.

      a. Dumping is the sale of imported goods at less than fair value or below the price of the goods in the exporting country.

      b. Antidumping duties or tariffs may be assessed on such goods.

      c. The International Trade Commission (ITC) assesses the effect of dumping on U.S. domestic business and makes recommendations to the President concerning temporary import restrictions.

      d. The International Trade Administration (ITA) of the U.S. Department of Commerce determines if import sales were at less than fair value and, if so, the amount of antidumping duties. (Such duties are set equal to the difference between the price charged in the U.S. and the price charged in the exporting country and may be retroactive to cover past dumping.)

D. The General Agreement on Tariffs and Trade (GATT) and the World Trade Organization (WTO). [See Appendix P.]

   1. The purpose of these international agreements has been to reduce trade barriers among nations.

2. In 1994, the GATT was replaced by the WTO as a result of the Uruguay Round agreement.

2. Each member of the WTO must grant other WTO members "most-favored-nation" status and, therefore, treat other WTO members at least as well as it treats the country that receives its most favorable treatment with regard to imports or exports.

E. The European Union (EU).

1. In 1951, the European Coal and Steel Community (ECSC) was established; in 1957, the European Atomic Energy Community (Euratom) was established and the European Economic Community (EEC) was created by the Treaty of Rome.

   a. The Treaty of Rome outlined the goals of preserving European peace, establishing a European common market in which goods, capital, and labor could move freely among countries, and forming a politically unified Europe.

   b. Under the Merger Treaty of 1965, the ECSC, Euratom, and EEC agreed to operate common institutions and, thereafter, were referred to collectively as the European Community or EC.

   c. The EC countries eliminated most tariffs within the EC by 1968 and, in 1986, ratified the Single European Act that furthered the objective of attaining a unified European market by 1994.

2. The EC, now known as the European Union (EU), had become a single integrated European trading unit made up of sixteen European nations.

F. The North American Free Trade Agreement (NAFTA) became effective in 1994. [See Appendix Q.]

1. The NAFTA created a regional trading unit consisting of the U.S., Canada, and Mexico with the objective of eliminating tariffs among these nations on substantially all goods within 20 years, while permitting the three countries to retain tariffs on goods imported from outside the NAFTA trading unit.

2. The NAFTA is designed to eliminate trade barriers that prevent the cross-border movement of financial, transportation, and other services.

V. United States laws in a global setting.

A. United States antitrust laws. [See also Chapter 47.]

1. Section 1 of the Sherman Act (1890) prohibiting contracts, combinations, and conspiracies that restrain interstate or foreign trade applies to foreign nationals and foreign governments.

    a. The Sherman Act applies only to those agreements, contracts, and conspiracies in restraint of trade that have substantial effects on commerce in the U.S.

    b. A *per se* violation (e.g., price fixing, quota allocations, resale price maintenance, and tying agreements) may occur if a domestic firm joins a foreign cartel that controls price, production, or distribution of products if there is a "substantial restraining effect" on commerce in the U.S.

2. People in foreign nations may be sued because of violations and may sue if they have been injured as a result of a violation of the U.S. antitrust laws.

3. The Foreign Trade Antitrust Improvements Act (1982) exempts from U.S. antitrust law conduct that does not have a direct, substantial, and reasonably foreseeable effect upon domestic trade within the U.S., on import trade, or on U.S. export trade.

4. Extraterritorial effects of U.S. antitrust laws — The U.S. antitrust laws explicitly cover restraints of trade in international commerce; even if a clear antitrust violation occurs in another country, a U.S. court may be able to enforce federal antitrust statutes.

B. United States iscrimination laws — Federal statutes prohibits discrimination in employment because of race, color, gender, religion, age, disability, or national origin. [See Chapter 36.]

1. These laws apply extraterritorially to U.S. employees working for U.S. employers abroad unless to do so would violate the laws of the country in which their workplace is located. (This "foreign laws exception" allows employers to avoid being subjected to conflicting laws.)

2. Foreign employers may "choose citizens of their own nation as executives" of their firms in the U.S.

VI.   Resolving international contract disputes.

A. Arbitration. [See Chapter 3.]

1. Frequently, parties to an international transaction include arbitration clauses in their contracts and agree to be bound by the decision of a specified third neutral person (or panel) if a dispute should arise.

2. Arbitration services for international disputes are available through the International Chamber of Commerce, the American Arbitration Association, and other organizations.

3. Court enforcement of arbitration clauses is governed by the U.N. Convention on the Recognition and Enforcement of Foreign Arbitral Awards (1958).

B. Litigation — Litigation in connection with an international transaction may occur if the parties' contract does not contain an arbitration clause.

   1. If forum-selection and choice-of-law clauses are included in a contract (specifying what nation's courts will have jurisdiction over and what nation's law will apply in a dispute), any lawsuit will be heard by a court in the specified country (or state in the U.S.) and the specified substantive law will be applied. [See Chapter 21.]

   2. If no such forum-selection and/or choices-of-law clauses are included in a contract, litigation may take place in different countries with each court applying its own rules in order to determine which substantive law should apply.

   3. Often, because of the principle of comity, nations give effect to the laws of other nations so that a judgment in a lawsuit litigated in the plaintiff's country may be enforced in the defendant's country.

VII. The bribery of foreign officials.

A. The Foreign Corrupt Practices Act (FCPA) of 1977, as revised in 1988, is administered by the Securities and Exchange Commission (SEC) and the Justice Department.

B. Major provisions of the FCPA.

   1. The FCPA makes it unlawful for a company or its directors, officers, shareholders, agents, or employees to use the mails or any instrumentality of interstate or foreign commerce in order to offer or give (corruptly) anything of value to foreign officials or political parties for purposes of influencing decisions if the objective is to obtain or retain business.

   2. The FCPA does not prohibit:

      a. Payments of substantial sums ("grease") to minor foreign officials whose duties are ministerial, provided that such payments are lawful within the foreign country and are intended to facilitate administrative services.

      b. Payments by U.S. firms to foreign private companies or other third parties, provided that such payments are not passed on to a foreign government official in violation of the FCPA.

   3. All companies must develop and maintain strict systems of internal accounting controls that produce accurate financial statements that will alert them if prohibited payments are made.

   4. The FPCA provides that firms that violate the FPCA may be fined up to $2 million, and individual officers or directors who violate the FCPA may be

imprisoned for up to five years and/or fined up to $100,000. (A fine may not be paid by the officer's or director's company)

C. Multinational initiatives that occurred in 1996.

    1. The Organization for Economic Cooperation and Development called upon its 26 members to criminalize bribery of foreign officials and to eliminate tax deductibility of bribes.

    2. The International Chamber of Commerce updated its rules to prohibit the payment and receipt of bribes by business firms.

    3. The General Assembly of the United Nations adopted the "Declaration against Corruption and Bribery in International Commercial Transactions."

KEY WORDS AND PHRASES IN TEXT

international law
international customs
treaty
bilateral international agreement
multilateral international agreement
European Union (EU)
Association of Southeast Asian Nations
Andean Common Market
international organizations
United Nations and its organizations
United Nations Commission on International Trade Law (UNCITRAL)
Convention on Contracts for the International Sale of Goods (CISG)
principle of comity
act of state doctrine
expropriation of private property
confiscation of private property
doctrine of sovereign immunity
Foreign Sovereignty Immunities Act
export
direct and indirect exporting
foreign agent
foreign distributor
distribution agreement
exclusive distributorship
technology licensing

franchising
wholly owned subsidiary company
joint venture
investing in foreign nations
Export Administration Act of 1979
Export Trading Company Act of 1982
Export-Import Bank
import controls
quotas and tariffs
dumping
International Trade Commission, an independent administrative agency
International Trade Administration in the Department of Commerce
antidumping duties
General Agreement on Tariffs and Trade (GATT)
World Trade Association (WTO)
most-favored nation treatment
North American Free Trade Agreement (NAFTA)
extraterritorial effect of U.S. antitrust laws
extraterritorial effect of U.S. employment discrimination laws
bribery of foreign officials
Foreign Corrupt Practices Act (FCPA)

FILL-IN QUESTIONS

1.   Article II, Section 2 of the _____ confers the power to enter into treaties with foreign countries upon the President. Before any treaty entered into by the President becomes the law of the land, however, the treaty must be approved of, or ratified, by at least a two-thirds vote in the United States _____.

2.   Generally accepted practices that have evolved over time among nations, which are not formally incorporated into international treaties or agreements, are referred to as international _____. These international _____, or practices, are not recognized as the law of the land under the United States Constitution.

3.   When a court in another nation states that it will defer to and enforce a judgment of a United States District Court because the law and the judicial decision are consistent with its law, the court is applying the principle of _____.

4.   Courts in the United States are precluded from inquiring into the validity of governmental acts of a foreign government when the acts occurred within the territory of the _____ because of the act of state doctrine.

5.   A foreign nation is not subject to the jurisdiction of a court in the United States because of the doctrine of _____ unless the foreign nation consents to such jurisdiction being exercised by the court in the United States.

6.   A U.S. manufacturing firm may sell its products directly to purchasers in other countries or, for purposes of marketing its products abroad, establish a relationship with a foreign firm. The foreign firm may be an agent or a distributor. A foreign agent is authorized to enter into contracts on behalf of the U.S. firm. When goods are shipped to a foreign agent, the U.S. company retains _____ to the goods and bears the risk of loss. A foreign distributorship is formed when the U.S. company and a foreign firm enter into a _____. When goods are received by a foreign distributor, _____ to the goods and the risk of loss shifts to the distributor.

7.   As an alternative to exporting goods produced in the U.S., a U.S. corporation may establish facilities in which to manufacture goods in a foreign country by forming a _____ company under the laws of the foreign country. The U.S. corporation, or the _____ corporation, would own all of the ownership interests (shares of stock, or the equivalent) in the foreign _____ company and, therefore, be able to direct and control its operations.

8.   The United States government has attempted to control the practice of foreign firms selling products in this country at prices that are lower than the price at which such products are sold in the country from which the products are exported. This practice is referred to as _____.

9.   The Convention on Contracts for the International Sale of Goods (CISG) applies to an agreement for the international sale of goods when the parties (the buyer and seller) are residents of countries that have _____ the CISG. If the seller is a

corporation incorporated in Delaware and the buyer is a French company, the CISG will govern their agreement because the United States and France have _____ the CISG. The trading parties, however, may expressly specify that the terms of the CISG will not apply to their agreement and that the law of a particular country or, in the case of the United States, a specified state, will be applied to any _____ that the parties may have regarding the sales contract.

10. In general, Section 1 of the Sherman Antitrust Act and other antitrust laws apply to foreign nationals and foreign governments when their anticompetitive acts occur outside the United States, provided that such acts have a _____ _____ on commerce in the United States.

11. Today, a principal instrument for cooperation among nations in the area of international trade is the World Trade Organization (WTO), which replaced the General Agreement on Tariffs and Trade (GATT), a _____ agreement. The objectives of the WTO are to limit or minimize tariffs and reduce other _____ to world trade.

MULTIPLE CHOICE QUESTIONS

1. An official of a foreign nation is proven to have committed war crimes and crimes against humanity under the Charter of the United Nations. When the foreign official made numerous entries into the United States, he also concealed from the U.S. Immigration and Naturalization Service his membership in a national political party, which advocated the overthrow of the United States government. Such crimes and such concealment are felonies under U.S. statutes. The foreign official most likely is best protected from prosecution for these alleged crimes in the U.S. District Court because of:
A. the act of state doctrine.
B. the doctrine of sovereign immunity.
C. the principle of comity.
D. international customs.

2. Which of the following claims for compensatory damages requiring determinations of legal disputes voluntarily may be submitted to and resolved by the International Court of Justice in the Hague?
A. The claim of the wife of a citizen of the United States, who was killed by a terrorist organization, instituted against the terrorist organization.
B. The claim of former hostages, who are citizens of the United States and were held by a foreign government for over a year, instituted against the foreign government.
C. The claim of the government of the United States, on behalf of former hostages, who are citizens of the United States and were held by a foreign government for over a year, instituted against the foreign government.
D. All of the answers above are correct.

Questions 3, 4, and 5 are based on the following fact situation: The JR Oil Company of Dallas, Texas enters into an agreement with the Oil and Petroleum Exporting Community (OPEC), a syndicate of oil producing nations. The agreement provides that JR Oil

Company contracts to purchase one million barrels of oil from each syndicate member nation in order to augment JR Oil Company's depleted oil reserves and OPEC agrees not to sell any oil to Eaststar Oil Co. of Dallas, Texas, a fierce competitor of JR Oil Company.

3. Eaststar Oil Co. wishes to initiate a lawsuit against the government of one of the OPEC members for violating Sections 1 and 2 of the Sherman Antitrust Act. Which of the following statements is true?
    A. Eaststar Oil Co. may bring this action against the foreign nation in a Texas state court.
    B. Eaststar Oil Co. may bring this action against the foreign nation in the United States District Court in Dallas, Texas, provided that the U.S. State Department approves the institution of such an action.
    C. Eaststar Oil Co. may bring this action against the foreign nation in the United States District Court in Dallas, Texas, even if the U.S. State Department does not approve the institution of such an action.
    D. No court in the United States has jurisdiction over this matter because the acts affecting the commercial activity in dispute were carried on, in part, in a hotel in Switzerland.

4. The agreement between JR Oil Co. and OPEC probably:
    A. constitutes a *per se* violation of Section 1 of the Sherman Act.
    B. **cannot** be the subject matter of a lawsuit in courts of the United States because of the act of state doctrine.
    C. **cannot** be the subject matter of a lawsuit in courts of the United States because of the doctrine of sovereign immunity.
    D. constitute a violation of Article II, Section 2 of the United States Constitution.

5. Eaststar Oil Co. has commenced an action against one of the foreign nations that is a member of OPEC in the United States District Court in Dallas, Texas. The foreign nation intends to argue that the Foreign Sovereign Immunities Act of 1976 (FSIA) does not permit the U.S. District Court to exercise jurisdiction over the foreign nation because that nation has sovereign immunity. Which of the following arguments best supports the foreign nation's position under the FSIA?
    A. The act of state doctrine protects a nation against such an exercise of jurisdiction.
    B. The commercial activity in dispute, in effect, constitutes a governmental activity because the country's economy depends upon oil exports.
    C. Despite the substantial restraining effect that the activities have on commerce within the United States, the acts in dispute were based upon commercial activities that were carried on outside the United States.
    D. The foreign nation did **not** waive immunity explicitly or by implication.

6. ET Sales, Inc. has imported electronic typewriters from a Japanese manufacturer for distribution and sale of the typewriters in the United States at a price of approximately $333. The typewriters with type that conforms to Japanese characters are sold in Japan at a price that is equivalent to $399.
    A. The International Trade Commission probably will determine that the typewriters are being sold at less than fair value and impose an extra tariff on the typewriters.
    B. Because the typewriters on being sold at less than fair value, an antidumping duty may be assessed on the typewriters.

C. Because the type on the typewriters imported into the United States is different from the type on otherwise comparable typewriters in the Japanese market, the products are different, and the antidumping laws of the United States, therefore, do **not** apply.

D. Because the type on the typewriters imported into the United States is different from the type on otherwise comparable typewriters in the Japanese market, the International Trade Administration will **not** impose an extra duty on the typewriters imported into this country.

7. The Foreign Corrupt Practices Act prohibits bribery of officials of foreign nations. The Foreign Corrupt Practices Act:

A. applies only to corporations that are incorporated in states of the United States and own subsidiary companies in foreign countries.

B. applies to corporations that are incorporated in states of the United States and engage in interstate and foreign commerce.

C. applies only to corporations whose securities are required to be registered with the Securities and Exchange Commission under the securities laws of the United States.

D. provides that a person who has been injured as a result of the bribe to a foreign official may sue a corporation that was incorporated in one of the states of the United States and recover treble damages.

8. A furniture manufacturer located in Sweden enters into a contract with Uranus Co., a Delaware corporation. The contract provides that the Swedish manufacturer appoints Uranus Co. for three years as its sole agent in the United States for the purpose of entering into contracts for the sale of furniture to retail purchasers in the U.S.

A. The Swedish firm is a foreign agent for Uranus Co.

B. Uranus Co. is a foreign agent for the Swedish manufacturer.

C. The agreement between the Swedish firm and Uranus Co. is an exclusive distribution agreement.

D. When the Swedish firm ships furniture to Uranus Co., Uranus Co. takes title to the furniture.

9. Copper Fields Corp., a New Mexico corporation, which produces mining equipment in the U.S. enters into an agreement with ZMB Ltd. and BMZ Ltd., two Zambian firms. The agreement calls for construction by ZMB Ltd. of a plant in Zambia for the manufacture of mining equipment. The construction cost is to be borne equally by Copper Fields Corp. and BMZ Ltd. The three parties agree that the plant will be jointly owned and operated, and that profits and losses be shared equally. The effect of their agreement is to establish:

A. a franchise. Copper Fields Corp. is the franchisor; ZMB Ltd., and BMZ Ltd. are the franchisees.

B. a technology license. Copper Fields Corp. is the licensor, and ZMB Ltd. and BMZ Ltd. are the licensees.

C. an agency relationship. Cooper Fields Corp. is the principal, and ZMB Ltd. and BMZ Ltd. are agents.

D. a joint venture. Cooper Fields Corp., ZMB Ltd., and BMZ Ltd. are joint venturers.

Chapter 56
Law for Entrepreneurs

This Chapter highlights significant areas of law that are covered in many of the previous 55 chapters (to which cross references of supplied) and are relevant for people who may contemplate starting a business enterprise.

THINGS TO KEEP IN MIND

Few people embarking on a business venture succeed without understanding and being able to respond to legal issues. In addition, often they underestimate the importance of having legal counsel.

OUTLINE

I. The importance of legal counsel — People who contemplate starting their own businesses should recognize that it is essential to have legal advice from a knowledgeable attorney.

    A. Finding an attorney — In selecting attorneys, entrepreneurs rely on referrals from friends, business associates, other entrepreneurs, chambers or commerce, bar associations, yellow pages in telephone books, and the *Martindale-Hubbell Law Directory.*

    B. Interviewing and evaluating attorneys — A person who contemplates starting a business should meet with and interview one or more attorneys in order to select an appropriate, knowledgeable attorney.

    C. Retaining an attorney — There are various arrangements that can be made for paying for legal services; for example, businesspersons may have a retainer agreement that provides for a monthly (or annual) payment to the attorney who will handle legal matters and be available for advise during the month (or year).

II. Selecting an appropriate business form — See Chapter 37, in which the various forms of business organizations are described and compared as well as the other Chapters in Unit Eight in which certain types of organizations are covered in greater detail.

    A. Limitations on liability.

        1. Sole proprietors and general partners in partnerships are liable personally for all business debts and obligations.

2. In order to avoid personal liability for business obligations and debts, people engaging in business may form corporations, limited partnerships, limited liability companies, and, in some states, limited liability partnerships.

B. Tax considerations.

1. Sole proprietors and partners pay taxes only on profits.

2. If the corporate form of organization is used, the corporation pays taxes on its profits and shareholders pay taxes on dividends (distributed profits) unless the corporation is an S corporation or a limited liability company.

C. Continuity of life — Unlike sole proprietorships and partnerships, corporations have continuity of life.

D. Legal formality and expense — When starting a business, entrepreneurs often underestimate the formalities that may be necessary and the initial costs, such as expenses of incorporation, licensing, registration, and compliance with other requirements.

III. Creating the business entity — Written, signed agreements with business associates should be prepared with care.

A. Choosing a corporate name — A corporate name must be different from the names of other existing firms and filed with a state official (e.g., the secretary of state) in the state of incorporation and other states in which the firm conducts business.

B. Articles of incorporation, bylaws, and initial meetings.

1. Articles of incorporation requirements and contents — See Chapter 40.

2. Bylaws are governing rules that can be changed more easily than articles of incorporation.

3. The first meeting of the board of directors designated in the articles of incorporation is held after the corporation comes into existence — See Chapter 40.

C. Creating a corporate records book — Documents, including the articles of incorporation, bylaws, minutes of directors' and shareholders' meetings, and, when applicable, a copy of the form of stock certificate, and an impression of the corporate seal are maintained in the corporate records book.

IV. Intellectual property — See Chapter 9.

A. Choosing and protecting your trademark.

1. Choosing your trademark.

      a. A trademark or service mark is a word, phrase, symbol, etc., that distinguishes the user's products or services from goods or services of other firms and may be the same as a trade name; trademarks may be registered with the U.S. Patent and Trademark Office (PTO).

      b. Usually, the first user of a distinctive trademark or service mark can prevent other people from using the mark in an infringement suit.

  2. Undertaking a trademark search — Sources of information include telephone books in the local areas, *Gale's List of Tradenames*, the PTO, and TrademarkScan on the Internet.

  3. Registering your trademark in the state and in the PTO.

  4. Protecting your trademark.

      a. The symbol ® may be used for marks registered with the PTO and the symbol ™ for unregistered marks.

      b. If a mark is abandoned intentionally, the mark can be used by others.

B. Protecting trade secrets.

  1. Trade secrets may make a firm unique and are protected under common law.

  2. In order to protect trade secrets, employers may include covenants not to compete or reveal trade secrets in employment contracts with employees.

V.   Raising financial capital — If a new enterprise is successful, external sources of capital (which initially were not available) may be accessible by borrowing funds and issuing stock. [See Units Four and Five.]

A. Loans — The Small Business Administration provides small loans.

B. Venture capital — Venture capitalists may provide funds in exchange for stock (equity) and some measure of control; usually, a venture capitalist will require that the entrepreneur furnish an accurate business plan.

C. Securities regulation — Federal securities acts and state blue sky laws regulate the issuance and trading in (debt and equity) securities. [See Chapter 43.]

  1. Private offerings of securities may be exempt from regulation.

  2. Public offerings are regulated under federal and state laws.

VI.   Buy-sell agreements and key-person insurance.

A. Shareholder agreements — A shareholder agreement specifies the rights and obligations of principals in the firm.

1. Shareholders can include buy-sell provisions specifying how the price to be paid for a shareholder's interest is to be determined upon the happening of specified events, such as the death, divorce, or bankruptcy of the shareholder.

2. Sole proprietors, partners, and shareholders in closely held corporations may enter into business continuation contracts providing that a deceased proprietor's, partner's, or shareholder's interest may be purchased at a specified price by a family member, other partner (or partners or the partnership), or other shareholders (or the corporation) respectively; typically, the purchase of the ownership interest is funded by the proceeds of life insurance.

B. Key-person insurance — Because an employer has an insurable interest in the continued life of a key employee, an employer can obtain life or disability insurance on the life of the employee; if the employee dies or becomes disabled, the proceeds of the policy are used to cover short-term losses and the expenses incurred in finding and training a replacement for the deceased or disabled employee. [See Chapter 52.]

VII. Contract law and the entrepreneur — Understanding of the law of contracts and agency is essential for entrepreneurs. [See Units Two and Six.]

VIII. Credit and payment — In many lines of business, credit is extended to customers and firms may have difficulty in obtaining payment.

A. Consumer protection laws are discussed in Chapter 45.

B. Methods that are used by creditors in order to obtain payment include use of negotiable instruments (covered in Unit Four) and secured transactions (covered in Chapter 30). In addition, see Chapters 24, relating to remedies for breach of contracts for the sale or lease of goods and Chapters 31 and 32 dealing with creditors' rights.

IX. Employment issues — See Units Six and Seven.

A. Hiring employees — Issues that should be considered when hiring employees

1. Did the applicant for a position agree with a prior employer that he or she would not compete with or disclose trade secrets of the prior employer?

2. What screening tests should potential employees be required to take?

3. Have you verified applicant's qualifications, experience, letters of recommendation, and citizenship status, and obtained other relevant information?

4. Have you consulted with an attorney regarding employment contracts?

5. Will an employee be an employee for a specified period of time or an at-will employee?

6. Have you complied with laws relating to employment discrimination?

B. Employee compensation — See Chapter 35 regarding wage and hour laws.

C. Workers' compensation insurance — Because employers are strictly liable to employees who incur injuries or illnesses while acting in the course of their employment (Chapter 35), employers obtain workers' compensation insurance (Chapter 52).

D. Unemployment compensation — See Chapter 35.

E. Firing employees.

1. Employers should maintain records for each employee containing documents, such as job applications and performance reviews.

2. Review material in Chapters 35 and 36 relating to wrongful discharge of employees.

F. Covenants not to compete — See Chapter 17.

G. Using independent contractors — See Chapter 33.

KEY WORDS AND PHRASES IN TEXT

legal counsel

retainer arrangement with an attorney

personal liability

corporate bylaws

trademark and trade name protection

trade secret protection

venture capitalist

buy-sell agreement

key-person insurance

UNIFORM CPA BUSINESS LAW AND PROFESSIONAL RESPONSIBILITIES EXAMINATION INFORMATION

In order to be certified, public accountants must fulfill certain requirements that are prescribed by state examining boards. A requisite in every state is successfully passing the Uniform Certified Public Accountant (CPA) Examination that is prepared and graded by the American Institute of Certified Public Accountants (AICPA). The Uniform CPA Examination is administered twice a year (in May and November) and contains four sections — (1) accounting and reporting (taxation, managerial, and governmental and not-for-profit organizations), (2) financial accounting and reporting (business enterprises), (3) auditing, and (4) business law and professional responsibilities.

The business law and professional responsibilities portion of the CPA Examination is a three hour test composed of objective and essay questions. It is administered on the first morning of the examination (a Wednesday) from 9:00 a.m. until noon. Between 50% and 60% of the examination is based upon a series of 50 to 60 four-option multiple choice questions, from 20% to 30% on other types of objective questions, and from 20% to 30% on essays.

The multiple choice questions are similar to those found at the end of the chapters in this *Study Guide*. Occasionally, correctly answering a multiple choice question requires knowledge of more than one area of law. The other types of objective questions may be matching questions or yes-no questions. Samples of such objective questions are included in several chapters in this *Study Guide*.

Each answer to an essay question is given a value of ten points. Often, essay questions have two or more parts that test candidates' knowledge of different business law and professional responsibilities topics. A typical essay question includes a statement of a fact situation involving a number of legal issues. Candidates are expected to discuss these issues in determining the liability of the parties. Five percent of the law and professional responsibilities section of the Uniform CPA Examination is allocated to effective writing skills evidenced by answers to the essay questions. Writing skills are based upon the following criteria: coherent organization, conciseness, clarity, use of standard English, responsiveness as to the requirements of the question, and appropriateness for the reader.[1]

Extensive in-depth knowledge of business law is necessary in order to pass the Uniform CPA Examination. Detailed information about the subject matter content and the approximate percentage of the examination devoted to each of seven broad areas of law is

---

1. AMERICAN INSTITUTE OF CERTIFIED PUBLIC ACCOUNTANTS, INC., INFORMATION FOR CPA CANDIDATES, Effective May 1997 at 29-30 (13th ed. 1996).

provided in specifications adopted by the Board of Examiners of AICPA. The current content specifications became effective in May 1997 and state:

> The business law & professional responsibilities section tests candidates' knowledge of a CPA's professional responsibilities and of the legal implications of business transactions, particularly as they relate to accounting and auditing. Content covered in this section includes a CPA's professional responsibilities, business organizations, contracts, debtor-creditor relationships, government regulation of business, the Uniform Commercial Code, and property. Candidates will be required to

> - Recognize relevant legal issues
> - Recognize the legal implications of certain business situations
> - Apply the underlying principles of law to accounting and auditing situations.

> This section deals with federal and widely adopted uniform laws. If there is no federal or uniform law on a topic, the questions are intended to test knowledge of the law of the majority of jurisdictions. Professional ethics questions are based on the AICPA *Code of Professional Conduct* because it is national in its application, whereas codes of other organizations and jurisdictions may be limited in their application.

Business law & professional responsibilities content specification outline

    I.   Professional and legal responsibilities (15%)

        A. Code of professional conduct
        B. Proficiency, independence, and due care
        C. Responsibilities in other professional services
        D. Disciplinary systems within the profession
        E. Common law liability to clients and third parties
        F. Federal statutory liability
        G. Privileged communication and confidentially

    II.   Business Organizations (20%)

        A. Agency

            1. Formation and termination
            2. Duties of agents and principals
            3. Liabilities and authority of agents and principals

        B. Partnerships and joint ventures

            1. Formation, operation, and termination
            2. Liabilities and authority of partners and joint owners

        C. Corporations

            1. Formation and operation
            2. Stockholders, directors, and officers
            3. Financial structure, capital, and distributions
            4. Reorganization and dissolution

      D.   Estates and trusts

          1. Formation, operation, and termination
          2. Allocation between principal and income
          3. Fiduciary responsibilities
          4. Distributions

III. Contracts (10%)

      A.   Formation
      B.   Performance
      C.   Third party assignments
      D.   Discharge, breach, and remedies

IV. Debtor-creditor relationships (10%)

      A.   Rights, duties and liabilities of debtors and creditors
      B.   Rights, duties and liabilities of guarantors
      C.   Bankruptcy

V. Government regulation of business (15%)

      A.   Federal securities acts
      B.   Employment regulation
      C.   Environmental regulation

VI. Uniform commercial code (20%)

      A.   Negotiable instruments
      B.   Sales
      C.   Secured transactions
      D.   Bailments and documents of title

VII. Property (10%)

      A.   Real property
      B.   Personal property
      C.   Fire insurance [2]

The AICPA specifications do not indicate the relative emphasis that may be placed upon the various topics within the seven major areas of business law. This is expected to fluctuate on future examinations as it has in the past.

---

2.   The Business Law & Professional Responsibilities Content Specification Outline for the Uniform Certified Public Accountant Examination (Effective May 1997), Copyright © 1996 by the American Institute of Certified Public Accountants, Inc., New York, NY 10036-8775, is reprinted with permission.

SOME CONCLUSIONS

The importance of contract law to accountants and, therefore, Unit Two in *West's Business Law: Seventh Edition* and this *Study Guide*, cannot be over stressed. Approximately 10% of the CPA Business Law and Professional Responsibilities Examination is devoted to specific topics relating to contracts. One must realize, however, that contract law provides the foundation for what normally are considered other, separate areas of business law.

With regard to the area referred to as Professional Responsibilities, information relating to this subject is presented in Chapter 54 of the textbook and this *Study Guide*. (In addition, see material dealing with torts in Chapter 6, contracts in Unit Two, and security regulations in Chapter 43.) Usually, this subject is also covered in accounting courses, such as auditing and taxation.

In addition to contracts and the CPA's professional and legal responsibilities, topics that have received significant treatment on past CPA examinations have included commercial paper, corporations, partnerships, sales, secured transactions, and federal securities laws.[3]

FUTURE CPA EXAMINATIONS

1998 — May 6 and 7 November 4 and 5	2001 — May 2 and 3 November 7 and 8
1999 — May 5 and 6 November 3 and 4	2002 — May 8 and 9 November 6 and 7
2000 — May 3 and 4 November 1 and 2	2003 — May 7 and 8 November 5 and 6

Students, who plan to sit for the examinations, are encouraged to obtain copies of *Information for CPA Candidates* issued by AIPCA.[4] In their preparation, CPA candidates will find the outlines and other materials in this book useful for review purposes. For this reason, cross references to the *Study Guide to Accompany West's Business Law: Seventh Edition* (which correspond to the textbook) are provided in the Table (on the next page) for the subjects that are covered on the Uniform CPA Examination.

---

3.   Knowledge concerning the federal securities laws is tested specifically and also in conjunction with a certified public accountant's statutory liability.

4.   Copies of publications of The American Institute of Certified Public Accountants, Inc. (AICPA) may be obtained from:

> Order Department
> American Institute of Certified Public Accountants
> P.O. Box 2209
> Jersey City, NJ 07303-2209
> 1-800-862-4272

TABLE OF CROSS REFERENCES

Subjects Covered on Uniform CPA Examination - Chapters in Study Guide

AREA, AICPA PERCENTAGE & GROUP	STUDY GUIDE CHAPTERS
PROFESSIONAL AND LEGAL RESPONSIBILITIES (15%)	See also AICPA *Code of Professional Conduct*
A. Code of Professional Conduct	54
B. Proficiency, Independence, and Due Care	6 and 54
C. Responsibilities in Other Professional Services	33 and 54
D. Disciplinary Systems Within the Profession	
E. Common Law Liability to Clients & Third Parties	6, 18, 19, 20, and 54
F. Federal Statutory Liability	43 and 54
G. Privileged Communications and Confidentiality	54
BUSINESS ORGANIZATIONS (20%)	
A. Agency	33 and 34
B. Partnerships and Joint Ventures	37, 38, and 39
C. Corporations	40, 41, and 42
D. Estates and Trusts	53
CONTRACTS (10%)	
A. Formation	12, 13, 14, 15, 16, and 17
B. Performance	19
C. Third-Party Assignments	18
D. Discharge, Breach, and Remedies	19 and 20
DEBTOR-CREDITOR RELATIONSHIPS (10%)	
A. Rights, Duties, & Liabilities of Debtors and Creditors	31
B. Rights, Duties, & Liabilities of Guarantors	31
C. Bankruptcy	32
GOVERNMENT REGULATION OF BUSINESS (15%)	
A. Federal Securities Acts	43
B. Employment Regulation	35 and 36
B. Environmental Regulation	46
UNIFORM COMMERCIAL CODE (20%)	
A. Negotiable Instruments	26, 27, 28, and 29
B. Sales	21, 22, 23, 24, and 25
C. Secured Transactions	30
D. Bailments and Documents of Title	49
PROPERTY (10%)	
A. Real Property	50 and 51
B. Personal Property	48
C. Fire Insurance	52

Business Law Partner 3.0
Study Guide
Questions and Exercises

EXERCISE 1

HOW DO I CLOSE ON A HOUSE WHEN I'M OUT OF THE COUNTRY?
POWERS OF ATTORNEY

Text References: Chapters 33 and 34

Nancy Travis, a photographer for *National Geographic*, lives in Scarsdale, New York. The National Geographic Society has just given Nancy an assignment in the Andes that will run from June 1, 1998 until July 14, 1998. Nancy will depart on May 29, 1998 for South America.

Nancy is single and has just purchased a house. The closing on her house is scheduled for June 15, 1998 and because of title searches and mortgage paperwork, she has learned that this date is the earliest she can expect for the closing. In addition, Nancy will be receiving an inheritance of 22,000 shares of IBM stock from her late uncle's estate which is scheduled for a final distribution hearing on June 20, 1998.

Nancy is concerned because she can't handle all of these personal transactions when she is out of the country working. "But, they'll need my signature on documents for the closing and the stock transfer. And the papers aren't even completed yet so I can't sign them in advance. There won't even be an papers for the stock until the judge signs them after the hearing. How can I sign for the shares then?"

Jake Truitt, a life-time friend of Nancy's, has offered to help in whatever way he can to handle the transactions while Nancy is gone but notes, "I just can't see that they will accept my signature."
Review the materials on agency in Chapters 33 and 334. Then turn to the Quicken Business Law Partners Program and refer to the power of attorney documents.

1. What authority does a general power of attorney give?

_____

_____

_____

_____

_____

2. According to the agreement, is Jake entitled to compensation?_____

3. Can Jake serve under the power of attorney without compensation?_____

_____

4. Can Nancy revoke the power of attorney?_____

_____

Refer to the special power of attorney in the Quicken business law partners documents.

5. What is the distinction between this document and the general power of attorney?

_____

_____

6. Is the agent entitled to compensation?_____

_____

INSTRUCTOR EXERCISES:

Can you help Nancy with her dilemma? Explain the pros and cons of a power of attorney to Nancy. Using the information you have been given, draft a power of attorney for Nancy.

NOTE: Exercises 2 through 8 are based on the following fact pattern.

EXERCISE 2
THEY SCRATCHED MY WIDE-SCREEN TV, NOW WHAT?
BREACH OF CONTRACT AND WITHHOLDING PAYMENT

Text References: Chapters 6, 20 and 29

David and Joan Woods contracted with Tolleson Carpet for the purchase and installation of carpet in their home for a total price of $4281. While the installers were moving the furniture in the Woods' family room in order to remove the old carpet and install the new, one worker swung a roll of carpet around in such a way that it hit the screen of the Woods' wide-screen television. Joan Woods witnessed the screen being scraped by the roll of carpet but could not get close enough to inspect the television screen when it happened.

After the carpet installation was complete, both David and Joan noticed a scratch on their wide-screen television. Joan told David, "That's just where that worker scraped the roll of carpet when they were moving the furniture." The Woods' television was two months old at he time of the carpet installation. The Woods had a repair service examine the screen. Replacement cost for the screen, including labor, was estimated at $671.

Joan called Tolleson's manager, Frank Fairbanks and explained the problem with the television screen. "Look," Fairbanks responded, "you can't prove we did that. That's not our problem. Besides, read your contract, it says right in there that we have no liability for any damages to your house or furniture that occurs while we're installing your carpet." Joan hung up and told David, "I guess I could put it all in writing and maybe the company could respond.

Refer to the BBB/Attorney General Letter of Complaint provided in the Quicken Business Law Partner documents.

1. What details will Joan and David need to fill in to draft the complaint?

_____

_____

2. What documents do you think they should attach to their complaint?

_____

_____

3. Can you think of means of alternative dispute resolution that might help Joan and David and Tolleson to resolve their differences?

_____

_____

_____

INSTRUCTOR EXERCISE:

Help Joan draft a letter of complaint using the form provided in the Quicken Business Law Partner documents. Do you have all the information you need?

EXERCISE 3

WE NEED TO GET THAT CHECK BACK
STOP PAYMENT ORDERS

Text Reference: Chapter 29

David has just given Tolleson a check for $2,281, the balance due on the carpet contract. "I wonder if there is anything I can do to get my money back until this issue with the television screen is resolved," wondered David.

Review Chapter 29 in the text and determine whether David can take any action with the check to Tolleson. Refer to the Quicken Business Law Partner credit documents, the stop payment on a check form, and answer the following questions:

1. Can the Woods rightfully stop payment on the check to Tolleson?

_____

_____

2. Must the drawer give a reason for the stop payment?_____

3. According to the stop payment form, who will pay the costs and fees for stopping payment?

_____

4. Will the bank be held liable if the stop payment order should not have been requested by the drawer?_____

5. Who will be held liable if the stop payment order was wrongfully issued?

_____

IINSTRUCTOR EXERCISES:

Review Chapters 6 and 17 and discuss the validity of Tolleson's disclaimer for damages that occur while they are installing carpet.

What information would the Woods need to stop payment on the check?

Draft a stop payment order for the Woods and be sure to customize it for their fact circumstances.

EXERCISE 4

THE SAGA OF THE WIDE-SCREEN TV CONTINUES
NOTICE OF DISHONOR

Text Reference: Chapter 29

After Tolleson deposited the Woods' check, it is notified that the check has been dishonored by the Woods' bank. Review Chapter 29 and determine Tolleson's rights. Answer the following questions:

1. Is Tolleson required to notify the Woods of the bank's dishonor of the check?

_____

Turn to the Quicken Bad Check Notice under the credit document section, and answer the following questions:

2. According to the notice, what will happen if payment is not made immediately?

_____

_____

3. Is interest accruing?_____

INSTRUCTOR EXERCISE:

Help Tolleson by also drafting a follow-up letter to the Woods with a demand for payment.

EXERCISE 5

COLLECTION EFFORTS FOR THE CARPET BEGIN
COLLECTION ACTIVITIES

Text Reference: Chapter 45

With no response from the Woods, Tolleson has referred the matter to a collection agency. The collection agency has contacted the Woods and demanded payment. The letter from the collection agency includes the following paragraph:

Tolleson Carpet has made repeated demands for payment on your carpet contract. Please pay the amount due ($2281.00) today so that your credit rating is not affected by your non-payment of this binding obligation.

If payment is not received within 10 days, we shall proceed with all rights and remedies afforded Tolleson by law.

Review Chapter 45 and the Quicken Business Law Partners Credit Documents and answer the following questions:

1. Has the collection agency violated any laws with it demand letter?

_____

_____

2. What rights could Woods assert?

_____

_____

INSTRUCTOR EXERCISE:

Help the Woods respond to the collection agency's demand for payment. What rights could the Woods assert? Has the collection agency violated any laws with its demand letter?

EXERCISE 6

NOW THE SCREEN SCRATCH MIGHT AFFECT MY CREDIT RATING
CREDIT REPORTS

Text Reference: Chapter 45

The Woods are concerned that their problems with Tolleson may have resulted in a blemish on their previously flawless credit report. Review Chapter 45 and the Quicken Business Law Partner Credit Documents. Refer to the request for a credit report and answer the following:

1. What must be included with a request for a credit report in order for the report to be furnished?

_____

_____

2. Why would the inclusion of a social security number be important?

_____

_____

INSTRUCTOR EXERCISES:

Help the Woods make the appropriate request.

Be sure to list any additional information you would need in order to make the request.

EXERCISE 7

THE LAW SUIT FOR THE CARPET PAYMENT
SMALL CLAIMS COURT

Text References: Chapters 1 and 20

Suppose that the Woods still have not paid the remaining balance for the carpet and Tolleson wishes to proceed with a suit to recover the amount due from the Woods. Refer to the Quicken Business Law Partners Credit Documents and the small claims worksheet and answer the following questions:

1. Go to the list of state small claims limits in the document. Does the claim against the Woods qualify for small claims court in your state? Suppose that the Woods have paid all but the $671 for the television screen, would the Tolleson suit then qualify for small claims court in your state?

_____

_____

2. What additional information do you need to complete the checklist?

_____

_____

3. Who is the plaintiff in this suit? Who is the defendant?

_____

4. Which state has the highest small claims court maximum?

_____

INSTRUCTOR EXERCISE:

Complete the small claims checklist for Tolleson.

EXERCISE 8

THE SUIT FOR THE TELEVISION SCREEN SCRATCH
FILING A LAW SUIT

Textbook Reference: Chapters 1 and 20

Suppose that the Woods make the $2,281 payment to Tolleson and then file suit against Tolleson to collect the $671 for the repair of their television screen. Refer to the Quicken Business Law Partners Credit Document and the portion on Defending A Lawsuit - Business and answer the following questions:

1. In this situation, who is the plaintiff? Who is the defendant?

_____

2. What additional information do you need to complete the form?

_____

_____

INSTRUCTOR EXERCISE:

Complete the checklist as thoroughly as you can for Tolleson with the information you have been given.

EXERCISE 9

CREDIT APPLICATIONS AND DENIAL

Text References: Chapter 45

Assume you have been denied a loan for the purchase of a car. Refer to Chapter 45 and the Challenge to a Denial of Credit in the Quicken Business Law Partners program.

What requests for information are made in the letter?

_____

_____

EXERCISE 10

THE DEFECTIVE APARTMENT

Textbook Reference: Chapter 51

The heating in your apartment does not work, and it is February in North Conway, New Hampshire. Refer to Chapter 51 and the Complaint to the Landlord in Quicken Business Law Partners.

1. What two things does the note to the landlord accomplish?

_____

_____

2. What rights do tenants have generally regarding the conditions of their leased premises?

_____

_____

INSTRUCTOR EXERCISE:

Draft a letter of complaint for a problem in your own apartment.

EXERCISE 11

COMMERCIAL REAL ESTATE LEASES

Textbook References: Chapter 51

Refer to Chapter 51 and the Real Estate Lease-Commercial in the Quicken Business Law Partners and answer the following questions:

1. When is the rent due under the lease?

_____

2. Who is responsible for insurance on the property?

_____

3. How does either party give notice to the other according to the lease?

_____

4. What happens if a portion of the lease agreement is unenforceable?

_____

EXERCISE 12

RESIDENTIAL LEASES

Textbook Reference: Chapter 51

Refer to the Residential Lease in the Quicken Business Law Partner and Chapter 51 and answer the following questions:

1. What provisions do you see in the residential lease that are not found in the commercial lease?

_____

_____

2. What is the habitability clause and what does it do for the tenant?

_____

_____

EXERCISE 13

RENTAL APPLICATION

Textbook Reference: Chapter 51

Refer to the Rental Application in the Quicken Business Law Partner and answer the following questions:

1. What happens if a tenant submits an application and is approved by the landlord and then fails to rent the premises?

_____

2. Will the landlord be permitted to do a credit check?_____

_____

3. List the grounds on which the landlord can't discriminate.

_____

_____

4. What rights does the tenant have if rejected by the landlord?

_____

_____

INSTRUCTOR EXERCISE:

What problem questions do you see in the application?

EXERCISE 14

THE RENTAL PROPERTY INSPECTION

Textbook Reference: Chapter 51

Refer to the Renter's Inspection Worksheet in the Quicken Business Law Partners and answer the following questions:

1. What are the general standards for the condition of the premises that the parties confirm through sign-off on this inspection sheet?

_____

_____

2. What effect does this checklist have on termination rights of the tenant?

_____

_____

3. What defects does the tenant assume the risk for?

_____

4. What does the tenant agree to do with respect to the smoke detector?_____

_____

EXERCISE 15

BILL OF SALE

Textbook References: Chapters 22 and 25

Refer to the Bill of Sale in the Quicken Business Law Partner and answer the following questions:

1. What does property sold "AS IS" mean?

_____

_____

2. What does a bill of sale do?

_____

3. Is a bill of sale different from a document of title?

_____

_____

EXERCISE 16

BILL OF SALE FOR MOTOR VEHICLES

Textbook References: Chapters 22, 25 and 45

Refer to the Bill of Sale-Motor Vehicles in the Quicken Business Law Partner and answer the following questions:

1. What differences are there between the bill of sale and the bill of sale for motor vehicles?

_____

_____

2. What happens if the seller makes a false statement regarding the vehicle's mileage?

_____

3. What promise does the seller make in the bill of sale about the vehicle's odometer?

_____

_____

EXERCISE 17

EQUIPMENT LEASE

Textbook References: Chapters 21, 23 and 24

Refer to the Equipment Lease in the Quicken Business Law Partner and answer the following question:

1. When is the rent due?

_____

2. Who has the risk of loss or is responsible for damage to the equipment?

_____

3. Can the lessee make alterations to the equipment?_____

4. Who pays for repairs to the equipment?_____

5. Can the lessor see the equipment during the term of the lease?_____

_____

6. What options are given to the lessee when the lease ends?

_____

_____

7. Does the lessor make any warranties about the property?_____

8. Is the lessor's disclaimer valid?_____

_____

9. Can the lessee assign the lease?_____

10. How will disputes be settled?_____

_____

EXERCISE 18

THE ROLE OF GUARANTORS

Textbook References: Chapter 31

Refer to chapter 31 and the Guaranty in the Quicken Business Law Partner and answer the following questions:

1. What type of guaranty is this?_____

_____

2. How long does the guaranty last?_____

_____

3. Does the creditor have to notify the guarantor if the debtor defaults?_____

4. Does the creditor have to notify the guarantor if he loans more money to the debtor?

_____

5. Does the creditor have to show diligence in collection before turning to the guarantor?

_____

6. What can the creditor change without notice to the guarantor?

_____

7. Is the guarantor released if the creditor does change terms?_____

EXERCISE 19

A LICENSE AGREEMENT

Textbook References: Chapter 9

Refer to Chapter 9 and the License Agreement in Quicken Business Law Partner and answer the following questions:

1. What types of arrangements would this agreement cover?

_____

2. What is the compensation under the agreement?

_____

EXERCISE 20

PROMISSORY NOTES

Text Reference: Chapter 26

Refer to the Promissory Note in the Quicken Business Law Partner documents and answer the following questions:

1. How are payments applied?

_____

2. In what currency is the note payable?

_____

3. Review Chapter 26. Is it possible to have a negotiable promissory note in the United States when the note is not payable in U.S. currency?

_____

_____

EXERCISE 21

ARTICLES OF INCORPORATION

Text References: Chapters 40 and 41

Review the Articles of Incorporation in the **Quicken Business Law Partner** and answer the following questions:

1. List the information needed for incorporation using this document.

_____   _____

_____   _____

_____   _____

2. Is this same information required under the MBCA? Refer to Chapter 40

_____

_____

3. Will the corporation provide indemnity for its officers and directors?

_____

4. Refer to Chapter 41. What does indemnity for officers and directors mean?

_____

_____

INSTRUCTOR EXERCISE:

Have the students draft their own articles of incorporation.

EXERCISE 22

CORPORATE BYLAWS

Text References: Chapters 40 and 41

Review the Corporate Bylaws in the Quicken Business Law Partner and answer the following:

1. How often will meetings of shareholders be held?

_____

2. Who can call a special meeting?_____

_____

3. When must notice of a meeting be given?_____

_____

4. What constitutes a quorum for meetings?_____

_____

5. Can a quorum be met with proxy representation?_____

6. Can a director be removed without cause?_____

7. List the offices provided by the bylaws.

_____   _____

_____   _____

8. Who elects the officers?_____

9. How are the bylaws amended?_____

_____

10. Can you own shares in the corporation without actually having stock certificates?

_____

EXERCISE 23

CORPORATE PROXY

Text Reference: Chapter 41

Review the corporate proxy in the Quicken Business Law Partner and answer the following:

1. Does this proxy revoke prior proxies?_____

2. Review Chapter 41 and explain why a proxy might be necessary._____

_____

3. Is there a provision for designating votes?_____

_____

EXERCISE 24

EMPLOYMENT/AGENCY
CONFIDENTIALITY AGREEMENT

Text References: Chapter 33

Review the Confidentiality Agreement in the Quicken Business Law Partner and answer the following:

1. What is the definition of confidential information given?

_____

_____

2. What kinds of information would you list as being confidential? Refer to Chapter 33.

_____   _____

_____   _____

_____   _____

EXERCISE 25

EMPLOYMENT/AGENCY
CONSULTING AGREEMENT

Textbook References: Chapters 33, 34, 35 and 36

Review the Consulting Agreement in the Quicken Business Law Partner and answer the
following:

1. Will the consultant be an independent contractor or an employee?

_____

2. Why is this distinction important? What differences exist between hiring an independent
contractor and hiring an employee? Refer to Chapters 33-36.

_____

_____

_____

_____

EXERCISE 26

EMPLOYMENT/AGENCY
EMPLOYMENT AGREEMENT

Text References: Chapters 33 and 34

Review the Employment Agreement in the Quicken Business Law Partner and answer the following:

1. How long will the employment last?_____

_____

2. Is an employment of this length legal?_____

_____

_____

3. How are the parties to the agreement to give notice?_____

_____

EXERCISE 27

EMPLOYMENT/AGENCY
LETTER OF ACCEPTANCE

Text References: Chapters 13 and 33

Review the Quicken Business Law Partner Letter of Acceptance under Employment and answer the following:

1. Prior to the time of the use of this document, what interaction had the parties had regarding employment?

_____

2. How would a letter like this help the employee? Be sure to review Chapters 13 and 33.

_____

_____

_____

EXERCISE 28

NON-COMPETE AGREEMENT
ANTITRUST AND EMPLOYMENT

Text References: Chapter 17

Review the Non-Compete Agreement in the Quicken Business Law Partner and answer the following:

1. What types of activities does the agreement prohibit?

_____   _____

_____   _____

2. What remedies are given for violation of the agreement?

_____

3. Refer to Chapter 17 and discuss why and when this type of an agreement would be necessary.

_____

_____

_____

_____

EXERCISE 29

CONSIGNMENT AGREEMENT
SALES - UCC ARTICLE 2

Text References: Chapters 22 and 49

Review the Consignment Agreement in the General Business document section of Quicken Business Law Partner and answer the following:

1. What is a consignment arrangement?_____

_____

2. Who is the consignee?_____

3. Who is the consignor?_____

4. How will the consignee be compensated for the sale of the goods?_____

_____

5. Who has title to the goods during the consignment?_____

6. Who has the risk of loss during the consignment?_____

7. What is the difference between a bailment and a consignment?_____

_____

_____

EXERCISE 30

COPYRIGHT APPLICATION
INTELLECTUAL PROPERTY

Text References: Chapter 9

Review the Copyright Application in the Quicken Business Law Partner and answer the following:

1. List the types of works that can be copyrighted.

_____   _____

_____   _____

_____   _____

2. If a book is written by an employee during the course of employment, who has the right to the copyright?_____

_____

EXERCISE 31

GENERAL CONTRACT - PRODUCTS
SALES/ARTICLE 2

Text References: Chapters 21, 22, 23, 24, and 25

Review the General Contract-Products in the General Business documents of Quicken Business
Law Partner and answer the following:

1. What happens in the buyer fails to make a payment?

_____

2. What is the time given for delivery?

_____

3. Who pays the costs if improper packaging produces damages to the goods?

_____

4. Who pays the taxes in this transaction?_____

5. What are the inspection rights under the contract?_____

_____

6. Are these inspection rights different from those given under the UCC?

_____

_____

7. What is force majeure?_____

_____

8. Give examples listed as force majeure.

_____   _____

_____   _____

_____   _____

_____   _____

_____   _____

9. What do the parties agree to do in the event there is a dispute between them?

_____

_____

_____

10. What is the pledge of confidentiality?_____

_____

11. Is an assignment of this contract permitted?_____

EXERCISE 32

TRADEMARK VIOLATION
INTELLECTUAL PROPERTY/TRADEMARKS

Text References: Chapters 9

Review the Trademark Violation letter in the Quicken Business Law Partner and answer the following:

1. What is the demand made in the letter?_____

_____

2. If the recipient of the letter complies with the demands, what will happen?_____

_____

INSTRUCTOR EXERCISE:

Have the students see if they can, through observation, find a trademark violation in the newspaper, on television, in ads or in business names. Have them describe it, the appropriate remedy and why it is important for the owner of the trademark to take action.

EXERCISE 33

GOVERNMENT RECORDS

Text References: Chapters 5 and 44

Review the Request for FBI and CIA Records in the Government section of the Quicken Business Law Partner and answer the following:

1. If you used this letter request, what would you obtain?_____

_____

_____

2. If the agency indicates it will withhold the records you have requested, what information must the agency give?

_____

INSTRUCTOR EXERCISE

Have the students write and make a request for their own records.

EXERCISE 34

FREEDOM OF INFORMATION REQUEST
ADMINISTRATIVE LAW

Text Reference: Chapter 44

Review the FOI Request in the Quicken Business Law Partner and answer the following:

1. What information does the requestor need to provide to the agency?

_____

_____

2. What does the letter request if your request is not addressed to the proper agency?

_____

EXERCISE 35

EMPLOYMENT LAW
REGULATION OF EMPLOYMENT

Text Reference: Chapter 35

Review the Social Security-Earnings Benefit Request in the Quicken Business Law Partner and answer the following:

1. What information is this request designed to obtain for you?

_____

_____

2. What are the penalties for making a request to obtain this information about someone other than yourself without their permission?

_____

INSTRUCTOR EXERCISE:

Have the students write and obtain their own SS-Earnings benefit statement.

Business Law Partner 3.0 Study Guide Answers

EXERCISE 1 - ANSWERS

1. A general power of attorney gives Jake full authority to run Nancy's business affairs. He can open, maintain and close bank accounts and securities accounts. He is given full access to safe deposit boxes. He can sell, exchange, buy, invest, and reinvest assets. He can purchase insurance and collect debts. He can enter into binding contracts on Nancy's behalf. He can exercise her stock options, employ help and sell, mortgage and lease property. If Nancy had any kind of business operations, he could run them with full authority. He can prepare, sign and file government documents on Nancy's behalf.

   This general power of attorney is an enormously broad one that gives Jake full and complete authority over any of Nancy's property and legal issues. In this case, a general power of authority may be more than Nancy wishes to give to Jake.

2. Yes, Jake is entitled to reasonable compensation plus reimbursement for expenses, but the parties can decide that Jake will serve as a gratuitous agent.

3. Yes, Jake could serve as a gratuitous agent. Because Jake is helping Nancy as a friend, they will need to change this portion of the form.

4. Yes, Nancy can revoke the power of attorney at any time. Nancy may want to put a time limitation on the power of attorney. Nancy could also put a transaction limitation on it in that she could direct the transactions for which Jake has authority.

5. The special power of attorney in the Quicken Business Law Partner requires that the specific matters for which there is authority be spelled out; the power of attorney is limited in scope in that transactional limitations are placed on the delegated authority.

6. Yes, Jake is entitled to compensation, but he can also serve as a gratuitous agent if he and Nancy agree.

EXERCISE 2 - ANSWERS

1. Joan and David will need to tell their story in their letter as it is reflected in the facts. They will need to spell out their issues about the carpet layers and the television screen.

2. Copies of the documents Joan and David should attach are: the carpet contract; the purchase contract for the television (to show it was a relatively new purchase at the time of the carpet problem); and the estimate for the repair. Joan and David could attach affidavits from people who had seen the screen before the installation (including themselves) that attest to the fact the screen was not scratched prior to the installers' conduct.

3. Joan and David and the Tollesons could sit with a mediator and try and work out a fair solution such as perhaps at least splitting the cost of the screen repair. They could also try arbitration in which the arbitrator could propose a solution.

EXERCISE 3 - ANSWERS

1. Yes, the Woods can stop payment on the check. Stopping payment on the check is not a final determination for the contract rights that might exist between the parties. Stopping payment on the check is simply a means for the Woods to gain leverage in terms of resolution of the dispute. By stopping payment, they are not in the position of having to seek money from Tolleson. Tolleson will be forced to deal with the issues the Woods have raised in order to obtain payment.

2. While the drawer may not be required to give a reason for a stop-payment order, they must still have a valid legal ground for issuing such an order; otherwise, the holder can sue the drawer for payment. In this case, Woods would simply explain that they are stopping payment because of a contract dispute.

3. Though Quicken provides the option, most banks will insist that the drawer bear the cost of stopping payment on a check.

4. No, the bank is not liable because the bank has no way of knowing whether the contract complaint is legitimate. The bank puts a clause in its stop payment forms to protect it — the bank stops the payment at the customer's direction but does not agree to assume the liability if the bank is wrong.

5. The drawer has full liability to the payee for a wrongful stop payment order. This liability rests where it should because the stop payment order is the result of a dispute between the drawer and the payee. To the extent the drawer is wrong, the parties' contractual liability will take over and determine damages.

EXERCISE 4 - ANSWERS

1. Yes, Tolleson is required to notify the Woods because the primary party, or at least the first party for presentment of the instrument, the bank, has refused to pay. In order to attach liability of the secondary party (the drawer), the payee must give notification of dishonor.

2. If payment of the amount of the check is not made immediately, Tolleson will make an additional charge and there will be no further credit extended to the Woods.

3. Yes, interest accrues during the entire time that Tolleson attempts to collect the amount from the Woods unless their agreement says otherwise.

EXERCISE 5 - ANSWERS

1. The collection agency has not violated any of the provisions of the Fair Debt Collections Practices Act assuming that the notice is given privately. The notice contains a classic collector's hedge in that it does not threaten a suit directly in case the creditor or the agency decides not to proceed with such action. The notice is broad enough that any additional action could be taken, but not so specific that the agency would be making a threat it would not carry out which is a violation of the FDCPA.

2. The Woods could respond that they wish to have no further contact from the collection agency and the contact would have to stop. If the Woods do assert their rights to no further contact, the issue about the scratched screen will come to a head because it is intertwined with the issue of payment and any legal action by Tolleson to collect the amount due will enable the Woods to respond with their claim for damages to their TV.

EXERCISE 6 - ANSWERS

1. Personal ID (copy), the appropriate fee, social security number and addresses for the last five years.

2. The social security number is included because mix-ups between individuals with the same names can be avoided when the SS# is used. Also, phoney requests are at least reduced because the SS# is more difficult to come by than a name and address. The additional information on addresses is also requested to match persons with reports correctly. Because of numerous lawsuits over the past few years of mix-ups in identification, credit reporting agencies take additional precautions with respect to data and the released of credit reports.

EXERCISE 7 - ANSWERS

1. Simply review the chart provided in the Quicken small claims worksheet and match it to your state. In most states the $671 qualifies for small claims court.

2. To complete the small claims checklist, you will need an address for Tolleson as well as its business status, i.e., is it a corporation or sole proprietorship, etc.

3. Tolleson is the plaintiff and the Woods would be the defendants.

4. Florida and Delaware, with a maximum of $15,000 have the highest small claims court jurisdiction.

EXERCISE 8 - ANSWERS

1. In this factual situation, the Woods will be the plaintiffs and Tolleson will be the defendant.

2. Tolleson will need to check with its employees or contractors who installed the carpeting to see what happened. Tolleson will need to find and provide any documentation it has with respect to the incident.

EXERCISE 9 - ANSWERS

1. The information requested in the Quicken form is whether a consumer reporting agency was used, and, if not, what was the other source. The letter also requests a description of the nature of the investigation conducted by that other source.

   An important tip in checking a credit denial is to be certain that the creditor had the information on you — did the have the right credit report and the right person?

EXERCISE 10 - ANSWERS

1. The letter serves two very important purposes: the landlord is put on notice of a heating problem in the apartment: and the landlord is given a time within which to solve the problem

2. Most states gives residential tenants a warranty of habitability which means that the premises are fit and habitable at the time of the lease. The Uniform Residential Landlord Tenant Act (URLTA) also provides tenants with rights in the event the basic essentials of habitation (such as heat, water, and, in some circumstances, air conditioning) cease to work. Those rights include the right to make a demand for repair (which is what this Quicken letter is designed to do), and then the right to self-help or making the repairs themselves and then billing the landlord or deducting that amount from their rent. However, all these rights begin with the notice to the landlord of the problem.

EXERCISE 11 - ANSWERS

1. The rent is due on whatever day the landlord and the tenant agree to.

2. Both the landlord and the tenant are responsible for carrying insurance on their respective properties. Tenants would have to carry their own insurance, for example, on their furniture. Landlords would carry an owner's policy on the property. Although, the tenant and the landlord can contractually agree to make insuring both parties' interests a responsibility of the tenant's.

3. Notice must be given in writing.

4. If one portion of the lease is unenforceable, it is to be struck from the lease so that the remainder can be enforced.

EXERCISE 12 - ANSWERS

1. Some of the provisions in the residential lease not found in the commercial lease include the condition of the dwelling unit, absences for extended periods of the tenant from the property, and the rights and obligations with respect to the keys.

2. The habitability clause simple puts into the official language of the lease the rights most tenants have in most states: that the premises are in habitable condition at the commencement of the lease.

EXERCISE 13 - ANSWERS

1. Unless the agreement states otherwise, the tenant whose application is approved by the landlord and who fails to enter into a lease agreement will lose his or her application fee. The reason for such damages is that the landlord does expend time and effort (and in some cases fees for the credit report) in processing an application.

2. Yes, the application form authorizes the landlord to do a credit check, although, the landlord may opt to leave this term out.

3. The grounds on which a landlord can't discriminate are race, religion, national origin, age, and disability.

4. If the applicant makes a written request for the reason for rejection of the application, the landlord has 60 days within which to respond to the applicant.

EXERCISE 14 - ANSWERS

1. The general standards that the checklist is intended to confirm are that the premises are in good, clean, sanitary order and in good condition and repair.

2. The tenant, by signing off on the inspection sheet, agrees to return the premises to the landlord in the same condition as when the inspection occurs.

3. The tenant assumes the risk for any defects in the rental property that he knew of or should have known of through inspection of the property.

4. The tenant agrees to test the smoke detector at agreed intervals and to be certain that it has an alkaline battery that is in working order.

EXERCISE 15 - ANSWERS

1. When the phrase "AS IS" appears in a contract it means that both the implied warranty of merchantability as well as the implied warranty of fitness for a particular purpose are disclaimed. The goods are sold with all their defects and the buyer assumes the risk of those defects. Subsequently discovered defects cannot be a basis for suit or liability against the seller.

2. A bill of sale is evidence of a transfer of title.

3. A bill of sale is evidence of a transfer of title. It is not, however, a document of title.

EXERCISE 16 - ANSWERS

1. A bill of sale for motor vehicles has more details including a description of the car (make, model, etc) as well as the mileage.

2. A false statement about the mileage on the car is a federal offense and can result in fines and/or imprisonment.

3. The seller promises that the odometer is in good working order and that it has not been tampered with so as to affect the recorded mileage on the car.

EXERCISE 17 - ANSWERS

1. The rent on the leased equipment is due either periodically or when the equipment is returned.

2. The lessee agrees to assume the risk of loss and responsibility for damage to the property.

3. No, the lessee is usually not permitted to make alterations to the equipment.

4. The lessee is usually responsible for repairs to the equipment.

5. Yes, if the lessor retains the rights of inspection of the equipment during the term of the lease.

6. When the lease agreement ends, the lessee could be given the option of renewing the lease agreement or purchase the leased property according to stated financial terms

7. Yes, the lessor can also specifically disclaim any warranties about the leased equipment.

8. This disclaimer may create problems since it is, in essence, an exculpatory clause that permits the lessor to lease defective property that could injure the lessee and others. It is against public policy to hold oneself immune from liability for one's own negligence. While many lease agreements contain such provisions, they can be successfully challenged on the grounds of unconscionability.

9. No, assignment by the lessee is prohibited unless the agreement specifically permits it.

10. The lease agreement can provide that any disputes between the parties will be settled through binding arbitration.

EXERCISE 18 - ANSWERS

1. This is an absolute and unconditional guaranty, but a change in the language in the "Obligations" paragraph can make this a conditional guarantee.

2. There can be no revocation of this guaranty. The length of this guaranty depends upon what the parties to the lease agreed to. Among the possibilities for the length of a lease are: 1) until all conditions under the original credit contract are satisfied; 2) until there is written notice to the creditor; 3) until a specified date; or 4) the guaranty is only for a specified period of time.

3. No, typically in most guaranty contracts, the creditor need not notify the guarantor of the debtor's default.

4. Usually no, the creditor need not notify the guarantor if additional loans are made by the creditor to the debtor, although, the parties can contract otherwise as they see fit.

5. No, the creditor need not show due diligence in collection because this guaranty is an unconditional guaranty of payment. Only in a guarantor of collection situation must a creditor establish due diligence before demanding payment from the guarantor.

6. The creditor can change the payment terms of the credit agreement and release the collateral without giving notice to the guarantor.

7. No, the guarantor is not released if the creditor changes the terms.

EXERCISE 19 - ANSWERS

1. This license agreement would cover any type of use of intellectual property such as the right to use a song or software.

2. The compensation to the owner of the intellectual property will be payment of royalties which is a percentage of total sales as when a songwriter is given a percentage of record sales in exchange for the artist's right to record the song.

EXERCISE 20 - ANSWERS

1. Payments under the note are applied first to accrued interest and then to principal.

2. The note is payable in U.S. currency.

3. Yes, a note can still be negotiable even though it is payable in a currency that is foreign to the country in which the note is made or either party is located. So long as the note is payable in a medium of exchange recognized by some country, it is negotiable and valid.

EXERCISE 21 - ANSWERS

1. Under these sample incorporation documents, the information needed is the total # of shares, the registered agent for the corporation, the purpose of the corporation and the directors.

2. No, the MBCA does not require all the information noted in these articles of incorporation. These articles require more information which is permitted and possibly desirable from the standpoint of the parties' rights.

3. Yes, the corporation's officers and directors enjoy the protection of indemnity from the corporation provided that the corporation's Articles of Incorporation limit these officers' and directors' liability.

4. Indemnity means that the officers and directors can be reimbursed for the expenses they incur in defending their conduct with respect to the corporation. There can be some exceptions such as when the directors and officers engage in fraud.

EXERCISE 22 - ANSWERS

1. The shareholders will hold meetings at least once each calendar year.

2. A special meeting of shareholders can be called by the president, the board or a majority of the outstanding shareholders of voting shares.

3. Notice of a meeting must be given no later than 10 days prior to the meeting. The time can be measured from the time the notice is mailed and not when it actually is received by the shareholders.

4. A quorum is the majority of the outstanding voting shares.

5. Yes, proxies can be used to make up a quorum.

6. Yes, a director can be removed with or without cause.

7. The offices provided in these bylaws include the president, vice president, secretary and treasurer. More than one office can be held by a single person.

8. The officers are elected by the directors.

9. The bylaws can be amended by the directors or the shareholders by a majority of a quorum of voting shares.

10. Yes, you can own shares in the corporation without having to have certificates as evidence.

EXERCISE 23 - ANSWERS

1. Yes, all prior proxies are revoked.

2. Proxies are needed because the majority of shareholders are unable to attend the annual meeting yet they want to have a voice in corporate governance. They designate a representative as well as their voting choices.

3. Yes, a segment of the proxy allows the shareholder to dictate how votes should be made.

EXERCISE 24 - ANSWERS

1. The definition of confidential information given in the document is proprietary information not generally known to the public.

2. Information about customers including customer lists, new products, strategies, supply chain management techniques, planned ad campaigns, etc.

EXERCISE 25 - ANSWERS

1. The consultant will be an independent contractor.

2. This distinction is important because of wage tax issues and liability issues and worker's compensation coverage issues. For an employee, an employer must pay wage taxes, if fully liable for acts within the scope of employment and subjects the employee to worker's compensation system rules. An independent contractor pays his or her own wage taxes and is not covered by worker's compensation. The employer would also not be liable for the torts of an independent contractor.

EXERCISE 26 - ANSWERS

1. Most employment agreements are "at will" — it can be terminated at any time. However, the parties can also agree to contract for employment over a specific term that cannot be terminated "at-will."

2. Yes, "at-will" employment is legal. There are some exceptions such as terminating a whistle-blower that would prevent termination because such a termination would be retaliatory in nature.

3. Termination notices are usually given in writing so as to protect the employer.

EXERCISE 27 - ANSWERS

1. From the document, we can conclude that the parties had a conversation about a contract for employment.

2. A letter such as this would help the employee prove that some type of a contract exists. It would be contemporaneous evidence of discussions of employment. It also serves as a formal acceptance of an oral offer. Further, the failure of the employer to correct any misunderstandings about the conversation and offer of employment would allow the employee to rely on the oral

promise and begin the process of terminating another job or moving.

EXERCISE 28 - ANSWERS

1. The types of activities prohibited under the agreement are: competing directly' competing indirectly; soliciting customers for business; inducing employees to leave; revealing confidential business information.

2. Monetary remedies as well as injunctive relief are afforded under the agreement.

3. This type of an agreement is necessary to prevent employees from obtaining proprietary information and then using it to start their own businesses or taking it to other employers who are competitors.

EXERCISE 29 - ANSWERS

1. A consignment is an arrangement whereby the property owner transfers property to a consignee for purposes of selling that property in exchange for a fee or a commission. For example, a consignment furniture store is filled with the used furniture of others that can be sold for a price below new and in exchange for a percentage to the consignee.

2. The consignee is the party who has possession of the property and agrees to sell it for a fee.

3. The consignor is the owner of the property who transfers possession.

4. The consignee is usually entitled to a fee or percentage for the sale of the goods.

5. The consignee.

6. The consignee.

7. A bailment is a temporary transfer of possession. A consignment is the transfer of possession for purposes of sale with the authority to transfer title to another. Until the terms of the consignment arrangement end, the title is held by the consignee. A bailee does not hold title in any type of bailment.

EXERCISE 30 - ANSWERS

1. The types of works that can be copyrighted are music, books, movies, television shows, magazines, newspapers, periodicals and software.

2. The employer has the right to the copyright because the employer provided the resources for its development.

EXERCISE 31 - ANSWERS

1. The failure of the buyer to make a payment is considered a material breach.

2. "Time is of the essence" is the time given for delivery — ASAP would be the standard.

3. In this case, the seller absorbs the loss if the goods are damaged due to improper packaging.

4. In this case the buyer is to pay the taxes.

5. The inspection rights include the opportunity to inspect the Goods to determine if they conform to the conditions of the contract.

6. The inspection rights afforded under the contract are about the same as those given under Article 2 with the exception that the buyer must give written notice of rejection and the reasons for such rejection.

7. A force majeure is an event that interferes with the performance of the contract that is beyond the parties' control and was not anticipated by them.

8. Examples of force majeure in the contract include: acts of God; fire; explosion; vandalism; storms; riots; military action; wars, insurrections.

9. If the matter has not been resolved in the time the parties originally agreed to in the contract, they then agree to go to binding arbitration.

10. A pledge of confidentiality is an agreement not to disclose the terms of the agreement or any proprietary information regarding the product.

11. No, assignment of the contract is usually not permitted. However, the parties may contract to allow such an assignment if it suits their needs.

EXERCISE 32 - ANSWERS

1. The demand is that the use of the trademark stop.

2. If the recipient complies, the owner of the trademark will take no further action and will not seek any damages. However, the owner of the trademark did not have to offer this inducement to cease use of his mark. He could have made this same demand without the offer and while seeking redress for the infringement.

EXERCISE 33 - ANSWERS

1. All information about you held by the FBI and CIA with certain exceptions such as information related to any ongoing investigations.

2. The agency must disclose why the information is being withheld.

EXERCISE 34 - ANSWERS

1. The requestor must provide what documents he/she is looking for and for what period.

2. That the request be forwarded to the proper agency.

EXERCISE 35 - ANSWERS

1. Your history of wages and applicable social security withholding as well as what benefits you could expect under SS programs.

2. Making a request for another without their permission is a violation of federal law that carries fines and/or imprisonment.

Notes

Notes

Notes

Notes

Notes

Notes

Notes

Notes

Notes

Notes

Notes